名家抒情詩評賞

（漢英對照）

Appraisal of Lyric Poems by Famous Artists (Chinese-English)

林　明　理著

Author: Dr. Lin Mingli

張智中　教授英譯

Translator:
Prof. Zhang Zhizhong

現代文學研究叢刊

文史哲出版社印行

國家圖書館出版品預行編目資料

名家抒情詩評賞 / 林明理著. 張智中英譯.
初版 -- 臺北市：文史哲出版社, 民 113.06
面； 公分.--（現代文學研究叢刊；51）
ISBN 978-986-314-675-9（平裝）

1.CST: 抒情詩 2. CST: 詩評

812.18   113009133

現代文學研究叢刊   51

名家抒情詩評賞

著　　　者：林　　　　明　　　　理
譯　　　者：張　　　　智　　　　中
出 版 者：文　史　哲　出　版　社
　　　　　http://www.lapen.com.tw
　　　　　e-mail：lapen@ms74.hinet.net
登記證字號：行政院新聞局版臺業字五三三七號
發 行 人：彭　　　正　　　雄
發 行 所：文　史　哲　出　版　社
印 刷 者：文　史　哲　出　版　社
臺北市羅斯福路一段七十二巷四號
郵政劃撥帳號：一六一八〇一七五
電話886-2-23511028 · 傳真886-2-23965656

定價新臺幣一二八〇元

二〇二四年（民一一三）六月初版

前 序

　　本書是爲協助英語系教師與學生進行「現代詩評賞」課程而設，透過英語翻譯評析全文，以期海內外讀者或詩歌學習者更深入瞭解書裡的每位詩人的內在世界，進而感受這些中外詩家詩韻優美的作品；也期望能在賞讀中，引導學生思考及從不同的文化與詩歌研究的情境中學習。這是本書出版的最重要的期許與價值所在。

張智中教授於 2024 年 02 月 21 日
南開大學博士班導師研究室

Author's and Compiler's Introduction

　　Scholar and poet Lin Mingli selects and combines what she feels and the experience and memories of reading ancient poems, and wants to add new poems created by her to the compiled ancient poems, hoping that readers can feel and understand the world of poetic beauty more closely.

　　And I think that if the study of ancient poetry and new poetry can be synchronously supplemented, the meaning of translated poetry will become more lively, so that students will have greater interest in appreciation and study of poetry, which is the most important value of this book , It can also deepen the sensibility and understanding when reading, which is also my expectation. This is the most important expectation and value of publishing this book.

Professor Zhang Zhizhong on February 21, 2024
Nankai University Doctoral Tutor Research Office

明闢理精

　恭賀

林明理博士著、張智中教授譯詩論集

《名家抒情詩評賞》面世。

文史哲出版社發行人

彭正雄　謹識

二〇二四年六月四日

名家抒情詩評賞

目 次 CONTENTS

中英對照 Chinese-English

一、外國詩人 1. International poets

1. 真樸的睿智：狄金森詩歌研究述評 2

1. Genuine Wisdom：Studies of Emily Dickinson's Poetry ...3

2. 愛倫・坡的詩化人生..28

2. Edgar Allan Poe's Poetic Life...................................29

3. 一隻慨然高歌的靈鳥：讀普希金詩 50

3. A Soul Bird Sings With Deep Feeling：Reading
   Alexander Pushkin's Poetry...51

4. 傑克・裴外詩歌的意象藝術探微 76

4. Exploring the Art of Imagery in Jacques Prévert's Poetry 77

5. 論布洛克詩歌中的象徵意蘊 106

5. On the Symbolic Meaning of Blok's Poetry 107

6. 孤獨的行吟 ： 讀里爾克的詩 142

6. Solitary Troubadour：Reading Rilke's Poems 143

7. 雅羅斯拉夫・塞弗特的詩歌藝術 158

7. The Art of Poetry by Jaroslav Seifert 159

8. 約瑟夫・布羅茨基的生平・及其詩藝成就 176

8. The Life and Poetic Achievements of Joseph Brodsky 177

9. 讀葉慈詩歌的意象藝術 190

9. The Art of Imagery in Reading W. B. Yeats Poetry 191

10 淺析希克梅特詩歌中的深情抒寫 202

10. An Analysis of Affectionate Writing in

　　 Hickmet's Poems 203

11. 試析佛洛斯特抒情詩四首 242

11. Analysis of Four Lyric Poems by Robert Frost 243

12. 淺析瑞典詩人川斯綽莫的詩世界 252

12. A Brief Analysis of the Poetic World of Swedish

　　 Poet Tomas Transtroemer 253

13. 試析巴爾蒙特詩二首 264

13. Analysis of Two Balmont Poems 265

14. 淺析約瑟夫·布羅茨基的詩 278

14. A Brief Analysis of Joseph Brodsky's Poems 279

15. 讀 Prof. Ernesto Kahan 的一首詩〈Mnemosyne

　　 And My Trip〉 294

15. Read a Poem *Mnemosyne And My Trip* by

　　 Prof. Ernesto Kahan 295

16. 論費特詩歌的藝術美 304

16. Title: On the Artistic Beauty of Fet's Poetry 305

17. 論丘特切夫詩歌的藝術美 340

17　On the Artistic Beauty of Tyutchev's Poetry 341

18. 簡論米蘭・裏赫特《湖底活石》的自然美學思想 380

18.　On the Aesthetic Thoughts of ature Milan Richter's
　　 Living Stones in the Bottom of the Lake 381

19. 論阿赫馬托娃的詩歌藝術 400

19.　On the Poetic Art of Akhmatova 401

20. 布邁恪抒情詩印象 436

20.　Impressions of Michael Bullock's Lyric Poetry 437

21. 試析康拉德・艾肯的詩〈先林的晨歌〉 448

21.　Analysis of Conrad Aiken's Poem *Morning
　　 Song of Senlin* 449

22. 一座沉思的雕像：讀若澤·薩拉馬戈的詩 462

22. A Contemplative Statue：Reading José Saramago's
　　 Poems 463

23. 讀秦立彥譯《華茲華斯抒情詩選》 476

23.　Reading Selected Lyric Poems of William
　　 Wordsworth Translated by Qin Liyan 477

24. 庫爾特•F•斯瓦泰克的詩歌藝術 486

24.　The Art of Poetry by Kurt F. Svatek 487

25. 試析喬凡尼・坎皮西抒情詩三首 496

25. Analysis of Three Lyrical Poems by Giovanni Campisi.. 497

26. 米拉・洛赫維茨卡婭抒情詩印象 506

26. Impressions of Mila Lokhvitskaya's Lyrical Poems 507

27. 真摯的詩情與崇高美的融合：讀倫扎・阿涅利 520

（Renza Agnelli）的詩 520

27. A Fusion of Sincere Poetry and Sublime Beauty

：Reading the Poems by Renza Agnelli 521

28. 追求光明的勇者Sara Ciampi 的詩世界 532

28. The Warrior-Pursuer of Light：The Poetic World

of Sara Ciampi.. 533

29. 托馬斯特蘭斯特羅默《巨大的謎語》賞析 546

29. Appreciation of The Great Riddle by Tomas Transtromer547

二、中國大陸、台灣詩人

2. Poets from Mainland China and Taiwan

1. 一棵冰雪壓不垮的白樺樹：淺釋北島的詩 560

1. A White Birch Which Can Never Be Bent by Ice or Snow:

An Interpretation of Bei Dao's Poetry 561

2. 一棵挺立的孤松：淺釋 艾青的詩 582

2. A Lone Pine Standing Erect：A Brief Analysis

of Ai Qing's Poetry 583

3. 夜讀張智中的詩 624

3. Reading Zhang Zhizhong's Poems at Night 625

4. 讀盧惠餘《聞一多詩歌藝術研究》.............................632

4. Reading Lu Huiyu's A Study of Wen Yiduo's Poetic Art....633

5. 沉雅與靜穆：讀牛漢〈落雪的夜〉〈根〉〈海上蝴蝶〉.......662

5. Elegance and Serenity：Reading Niu Han's *Night of Falling Snow*, *Root*, and *Butterfly on the Sea*.............663

6. 陳義海詩歌的思想藝術成就 680

6. The Ideological and Artistic Achievements of Chen Yihai's Poems 681

7. 清靜淡泊的詩音 ： 秦立彥詩歌的另類讀法.................702

7. Quiet and Indifferent Poetry：An Alternative Reading of Qin Liyan's Poems...................................703

8. 簡潔自然的藝術風韻：讀余光中的鄉土詩.................712

8. Concise and Natural Artistic Charm：Reading the Local Poems of Yu Guangzhong...................................713

9. 最輕盈的飛翔：淺釋鍾鼎文的詩.................................724

9. The Lightest Flying：An Analysis of Zhong Dingwen's Poems...................................725

10. 鄭愁予—站在中西藝術匯合處的詩人.......................740

10. Zheng Chouyu：A Poet Standing at the Confluenceof Chinese and Western Art...................741

11. 論周夢蝶詩中的道家美學：以〈消遙遊〉〈六月〉二詩為例...758

11. On the Taoist Aesthetics in Zhou Mengdie's Poems:....759

12. 追尋深化藝術的儒者：楊牧詩歌的風格特質 786

12. Pursuing Confucianists：Who Deepened Art 787

13. 洛夫詩中的禪道精神 798

13. The Zen Spirit in Luo Fu's Poems 799

14. 席慕蓉的詩歌藝術 824

14. The Art of Xi Murong's Poetry 825

15. 夜讀鍾玲詩集《霧在登山》 854

15. Night Reading of Zhong Ling's Poetry Collection 855

16. 一棵不凋的樹：試析穆旦的詩三首 870

16. An Unfading Tree：Analysis of Three Poems by
    Mu Dan 871

林明理專書書目及封面書影 891

名家抒情詩評賞

一、外國詩人

1. International poets

1. 真樸的睿智—狄金森詩歌研究述評

摘要： 艾米莉·狄金森既是美國十九世紀最富傳奇性、傑出的天才，又是最孤獨羞澀、深居簡出的女詩人。在她所創造的詩歌中，常可發現不為人所理解的多層意義與智慧。本文從非馬博士翻譯其作品中，淺析她如何將純真與經驗的意象並置或矛盾對立的統一與釋放所產生的雙重視野，成為一個她所追逐的絕對純潔的文學表現。

關鍵字： 艾米莉·狄金森；非馬；詩歌；精神之美；自我救贖

一、其人其詩

　　一個多世紀以來，生於麻塞諸塞州的阿莫斯特(Amherst)且幾乎不曾離開故鄉生活的艾米莉·狄金森〈Emily Dickinson〉〈1830-1886〉始終是美國文學史上偉大的女詩人。她擅寫短詩、情感細膩，意象深切；一生大部分的詩都在她死後才被發現，結集出版後才重現光芒。

1. Genuine Wisdom – Studies of Emily Dickinson's Poetry

Abstract: Emily Dickinson is not only the most legendary and outstanding genius, but also an exceedingly solitary and reclusive poetess. In her poems, one can often find layers of meanings and wisdom that are hard to comprehend. This article tries to analyze some of her poems through the Chinese translation by Dr. William Marr (Fei Ma), to see how she manages to unite her images of innocence and experience, and her contradictory or opposite concepts, to produce a double vision, a pure literary expression which she is constantly after.

Key words: Emily Dickinson, William Marr, poetry, spiritual beauty, self-salvation

1. Her People and Her Poems

For over a century, Emily Dickinson (1830-1886), born in Amherst, Massachusetts who hardly ever left her hometown, has always been a great female figure in the history of American literature. She is good at writing short poems with delicate emotions and deep images; most of her poems written through her life were discovered after her death, and only after they were collected and published did they begin to regain brilliance.

　　狄金森求學時曾就讀於阿莫斯特學院，和一年時間讀聖尤奇山(Mount Holyoky)神學院。而她深鎖在盒子裏的詩篇，能展現純真、聖潔、簡樸、有深刻思想的美德。她為世人留下了一千八百首詩，凝聚著深厚的情感和創造性的智慧。在她 28 歲後七年，這段期間，可說是狄金森詩歌創作生涯的巔峰時期。尤以 32 歲前後是創作的高峰，在此期間她大量創作出反映死亡、永恆、自然與愛情等主題的詩歌，能夠揭示詩人在經歷了心靈創傷、掙扎於精神崩潰邊緣之際，如何以詩歌藝術逐漸實現心靈的「自我救贖」的過程。她的秘密日記寫下了自己一生的生死愛恨，在她去世二十多年後，才被一位整修她舊居的木匠發現，但因其私心作祟，再度埋沒了近八十年才輾轉問世。

　　狄金森是個優雅、擁有高遠的理想、愛追求自由和夢想但個性強烈的詩人。即便是年華已逝、深居簡出的她，也散發著清純氣韻，性格易害羞，卻始終保持著少女的純真，但對感情方面較為敏感。有很強的獨立精神和豐富的想像力，在平凡的生活中，安於孤獨自由的和靈光乍現的機智，常會使讀者驚歎不已。本文從旅美非馬博士的幾首譯詩〈註〉中，嘗試探索狄金森詩歌的藝術表現；其天真和孤獨精神的靈思，常可發現不為人所理解的多層意義與智慧。壓抑在內心深處的「自卑情結」，在表現自我的層面上，也從而獲得了對現實的超越和自我拯救。

Dickinson attended Amherst College, spending a year at Mount Holyoky Theological Seminary. And thedes apoems she locked in the box show the virtues of innocence, holiness, simplicity, and deep thinking. She left behind her 1,800 poems for the world, embodying profound emotions and creative wisdom. The seven years after she turned 28 can be said to be the peak of Dickinson's poetic career. Especially around the age of 32 was the peak of her creation. During this period, she has written a large number of poems on the themes of death, eternity, nature and love, which reveal how the poet uses poetry when he has experienced trauma, struggling on the verge of mental breakdown. In art she gradually realizes the process of "self-salvation" of the soul. Her secret diary is a record of her love and hatred in her life. It was discovered by a carpenter renovating her old house more than 20 years after her death, but because of her selfishness, she was buried again for nearly 80 years before being published.

pure charm, with a shy personality, but she always maintains the innocence of a girl, but she is more sensitive to emotions. With a strong independent spirit and rich imagination, in the ordinary life, she rests content with loneliness and freedom, and her quick wit often surprises readers. This article attempts to explore the artistic expression of Dickinson's poems from several translated poems by Dr. William Marr who lived in the United States; in her innocence and lonely spiritual thoughts, we can often find multi-layered meanings and wisdom that are not understood by people. The "inferiority complex" repressed deep in the heart, on the level of self-expression, has also obtained the transcendence of reality and self-salvation.

二、狄金森詩歌的意象與内涵

　　詩美意識是形而上的藝術直覺，是以人的靈性去體驗到的一種本原的、悠遠的意境之美；從而展現出詩人獨特的審美理念和藝術開拓。如何凸顯審美觀是詩發展需要反思其深度根源與現代含義的一項創新的視域。更為重要的是，必須揭示出詩的意象及心理學解讀，才能昇華當代新詩的審美體驗，藉以反映出詩人的精神本性，探索其內心的情感世界。艾米莉·狄金森是個感覺經驗強烈而靈敏的詩人，儘管外界事物多變與永恆不變的理型相區別；然而，在狄金森的詩歌中，其心靈恆處於嚮往真理的狀態，因之，思想之船槳常能與心志相契合。接著來看她的這首〈懸宕〉，強調語言的精巧，也反映出作者對「生死」的世間法則，有種恢宏氣勢的感覺：

> 天堂遙遠得有如
> 到最臨近的房間，
> 要是那房裡有一位朋友在等待
> 幸福或災難
>
> 何等的剛毅，
> 使靈魂經受得了
> 一隻來腳的重音，
> 一扇門的開啓！

2. Imagery and Connotation of Dickinson's Poems

Poetic beauty consciousness is metaphysical artistic intuition, a kind of original and distant beauty of artistic conception experienced by human spirituality; thus it shows the poet's unique aesthetic concept and artistic development. How to highlight the aesthetics is an innovative vision for the development of poetry that needs to reflect on its deep roots and modern meanings. More importantly, the poetic imagery and psychological interpretation must be revealed in order to sublimate the aesthetic experience of contemporary new poetry, so as to reflect the poet's spiritual nature and explore his inner emotional world. Emily Dickinson is a poetess with strong and sensitive sensory experience, although the changeable external things are different from the eternal ideal; however, in Dickinson's poems, her heart is always in a state of yearning for truth, so, the oars of thought can often match the mind. Next, look at her song *Suspense*, which emphasizes the delicacy of language, and also reflects the author's feeling of grandeur towards the worldly laws of "life and death":

ELYSIUM is as far as to
The very nearest room,
If in that room a friend await
Felicity or doom.

What fortitude the soul contains,
That it can so endure
The accent of a coming foot,
The opening of a door!

　　在第一個詩節，作者質疑自己所處的困境，她想從人類的制度的束縛中解脫出來，在現實中，無疑是不可能的；但這種對神的反抗導致了心靈的痛苦。因此，她試圖將世間所有懸而未決的人事物都歸於平靜；但又不禁期許博得上帝的垂愛，得到寄望中的生存空間。接著，她發現生死的關鍵不在上帝，不在遙遠的夢土；而是淳樸的生活裡試煉的心志。有了這個認知，她不再畏懼死亡、或紛歧是非；並能心悅誠服地突破生命的鐵門，接受自己命定的一切。

　　接著，這一首柔美的〈以一朵花〉，注重整體的抒情而非細節的描述，以打造愛情的想像空間：

> 我躲在我的花裡，
> 你，把它當胸戴起，
> 不提防地，也戴著我——
> 天使們知道其餘。
>
> 我躲在我的花裡，
> 那朵，在你的花瓶裡褪色，
> 你，不提防地，摸索我
> 幾乎是一種落寞。

　　詩句滲透了狄金森自己個性的傾向，感情色彩與主觀的想望，每一句都從心底湧出，且自然而然地融入了作者孤寂的情緒。彷彿驟然顛覆時空在我們也曾回眸一瞥百合時，這樣的美麗是隱而未現的脆弱、衝動、夢想、善變…其間的滋

In the first stanza, the author questioned her predicament. She wanted to free herself from the shackles of the human system. In reality, it was undoubtedly impossible; but this resistance to God led to spiritual pain. Therefore, she tried to calm all the unresolved people and things in the world; but she couldn't help but hope to win God's favor and get the expected living space. Then, she discovered that the key to life and death is not in God, nor in the distant dream land; With this understanding, she is no longer afraid of death, or disagreeing between right and wrong; and can break through the iron gate of life convincingly and accept everything she is destined for.

Then, this soft song *With a Flower* focuses on the overall lyricism rather than the description of details, so as to create the imagination space of love:

> *I hide myself within my flower,*
> *That wearing on your breast,*
> *You, unsuspecting, wear me too —*
> *And angels know the rest.*

> *I hide myself within my flower,*
> *That, fading from your vase,*
> *You, unsuspecting, feel for me*
> *Almost a loneliness.*

The verses are infiltrated with Dickinson's own personality tendency, emotional color and subjective desire, each sentence gushes out from the bottom of his heart, and naturally blends into the author's lonely mood. It seems that time and space are suddenly subverted. When we once glance back at Lily, this kind of beauty is the hidden fragility, impulsiveness, dream, fickleness... the taste in it is very

味迴腸盪氣。狄金森如愛神丘比特般的童真，將思念的憧憬
巨細靡遺地描繪出來；讓愛情的糾結悵然面貌及落寞的底
蘊，呼之欲出，呈現出不一樣的生命姿態，也見識到作者
嚮往超凡脫俗的愛情的悲傷。

　　這首〈我是個無名小卒！你呢？...〉，成功地創造了一個
虛擬的世界，藉此表達她對世人追逐名利的想法和其不同流
俗的心胸：

　　　　我是個無名小卒！你呢？
　　　　你也是個無名小卒？
　　　　那我們可成了對--別說出來！
　　　　你知道，他們會把我們放逐。

　　　　做一個名人多可怕！
　　　　眾目之下，像隻青蛙
　　　　整天哇哇高唱自己的名字
　　　　對著一個哐哐讚美的泥淖！

　　狄金森也是位常保赤子心的詩人，因真感情，才有真境
界。在這裡，她成功地找出一個具體意象，鼓勵人盡可能地
享受大自然的美好時光。所要闡述的，是在一片搶當名人的
爭戰聲中，請讓出心靈的空間吧。而人們所爭求的到最後都
是由單純變複雜，此詩則延伸了這一幅諷刺的縮圖：人類因
好勝心而爭個死去活來，不過只增多旁人的譏笑罷了。如果
不是狄金森的詩才超群，那麼她也不可能有感觸即興迸出，

soul-stirring. Dickinson's childlike innocence, like Cupid, depicts the longing and longing in detail; the tangled and sad appearance of love and the background of loneliness are ready to come out, showing a different life attitude, and seeing the author's yearning for the otherworldly. The sorrow of love.

This song *I'm Nobody! Who Are You...* successfully created a virtual world to express her thoughts on the world's pursuit of fame and fortune and her unconventional mind:

> *I'm nobody! Who are you?*
> *Are you nobody, too?*
> *Then there's a pair of us — don't tell!*
> *They'd banish us, you know.*
>
> *How dreary to be somebody!*
> *How public, like a frog*
> *To tell your name the livelong day*
> *To an admiring bog!*

Dickinson is also a poet who always maintains a pure heart, because of true feelings, there is a true realm. Here, she managed to find a specific image that encourages people to enjoy the good time in nature as much as possible. What I want to explain is that in the midst of the battle to become a celebrity, please make room for your soul. But what people strive for eventually changes from simplicity to complexity. This poem extends this satirical miniature: human beings fight to the death because of their

的強度，冀望著愛是「永恆、無限、純一」，讓人重新感知這
個世界：

　　　屋裡的忙亂
　　　在死亡過後的早晨
　　　是這塵世上
　　　最最莊嚴的勞動　，──

　　　把心掃起　，
　　　把愛收拾藏好
　　　我們將不再用得著
　　　直到永遠。

　　　在宗教領域裡，狄金森保持著更多自由。她一直希望找
到一條出路，從而自痛苦的樊籠中擺脫出來。在這裡，可明
顯地感受到作者將生與死的莊嚴、與忙亂的家人的意象並
陳；以探究愛情的深度與價值，進而說出內心深處的憂鬱，
以彌補過去對宗教方面失落的態度，情味綿緲。暗喻生命終
有結束的一天，因為我們知道它有盡頭，才會更積極把握現
有的…曾經擁有是幸福的，否則，那一切的一切盡都惘然。
當我們身臨其境，作者所能喚起的，就是在我們心中激發起
連我們都不曾料想的情感或某段經歷的記憶。這樣，過去，
風格在她身上產生了創作的動力，是偏於幽默性的舒緩愉悅

to express the intensity of life, hoping that love is "eternal, infinite, and pure", so that people can re-perceive this world:

The bustle in a house
The morning after death
Is solemnest of industries
Enacted upon earth, —

The sweeping up the heart,
And putting love away
We shall not want to use again....
Until eternity.

　　In the realm of religion, Dickinson maintained more freedom. She has always hoped to find a way out, so as to escape from the cage of pain. Here, it can be clearly felt that the author presents the solemnity of life and death, and the images of busy family members side by side; in order to explore the depth and value of love, and then express the melancholy deep in his heart, so as to make up for the past lost in religion, attitude and affection. It is a metaphor that life will end some day, because we know that it will end, so we will be more active in grasping what we have.... What is once possessed is happiness; otherwise, everything will be in vain. When we are on the scene, what the author can evoke is to arouse in our hearts emotions or memories of a certain experience that we have never expected. In this way, the past, present, future, fantasy and the distance of

現在，未來，幻想與時間的距離就串聯在一起了。

　　狄金森思想的深刻性不僅在於能一針見血地指出現實社會的弊病，而且還在於能在詩中把相互對立的情景組合在一起，出人意料地取得了某種特殊的意蘊。比如〈兩個泳者在甲板上搏鬥...〉就是首哲理的小詩，試圖解決人與人之間的敵對問題：

> 兩個泳者在甲板上搏鬥
> 直到朝陽東升，
> 當一個微笑著轉向陸地。
> 天哪，另一個！
>
> 路過的船隻看到一張臉
> 在水面漂蕩，
> 在死亡裡依然舉目乞求，
> 雙手哀懇地伸張。

　　無論這畫面是真是假，這裡作者的意識與外界的物象相交會，形成一種生命風貌的展現。它讓讀者感受親歷其境的一刻，既是作者個人對生之尊重所展現的風姿，也是讀者透過意象的圖騰所體悟的風貌。作者繼以擬人手法，描繪死亡的恐懼，既凸顯了不當的搏鬥所帶來的傷害後遺症，甚至使萬物之主也望之興歎。所以，清醒是很重要的。這種調侃式風

time are connected in series.

The profundity of Dickinson's thought lies not only in his ability to point out the ills of the real society, but also in his ability to combine opposite scenes in his poems, unexpectedly obtaining a special meaning. For example, *Two Swimmers Wrestled on the Spar...* is a short philosophical poem that tries to resolve the problem of hostility between people:

> *Two swimmers wrestled on the spar*
> *Until the morning sun,*
> *When one turned smiling to the land,*
> *O God, the other one!*
>
> *The stray ships passing spied a face*
> *Upon the waters borne,*
> *With eyes in death still begging raised,*
> *And hands beseeching thrown.*

Regardless of whether this picture is real or not, here the author's consciousness intersects with the external objects to form a display of life style. It allows readers to feel the moment of personal experience. It is not only the demeanor shown by the author's personal respect for life, but also the demeanor that readers understand through the totem of the image. The author continues to use anthropomorphic techniques to describe the fear of death, which not only highlighted the sequelae of injuries caused by improper fighting, but even made the Lord of all things sigh. Therefore, it is very important to be awake. This

格在她身上產生了創作的動力，是偏於幽默性的舒緩愉悅的
審美風格，非常自然又意趣橫生。

　　接著，〈如果我能使一顆心免於破碎…〉這首詩在平凡之
中鋪陳出不凡的喻意，浪漫的筆調，能喚起情感的亮度：

> 如果我能使一顆心免於破碎，
> 我便沒白活；
> 如果我能使一個生命少受點罪，
> 或緩和一點痛苦，
> 或幫助一隻昏迷的知更鳥
> 再度回到他的窩，
> 我便沒白活。

　　成年的狄金森羞於表現自己的幻想，並且也向其他人隱瞞
自己的幻想。她常運用自己的奇異感去凝視這普通又多情的
世界，賦予簡單的生活中醇厚的詩味。在這首詩裡，視覺已
鋪墊了愛戀的氛圍，充分展現了詩作的自由性與聯想力。一
方面，作者表達出她對愛情孤獨的悲嘆，一方面道出她所關
心的是對人類的愛、自然的愛，鮮活地刻劃出作者心境的變
化。再由知更鳥的「昏迷」與作者的呵護回「窩」串聯的意
象，化靜為動，更添一種詩的興味。其詩心的靈巧，令人咀
嚼。

sarcastic style has inspired her to create. It is a soothing and pleasant aesthetic style that is biased towards humor, which is very natural and interesting.

Then, *If I Can Stop One Heart from Breaking*... the poem lays out the extraordinary in the ordinary, romantic in tone, and able to evoke emotional brightness:

If I can stop one heart from breaking,
I shall not live in vain;
If I can ease one life the aching,
Or cool one pain,
Or help one fainting robin
Unto his nest again,
I shall not live in vain.

The adult Dickinson was shy about expressing her fantasies, and also kept them from others. She often uses her sense of strangeness to gaze at this ordinary and passionate world, endowing the simple life with a mellow poetic flavor. In this poem, the vision has paved the way for the atmosphere of love, fully demonstrating the freedom and association of the poem. On the one hand, the author expresses her lament for the loneliness of love, and on the other hand, she expresses that what she cares about is the love for human beings and nature, vividly depicting the changes in the author's mood. Then, the imagery connected by the robin's "coma" and the author's care and return to the "nest" turns static into dynamic, adding a poetic interest. The dexterity of its poetic heart is chewing.

最後介紹這首〈有某種斜光。。。〉，羅織出作者心靈圖象，意味深長：

> 有某種斜光 ，
> 在冬日午後 ，
> 壓迫 ，如教堂曲調般
> 沉重。
>
> 它給了我們天大的斲害；
> 我們找不到傷痕 ，
> 除了內部的差異
> 標示意義所在。
>
> 沒有東西能教給它什麼 ，
> 它是封緘 ，絕望 ，——
> 一個龐大的痛苦
> 由天而降。
>
> 當它來到 ，山水傾聽 ，
> 陰影屏息；
> 當它離去 ，就如死亡
> 凝視的距離。

Finally, I will introduce this song *There's a Certain Slant of Light...*, Luo weaves the author's spiritual image, which is meaningful:

There's a certain slant of light,
On winter afternoons,
That oppresses, like the weight
Of cathedral tunes.

Heavenly hurt it gives us;
We can find no scar,
But internal difference
Where the meanings are.

None may teach it anything,
'T is the seal, despair, —
An imperial affliction
Sent us of the air.

When it comes, the landscape listens,
Shadows hold their breath;
When it goes, 't is like the distance
On the look of death.

詩中，作者所流露的孤獨與感傷有別於其他浪漫派詩人，她解釋愛情與失去間如何妥協，理出她對自然界特殊的敏覺與感性。詩人面對坎坷人生的智慧，讓我們瞭解到，希望中的快樂是比實際享受快樂更有福的。此詩暗喻作者勇於孤寂的生活時心中的悲嘆，而人生到處是死亡、變化的意象，亦充滿著內心情感的寄盼。其實，愛情是一種等待的時間越長久，在記憶中的痕跡就越活躍和清晰的莫名思緒。當我們在她詩歌意象的聯想中流連時，就能喚起了我們的期待。

三、孤獨的精神：艾米莉·狄金森

無疑，對一個詩人來說，憂鬱是很自然的。狄金森對藝術美學的感知，源自於求學期間的汲取及天賦的智能。當她用豐富的想像力喚醒自我靈魂的時候，在那裡精神也獲得了生命。誠然，生命是短促的，然而在她孤獨的靈魂裡頭，深藏著美好的精華，也有一顆勇敢的心靈。儘管當時外界批評之語有些混亂，她還是帶著一種清新、平和的心情醒過來了。她的智慧越是遮掩，越是明亮；其無言的純樸所煥發出的情感，是純真的，也是詩歌藝術最大的遺產之一。

事實上，狄金森對世間萬物的一切，從未棄擲，她創作時的思考重點已經轉移到新近獲得智慧的意識之流，正義與真

In the poem, the loneliness and sentimentality expressed by the author are different from other romantic poets. She explains how to compromise between love and loss, and sorts out her special sensitivity and sensibility to the natural world. The poet's wisdom in facing the ups and downs of life allows us to understand that the happiness in hope is more blessed than the actual enjoyment of happiness. This poem is a metaphor for the lament in the author's heart when he bravely lives a lonely life. Life is full of images of death and change, and it is also full of inner emotional hope. In fact, love is an inexplicable thought that the longer you wait, the more active and clear the traces in memory will be. As we linger in associations of her poetic imagery, it arouses our anticipation.

3. The Spirit of Solitude: Emily Dickinson

Doubtless melancholy is natural to a poet. Dickinson's perception of artistic aesthetics comes from her learning and innate intelligence during her studies. When she awakens her own soul with her rich imagination, the spirit also gains life there. It is true that life is short, but in her lonely soul, there is a beautiful essence and a brave heart. Despite the confusion of the criticism from the outside world at the time, she woke up with a fresh and peaceful mood. The more veiled her wit is, the brighter it is; and the emotion radiated by its unspoken simplicity is that of innocence and one of the greatest legacies of the art of poetry.

In fact, Dickinson has never abandoned everything in the world. The focus of her thinking has shifted to the

理才是她高尚人格的真實標誌。當她在隱居中，仍保持最純潔的德性，以避開外界的誹謗之音。狄金森成功地讓感情屈服於創作上的支配並且發揮詩歌的自由表達。在她的潛意識中，她仍然被帶有自閉或自卑心結的色彩的批評眼光繫在她的身上。對此，一個感情的動機導致她寫下了這些日記，它使得那些詩歌的背景的意義清晰了。也唯有透過她遺留的秘密日記的進一步探討，或可瞭解她孤獨的精神的可能性變為確定性。但這並不是試著從她的微小弱點或個性的孤僻出發，來解答她的精神生活中的問題。

　　狄金森童年時生長在優渥的家庭，既聰明又清純。她的父親為名律師及議員，但將其興趣都投注到他的事業上，且偏愛於狄金森的哥哥奧斯汀。由於家庭因素，她在少女時代就必須照料生病的母親；長期的不安與父母兄妹間的關係變得敏感而疏離。因此，在她心靈投下了痛苦的陰影。加以 25 歲時，她暗戀著一位有婦之夫的牧師。雖未有結果，然而此痛苦經歷，招致周遭眾人對她的不解與誤會。在精神打擊下，遂而選擇遠離生活，遠離人群。她對外界的記憶變成深沉的

stream of newly acquired wisdom in her creation. Justice and truth are the true symbols of her noble personality. When she is in seclusion, she still maintains the purest virtues to avoid the slander of the outside world. Dickinson succeeds in subjugating emotion to creative domination and exploiting poetic freedom. In her subconsciousness, she still has a critical eye attached to her that may tinge with autism or an inferiority complex. For this, an emotional motive led her to write these diaries, which make clear the meaning of the background of those poems. Only through further exploration of the secret diary she left behind, the possibility of understanding her lonely spirit becomes certain. But this is not an attempt to answer questions about her spiritual life in terms of her minor weaknesses or eccentricities of personality.

Dickinson grew up in a wealthy family when she was a child, and she was both smart and pure. Her father was a lawyer and a member of Parliament, but she devoted her interests to her career, favoring Dickinson's older brother Austin. Due to family factors, she had to take care of her sick mother when she was a girl; the long-term anxiety and the relationship between parents and siblings became sensitive and alienated. Thus cast a shadow of pain upon her soul. When Jia was 25 years old, she had a crush on a married pastor. Although there was no result, this painful experience led to confusion and misunderstanding from the people around her. Under the mental blow, she chose to stay away from life and the crowd. Her memory of the

遺忘，但她似乎也明白，當她被壓抑的情感復甦時，詩歌就在壓抑力量中誕生了。

以心理學論，人類在心理生活中，唯一有價值的是感情。因此，一首詩的力量如不具有喚起情感的特徵，那麼它就無任何意義了。狄金森生前在詩歌的舞臺上，並不是一個悲劇的英雄；其創作的目的，是為了通過需要有精神痛苦的環境來認識精神痛苦，而企圖完成靈魂的自我救贖的。人生其實不複雜，也沒有任何規則；它只是一場追尋，凡事都有可能沒有人會永遠完美的。狄金森在人格的一二缺陷，也無法掩蓋住她的全部優點。上天是公正的，在她逝世後，她唯一留給世人的一張照片，是端莊又素靜的容貌，隱藏在她詩一般的微笑下，她的詩歌的美卻隨著時間而變得更有價值。或許，正是這個不尋常的有獨特魅力的神秘步態，引起了詩界的興趣。我彷彿看到一個淡淡的影子、自覺地生活，消失在湖畔盡頭，而雕像捕捉的正是她沉碧如湖的眼睛，正靜靜地坐在那兒的姿態。以上似乎是筆者從非馬博士對狄金森翻譯的詩

outside world has become a deep oblivion, but she also seems to understand that when her repressed emotions are revived, poetry is born in the repressed power.

According to psychology, in the psychological life of human beings, the only value is emotion. A poem, therefore, would be meaningless if its force were not to be characterized as evocative. Dickinson was not a tragic hero on the stage of poetry during his lifetime; the purpose of his creation was to realize the spiritual pain through the environment of mental pain, and attempt to complete the self-salvation of the soul. Life is not complicated, and there are no rules; it is just a quest, everything is possible, and no one is perfect forever. Dickinson's one or two flaws in personality cannot cover up all her strengths. God is just. After her death, the only photo she left to the world is a dignified and quiet appearance, hidden under her poetic smile, but the beauty of her poetry has become more and more beautiful with time, and more valuable. Perhaps it is this unusual and mysterious gait with unique charm that has aroused the interest of the poetic world. I seem to see a faint shadow, living consciously, disappearing at the end of the lake, and what the statue captures are her eyes as deep as the lake, and she is sitting there quietly. The above seems to be an insufficient but bold conclusion drawn by the author from Dr. William Marr's translation of Dick

歌資料中得出一個不夠充分、卻很大膽的結論。但我深信，
研究狄金森的意義會隨著我們繼續深入的研究而增加。

> 註・《讓盛宴開始---我喜愛的英文詩 Let the Feast
> Begin 》，英漢對照，非馬編譯,書林出版社，1999
> 年 6 月一版。

－ 2010.10.13 作

－湖北省武漢市華中師範大學文學院主辦《世界文學
評論》／《外國文學研究》〈AHCI 期刊〉榮譽出
品，2011 年 05 月，第一輯〈總第 11 輯〉，頁 76-78。

inson's poetry materials. But I firmly believe that the significance of studying Dickinson will increase as we continue to study in depth.

Note ‧ Let the Feast Begin — My Favorite English Poems, bilingual in English and Chinese, compiled by Dr. William Marr, Shulin Publishing House, June 1999 edition.

2. 愛倫·坡的詩化人生

摘要：埃德加·愛倫·坡由於在世界文學中占有獨特的地位，其詩歌運用的語言和比喻十分巧妙。他用心血培育出一株柯椏枝葉都長得恰到好處的詩美之樹，迄今仍在陽光雨露下滋長；其不朽的生命力，也正是他詩意人生的寫照。本文試從幾首翻譯的詩歌中，嘗試對愛倫·坡的生命詩學進行探索。

關鍵詞：埃德加·愛倫·坡，詩人，浪漫主義，象徵主義

詩人側影

埃德加·愛倫·坡（Edgar Allan Poe，1809-1849）生於美國波士頓，是一位天才的悲劇詩人、文學評論家；他的生命並不長，只活了 40 歲。四歲時，即失去父親，由親戚撫養，曾在維吉尼亞大學短暫就讀。因與養父的關係不合，遂而離家謀生；從事軍職後，就離開了養父母。他一生儘管失意潦倒、為酗酒所折磨，詩歌也不算多，只發表了大約五十首；但因其文才橫溢，從二十世紀初，愛倫·坡在世界文學中的地位才被重新評價。愛爾蘭詩人葉慈〈William Butler Yeats，1865-1939〉曾把愛倫坡譽為「美國最偉大的詩人」，法國象徵派詩歌先驅波德萊爾（Charles Pierre Baudelaire，1821－

2. Edgar Allan Poe's Poetic Life

Abstract: Edgar Allan Poe occupies a unique place in world literature. His poetic use of language and metaphor is very artful. His efforts fostered a tree of poetry which has a perfect look and is still growing. The enduring vitality of the tree is also the portrayal of his poetic life. This article tries to explore Allan Poe's life poetics from some of his translated poems.

Key: words: Edgar Allan Poe, poet, Romanticism, Symbolism

Silhouette of the Poet

Edgar Allan Poe (1809-1849) was born in Boston, USA. As a talented tragic poet and literary critic, his life was not long, only 40 years old. At the age of four, he has lost his father and was raised by his relatives. He studied briefly at the University of Virginia. Because of a disagreement with his adoptive father, he left home to make a living. Afflicted by alcoholism, there were not many poems, and only about fifty poems were published; but owing to his literary talent, Edgar Allan Poe's status in world literature was re-evaluated from the beginning of the twentieth century. Irish poet Yeats William Butler Yeats (1865-1939) once praised Poe as "the greatest American poet", and Charles Pierre Baudelaire (1821-1867), the

1867）還翻譯了愛倫·坡的《怪異故事集》和《怪異故事續集》。英國重要詩人斯溫伯恩（Algernon Charles Swinburne，1837-1909），愛爾蘭劇作家蕭伯納（George Bernard Shaw，1856 年—1950 年）及美國推理小說作家勞倫斯·布拉克〈Lawrence Block，1938-〉等也給予高度的評價；二次大戰後，其作品更是風靡歐洲和拉丁美洲，被稱譽為唯美主義文學的先驅、象徵主義的鼻祖之一、偵探小說和幻想小說的開拓者，尤以詩歌倍受推崇。

　　所謂哥特式文學〈Gothic Literature〉，係盛行於 18、19 世紀的西方世界，旨在描摹發生於「神秘」與「恐怖」氛圍中的傳奇經歷。而愛倫·坡的短篇小說隱有著哥特式的寫作風格——推理、夢幻、神秘、驚悚，其詩作也有哥特元素的神奇色彩——超自然、死亡、頹廢和黑暗。後來愛倫·坡自費出版詩集後，隨即昂然奮起，開始了他創作的生涯，寫下了著名的詩篇。1845 年 1 月，愛倫·坡發表了名詩《烏鴉》，二年後其妻死於肺癆；四年後他就逝於巴爾的摩。愛倫·坡生前作品除了影響於宇宙學、密碼學等科學領域，也常現於文學、音樂、影視等流行文化中；亦擅長於死亡驚悚、推理偵探、科幻和幽默諷刺等四種小說，約莫寫了將近 70 篇。他用心血培育出一株柯椏枝葉都長得恰到好處的詩美之樹，迄今仍在陽光雨露下滋長；其不朽的生命力，也正是他詩意人生的寫照。本文試從幾首翻譯的詩歌中，嘗試對愛倫·坡的生命詩學進行探索。

pioneer of French symbolist poetry, also translated Poe's "Strange Tales" and "Strange Stories Sequel". Important British poet Algernon Charles Swinburne (1837-1909), Irish playwright George Bernard Shaw (1856-1950) and American mystery writer Lawrence Braque (1938-) etc., all gave him high praises; after World War II, his works became more popular in Europe and Latin America, known as the pioneer of aestheticism literature, one of the originators of symbolism, detective novels and fantasy novels. He is especially respected for his poetry.

The so-called Gothic Literature was popular in the Western world in the 18th and 19th centuries, aiming to depict legendary experiences that took place in an atmosphere of "mystery" and "horror". And Poe's short stories have Gothic writing style — reasoning, dream, mystery, thriller, and his poems also have the magical color of Gothic elements — supernatural, death, decadence and darkness. Later, after Edgar Allan Poe published his collection of poems at his own expense, he immediately rose up and started his creative career, writing famous poems. In January 1845, Edgar Allan Poe published the famous poem *The Raven*. Two years later, his wife died of tuberculosis; four years later, he died in Baltimore. Edgar Allan Poe's works during his lifetime not only influenced scientific fields such as cosmology and cryptography, but also often appeared in popular culture such as literature, music, film and television. He wrote about 70 articles. With his painstaking efforts, he cultivated a tree of poetic beauty with its branches and leaves growing just right, and it is still growing under the sun and rain; its immortal vitality is also a portrayal of his poetic life. This article attempts to explore Poe's life poetics from several translated poems.

愛倫·坡的詩藝主張

　　愛倫·坡曾提出過在詩歌中只有創造美——超凡絕塵的美才是引起樂趣的正當途徑的主張。即是要求自己詩歌創作的原則是音樂感和憂鬱美，力求視覺和聽覺、節奏和音韻、想像和情感間的和諧統一，以造成獨特的審美感受。而他所主張「爲藝術而藝術」，及聲稱「一切藝術的目的是娛樂，不是真理。」凡此種種想法，皆是愛倫坡在詩歌創作達到成熟期的經驗之談；也引發了一波「純藝術」、「純詩歌」的風潮。事實上，詩歌從來不是愛倫·坡自己官感的享受，反而是他本人真實的生活中，包括情感、夢想這些超官感的寫照。他的詩歌是自己心靈的獨白，並以美爲其靈魂的震顫。愛倫·坡在捕捉詩歌的靈感時，不僅僅侷限於一種特殊的音樂美或憂鬱美，或是視覺與聽覺的感受；而是通過一種現實和超感覺的純粹主觀思維的過程，用全心靈的觀照，從而把詩美體現出來，達到「純粹美」的境界。

　　在愛倫·坡的詩學理論中，他把詩歌的創作形容爲一個精確的「數學過程」，並且始終遵循著「令心靈顫動」的美學原則。他曾表示，詩歌的最好主題是死亡，尤其是年輕美女的死亡，將是世界上最具詩意的主題，因爲美麗與死亡是密切相關的。在他各個不同的作品中，尤以詩歌藝術最能激活讀者的審美感情；因為其詩歌富於韻律美，是時空藝術的綜合；他始終認為，美是詩的唯一正統的領域，而這種美是「一種效果」，即在作品的「刺激」下，「靈魂昇華」的效果。

Edgar Allan Poe's Poetry

Edgar Allan Poe once argued that in poetry only the creation of beauty — beauty beyond the ordinary — is the only legitimate path to pleasure. That is to say, the principle of my own poetry creation is the sense of music and the beauty of melancholy, and efforts shall be made for the harmony and unity between vision and hearing, rhythm and rhyme, imagination and emotion, so as to create a unique aesthetic feeling. And he advocated "art for art's sake" and claimed that "the purpose of all art is entertainment, not truth." All these ideas are all Poe's experience in poetry creation when he reached a mature stage; the trend of "pure art" and "pure poetry". In fact, poetry has never been the enjoyment of Poe's own senses, but rather a portrayal of his real life, including emotions and dreams. His poems are the monologues of his own soul, and beauty is the vibration of his soul. When Edgar Allan Poe captures the inspiration of poetry, he is not limited to a special musical beauty or melancholy beauty, or visual and auditory feelings; in order to reflect the beauty of poetry and achieve the realm of "pure beauty".

In Edgar Allan Poe's poetics theory, he described the creation of poetry as a precise "mathematical process" and always followed the aesthetic principle of "making the soul vibrate". He once said that the best theme of poetry is death, especially the death of young beauties, which will be the most poetic theme in the world, because beauty and death are closely related. Among his different works, the art of poetry is the most able to activate readers' aesthetic feelings; because his poetry is full of rhythmic beauty and is a synthesis of time and space art; he always believes that beauty is the only orthodox field of poetry, and this kind of Beauty is "an effect", that is, the effect of "soul sublimation" under the "stimulation" of the work. In other

或者說，「一首詩必須刺激，才配稱作一首詩」；也曾說，美，應該通過傷感的手段來體現的。為此，愛倫·坡的詩歌色彩偏向於浪漫、鬱暗的，他常表達出對愛情幻想的追求而不可得的傷感或死亡的淒愴。因為，世上沒有一種悲哀比起自己真心的愛人死去那時候更使人心碎了，所以，愛倫·坡設想自己沉重的心，卻也生出了翼翅。

比如，The Raven 這首《烏鴉》，詩人於 1845 年首次發表，全詩共 108 行，雖然在其《創作的藝術》書中曾說過，此詩內容是純屬虛構的，但仍被認為是愛倫·坡詩歌的代表作。詩裡含蘊兩個重要形象：年輕男子與烏鴉。詩人用超感官的靈視，使整首詩的基調是傷感的，並藉由象徵和隱喻的手法來沖淡他對死去愛人的悲痛。或者說，愛倫·坡在感情上並不是一帆風順的，此詩卻已傳遞出他想像與愛人的重逢與懷戀之情；即使想追隨烏鴉，這象徵不祥之鳥的黑暗使者，跟著愛人到冥河深處，但現實中外力的阻礙，使詩人絕望地意識到，只是痛苦的回憶是格外長的。那愛人的身影比天風還輕，更輕，怕是永遠追尋不到的。這首經典處在於使讀者也陷入詩人的幾近崩潰的沉哀氣圍中，詩人在此低沉的原音中所產生的悲涼之感與自我折磨是渲染到高點了。

愛倫·坡對自己妻子的愛也是無可厚非的，因而在她死後，也寫了一首力作 Annabel Lee《安娜貝爾·李》，並發表於 1844 年 10 月 9 日，這首詩通常被認定是詩人的最後遺作，因為是在愛倫·坡逝世後的第三天才公諸於世。內容多以一種象徵和暗示，表達了對自己愛情故事的追緬與不願相信愛妻

words, "a poem must be stimulating to be called a poem"; it was also said that beauty should be expressed through sentimental means. For this reason, Edgar Allan Poe's poetry tends to be romantic and gloomy, and he often expresses the unattainable sadness of pursuing the fantasy of love or the sadness of death. Because there is no sorrow in the world that breaks the heart more than the death of a true love, so Edgar Allan Poe imagined that his heavy heart also sprouted wings.

For example, The Raven's *The Raven*, which the poet first published in 1845, has 108 lines in total. Although he said in his book *The Art of Creation* that the content of this poem is purely fictional, it is still considered as a representative work of Edgar Allan Poe. There are two important images in the poem: the young man and the crow. The poet uses supersensory vision to make the tone of the whole poem sad, and uses symbols and metaphors to dilute his grief for his dead lover. In other words, Edgar Allan Poe was not all smooth sailing emotionally, but this poem has conveyed the reunion and nostalgia he imagined with his lover; even if he wants to follow the crow, the dark messenger that symbolizes the ominous bird, to follow his lover to hell. The depths of the river, but the obstacles of external forces in reality, make the poet realize desperately, but the painful memories are extraordinarily long. That lover's figure is lighter and lighter than Tianfeng, and I'm afraid I will never be able to find it. This classic is to make readers fall into the poet's almost collapsed mournful atmosphere, and the poet's sense of desolation and self-torture in this low original sound are exaggerated to a high point.

Edgar Allan Poe's love for his wife is also understandable, so after her death, he also wrote a masterpiece *Annabel Lee* and published it on October 9, 1844. This poem is usually regarded as the poet's last posthumous work, because it was not made public until the third day after the death of Edgar Allan Poe. The content mostly uses a kind of symbol and hint to express the memory of one's own love story, the melancholy of no wanting

已死的惆悵，最後在墓前發誓的癡情，使人感受到愛情崇高而深遠的美感。

譯詩選讀

時至今日，海內外仍不乏翻譯愛倫·坡詩歌的愛好者；數以千計的作家或學者為他著書，研究論文更是不勝枚舉。其中，吳鈞〈註 1〉教學外，勤於詩歌翻譯等研究；對愛倫·坡的詩歌翻譯之筆輕靈、俊逸，獨樹一幟。比如這首《十四行詩－－致科學》，詩句情象的流動，技巧繁富：

科學！你是漫長古遠歷史的真正兒女，
你那細審一切的目光改變著萬物，
你那乏味的現實如兀鷹的雙翼，
怎教詩人愛你，欣賞你的才智？
你不會任我去漫遊遐思，
到那鑲滿寶石的夜空去尋求珍奇，
儘管詩魂無畏地展翅翱翔，
你還是把狄安娜從她的月車中拽出，
把海墨諸德從樹叢中拖向
更幸福的星球去尋找歸宿。
你也曾把娜愛達從洪峰頂上扯下，
將綠草叢中的小精靈驅逐，
且把我從羅望子樹蔭中
沉沉的酣睡中驚醒。

to believe that the beloved wife is dead, and the infatuation of swearing in front of the grave at the end, which makes people feel the lofty and profound beauty of love.

Selected Readings of Translated Poems

Today, there are still many lovers of Poe translation at home and abroad; thousands of writers or scholars have written books for him, and there are too many research papers. Among them, Wu Jun <Note 1> is diligent in poetry translation research besides her teaching; she is unique in her translation of Edgar Allan Poe's poetry with lightness and elegance. For example, this *Sonnet — To Science*, the flow of emotion and imagery in the poem is rich in skills:

> science! You are true sons and daughters of long and
>   ancient history,
> Your scrutinizing gaze changes all things,
> Your dull reality is like the wings of a vulture,
> How to teach poets to love you and appreciate your intelligence?
> You won't let me wander in reverie,
> To the gem-studded night sky to seek the rare,
> Although the soul of poetry soars fearlessly,
> You still drag Diana out of her moon chariot,
> dragged Haimo Zhude from the bushes to
> A happier planet to find a destination.
> You also tore Naida from the top of the flood peak,
> To expel the elf in the green grass,
> And save me from the shade of the tamarind tree
> Waking up from a deep sleep.

　　愛倫·坡的這首十四行詩，韻律優美、科學形象的比喻十分巧妙，這和他豐富的想像力特徵概括無遺，令人感覺到詩歌可以像繪畫、音樂般無國界限制而能流通於世的魅力。詩句一開始，相當經典的呈現了科學是「漫長古遠歷史的真正兒女」與「那細審一切的目光改變著萬物」的視覺性相當突出，表達抽象浪漫〈Romance〉的情思，絕非工筆可素描的。然後再滿涵深意地營造出科學「那乏味的現實如兀鷹的雙翼」，這正是詩人對於他所生存的真實空間的感知與領受；亦或對自然的厚賜與人文交織所觀照的世界用情至深。

　　題旨暗喻詩人的心理動向是渴望大自然的清新與生活的幽靜，不巧，讓科學的發展如兀鷹的出現，驚擾了其周遭環境安寧而造成一種「龐雜的感受」的心情。之後，詩人開始不悅又忍不住俏皮地責怪它，科學絕對「不會任我去漫遊遐思」，讓愛倫·坡想「到那鑲滿寶石的夜空去尋求珍奇」；儘管詩海浩瀚無窮，但還是抵不住科學的實事求是精神，因而就連月亮女神狄安娜、樹神海墨諸德、水仙娜愛達及草叢中的小精靈都因科學的廣泛普遍意識而被逐出了靜謐的家園。在最後兩行詩句裡，詩人想像自己正在羅望子樹蔭中酣睡，大做科學與人文的論辯之夢，却被「科學」——這振翼飛來的巨鷹從文學浪漫的遐思中拖回到現實世界。全詩比喻生動豐富是其突出的特點，且已構築了詩人一個獨立自主的第三自然的精神世界。

　　另一首《致一位在天堂者》，也是難得的佳作：

This sonnet of Edgar Allan Poe has beautiful rhythm and clever metaphors of scientific images, which can be summed up with his rich imagination. It makes people feel that poetry can be circulated in the world without borders like painting and music. At the beginning of the verse, it is quite classic to present that science is "the true son and daughter of the long and ancient history" and "the eyes that scrutinize everything change everything". And then to create a scientific stuff "that boring reality like the wings of a vulture" full of meaning, which is exactly the poet's perception and understanding of the real space in which he lives; or the interweaving of nature and humanity The world is deeply affectionate.

The title implies that the poet's psychological trend is longing for the freshness of nature and the tranquility of life. Unfortunately, the development of science is like the appearance of vultures, which disturbs the tranquility of his surrounding environment and creates a "complex feeling" mood. Afterwards, the poet became displeased and couldn't help but blame it playfully. Science would never let me wander in my reveries, making Edgar Allan Poe think of "going to the jewel-studded night sky to seek rare things"; although the sea of poetry is vast and infinite, still it cannot resist the spirit of seeking truth from facts, so even the moon goddess Diana, the tree god Haimozhude, Narcissus Naida and the elves in the grass are driven out of the quiet because of the broad and general consciousness of science. In the last two lines of verses, the poet imagines that he is sleeping soundly in the shade of a tamarind tree, dreaming of debates about science and humanities, but is dragged away from his literary and romantic reverie by "science" — the giant eagle flying over with wings , back to the real world. The vivid and rich metaphors in the whole poem are its outstanding features, and have built an independent spiritual world of the third nature of the poet.

Another song *To a Man in Heaven* is also a rare masterpiece:

獻上我所有的愛，
我的心靈之所望，
你如那蒼茫大海中一綠洲，
似那清澈的噴泉與聖堂，
用碩果鮮花將你覆蓋，
我奉上所有的芳香。
啊！迷夢太美好而消逝！
正道是夜璀燦，却已烏雲密布！
來自未來的聲音在呼喚，
"來吧！來吧！"—却聲聲迴盪在過去。
（陰暗的深淵）徬徨、沉寂、木然、恐懼！
啊！我的生命之光已經逝去，
再不會—再不會—再不會—
（這樣悲怨的呼喊掀起拍擊沙岸的憂鬱的海浪）
被雷擊的樹再不會花朵綻開，
受傷的鷹再不能展翅雲端。
沉沉昏睡於白晝，
跚跚漫步於夜夢，
充滿你閃亮的黑眼睛，
響徹你匆匆的腳步聲，
融化在你如仙的歌舞中，
追隨你永恒的溪流。

　　此詩據說是愛倫·坡爲他青年時代的戀人羅絲小姐而寫
的，在 1845 年收集成詩冊之前，他將自己喜愛的這首輓歌，

give all my love,
the desire of my heart,
You are like an oasis in the vast sea,
Like clear fountains and sanctuaries,
Cover you with fruit and flowers,
I offer all the fragrances.
what! Dreams are too good to pass away!
The righteous way is bright at night, but it is
　　already covered with dark clouds!
A voice from the future is calling,
"Come on! Come on!"—but the voice echoed in the past.
(Dark abyss) Hesitation, silence, numbness, fear!
what! The light of my life is gone,
never again — never again — never again —
(Such mournful cries set off melancholy waves that
　　beat on the sandy shore)
The tree struck by lightning will no longer bloom,
A wounded eagle can no longer spread its
　　wingstothe clouds.
deep in sleep in the day,
Staggering through night dreams,
Fill your shining black eyes,
Resounding through the sound of your hasty
　　footsteps,
Melted in your fairy song and dance,
Follow your eternal stream.

The poem is said to have been written by Poe for his youthful lover, Miss Rose, and he published his favorite elegy in six different editions before collecting it in a volume in 1845. The whole poem is divided into four

發表在六種不同的版本中。全詩分四段，愛倫·坡以「綠洲」生動地比喻出自己的蒼茫；以「噴泉與聖堂」來安慰戀人是在天上；以「碩果鮮花」覆蓋塵間所有喧聲讓亡靈得以庇護；以他所有的愛獻以詩的「芳香」。至此，愛倫·坡的憂傷全然是自己獨有的，當言語的風兒輕輕吹動時；他的愁人之眼總是像他的愛一樣，留下悲痛的餘音在空中顫動。

　　接著，在第二段裡，詩人的悲觀是基於現實，他以「迷夢太美好」道盡了期待魂夢一見的百般無奈與幻滅；以原是璀燦的夜，心中卻已「烏雲密布」來直接投訴於視覺性的象徵。那希望與美好的期盼戀人的回聲，亦圍繞於讀者糾葛的心靈：那陰暗的深淵處，是否也跟詩人一樣流著「徬徨、沉寂、木然、恐懼」之淚，亦或真愛的召喚聲？第三段，詩人進而悲怨地發出「再不會 —— 再不會 —— 再不會 —— 」的哀鳴，讓詩的建築特性有了強音。再自喻為「被雷擊的樹」，再不想有愛情的奇垛；一如「受傷的鷹」，再不能展翅於長空，逝愛之痛也表現得十分貼切傳神。末段，與其全詩，做了有機的組合。詩人為愛消瘦，長若雪河，他昏睡於白晝，「跚跚漫步於夜夢」，痴心於夢中閃現那唯一的戀人的「黑眼睛」或匆匆的腳步聲；但終歸是南柯一夢，消失在每一夢中的清姿舞影…。此詩擅用重覆與對仗手法，頭韻和中間韻節奏分明，尾韻整齊、音樂性高；能將愛倫·坡詩性智慧與提倡詩歌的象徵、比喻做了完美的展現，是自然地發自內心的謳歌，誰又能對其悲哀一笑置之？

sections. Edgar Allan Poe used "oasis" to vividly describe his own confusion; he used "fountain and sanctuary" to comfort his lovers in heaven; ; with all his love to offer the "fragrance" of poetry. So far Poe's melancholy was all his own, when the wind of words blows gently; and his sad eyes always, like his love, leave an echo of grief quivering in the air.

Then, in the second paragraph, the poet's pessimism is based on reality. He expresses all kinds of helplessness and disillusionment in waiting for the dream to be seen with "dreams are too beautiful"; to complain directly to visual symbols. The echoes of hope and good looking forward to lovers also surround the readers' entangled hearts: whether there are tears of "hesitation, silence, numbness, fear" like the poet in the dark abyss, or the call or voice of true love? In the third paragraph, the poet utters a mournful moan of "never—never—never—", which strengthens the architectural features of the poem. It also refers to itself as a "tree struck by lightning", and no longer wants to have strange piles of love; like a "wounded eagle", it can no longer spread its wings in the sky, and the pain of dying love is also expressed very vividly. The last paragraph, with the whole poem, has been organically combined. The poet is thin because of love, as long as a snow river, he sleeps in the daytime, "staggers and walks in the night dream", obsessed with the "black eyes" or the hurried footsteps of the only lover flashing in the dream; but it is a fond dream, disappearing in the dream, the dancing shadows in every dream... This poem is good at repetition and antithesis, alliteration and middle rhyme with distinct rhythms; the end rhyme is neat, and the music is high; it can perfectly display Edgar Allan Poe's poetic wisdom and the symbols and metaphors that advocate poetry, which is natural praise from the heart, who can laugh at its sorrow?

愛倫·坡詩歌的審美意義

　　通過上述兩首翻譯詩歌的賞讀後，對再深入研究二十一世紀東西方文界對愛倫·坡詩歌的迴響是十分必要的。從詩學原理到創作方法、美學上，愛倫·坡的詩歌已自成體系、風格；他的詩學理論建樹是建立在自己創作的基礎之上，而這也是他對自己內心、精神的微觀世界。雖然有些詩流派稱愛倫·坡為西方頹廢文學的鼻祖；但他的詩歌膾炙人口，他的小說常能引人入勝。至於他的純詩理論，應用在音律美的詩藝上，都有很好的論證，無疑地，也豐富了世界詩歌史的藝術寶庫。

　　愛倫·坡也是個敏感的詩人，作為美國哥特式文學的開拓者，正因其作詩的初衷，不正是要從醜陋、貧困、痛苦、疾病之中發掘詩美，藉以獨特地、完美地顯示自己的精神境界嗎？所以，他的心中有著永恆的理想，不願在命運面前低頭。至於其創作結構之巧妙，當然是含有文學的、美學的意義，也就是藝術。他必須開拓詩美的世界，以顯出自己的獨創性。

　　愛倫·坡深知，一首好詩，得承擔著某種救贖功能，它是神聖的。因而，愛倫·坡在創作過程中有著自己的審美意識。

The Aesthetic Significance of
Edgar Allan Poe's Poems

After appreciating and reading the above two translated poems, it is necessary to further study the echoes of Edgar Allan Poe's poems in the Eastern and Western literary circles in the 21st century. From the principles of poetics to creative methods and aesthetics, Poe's poetry has its own system and style; his poetic theory is based on his own creation, which is also his own heart and spiritual microcosm. Although some schools of poetry call Edgar Allan Poe the originator of Western decadent literature, his poems are popular and his novels are often fascinating. As for his pure poetic theory, it has been well demonstrated when applied to the poetic art of rhythmic beauty, and undoubtedly enriched the art treasure house of the history of world poetry.

Edgar Allan Poe is also a sensitive poet. As the pioneer of American Gothic literature, because of his original intention of writing poems, isn't it just to discover the beauty of poetry from ugliness, poverty, pain, and disease, so as to uniquely and perfectly express the poetic beauty? Show your spiritual realm? Therefore, he has an eternal ideal in his heart, unwilling to bow his head in front of fate. As for the ingenuity of its creative structure, of course it contains literary and aesthetic meanings, that is, art. He must open up the world of poetic beauty in order to show his originality.

Edgar Allan Poe knew that a good poem has to undertake some kind of redemptive function, and it is sacred. Therefore, Poe has his own aesthetic consciousness

在此歸納為三個象徵意義：（一）獨特的美學詩觀：愛倫·坡在詩歌具像與內在情志有同構之處時，擅用象徵與比喻的手法在合理、貼切的同時求新、求奇。他曾說，深深地埋藏在人類靈魂深處的永恒的本能就是對美的感受力；而真正的詩歌是由永恒性的元素構成的美的創造，它使人們竭盡全力去獲得天上的美，而不是眼前的美。他的詩從本質上，常以「不幸」的憂鬱美，追求事物與主體神秘的交感，常關心生與死的問題，意象幽深、抑鬱，帶有神秘或夢幻的色彩，也蘊涵著玄思與感慨。（二）音律美是詩的基本審美單元：他認為詩歌能够喚醒人們對美的認知與崇高和神秘事物的感悟。欣賞愛倫·坡的詩歌，則是端視其音樂性的力度是否與情感的濃烈相一致，還要欣賞其崇高美意象創造中的智慧，從而抵達統一的美好境界。（三）終極追求對死亡的反思與完整人性的呼喚：愛倫·坡的詩歌作用於人的感官層次，極易引起人的情感共鳴。他透過書寫時間來直面死亡，以獲得形而上學的美，或愛的回應和自我反思，這是他在美學表述中以審美救贖人生的積極探索。對我而言，能研究愛倫·坡詩歌的確也展現了一個全新的視野；因為，也讓我瞭解到，把握了詩的意象，才能走進詩人的內心，期在未來有更多的研究者能上下

in the process of creation. It is summarized here as three symbolic meanings: (1) unique aesthetic poetic view: when Edgar Allan Poe's poetry has the same structure as the image and the inner emotion, he is good at using symbols and metaphors in a reasonable and appropriate way. At the same time, to seek novelty and curiosity. He once said that the eternal instinct deeply buried in the human soul is the beauty composed of eternal elements, which makes people try their best to obtain the beauty of heaven, and not the beauty in front of you. In essence, his poems often use the melancholic beauty of "unfortunate", pursue the mysterious sympathy between things and the subject, and are often concerned with the issues of life and death with emotion. (2) The beauty of rhythm is the basic aesthetic unit of poetry: he believes that poetry can awaken people's awareness of beauty and the perception of lofty and mysterious things. To appreciate Edgar Allan Poe's poems is to see whether the strength of music is consistent with the intensity of emotion, and also to appreciate the wisdom in the creation of his sublime and beautiful images, so as to reach the beautiful state of unity. (3) The ultimate pursuit of reflection on death and the call for complete humanity: Poe's poems act on people's sensory level, and can easily arouse people's emotional resonance. He confronts death by writing time to obtain metaphysical beauty, or the response of love and self-reflection. This is his active exploration in aesthetic expression to redeem life through aesthetics. For me, being able to study Edgar Allan Poe's poems has indeed shown a new perspective; because it also made me understand that only by grasping the imagery of the poem can we enter the poet's heart. It is hoped that more research be made in the future, so readers can search

求索和理解愛倫·坡的思想性和藝術性。

　　　　註 1. 吳鈞，文學博士，現任中國山東大學外國語學
　　　　　院教授，碩士生導師，中國翻譯協會專家會員。

　　　　作者林明理 1961 年生，女，台灣雲林縣人，法學碩士，
　　　　　曾任臺灣省立屏東師範大學講師，現任中國文藝協
　　　　　會理事。

　　　　--2012.2.12 作

　　　　──寧夏省《寧夏師範學院學報》，2012.第 02 期，第
　　　　　33 卷，總第 160 期，頁 27-30。

up and down to understand Poe's thought and artistry.

Note 1. Wu Jun, Ph.D., is currently professor at the College of Foreign Languages, Shandong University, a master supervisor, and an expert member of the Translators' Association of China.

Author: A poetess and a critic, Lin Mingli, the author of this book, was born in Yunlin county of Taiwan province in 1961. She got received her LLM in 19xx and was a lecturer in Pingdong Normal University of Taiwan Province.

February 12, 2012

3. 一隻慨然高歌的靈鳥
—讀普希金詩

摘要：普希金以詩真實地反映內心的深沉思想及豐沛感情與當年俄國社會背景嚴酷的真實境遇；作品無不至情至性，深具魅力。其中蘊含的溫柔、豐盛與美好，正如他自己流星般燦爛卻短暫的一生，給予人無限遐思；也表達了他深信光明必勝黑暗，人類的博愛必能戰勝奴役和壓迫的反抗精神和崇尚自由的詩意生活。

關鍵詞：普希金，詩人，俄羅斯，詩歌

傳　略

　　普希金〈Aleksandr Pushkin 1799-1837〉是享譽世界的俄國詩人、最偉大的文豪。1799 年生於莫斯科一個富有詩文修養的貴族家庭，八歲即能以法文寫詩，十五歲寫下詩歌〈沙皇村回憶〉，清新雋永，展現他非凡的天賦，獲老詩人德札文〈Gavriil Romanovic Derzavin, 1743-1816〉激賞。1817 年畢業後入外交部任職，開始與十二月黨人（註 1）文藝圈接近；當時因俄國民族意識高漲，遂而寫了多首政治抒情詩，

3. A Soul Bird Sings With Deep Feeling
— Reading Alexander Pushkin's Poetry

Abstract: Pushkin used his poems not only to reflect his deep thought and rich feeling, but also to portrait the cruel reality of the Russian society of his time. With great sincerity and compassion, his works are full of artistic charm. Just like his brilliant yet short life like a shooting star, the gentleness, richness and goodness imbedded in his works captivated the imagination of the readers. His works also expressed his firm belief that light would conquer darkness, and that universal love would overcome enslavement and oppression, leading to a poetic life of freedom.

Key words: Pushkin, poet, Russia, poetry

Biography

Aleksandr Pushkin (1799-1837) is a world-renowned Russian poet and the greatest writer. Born in a noble family in Moscow in 1799, he was able to write poems in French at the age of eight. At the age of fifteen, he wrote the poem *Memories of Tsarist Village*. Romanovic Derzavin, 1743-1816 Excellent award. After graduating in 1817, he worked in the Ministry of Foreign Affairs, and began to get close to the literary and artistic circles of the Decembrists〔Note 1〕. At that time, because of the high national consciousness in Russia, he wrote many political

如〈致查阿達耶夫〉（1818）、〈自由頌〉（1817）等，是貴族革命運動在文學上的反映。不料，在 1820 年，竟因此遭到遠調南俄。然而，高加索 Caucasus 與克里米亞 Crimean 的美麗而寧靜的山水景物與豪邁風情，卻引起了普希金崇仰自由的情感，在那裡生活了四年，也完成多首長篇敘事詩、戲劇及讚美了純潔的愛情詩和美妙的大自然。

　　1824 年，普希金在南方期間，因愛上敖德塞 Odessa 總督沃隆佐夫之美貌的妻子伊莉莎白，與總督發生衝突，又被沙皇革職，轉而幽禁於其父親領地米哈夫斯特村兩年。由於幽禁地係普希金童年故鄉，那裡樸實的鄉村生活，促使他的心境趨於沉穩並專於寫作。他開始接近勞動人民，也搜集民歌、格言、諺語，開啟了研究俄國歷史的機遇。這期間他留下許多豐富成果。包括抒情詩、童話詩、敘事詩及 1825 年寫下著名的歷史劇《鮑里斯‧戈杜諾夫》〈俄語：Борис Годунов〉，它取材於十六世紀末至十七世紀初俄國歷史上的真實事件。還有長篇詩體小說《葉甫蓋尼‧奧涅金》是普希金整整用了八年時間完成的重要作品，其筆下的奧涅金厭惡上流社會的虛偽生活，可又無自己的生活目標，這個形象恰好表現了當時俄國進步的貴族青年思想上的鬱悶；因詩體音韻輕巧、優美，被名作曲家柴可夫斯基〈1840-1893〉譜為歌劇，致使此詩廣為流傳。

lyric poems, such as *To Cha Adayev* (1818), *Ode to Liberty* (1817), etc., are the literary reflections of the aristocratic revolutionary movement. Unexpectedly, in 1820, he was transferred to southern Russia because of this. However, the beautiful and serene landscapes and heroic style of Caucasus and Crimean aroused Pushkin's admiration for freedom. He lived there for four years and completed many long narrative poems, dramas and praises of purity. He loves poetry and wonderful nature.

In 1824, when Pushkin was in the South, because he fell in love with Elizabeth, the beautiful wife of Odessa governor Vorontsov, he had a conflict with the governor, was dismissed by the tsar, and was imprisoned in Mihavs, his father's territory. Special village for two years. Because the place of confinement is Pushkin's childhood hometown, the simple rural life there made him calm down and concentrate on writing. He began to get close to the working people, and also collected folk songs, aphorisms, and proverbs, which opened up the opportunity to study Russian history. During this period, he has made many fruitful achievements. Including lyric poems, fairy tale poems, narrative poems and the famous historical drama *Boris Godunov* (Russian: Борис Годунов) written in 1825, which is based on real events in Russian history from the end of the sixteenth century to the beginning of the seventeenth century. There is also the long poetic novel *Evgeny Onegin*, which is an important work that Pushkin spent eight years completing. The Onegin in his works hates the hypocritical life of the upper class, but has no goals in life. This image just showed the ideological depression of the progressive young nobles in Russia at that time; because of the light and beautiful phonology of the poem, it was composed as an opera by the famous composer Tchaikovsky (1840-1893), which made this poem widely circulated.

　　此外，十餘篇敘事詩，多為 1820 至 1830 年間所作，取材包括俄羅斯民間故事、神異傳說及特殊的民族習俗、自然景致等。1831 年 2 月，普希金與 19 歲的奧斯科第一美少女娜塔莉亞結婚。1833 年秋，詩人再度回到其父親領地波爾金諾，在那裡完成了敘事詩〈青銅騎士〉，童話《漁夫和金魚的故事》，小說《黑桃皇后》等。其間，由於其妻美貌驚動彼得堡，甚至引起沙皇尼古拉一世注意，宮廷邀宴不斷的生活令普希金深感痛苦。普希金最後的重要作品是歷史小說《上尉的女兒》，在這小說裡，普希金又成功地塑造出一個自信又酷愛自由，深受人民擁戴的農民起義領袖普加喬夫的形象，同時，也譴責了沙皇的專制和殘暴；這在當時是極大膽的行徑。1837 年 1 月 27 日，普希金因妻子緋聞與流亡到俄國的法國保王黨人丹特士決鬥，兩天後，因傷重去世，年僅 38 歲。據說這是沙皇精心策劃的一個陰謀，為此，使全體俄羅斯人哀痛萬分，憤懣之士紛紛抗議，為之沸騰。

　　普希金一生的創作富有崇高的思想，他深信光明必勝黑暗，人類的博愛必能戰勝奴役和壓迫，因而在世界文壇引起許多共鳴。1829 至 1836 年，是普希金創作的巔峰期；其間創作了 12 部敘事長詩，其中，最主要的是〈魯斯蘭和柳德米拉〉、〈高加索的俘虜〉（1822）、〈青銅騎士〉（1833）等。普希金劇作並不多，最重要的是歷史劇《鮑里斯·戈杜諾夫》（1825）。去世前數年，其寫作重心已漸由韻文轉向

In addition, there are more than ten narrative poems, most of which were written between 1820 and 1830. The materials include Russian folk tales, mythical legends, special ethnic customs, and natural scenery. In February 1831, Pushkin married the 19-year-old Natalia, the first beautiful girl in Osko. In the autumn of 1833, the poet returned to Polkino, his father's territory, where he completed the narrative poem *The Bronze Horseman*, the fairy tale *The Story of the Fisherman and the Goldfish*, and the novel *The Queen of Spades*. During this period, because of his wife's beauty, he shocked Petersburg and even attracted the attention of Tsar Nicholas I. Pushkin was deeply distressed by the constant life of court invitations. Pushkin's last important work is the historical novel *The Captain's Daughter*. In this novel, Pushkin successfully created the image of Pugachev, the leader of the peasant uprising who is confident and loves freedom, and is deeply supported by the people. The despotism and brutality of the tsar were overthrown; this was a very daring act at the time. On January 27, 1837, Pushkin had a duel with Dantes, a French royalist in exile in Russia, due to his wife's scandal. Two days later, Pushkin died of serious injuries at the age of 38. It is said that this was a conspiracy carefully planned by the tsar. For this reason, all Russians were deeply saddened, and resentful people protested and boiled over it.

Pushkin's creations in his life are full of lofty thoughts. He firmly believes that light must overcome darkness, and human fraternity must overcome slavery and oppression, which has aroused many resonances in the world literary circle. From 1829 to 1836, it was the peak period of Pushkin's creation; during this period, he created 12 narrative poems, among which the most important ones were *Ruslan and Lyudmila*, *Captive of the Caucasus* (1822), *The Bronze Horseman* (1833), and so on. Pushkin did not have many plays, the most important being the historical drama *Boris Godunov* (1825). In the few years

非韻文。包括 1831 年《貝爾金小說集》裡有五篇散文故事，1834 年《黑桃皇后》，1836 年《上尉的女兒》等；內容人物真實親切，並以客觀的描寫取代主觀表述。他真是俄羅斯浪漫主義文學的傑出代表、現代文學的始祖；因而獲「偉大的俄國人民詩人」、「俄羅斯詩歌的太陽」等稱號。

賞　析

　　想認識俄國的詩，想了解俄國現代文學抒情的傳統，研究普希金是最好的入門；其詩歌語言洋溢著浪漫主義的繽紛色彩，讀來餘韻十足，也反映了詩人對自由的熱烈追求。如 1815 年寫下的〈我的墓誌銘〉，這首詩是年僅 16 歲的普希金作品，竟預言了自己流星般燦爛卻短暫的一生：

　　　　這裡埋著普希金；他畢生快樂，
　　　　結交年輕的繆思、愛神和懶散，
　　　　未曾有什麼善行，但蒼天為證，
　　　　是個好人。

　　從看似短小、簡潔的句中，彷彿看見了一個聰穎而充滿抱負的詩人在自我形象的塑造上，企圖要將心的夢田植入更多的意念，包含足以與繆思為友、追求愛情與自由、顛覆黑暗世界並嚮往光明的想法。而情感和願望是普希金經過痛苦

before his death, the focus of his writing has gradually shifted from verse to non-verse. Including five prose stories in *Belkin Collection* in 1831, *The Queen of Spades* in 1834, and *The Captain's Daughter* in 1836; he is really an outstanding representative of Russian romantic literature and the ancestor of modern literature; thus he was awarded the titles of "Great Russian People's Poet" and "Sun of Russian Poetry".

Appreciation

If you want to understand Russian poetry and the lyrical tradition of modern Russian literature, the best introduction is to study Pushkin; his poetic language is full of colorful colors of romanticism, and the aftertaste is full of aftertaste, which also reflects the poet's passionate pursuit of freedom. For example, *My Epitaph* written in 1815, this poem was written by Pushkin who was only 16 years old, and it predicted his brilliant but short life like a shooting star:

> *Here Pushkin is buried; he was happy all his life,*
> *Befriend young muses, cupids, and idlers,*
> *No good has been done, but heaven beholds,*
> *Is a nice guy.*

From the seemingly short and succinct sentences, it seems that an intelligent and aspiring poet tries to implant more ideas in the dream field of his heart in shaping his self-image, including being friends with muse, pursuing ideas of love and freedom, overturning the dark world and

的蛻變後，一切努力和創作的背後動力。需要明確的是，現
實主義作為普希金的精神內核仍有其極大影響。在這兒，我
們不妨欣賞一下這首 1818 年寫下的詩〈致查阿達耶夫〉，這
可以說是帶有某些浪漫主義色彩的現實主義作品。詩人用諷
刺、犀利的筆法描述出心中對沙皇制制度的憤懣，以正義的
界線去界開黑暗與光明，突出昂揚的激情：

> 愛、希望和虛名的
> 欺騙短暫愉悅了我們，
> 年少的歡樂已經消失，
> 如夢、如晨霧；
> 我們心中仍燃燒希望，
> 致命勢力的壓迫下，
> 我們以焦灼的心情
> 傾聽祖國的召喚。
> 我們懷著期待的折磨，
> 等候神聖的自由時刻，
> 如年輕的戀人
> 等候已訂的約會。
> 當我們為自由燃燒，
> 當心靈為榮譽活躍，
> 朋友，奉獻給祖國
> 我們至高的熱情吧！
> 同志，相信吧：將升起

yearning for the light. Emotion and desire are the driving force behind Pushkin's efforts and creations after his painful transformation. What needs to be made clear is that, as Pushkin's spiritual core, realism still has great influence. Here, we might as well appreciate this poem *To Cha Adayev* written in 1818, which can be said to be a realistic work with some romanticism. The poet uses ironic and sharp writing to describe his resentment against the tsarist system in his heart, divides darkness and light with the boundary of justice, and highlights the high-spirited passion:

> *Of love, hope and fame*
> *Deception pleases us briefly,*
> *The joys of youth are gone,*
> *Like a dream, like a morning mist;*
> *Hope still burns in our hearts,*
> *Under the oppression of deadly forces,*
> *We are anxious*
> *Listen to the call of the motherland.*
> *Tormented with anticipation, we*
> *Waiting for the holy moment of freedom,*
> *Like young lovers*
> *Waiting for booked appointments.*
> *When we burn for freedom,*
> *When the heart is active for honor,*
> *Friends, dedicated to the motherland*
> *Our highest enthusiasm!*
> *Comrade, believe it: will rise*

　　　　一顆醉人的幸福之星，
　　　　俄羅斯將自夢中驚醒，
　　　　在專制制度的廢墟上，
　　　　——鏤刻我們的姓名！

　　詩裡的查阿達耶夫〈1794-1856〉是歷史哲學家及出版家，
1816 年在沙皇村與普希金相識成為摯友。查阿達耶夫有強烈
愛國意識，政治思想傾向激進。1836 年因寫文批判當局而遭
沙皇尼古拉一世以精神病罪名入監拘禁。普希金既能滿懷深
深的同情去揭示俄羅斯被壓迫的知識青年遭受沙皇專制的苦
難，又能以無限的信心為光明的未來而高歌。因而，人們，
不能不為詩中的強烈情緒而感動。詩人在南俄的坎坷歲月，
使他同勞動人民的心靠得更緊了，而愛情也給他提供了取之
不盡的創作素材和詩的感受。如 1825 年寫下的〈假如生命欺
騙了你〉，詩中有著這樣感情炙人的句子：

　　　　假如生命欺騙了你，
　　　　莫悲傷，別生氣！
　　　　憂愁之日要克己，
　　　　要相信快樂會降臨。

　　　　心靈憧憬著未來，
　　　　眼前的總令人沮喪：
　　　　一切將轉眼不在，

A star of intoxicating happiness,
Russia will wake up from its slumber,
On the ruins of despotism,
Engraving our names one by one!

Chaadaev (1794-1856) in the poem is a philosopher of history and a publisher. He met Pushkin in Tsarist Village in 1816 and became a close friend. Chaadaev has a strong sense of patriotism, and his political ideology tends to be radical. In 1836, he was imprisoned by Tsar Nicholas I on charges of insanity for writing articles criticizing the authorities. Pushkin can not only reveal the sufferings of Russia's oppressed intellectual youths under the tsarist tyranny with deep sympathy, but also sing with boundless confidence for a bright future. Therefore, people cannot but be moved by the strong emotions in the poem. The poet's ups and downs in southern Russia made him closer to the working people, and love also provided him with inexhaustible creative materials and poetic feelings. For example, *If Life Deceives You* written in 1825, there are such emotional lines in the poem:

If life deceives you,
Don't be sad, don't be angry!
Deny yourself in a day of sorrow,
Believe that happiness will come.

The mind looks forward to the future,
It's always depressing to see:
Everything will be gone in a blink of an eye,

　逝去的常令人懷想。

　面對著瞬息變幻的現實，普希金必須說出自己的心裡話。
在這兒，詩人沒有直接抨擊和批評被沙皇遠調南俄的惡行，
而是攫取一段關於愛遭遇了無法克服之障礙，揭露自己苦心
尋找思想和以強烈的火樣的熱情去擁抱生活的心情。然而，
在他捕捉生活，創作的同時，不僅僅局限於視覺或聽覺的感
受，而是通過全心靈的觀照。像詩人在 1828 年寫下的〈冷風
依然吹颳〉一詩那樣，把詩美體現出來：

　　冷風依舊吹颳，
　　送來凌晨的寒。
　　春雪初融的地上，
　　冒出早生的小花。
　　彷彿來自蠟世界，
　　從芳香的蜜室
　　飛出第一隻蜂，
　　飛向初開的花
　　探問春的訊息：
　　貴客是否就要駕臨，
　　草地是否就要轉綠，
　　白樺是否就要茂密，
　　嫩葉是否就要綻放，
　　稠李是否就要開花？

The past is often nostalgic.

Facing the rapidly changing reality, Pushkin must speak his mind. Here, the poet did not directly criticize and criticize the evil deeds of being transferred to southern Russia by the tsar, but seized a paragraph about love encountering an insurmountable obstacle, revealing his painstakingly searching for ideas and embracing life with strong fire-like enthusiasm. However, when he captures life and creates, he is not limited to the visual or auditory experience, but through the observation of the whole soul. Like the poem *The Cold Wind Still Blows* written by the poet in 1828, it reflects the beauty of poetry:

The cold wind still blows,

Send the morning cold.

On the ground where the spring snow has just melted,

Early florets emerge.

As if from the world of wax,

from the fragrant honeycomb

Flew the first bee,

Flying to the first blooming flowers

Inquiring about spring's message:

Is your guest coming soon?

Will the grass turn green,

Will the birch be dense,

Are young leaves about to bloom,

Is thick plum about to bloom?

此詩情象的流動，雖帶有一點淒涼的色彩，但其多彩的
形象和那有意的重複，增添了對愛情無限的惆悵和懷舊的情
緒，這都是在詩人感情的催動下展現的。再試看這首在 1828
年標誌著詩人感情生活的〈回憶〉，很有神韻：

　　　當喧囂的白晝如死者靜默，
　　　　　城市無聲的街道
　　　覆蓋半透明的夜影
　　　　　與睡夢，日間辛勤的酬報，
　　　痛苦的失眠在
　　　　　靜寂中牽曳，
　　　寂寥的夜裡燃燒我的心，
　　　　　彷彿蛇在嚙咬；
　　　幻想沸騰，憂思壓抑的智慧
　　　　　擠迫過剩的沉重思維；
　　　回憶在我眼前默默
　　　　　伸展長長的畫卷；
　　　我厭惡地閱讀自己的生命，
　　　　　我顫抖，我詛咒，
　　　流著熱淚，痛苦抱怨，
　　　　　洗不去悲哀的詩行。

　　其實，普希金短暫的人生是複雜的。他在詩中歌詠過窮
苦的勞動大眾，詛咒過沙皇給人民帶來的苦難和專政的罪行，

Although the flow of emotional images in this poem has a bit of desolation, its colorful images and intentional repetition add infinite melancholy and nostalgic emotions to love, which are all displayed under the urging of the poet's emotions. Let's try this song *Memories* which marked the poet's emotional life in 1828, which is very charming:

When the tumultuous day is as silent as the dead,
Silent city streets
Overlay translucent night shadow
And sleep, the reward of the day's toil,
Painful insomnia in
Dragging in the silence,
Burn my heart in the lonely night,
Like a snake biting;
Fantasies seethe, thoughts depress wisdom
Overcrowded heavy thinking;
Memories silently before my eyes
Stretch the long scroll;
I read my life with disgust,
I tremble, I curse,
Weeping, complaining bitterly,
Can't wash away sad lines.

In fact, Pushkin's short life was complicated. In his poems, he sang of the poor working people, cursed the suffering and dictatorship crimes brought by the tsar to the people,

還悼念過為批評專政而犧牲的友人，為人民立下了一個勇敢嘗試的榜樣。可是，在感情上，詩人也是一種癡鳥，是一個以自己的感情慨然高歌著大自然的美與人類的希望之鳥。如同印度詩人泰戈爾（1861-194）所說一般：「生命從世界得到資產，愛情使它得到價值。」（註2），普希金在 1829 年的另一首名詩〈愛過妳〉，亦從另一段愛情體驗受著痛苦的煎熬，這當然有些絕望之感，但也表明了愛情的到來是要勇於付出代價的：

愛過妳：也許，愛火
在我心裡未完全隕熄；
但它不再煩擾妳，
不願再惹妳憂傷。
絕望無言地愛妳，
有時羞澀，有時妒忌。
懇切溫存地愛妳，
願他對妳一樣珍惜。

此詩是普希金獻給愛人安娜·阿列克謝耶夫娜·奧列尼娜（1808-1888）的。奧列尼娜（乳名安涅塔）是彼得堡公共圖書館館長、考古學家奧列寧的千金小姐。奧列尼娜和普希金接觸之後，隨即墜入愛情，普希金對她也充滿了情意。1828年夏，普希金很想和奧列尼娜結為夫妻，但卻遭到了她的父親的拒絕；因而傷心地離開了彼得堡。後來，普希金與奧列尼娜一家關係大大疏遠的另一原因，是她的父親越來越靠近

and mourned the friends who died for criticizing the dictatorship, setting a brave example for the people. However, emotionally, the poet is also a kind of idiot, a bird that sings the beauty of nature and the hope of human beings with his own feelings. As the Indian poet Rabindranath Tagore (1861-1941) said: "Life gets assets from the world, love makes it worth." <Note>, another famous poem *Love You* by Pushkin in 1829, also from another love experience, suffering from pain. Of course, there is a sense of despair, but it also shows that the arrival of love requires the courage to pay the price:

Love you: maybe, love fire

Not quite extinguished in my heart;

But it doesn't bother you anymore,

I don't want to make you sad anymore.

love you hopelessly,

Sometimes shy, sometimes jealous.

I love you earnestly and tenderly,

May he cherish you as much.

This poem is dedicated by Pushkin to his lover Anna Alexeyevna Olenina (1808-1888). Olenina (child name Annetta) is the daughter of Olenin, director of the Petersburg Public Library and archaeologist. After Olenina and Pushkin came into contact, they immediately fell in love, and Pushkin was also full of affection for her. In the summer of 1828, Pushkin wanted to marry Olenina, but was rejected by her father; thus sadly left Petersburg. Later, another reason for the estrangement between Pushkin and Olenina's family was that her father was getting closer and

沙皇，且對普希金的諷刺短詩極為不滿。這期間，普希金在
1828 年左右寫下許多愛情詩，如〈她的眼睛〉、〈你和您〉、
〈美人兒啊，不要在我面前唱起〉、〈豪華的京城，可憐的
京城〉、〈唉，愛情的絮絮談心〉等，應該是由奧列尼娜引
發出來的，這不能不說是詩人在表達詩情上的苦心經營。

　　詩人他一生追求理想，追求愛情，也追求藝術上的創新。
但時時遇到挫折，使他感到迷惘與苦悶。失去愛後，1829 年
普希金又認識娜塔莉亞・岡察洛娃，這是詩人在一次旅途中
寫下對她的思念的詩〈夜霧瀰漫在格魯吉亞山崗上〉，節奏
和韻律都是和詩相吻合的，這就增加了此詩的音律美：

　　　　夜霧瀰漫在格魯吉亞山崗上，
　　　　阿拉戈河在我眼前喧響。
　　　　我憂鬱輕快，我的哀思發亮；
　　　　妳的麗影充塞我的愁腸。
　　　　妳，只有妳……沒有什麼
　　　　能驚動我的悲傷。
　　　　心再度燃燒再要愛──因為
　　　　不能不把妳愛上。

　　小小的一首八行詩，便把讀者的心抓住了。詩人借景抒
情，他站在格魯吉亞山崗上，從夜霧瀰漫的畫面中，使人看
到了詩人悲喜交感又期盼的心；這就使他的愛情詩更為絢麗
多姿。在那個年代，普希金如果對人民的痛苦漠不關心，只

closer to the Tsar and was extremely dissatisfied with Pushkin's satirical short poems. During this period, Pushkin wrote many love poems around 1828, such as *Her Eyes*, *You and You*, *Beauty*, *Don't Sing in Front of Me*, *Posh Capital*, *Poor Capital*, *Alas, the Heart-to-Heart Talk of Love* and so on should be triggered by Olenina, which cannot but be said to be the poet's painstaking efforts in expressing poetic feelings.

The poet pursues ideals, love, and artistic innovation all his life. But he encountered setbacks from time to time, which made him feel confused and depressed. After losing love, Pushkin met Natalia Goncharova again in 1829. This is a poem *Night Fog Over the Georgian Hills* written by the poet about her thoughts during a journey. The rhythm and rhythm are harmonious. The poem coincides, which increases the rhythmic beauty of this poem:

> *The night mist hangs over the Georgian hills,*
> *The Arago River roared before my eyes.*
> *I am melancholy and light, my mourning is bright;*
> *Your beautiful shadow fills my heart with sorrow.*
> *you, just you... nothing*
> *Can disturb my sadness.*
> *The heart burns again and loves again ——*
> *I can't help but put you on.*

A small eight-line poem grabs the reader's heart. The poet used the scenery to express his emotions. He stood on the hills of Georgia, and from the foggy night scene, people could see the poet's sympathetic and hopeful heart; Pushkin was indifferent to the suffering of the people and

關在象牙塔裡自我吟醉，就算不上是個真正的詩人；同樣，在沙皇處心積慮的重壓下，只有悲苦地呻吟或憤恨，而無法向人民昭示出光明的前途，或為祖國人民爭取自由和幸福而奮鬥，也不會成為偉大的文學家。普希金的可貴之處，恰恰在於：他對人民苦難的同情和對光明的渴求是他鮮明的思想傾向。如詩人在 1834 年寫下的〈是時候了，朋友，是時候了！〉一詩，他對愛情帶來的痛苦與渴望心的平靜，他的正義與犧牲的精神，正代表了他悲苦而璀璨的命運，給人們寄予了無限的同情：

> 是時候了，朋友，是時候了！心要求平靜，
> 歲月一天天飛去，每一片刻帶走
> 一部分生命，我倆
> 準備共同生活⋯⋯一看，已將死去，
> 世間沒有幸福，但有安寧與自由。
> 我曾夢想令人欣羨的命運——
> 我，疲倦的奴隸，早已盼望逃去
> 辛勤勞作與真正安逸的遙遠居所。

詩人雖抒發了一種又恨又愛的複雜感情，並表達了一種要使勞動人民新生的渴望。這表面上寫的是朋友，但實際上卻都是在象徵處於反抗俄皇鬥爭中的俄國人民的互相團結；正是靠了這種在心靈深處的互相共鳴與攜手，才能讓普希金向他所熱愛的祖國和人民捧出了許多堅實的、閃耀著灼人的光芒的文學作品。

only chanted himself in an ivory tower, he would not be considered a real poet; similarly, under the pressure of the tsar's deliberate deliberation, he could only groan or resent, but could not express his gratitude to him. The people who show a bright future, or fight for the freedom and happiness of the people of the motherland, will not become great writers. The value of Pushkin lies precisely in that his sympathy for the suffering of the people and his desire for light are his distinct ideological tendencies. As the poet wrote in 1834, *It's time, friends, it's time!* A poem, his pain and longing for the peace of mind brought by love, his spirit of justice and sacrifice, just represent his miserable and bright destiny, and send infinite sympathy to people:

> *It's time, friends, it's time! The heart asks for peace,*
> *Years fly by day by day, every moment takes away*
> *part of life, both of us*
> *Ready to live together... Look, dying,*
> *There is no happiness in the world, but there is peace and*
> *   freedom.*
> *I dreamed of an enviable fate —*
> *I, tired slave, longed to escape*
> *A remote abode for hard work and true ease.*

Although the poet expressed a complex feeling of hatred and love, and expressed a desire to be reborn as one of the working people. On the surface, they are written as friends, but in fact they all symbolize the mutual unity of the Russian people in the struggle against the Russian emperor; the beloved motherland and people have light. Produced many solid literary works shining with scorching

浪漫與睿哲的肖像：普希金

　　記得唐代詩人劉禹錫的《秋詞》裡寫道：「晴空一鶴排雲上，便引詩情到碧霄。」夜讀普希金詩，思索之後，心情也像是看到：秋天晴朗的天空中一隻仙鶴排開雲層，不停不息地在微光中飛翔；而我的詩興也隨它到了蔚藍的天上，愛上了它一樣，也可感覺到他離開塵世的自由了。這位曾舉著「火把」，迎向「太陽」的歌手，他雖不怨天，在沙皇專政時期又經過種種挫折和磨難中；卻奇蹟地活出極強的藝術生命力。其藝術的主要使命，在於將情致深摯而見於文字的意象保持一種高貴的情操及純真的美。他在大量地寫下抒情詩的同時，也雙寫了十四首長篇敘事詩，這是他詩歌創作中最豐盛的階段。這些詩歌是普希金的本真，是靜默的沉思；大致洋溢著浪漫主義的繽紛色彩，也反映了詩人對自由的熱烈追求。

　　再者，普希金詩的語言精練程度也很高，尤以其中的〈高加索俘虜〉等詩作，更可視為詩體長篇小說《葉甫蓋尼·奧涅金》的補充。確實，他是俄羅斯近代文學的奠基者和俄羅斯文學語言的創建者。他促使俄羅斯文學走上了現實主義的道路，給詩歌以血液和呼吸！其詩歌不但體現了詩人的一種胸襟，一種浩然之氣的人格；而所要表達的主題思想，又造成

Portrait of Romance and Wisdom: Pushkin

I remember that Tang Dynasty poet Liu Yuxi wrote in *Ode to Autumn*: "A crane flying in the clear sky will lead the poetic sentiment to the blue sky." After reading Pushkin's poems at night, after thinking about it, I feel like I saw: in the clear sky of autumn, a crane was parting the clouds and kept flying in the twilight; and my poetic spirit followed it to the blue sky, as if I fell in love with it, and I could feel the freedom of him leaving the world. The singer who once held the "torch" to meet the "sun", although he did not complain about the sky, he went through all kinds of setbacks and tribulations during the tsarist dictatorship; however, he miraculously lived out a strong artistic vitality. The main mission of his art is to maintain a noble sentiment and pure beauty in the imagery that is deeply emotional and can be seen in words. While writing down a great number of lyric poems, he also wrote fourteen long narrative poems, the most abundant stage in his poetry creation. These poems are the true nature of Pushkin, and they are silent meditations; they are generally filled with colorful romanticism, and also reflect the poet's passionate pursuit for freedom.

Furthermore, the language of Pushkin's poems is also very concise, especially the "Caucasian Prisoner" and other poems, which can be regarded as a supplement to the poetic novel *Evgene Onegin*. Indeed, he is the founder of modern Russian literature and the creator of the Russian literary language. He pushed Russian literature onto the path of realism, giving poetry its blood and breath! His poems not only embody the poet's mind, an awe-inspiring

了一個完整的藝術境界，有如黎前的黑暗——是偉大的，這就與西方的一些純意象派詩大不同。它總是通過人民群眾最熟悉的事物，或敘事，或抒情，或描寫，或比興；給讀者打下深刻的印象。詩人把理想和愛寄托於無際的星空，就像隻靈鳥不停地鳴唱，早已贏取天國之永恆；其不朽的一生，也傳聞於世，對世界文學的繁榮是有極大促進作用的。

註 1. 1825 年，俄國貴族革命家發動了反對農奴制度和沙皇專制制度的武裝起義，因起義時間是俄曆 12 月，所以領導這次起義的俄國貴族革命家在俄國歷史上被稱為「十二月黨人」，即 Decembrist。

註 2‧《泰戈爾經典詩選：生如夏花》，譯者：鄭振鐸，臺灣，遠足文化，2011‧12，頁 84。

--2013.03.04 作

--臺灣《新原人》季刊，2013 春季號，第 81 期，頁 164-173。

personality; but the theme to be expressed creates a complete artistic realm, just like the darkness before dawn — it is great, which is different from some pure imagery in the West. Pai poetry is very different. It always leaves a deep impression on readers through the things most familiar to the masses, or narrative, or lyric, or description, or metaphor. The poet entrusts his ideals and love to the boundless starry sky, just like a spiritual bird singing non-stop, he has already won the eternity of heaven; his immortal life is also rumored in the world, which greatly promotes the prosperity of world literature.

Note 1. In 1825, Russian aristocratic revolutionaries launched an armed uprising against serfdom and tsarist autocracy. Because the uprising took place in December of the Russian calendar, the Russian aristocratic revolutionaries who led this uprising were called "December" in Russian history. Partisan, that is, Decembrist.

Note 2. *Selected Classic Poems of Tagore: Life Like Summer Flowers*, translated by Zheng Zhenduo, Taiwan, Hiking Culture, 2011.12, p. 84.

Author : A poetess and a critic, Lin Mingli, the author of this book, was born in Yunlin county of Taiwan province in 1961. She received her LLM in 1987 and was a lecturer at the Pingdong Normal University in Taiwan.

4. 傑克‧裴外詩歌的意象藝術探微

摘要：傑克‧裴外(Jacques Prévert，1900-1977)是法國卓著的詩人兼劇作家，其詩歌內容廣泛，形式新穎、語言精煉。本文嘗試從其語言特色、詩歌意象藝術及其審美價值等方面進行論述。

關鍵詞：傑克‧裴外，詩歌、寫實主義、超現實主義

行吟詩人：傑克‧裴外

傑克‧裴外(Jacques Prévert，1900-1977) 成長於巴黎近郊的諾伊理(Neuilly)，是法國家喻戶曉的詩人；性喜熱鬧、節慶，幽默且善談。他從二零年代末期開始發表詩作，藉以抒發其強烈的感情和表明心志。1945 年，詩人將最為人所知的詩集《話（語）》（Paroles）一出版，就以驚人的銷售量響徹了法國詩壇。繼而 1951 年的《演出》(Spectacle) 及 1955 年的《雨與晴天》(La Pluie et le beau temps)，也持續迴響。此外，他也積極推動民間劇團的工作，熱衷於電影編劇。在三零年代、或二次大戰期間的法國經典名片裡，由他參與的編劇中，如《天堂的小孩》（Les enfants du paradis）〈1944〉、《夜訪者》（Les visiteurs du soir）、《夜之門》（Les portes de la nuit）、《破曉》（Le jour se lève）等劇本或影片裡的獨白，如風吹拂過樂器那般「寫實詩意」，對後世影響極大。

4. Exploring the Art of Imagery in Jacques Prévert's Poetry

Abstract: Jacques Prévert is a distinguished French poet and playwright. With an original form and refined language, his poetry covers a wide range of subjects. This paper attempts to discuss his poetry from various aspects such as his language features, poetic imagery and its aesthetic value.

Key words: Jacques Prévert, poetry, realism, surrealism

Troubadour: Jack Prévert

Jacques Prévert (1900-1977) grew up in Neuilly, a suburb of Paris. He is a well-known French poet; he began to publish poems in the late 1920s to express his strong feelings and express his will. In 1945, as soon as the poet published his most well-known collection of poems, *Paroles*, which resounded through the French poetry circle with an astonishing sales volume. Then *Spectacle* in 1951 and *La Pluie et le beau temps* in 1955 continued to work of folk theater troupes and is keen on film screenwriting. In the French classic business cards in the 1930s or during World War II, among the screenwriters he participated in, such as *Les enfants du paradis* (1944) and *Night Visitor* (Les visiteurs du soir) , *Les portes de la nuit*, *Le jour se lève* and other scripts or monologues in films are as "realistic and poetic" as the wind blowing through musical instruments, which has a great influence on later generations.

　　傑克・裴外詩歌有三個表徵，其一、通曉音律：詩清逸可頌，多被譜成曲或為電影而寫，如法國名歌者如 Edith Piaf、Yves Montant 幾乎都唱過他的詩歌，〈落葉〉（Les feuilles mortes）或是〈芭芭拉〉（Barbara）流傳久遠；很多詩也被柯士瑪(Joseph Kosma)譜曲成流行的法國香頌。其詩的語言，如繆斯之聲音或是神的恩典般純潔，藝術感染力強。其二、語言精煉傳神、形式新穎：詩境的進展，常能震撼著讀者的思緒。尤以對廣泛存在的生活主題及人物形象的巧喻〈conceit〉，情感真摯，可直接表達出詩人的想像狂放。他痛恨戰爭，也曾攻擊過宗教的虛偽；體內有熾熱的血氣、也有童稚、風趣的一面。另一方面，以善於寫大自然、純真的人，動物及鳥著稱；詩歌力求擺脫用語綺靡，通俗易懂，能以簡單的詩詞就觸人心弦。他常關心世上可憐人，反對強權、能映照出現實人生中情感疏離與淪喪的現象。雖然有的詩篇受到情感的驅使，才會道出對壓迫者或對社會諷刺的聲音；然而，以詩表達心中意念，處處隱藏著詩人對生命的愛與樂觀的幻想，不知撫慰了多少頹喪的心靈。其三、詩歌視覺性與故事性強：他的詩歌類似電影蒙太奇的手法，意象跳躍性大，常能客觀敏銳地觀察生命，從中粹取出各個層面主題的靈感。比如對人性的剖析或邪惡社會所帶來的不平等，能以挪揄幽默的口吻來書寫人生百態，或大膽地利用超現實的筆調，以反映出社會惡勢力的具形化；而意象所涵蓋的多重意義，也為生活的雋永〈wit〉，提供了很深的著墨，因而被譽為中世紀行吟詩人以來口語詩的承繼者。

There are three characteristics of Jack Prévert's poems. First, he is proficient in rhythm: his poems are clear and eulogizing, and most of them are composed into music or written for movies. For example, famous French singers such as Edith Piaf and Yves Montant have almost sung his poems. *Les feuilles mortes* or "Barbara" have been handed down for a long time; many poems were also composed by Joseph Kosma into the popular French chanson. The language of his poems is as pure as the voice of the Muse or the grace of God, and his artistic appeal is strong. Second, the language is refined and vivid, and the form is novel: the development of the poetic realm can often shake the reader's thoughts. In particular, the ingenious metaphor <conceit> of widespread life themes and characters is sincere and can directly express the wild imagination of the poet. He hates war and has attacked the hypocrisy of religion; he has a fiery blood in his body, but also has a childish and funny side. On the other hand, he is famous for being good at writing about nature, innocent people, animals and birds; his poetry strives to get rid of the extravagant language, is easy to understand, and can touch people's hearts with simple poems. He often cares about the poor people in the world, opposes power, and can reflect the phenomenon of emotional alienation and loss in real life. Although some poems are driven by emotion, they will express their satirical voice to the oppressor or society; however, expressing the thoughts in the heart with poetry hides the poet's love for life and optimistic fantasy everywhere, which comforts many depressed minds. Third, his poems are highly visual and storytelling: his poems are similar to the technique of movie montage, and the imagery is very jumpy. He can often observe life objectively and keenly, and extract inspiration from it at various levels. For example, the analysis of human nature or the inequality brought about by an evil society can be written in a teasing and humorous tone to describe the various aspects of life, or boldly use a surreal style of writing to reflect the concretization of evil forces in society. The multiple meanings covered also provide a deep inkling for the meaningful <wit> of life, so it is known as the successor of spoken poetry since the troubadours in the Middle Ages.

　　百年多來，法國對於裴外詩歌的風靡經久不衰，雖然九七年法國才爲裴外舉行過逝世二十周年盛大紀念活動，而百年冥誕時仍有舉辦多項節目，連他住過二十年的巴黎蒙馬特〈Montmartre〉區也動員了全社區爲裴外個人舉辦過「拼貼」展、遊街慶祝等活動。著名的傳記作家 Yves Courrière 也曾寫下《傑克‧裴外》傳。為此，本文試圖結合其詩歌意象藝術，來進一步論證其在世界文學史的地位，加深讀者對傑克‧裴外詩歌的理解和支持。

詩歌的意境分析

　　在裴外的詩裡，有許多首以動物為主題。其中，關於鳥的詩歌就將近 20 首。而〈畫小鳥畫像〉是傑出的代表作：

> 首先畫一個鳥籠有個敞開的門
> 然後畫
> 一些漂亮的東西
> 一些簡樸的東西
> 一些美麗的東西...
> 為鳥
> 然後把畫布靠放在一棵樹上
> 在花園裡
> 在樹林裡
> 或在森林裡
> 躲在樹後

For more than a hundred years, the popularity of Prévert's poetry in France has lasted for a long time. Although France only held a grand commemorative event for the 20th anniversary of Prévert's death in 1997, many programs were still held on the centenary of his birthday. The Montmartre district of Paris for ten years has also mobilized the whole community to hold "collage" exhibitions, street parades and other activities for Prévert himself. The famous biographer Yves Courrière also wrote the biography of *Jack Prévert*. For this reason, this article attempts to combine his poetic image art to further demonstrate his status in the history of world literature and deepen readers' understanding and support for Jack Prévert's poems.

Analysis of Poetry's Artistic Conception

Among Prévert's poems, there are many with animals as the theme. Among them, there are nearly 20 poems about birds. And *Painting a Portrait of a Bird* is an outstanding representative work:

First draw a birdcage with an open door
Then draw
Something nice
Something austere
Something beautiful...
For the bird
Then lean the canvas against a tree
In the garden
In the woods
Or in the forest
Hide behind a tree

不說
不動...
有時鳥會很快到來
但他也可能花好幾年的長時間
去下決心
不要氣餒
等
等上幾年如果必要
鳥來的快慢
同畫的成敗
沒有關係
當鳥來了
如果他來了
保持極度蕭靜
等鳥進籠
當他進去了
輕輕地把門關上以一支畫筆
然後
把所有鐵條一根根塗掉
小心翼翼不踩到鳥的羽毛
然後畫樹的像
挑它枝椏中最美麗的
為鳥
同時畫上綠葉與風的清新
太陽的微塵

*At the same time, draw the freshness of green
　leaves and wind
Motes of the sun
Do not say
Do not move...
Sometimes birds come quickly
But he could also spend years
To make up your mind
Do not be discouraged
Wait
Wait a few years if necessary
Birds come fast
The success or failure of the same painting
It doesn't matter
When the bird comes
If he comes
Keep quiet
Wait for the bird to enter the cage
When he went in
Softly close the door with a paintbrush
Then
Paint all the iron bars one by one
Be careful not to touch the bird's feathers
Then draw the image of the tree
Pick the most beautiful of its branches
For the bird*

還有草裡蟲豸的喧囂在夏熱裡
然後等鳥去決定唱歌
如果鳥不唱
那是壞的表示
表示畫得不好
但如果他唱了那是好的表示
表示你可簽名
所以你便輕輕拔下
鳥的一根羽毛
把你的名字寫在畫像的一角

　　此詩情景交融，一開始，裴外沒有使用花俏的意象或矯飾；而以寫實主義手法來描繪出畫家想要畫小鳥的細節，含有強烈的詼諧成分，予人以飄逸輕靈，也有許多戲劇性的色彩。句中的「鳥」，象徵著「自由」或「靈思湧現」；詩人讓畫家的靈感和畫鳥過程進行了一段有趣的邂逅。在詩中，動與靜、鳥兒對美麗風景的嚮往與畫家跟著揣摩鳥兒的苦思與細心呵護的矛盾，都構成了明朗和深刻的對比。首先畫家刻意地畫出牠的籠子，再以敏銳而富於同情的態度，畫出牠重獲自由的想像。到底畫家該如何才能讓鳥兒欣然而歌呢？接著，畫家小心翼翼地把籠子塗掉，再畫以大自然、樹、綠葉、風和草叢，並回頭來看看鳥的表情，是否如一個天真、快樂的小孩，決定可以唱歌了？因為詩裡只提到畫家自己的遐思，並沒有交待最後這畫家是否滿意地簽下名；這結果，反而使我們產生濃烈的興趣和純樸的好奇心，做到意在言外，讓讀者費神去猜度。

And the clamor of insects in the grass in the summer heat
Then wait for the bird to decide to sing
If the birds don't sing
That's a bad sign
Indicates that the drawing is not good
But if he sings that's a good sign
Means you can sign
So you gently unplug
Bird's feather
Write your name in the corner of the picture

This poem blends scenes and scenes. At the beginning, Prévert did not use fancy imagery or pretense; instead, he used realism to describe the details of the bird that the artist wanted to paint, which contained a strong humorous element, giving people an elegant and light spirit. Dramatic color. The "bird" in the sentence symbolizes "freedom" or "emergence of inspiration"; the poet made an interesting encounter between the artist's inspiration and the process of painting birds. In the poem, there is a clear and profound contrast between movement and stillness, the bird's longing for the beautiful scenery, and the painter's hard thinking and careful care of the bird. First, the artist deliberately draws its cage, and then, with a keen and sympathetic attitude, draws the imagination of its freedom. How can the painter make the birds sing happily? Then, the artist carefully painted out the cage, and then painted nature, trees, green leaves, wind and grass, and looked back at the expression of the bird. Is it like an innocent and happy child who decides to sing? Because the poem only mentions the artist's own reverie, and does not explain whether the artist is satisfied with the signature at the end; this result, on the contrary, arouses strong interest and simple curiosity in us, so that the meaning is beyond the words, and readers are troubled to guess.

　　我們不妨再引這首〈歌〉，看看它意象的組合及詩人想
表達的情趣，是否有異曲同工之妙：

　　　　這是什麼日子
　　　　這是每天
　　　　我的朋友
　　　　是一生
　　　　我的愛
　　　　我們彼此相愛且我們過活
　　　　我們過活且彼此相愛
　　　　而不知這生命是什麼
　　　　而不知這日子是什麼
　　　　而不知這愛情是什麼

　　讀這首詩，猶如透過「戲劇獨白」把自己和空間的距離
拉開；一方面讓讀者的猜測懸宕未解，一方面揭露人性矛盾
與猜疑的一面。然後就可以理解裴外在變動的年代裡，想發
出那無法捕捉的、卻又縈迴心頭的聲響，勾勒出一幅全然不
同的愛情樣貌。如此看來，裴外常對日常事物做精細的探微，
十分符合對一般百姓關懷的美麗象徵；甚至連死亡也能成為
一個愛的形象，如這首短詩〈秋〉：

　　　　一匹馬倒斃在一條巷子中央
　　　　　葉子落在牠身上
　　　　　　我們的愛顫慄
　　　　　　　太陽也一樣

We might as well quote this "song" again to see if there are similarities in the combination of its images and the taste the poet wants to express:

> What day is this
> This is every day
> My friend
> This is a lifetime
> My love
> We love each other and we live
> We live and love each other
> I don't know what this life is
> I don't know what day it is
> I don't know what this love is

Reading this poem is like opening the distance between yourself and space through a "dramatic monologue". On the one hand, it keeps readers' guesses unsolved, and on the other hand, it exposes the contradictions and suspicions of human nature. Then it can be understood that Prévert wanted to make that uncapturable but lingering sound in the changing age, and outline a completely different love appearance. From this point of view, Prévert often makes detailed explorations of everyday things, which is very in line with the beautiful symbol of caring for ordinary people; even death can become an image of love, as in this short poem *Autumn*:

> A horse lay dead in the middle of an alley
> Leaves fall on it
> Our love trembles
> The sun too

　　這可說是一首表達對四季幻逝的詩。儘管只有短短的四
句，超現實的圖像具體呈現出抽象概念，並逐漸延伸為秋天
蕭瑟的圖像，易觸動了人們心靈的深處。我們看到了詩歌帶
有浪漫色彩的基調，它也告訴我們詩人對秋天癡愛的頓悟，
如同觀賞葉的飄落、萬物的死亡一般感到莫有的淡傷。裴外
對愛情理想的特點，在於不願以營造的、主觀的哀傷情緒為
假象，而以昇華為普遍的存在現象或經驗，表現出獨特的詩
學品味。如這首〈在夜裡擁抱的男女〉，表現出裴外如何利
用詩裡的人物，繪製出愛情的意象「並非正確的公式」的本
質，也無法用「道德的流失或指指點點」為批判，唯一可以
解釋的，是映照出每個人心裡頭存有過的感覺，訴說著男女
之間看是「似是而非的矛盾關係」。全詩把戀愛中旁若無人
的感覺幻化為一種狡點而可愛的形象，極為生動。而那「初
戀的星光」，既薄弱卻恆久綿長，也表現出詩人想要表達的
情趣：

在夜裡擁抱的男女

靠在幽暗的走道上

過路的人指指點點

但戀愛的男女

不是為別人而擁抱

只熔成一個影子

在黑暗裡扭動

引起路人的憤怒

他們憤怒他們指責他們笑話他們嫉妒

但男女們不是為別人而擁抱

在他們初戀的星光下

他們比黑夜輕

他們比白日遠

This can be said to be a poem expressing the illusion of the four seasons. Although there are only four short sentences, the surreal image concretely presents an abstract concept, and gradually extends to the image of bleak autumn, which easily touches the depths of people's hearts. We have seen the romantic tone of the poem, and it also tells us the poet's epiphany about autumn's infatuation, just like watching the falling of leaves and the death of all things, he feels the unique sadness. The characteristic of Prévert's ideal of love is that he does not want to use artificial and subjective sadness as an illusion, but sublimates it into a common phenomenon or experience, showing his unique poetic taste. For example, this poem *Man and Woman Embracing at Night* shows how Prévert used the characters in the poem to draw the essence of the imagery of love, which is "not the correct formula", and cannot be criticized with "the loss of morality or pointing fingers". The only thing that can be explained is to reflect the feelings that everyone has had in their hearts, telling what seems to be a "paradoxical relationship" between men and women. The whole poem transforms the feeling of being alone in love into a cunning and lovely image, which is extremely vivid. And the "starlight of first love", which is weak but long-lasting, also shows the taste that the poet wants to express:

> *Man and woman hugging at night*
> *Leaning on the dark walkway*
> *Passersby pointing*
> *But men and women in love*
> *Not hugging for others*
> *Only melted into a shadow*
> *Writhing in the dark*
> *Arouse the wrath of passers-by*
> *They're angry they accuse them of laughing they're jealous*
> *But men and women don't embrace for others*
> *Under the starlight of their first love*
> *They are lighter than night*
> *They are farther than the day*

　　雖然愛情的千種面貌，成了裴外不斷重複歌頌的主題，使他的詩歌藝術展現了愛情的強度，如這首〈亞利坎塔〉，唯美的風格才能呈現深切悽情。暗示愛情的甜蜜與生命的溫馨，恰如時光的流逝，夜的清涼般自然：「一個桔子在桌上／妳的衣服在地毯上／而你在我床上／現在甜蜜的禮物／夜的清涼／我生命的溫馨」。接著，〈直路〉是裴外經由知性和思考得來的巧喻，有教化和愉悅〈delight〉的涵義：

　　　　每一里

　　　　　　每一年
　　　　　　拉長臉的老頭們
　　　　　　給孩子們指路
　　　　　　以鋼筋水泥的手勢

　　暗喻我們雖然無法改變前路的方向，卻可盡所能地踏穩每一腳步。循著長者的指示，一切責難，並不是毫無根據，儘管是求好心切，倚老賣老或站不住腳、滿腹嘮叨；但只要走得直，哪怕走得再久再遠，總會有了心中的答案。傑克・裴外詩歌的重要課題，亦即厭惡暴力、戰爭、偽善者，因而寄望從這首〈和平演講〉中尋求自我靈魂的救贖與慰藉：「在一個極端重要的演講接近尾聲時／那大人物被／一個漂亮空洞的詞句絆了一跤／倒在它上面／沒講完張著嘴／喘著氣／咧著牙／而他和平論調的蛀牙／暴露了戰爭的神經／金錢的微妙」，此詩敘事邏輯上，能證明裴外如何運用精心設計的戲劇性，來打造戰爭的荒謬與金錢的疏通、強權與被壓迫者之間的對立，讓再多漂亮空洞的詞句也挽不回為和平所付出

Although the thousands of faces of love have become the theme of Prévert's repeated praises, making his poetry art show the intensity of love, such as this song *Alicanta*, only the beautiful style can present deep sadness. It implies the sweetness of love and the warmth of life, just as time goes by, and the coolness of night is as natural: "An orange is on the table / Your clothes are on the carpet / And you are in my bed / Now sweet gift / The coolness of the night / I The sweetness of life". Next, "Straight Road" is a clever metaphor that Prévert acquired through his understanding and thinking, and it has the meaning of enlightening and delighting *Delight*:

> *Every mile*
> > *Every year*
> > *Long-faced old men*
> > *Show the way to the children*
> > *Gesture with reinforced concrete*

It is a metaphor that although we cannot change the direction of the road ahead, we can try our best to keep every step steady. Following the instructions of the elders, all accusations are not groundless, although they are eager to seek good things, rely on the old to sell the old, or are untenable, full of nagging; but as long as you walk straight, no matter how long you walk, there will always be answer in mind. The important subject of Jacques Prévert's poems is that he hates violence, war, and hypocrites, so he hopes to seek salvation and comfort for his soul from this *Peace Speech*: "At the end of an extremely important speech/The big man Stumbled / on a pretty empty phrase / fell on top of it / opened his mouth / gasped / grinned / and the decay of his peace talk / exposed the nerves of war / the subtleties of money", In terms of the narrative logic of this poem, it can prove how Prévert uses carefully designed drama to create the opposition between the absurdity of war and the smooth flow of money, the power and the oppressed, so that no amount of beautiful and empty words can bring back peace The price paid and innocent lives.

的代價及無辜的生命。另一首〈花束〉，同樣也是裴外抒寫
戰爭的後遺症或因之受難者親友的痛苦遭遇，真摯感人：

> 妳在幹什麼小女孩
> 帶著那些新摘的花
> 妳在那裡幹什麼年輕的女孩
> 帶著那些花枯乾的花
> 妳在幹什麼漂亮的婦人
> 帶著那些凋謝的花
> 妳在那裡幹什麼老婆婆
> 帶著那些瀕死的花
>
> 我等著勝利者

〈為妳我的愛〉也是首愛情詩，透過畫面具體的形象及
詳實的動作，表達了詩人對戰後榮衰無常、愛人消沓不復可
尋的感嘆，也讓為愛寧願奔波、飛馳的想像躍然紙上：

> 我到鳥市場去
> 買了些鳥
> 為妳
> 我的愛
> 我到花市場去
> 買了些花
> 為妳

Another song *Bouquet of Flowers* is also written by Prévert about the aftermath of the war or the painful experiences of the relatives and friends of the victims, which is sincere and touching:

> *What are you doing little girl*
> *With those freshly picked flowers*
> *What are you doing there young girl*
> *With those flowers withered*
> *What are you doing beautiful woman*
> *With those withered flowers*
> *What are you doing there old woman*
> *With those dying flowers*
>
> *I wait for the winner*

My Love For You is also a love poem. Through the specific images and detailed actions on the screen, it expresses the poet's lament for the impermanence of prosperity and decline after the war, and the disappearance of his lover. Imagine jumping on paper:

> *I go to the bird market*
> *Bought some birds*
> *For you*
> *My love*
> *I go to the flower market*
> *Bought some flowers*
> *For you*

我 的 愛
我 到 鐵 市 場 去
買 了 些 鏈 條
沉 重 的 鏈 條
為 妳
我 的 愛
然 後 我 到 奴 隸 市 場 去
找 妳
但 找 不 到 妳
我 的 愛

另外，下面這首〈向日葵〉是詩人裴外的名作之一，讀來情真意切，十分感人：

星 期 中 的 每 一 天
冬 天 及 秋 天
在 巴 黎 的 天 空 上
工 廠 的 烟 囪 只 吐 灰 色

但 春 天 來 了 ，一 朵 花 在 他 耳 上
在 他 臂 上 一 個 漂 亮 的 姑 娘
向 日 葵 向 日 葵
那 是 花 的 名 字
姑 娘 的 渾 名
她 沒 有 名 也 沒 有 姓

My love
I'm going to the iron market
Bought some chains
Heavy chain
For you
My love
Then I go to the slave market
Looking for you
But can't find you
My love

In addition, the following song *Sunflower* is one of the famous works of the poet Prévert. It is very touching when I read it:

Every day of the week
Winter and autumn
On the Paris sky
Factory chimneys spit gray

But spring came and a flower was in his ear
On his arm a beautiful girl
Sunflower sunflower
That is the name of the flower
Girl's nickname
She has no name or surname

在街角跳舞
在貝維爾及塞維爾

向日葵向日葵向日葵
街角的華爾茲
而陽光的日子來到
帶著甜蜜的生活

巴士底獄的精靈們吸著藍煙
在塞維爾天空貝維爾天空
的香氣裡
甚至別處
向日葵向日葵向日葵
那是花的名字
姑娘的渾名

　　這種超然於現實的富有音韻的詩，其產生背景不外有兩種原因：一是大時代的動盪造成詩人精神的空虛促使他走入某種對現實世界的虛幻反映；二是詩人欲體現出光明與在監獄黑暗搏鬥中，一個長期在巴士底獄的受刑人燃起一根煙，思緒衍生出一種生命渴望愛人的激想。詩人以監獄之束縛來對比天空的自由，讓讀者去體會超越時空的生命自由與愛。

　　同樣，生活在巴黎天空下的詩人，其親眼經歷的社會矛盾與心靈的苦惱也不少，比如這首〈禮拜天〉，詩人運用了

Dance on a street corner
Bayville and Seville

Sunflower sunflower sunflower
Street corner waltz
And the sunny day comes
With the sweet life

The elves of the Bastille smoke blue smoke
Beville Sky at Seville Sky
In the aroma
Even elsewhere
Sunflower sunflower sunflower
That is the name of the flower
Girl's nickname

There are two reasons for the background of this kind of rhyme-rich poems that are detached from reality: one is that the turmoil of the great era caused the spiritual emptiness of the poet and prompted him to enter into some kind of illusory reflection of the real world; In the struggle between coming out of the light and being in the darkness of the prison, a prisoner who had been in the Bastille for a long time lit a cigarette, and his thoughts derived a kind of excitement of life longing for a lover. The poet compares the freedom of the sky with the shackles of the prison, allowing readers to experience the freedom and love of life beyond time and space.

Similarly, poets who live under the sky of Paris have experienced many social contradictions and spiritual distress. For example, in this poem *Sunday*, the poet uses

許多現代詩的藝術手法，為隱喻、通感和幻覺：

> 在栗樹排立的廣場裏
> 一座石像牽著我的手
> 今天是禮拜天電影院都客滿
> 鳥在他們的樹上看著人們
> 石像擁抱我但沒有人看到
> 除了一個盲童指點的手

　　在巴黎都會上層階級的浮華與禮拜天在空曠的廣場上散步的詩人，力圖找出一塊安靜的歇地卻無意中看到盲童的一種空靈感，而鳥在樹上看著匆忙的人們，畫面也超然的寂靜。

　　裴外的詩歌並非固定傳統的頑冥不化者，他不老的詩心仍像小孩一樣純真。且看這首〈失時〉：

> 在工廠的大門口
> 那工人突然停步
> 為這好天氣所絆住
> 他轉身看著太陽
> 紅而圓
> 在他封閉的天空裡微笑
> 他眨了眨一隻眼——
> 喂，太陽同志
> 那豈不是天大的損失

many artistic techniques of modern poetry, such as metaphor, synaesthesia and hallucination:

> *In the square lined with chestnut trees*
> *A stone statue holds my hand*
> *It's Sunday and the movie theaters are full*
> *birds watching people from their trees*
> *The statue hugs me but no one sees*
> *Except for the pointing hand of a blind child*

In the pomp of the Paris metropolitan upper class and the poet who walks in the empty square on Sunday, trying to find a quiet resting place, accidentally sees an ethereal idea of a blind child, while the bird watches the people in a hurry from the tree, the screen is also detached and silent.

Jacques Prévert's poetry is not a stickler for fixed traditions, his ageless poetic heart is still as pure as a child. Let's look at this song *Lost Time*:

> *At the gate of the factory*
> *The worker stopped suddenly*
> *Stumped by the good weather*
> *He turned to look at the sun*
> *Red and round*
> *Smiling in his closed sky*
> *He blinked one eye —*
> *Hello, Comrade Sun*
> *Wouldn't that be a huge loss*

　　　把這麼美好的一天
　　　送給上司」

　　這首可以說是自由體的韻詩，正是由於詩人心態的悲憫和美學觀念的變化造成的。在我看來，不完整、看似平淡的街景或勞動者對上司的不同心聲、童趣又真性的語言才是一種真正的意象藝術；反之則僵化、定型。

　　最後，這首〈不可〉是對現實世界中某些知識份子庸俗無聊卻自以為是的幽默諷刺和對黑暗醜陋事物的否定：

　　　不可讓知識份子玩火柴
　　　因為要是不管他們
　　　這些先生們的精神世界
　　　便一點兒都不靈光
　　　一但獨處
　　　便胡亂來
　　　為他們自己造
　　　一座自我碑
　　　並且自命慷慨為建造者
　　　慶功
　　　讓我們再說一遍
　　　要是不管這些先生們
　　　他們的精神世界
　　　便要豎起
　　　紀念碑

Make such a beautiful day
To the boss

This rhyme, which can be said to be in free style, is precisely due to the poet's compassion and changes in aesthetic concepts. In my opinion, incomplete and seemingly plain street scenes or laborers' different voices to their bosses, childlike and authentic language is a real image art; otherwise, it is rigid and stereotyped.

Finally, this song *Unable* is a humorous satire on some vulgar and boring but self-righteous intellectuals in the real world and a denial of dark and ugly things:

Intellectuals are not to be allowed to play with matches
Because if they don't
The spiritual world of these gentlemen
It's not bright at all
Once alone
So random
Make for themselves
A self monument
And call themselves generous builders
Celebrate
Let's say it again
If these gentlemen
Their spiritual world
Will be erected
Monument

詩人以超驗象徵為邏輯起點恰恰是一種新人文精神的反照。暗喻我們的時代變化萬端，知識份子應覺醒、要伸張正義，是要付出血的代價的；當然這種智性思維並非排斥詩人的感情；反而是詩人欲深刻地揭示出那顛倒黑白的年代對人性的探索。

斐外詩歌的審美價值

傑克・斐外主觀感情之烙印，常構成詩歌裡獨具的意象，且思想容量極大。古人云，「語不接而意接」，斐外以高度的詩化語言，擴大並進一步努力形成自己的特色，能夠獨立地屹立在世界詩壇上百年之因，在於其語言風格脫去柔媚氣質，保有濃郁的現代意識，意象不撲朔迷離且能張揚民族精神、創造出一種超現實的景觀與寫實並濟的風格。我們由以上的賞析中，便可以找到斐外詩歌審美價值的答案。

一、自由聯想的風格美：擅於運用奇特的遐想，表達其嘲弄又叫人覺得滑稽，富有戲劇色彩的幽默感。二、打破時空限制的形象美：詩人對宇宙萬類的印象都活動在腦海裡，使詩歌意象鮮活，那可觸性的形象詩句，常給人以藝術的美感。三、繪畫美給人帶來希望的景像：詩句不但有形態，還有多彩的畫面，可以陶冶讀者的情愫。總之，斐外生命裡的

The poet's logical starting point of transcendental symbols is just a reflection of a new humanistic spirit. It is a metaphor that our times are changing, and intellectuals should wake up and uphold justice at the cost of blood; of course, this kind of intellectual thinking does not exclude the poet's feelings; The exploration of human nature.

The Aesthetic Value of Jacques Prévert's Poetry

The imprint of Jacques Prévert's subjective feelings often constitutes a unique image in his poems, and his thinking capacity is huge. The ancients said, "words don't connect but meaning connects." Prévert used highly poetic language to expand and further strive to form his own characteristics. The reason why he can stand independently in the world poetry circle for hundreds of years is that his language style has lost its femininity, retaining a strong sense of modernity, the images are not confusing and can promote the national spirit, creating a surreal landscape and a realistic style. From the above appreciation and analysis, we can find the answer to the aesthetic value of Prévert's poems.

(1) The style beauty of free association: Good at using strange reverie, expressing its mockery and making people feel funny, with a sense of humor rich in drama. (2) Image beauty that breaks the constraints of time and space: the poet's impressions of all kinds of the universe are active in his mind, making the poetic imagery vivid, and the palpable image lines often give people an artistic sense of

愛與快樂、痛苦與希望是渾成一片的。詩人用想像之花，結成形象之果，他用寫實主義同超現實手法的融合，更能抒發真情和對美好理想的追求，常能激起人們感情的共鳴。他對詩美的精湛創造已響譽整個法國，其詩歌的審美價值與取得的編劇成就也是令世界文壇所矚目的。

> 註；文中譯詩選自非馬譯《裴外的詩》，臺灣，大舞臺書苑出版社，1978 年 1 月 15 日初版，收錄法國詩人傑克・裴外的 47 首詩，由英譯本(美國詩人佛苓蓋蒂(Lawrence Ferlinghetti, 1919-) 的英譯本《話》(PAROLES) 移譯。

--2012.2.17 作

--臺灣《大海洋》詩雜誌，第 87 期，2013.07，頁 2

joy, pain and hope in Prévert's life are all integrated. The poet uses the flowers of imagination to form the fruit of images. He uses the fusion of realism and surrealism to express his true feelings and pursuit of beautiful ideals, and often arouses people's emotional resonance. His exquisite creation of poetic beauty has been well-known throughout France, and the aesthetic value of his poems and his achievements in screenwriting have also attracted the attention of the world's literary circles.

Note：Chinese translation of poems is selected from Dr. WilliamMarr's translation of *Jacques Prévert's Poems*, Taiwan, Grand Stage Shuyuan Publishing House, first edition on January 15, 1978, including 47 poems by French poet Jack Prévert, translated from English; American poet Lawrence Ferlinghetti (1919-)'s English translation *PAROLES*.

5. 論布洛克詩歌中的象徵意蘊

內容提要：亞歷山大‧布洛克的創作將象徵主義浪潮，推展至顛峰，其詩歌中的象徵意蘊已經作了高度發揮。本文將其反映生活和抒情狀物的特點嘗試做一分析。

關鍵詞：布洛克，象徵主義，意象，俄羅斯

一、引言

在俄國文學中，亞歷山大‧布洛克(Alexander Blok,1880－1921)被當代批評家譽為俄國詩史上有重大影響的象徵主義詩人。他父親是教授，外祖父曾任彼得堡大學校長，學生時就開始寫詩，尤其喜愛朱可夫斯基(VasiljAndreeviéZukovski,1783-1852)具有溫柔甜蜜和遁世的憂鬱的浪漫詩歌，並且認識了象徵主義的先驅、詩人索洛維約夫(Vladimir Solovev , 1853 - 1900)的神秘宗教哲學。同索洛維約夫一般，他使俄國詩歌有了自己獨立的語言和獨特的表達形式，進而結束了俄國哲學僅僅靠散文、札記等方式表達自己情感及思想的時代。

1890 年以後，象徵派興起，詩歌在俄羅斯文學中重獲主流地位。但這時期的象徵派作品都刊登於小雜誌上，直到《北方通訊》才成為象徵派的機關刊物，此刊物於 1898 年停刊後，

5. On the Symbolic Meaning of Blok's Poetry

Abstract: Alexander Blok's work pushed the wave of symbolism to its peak. Symbolism played a big role in his poetry. This article is an attempt to analyze and reflect on his life and lyrical characteristics of his poetry.

Key words： Alexander Blok; symbolism; image; Russia

1. Introduction

In Russian literature, Alexander Blok (1880-1921) is hailed by contemporary critics as a symbolist poet with great influence in the history of Russian poetry. His father was a professor, and his maternal grandfather was the president of Petersburg University. He began to write poetry when he was a student. He especially liked Zhukovsky's (Vasilj Andreevié Zukovski, 1783-1852) romantic poetry with tenderness, sweetness and secluded melancholy, and he knew the pioneer of symbolism. The mystical religious philosophy of the poet Solovyov (Vladimir Solovev, 1853-1900). Like Solovyov, he gave Russian poetry its own independent language and unique form of expression, and thus ended the era when Russian philosophy only expressed its emotions and thoughts in prose and notes.

After 1890, symbolism emerged, and poetry regained its mainstream status in Russian literature. However, the works of the Symbolists during this period were all published in small magazines, and it was not until the "Northern Newsletter" that it became the official publication of the Symbolists. After this publication ceased publication in 1898, the magazine *Fine Arts* issued

緊接著在 1899 年發行的雜誌《美術界》，開始有優秀的畫家和詩人為此撰稿，但還是延續到 1904 年即停刊。1903 年，批評家弗羅梭霍夫和作家、詩人米列日柯夫斯基在彼得堡主編發行了雜誌《新道路》，熱烈提倡宗教哲學的新思想。1905 年《新道路》改編成《人生問題》，但經營一年即停刊。

　　在這期間，莫斯科有一群青年作家崛起，他們在詩歌、評論、小說各方面均有表現，作品的思想深刻，詩歌典雅華麗、民族性強，對日後俄國文藝界貢獻良多。其中，巴爾蒙特（1867-1942）、勃留索夫（1873-1924）、米列日柯夫斯基、吉皮烏斯女詩人（1869－1945）、索羅古勃等人被認為是俄國現代主義之星，之後，伊凡諾夫、別雷（1880-1934）、果洛丁茲基、布洛克、庫茲明（1872-1936）等年輕詩人則代表一種新思想。因此，俄國的批評家稱前者為前期現代派，稱後者為後期現代派。至此，俄國的象徵派詩人努力通過宗教、科學和藝術的綜合，創造出新的人生觀。

　　著名的巴爾蒙特十分重視詩歌的音樂性，他為俄國詩壇開創了很多獨特的韻律方式。他在《詩即魔法》一書中寫道，「詩即有節奏的語言表達出來的內在音樂。」這是象徵派詩人所追求的藝術境界。在俄羅斯文學群星璀璨的「白銀時代」最大的成就，當屬詩歌。但這時期的詩人，有的是多災多難的。如古米廖夫被無罪處決，而承受著苦難的女詩人阿赫馬托娃則選擇留在祖國俄羅斯，還有早逝的馬雅可夫斯基等詩人。

in 1899 began to publish Excellent painters and poets contributed to it, but it continued until 1904 when it ceased publication. In 1903, the critic Vrosokhov and the writer and poet Mirezhkovsky edited and published the magazine *The New Way* in Petersburg, enthusiastically advocating new ideas of religious philosophy. In 1905, *The New Way* was adapted into *The Problem of Life*, but it ceased publication after one year of operation.

During this period, a group of young writers rose up in Moscow. They performed in all aspects of poetry, commentary, and novels. Among them, Balmont (1867-1942), Bryusov (1873-1924), Mirezhkovsky, Gippius Poetess (1869-1945), Sorogub and others are considered to be Russian The star of modernism, after that, young poets such as Ivanov, Bely (1880-1934), Golodinsky, Blok, Kuzmin (1872-1936) and other young poets represented a new kind of thinking. Therefore, Russian critics call the former the early modernists and the latter the late modernists. So far, Russian Symbolist poets have tried to create a new outlook on life through the synthesis of religion, science and art.

The famous Balmont attached great importance to the musicality of poetry, and he created many unique rhythmic methods for the Russian poetry circle. He wrote in the book *Poetry is Magic*, "poetry is the inner music expressed by rhythmic language." This is the artistic realm pursued by symbolic poets. In the "Silver Age" of Russian literary stars, the greatest achievement was poetry. But some poets in this period were troubled by disasters. For example, Gumilyov was executed without charge, while the suffering female poet Akhmatova chose to stay in her motherland, Russia, and there were poets such as Mayakovsky who died young.

　　同樣作為一個詩人，布洛克的思想也影響到文學、哲學、歷史、美學等層面，那些廣泛奇巧的學識，超人的智慧包羅於其詩中。俄國詩評家日爾蒙斯基 (В. Жирмунский)說：

　　「布洛克是個隱喻詩人，他將世界隱喻知覺確認為詩人基本屬性。對詩人而言，依照隱喻的幫助，可對世界進行浪漫的變形；但這不是一個隨心所欲的詩歌游擊，而是對生活神秘本質的真正領悟。」

　　可見，這位書香世家、具有超脫風範的詩人，他喜歡超越現代一切現象，時時睜開眼睛睨視世界。他的早期詩歌具有一種令人着魔般的手法，主觀性特別強烈。他所描繪的世界是朦朧的、神秘的，一個無定形的世界。他注重抒寫自己的內心世界，常沉浸在某種夢幻般依稀的氣氛中，心裡充滿著中世紀騎士的宗教情緒。然而，富於幻想也是俄國象徵主義的特徵。他以清新、無邪的幻想的詩眸縱觀宇宙，去感受、要得到一切實在事物的印象。詩音流暢，韻律豐富；同時，思想的朦朧，盤旋在心中的憂愁和對現實的絕望等等，在詩歌意蘊中和浪漫主義之間仍存在著某種聯繫，並且，在冥想中往往會不自覺地產生一種聖潔的宗教情操。布洛克的詩本質上與西方象徵派相溝通，後期之作轉為抒寫熱烈的祖國愛，常以社會和人生為對象，抒寫「不幸」的憂鬱美。他把表象世界運用暗示、隱喻等手法和此世界中夢樣神奇的幻滅冶於一爐，從而將自我的感情展示出來。他也追求事物與主體神秘的交感，關心革命與人民生與死的抽象問題，意象憂鬱、幽深而神秘，為俄國象徵主義作了高度發揮。他真正稱得上

Also as a poet, Blok's thoughts also affect literature, philosophy, history, aesthetics and other aspects. Those extensive and ingenious knowledge and superhuman wisdom are included in his poems. Russian poetry critic Zhiermensky (В. Жирмунский) said:

"Bloch is a poet of metaphors, and he affirms the metaphorical perception of the world as an essential attribute of poets. For poets, with the help of metaphors, the world can be romantically deformed; but this is not a poetic guerrilla at will, but the mystery of life true understanding of nature."

It can be seen that this scholarly and detached poet likes to transcend all modern phenomena and always open his eyes to see the world. His early poems have an obsessive approach and are particularly subjective. The world he depicts is hazy, mysterious, an amorphous world. He pays attention to expressing his inner world, and is often immersed in a dreamlike atmosphere, full of religious emotions of medieval knights. However, fantasy is also characteristic of Russian symbolism. He looks at the universe with fresh, innocent and imaginative poetic eyes, to feel and get the impression of all real things. The sound of the poem is smooth and the rhythm is rich; at the same time, there is still a certain connection between the implication of poetry and romanticism, such as hazy thoughts, lingering sorrow in the heart and despair of reality, etc., and often unconsciously in meditation. to produce a holy religious sentiment. Blok's poems are essentially in communication with the Western symbolism, and his later works turned to expressing passionate love for the motherland, often using society and life as objects, and expressing the melancholy beauty of "unfortunate". He combines hints, metaphors and other techniques in the representational world with the magical disillusionment of dreams in this world, so as to show his own feelings. He also pursues the mysterious sympathy between things and the subject, and cares about the revolution and the abstract issues of people's life and death. His images are melancholy, deep and mysterious, and he has made great

是不朽的詩人，也是俄國文學改革者，因而贏得了人民的頌
揚與欽讚。

二、布洛克詩歌──象徵意蘊

　　什麼是象徵？象徵一詞從西方語源說源自於古希臘，歷
來有各種各樣的說法。美國學者勞•坡林 Lawrence Perrine 把
象徵表述為：「象徵的意義可以粗略說成某種東西的含義大
於其本身。」（註）簡言之，它是一種藝術方法，即通過具
體的、感性形式傳達出它所暗示的普遍性意義。例如，我們
一提到太陽，就會聯想到希望、生機，溫暖和光明。太陽是
具體的，但當它放進一個象徵結構中，它就傳達出巨大的理
性內容。西方哲學思潮的湧入，也為俄羅斯詩人提供了新的
理論與視角，促進了俄國十九世紀末至二十世紀初的文化繁
榮，一般稱為「白銀時代」（1890-1920），約有三十多年的
時間出現在俄國文學上，而俄國象徵主義正是此時代最先出
現的新流派，在詩藝創作與理論批評上都有卓越的成就。

　　在布洛克詩歌中象徵意象所包含的象徵意蘊十分豐厚，
往往不是單層的，而是多層的；往往不是清晰的，而是隱喻、
神秘的。他在 1904 年出版的第一本詩集《美女詩篇》（Стихи
о прекрасной даме），這是詩人早期重要之作，內心充滿著
對美好理想的追求，與其生活、情感方面有緊密相關。在這
部詩裡 他表現了對於未來妻子門捷諾娃甜蜜或苦澀的愛情，
也表現了受俄國詩人哲學家索諾維約夫的思想影響極深，文

use of Russian symbolism. He was truly an immortal poet and a reformer of Russian literature, and thus won the admiration of the people.

2. Bloch's Poetry — Symbolism

What is a symbol? The word symbol originated from ancient Greece in Western etymology, and there have been various sayings throughout the history. American scholar Lawrence Perrine expressed symbolism as: "The meaning of a symbol can be roughly said to mean that something has a meaning greater than itself." (Note) In short, it is an artistic method, that is, through concrete, perceptual Form conveys the universal meaning it implies. For example, when we mention the sun, we think of hope, vitality, warmth and light. The sun is concrete, but when placed into a symbolic structure, it conveys enormous intellectual content. The influx of Western philosophical thoughts also provided new theories and perspectives for Russian poets, and promoted the cultural prosperity of Russia from the end of the 19th century to the beginning of the 20th century, generally known as the "Silver Age" (1890-1920), about three years It has appeared in Russian literature for more than ten years, and Russian symbolism is the first new genre to appear in this era, with outstanding achievements in poetic creation and theoretical criticism.

The symbolic meaning contained in the symbolic imagery in Blok's poems is very rich, often not single-layered, but multi-layered; often not clear, but metaphorical and mysterious. His first collection of poems, "Beauty Poems" (Стихи о прекрасной даме), published in 1904, was an important early work of the poet, filled with the pursuit of beautiful ideals, and closely related to his life and emotions. In this poem, he expresses his sweet or bitter love for his future wife Mendenova, and also shows that he is deeply influenced by the thoughts of the Russian poet

字的琢磨，幾乎是字字珠璣。從索諾維約夫倡導宗教——哲學協會起，他們就把哲學問題同文學評論有機地結合起來。於此階段中，布洛克認為唯有藝術的象徵才能表達無法言語的世界奧秘，一心渴求臻於完善、柔美的崇高境界。他運用閃動的意象及抽象的象徵手法表達靈魂對於另一個世界的嚮往，而詩裡所指的「美女」自然成為世界靈魂及理想世界的象徵，給人無限的聯想。同其他象徵派詩人，尤其是知識份子，普遍的感受一般，他一方面對於現實感到不滿，一方面又無法從日漸沉落的社會中，把人民從絕望的邊緣上拉回，置入希望的道路上。故而，其思想常處於生之寂寞的狀態。於《美女詩篇》詩集中，詩人以神秘、浪漫愛情為主旋律，許多方面可能是受索諾維約夫以美為基礎改造世界的烏托邦理想的影響。他認為，現實世界是污濁痛苦的，也因此於詩人的心中建構出另一個彼岸的理想世界。於這理想的世界中，他運用神祕且朦朧的情境來寄託自己的情感。

到了布洛克的第二本詩集《意外的歡樂》，則詩韻較為活潑，沉浸在都會中美妙的氛圍裡，詩人從巴黎的遊樂場或彼得堡的列斯特蘭這類地方獲得了靈感。隨著西歐都會文明和市民運動波及俄羅斯，都會文學終於取代了以往的田園文學。而這一轉折過程中的重要詩人就是亞歷山大・布洛克。

如這首 1901 年的（上蒼不能以理性測量）是世紀末的苦悶、迷醉，現實社會裡的特質。二十一歲的詩人企圖從中尋找出一種新的領悟，或表達我們無法以文字表達的某種體驗：

and philosopher Sonovyov, and he ponders the words almost every word. pearls. Since Sonovyov advocated the Religion-Philosophy Association, they have organically combined philosophical issues with literary criticism. At this stage, Blok believes that only the symbols of art can express the unspeakable mysteries of the world, and he is eager to reach the lofty realm of perfection and softness. He uses flickering images and abstract symbolism to express the soul's longing for another world, and the "beauty" referred to in the poem naturally becomes a symbol of the soul of the world and the ideal world, giving people infinite associations. Like other symbolic poets, especially intellectuals, he is dissatisfied with the reality on the one hand, and on the other hand, he cannot pull the people back from the brink of despair and put them in hope from the sinking society. on the road. Therefore, their thoughts are often in a state of loneliness in life. In the collection of poems "Beauty Psalms", the poet focuses on mysterious and romantic love, which may be influenced by Sonovyov's utopian ideal of transforming the world based on beauty in many aspects. He believes that the real world is dirty and painful, and therefore constructs another ideal world on the other side in the poet's heart. In this ideal world, he uses mysterious and hazy situations to pin his emotions.

In Blok's second collection of poems *Unexpected Joy*, the rhyme is more lively, immersed in the wonderful atmosphere of the city. The poet got inspiration from places such as the playground in Paris or Listland in Petersburg. As Western European urban civilization and citizen movements spread to Russia, urban literature finally replaced pastoral literature. And the important poet in this turning process is Alexander Blok.

For example, this song from 1901 (God cannot measure it rationally) is the depression and intoxication at the end of the century, which are the characteristics of the real society. The 21-year-old poet tries to find a new understanding from it, or express some kind of experience that we cannot express in words:

上蒼不能以理性測量，
藍天隱藏在智慧之外。
只有時六翼天使帶給
世間特選者神聖之夢。

俄羅斯女神在我夢裡出現，
她披覆著厚重長袍，
純潔而沉靜，不盡的悲愁，
面容中──安詳的夢。

她並非初次下降凡塵，
卻是第一次簇擁著
不是那些勇士，而是其他英雄……
深眸中的光澤奇異……

　　詩裡的撒拉弗（Seraphim）又稱六翼天使，有六個翅膀。
他是神最親近的御使，也是天使之首熾天使，其唯一的使命
就是歌頌神。在天使群中甚持威嚴和名譽，被稱為是「愛和
想像力的精靈」。「俄羅斯女神」既是詩人觀察都會生活中
的心儀對象，並將這些朦朧的印象象徵化，也是索洛維約夫
宗教理想中的熾天使。他的早期詩歌裡，幻想和現實參差交
錯，常編織出神奇的都會氣氛。這種把自己宗教性的渴望之
情加以象徵化，六翼天使恰如朦朧的幻影在讀者面前掠過，

God cannot measure with reason,
The blue sky is hidden from wisdom.
only time seraphim brings
The divine dream of the Chosen One.

The Russian goddess appeared in my dreams,
She is draped in a heavy robe,
Pure and silent, endless sorrow,
In the face — a peaceful dream.

It is not the first time she has descended into the
　mortal world,
It's the first time surrounded by
Not those warriors, but other heroes...
The luster in the deep eyes is strange...

The Seraphim in the poem, also known as the seraphim, has six wings. He is God's closest envoy and the head of the angels, Seraphim, whose sole mission is to sing praises to God. It holds majesty and reputation among the angels, and is called "the elf of love and imagination". The "Russian Goddess" is not only the favorite object of the poet to observe the urban life and symbolize these hazy impressions, but also the Seraphim in Solovyov's religious ideal. In his early poems, fantasy and reality are intertwined, often weaving a magical urban atmosphere. This symbolization of one's own religious longing, the seraph flits before the reader like a hazy phantom, has

祂已成為融合整個俄羅斯人民為愛所苦的美的象徵。祂，沒有固定的姓名，又有所有的名字。

　　就如同 1902 年寫的另一首（我步入幽暗的教堂(Вхожу я в темные храмы)詩中寫道：

> 我步入幽暗的教堂，
> 完成一次空泛的儀式。
> 在那裡我等待美女
> 在紅燈的微弱顫抖中。
>
> 在高高圓柱陰影裡，
> 門的吱咯令我哆嗦。
> 唯有那聖容，唯有對她的憧憬，
> 閃爍著，直視我的臉。
>
> 啊，我已熟悉這位
> 莊嚴永恆女神的法衣！
> 教堂窗簷上高飛著
> 微笑、神話與夢想。
>
> 啊，女神，燭光多麼溫柔，
> 妳的聖容多麼令人振奮！
> 我聽不見話語和聲音，
> 但我相信：親愛的，那是妳。

become a symbol of beauty that unites the entire Russian people suffering from love. He has no fixed name, but has all names.

As in another poem written in 1902 (I stepped into the dark church (Вхожу я в темные храмы)) wrote:

I step into the dark church,
Complete an empty ritual.
where I wait for the beauty
In the faint trembling of the red light.

In tall cylindrical shadows,
The creaking of the door made me shiver.
Only that holy face, only the longing for her,
Blinking, looking straight into my face.

Ah, I'm familiar with this
The vestments of the majestic Eternal Goddess!
Flying high above the church window cornices
Smiles, myths and dreams.

O Goddess, how gentle the candlelight is,
How uplifting is your countenance!
I cannot hear words and voices,
But I believe: Honey, it's you.

　　這訥喊是短促的、嚴肅的，但也帶有幾分浪漫的靈魂的意蘊，意象的情感內涵增強了。詩裡美人的意象和俄羅斯女神及大自然的意象合而為一，充滿神秘與聖美。雖然她是宇宙的靈魂，是世界的主宰，但對詩人而言，她是令人難以捉摸的，也期待著他心中如夢似幻的女神的降臨。幾乎在布洛克之前，俄羅斯象徵派還沒有人寫過如此偉構的詩。他的詩歌常跳脫俄詩的格律常規 將都會文明嵌入世界生活的畫框，而且象徵化地再現了都市人民的生活狀態及反映出詩人心靈不斷被喧嘩和光波衝擊著的內心世界。他也是一個浪漫主義者，然而在布洛克的浪漫主義裡，技巧上是師承了象徵派而又揉合了諸多宗教哲學上的成就。行動上也為了詩人的熱愛和神的讚美而寫的。在這些主題中，他都不是像抒情詩那樣容易捉摸，或者一氣呵成，而是經過一段時間的沉思，然後把都市特有的瞬即意象揉進詩裡。因此，他的詩裡描繪的是馬車、電車的聲響和煤氣燈、電燈、昏暗的光芒等現實生活中不可或缺的影像，而這些景色輝映著他的生命。

　　再如 1905 年寫的（秋的自由）一詩裡：

　　　　我走上眼前的道路，
　　　　風屈折彈性的灌木，
　　　　碎石仰臥斜坡道上，
　　　　黃土鋪覆貧瘠岩層。

　　　　秋氾濫潮濕的山谷，
　　　　裸露大地的墓。

This shout is short and serious, but it also has a romantic soul meaning, and the emotional connotation of the image is enhanced. The image of the beauty in the poem and the image of the Russian goddess and nature are combined into one, full of mystery and beauty. Although she is the soul of the universe and the master of the world, for the poet, she is elusive, and she is also looking forward to the coming of the dreamlike goddess in his heart. Almost before Bloch, no one of the Russian Symbolists had written such a magnificent poem. His poems often break away from the metrical conventions of Russian poetry, embedding urban civilization into the frame of world life, and symbolically reproduce the living conditions of urban people and reflect the poet's inner world that is constantly impacted by noise and light waves. He is also a romanticist, but in Blok's romanticism, technically he inherited the symbolism and combined many religious and philosophical achievements. Deeds are also written for the love of poets and the praise of God. Among these themes, he is not as elusive as lyric poems, or completed in one go, but after a period of meditation, he then rubs the city's unique instantaneous imagery into the poems. Therefore, his poems depict the sounds of carriages and trams, gas lamps, electric lights, and dim lights, which are indispensable in real life, and these scenes reflect his life.

Another example is in the poem (Autumn Freedom) written in 1905:

> I walked the path before me,
> wind-bending springy shrubs,
> The gravel lies supine on the ramp,
> Loess covers barren rock formations.
>
> Autumn floods the damp valleys,
> The tomb of the bare earth.

沿途的村落中，
花揪揚起濃濃的紅。

看啊，我的歡悅，它舞著，
響著，響著，跌入灌木中。
你五彩斑斕的衣袖，
在遠方，在遠方揮舞。

誰誘我來到這路，
向著牢獄之窗冷笑？
是拖曳在石道上
吟唱讚美詩的乞兒？

不，我走上無人呼喚的道路，
大地如是輕盈，
我將諦聽俄羅斯的醉語，
我將在酒店屋簷下歇息。

我將歌頌自己的幸福，
唱我酩酊中毀去青春。
我將哭你田園的淒涼，
也將永遠愛你的遼闊。

許多人——奔放的，青春的，優雅的
不曾愛，便將死去……
在天涯盡處收容他們吧！
沒有你如何活？如何哭？

In the villages along the way,
Rowan raised a thick red.

Behold, my joy, it dances,
Ring, ring, fall into the bushes.
Your colorful sleeves,
In the distance, waving in the distance.

Who lured me down this road,
Sneering at the prison window?
is dragged on the stone road
A beggar who sings hymns?

No, I go on the road that no one calls,
The earth is so light,
I will listen to the drunken language of Russia,
I will rest under the roof of the hotel.

I will sing of my happiness,
Sing that I ruin my youth while drunk.
I will weep for your pastoral desolation,
And will always love your expanse.

Many people — unrestrained, youthful, elegant
If you don't love, you will die...
Take them to the ends of the earth!
How can I live without you? how to cry

　　這裡，布洛克所表現的就是他在都市中的青春，他認為
象徵比形象更能有效地反映世界的真實;但他在接受了西方
象徵主義者許多美學觀點的同時，又富有社會敏感和生活激
情，關注對俄羅斯受難人民生活與社會現實的思考與觀察。
此詩，他把自己的身心整個溶化在大自然氣氛中，灌木、山
谷、牢獄之窗、酒店、田園等這些意象裡，時間彷彿暫時休
止，在詩中重新撿拾他對青春的感覺。布洛克是個高度的感
覺性詩人，他的詩多以有力的語言，借助清新的、敏感的形
象，勾勒出了一顆孤獨心靈的全部體驗。

　　但 1905 年俄國第一次革命對布洛克的創作道路起了關
鍵性的影響，他開始關注起貧困的人民及受難者的痛苦世界。
此階段的作品以詩集《城市》(Город)為主。這是布洛克詩歌
創作的轉折期。這時整個社會已動盪不安，詩人放棄了索羅
維約夫的神祕主義，轉而寫出反映現實生活和現實的題材。他
也富有民主思想，對俄羅斯人民的貧困不安、懷疑、底層的蒼
涼、囚犯的悲傷、都會的歡樂或愛的輕愁都獨具慧眼。例如在
1908 年寫的（俄羅斯），這就是對祖國愛的真諦一種詮釋：

　　　　又是，彷彿在黃金年代，
　　　　拖動破舊套繩的三頭馬車，
　　　　五彩的木輪陷入
　　　　鬆動車道……

　　　　俄羅斯，貧窮的俄羅斯啊，
　　　　妳的晦暗農舍，

Here, what Blok expresses is his youth in the city. He believes that symbols can reflect the reality of the world more effectively than images. Passionate, focusing on the thinking and observation of the lives of the suffering people in Russia and the social reality. In this poem, he melts his body and mind into the atmosphere of nature. In the images of bushes, valleys, prison windows, hotels, fields, etc., time seems to stop temporarily, and he regains his feeling of youth in the poem. Blok is a highly sensual poet. Most of his poems outline the whole experience of a lonely soul with powerful language and fresh and sensitive images.

However, the first Russian revolution in 1905 had a key impact on Blok's creative path, and he began to pay attention to the world of suffering of the poor and the victims. The works at this stage are dominated by the poetry collection "City" (Город). This is a turning point in Blok's poetry creation. At this time, the whole society was in turmoil, and the poet gave up Solovyov's mysticism and turned to write themes that reflected real life and reality. He is also rich in democratic ideas, and has a unique insight into the poverty and anxiety of the Russian people, doubts, the desolation of the bottom, the sorrow of prisoners, the joy of the city or the melancholy of love. For example written in 1908 (Russia), this is an interpretation of the true meaning of love for the Fatherland:

Again, as in the golden age,
Pulling the troika of worn nooses,
Multicolored wooden wheels sinking
loosing driveway...

Russia, poor Russia,
your dark farmhouse,

妳的風中歌聲——
恰似我的初戀之淚！

我不善憐惜妳，
只能背起十字架……
隨妳把粗獷美色
交付給巫術師！

儘管他誘惑欺騙，——
妳不隱沒，不消失，
只是憂愁遮掩了
妳的嬌容……

那又怎樣？唯有愁更多——
唯有淚河更洶湧，
而妳依舊——森林、曠野，
花巾覆上秀眉……
於是萬難盡去，
長路輕盈。
而路的那端，
花巾下秋水盈盈，
而車夫的蒼涼之歌，
唱著囚犯的悲情。

Your singing in the wind —
Just like the tears of my first love!

I don't take pity on you,
Just take up the cross...
rough and beautiful
Delivery to the wizard!

Though he tempts and deceives, —
You don't disappear, you don't disappear,
just covered by sorrow
your beauty...

So what? only worry more —
Only the river of tears is more turbulent,
And you still — the forest, the wilderness,
The flower scarf covers the beautiful eyebrows...
So all is lost,
The long way is light.
And on the other side of the road,
Under the flower scarf, the autumn water is full,
And the desolate song of the coachman,
Singing the pity of the prisoner.

　　這是多悲傷的嘆息，詩人對俄羅斯抱著無限的依戀，而又面臨革命的聲音一步一步靠近來的迫切時，這是令人愁苦而不安的。他用他的眼淚哭泣在哀戚的長路之中，去為死去的囚犯悲悼，為貧窮的俄羅斯人民沉痛的背起十字架的枷鎖。在俄羅斯的傳統文化中，大地也被看成是一位偉大的女性，是孕育一切生命之物的母親。在這裡，詩人也以「妳」稱呼俄羅斯大地之母，歌頌她的潤澤與愛，也歌頌她的苦痛與悲傷。俄國詩人布留索夫(В. Брюсов)曾說，「布洛克的詩是白晝的、不是夜間的，是色彩、不是色調，是豐富的聲音，不是叫喊與沉默」。而此詩，除了色彩的意象外，也能喚起人們的聽象上極強的藝術力量。他用「五彩的木輪陷入／鬆動車道……」創造出馬車在貧瘠鄉路的聽象，用「妳的風中歌聲──／恰似我的初戀之淚！」創造出俄羅斯大地痛苦私語的聽象。用「花巾下秋水盈盈」疊字詞摹聲創造出俄羅斯婦女哭泣的神情，用車夫的蒼涼及囚犯的悲情傳達出他們內心交織變化的痛苦情狀。如果我們再三的研讀這段話之後，我們會發現這時期的布洛克一心只想引導混亂的世界重新走向統一的和諧。除了此詩以外，他開始創作以俄羅斯命運為主體的詩歌，如〈祖國〉以及長詩《Двенадцать》（十二），這是以十二名俄國士兵象徵基督的十二門徒，藉以歌誦偉大的十月革命，揭示舊世界的真面目。他的理想已遠超過同期的象徵派詩人的感性形式。他的詞句轉而更聖潔凝鍊，可說是一個道地的俄羅斯文學家。譬如他在 1912 年寫的〈黑夜、馬路、街燈、藥房〉一詩，則有更深奧的意義存在：

This is a sad sigh. When the poet has an infinite attachment to Russia and faces the urgency of the voice of revolution approaching step by step, it is distressing and disturbing. He wept with his tears on the long road of mourning, mourning for the dead prisoners, and sadly bearing the shackles of the cross for the poor Russian people. In Russian traditional culture, the earth is also regarded as a great woman, the mother who conceives all living things. Here, the poet also uses "you" to call the mother of the Russian land, singing her praises of her nourishment and love, as well as her pain and sorrow. The Russian poet Bryusov (В. Брюсов) once said, "Bloch's poetry is daytime, not nighttime, color, not tone, rich sounds, not shouts and silence." And this poem, in addition to the imagery of color, can also arouse people's strong artistic power in hearing. He used "multicolored wooden wheels sinking / loosening the driveway..." to create the sound of a carriage on a barren country road, and used "your singing in the wind — / Just like the tears of my first love!" to create the painful whispers of the Russian land. The expression of Russian women weeping is created by using the repeated words of "autumn water under the flower scarf" to imitate the sound, and the desolation of the coachman and the sadness of the prisoners are used to convey the intertwined and changing pain in their hearts. If we study this passage time and again, we will find that Blok in this period only wants to lead the chaotic world back to unity and harmony. In addition to this poem, he began to write poems about the destiny of Russia, such as (Fatherland) and the long poem "Двенадцать" (Twelve), which uses twelve Russian soldiers to symbolize the twelve disciples of Christ, in order to sing the great October Revolution which revealed the true face of the old world. His ideals have far surpassed the sensual forms of the Symbolist poets of the same period. His words turned more holy and coherent, which can be said to be a true Russian writer. For example, his poem *Night, Road, Streetlight, Pharmacy* written in 1912 has a deeper meaning:

> 黑夜、馬路、街燈、藥房，
> 混沌昏暗的燈光。
> 縱使你再活四分之一世紀，
> 一切仍將這樣，沒有出路。
>
> 你死去──將重新開始，
> 一切重複，如從前一樣：
> 黑夜、運河冰封的漣漪、
> 藥房、馬路、街燈。

　　他喜歡運用相關語，保持著對社會與人生的高度觀察力，運用其沉靜的理性，將一個或幾個意象的種種意義經常在一節裡面反射出來。經過詩人的感情活動而創造出來的獨特意象「運河冰封的漣漪」這是一種賦予更多主觀情感色彩的具體藝術形象。如能掌握詩歌意象，就能更進一步了解詩人蘊涵於詩歌中的覆述「黑夜、藥房、馬路、街燈」的意思。詩人話語當中對社會的處境已不再是掙扎與混亂，而是心情平靜的沉默，可令讀者意識到詩人內心一種新的感情，那是非常寧靜和非常感傷的，幾乎像他血管中輕唱的血液，又似細石上掠過的溪流。為了使詩中所描繪的形象更具體化、生動化，感官度的傳達及文字意象的形成就很重要。他的感情與情緒，都依附在他所創作的色彩中。

　　我們讀布洛克的詩，像看抽象畫一般，它使人迷惑，但

The night, the road, the street lights, the pharmacy,
Chaotic dim lighting.
Even if you lived another quarter of a century,
Everything will remain as it is, with no way out.

You die — will start again,
Everything repeats, as before:
The night, the frozen ripples of the canal,
Pharmacies, roads, street lights.

He likes to use related words, maintains a high degree of observation on society and life, uses his quiet reason, and often reflects the various meanings of one or several images in a section. The unique image "ripples in the frozen canal" created by the poet's emotional activities is a specific artistic image that gives more subjective emotional color. If you can grasp the poetic imagery, you can further understand the meaning of the poet's repetition of "night, pharmacy, road, street lamp" contained in the poem. The social situation in the poet's words is no longer struggle and chaos, but a calm silence, which can make readers realize a new feeling in the poet's heart, which is very peaceful and sentimental, almost like singing in his veins. The blood is like a stream passing over fine stones. In order to make the images depicted in the poems more specific and vivid, it is very important to convey the sensuality and form the imagery of words. His feelings and emotions are attached to the colors he creates.

When we read Bloch's poems, it is like looking at an

又有非看下去不可的魅力,這就是他憂鬱中給人稀有的快感。如這首在 1914 年寫的（啊,我願瘋狂地活下去!）一詩:

> 啊,我願瘋狂地活下去!
> 讓真實的永遠保存,
> 讓非人的呈現人性,
> 讓未實現的化為現實。
>
> 縱使生活的沉夢令人窒息,
> 縱使我在這夢中氣喘吁吁,
> 也許,會有快樂的青年
> 在未來將我提起:
>
> 我們原諒他的憂鬱——難道
> 這不是他潛在的動力?
> 他是善與光之子,
> 他是自由的勝利!

　　這是一種感覺性的詩,藝術感染力大,內裡包含著詩人的悲、樂、美等多邊形的人生觀。至此時期,他已找回自我的存在,以自我的情意來透視事象。從他年青的強烈的情感和優美的詩篇中,他的力量是源自於他的聰穎或者憂鬱的藝術一直昇華到足以溝通他的特殊思維的形態。而他所追求的詩的特質,也是他固執著堅持藝術是一種純粹的表現,是難以用恰當的語言來表達出他濃郁的情感和愛憐。由此而知,

abstract painting. It confuses people, but it also has the charm that must be read. This is the rare pleasure in his melancholy. As in this poem written in 1914 entitled *Oh, I Would Live Madly!*:

Ah, I would live madly!
Let the truth be preserved forever,
Let the inhuman appear human,
Turn the unrealized into reality.

Though life's heavy dream is suffocating,
Even though I'm out of breath in this dream,
Perhaps, there will be happy youth
Bring me up in the future:

We forgive his melancholy — does it
Isn't that his underlying motivation?
He is the son of good and light,
He is the triumph of liberty!

　　This is a sensual poem with great artistic appeal, which contains the poet's polygonal outlook on life such as sadness, joy, and beauty. So far, he has recovered his own existence and used his own affection to see things through. From the strong emotions of his youth and the beauty of his poetry, his strength is derived from his witty or melancholic art until it is sublimated enough to communicate his peculiar thought-forms. And the characteristic of poetry he pursues is also his stubborn insistence that art is a kind of pure expression, and it is difficult to express his strong emotion and love with appropriate language. From this we can see that the image

神的意象也一直是布洛克詩歌的靈魂。他曾說:「詩人的職責首先在於揭開外面表面的覆蓋,挖掘心靈的深處,詩人必須放棄世俗一切的羈絆」。他把詩歌作為神性的傳達,它的魅力不僅在於詩歌擁有生動形象的敘事,也有深刻動人的詩情,且能滲入到俄羅斯農工階級及底層人民的生活和意識中。但是不可否認的是,他在追尋心目中想要遠離世俗塵囂所高築起來的理想國度,其實都屬於精神上的。然而,其詩歌仍有十分長久的影響性,在俄羅斯詩史上也獲得了永恆的意義。

三、布洛克獨特風格的成因

最後,我想探索一下,布洛克的這種藝術風格的成因。誠然,十九世紀末、二十世紀初,俄羅斯由農業社會逐漸過渡到工業社會。在新社會的秩序尚未建立之前,俄羅斯的知識份子在不安的社會氛圍下,紛紛投向精神的探索,由此萌生了一些思想流派,而象徵派就是個中的翹楚。他們強調藝術有三大要素:神祕主義的內容、象徵的手法、藝術感染力的擴大。在年青詩人中,布洛克是俄國象徵主義詩潮的傑出代表,其詩歌創作繼承了俄羅斯沉鬱、憂傷和哲理抒情詩傳統,但又以神秘、柔美、朦朧、絕望、冥想的筆觸及音樂性的旋律,成為俄羅斯象徵派詩歌的大師。其詩歌之可貴,是因為它描摹的畫面裡,捕捉著現代精神的複雜的形象。他曾說「現代都會人的精神,充滿著來自歷史和現實生活的連續不斷的印象,並且,在懷疑和矛盾中變得軟弱,被漫長的憂傷苦悶所侵蝕。儘管這種苦悶令人倦怠,可一旦因歡樂而興

of God has always been the soul of Blok's poetry. He once said: "The duty of a poet is first of all to uncover the cover of the outer surface and dig into the depths of the soul. A poet must give up all the fetters of the world." He regards poetry as the transmission of divinity. Its charm lies not only in its vivid narrative, but also its profound and moving poetic sentiment, which can penetrate into the life and consciousness of the Russian peasant and working class and the people at the bottom. But it is undeniable that the ideal country he built in his mind to stay away from the hustle and bustle of the world is actually spiritual. However, his poems still have a very long-lasting influence and have gained eternal significance in the history of Russian poetry.

3. The Cause of Blok's Unique Style

Finally, I would like to explore the origin of Blok's artistic style. It is true that at the end of the nineteenth century and the beginning of the twentieth century, Russia gradually transitioned from an agricultural society to an industrial society. Before the new social order was established, intellectuals in Russia devoted themselves to spiritual exploration in an uneasy social atmosphere, which gave birth to some schools of thought, among which the symbolism school was the leader. They emphasized that art has three major elements: the content of mysticism, the technique of symbolism, and the expansion of artistic appeal. Among the young poets, Blok is an outstanding representative of Russian symbolist poetic trend. His poetic creation inherits the tradition of Russian melancholy and philosophical lyric poetry, but also uses mysterious, soft, hazy, desperate, meditative strokes and musical melody, to become a master of Russian Symbolist poetry. The value of his poetry lies in the complex images of the modern spirit captured in the pictures it depicts. He once said that "the spirit of modern urbanites is full of continuous impressions from history and real life, and, weakened by doubts and contradictions, is eroded by long-term sorrow and depression. Although this depression

奮時，他們就會手舞足蹈、歡騰雀躍，不斷創造著夢幻和傳說，秘密和謎語。」由此可知，他在革命前的動盪接觸到生活的現實之後，寫詩是隨著不同時期的心境轉變及社會環境的變化，於作品中將許多想要表達的思想心情反映在詩歌的意象變化中，並賦予詩中的意象更多元的象徵意義。

對布洛克而言，俄國處於激烈動盪的經歷與人民困厄的現實帶給他的苦悶不滿從而造成一種憂鬱的性格，可說是形成他的藝術風格的基礎。但更重要的還是他在藝術上受到的主要影響和他的美學觀點的制約。誠如布洛克在《野蠻人》詩中提到：「俄羅斯是個難解的謎。」有人說，俄國浪漫文學是十八世紀西歐文學的晚輩。事實上，俄國自詩聖普希金去世，詩歌的黃金時代暫告終止。而布洛克在俄國文學史的重要性並不下於普希金、托爾斯泰等詩人。他詩歌裡的哀傷或沉思冥想，絲毫沒有矯揉造作之感。他對俄羅斯文學創作和發展也提供了方法和思路 詩人曾自己介紹他的創作過程，首先是他在 1911 致別雷(A. Белый2)的信上說：「我全部詩篇加在一起，乃成為「人形成過程的三部分」：從一瞬間極度燦爛的閃亮開始，通過必經的沼澤森林，走向絕望、詛咒、報復……到誕生一個社會的人，一個藝術家，他勇敢地放眼世界，他有權去研究諸多形式，去審視善與惡的雛形…」他由俄羅斯革命動盪的痛苦和磨難中，學會用一雙嚴肅又感傷的眼睛去看社會人生，而且，以敏感的神經去感受人民生活的苦楚，以強烈的火樣的熱情去擁抱祖國，以正義的界線去界開黑暗與光明，真理與罪惡。總之，他是善與光之子，他關心祖國飢餓的人民或遭禁的囚犯，而所造成的衝突、悲劇、

is languid, But once they are excited by joy, they will dance and jump for joy, constantly creating dreams and legends, secrets and riddles." From this, it can be seen that after the turmoil before the revolution came into contact with the realities of life, his poetry writing followed the changes in mood and social environment in different periods, to reflect many thoughts and moods to be expressed in the changes in the imagery of the poems, and give the images in the poems more symbolic meanings.

For Blok, Russia's experience of intense turmoil and the reality of people's distress brought him a melancholy character, which can be said to be the basis of his artistic style. But what is more important is the main influence he received in art and the constraints of his aesthetic point of view. As Blok mentioned in his poem "the Barbarian", "Russia is an insoluble mystery." Some people say that Russian romantic literature is the younger generation of Western European literature in the eighteenth century. In fact, the golden age of poetry in Russia came to an end temporarily after the death of the poet St. Pushkin. The importance of Blok in the history of Russian literature is no less than that of Pushkin, Tolstoy and other poets. There is nothing artificial about the mournful or the brooding in his poetry. He also provided methods and ideas for the creation and development of Russian literature. The poet himself introduced his creative process. First, he said in a letter to Farewell Ray (A. Белый 2) in 1911: "All my poems are added together to become three parts of the process of human formation": from the moment to the extreme The brilliant and shining beginning, through the necessary swamp forest, towards despair, curse, revenge..., until the birth of a social person, an artist, he bravely looks at the world, he has the right to study many forms, to examine good and evil from the pain and suffering of the turmoil of the Russian Revolution, he learned to look at social life with a pair of serious and sentimental eyes, and to feel the suffering of the people's life with sensitive nerves, and to read it with strong fiery enthusiasm. To embrace the motherland and divide darkness and light, truth and evil with the boundaries of

沮喪、渴望也隱喻在詩創作中。他在詩歌創作和理論上既汲取了法國象徵主義的養分，又從俄羅斯詩人、哲學家索洛維約夫的宗教哲學思想中吸取精華，他也注重對理性的運用，在一定程度上使俄國的哲學從內容和形式上完全擺脫了具有粗糙、隨意、神秘的特點。至此，布洛克的思想和人生觀已經找到了自己的固定位置，也終於走出了屬於自己風格的象徵之路。因而，他的詩才獲得了自己的風格。

其次，是布洛克對詩歌藝術多方面的探索及美學觀點的形成。他說，他曾受過朱可夫斯基詩歌的影響。朱可夫斯基是位優秀的詩歌譯家，他翻譯了許多英文和德文詩歌，譯文的選字與技巧皆使原詩更出色，詩的基調是憂鬱而浪漫；此外，他也深入研究俄國風俗和信仰，將民間藝術融入詩歌，使詩句更活潑而有韻律感。他的詩像仙樂般柔美，像美夢。這就大大影響了布洛克早期詩歌也蘊聚了帶有朦朧神秘與幻想悠遠的色彩，以及那滿腹的情絲，細緻優雅的格調。因此，除了詩人的身份，布洛克也是個劇作家，翻譯家，文學評論者和有著深刻的思想及深沉的愛國主義感情的政治家。在他誕辰百年時，聯合國教科文組織將他列為世界重點紀念的文化名人之一。綜上所述，未來對布洛克詩歌的研究亦將呈逐漸深化的趨勢，而其詩歌的成就也已獲得了永恆的精神終極追求。

justice. In short, he is the son of goodness and light. He cares about the hungry people of the motherland or the prisoners, and the conflicts, tragedies, depressions, and longings caused by them are also metaphors in his poems. In his poetry creation and theory, he not only absorbed the nutrients of French symbolism, but also absorbed the essence from the religious philosophy of Russian poet and philosopher Solovyov. He also paid attention to the use of reason, which to a certain extent made Russia Philosophy rid of the features of roughness, randomness and mystery in content and form. So far, Blok's thoughts and outlook on life have found their own fixed position, and finally walked out of the symbolic road of their own style. Therefore, his poems have acquired their own style.

Secondly, it is Blok's exploration of the various aspects of poetic art and the formation of aesthetic views. He said he had been influenced by Zhukovsky's poetry. Zhukovsky was an excellent translator of poetry. He translated many English and German poems. The choice of words and skills in the translations made the original poems better. The tone of the poems was melancholy and romantic; faith, integrating folk art into poetry, makes the lines more lively and rhythmic. His poems are as soft as fairy music, like dreams. This has greatly influenced Blok's early poems, which also contain the color of hazy mystery and fantasy, as well as full of love and delicate and elegant style. Therefore, in addition to being a poet, Blok is also a playwright, translator, literary critic and politician with deep thoughts and deep patriotic feelings. On the centenary of his birth, UNESCO listed him as one of the world's key cultural celebrities. To sum up, the future research on Blok's poetry will also show a gradual deepening trend, and the achievements of his poetry have also obtained the eternal spiritual ultimate pursuit.

註 .美國勞・坡林 Lawrence Perrine《談詩的象徵》，
載耿建華著，《詩歌的意象藝術與批評》，頁
49，山東大學出版社，2010 年版。--2016.6.17

--湖北省武漢市華中師範大學文學院主辦《世界文
學評論》／《外國文學研究》〈AHCI 期刊〉榮
譽出品，2016 年第 03 期，詩評，頁 123-128。

Note. Lawrence Perrine of the United States, "On the Symbolism of Poetry", contained in Geng Jianhua, "The Art and Criticism of Poetry Imagery", page 49, Shandong University Press, 2010 edition. — June 17, 2016.

—Honorary publication of "World Literature Review"/"Foreign Literature Research" <AHCI Journal>, sponsored by the School of Literature, Central China Normal University, Wuhan, Hubei Province, Issue 03, 2016, Poetry Review, pp. 123-128.

6. 孤獨的行吟——讀里爾克的詩

奧地利詩人里爾克（Rainer Maria Rilke，1875-1926）無疑是世上具有魅力的詩人之一，他生於布拉格一個鐵路工人家庭，九歲時父母離異，自幼即展露文藝天分，個性纖細善感，童年缺少樂趣和歡笑。十一歲時，被送進軍事學校，因體弱多病而轉到一所商業學校，但第二年因戀愛事件而退學。在此期間，他已在報紙上發表了第一首詩，並開始頻繁地寫作。1895 年，入布拉格大學攻讀哲學，次年遷居慕尼黑，從事寫作，也開始了他的流浪生活。1897 年後懷著孤獨的心情遊歷各國。會見過托爾斯泰，給雕塑家羅丹當過秘書，並深受法國象徵派詩歌先驅波德萊爾（1821-1867）等人的影響。

一次世界大戰時，里爾克曾應徵入伍，1919 年六月間，他從慕尼克來到了瑞士蘇黎世。表面上看來是應蘇黎士地方邀請前往講學，實際上是里爾克想逃脫戰後的混亂以及離棄這個耽誤他多年寫作工作之地，重新開始《杜伊諾哀歌》的創作。1922 年二月，里爾克在短短的幾個星期內靈感迸發，完成了長達十年的《杜伊諾哀歌》的創作，並且在這段時間完成了另一部著作《致奧爾弗斯的十四行詩》。

他是繼歌德（Johann Wolfgang von Goethe，1749-1832）之後，二十世紀德語國家中最重要的詩人；除了德語、法語，

6. Solitary Troubadour ── Reading Rilke's Poems

The Austrian poet Rainer Maria Rilke (1875-1926) is undoubtedly one of the most charming poets in the world. He was born in a family of railway workers in Prague. His parents divorced when he was nine years old. He showed his talent for literature and art when he was a child, and his personality was delicate and sensitive, his childhood lack of fun and laughter. At the age of eleven, he was sent to a military school and transferred to a commercial school due to infirmity, but dropped out the following year due to a love affair. During this time, he had published his first poems in newspapers and began to write frequently. In 1895, he entered the University of Prague to study philosophy, moved to Munich the next year, engaged in writing, and began his wandering life. After 1897, he traveled around the world in loneliness. He met Tolstoy, worked as a secretary to the sculptor Rodin, and was deeply influenced by Baudelaire (1821-1867), the pioneer of French Symbolist poetry.

During World War I, Rilke was drafted into the army. In June 1919, he came to Zurich, Switzerland from Munich. On the surface, it seems that he was invited by Zurich to give lectures. In fact, Rilke wanted to escape the chaos after the war and leave this place that had delayed his writing work for many years, and restarted the creation of *Duino Elegies*. In February 1922, Rilke had a burst of inspiration in just a few weeks and completed the creation of the ten-year-long

After Goethe (Johann Wolfgang von Goethe, 1749-1832), he is the most important poet in the German-speaking countries in the 20th century; in addition

俄語與義語也成為他寫詩的語言。早期詩歌，令人感到一種浪漫的布拉格地方色彩和富有波希米亞式的飄逸與不羈，流露出流浪的欲望與詩人的氣質；詩集內容也偏重神秘、夢幻與哀傷。周遊歐洲列國，甚至還曾抵達埃及之後，他改變了偏重主觀抒情的浪漫風格，寫出以直覺形象象徵人生和表現自己思想感情的作品。其中，《時禱書》常予人多愁善感、虔誠敬神的印象，但藝術造詣很高。其詩歌不但開啟了存在主義的先河，對後期的象徵主義也產生了極大的影響。除了創作詩歌外，他還撰寫小說、劇本等多種，而書信也是重要的文學作品之一，對十九世紀末的詩歌影響深遠。

　　我們舉一首里爾克寫於 1903 年的名作〈豹〉，，詩情澎湃，有明顯的象徵主義風格，而且形象性很強。此時，詩人與結縭一年又四個月的女雕刻家克拉拉（Clara Westhoff，1878-1954）協議分手，心情憂鬱。一天，他在法國巴黎植物園與一隻豹相遇時，心中激起了無限感慨：

　　　　它的目光被那走不完的鐵欄
　　　　纏得這般疲倦，什麼也不能收留。
　　　　它好像只有千條的鐵欄杆，
　　　　千條的鐵欄後便沒有宇宙。

　　　　強韌的腳步邁著柔軟的步容，
　　　　步容在這極小的圈中旋轉，
　　　　彷彿力之舞圍繞著一個中心，
　　　　在中心一個偉大的意志昏眩。

to German and French, Russian and Italian have also become the languages of his poetry. In his early poetry, people feel a kind of romantic Prague local color and full of bohemian elegance and uninhibitedness, revealing wandering desire and poetic temperament; the content of the poetry collection also focuses on mystery, dreams and sadness. After traveling around European countries and even arriving in Egypt, he has changed his romantic style, which emphasized subjective lyricism, and wrote works that symbolize life to express his own thoughts and feelings with intuitive images. Among them, *The Book of Hours* often gives people the impression of being sentimental and pious, but it has high artistic attainments. His poems not only pioneered existentialism, but also had a great influence on later symbolism. In addition to writing poetry, he also wrote novels, plays, etc., and letters are also an important literary works for him, which had a profound influence on poetry at the end of the nineteenth century.

Let's take a famous work *Leopard* written by Rilke in 1903, which is full of poetic emotion, obvious symbolism style, and strong imagery. At this time, the poet and the female sculptor Clara (Clara Westhoff, 1878-1954), who had been married for one year and four months, agreed to break up, feeling depressed. One day, when he met a leopard in the Botanical Garden of Paris, France, his heart was filled with emotion:

Its eyes are caught by the endless iron bars
I'm so tired of entanglement, I can't hold anything.
It seems to have only a thousand bars of iron,
There is no universe behind a thousand iron bars.

With strong steps and soft steps,
Steps spin in this tiny circle,
As if the dance of power revolved around a center,
In the center a great will stuns.

只有時眼簾無聲地撩起——
於是有一幅圖像浸入，
通過四肢緊張的靜寂——
在心中化為烏有。

　　從詩的全意看，首先，他從豹的目光中，觀察到牠日夜
的踱步，時時刻刻想逃卻無法逃離的處境。他用鐵欄象徵無
奈和令人煩躁的生活。第二段寫的是豹子內在的苦楚，牠本
身具有的高貴和神性，卻無法避免羞辱，因而反抗的心就日
益強烈內聚。詩人感到那鐵欄背後有顆被壓抑得疲憊的心，
就好似自己，一個受挫的詩人精神的鬱悶。他用昏眩或者靜
寂來表現詩人雖有勃發的詩情，也只能像那隻豹子在極小的
圈子裡旋轉，詩人的境遇是何等的相似。而自己圍著那個中
心打轉，是詩人人格的化身和自我形象的塑造。詩人眼中的
豹子就是自己的化身，豹子的境遇就是詩人生活的象徵。當
他與之對視，那靜靜的目光，那悠然的心靈，在放鬆的靜寂
中，憑藉豹的靈魂，而帶給自己些許的安慰和生活的啟示。
這飛動的詩思似乎超越了鐵欄，超越了生活的繁瑣和局促；
也顯示里爾克之所以會成為偉大的詩人，在於他內心的孤寂
以外，仍有著深遠的夢想。在這首詩裡，他使情和形象得到
了最完美的結合，給人一種壯懷盡展的美感力。

　　而這首（秋日），是詩人獨自在異鄉寫下個人感情的湧
動，寫愛情的逝去，寫自己的生活所思，一切都在筆下自然
地流出：

Only when the eyelids lift silently —
So an image dips in,
Through the tense silence of the limbs —
Disappeared in the mind.

From the whole point of view of the poem, first of all, from the eyes of the leopard, he observes its pacing day and night, and the situation that it wants to escape but cannot escape all the time. He used iron bars to symbolize the helpless and irritating life. The second paragraph is about the inner pain of the leopard. It has nobility and divinity, but it cannot avoid humiliation, so the rebellious heart becomes increasingly cohesive. The poet feels that there is a tired and suppressed heart behind the iron bars, just like himself, the depressed spirit of a frustrated poet. He uses dizziness or silence to show that although the poet has vigorous poetic sentiment, he can only rotate in a very small circle like the leopard. How similar the situation of the poet is, and I revolve around that center, which is the incarnation of the poet's personality and the shaping of his self-image. The leopard in the poet's eyes is his own incarnation, and the situation of the leopard is the symbol of the poet's life. When he looked at him, the quiet eyes, the leisurely heart, in the relaxed silence, with the leopard's soul, brought him a little comfort and enlightenment of life. This flying poetic thought seems to have surpassed the iron bars, and surpassed the tedious and cramped life; it also shows that the reason why Rilke became a great poet lies in the fact that he still has far-reaching dreams beyond his inner loneliness. In this poem, he perfectly combined emotion and image, giving people a full-bodied beauty.

And this song *Autumn Day* is a poem in which the poet writes about the surge of his personal feelings, the passing of love, and his thoughts about life in a foreign land alone. Everything flows naturally from his pen:

主啊，是時候了，夏日曾經很盛大。
把你的陰影落在日規上，
讓秋風刮過田野。

讓最後的果實長得豐滿，
再給它們兩天南方的氣候，
迫使它們成熟，
把最後的甘甜釀入濃酒。

誰此時還沒有房子，就不會再建造。
誰此時還獨自一人，就會有很長一段時間如此，
將會醒來，讀書，寫長信
與心神不寧地在林蔭道上
來回遊蕩，當落葉紛飛時。

全詩已預示了詩人與克拉克分手後，選擇孤獨地四處漂泊、創作、讀書、寫信，是生活的重心。詩人早期的詩作可說是體現了濃郁的詩情與細膩的心靈感受相結合，創造出許多優美的意象與一種恬淡或飄逸清麗的意境。此外，其抒情的手段亦不斷變化，能多面地展示內心世界的情愫和感覺，給人以強烈的藝術感染力。如這首（挖去我的眼睛，我仍能看見你）：

未和愛情絕緣，往往通過回憶的方式展現出來，仍執著地去追尋挖去我的眼睛，我仍能看見你，／堵

Lord, it's time, summer was once grand.
Cast your shadow on the sundial,
Let the autumn wind blow across the fields.

Let the last fruit grow full,
Give them another two days of southern climate,
Forcing them to mature,
Brew the last sweetness into strong wine.

Whoever does not have a house at this time will
　not build any more.
Whoever is alone now, will be for a long time,
Will wake up, read, write long letters
Restlessly on the boulevard
Wandering back and forth, when the fallen leaves
　are flying.

The whole poem has foreshadowed that after the poet broke up with Clark, he chose to wander around alone, creating, reading, and writing letters are the focus of his life. The poet's early poems can be said to reflect the combination of rich poetic feelings and delicate spiritual feelings, creating many beautiful images and a tranquil or elegant artistic conception. In addition, his lyrical methods are also constantly changing, which can show the emotions and feelings of the inner world in many ways, giving people a strong artistic appeal. Like *Gouge Out My Eyes and I Can Still See You*:

Take out my eyes and I can still see you, / Stop my ears and I can still hear you; / Without feet, I can walk to you, / Without a mouth, I can still beg you. / Break my

我住我的耳朵，仍能聽見你；／沒有腳，我能夠走到你身旁，
／沒有嘴，我還是能祈求你。／折斷我的雙臂，我仍將擁抱
你——／用我的心，像用手一樣。／箝住我的心，我的腦子不
會停息；／你放火燒我的腦子，／我仍將托負你，用我的血液。

　　這些感人的抒情詩句，是詩人的自敘，但也是在啟示他
人：在心的年輪上不要刻下為愛而悔恨的遺憾，要誠摯地面
對愛情。他說：「愛意謂獨處」，「愛情——最神聖的嚴肅，
然而亦是所有遊戲當中最美麗的。」（註）其實，里爾克心
的年輪也有種種痕跡，這些使人心靈顫抖的詩句，是一種象
徵和暗示，正昭示了詩人悲苦愁悶的心境，也表達了對愛情
追求而不可得的惆悵情懷。另一首〈在春天或者在夢裡〉，
亦典型地體現了詩人的美學追求：

　　　　在春天或者在夢裡／我曾經遇見過你／而今我們
　　　　一起走過秋日／ 你按著我的手哭泣／你是哭急
　　　　逝的雲彩 ／還是血紅的花瓣？／ 都未必／ 我
　　　　覺得：你曾經是幸福的 ／在春天或者在夢裡。

　　這首詩從春夜詩人瞬間的心緒展開聯想，跨越時空的限
制，透露出詩人的一種淡淡的愁緒。而這種意象詩，也是情
象流動的詩，寫得相當含蓄而朦朧。但細細揣摩，就可道出
其中奧妙，也可理解為對喜歡的人離別後成為遙遠的旅愁的
憑藉吧。尤以最後兩句，讓詩人感情的浪峰掀起，而後又回

arms, and still I will embrace you — / With my heart, as with my hands. / Clamp my heart, my brain will not rest; / You set fire to my brain, / I will still entrust you with my blood.

These touching lyric lines are the poet's self-narration, but they are also inspiring others: don't engrave regrets for love on the annual rings of your heart, but face love sincerely. He said: "love means being alone", "love — the most sacred solemnity, but also the most beautiful of all games." (Note) In fact, the annual rings of Rilke's heart also have various traces, which make people's hearts tremble. The verses are a kind of symbol and hint, which just shows the poet's sad and depressed state of mind, and also expresses the melancholy feeling that the pursuit of love cannot be obtained. Another song *In Spring or In a Dream* also typically embodies the poet's aesthetic pursuit:

> *In spring or in a dream / I met you before / Now we walk through the autumn together / You hold my hand and weep / Are you crying a dying cloud / Or blood-red petals? / Not necessarily / I think you were happy / in spring or in a dream.*

This poem unfolds associations from the poet's momentary mood on a spring night, transcending the constraints of time and space, revealing a faint melancholy of the poet. And this kind of imagery poem is also a poem with flowing emotions and images, written quite implicitly and hazily. But if you think about it carefully, you can tell the mystery, and it can also be understood as a source of sorrow for distant travel after parting with the person you like. Especially in the last two sentences, the wave of the poet's emotion rises, and then returns to a gentle level,

歸平緩，形成一道道水紋，使人回味。或許，如詩人自己所言：「過往的事物並未逝去，僅只轉變了而已。」他並那片純淨的浪漫星空。

　　里爾克人生的創作高峰發生在 1912 年至 1922 年之間，其中的著作《杜伊諾哀歌》抒寫較多的是苦難與死亡，而《致奧爾弗斯的十四行詩》書中則是歌頌著世間萬物。我認為，里爾克的詩，總給人們的官能上造成一種舒緩縈繞的浪漫旋律，有著詩情畫意的契合與交融，使人如置身其中。如這首（寂寞），是詩人把內心的隱痛溶入一場雨、黃昏、深巷等帶感情色彩的意象中：

　　　　孤寂好似一場雨。
　　　　它迎著黃昏，從海上升起；
　　　　它從遙遠偏僻的曠野飄來，
　　　　飄向它長久棲息的天空。
　　　　從天空才降臨到城裡。

　　　　孤寂的雨下個不停，
　　　　在深巷裡昏暗的黎明，
　　　　當一無所獲的身軀分離開來，
　　　　失望悲哀，各奔東西；
　　　　當彼此仇恨的人們
　　　　不得不睡在一起：
　　　　這時孤寂如同江河，鋪蓋大地……

Perhaps, as the poet himself said: "things in the past have not passed away, they have only changed." He is not insulated from love, and often shows it through memories, and still persistently pursues the pure romantic starry sky.

The creative peak of Rilke's life occurred between 1912 and 1922. Among them, *Duino Elegy* described more suffering and death, while *Sonnets to Orpheus* sings the praises of all things in the world. In my opinion, Rilke's poems always create a soothing and lingering romantic melody for people's senses, with a poetic and picturesque fit and blend, making people feel like they are in it. For example, in *Loneliness* the poet dissolves the hidden pain in his heart into emotional images such as rain, dusk, and deep alleys:

Loneliness is like rain.
It rises from the sea against the dusk;
It floats from far and remote wilderness,
Floats to the sky where it has long lived.
From the sky came down to the city.

The lonely rain keeps falling,
In the dim dawn in the alley,
When the body with nothing to gain is separated,
Disappointed and sad, go their separate ways;
When people who hate each other
Had to sleep with:
At this time, loneliness is like a river, covering the
*   earth...*

　　這裡，用馳騁的想像、沉哀的筆調，恰切地表達出詩人把悲傷往心的深處埋藏，並把它濃縮，壓擠，使之變形，滲入到一個獨特的藝術境地，我們從中可以體會到一種情緒上的消長和抑揚頓挫。然而，因大量的創作，耗費許多體力，四十八歲的里爾克不得不在療養院度日。隨後的兩年時間一直在法國和瑞士停駐，直到 1925 年 8 月，里爾克已無法擺脫病魔的束縛，終於在 1926 年 12 月與世長辭，享年五十歲。里爾克被安葬在瑞士瓦萊州（Kanton Wallis）西邊的小鎮拉龍（Raron），墓誌銘則出自其手。因里爾克的死因是白血病，但有一說是由於被玫瑰針刺感染。最後，他在墓誌銘中訴說著自己的心願：

Rose, oh reiner Widerspruch, Lust,

Niemandes Schlaf zu sein unter soviel

Lidern.

玫瑰，噢，純粹的矛盾呦，欲願，

旁若無人地長眠於眾人的眼瞼下。

　　這也正表現出這位偉大詩人的不同凡響。總之，里爾克的詩歌是用他自己的整個生命去歌唱，其所創造的形象孵育了一切藝術手法：意象、象徵、想像、聯想……使宇宙萬物在詩人的眼前互相呼應，這就使人看到了里爾克富有特色的抒情方式。詩人精湛的詩藝，確實已獲得長久的生命了。

Here, with galloping imagination and mournful style of writing, it is apt to express that the poet buries the sadness deep in the heart, condenses, squeezes, deforms it, and infiltrates it into a unique artistic situation, from which we can learn experience in emotional ups and downs. However, due to a lot of creations and a lot of energy, the forty-eight-year-old Rilke had to spend his days in a sanatorium. For the next two years, he stayed in France and Switzerland until August 1925. Rilke could no longer shake off the shackles of illness, and finally died in December 1926 at the age of fifty. Rilke was buried in Raron, a small town in the west of the Swiss canton of Valais (Kanton Wallis), and the epitaph was written by him. The cause of death was leukemia, but one theory is that it was infected by rose needles. Finally, he expressed his wish in the epitaph:

Rose, oh reiner Widerspruch, Lust,
Niemandes Schlaf zu sein unter soviel
Lidern.

This also shows the extraordinariness of this great poet. In short, Rilke's poetry is to use his whole life to sing, and the images he creates nurture all artistic techniques: imagery, symbolism, imagination, association... making the universe and everything echo each other before the poet's eyes, which makes people see Rilke's characteristic lyrical way. The poet's superb poetic skills have indeed gained a long life.

註. 參見里爾克著，唐際明譯，《慢讀里爾克》，
台北，商周出版，2015 年，121 頁及 115 頁。

—— 2016.9.9 作

—— 臺灣《海星》詩刊，2017.03，第 23 期春季號，
頁 15-18。

Note. See Rilke, translated by Tang Jiming, "Slow Reading Rilke", Taipei, Shang Zhou Publishing, 2015, pages 121 and 115.

7. 雅羅斯拉夫·塞弗特的詩歌藝術

　　2016 年九月十五日起連續五天在布拉格舉行第 36 屆世界詩人大會，這是由美國《世界藝術文化學院》和《捷克國家筆會》等主辦的一場文化饗宴，會中主席是楊允達博士及副主席 Prof.Ernesto Kahan。此大會是為紀念捷克最負盛名的詩人雅羅斯拉夫·塞弗爾特（Jaroslav Seifert，1901—1986）的 115 周年誕辰。他生於布拉格一個工人家庭，中學還未畢業就步入社會，投身於新聞工作和文學創作活動。除詩歌外，他還撰寫了有關文學、戲劇、電影和美術的評論文章及小品雜文。

　　早期詩作主要歌咏了詩人對勞苦的勞動大眾，對美好理想的追求，抒發細膩感人的真實情懷和故鄉的面貌。一九三六年後，由於納粹德國的威脅和《慕尼克協定》的簽訂，他的祖國處於危難之中，遂而激發詩人的愛國主義熱情。其中《祖國之歌》被認為是 Seifert 最優秀的愛國主義詩篇。其他幾部詩集也都表達了詩人對祖國、對捷克民族文化傳統的讚

7. The Art of Poetry by Jaroslav Seifert

The 36th World Poets Conference will be held in Prague for five consecutive days from September 15, 2016 onward. This is a cultural feast hosted by the American "World Academy of Arts and Culture" and "Czech National PEN". The chairman of the meeting is Dr. Yang Yunda and Vice Chairman Prof. Ernesto Kahan. This conference commemorates the 115th anniversary of the birth of Jaroslav Seifert, the most famous Czech poet (1901-1986). Born in a worker's family in Prague, he entered the society before graduating from a middle school and devoted himself to journalism and literary creation. In addition to poetry, he has written critical essays and short essays on literature, theatres, films, and fine arts.

The early poems mainly sang the poet's pursuit of the hardworking working people and the beautiful ideals, expressing delicate and touching true feelings and the appearance of his hometown. After 1936, due to the threat of Nazi Germany and the signing of the "Munich Agreement", his country was in danger, which aroused the poet's patriotic enthusiasm. Among them, *Song of the Fatherland* is considered Seifert's best patriotic poem. Several other anthologies also aspirations of the people. After about forty-eight, Seifert had expressed the poet's praise of the motherland and the Czech

頌，唱出了人民的共同心願。大約四十八歲以後，Seifert 已
成為專業詩人。晚期的詩作，有對青少年時代的回憶，對親
友的懷念及對祖國和首都布拉格的讚美，也有對愛情的歌頌
和對女性的愛慕，對人生的回顧和對死亡的想像。這些作品，
都融匯了詩人飽經滄桑後的深思及對使命的真誠體會。詩風
平穩，語言明晰，平易中還帶有一點幽默。

塞弗爾特從事文學創作六十餘年，著作多種，還翻譯過
俄國詩人勃洛克和法國詩人阿波利奈爾等人的作品。正如瑞
典學院授予諾貝爾文學獎的授獎詞中所說，「他的詩富於獨
創性、新穎、栩栩如生，表現了人的不屈不撓精神和多才多
藝的渴求解放的形象。」為了表揚他在詩歌創作上的成就和
對捷克詩歌所作出的貢獻，1966 年，捷克斯洛伐克社會主義
共和國政府曾授於他「民族藝術家」的光榮稱號。1981 年，
詩人八十壽辰之際，共和國總統古斯塔夫·胡薩克給 Seifert
發去賀信。在布拉格民族大街詩人聚會的酒店裡，人們還為
塞弗爾特舉辦了盛況空前的新詩朗誦會。他代表著自由、熱
情和創造性，他歌頌愛情，歌頌布拉格春天。無論是溫柔、
憂傷、快樂、幽默、欲望以及所有那些人們之間的愛產生的
感情，都是他寫詩的主題。且看這首（最後的歌）：

national cultural traditions, and sang the common become a professional poet. In his later poems, there are memories of youth, nostalgia for relatives and friends, and praise to the motherland and the capital Prague, as well as praises of love, admiration for women, review of life and imagination of deatThese works are a fusion of the poet's deep thinking after vicissitudes of life and his sincere understanding of the mission. The poetic style is stable, the language is clear, and there is a little humor in the simplicity.

Seifert has been engaged in literary creation for more than 60 years and has written various literary works. He has also translated the works of Russian poet Blok and French poet Apollinaire. As stated in the awarding speech of the Swedish Academy for the Nobel Prize in Literature, "his poems are full of originality, novelty, and lifelikeness, expressing the image of people's indomitable spirit and versatile desire for liberation." In order to praise his poetry creation for his achievements and contributions to Czech poetry, in 1966, the government of the Czechoslovak Socialist Republic awarded him the honorable title of "National Artist". In 1981, on the occasion of the poet's eightieth birthday, the President of the Republic, Gustav Husak, sent a congratulatory letter to Seifert. In the hotel where the poets met on National Street in Prague, an unprecedented reading of new poems was held for Seifert. He represents freedom, enthusiasm and creativity, he sings love, sings the praises of Prague spring. Tenderness, sadness, joy, humor, desire, and all those emotions that arise from the love between people are the themes of his poems. Let's look at *The Last Song*:

　　請聽：這是有關小亨戴莉的。
昨天她回到了我身邊，
假如在白色的聖喬治大教堂
突然起火，

　　但願不要這樣，
大火後它的牆壁會呈玫瑰色。
　　甚至它的雙子塔（亞當和夏娃）也會如此。
　　更纖細的那座是夏娃，正如女性通常那樣，

雖然這只是一種毫無意義的
　　性別的榮耀。
　　猛烈的火焰也會使石灰岩泛紅。
　　正如年輕的女孩
初吻之後。

她已經二十四歲，
　　美麗得彷彿書拉密*。

　　她穿一件淺灰色松鼠皮衣，
　　戴一頂俏麗的小帽，
　　脖上繫了一條
白煙似的圍巾。

　　亨戴莉啊，這裝扮真適合妳！
　　我原以為妳已死去，
不想妳出落得如此美麗。
　　我真高興妳能回來！

　　你錯得離譜啦，親愛的朋友！
　　我已死了二十年，
你很清楚。
　　我只是回來看看你。

*書拉密（Shulamite），《聖經·雅歌》中讚美的新娘。

Listen: This is about Henry Daly.
She came back to me yesterday,
If in white St George's Cathedral
　Burst into flames,

　I hope not,
　Its walls will be rose-colored after a fire.
Even its twin towers (Adam and Eve) will.
The slender one is Eve, as women usually do,

　Although this is just a meaningless
　　The glory of sex.
Fierce flames can also redden limestone.
Like a young girl
　After the first kiss.

　She is twenty-four years old,
　As beautiful as a Shulammite.

　She wore a light gray squirrel fur coat,
　Wearing a pretty little hat,
　Tied around the neck,
　　Scarf like white smoke.

Hendelle, this outfit really suits you!
I thought you were dead,
I don't want you to be so beautiful.
I'm so glad you're back!

How wrong you are, my dear friend!
I have been dead for twenty years,
　You are very clear.
　I just came back to see you.

*Shulamite, the bride praised in the Bible Song of Solomon.

在詩中，詩人所描繪的那美麗的女孩，帶有烏托邦的色彩，卻給人以真實的具體感受；但結尾處雖帶有較濃重的悲傷色彩，又不同於某些浪漫主義詩人的直抒胸臆。而這一手法的展現，是詩人將兩個時空交替的對話融匯在一起的畫面來呈現出追憶的情懷，這不能不說是詩人在詩情上的用心經營。詩人也往往採用一些局部的象徵來表達他的思想感情，如這首（一九三四年）：

> 回憶青春年華
> 　是愉快的。
> 　　惟有河流不會老。
> 　風磨傾圮，
> 　任性的風
> 　打著口哨，漠不關心。
>
>
> 　一具令人悲傷的十字架留在路邊。
> 　　矢車菊花如無鳥的空巢
> 　落在基督的肩頭，
> 　　青蛙在蘆葦叢呱呱叫嚷。
> 　垂憐我們吧！
> 　苦澀的時日已經來到
> 　甜蜜的河邊，
> 　工廠兩年空氣無一人
> 　　孩子們坐在母親的膝上
> 　學會饑餓的語言。

In the poem, the beautiful girl depicted by the poet has a utopian color, but it gives people a real and concrete feeling; but although the ending has a strong sad color, it is different from the direct expression of some romantic poets. And the presentation of this technique is the poet's fusion of two alternate time and space dialogues to present the feelings of reminiscence, which cannot but be said to be the poet's careful management of poetic sentiment. Poets also often use partial symbols to express their thoughts and feelings, such as this poem (1934):

Reminiscing about my youth
　Be pleasant.
　　Only the river is not old.
The wind grinds,
Wayward wind
Whistling and indifference.

A sad cross was left by the side of the road.
　Cornflowers bloom like empty nests without birds
On the shoulders of Christ,
　Frogs croaked in the reeds.
Have mercy on us!
Bitter times have come
By the sweet river,
The factory has had no one in the air for two years
　Children sitting on mother's lap
Learn the language of hunger.

　　而他們的笑聲仍然銀鈴般響起
又在柳樹下淒然地沉寂下去
在它的銀色裡。

但願他們為我們安排的晚年
比我們給他們準備的童年幸福！

　　此詩採用象徵手法創造的藝術境界，並非現實中的真實存
在，而是詩人虛擬的一種精神上的昇華。如詩裡提到的，那
任性的風，悲傷的十字架，矢車菊花如無鳥的空巢，苦澀的
時日，甜蜜的河邊，都是詩人頭腦中的象徵體。詩裡當然對
時下的社會有些失望之感，但也表明了未來的美好生活是要
付出努力代價的。再如〈告別曲〉也都採用了含蓄的象徵手
法，內裡有無限的弦外之音，令人思索：

　　給這世界億萬的詩，
我只增添了寥寥幾行。
或許不比蟋蟀的叫聲高明。
我知道。請原諒。

　　我就要收場。

　　它們甚至不及月球塵埃
最初的腳印。
如果它們間或也發出了一閃

And their laughter still rings like silver bells
Under the willow tree fell silent again
In its silver.

I hope they arrange for our old age
Happier than the childhood we prepared for them!

The artistic realm created by symbolism in this poem is not a real existence in reality, but a kind of spiritual sublimation imagined by the poet. As mentioned in the poem, the willful wind, the sad cross, the cornflower flowers like an empty nest without birds, the bitter days, and the sweet riverside are all symbols in the poet's mind. Of course, the poem is a little disappointed with the current society, but it also shows that a better life in the future will come at the price of hard work. Another example, *The Farewell Song*, also uses implicit symbolism, and there are infinite overtones which makes people think:

A million poems to the world,
I only added a few lines.
Perhaps no louder than the crickets.
I know. please forgive.

I'm going to close.

They're not even as good as moon dust
Initial footprints.
If they also flash now and then

並非它們自己的光亮。
我熱愛過這語言。

那使沉默的嘴唇
顫動的
仍將使年輕的情侶們親吻
當他們漫步於霞光鍍金的原野
那裡的夕陽
比在熱帶墜落得還要緩慢。

詩歌亙古與我們同在。
如同愛情，
饑餓，瘟疫，和戰爭。
有時我的詩句令人難堪地
愚蠢。

但我並不因此尋求原諒。
我相信對美的詞語的尋求
勝過
屠戮和謀殺。

　　此詩象徵開始在歲月不饒人的冷酷中褪色、凋零的心緒，
而後因詩人相信對美的詞語的尋求勝過戰爭的屠戮和謀殺，
這裡象徵著詩人開始振醒又變得鮮明的靈魂。他的詩句，正
蘊含著詩人理想中的新的社會。詩人有時為了造成一種音樂

Not their own light.
I have loved this language.

Lips that silence
Quivering
Will still make young couples kiss
As they walk across the gilded fields
Where the sunset
Slower than falling in the tropics.

Poetry is with us forever.
Like love,
Hunger, plague, and war.
Sometimes my lines are embarrassingly
Madness.

But I don't seek forgiveness for that.
I believe in the search for beautiful words
Outperform
Slaughter and murder.

This poem symbolizes the mood that began to fade and wither in the relentless coldness of the years, and then because the poet believes that the pursuit of beautiful words is better than the slaughter and murder of war, it symbolizes the poet's soul that has begun to wake up and become vivid. His verses contain the poet's ideal new society. Poets sometimes imitate a special picture in order

氣氛，還常模擬出一種特殊的畫面，以增添詩的獨特表現力。
如他的短詩〈壁毯之歌〉：

> 布拉格！
> 哪怕你只見過她一面，
> 那她的名字就會在你的心中
> 唱個不息。
> 她自己就是譜寫在時間裡的樂章，
> 我們愛她。
> 願她永遠響徹雲霄！
> 當我青春年少時，
> 做過一個美夢，
> 那是我甜蜜幸福的初夢，
> 它們像飛碟一樣
> 在她屋頂上空閃閃發光，
> 而後便消失在鬼才知道的什麼地方。
> 一次，我把臉龐
> 貼在赫拉恰尼古堡庭院下面
> 舊城牆的石頭上，
> 我的耳膜突然被陣陣
> 沉悶的轟鳴振響。
> 這是那遙遠世紀的隆隆聲。
> 然而，那來自「白山戰役」的
> 濕潤、柔軟的泥灰土卻
> 親切細語地在我耳邊響起：

to create a musical atmosphere, so as to add the unique expressiveness of the poem. As in his short poem *Song of the Tapestry*:

Prague!
Even if you only saw her once,
Then her name will be in your heart
Sing all the time.
She herself is the music written in time,
We love her.
May she resound forever in the sky!
When I was young,
Had a sweet dream,
That was my sweet and happy first dream,
They are like flying saucers
Glittering over her roof,
And then disappeared into who knows where.
Once I put my face
Posted under the courtyard of Hracani Castle
On the stone of the old city wall,
My eardrums were suddenly burst
A dull roar resounded.
This is the rumble of that distant century.
However, that from the "Battle of White Mountain"
Moist, soft marl
Kindly whispered in my ear:

　　去吧，你將幸福至極。

　　歌唱吧，人們對你有所期待。

　　你可不能說謊啊！

　　我走了，我沒有說謊。

　　可我僅僅對您，我的愛，

　　說了一丁點兒。

　　自白山戰役（1620 年 11 月 8 日）失利後，布拉格全面衰敗，十七世紀上半葉，中產階級紛紛移居他鄉。直到 1623 年，19 世紀捷克著名音樂家安東甯・德沃夏克著名的作品《白山的子孫》即是紀念這場戰役而譜寫的。這場戰役標誌著捷克作為一個獨立的國家消失了整整三百年之久，直到第一次世界大戰結束時才重現獨立。而詩人 Seifert 寫下當時的心中感慨，也讓捷克人民看到了改革與自由的希望之光。

　　賽弗爾特一生經歷過兩次世界大戰，青少年時代是在貧困、飢餓和戰爭中度過的。他看見了世界的苦難，也看見了人間的罪惡。但在戰爭的血腥和貧困的現實中，他仍沒有放棄希望、放棄愛。其詩歌在藝術上的感人之處，是作品主題始終圍繞著愛情，藝術，和對祖國的熱愛，這是一個民族詩人的典範。他在一九八四年榮獲諾貝爾文學獎時已重病在身，兩年後便與世長辭，享年八十六歲。一生著有詩集，小說，散文集和回憶錄等多種，作品不僅對捷克文學有深遠影響，更受到一般人民的喜愛。賽弗爾特也寫了很多愛情詩或描繪女性的作品，如在《自傳》中詩裡曾寫下這樣感性的句子：

Go, you will be very happy.
Sing along, people expect something from you.
You can't lie!
I'm gone, I'm not lying.
But to you only, my love,
Said a little bi

(November 8, 1620), Prague was in total decline, and the middle class emigrated in succession in the first half of the seventeenth century. Until 1623, Antonin Dvořák, a famous Czech musician in the 19th century, wrote the famous work *Children of the White Mountain* to commemorate this battle. The battle marked the disappearance of the Czech Republic as an independent country for three hundred years, which was not regained until the end of the First World War. The poet Seifert wrote about his emotions at the time, and let the Czech people see the light of hope for reform and freedom.

Seifert lived through two world wars in his life, and spent his youth in poverty, hunger and war. He saw the suffering of the world, but also saw the evil in the world. But in the reality of bloody war and poverty, he still did not give up hope and love. The artistic touch of his poems is that the themes of his works always revolve around love, art, and love for the motherland. This is a model of a national poet. He was seriously ill when he won the Nobel Prize in Literature in 1984, and died two years later at the age of eighty-six. He has written a variety of poetry collections, novels, essay collections and memoirs throughout his life. His works not only have a profound impact on Czech literature, but are also loved by ordinary people. Seifert also wrote a lot of love poems or works depicting women, such as the emotional sentence written in the poem in *Autobiography*:

當我第一次看到
一個女人的裸體像時，
我開始相信奇蹟。

從這裡看出，他不只描寫大時代下心中的痛苦與不屈服的精神，而且熱烈地謳歌未來美好的憧憬與期待。此外，他也試圖告訴我們，愛並非是某一感官的享樂，而是超官感的感覺；不僅是互持，也包括傾慕與關懷。他在詩藝與詩美上的探索，對國際新詩的發展確實是具有很大貢獻的，因而，廣為捷克官方與人民及世界詩人所歌頌與紀念。

－2016.9.19 作

－臺灣《新文壇》季刊，第 46 期，2017.01，
頁 31-40.

When I first saw
When a woman is nude,
I started to believe in miracles.

From this, it can be seen that he not only describes the pain and unyielding spirit in the heart of the great era, but also enthusiastically eulogizes the vision and expectation of the bright future. In addition, he also tried to tell us that love is not a sensual pleasure, but a super-sensual feeling; not only mutual support, but also admiration and care. His exploration of poetic art and poetic beauty has indeed made a great contribution to the development of international new poetry, so he is widely praised and commemorated by Czech officials and people as well as poets around the world.

8. 約瑟夫·布羅茨基的生平 及其詩藝成就

　　約瑟夫·布羅茨基（Joseph Brodsky，1940-1996）是美籍蘇聯詩人，在他四十七歲時，以其詩作「出神入化」、「韻律優美」，「如交響樂般豐富」和「為藝術英勇獻身的精神」榮獲 1987 年度諾貝爾文學獎，成為最年輕的諾貝爾文學獎得主之一。他誕生在蘇聯一個猶太知識份子家庭，父親原為海軍軍官，因是猶太人被迫退役，靠母親掙錢養家。由於他家庭的環境，自 15 歲起，即輟學謀生，先後做過車工、水手等工作，詩作通過詩朗誦和手抄本形式流傳於社會，除繼承了古典主義優秀傳統，也深受西方現代主義詩歌的影響，遂成為「不斷更新表現手法的高手」，深受俄羅斯重要詩人阿赫瑪托娃（Akhmatova）的賞識。

　　Brodsky 從 22 歲起，即被蘇聯公安部門監視，兩次被關進精神病院，遭受慘無人道的折磨。23 歲時，他發表著名長詩《悼約翰·鄧》，同年年底被捕，被法庭判服苦役五年。在阿赫瑪托娃等知名人士及西方作家的呼籲下，才使得服刑十八個月的他提前獲釋，獲准回到列寧格勒。他的作品陸續在國外出版，但仍在 32 歲被剝奪蘇聯國籍並驅逐出境。在離開祖國前，他給勃列日涅夫寫信裡說：

8. The Life and Poetic Achievements of Joseph Brodsky

Joseph Brodsky (1940-1996) was an American Soviet poet. At the age of forty-seven, he won the 1987 Award for his poems *Supernatural, Beautiful Rhythm"*, *Rich as a Symphony* and *Heroic Dedication to Art*; the annual Nobel Prize in Literature, becoming one of the youngest Nobel Prize winners in Literature. He was born in a Jewish intellectual family in the Soviet Union. His father was a naval officer. He was forced to retire because he was a Jew, and his mother earned money to support the family. Due to his family's environment, he dropped out of school to make a living from the age of 15 onward, and worked successively as a lathe worker and a sailor. His poems were spread to the society through poetry recitation and manuscripts. In addition to inheriting the excellent tradition of classicism, he was also deeply influenced by modern Western culture. Under the influence of socialist poetry, he became a "master of constantly updating expression techniques", and was deeply appreciated by the important Russian poet Akhmatova.

At the age of 22, Brodsky was monitored by the Soviet public security department, and he was imprisoned in a mental hospital twice and suffered inhumane torture. At 23, he published the famous long poem *Mourning John Deng*. At the end of the same year, he was arrested and sentenced to five years of hard labor by the court. Under the appeal of Akhmatova and other famous people and Western writers, he was released early after serving 18 months in prison and was allowed to return to Leningrad. His works were published abroad one after another, but he was still deprived of Soviet citizenship and deported at the age of 32. Before leaving the country, he wrote to Brezhnev:

「我雖然失去了蘇聯國籍，但我仍是一名蘇聯詩人。我相信我會歸來，詩人永遠會歸來的，不是他本人歸來，就是他的作品歸來。」

之後，Brodsky 受聘於美國密執安大學，擔任駐校詩人，開始了他在美國的教書、寫作生涯，也在其他大學任訪問教授，直到 37 歲才加入美國籍，任美國藝術與科學學院和全國藝術與文學學會會員，巴伐利亞科學院通訊院士。一生著有詩集、散文集《小於一》、《論悲傷與理智》及長詩《悼約翰·鄧及其他》等多種。最終他在紐約因心臟病突發於睡夢中離世，享年僅 56 歲。

Brodsky 早期詩作題材多為愛情、離別或孤獨；在經歷審判、監禁之後，於 32 歲時被迫流亡海外，此生再未踏上故土。因此，回憶不可避免地成為了他的文集的主題。當他抵達西方，從貧瘠封閉的蘇聯來到後現代美國，其作品轉為醉心於具體描寫，詩作不刻意去營造高潮，而是從「微妙關係」來看。他強調語言的超越性功能，認為詩歌是探索語言極限，詩歌是一種加速的思想，而韻律是完成這個工作的關鍵。詩作風格多變，可以寫得深沉廣闊，也可輕鬆諷刺；有時寫得很日常化，有時也可以進行玄思冥想。在詩行的安排方面，他既可以工整嚴格，又可以長短不一；在意象方面則運用自如。總之，布羅茨基的詩繼承了俄古典主義傳統，又汲取了英國詩歌的精華，形成自己的獨特風格。在散文寫作中形成富於原創性的語氣和語體，往往也超越一般的意識形態控訴和傷痛展示，極耐人尋味。

"Although I have lost my Soviet citizenship, I am still a Soviet poet. I believe that I will return, and poets will always return, either in person or in his works."

After that, Brodsky was employed by the University of Michigan as a poet-in-residence. He began his teaching and writing career in the United States, and also served as a visiting professor in other universities. He did not become an American citizen until he was 37 years old. Member of the National Academy of Arts and Letters, Corresponding Member of the Bavarian Academy of Sciences. In his life, he wrote a collection of poems and essays *Less Than One, On Sorrow and Reason* and a long poem *Mourning John Deng and Others*. In the end, he died of a heart attack in his sleep in New York at the age of 56.

Brodsky's early poems were mostly about love, parting or loneliness; after being tried and imprisoned, he was forced into exile at 32, and never set foot on his homeland again in this life. Therefore, memory inevitably became the theme of his essays. When he arrived in the West, from the barren and closed Soviet Union to the post-modern United States, his works became obsessed with specific descriptions, and his poems did not deliberately create a climax, but from the "subtle relationship". He emphasizes the transcendent function of language, and believes that poetry is to explore the limits of language, poetry is an accelerated thought, and rhythm is the key to accomplish this works. The style of poetry is changeable, it can be written in a profound and broad way, or it can be light and satirical. In terms of the arrangement of lines of poetry, he can be neat and strict, and can also be of different lengths; in terms of imagery, he can use them freely. In short, Brodsky's poems inherited the tradition of Russian classicism and absorbed the essence of British poetry to form their own unique style. Forming an original tone and style in prose writing often surpasses general ideological accusations and pain display, which is extremely intriguing.

先說 Brodsky 早期詩作。在（快從這裡飛走吧，白色螟蛾……）中寄托了不少童年的回憶，寫得很美，也有悲憫氣息：

> 快從這裡飛走吧，白色螟蛾，
> 我給你留下活命。這是顧及到
> 你的道路並不長久。快飛吧。
> 你要當心吹來的風。在你之後
> 我本人很快也將喪失性命。
> 快飛吧，飛過光禿禿的花園，
> 飛吧，親愛的。最後我要提醒：
> 飛過電線的時候，多加小心。
> 好吧，我託付給你的並非資訊，
> 而是我始終不渝的夢想：
> 或許你就是那種小小的生靈
> 在輪回的大地上可以轉生。
> 當心，千萬別撞到車輪之下，
> 躲避那些飛鳥，動作要巧妙，
> 在空空的咖啡廳，在她面前
> 描畫我的面貌。在茫茫的霧氣中。

這些細節描繪，讓人有親臨其境之感。看來 Brodsky 少年時光的生活，對他的影響是深刻的，因而，抒情詩寫起來

Let me talk about Brodsky's early poems first. In *Fly Away From Here, White Moth...*, I entrusted a lot of childhood memories, it is beautifully written, and there is also a sense of compassion:

Fly away from here, white borer moth,
I leave you alive. This is taking into account
Your path is not long. fly fast.
You have to watch out for the wind blowing, after you
I myself will soon lose my life.
Fly, fly over the bare garden,
Fly, dear. Finally, I would like to remind:
Be careful when flying over wires.
Well, I don't entrust you with information,
But my unswerving dream:
Maybe you're one of those little creatures
In the land of reincarnation, you can reincarnate.
Be careful not to run under the wheel,
Dodge the birds with skill,
In the empty cafe, in front of her
Paint my face. In the vast mist.

These detailed descriptions give people a sense of being there. It seems that Brodsky's youthful life had a profound impact on him, so the lyric poems can be touched

可觸可感。同樣，Brodsky 在 1960 年代的作品（冬天已經過
去……）抒寫心裡的憂傷，也有獨特的體會，所以，在詩的
結尾寫出這樣有概括力，又能讓人動情的詩句：

　　冬天已經過去。春天
　　還很遙遠。花園裡
　　池塘當中三股噴泉
　　尚未從水底噴湧翻捲。

　　而飽含憂慮的視線
　　猶如纖細的蛛絲
　　投向朋友們的藍天，
　　他們早已死亡腐爛。

　　那裡空中的押送隊
　　在顏色暗紅的區域
　　除了兩隻紅腹灰雀
　　都變成了一片深藍。

　　這首韻律整齊和諧，當然，這些是 Brodsky 藝術上比較
早期的作品，但在節奏的安排上也很精當的。在這裡，他哀
悼美好光明事物的沉落，象徵性強。另外，如 1983 年的（你
是風，我是你的樹林……），也很傳神，詩作跳出了只寫眼
前冬景、繼而再抒發情懷的老調，而是展開豐富的藝術想像，

and felt. Similarly, Brodsky's works in the 1960s, like
Winter Has Passed..., express the sadness in his heart, and
he also has a unique experience. Therefore, at the end of
the poem, he wrote such a general and emotional line:

> *Winter is over, spring*
> *It's still far away; in the garden*
> *Three fountains in the pond*
> *It has not yet rolled over from the bottom of the*
> *water.*

> *With worried eyes*
> *Like slender spider silk*
> *Into the blue sky of my friends,*
> *They are long dead and rotten.*

> *The escort team in the air*
> *In dark red areas*
> *Except for two bullfinches*
> *All turned into a deep blue.*

The rhythm of this song is neat and harmonious. Of
course, these are Brodsky's earlier works in art, but the
rhythm arrangement is also very precise. Here, he mourns
the fall of good and bright things, symbolically. In
addition, as in 1983, *You Are the Wind, I Am Your Forest...*,
it is also very expressive. The poem jumped out of the old
tune of only writing about the winter scene in front of you,
and then expressing your feelings. Instead, it unfolded rich
artistic imagination, grasped the most prominent features
of each scene are described, and the wind and leaves are

抓住每一景物最突出的特點加以描繪，以風和樹葉暗喻不可分割的愛情心情，雖帶有一點淒涼的色彩，但彰顯愛情的悲傷同眼前景物融為一體，也使人沉浸在一種誘人的氣圍中：

> 你是風，我是你的樹林。
> 我渾身顫抖樹葉亂紛紛，
> 一封封書信毛毛蟲
> 咬嚙得樹葉千瘡百孔。
> 北風越是憤怒地襲來，
> 樹葉的顏色越發慘白，
> 就連冬天裡的神靈
> 也替樹葉哀求北風。

　　詩人充滿著愛與期盼的感情，隨著詩句的變化而展現出來。內裡含著詩人在遙遠的旅途上奔波的感嘆，蘊聚著深深的詩情。Brodsky 晚年在 1990 年發表的警世遺言（我為自己樹座別樣的紀念碑…），這就成了詩人藝術主張的最後宣言：

> 我背向著那個可恥的世紀。
> 我面對著自己失落了的愛。
> 胸膛像個滾滾的自行車輪。
> 屁股對準真真假假的事海。
> 不管包圍我的是何種景象，

used to imply the inseparable love mood. Although there is a bit of desolation, the sadness that shows love is integrated with the foreground, and it also makes people immerse themselves in a seductive mood. In the atmosphere:

> *You are the wind; I am your forest.*
> *I tremble and the leaves are scattered,*
> *A letter to a caterpillar*
> *The leaves are riddled with bites.*
> *The north wind blows more and more angrily,*
> *The leaves grow paler,*
> *Even the gods in winter*
> *And beg the north wind for the leaves.*

The poet is full of feelings of love and expectation, which are revealed with the changes of the lines. It contains the poet's exclamation on the distant journey, and it contains deep poetic feelings. Brodsky's warning last words published in 1990 in his later years, *I Set up a Different Kind of Monument for Myself...*, which became the final declaration of the poet's artistic proposition:

> *I turn my back on that shameful century.*
> *I confronted my lost love.*
> *The chest is like a rolling bicycle wheel.*
> *The butt is aimed at the sea of true and false things.*
> *No matter what vision surrounds me,*

不管我必須對什麼事諒解，
我不會將自己的面目更改。
我可以的只是那高度和姿態，
疲勞把我高高舉向了這境界。
你，繆斯，不要因為如今
我的智能像一隻漏空的篩子，
並非注滿神靈的容器而責怪我。
任憑人們把我推倒、拆毀吧，
任憑人們責罵我、我行我素吧，
任憑人們把我毀掉、肢解吧，
在一個孩子們高興的大國裡，
我從院子裡的一個石膏半身像，
穿過這一對失明的白色的眼睛，
把噴湧而出的淚泉濺灑到天上。

　　此詩充滿了俄羅斯風味，特別是流亡到美國之後，鄉愁成為他的重要詩歌主題之一。事實上，Brodsky 到美國以後，也結識了漢學家塔奇雅娜•阿伊斯特，詩人跟她學習漢語，曾翻譯過李白的《靜夜思》、孟浩然的《春曉》和王維的《鹿柴》，也研究過《道德經》。在他一生複雜曲折的經歷之後，又昂然奮起，年過半百的 Brodsky 用一雙最嚴肅的眼睛去看人生，而且，以強烈的火樣的熱情去擁抱生活。他曾在著作《文明的孩子》說：「一首愛情詩就是一個人啟動了的靈魂。」他不但把詩作描繪得飛動起來，而且更具濃重的感情色彩，給人深刻的

Whatever I must forgive,

I will not change my face.

All I can do is that height and posture,

Fatigue lifted me aloft to this realm.

You, Muse, don't because now

My intelligence is like a leaky sieve,

Not to blame me for filling the vessel of the gods.

Let people push me down and tear me down,

Let people scold me and do my own way,

Let people destroy and dismember me,

In a great country where children rejoice,

From a plaster bust in the yard,

Through these blind white eyes,

Splash the welling fountain of tears into the sky.

This poem is full of Russian flavor, especially after being exiled to the United States, nostalgia has become one of his important poetic themes. In fact, after Brodsky arrived in the United States, he also got to know the sinologist Tatiana Ayster, and the poet learned Chinese from her. Chai, also studied the *Tao Te Ching*. After the complex and tortuous experience of his life, Brodsky, who is over half a century old, looks at life with the most serious eyes, and embraces life with strong fire-like enthusiasm. He once said in the book *Children of Civilization*: "A love poem is a person's activated soul." He not only portrayed the poems as flying, but also had a stronger emotional color, giving people profound ideological enlighte

思想啟迪和美的享受。因而，他的詩才獲得了自己的風格。如同俄羅斯總統葉利欽曾熱烈地讚揚 Brodsky，說他是：

　　「俄羅斯詩歌的太陽，是繼普希金之後最偉大的俄羅斯詩人」。

　　蘇聯為紀念約瑟夫·布羅茨基誕辰 70 周年，俄羅斯首都莫斯科畫廊曾舉辦「浮水印」展，主要展出布羅茨基生前最喜愛的城市義大利威尼斯的寫生畫和威尼斯風光圖片。而彼得堡市政府也建成布羅茨基故居博物館於 2015 年 5 月 24 日詩人誕辰 75 周年前夕向公眾開放。由此，可看出 Joseph Brodsky 在詩藝上的刻苦追求和偉大的藝術成就，終於能經幾十年甚至上百年的歌頌而不衰。

— 2016.9.23 作

— 臺灣《大海洋》詩雜誌，第 104 期，
　2022.01，頁 109-110。

and beautiful enjoyment. Therefore, his poems have acquired their own style. As Russian President Yeltsin once raved about Brodsky, saying he was

"the sun of Russian poetry is the greatest Russian poet after Pushkin."

To commemorate the 70th anniversary of the birth of Joseph Brodsky in the Soviet Union, the Moscow Art Gallery in the Russian capital once held the "Watermark" exhibition, which mainly exhibited sketches and photograms of Venice, Italy, which was Brodsky's favorite city during his lifetime. The Petersburg Municipal Government also built the Brodsky House Museum and opened it to the public on May 24, 2015, on the eve of the 75th anniversary of the poet's birth. From this, it can be seen that Joseph Brodsky's assiduous pursuit of poetic art and great artistic achievements can finally be praised for decades or even hundreds of years to come.

9. 讀葉慈詩歌的意象藝術

　　細讀楊牧編譯《葉慈詩選》文本之後我們就會發現，葉慈（W. B.Yeats，1865-1939）是愛爾蘭著名詩人、劇作家和散文家，也是 1923 年榮獲諾貝爾文學獎得主。正如他在得獎時的感言：「現在我已經蒼老，而且疾病纏身，形體不值得一顧，但我的繆斯卻因此而年輕起來。」這表明他不僅從事詩歌創作，而且希望借助一個獨特視角，刻劃出深刻而豐富的創作思想或展現出更多采的生活內容。

　　葉慈從小就喜讀愛爾蘭神話和民間故事，對繆斯充滿無限的嚮往。詩就是他的夢，故而早期的作品多反映對故鄉的思戀情緒或抒發愛情苦澀的喜樂，細膩地刻劃了他的內心世界。取材則源於愛爾蘭鄉土為背景的傳說與歌謠，音韻柔美、能表現一種憂鬱的抒情及夢幻般玄秘的氛圍，頗具浪漫主義的華麗風格，筆觸頗似雪萊，就像在欣賞一幅幅色彩清麗的畫。

　　其詩所述人物多為愛爾蘭神話與傳說中的英雄、智者或詩人及魔術師等。中期創作的詩歌，不僅描繪出他對愛爾蘭政治的悲觀與失望，同時也因熱烈地投入愛爾蘭民族解放運

9. The Art of Imagery in Reading W. B. Yeats Poetry

After carefully reading the text of *Selected Poems of Yeats* compiled by Yang Mu, we find that W. B. Yeats (1865-1939) is a famous Irish poet, playwright and essayist, and also the winner of the Nobel Prize in Literature in 1923. Just as he said when he received the award: "Now I am old and sick, and my body is not worth looking at, but my muse is young because of it." This shows that he is not only engaged in poetry creation, but also hopes to adopt a unique perspective to depict the deep and rich creative thought or to show more colorful life content.

Yeats liked to read Irish myths and folk tales when he was a child, and he was full of infinite yearning for the muse. Poetry is his dream, so his early works mostly reflected his nostalgia for his hometown or expressed the bitter joy of love, delicately depicting his inner world. The material is based on the legends and ballads of the Irish countryside. The rhyme is soft and can express a melancholic lyric and dreamlike mysterious atmosphere. It has a romantic and gorgeous style, with brightly colored painting.

Most of the characters described in his poems are heroes, wise men, poets and magicians in Irish myths and legends. The poems he created in the middle period not only portrayed his pessimism and disappointment in Irish politics, but also because he believed that violence and

動後，他認為，暴力、內戰並非愛國的表現，也以激昂的筆調趨使詩歌風格更趨近現代主義。而後期詩歌在措詞上，展現新的樸實無華、具體的風格，多取材於詩人個人生活及現實生活中的細節，且多以死亡和愛情為題，以表達某種情感和對東方玄秘學理的思索。

葉慈詩歌從早期的苦澀感傷，到晚年的沉思凝練，已無可避免地讓讀者通過他的記憶去追尋愛爾蘭民族的精神家園。1938 年愛比劇場演出他的戲（Purgatory），又發表了最後一場公開演講，同時出版自傳後不久即逝世，長眠於他童年故鄉的不遠處，享年七十四歲。

這首（白鳥），正是經典之作，在詩行當中穿梭著詩人抒情般的陳述：

> 我但願我們，愛人，是海波上的白鳥！
> 厭倦了流星它熄滅，消逝以前的火焰，
> 和暮色裏藍星的光彩低低垂落在天一邊，
> 心中凜凜蘇醒，愛人，一種揮不去的愁。

> 困頓來自露水打溼的夢魂那百合與薔薇。
> 啊不要夢那些，愛人，那流星火燄會消滅，
> 而藍星的光彩低垂當露水降落時正猶疑告別：
> 而我但願我們變成流波上的白鳥：我和你。

enthusiastically participated in the Irish National Liberation Movement. Approaching modernism. In terms of diction, the poems in the later period showed a new unpretentious and specific style, mostly based on the details of the poet's personal life and real life, and most of them took death and love as the theme to express certain emotions and the mystery of the East.

Academic thinking. Yeats's poems, from his bitter and sentimental early years to his later contemplative and condensed years, inevitably allow readers to search for the spiritual home of the Irish nation through his memory. In 1938, he performed his play *Purgatory* at the Abbey Theater and gave his last public speech. At the same time, he died shortly after publishing his autobiography, and died not far from his childhood hometown at the age of seventy-four.

This poem *White Bird* is a classic, with the poet's lyrical statements running through the lines:

> *I wish we, lovers, were white birds on the waves!*
> *Tired of shooting stars it extinguishes, fades the former flames,*
> *And in the twilight the blue star's brilliance hangs low on one side of the sky,*
> *Awake in the heart, love, a kind of sorrow that can't be shaken off.*
>
> *Difficulty comes from the lilies and roses of the dream soul wet with dew.*
> *Oh don't dream those, love, the meteor fire will die,*
> *And the blue star's brilliance hangs low and hesitantly bids farewell when the dew falls:*
> *And I wish we were white birds on the waves: me and you.*

> 我心縈繞無數的島嶼，和許多丹黯海灘，
> 那裏時間將把我們遺忘，憂鬱也不再來接近，
> 很快我們就要遠離薔薇和百合，和火燄煩心，
> 假若我們果然是白鳥，愛人，在海波上浮沉。

　　詩的情感節奏是內在的，韻律性也強，歌裡盡是愛意。在詩人筆下，白鳥飛迴，聚散匆匆，也暗含著愛情的矛盾性與痛楚。細讀此詩，需要讀者解謎的智慧，也需要調動自己的情感經驗；海波、白鳥、流星構成了神秘朦朧的意境。這些被詩人靈性照亮的詩句是其生命中的閃現，竟如此心痛心憂。同樣的，（葉落）一詩也通過類似講故事的方式披露愛情的記憶歷久彌堅：

> 秋天附著修長的葉子葉子愛我們，
> 守住一些田鼠在成捆的麥穗；
> 山楸樹葉都黃了，高過我們頭頂，
> 還有那潮濕的葉也黃，那野草莓。
>
> 愛情衰蝕的時刻竟已經襲到了，
> 我們憂傷的靈魂是困頓而且疲憊；
> 無須等激情的季候遺棄，讓我們
> 就此吻別，淚滴落你低垂的眉。

　　由山楸樹綠葉枯黃、掉落，成捆的麥穗，引我們進入到空曠浩蕩的大地裡。詩人靜觀宇宙萬物，落葉與憂傷相照，

My mind haunts countless islands, and many Danian beaches,
Where time will forget us, and melancholy will not come near,
Soon we shall be far from the rose and the lily, and troubled
　by the flame,
If we were indeed white birds, lovers, bobbing and sinking
　on the waves.

The emotional rhythm of the poem is internal, the rhythm is also strong, and the song is full of love. In the poet's writing, the white bird flies back and gathers and disperses in a hurry, which also implies the contradiction and pain of love. Careful reading of this poem requires the reader's wisdom in solving puzzles, as well as mobilizing his own emotional experience; sea waves, white birds, and meteors constitute a mysterious and hazy artistic conception. These verses illuminated by the poet's spirituality are flashes in his life, which are so heart-wrenching. Similarly, the poem *Falling Leaves* also uses a similar storytelling method to reveal that the memory of love has become stronger over time:

Autumn clings to its slender leaves The leaves love us,
Hold some voles in the sheaves;
The mountain cath tree leaves are yellow, high above our heads,
And the damp leaves are yellow too, the wild strawberries.

The hour of love's decay has come,
Our sad souls are weary and weary;
Without waiting for seasons of passion to abandon, let us
Kiss me goodbye, tears fall down your drooping brows.

The withered and fallen green leaves of the mountain catalpa and the bundles of wheat ears lead us into the vast and empty land. The poet quietly observes everything in

在愛情衰蝕的時刻也孕育著對生命無常的慨嘆，如季節的遞變，蒼涼中又透射出達觀。詩人立在宇宙中，無論是愉快或痛苦的記憶，都是生命過程的環節，而在他解讀記憶影像空間和時間的交錯中已進行了心與物交融，使意象具有多重內涵，其蘊藉的藝術精神亦得到了張揚。

葉慈詩歌構建於愛爾蘭歷史的厚重與冥默的思維之上，但作為對故鄉革命事業最關注的詩人，他始終表現出強烈的革命意志不改。在二十世紀的前三十年間，愛爾蘭因長期處於不安，他的詩歌則見證了歷史傷痛的經歷，激發讀者對往事的闡釋和想像。再如（催眠曲），詩質很堅實，從而創造出富有張力的意象：

> 我愛，願你的睡安穩香甜
> 在往日哺乳處找到一點。
> 世界上所有那些警戒信號
> 與勇敢的巴里士有何相干？
> 當他在金鏤的床上，初夜破曉
> 在海倫的臂彎裏找到他的睡。
>
> 睡，我愛，睡一個像
> 狂蕩的特利斯坦中心明白的

the universe, and the fallen leaves and sorrows reflect each other. At the moment of love decay, he also laments the impermanence of life, such as the gradual change of seasons, and the desolation reveals optimism. The poet stands in the universe, whether it is a pleasant or painful memory, is a link in the life process, and in the interlacing of space and time in his interpretation of the memory image, he has already carried out the fusion of mind and matter, making the image have multiple connotations. The artistic spirit has also been promoted.

Yeats's poems are built on the thick and silent thinking of Irish history, but as a poet who is most concerned about the revolutionary cause in his hometown, he has always shown a strong revolutionary will. In the first three decades of the twentieth century, Ireland was in constant turmoil, and his poems witnessed the painful experience of history, stimulating readers' interpretation and imagination of the past. Another example is *Lullaby*, the poetic quality is very solid, thus creating an image full of tension:

> *I love, may your sleep be safe and sound*
> *Find a little bit at Past Nursing.*
> *All those warning signs in the world*
> *What has it to do with brave Parish?*
> *When he was on Jin Lou's bed, the first night dawned*
> *Find his sleep in Helen's arms.*
>
> *Sleep I love sleep a like*
> *Slutty tristan center understands*

那種睡，當愛底醍醐已過藥效，
小麂在奔跑鹿牝在跳躍；

在橡樹和山毛櫸的枝枒下，
小麂在跳躍鹿牝在奔跑；

像那樣的睡安穩香甜如同
那神鳥滑落到尤蘿大芊芊的
河岸，當他終於完成了
命定執行的任務，在那裏，
遂脫開麗妲的肢體下沉，
但不會失去她的繾綣呵護。

　　詩人對當時政治的局面雖然失望卻從來沒有絕望，詩歌中的堅強詩意是葉慈掛念著故鄉的土地，常伴以痛感，也是愛爾蘭人民不可或缺的靈魂安慰力量。他以詩回報大地的滋養，才能不斷超越政治的現實。對葉慈來說，隨著年紀不斷增大，他對生命流逝的感悟與自由的嚮往超越常人。正如他寫的（睿智隨時間）所言：

樹葉雖然很多，根柢惟一。
青春歲月虛妄的日子裏
陽光中我將葉子和花招搖；
如今，且讓我枯萎成真理。

That kind of sleep, when love's cure is over,
The young deer are running and the female is jumping;

Under the boughs of oak and beech,
The young deer are jumping and the female is running;

Sleeping like that is safe and sweet like
The divine bird slipped onto Yuluo Daqianqian's
Bank, when he finally finished
Destined to perform the task, there,
Then she broke free from Lita's limbs and sank,
But she will not lose her care.

uation at that time, he never despaired. The strong poetic flavor in the poems made Yeats miss his hometown, often accompanied by pain, and it was also an indispensable soul comfort force for the Irish people. He repays the nourishment of the earth with poetry, so that he can constantly surpass the political reality. For Yeats, as he grows older, his perception of the passing of life and his yearning for freedom surpass ordinary people. As he wrote *Wisdom Over Time*:

Although there are many leaves, there is only one root.

In the vain days of youth

In the sun I shake leaves and flowers;

Now, let me wither into truth.

　　這首短詩別出心裁，也蘊涵哲思，但哲思又隱藏於詩意象之中，讓我看到了一個迎風獨立的堅強靈魂。他是詩美的探求者，其成就在於那豐富的題材與想像。詩，是他飛翔的翅膀。既柔美又剛烈，既浪漫又孤絕。歲月雖逝，在 2015 年，葉慈誕辰 150 周年期間，從他的故鄉小鎮斯萊戈到愛爾蘭首都都柏林再到南美甚至非洲，喜愛葉慈的讀者先後發起了一系列的活動來紀念這位諾貝爾文學獎得主和偉大的浪漫主義詩人。他的詩歌已扎根於愛爾蘭人民居住的遼闊土地，並帶來廣泛的影響，這可以從《葉慈詩選》書裡看出其中端倪，也能給我們啟示。

— 2017.02.07 作

— 臺灣《海星》詩刊，2017.06，第 24 期夏季號，頁 15-18。

This short poem is ingenious and contains philosophical thinking, but the philosophical thinking is hidden in the imagery of the poem, allowing me to see a strong and independent soul facing the wind. He is a seeker of poetic beauty, and his achievement lies in the rich themes and imagination. Poetry is his flying wings. Both soft and strong, both romantic and lonely. Although the years have passed, in 2015, during the 150th anniversary of Yeats's birth, from his hometown of Sligo to Dublin, the capital of Ireland, to South America and even Africa, readers who love Yeats launched a series of activities to commemorate Yeats as Winner of the Nobel Prize in Literature and a great romantic poet. His poetry has taken root in the vast land inhabited by the Irish people and brought extensive influence, which can be seen from the book *Selected Poems of Yeats* and can also enlighten us.

10. 淺析希克梅特詩歌中的深情抒寫

摘要：土耳其文學界巨人，詩人作家納奇姆·希克梅特（Nazim Hikmet，1902-1963），其現代詩創作中不僅傳達著處於惡劣環境中獨特的深覺，更帶有向上向善的鼓舞力量，這與他傳奇的一生和純真勇毅的氣質恰恰切合。本文嘗試從翻譯的詩選中，聆聽其詩音情思，以體認其詩歌令人感動的成果。

關鍵詞：納齊姆·希克梅特　現代詩　土耳其詩人

當我讀到希克梅特那首在 1928 年的詩作《鐵籠裡的獅子》，對於時序已進入二十一世紀冬至初春，卻仍然保有無名的感動：

> 看那鐵籠裡的獅子，
> 深深看進它的眼裡去：
> 像兩支出鞘的匕首
> 閃著怒光。
> 但它從未失去它的威嚴
> 雖然它的忿怒
> 來了又去

10. An Analysis of Affectionate Writing in Hickmet's Poems

Abstract: Nazim Hikmet (1902-1963), a Turkish literary giant and poet and writer, not only conveys his unique deep consciousness in a harsh environment, but also encourages him to be good power, which is exactly in line with his legendary life and innocence and courage. This article attempts to select from the translated poems, listen to their poetic sounds and emotions, and realize the moving results of their poems.
Key words: Nazim Hikmet, modern poetry, Turkish poet

When I read Hikmet's poem *The Lion in the Iron Cage* in 1928, I was still moved by the nameless fact that the time sequence has entered the winter solstice and early spring of the 21st century:

Look at the lion in the cage,

Look deeply into its eyes:

Like two sheathed daggers

Glowing with anger.

But it never loses its majesty

Though its wrath

Comes and goes

來了又去
去了又來。

你找不到一個可繫項圈的地方
在它那厚而多毛的鬃上
雖然皮鞭的創痕/仍在它黃背上燃燒/它的長腿
延伸而終結/成兩隻銅爪。
它的鬃毛一根根豎起/繞著它驕傲的頭。
它的憤恨/來了又去/去了又來...

我兄弟的影子在地牢的牆上
移動
上上下下
　　上上下下

　　或者感嘆詩人在詩中所臻入逆風行進的身影，彷彿中，
我看見一道炯炯目光，唱起命運之歌，一個字，一個字地，
藏在詩人淚水中的孤獨與伴隨著溫情與自由的期望。

　　希克梅特生前是二十世紀土耳其歷史上備受爭議的詩
人，曾因政治性活動被逮捕，前後入獄加起來有十七個春秋。
其詩作因為刻畫了不同階層人物的生活和抒情真切而留名，
詩篇優美，具有豐富的想像力，凌駕於人類利益之上。後人
把他同智利詩人聶魯達（1904-1973）及西班牙詩人羅卡 36）

Comes and goes
Comes and goes.

You can't find a place to attach a collar
On its thick and hairy mane
Though the scars of the whip
Still burn on its yellow back,
Its long legs
Stretched and terminated
Into two copper claws.
Its mane stands
Around its proud head.
Its resentment
Comes and goes
Goes and comes...

My brother's shadow on the dungeon wall
Move
Up and down
Up and down

Or lament the figure of the poet walking against the wind in the poem, as if, I saw a piercing gaze, singing the song of fate, one word, one word, the loneliness hidden in the poet's tears and the love accompanied by expected warmth and freedom.

Hikmet was a controversial poet in the history of Turkey in the 20th century. He was arrested for political activities and spent seventeen years in prison. His poems are famous for depicting the lives of people from different classes and their lyricism. The poems are beautiful, rich in imagination, and above human interests. Later generations listed him together with the Chilean poet Neruda (1904-1973) and the Spanish poet Roca(1898-1936)

並列為二十世紀的重要詩人之林，曾獲得列寧國際和平獎金等殊榮，病逝於莫斯科。他在生前 1929 年發表的《八百三十五行》詩作，敏感地揭露時代的憂傷和吶喊，被當時的左派組織喻為「工人階級和社會主義的偉大詩人」，時至今日，有人稱他為愛國詩人，有人喜歡他的愛情詩。其實，他寫詩的目的很單純，是為了在面對監獄生活與親人分離之間找到一個平衡點，詩，成了救贖的窗口，寫作成了黑暗與陽光中冒出的晶瑩花朵，也鼓舞全世界為了更好的未來而努力以赴。他是享有國際聲譽的民族詩人，去世後，在文學史上的聲譽日趨高漲；其小說《我的同胞們的群像》及許多劇本，被視為不可多得的珍品，有的作品也被拍成電影或出版。在他百年誕辰之後，聯合國教科文組織宣佈 2002 年為「希克梅特年」，近些年來，土耳其境內組織也為他舉辦過各項紀念性活動。他的詩魂永遠縈繞在故土，受到大眾的尊崇。

真摯和純正：希克梅特的詩風

生於貴族世家的希克梅特，外曾祖父曾是土耳其軍總司令，也是詩人，而其父親是外交部官員，母親是畫家，外祖父是教育學家；在文藝氣息的熏陶與嚴格的家教下，遂而成就了他從年少時代起就喜歡讀詩、寫作。14 歲時，在一次家庭聚會上，他朗誦了一首歌頌英雄主義的詩歌，讓海軍部長大為賞識，並邀他到海軍學校上學。1919 年，他從海軍學校畢業後，在一艘巡洋艦上擔任見習軍官，因重病，在 1920 年 5 月間提前退役。在此期間，他已成為土耳其詩壇上的一顆新星。

as an important group of poets in the 20th century. He was awarded the Lenin International Peace Prize and other honors, and died of illness in Moscow. His poem *Eight Hundred and Thirty-Five Lines* published in 1929 sensitively exposed the sorrow and cry of the times, and was hailed by leftist organizations as "the great poet of the working class and socialism". As a patriotic poet, some people like his love poems. In fact, his purpose of writing poems is very simple, to find a balance between facing prison life and the separation of relatives. Poetry has become a window of redemption, writing has become crystal flowers emerging from darkness and sunshine, and also inspires The whole world is working hard for a better future. He is a national poet with international reputation. After his death, his reputation in the history of literature is increasing day by day; his novel *Portrait of My Compatriots* and many scripts are regarded as rare treasures, and some works have also been made into film or publishing. After his 100th birthday, UNESCO declared 2002 as the "Year of Hikmet". In recent years, organizations in Turkey have also held various commemorative activities for him. His poetic soul will always linger in his homeland and is respected by the public.

1. Sincerity and Purity: Hikmet's Poetic Style

Hikmet was born in an aristocratic family. His great-grandfather was the commander-in-chief of the Turkish Army and a poet. His father was an official of the Ministry of Foreign Affairs, his mother was a painter, and his maternal grandfather was an educator. Under the influence of literature and art and strict family education, which made him like reading poetry and writing since he was young. At the age of 14, at a family gathering, he recited a poem praising heroism, which was greatly appreciated by the Secretary of the Navy and invited him to the Naval Academy. After graduating from the Naval Academy in 1919, he served as a cadet officer on a cruiser, but due to serious illness, he retired early in May 1920. During this period, he has become a rising star in Turkish poetry.

　　1921 年初，希克梅特常與一些愛國詩人聚會，並開始撰寫號召青年為民族解放而戰的詩篇，因而受到過土耳其國父凱末爾（1881-1938）的接見。不久，他奉命到土耳其西北部的一個城市博盧擔任教師，為了深造，於 1921 年隻身前往莫斯科東方大學學習，因而結識了詩人馬雅可夫斯基（1893-1930），並深受蘇聯文學的影響。在那期間，他成為一個堅定的社會主義者，亦決心為土耳其人民的解放而奮鬥。他在 20 年代末 30 年代初，寫過許多優秀的詩篇。他在 1924 年回祖國土耳其後，在《光明雜誌》及其他單位工作，從事文學創作，並加入共產黨，仍因從事一些活動，遭到迫害和多次被捕入獄。

　　和所有愛國詩人一樣，他在早期詩中臻入的思想，大多抒發個人的感情；其詩風真摯而純正，處處流露出在囚禁陰影下感性的抒發和勇毅的堅決。例如，他在 1922 年寫的《赤足》，震憾我的心靈，也帶給勞動者心的力量：

> 太陽繞著我們的頭頂，
> 一條灼燙的頭巾；
> 乾裂的土地，
> 我們腳下的一雙涼鞋。
> 一個老農夫
> 比他的老馬
> 還像死
> 在我們近傍
> 不在我們近傍/但在我們燃燒的/血管內。

At the beginning of 1921, Hikmet often met with some patriotic poets, and began to write poems calling on young people to fight for national liberation, so he was received by Turkey's founding father Kemal (1881-1938). Soon, he was ordered to work as a teacher in Bolu, a city in northwestern Turkey. In order to further his studies, he went to Moscow Oriental University to study alone in 1921, where he met the poet Mayakovsky (1893-1930) and was deeply influenced by Soviet literature. During that time, he became a staunch socialist and determined to fight for the liberation of the Turkish people. He wrote many excellent poems in the late 1920s and early 1930s. After returning to his motherland, Turkey in 1924, he worked in Guangming Magazine and other units, engaged in literary creation, and joined the Communist Party. He was still persecuted and arrested and imprisoned many times because of some activities.

Like all patriotic poets, most of the ideas he developed in his early poems expressed his personal feelings; his poetic style is sincere and pure, showing emotional expression and courageous determination under the shadow of captivity everywhere. For example, he wrote *Barefoot* in 1922, which shocked my heart and brought strength to the hearts of laborers:

> *The sun circles our heads,*
> *A scorching turban;*
> *Cracked land,*
> *A pair of sandals under our feet.*
> *An old farmer/than his old horse*
> *Still like dead*
> *Near us*
> *Not near us / but in our burning veins / vessels.*

肩膀沒有厚披肩
手沒有皮鞭；
沒有馬，沒有車
沒有村警，
我們旅行過
熊穴般的村落
泥濘的城鎮，
在光禿禿的山丘上。
我們聽到聲音
自多石的土地
在病牛的淚裡；
我們看到土地
不能給黑犁
以金黃玉蜀黍的香氣。
我們還沒走出
如在夢中，
呵不！
一個垃圾堆便已到達另一個。
我們
知道
一個國家
的渴望。
這渴望輪廓分明
如唯物論者
的心態
而真的
這渴望
自有它的道理。

Shoulders without thick shawls
Hand without a whip;
No horses, no carts
No village police,
We traveled
Bear den villages
Muddy towns,
On the bare hills.
We hear voices
From rocky land
In the tears of sick cows;
We see land
Can not give black plow
With the aroma of golden corn.
We're not out yet
As in a dream,
Oh no!
One garbage dump has reached another.
We know
A country/desire.
This longing for chiseled
As materialist
State of mind
And really
This desire
It has its own reasons.

　　此詩堪稱是社會主義詩篇的楷模。詩人強烈的詩音，提昇了生命，也意謂著，為了民族解放的未來，為了勞動人民所受的苦，詩人不僅時時鞭策自己，也因渴望為土耳其民族奮鬥而引發的內心震動。然而，詩歌的激情是一個片刻，不受時空約束。在入獄期間，他也寫下《工作》一詩，詩裡對光明的渴望並未逝去，僅只轉換個方式抒寫而已：

　　　　當白天在我的牛角上破曉，
　　　　我用耐心與尊嚴犁地；
　　　　大地濕而暖觸摸我赤裸的腳底。

　　　　我的肌肉亮閃著火花
　　　　我捶擊熱鐵直到正午；
　　　　它的光芒替代了所有的黑暗。

　　　　葉上最鮮活的青綠
　　　　我在午後的炎熱裡採摘橄欖，
　　　　光照在我衣上、臉上、頭上、眼上。

　　　　每個黃昏我都有訪客：
　　　　我的門敞開
　　　　向所有美妙的歌曲。

　　　　夜裡我沒膝走入海中
　　　　開始收攏我的網；
　　　　我的撈獲：星與魚的混合。

This poem can be regarded as a model of socialist poetry. The strong poetic voice of the poet improves life, and also means that for the future of national liberation and the suffering of the working people, the poet not only spurs himself from time to time, but also causes inner shocks caused by his desire to fight for the Turkish nation. Yet the passion of poetry is a moment, unbound by time and space. During his imprisonment, he also wrote the poem *Work*. In the poem, the longing for light has not disappeared, but it has only been written in a different way:

When day dawns on my horns,
I plow with patience and dignity;
The earth is wet and warm to the soles of my bare feet.

My muscles are sparkling
I beat the hot iron till noon;
Its light replaces all darkness.

The freshest green on the leaves
I picked olives in the heat of the afternoon,
The light shines on my clothes, on my face, on my head,
and on my eyes.

Every evening I have visitors:
My door is wide open/to all the wonderful songs.

In the night I went knee-deep into the sea/Started to
draw my net;
My catch: a mix of stars and fis

　　我現在已變得該
　　對我身邊發生的事情負責，
　　對人類及大地
　　對黑暗與光明。

　　你能看到我陷沒在工作裡，
　　別用話來阻撓我，我的愛，
　　我在忙著同你相愛。

　　如同許多囚禁的愛國詩人一樣，希克梅特在獄中可能每天也得犁地或辛苦地勞動；然而，卻再也沒有什麼比工作中還能思想更自由的了——因此，他也試圖寫下詩句，像是正在從事一項偉大的工作一般，他必須把對祖國的愛，對民族與同胞的愛當作是精神的支柱，當祖國需要他的時候，他必須在。

二、詩性思維和情的聯結：家人和愛

　　什麼是詩性思維？對於詩人而言，它是透過想像力的一種特殊的精神活動，將強烈的感受到對於任何的人、物、事，以直覺方式去創造出具有詩化美感的主體境界。而希克梅特無論身體受到怎樣的痛楚，或身心糾纏於被迫害的問題，他為何還要堅持以詩歌及寫作將憂鬱排除於生命之外呢？這一切詩性思維究竟從何而來？而那些加諸於其身上的力量又是什麼？

I have now become
Take responsibility for what happens around me,
To humans and the earth
To darkness and light.

You can see me lost in work,
Don't stop me with words, my love,
I'm busy falling in love with you.

Like many imprisoned patriotic poets, Hikmet may have had to plow or toil every day in prison; however, there is nothing more free than thinking at work-so he also tried to write The next verse, as if he is doing a great job, he must regard the love for the motherland, the nation and the compatriots as a spiritual pillar, and when the motherland needs him, he must be there.

2. The Connection Between Poetic Thinking and Emotion: Family and Love

What is poetic thinking? For poets, it is a special spiritual activity through imagination, which will strongly feel any person, object, or event, and create a subjective realm with poetic beauty in an intuitive way. And no matter what kind of pain Hikmet suffered physically, or whether he was entangled in the problem of persecution, why did he insist on keeping depression out of his life through poetry and writing? Where did all these poetic thoughts come from? And what are the forces that are exerted on it?

　　我思索，再思索，最後，我得到這樣的結論，這可能跟
他對家人和祖國的愛相關，又或者他內心深處認為「情」與
其思維相近且密切，而「情」也正是詩歌創作中最必要的。
例如，他在 1933 年 11 月 11 日監獄裡寫下的這首《給我妻的
信》，真情流露是顯而易見的：

　　　　我的愛！
　　　　在你最近的信上你說，
　　　　「我的頭疼痛/我心驚悸。」
　　　　「如果他們吊你/
　　　　如果我失去你，」
　　　　你說，
　　　　「我不能活。」

　　　　但你能的，我的愛；
　　　　我的形相散佈風中
　　　　如一股濃而黑的煙。
　　　　當然你要活下去
　　　　我心上的紅髮姐妹；
　　　　哀悼死者
　　　　在二十世紀
　　　　頂多維持一年。

I thought and thought again, and finally, I came to the conclusion that this may be related to his love for his family and the motherland, or he believes that "love" is close and close to his thinking, and "love" is poetry most necessary in creation. For example, in this *Letter to My Wife*, which he wrote in prison on November 11, 1933, the truth is obvious:

My love!
In your most recent letter you said,
"My head hurts
I'm terrified."
"If they hang you/
If I lose you,
You say,
"I can't live."

But you can, my love;
My form is scattered in the wind
Like a puff of thick, black smoke.
Of course you have to live
The red-haired sisters of my heart;
Mourn the dead
In the twentieth century
At most one year.

死神：
一個死人在一根繩子的末端，蕩著 ──
但怪事
我的心不接受
這種死亡。
你必須
記住，我的愛人，如果一隻像黑蜘蛛般
可憐的吉普賽多毛的手
把繩子套
在我的脖子上──
那些等著在我的藍睛裡看到恐懼的人
將徒然地看著納京。

我
在我最後一個早晨的曙光裡
將看到我真心的朋友們和你，
而只有
一首被打斷的歌的激恨
我將帶進我的墳墓。

我妻！
我好心腸的
金蜂
有著比蜜還甜的眼睛
究竟為什麼我要告訴你
他們正催著把我吊死？
審判才剛剛開始
而他們並不真的摘你的腦袋
像一隻蘿蔔。

Grim Reaper:
A dead man swings at the end of a rope —
But strange things
My heart doesn't accept
This death.
You must
Remember, my love, if a black spider
Poor gypsy hairy hands
Put the rope on
On my neck —
Those who wait to see fear in my blue eyes
Will look at Nakin in vain.

I
In the light of my last morning
Will see my true friends and you,
And only
The rage of an interrupted song
I will take it to my grave.

My wife!
I am kind
Golden bee
With eyes sweeter than honey
Why on earth am I telling you
They're urging to hang me?
The trial has just begun
And they don't really take your head off
Like a radish.

來，別管那麼多。
那種可能性還渺茫得很。
要是你有錢
給我買條法蘭絨褲；
坐骨神經又開始痛了。
還有別忘記
一個囚犯的妻子要經常想
美麗的思想。

　　人間最幸福的，不是財富或家世的顯赫，而是成就於智慧的生成與愛的真摯。對於希克梅特而言，能收到愛妻的信件，哪怕是隻字片語，他仍讀了一遍又一遍，喜悅之心遠勝於相守的幸福。此詩最美好的，是讓讀者看到了希克梅特在堅強的心志之外，還保存著英雄柔情的純真。一般人，在獄中是怎樣地戰戰兢兢啊，但詩人已學會督促自己，盡全力以詩歌凝聚力量與固守自我崇高的靈魂。他必須寫詩，也必須有所成就，因為，在所有文字當中，以詩寫給妻子是最美麗的。例如，他在 1938 年也寫下這樣的詩句《今天是禮拜天》：

今天是禮拜天。
今天，頭一次，
他們把我帶到陽光裡
而在我一生中頭一次

Come on, don't worry about it.
That possibility is still very slim.
If you have money
Buy me a pair of flannel trousers;
The sciatic nerve started to hurt again.
And don't forget
A prisoner's wife has to constantly think,
Beautiful thought.

The happiest thing in the world is not wealth or illustrious family background, but the generation of wisdom and sincerity of love. For Hikmet, he still reads over and over again even if he received a letter from his beloved wife, and the joy is far greater than the happiness of staying together. The most beautiful thing about this poem is that it allows readers to see that Hikmet retains the innocence of heroic tenderness in addition to his strong will. Ordinary people are trembling in prison, but the poet has learned to urge himself to do his best to use poetry to gather strength and stick to his noble soul. He must write poetry, and he must achieve something, because, of all words, poetry to his wife is the most beautiful. For example, he also wrote this verse *Today is Sunday* in 1938:

Today is Sunday.
Today, for the first time,
They lead me into the sun
And for the first time in my life

我看著天空
驚奇於它是這麼遠
這麼藍
這麼遼闊。
我站著一動不動
然後必恭必敬地坐在黑地上，
把我的背緊緊靠著牆壁。
這時候，一點都沒想到死亡，
一點沒想到自由，或我的妻子。
大地，太陽與我.../我很快活。

此詩詩韻優美，表達了一種尋求自我超越的期許，一種攬抱遙遠的天空與內在的精神融合為一的思維。從藝術的角度看，疊句的復沓出現，透過沉吟，也讓詩人暫時獲得心靈的紓解。就像所有偉大的詩人，希克梅特詩中的悲痛與歡欣源於本身經歷愛、生存與困境，同時詠頌面對黑暗，尋求光明的途徑。在他所深愛的祖國和家人的不朽記憶裡，其生命之光，何等榮耀！例如，在 1945 年 9 月間，他寫給其妻派拉羿的詩，滿懷愛意與渴望，皆源自於他每絲微微的辛酸中：

九月二十一日
我們的兒子病了
他的父親在監牢裡
而你沉重的頭在你疲累的掌心上
我們共嘗世界的辛酸。

I look at the sky
Amazed how far it is
So blue
So vast.
I stand still
Then sit respectfully on the black ground,
Press my back against the wall.
At that time, I didn't think about death at all.
Didn't think about freedom, or my wife at all.
The earth, the sun and me.../I am happy.

This poem has a beautiful rhyme, expressing an expectation of seeking self-transcendence, a thinking that embraces the distant sky and merges with the inner spirit. From an artistic point of view, the repetition of refraining sentences also allows the poet to obtain temporary spiritual relief through meditation. Like all great poets, the grief and joy in Hikmet's poems come from his own experience of love, survival and difficulties, while singing the way to face darkness and find light. How glorious is the light of his life in the immortal memory of his beloved motherland and family! For example, in September 1945, he wrote a poem to his wife Pellaia, full of love and longing, all from his every trace of bitterness:

September 21
Our son is sick
His father in prison
And your heavy head on your tired palm
We taste the bitterness of the world together.

人們將相扶到較美好的日子
所以，我們的兒子會好起來
他的父親將出獄
而你金色的眼睛裡將再度微笑
共嘗世界的辛酸。

九月二十二日
我讀一本書：
你在其中/聽一首歌：
你在其中。
我坐下來吃我的麵包：
你面對著我。
我工作：
你面對著我。
雖然你無所不在
你無法同我說話
我們聽不見彼此的聲音——
你，我八歲的寡婦。

十月六日
雲層移過：載著新聞，沉重地。
我揉縐我還沒收到的你的信
而我有大叫的衝動：派拉羿
派——拉——羿。
在心型眼睫毛的尖端：
無邊的土地有福了。

People will hold each other to better days
So our son will be fine
His father will be released from prison
And your golden eyes will smile again
Taste the bitterness of the world together.

September 22
I read a book:
You're in/listening to a song:
you are in it.
I sit down and eat my bread:
You face me.
I worked:
You face me.
Although you are everywhere
You can't talk to me
We can't hear each other's voices—
You, my eight-year-old widow.

October 6
The clouds move past: carrying the news, heavily.
I crumpled your letter that I haven't received yet
On the tip of the heart-shaped lashes:
Blessed is the boundless land.
And I have the urge to yell:
Pella Yi Pai-la-yi.

十月九日
從櫃子裡取出
我頭一次看到你穿的裙子，
把康乃馨插上你的頭髮
那朵我從監獄裡送給你的
不管它現在有多乾枯。
打扮得好看起來，
像春天。

在像這樣的日子裡你絕不可顯得
悲傷絕望。
絕不可以！
在像這樣的日子裡
你必須抬頭而高貴地
走路，
你必須以納齊姆‧希克梅特
的妻子的自負走路。

　　希克梅特的詩歌是偉大的。當他勇敢地說出心中的這些
思念，也將以語言和行動來證實。他讓詩句與其思想對話，
而我不懷疑他對著空中向其妻喊叫，派一拉一羿，因為，那
聲音，讓讀者看到其眼眸閃爍的光芒；因為，人們喜歡愛情，

October 9
Take it out of the cabinet
I saw your dress for the first time,
Put carnations in your hair
That flower I gave you from prison
No matter how dry it is now.
Dress up and look good,
Like spring.

On a day like this you must never appear
Sad and hopeless.
Never!
On days like this
You must hold your head high and dignified
Walk,
You have to be Nazim Hikmet
Wife's ego walks.

Hikmet's poetry is great. When he bravely speaks out these thoughts in his heart, it will also be confirmed by words and actions. He let the lines talk to his thoughts, and I don't doubt that he shouted into the air to his wife, Pie-La-Ye, because, that voice, let the reader see the twinkle in his eyes; because, people love, that voice, made

那聲音，讓我的眼睛瞬間迷濛，也確實是首豪邁又柔情的史詩。他的詩性思維和情的聯結，大多源於家人和愛，沒有任何虛妄，因而能歷經百年依然為世人所傳頌。

三、希克梅特詩歌中最偉大的啓示

希克梅特早在蘇聯學習期間就認識了許多中國現代詩人，其中包括曾與毛澤東早年就讀小學和湖南師範學院時期的同學蕭三（1896-1983），他同情中國人民的革命鬥爭，因而他在詩裡多次提到中國，並展現其博大的胸懷。例如，他在 1948 年寫下《我的心不在這裡》，其中一段寫道：「鮮紅的血，我的血，同黃河一起奔流。我的心在中國，在那為正義的制度而戰的士兵的隊伍中間跳動。」詩裡飽含著透徹的靈魂，閃亮了東方的靈魂，就如雪松和大地輝耀；多少歲月過去了，而他的愛也已生長成中國土地上的星子。

當詩人在 1947 年寫下《自從我被投進這牢洞》這首名詩，他的眼神在獄中尋找，他注視同胞，他們被迫害，被推進死亡地獄。他在自由烈士的精神上尋找，回想往昔，為受難者流出的血與他熱愛的祖國，願為正義而謳歌：

自從我被投進這牢洞/地球已繞了太陽十圈。

如果你問地球，它會說，

「不值一提/這麼微不足道的時間。」

如果你問我，我會說，

my eyes instantly blurred, and it is indeed a heroic and tender epic. Most of his poetic thinking and emotional connections come from his family and love, without any falsehood, so he can still be praised by the world after a hundred years.

3. The Greatest Revelation in Hikmet's Poetry

Hikmet met many modern Chinese poets during his studies in the Soviet Union, including Xiao San (1896-1983), a classmate of Mao Zedong in elementary school and Hunan Normal University. He sympathized with the revolutionary struggle of the Chinese people, so China is mentioned many times in the poem and shows its broad mind. For example, he wrote *My Heart Is Not Here* in 1948, in which a passage reads: "The red blood, my blood, runs with the Yellow River. My heart is in China, where I am fighting for a just system. Jumping in the middle of the ranks of soldiers." The poem is filled with a thorough soul, shining the soul of the East, just like the cedar and the earth shine; how many years have passed, and his love has grown into stars on the land of China.

When the poet wrote the famous poem *Since I Was Thrown Into This Hole* in 1947, his eyes searched in prison, and he watched his compatriots, who were persecuted and pushed into the hell of death. He searched for the spirit of the free martyrs, recalled the past, shed the blood of the victims and the motherland he loved, and was willing to sing for justice:

> *The earth has circled the sun ten times since I was cast into this hole.*
> *If you ask the earth, it will say,*
> *"Not worth mentioning / Such an insignificant amount of time."*
> *If you ask me, I'd say,*

「我生命裡去掉了十年。」
我被囚禁的那天/我有支小鉛筆
不到一個禮拜我便把它用完。
如果你問鉛筆，它會說，
「我整整一生。」
如果你問我，我會說，
「又怎樣?只不過一個禮拜。」

奧斯曼，正為謀殺罪服刑
當我第一次進入這牢洞，
在七年半後出去；
在外頭享受了一陣生活
又為了走私案回來
而在六個月後再度出去。
昨天有人聽說，他結了婚
來年春天要有小孩。
那些在我被投入這牢洞的那天
受孕的小孩
現在正慶祝他們的十周歲。
那一天出世的
在它們細長腿上搖晃的小馬
現在必也已變成
擺蕩著寬臀的懶馬。
但年青的橄欖枝依然年青，
還在繼續成長。

"Ten years were removed from my life."
The day I was imprisoned / I had a little pencil
I used it up in less than a week.
If you ask the pencil, it will say,
"My whole life."
If you ask me, I'd say,
"So what? It's only been a week."

Osman, serving time for murder
When I first entered this prison,
Out after seven and a half years;
Enjoying life outside
Back again for the smuggling case
And go out again six months later.
Someone heard yesterday that he got married
There will be a baby next spring.
On the day I was thrown into this hole
Children conceived/now celebrating their tenth birthday.
Ponies born that day/Wagling on their slender legs
Now it must have become a lazy horse with wide hips swinging.
But the young olive branch is still young,
Still growing.

他們告訴我我來這裡以後
故鄉新造了個廣場。
我那小屋裡的家人
現在住在
一條我不認識的街上
另一座我無法看到的房子裡。

麵包白得像雪棉
我被投進這牢洞的那年
然後便開始了配給。
這裡，在牢室內，
人們互相殘殺
為一點點黑麵包屑。
現在情形比較好些
但我們的麵包，沒有味道。

我被投進這牢洞的那年
第二次世界大戰還沒開始；
在達考（註）的集中營裡/煤氣爐還沒被造起；
原子還沒在廣島爆裂。
呵，時間流著
像一個被屠殺的嬰孩的血。
現在這些都已成過去
但美元
早已在談論著
第三次世界大戰

They told me when I came here
A new square was built in my hometown.
My family in that cabin/living now
On a street I don't know
In another house I can't see.

The bread is as white as snow cotton
The year I was thrown into this hole
Then the rationing began.
Here, in the cell,
People kill each other
For a little brown breadcrumbs.
Things are better now
But our bread has no taste.

The year I was thrown into this hole
World War II has not yet begun;
In the concentration camp of Da Kao (Note)
The gas stove has not yet been built;
Atoms hadn't exploded in Hiroshima yet.
Oh, time goes by
Like the blood of a slaughtered baby.
It's all in the past now
But the dollar
Already talking about the book
World War III

都一樣，現在日子比
我被投進這牢洞裡時
明亮/從那天以後/我的同胞們半撐著肘
起來了；/地球已繞了太陽
十圈
但我用同樣熱切的期望重複
那我在十年前的今天
為我的同胞們寫的：
「你們多
如地上的螞蟻
海裡的魚
天上的鳥；
你們可能懦弱或勇敢
目不識丁或滿腹經綸。
而因為你們是所有事業
的創造者
或毀壞者，
只有你們的事蹟
將被記錄在歌裡。」
而別的，
諸如我十年的受難，
只不過是閒話。

　　在他多次入獄，接受社會主義的狂熱、嚮往自由的這段
時期，他寫下許多詩篇。直到 1950 年，土耳其民主黨頒佈了

All the same, now days
When I was thrown into this hole
Bright
Since that day
My countrymen half-bend their elbows
Arise;
The earth has circled the sun
Ten laps.
But I repeat with the same eager expectation
Then I was ten years ago today
For my fellow citizens:
"You are as numerous
As ants on the ground
Fish in the sea
Birds of the sky;
You may be cowardly or brave
Illiterate or knowledgeable.
And because you are the creators of all
Or destroyer,
Only your deeds/will be recorded in the song."
While others,
Like my ten years of suffering,
It's just gossip.

He wrote many poems during the period when he was imprisoned many times, accepted the fanaticism of socialism, and yearned for freedom. Until 1950, the

大赦法，希克梅特因此獲釋，但仍受到當局監視和迫害；在
親朋好友的相助下，他經羅馬尼亞逃亡蘇聯，於 1951 年定居
莫斯科。有時，回憶也是一種希望。例如在 1950 年間，他為
其妻寫的《歡迎，我的女人》一詩，以求療癒分離的痛苦：

> 歡迎，我親愛的妻子，歡迎！
> 你一定累了：
> 我怎能洗你的小腳？
> 我既沒有銀盆也沒有玫瑰水。
> 你一定渴了：
> 我沒有冰果汁可以奉獻你。
> 你一定餓了：
> 我無法為你擺筵席
> 在繡花的白桌布上——
> 我的房間同我的國家一樣窮。
>
> 歡迎，我親愛的女人，歡迎！
> 你一踏進我的房間，
> 那四十年的混凝土便成了草地；
> 當你微笑/窗上的鐵條便長出玫瑰花；
> 當你哭泣/我的手便盛滿了珍珠。
> 我的牢房變得像我的心一般富有
> 像自由一般明亮。
>
> 歡迎，我自己的，歡迎，歡迎！

Turkish Democratic Party promulgated the amnesty law, so Hikmet was released, but he was still monitored and persecuted by the authorities; with the help of his relatives and friends, he fled to the Soviet Union via Romania, and settled in Moscow in 1951. Sometimes, memory is also a kind of hope. For example, in the 1950s he wrote *Welcome, My Woman* for his wife as a cure for the pain of separation:

Welcome, my dear wife, welcome!
You must be tired:
How can I wash your little feet?
I have neither silver basin nor rose water.
You must be thirsty:
I don't have ice cream to offer you.
You must be hungry:
I can't make a feast for you
On the embroidered white tablecloth —
My room is as poor as my country.

Welcome, my dear woman, welcome!
As soon as you step into my room,
Those forty years of concrete became grass;
When you smile
The iron bars on the window grow roses;
When you cry
My hands are full of pearls.
My cell became as rich as my heart
As bright as freedom.

Welcome, my own, welcome, welcome!

　　詩篇有格律，毫無保留的吟哦他的企盼與痛苦。那隱藏的淚水，在讀者面前，彷彿也能擁抱我們的傷口，也終將換成今日令人目眩耀眼的詩花。晚年的他，在蘇聯積極參加社會活動，繼續從事文學創作，榮獲過「列寧國際和平獎」等殊榮。流亡期間，他寫了許多以維護和平為主題的詩歌，更多的作品，小說或劇本，則表達他對祖國的熱愛和思鄉的情懷。他在 1951 年起，任世界和平理事會理事，1960 年，任世界和平理事會國際和平獎評議委員會主席；在 1952 年九月至十月間，應邀訪問中國並稱讚新中國的革命和建設。但 1963 年 4 月 3 日，這位對祖國充滿憂患之情的民族詩人，便與世長辭在莫斯科，終年六十二歲。他被安葬在莫斯科著名的新聖女公墓，在黑色花崗岩豐碑上刻著他名震後世的影像。他的詩揉合著激昂、純真與柔情，並富音樂性。

　　對於這樣的一個愛國抒情主義的詩人，其詩歌中最偉大的啟示，是他宛若巨樹般地，詩意的矗立於風雨之中，在痛苦中淬鍊時，內心仍充滿光明。他對祖國懷著這樣的深情，讓詩美在故土腹地，在耕者鋤禾裡，令無數勞動者鼓舞，感動於心。他說過：「人的一生有兩種東西不會忘記，那就是母親的面孔和城市的面貌。」在這裡所指的母親，是廣義的，是他思念中的祖國；而其身影如朝霞般絢爛，是那麼熟悉，又那麼神奇，在風中傲然屹立，在鮮活的碑表上，也永遠刻著這位如同土耳其的莎士比亞之名。因而，閱讀希克梅特的詩，始終保持著崇敬；不僅多了一次深刻的記憶，也是心靈

The Psalm has a metric, unreservedly chanting his hopes and pains. The hidden tears, in front of readers, seem to be able to embrace our wounds, and will eventually be replaced by today's dazzling poetry. In his later years, he actively participated in social activities in the Soviet Union, continued to engage in literary creation, and won the "Lenin International Peace Prize" and other honors. During his exile, he wrote many poems on the theme of maintaining peace, and more works, novels or plays, expressed his love for the motherland and his homesickness. Since 1951, he has served as a director of the World Peace Council. In 1960, he served as the chairman of the International Peace Prize Review Committee of the World Peace Council. From September to October 1952, he was invited to visit China and praised the revolution and construction of New China. But on April 3, 1963, this national poet, who was full of worries about the motherland, died in Moscow at the age of sixty-two. He was buried in the famous Novodevichy Cemetery in Moscow, and his famous image is engraved on the black granite monument. His poems combine passion, innocence and tenderness, and are rich in music.

For such a patriotic and lyrical poet, the greatest inspiration in his poems is that he stands poetically like a giant tree in the wind and rain, and when he is quenched in pain, his heart is still full of light. He has such a deep affection for the motherland, so that Shimei is in the hinterland of his homeland, where the plowmen are hoeing, and countless laborers are inspired and moved in their hearts. He said: "There are two things in a person's life that will never be forgotten, that is, the face of the mother and the appearance of the city." The mother referred to here is in a broad sense, and it is the motherland he misses; and her figure is like the morning glow. It is so gorgeous, so familiar, and so magical, standing proudly in the wind, and the name of this Turkish Shakespeare will always be engraved on the vivid tablet. Therefore, reading Hikmet's poems always maintains reverence; not only has a deep memory, but also

上最豐富的饗宴。彷彿中，我看到希克梅特攜著美麗的夕陽
和唇邊的一朵微笑，在天宇間漫步，邊哼著歡樂的小曲了。

註：Dachau，納粹消滅猶太人的集中營。

參考文獻：本文譯詩均選自美國詩人非馬（Dr. William
Marr）編譯的《鐵籠裡的獅子--土耳其詩人希克梅
特的詩》。

— 臺灣《秋水》詩刊 187 期，2021.04，頁 58-64。

the richest feast for the soul. As if, I saw Hikmet walking in the sky with a beautiful sunset and a smile on his lips, humming a happy little song.

Note: Dachau, the concentration camp where the Nazis wiped out the Jews.

References: The translated poems in this article are selected from *The Lion in the Iron Cage-Poems of the Turkish Poet Hikmet* compiled by the American poet Dr. William Marr.

11. 試析佛洛斯特抒情詩四首

摘要：佛洛斯特詩歌已為學者廣泛關注，他們多將「抒情性」歸納為佛洛斯特詩歌的突出特點。筆者從非馬的譯作（註 1）中試圖對每一篇詩歌所設想的意境談談自己的聯想之見。

關鍵詞：佛洛斯特　美國詩人　抒情性

一、其人其詩

　　佛洛斯特＃生於美國舊金山，是二十世紀備受愛戴和尊榮的詩人之一；其詩歌特徵源於兒時便開始對寫詩的熱愛。他一生歷經許多艱辛和痛苦，十一歲喪父、之後隨母親遷居新英格蘭，家庭雖貧窮，但他勤奮筆耕，十六歲便開始學寫詩，那塊與他結下不解之緣的土地，更孕育了伴隨他一生的歡欣、孤獨、悲哀和寫作的想像力。日後他創作詩歌時，那些人物或動植物，巡更人、母親、小牛、馬兒、鳥兒、凋零的玫瑰或大自然和英格蘭北方的農民……甚至無生命的農舍、牧場等，從某種角度都可看出是被詩人賦予了生命、愛與情感的遐思。

11. Analysis of Four Lyric Poems by Robert Frost

Abstract: Robert Frost's poems have been widely discussed by scholars, and most of them summarize "lyricism" as the outstanding feature of Frost's poems. From William Marr's translation (Note 1), the author tries to talk about his own associations with the artistic conception envisaged in each poem.

Key words: Frost, American poet, lyricism

1. His People and His Poems

Robert Frost (1874-1963), born in San Francisco, USA, is one of the most beloved and honored poets of the 20th century; his poetic identity stems from a love of writing poetry that began at an early age. He experienced many hardships and pains in his life. He lost his father at the age of 11 and moved to New England with his mother. Although his family was poor, he worked diligently and began to learn to write poetry at the age of 16. The land also gave birth to the joy, loneliness, sorrow and imagination of writing that accompanied him throughout his life. When he wrote poems in the future, those characters or animals and plants, patrolmen, mothers, calves, horses, birds, withered roses, or nature and farmers in the north of England... even inanimate farmhouses, pastures, etc., came from a certain place. It can be seen from all angles that it is a reverie endowed with life, love and emotion by the poet.

　　他在年輕時當過工人、瓦匠、教師和記者等，後來考入
哈佛大學，卻因貧困而輟學，歸於務農。在他的理念中，寫
詩是他全部人生的結晶，在他最艱辛的階段上結出奇蹟似的
碩果。當他在出版第二部詩集後，詩人的名字已開始在美國
流傳，並在各地巡迴朗誦自己的詩歌。成名後的佛洛斯特受
聘於多所大學，經常疲於奔波。晚年的他，回到他的農莊，
繼續品味田園的純樸與孤獨。其詩質樸、清新，極具藝術感
染力；一生共出了十多本詩集，也獲得四次普立茲獎，這是
美國文學史上獲得此殊榮的第一人，享年八十九歲。

二、名作賞析

　　所謂抒情性，廣泛地說，是指作者表現個人美好情感的
一類文學活動，並充滿詩意的效果。筆者以為，佛洛斯特詩
歌最大的特點是語言質樸，但折射出哲人般的光芒；詩句意
象清新雋永，亦深藏著細膩的情感。這既是佛洛斯特對藝術
的追求，也是其詩歌迷人的所在。我們不妨來閱讀這首小詩
（牧場），便可體會其詩歌的扣人心弦和崇高：

> 我正要去清理牧場的泉水；
>
> 只去耙耙葉子
>
> （等著看水清，也許）
>
> 我不會待太久——你也來吧。

When he was young, he worked as a worker, a bricklayer, a teacher, and a reporter. Later, he was admitted to Harvard University, but he dropped out of school due to poverty and returned to farming. In his philosophy, writing poetry is the crystallization of his whole life, and it bears miraculous fruits in his most difficult stage. When he published his second collection of poems, the poet's name has begun to circulate in the United States, and he toured around to recite his poems. After becoming famous, Frost was employed by many universities and was often exhausted. In his later years, he returned to his farm and continued to taste the simplicity and loneliness of the countryside. His poems are simple, fresh, and highly artistic; he has published more than ten poetry collections in his lifetime, and won four Pulitzer Prizes. He is the first person to win this honor in the history of American literature. He died at the age of eighty-nine.

2. Appreciation of Masterpieces

The so-called lyricism, broadly speaking, refers to a kind of literary activity in which the author expresses his personal beautiful emotions, and is full of poetic effects. The author believes that the biggest feature of Frost's poetry is that the language is simple, but it reflects the light of a philosopher; the imagery of the poems is fresh and meaningful, and it also contains delicate emotions. This is not only Frost's pursuit of art, but also the charm of his poetry. We might as well read this little poem *The Pasture*, and then we can appreciate the excitement and sublimity of its poetry:

> *I'm going out to clean the pasture spring;*
> *I'll only stop to rake the leaves away*
> (And wait to watch the water clear, I may):
> *I sha'n't be gone long. — You come too.*

我正要去捉小牛
站在母親的身邊。那麼幼小
她用舌頭舔牠都會使牠站不穩。
我不會待太久——你也來吧。

　　當佛洛斯特開始轉向詩歌創作道路時，新英格蘭鄉野間常見的景物遂成他寫作的最愛，且每首詩的意象都是獨一無二的。此詩內含著詩人的溫暖情懷，寫得十分自然貼切，感人至深，也鐫刻著詩人浪漫的精神。而另一首小詩〈小鳥〉，卻有著難得的喜劇性的詩性表現，詩人與小鳥間的互動也體現出他呵護小動物稚嫩心靈的細膩情懷：

我曾希望一隻鳥飛開，
別儘在我屋旁磨他的聲帶；

在門口對牠大拍其手
當我到了忍無可忍的時候。

錯處必多少在我。
鳥的音調沒有罪過。

而想讓歌聲靜止
當然也有點謬誤。

I'm going out to fetch the little calf
That's standing by the mother. It's so young
It totters when she licks it with her tongue.
I sha'n't be gone long. — You come too.

When Frost turned to poetry, the common sights of the New England countryside became his favorites, and the imagery in each poem was unique. This poem contains the poet's warm feelings, written very naturally and appropriately, deeply touching, and engraved with the poet's romantic spirit. But another little poem entitled *Little Bird* has a rare comic poetic expression, and the interaction between the poet and the little bird also reflects his delicate feelings of caring for the immature hearts of small animals:

I have wished a bird would fly away,
And not sing by my house all day;

Have clapped my hands at him from the door
When it seemed as if I could bear no more.

The fault must be partly have been in me.
The bird was not blame for his key.

And of course there must be something wrong
In wanting to silence any song.

這是一首淋漓盡致的幽默詩，詩人雖然創作了不少抒情詩，但在其幽默的語言中，依然保存著一顆溫柔的童心且寓意深長，留給讀者更多的想像空間及心中懷著對此詩至純至深至厚的回味。眾所周知，佛洛斯特之所以擁有強烈的藝術感染力，除了他對詩歌的執著追求體現出美感的意象以及保持清新的高潔情懷外，他因為中年喪妻、老年喪子，以致其詩歌裡常隱含著一種孤獨美的形象塑造和靈魂開掘，且把所有的經歷化作創作的思路，也因而定下舒緩抒情的基調。比如這首〈夜的知心〉，充滿感傷和悲涼。因為詩人的快樂和幸福來得十分不易，此詩也映襯了其內心的寂寞與孤獨。

三、結　語

總而言之，佛洛斯特是一顆永不凋謝的明星，其詩歌中大量使用的比喻與其抒情語言是分不開的。他說過：「詩始於普通的隱喻，巧妙的隱喻和高雅的隱喻，適於我們所擁有的最深刻的思想。」閱讀其詩，一面可對於其一生總是努力以赴與其悲傷一面有了深刻理解，一面也加深對非馬英譯其詩歌的能力肯定。讓後學對探討佛洛斯特詩歌的傳承因而有了歷史的關聯性，也讓筆者理解到，佛洛斯特成為二十世紀地位高、影響大的詩人，確實是值得推崇與繼續研究的。

The poet described a scene in an empty and quiet snowy night without any concealment, and was confused by the turbulent world all day long, and it was difficult for people to calm down and find the beauty and tranquility of nature. Lü Jin said: "Poetry is an art with a strong spirituality, and its aesthetic point of view is an internal point of view, not an external point of view." (Note 2) Because Frost wandered in the prosperous cities of the United States in his early years, he returned to him in his later years. Finally, I can enjoy the beauty of nature infatuatedly. This poem combines the leaping weaving of Western aesthetic images with the "music" embodied in nature, and it is also his aesthetic expression of true feelings.

3. Conclusion

All in all, Frost is a star that never fades, and the metaphors that are used extensively in his poems are inseparable from his lyrical language. He said: "Poetry begins with ordinary metaphors, ingenious metaphors and elegant metaphors, suitable for the deepest thoughts we have." Reading his poems, on the one hand, he has always worked hard all his life, and on the other hand, he is sad. On the one hand, he gained a deep understanding, and on the other hand, he also deepened his affirmation of William Marr's ability to translate his poems into English. It makes the later scholars have historical relevance to discuss the inheritance of Frost's poetry, and also makes the author understand that Frost has become a poet with a high status and great influence in the 20th century, which is indeed worthy of praise and further research.

註 1.非馬編譯《讓盛宴開始--我喜愛的英文詩》，Let the Feast Begin, 英漢對照，書林出版有限公司，1999 年。

註 2.呂進著，《呂進詩學雋語》，臺北，秀威，2012

Note 1. *Let the Feast Begin—My Favorite English Poetry* compiled by William Marr, *Let the Feast Begin*, English-Chinese bilingual, Shulin Publishing Co., Ltd., 1999.

Note 2. Lü Jin, *Lüu Jin's Poetics*, Taipei, Xiuwei, 2012 edition, page 21.

12. 淺析瑞典詩人川斯綽莫的詩世界

　　二○一一年諾貝爾文學獎得主的瑞典詩人川斯綽莫（特朗斯特羅姆 Tomas Transtroemer）（1931－2015）一生著有詩集十餘卷，作品已被譯成六十多種文字，不僅造就了「為藝術而藝術」的創作風格，而且深深影響了象徵主義與超現實主義的創作方法，因而獲得了多項國際的文學類獎項及很高的聲譽。詩人非馬在英譯川斯綽莫的詩歌創作中引出的人生感慨與強烈情感，恰恰點明川斯綽莫的想像力往往帶著某種邏輯的創造力量，甚而不懈地創造一個令人激賞而奇幻的詩世界。

　　誠然，寫詩最需要的是真實情感及意境，尤以形象思維為重。英國詩人柯勒律治（Samuel Taylor Coleridge，1772-1834）就明確指出，「詩」是最佳語言的最佳安排。其實，川斯綽莫的詩歌大多是由開頭的「象徵」和其後的「聯想」相輔相成而得。在具體的詩作中，他也喜歡使用大膽的比喻，往往與自由的節奏情景交融，而音樂在其創作中也起了很重要的角色。

12. A Brief Analysis of the Poetic World of Swedish Poet Tomas Transtroemer

Swedish poet Tomas Transtroemer (1931-2015), winner of the Nobel Prize for Literature in 2011, has written more than ten poetry collections in his life, and his works have been translated into more than 60 languages. His style has deeply influenced the creative methods of symbolism and surrealism, and thus won many international literary awards and a high reputation. The life emotions and strong emotions elicited by the poet William Marr in the English translation of Transtramo's poetry just point out that Transtramo's imagination often has a certain logical creative power, and even unremittingly creates an exciting and fantastic poetic world.

It is true that what is most needed in writing poetry is true emotion and artistic conception, especially thinking in images. The British poet Samuel Taylor Coleridge (1772-1834) clearly pointed out that poetry is the best words in the best order. In fact, most of Transtroemer's poems are composed of the initial "symbol" and the subsequent "association". In specific poems, he also likes to use bold metaphors, often blending with free rhythmic scenes, and music also plays a very important role in his creation.

　　比如他寫過一首兼具思想藝術雙美的詩歌《徐緩的音樂》，語言精煉清醇，頗有神秘主義之風：

　　　　大廈今天不開放。太陽從窗玻璃擠入
　　　　照暖了桌子的上端
　　　　堅固得可負載別人命運的桌子。

　　　　今天我們來到戶外，在寬闊的長坡上。
　　　　有人穿暗色的衣服。你要是站在陽光裡
　　　　閉上眼睛，
　　　　你會感到像被慢慢地吹送向前。

　　　　我太少來海邊。可現在我來了，
　　　　在有寧靜背部的石子中間。
　　　　那些石子慢慢倒退著走出海。

　　這首詩不僅帶有一種撲朔迷離的神秘色彩，且反映出詩人想要探索自己的內心深處與外在世界的關係。詩句形象地概括出在那年代裡詩人逐漸關注把大自然的力量同處於一種超然狀態交融在一起，像是經受大海的撫慰，他找到了想表達心靈之感的藝術世界，並竭力運用了隱喻、象徵和幻覺來體驗現實世界，也體現了自己偏愛清靜又深情善感，給人一

For example, he wrote a poem *Slow Music* with both ideological and artistic beauty. The language is refined and mellow, with a touch of mysticism:

The building is closed today. The sun squeezes in through the window pane
Warmed the top of the table
A table strong enough to bear the fate of others.

Today we are outside, on a wide long slope.
Some people wear dark clothes. if you stand in the sun
Close your eyes
You will feel like being slowly blown forward.

I rarely come to the beach. But here I am,
Among the stones with a peaceful back,
The stones slowly walked backwards out of the sea.

This poem not only has a confusing and mysterious color, but also reflects the poet's desire to explore the relationship between his innermost being and the external world. The verse vividly summarizes that in that era, the poet gradually paid attention to blending the power of nature with a transcendent state, as if being comforted by the sea, he found an artistic world that wanted to express the feeling of the soul, and tried his best to use metaphors, symbols and hallucinations to experience the real world, also reflects his preference for quiet and affectionate,

種高境界之美。除了寫詩，川斯綽莫也在瑞典國家勞工部做工作方面的心理學家，同時也是一位業餘音樂家；其晚年詩集內容大多與死亡和社會體驗相關，曾被喻為「歐洲詩壇最傑出的象徵主義和超現實主義大詩人。」

　　再看這首《軌道》，顯然，詩人的描景記事，已構成了一個超越時空又異常恬靜的藝術境界，如詩中這樣以感情注入物象的繪畫美的句子：

　　　清晨兩點：月光。火車停在
　　　野外。遠處小鎮的燈光
　　　在地平線上冷冷地閃爍。

　　　如同一個人深深走進他的夢
　　　他將永不會記得他到過那裡
　　　當他再度回到他的房間。

　　　或者當一個人深深走入病中
　　　他的日子全成了幾粒閃爍的火花，一群，
　　　微弱冷漠在地平線上。

　　　火車完全靜止不動。
　　　兩點鐘：皎潔的月光，幾顆星星。

giving people a high-level beauty. In addition to writing poetry, Transstromo is also a psychologist at the Swedish National Labor Department and an amateur musician; most of his poetry collections in his later years are related to death and social experience, and he was once hailed as "the most important poet in Europe" and "an outstanding symbolist and surrealist poet".

Looking at this song *Orbit* again, it is obvious that the poet's description of scenery and events has formed an artistic realm that transcends time and space and is extremely peaceful, such as the sentence in the poem that injects emotion into the beauty of objects:

> *Two in the morning: moonlight. train stops at*
> *Field. Distant town lights*
> *Glittering coldly on the horizon.*

> *Like a man walking deep into his dream*
> *He will never remember he was there*
> *When he returned to his room again.*

> *Or when a person goes deep into illness*
> *His days were all a few flickering sparks, a crowd,*
> *Faint indifference on the horizon.*

> *The train is completely still.*
> *Two o'clo*
> *ck: bright moonlight, a few stars.*

　　眾所周知，川斯綽莫是目前第七位獲得諾貝爾文學獎的
瑞典人，也擁有「神秘主義大師」稱譽。在他優秀的詩篇中，
經常描繪些夢幻般的意識，其感情總是與具體可感的藝術形
象融為一體；只要把時間放慢，細細品味，便能慢慢瞭解他
想解析內在自我與歲月滄桑變遷的不勝感喟，這些作品都含
有深意。詩人先說，深夜靜寂，如冷鑄的時間分分秒秒的流
逝，驀然，有一個人潛入夢，詩人把病中的聯想濃縮成令人
感傷的藝術畫面，這種娓娓而言的傾訴是很有創見的，沒有
真切的體驗，是寫不出這樣奇特的詩句的。

　　雖然川斯綽莫是位心理學家，也有些詩作是以自己獨特
的抒情方式去描繪生命的悲苦或對故友親人的思念，但他總
能從寫作之中擁有自己的藝術發現。再如這首《哀歌》，說
它內裡寓含著對自己或是一個親友或傑出的文學家的悼念，
或許是可能的：

　　　他放下筆。
　　　他躺在那裡不動。
　　　他躺在那空無一物的空間裡不動。
　　　他放下筆。
　　　這麼多憋不住又寫不出來的東西！
　　　他的身體因某些在遠處發生的事而僵硬
　　　雖然那奇異的旅行袋搏動如心臟。

As we all know, Transtramo is currently the seventh Swede to win the Nobel Prize in Literature, and also has the title of "Master of Mysticism". In his excellent poems, he often depicts dreamlike consciousness, and his feelings are always integrated with concrete and sensible artistic images; as long as you slow down time and savor carefully, you can gradually understand that he wants to analyze the inner self with the vicissitudes of the years, and these works are full of deep meaning. The poet first said that the silence in the middle of the night, like the passing of cold casting time, suddenly, a person sneaked into the dream, and the poet condensed the association of his illness into a sad artistic picture. It is quite original, and without real experience, it is impossible to write such peculiar lines.

Although Transtramo is a psychologist, and some poems describe the misery of life or the longing for old friends and relatives in his own unique lyrical way, he always has his own artistic discovery from writing. Another example is *Elegy*. It may be possible to say that it contains mourning for myself, a relative, a friend, or an outstanding writer:

He puts down his pen.

He lay there motionless.

He lay motionless in that empty space.

He puts down his pen.

There are so many things that I can't hold back and can't write!

His body stiffened by something happening in the distance

Although that strange travel bag beats like a heart.

外頭，晚春。

來自枝葉間的一聲呼嘯——是人還是鳥？

而開花的櫻桃樹迎擁重卡車歸來。

幾個星期過去。

夜緩緩來臨。

飛蛾停落在窗玻璃上：

來自世界的蒼白的小訊息。

　　在一九九○川斯綽莫正值五十九歲那年，他因中風而影響到語言能力，但此詩仍以深沉舒緩的筆調把內心感情吐出，直到享壽八十三歲，他都繼續從心靈中綻放出奇異意象的詩花，共發表兩百餘首詩，被譽為「二十世紀最後一位詩歌巨匠」。僅從這一點看，就不難看出此詩已超出了純粹的完美主義，不能簡單地歸結為只是用了「象徵化」，而應看作是詩人通過感覺的變異，使自己與境中的景物更融合無間，才賦予病中的生活以醇厚之味。我認為，詩人在八十歲獲得諾貝爾獎是名至實歸的殊榮，其所追求的詩美創造，始終保留著一顆童心，心靈純淨，感情自然是真摯的，這點尤為可貴。難怪德國電台評論其詩「充滿了味道、顏色、振動和雜音」，而我卻為他獨具的思維方式及多層次地展現出來的藝術表現方式，深刻地印在我的心田裡。德國詩人里爾克（Rainer Maria Rilke 1875-1926）曾說：「天才總為他的時代帶來驚

Outside, late spring.
A whistling from among the branches-is it a man or a bird?
And the blossoming cherry trees welcome the return of
heavy trucks.

A few weeks passed.
Night came slowly.
Moths settle on the window panes:
Pale little messages from the world.

In 1990, when Trump was fifty-nine years old, he had a stroke that affected his language ability, but this poem still expressed his inner feelings in a deep and soothing style until he was eighty-three years old. They all continued to bloom poetic flowers of strange images from their hearts, published more than 200 poems in total, and were hailed as "the last poetic master of the twentieth century". From this point alone, it is not difficult to see that this poem has gone beyond pure perfectionism. It cannot be simply attributed to the use of "symbolization", but it should be regarded as the poet's ability to connect himself with the situation in the environment through the variation of his feelings. The scenery is more integrated, which gives life in illness a mellow taste. In my opinion, it is a well-deserved honor for a poet to win the Nobel Prize at the age of 80. The creation of poetic beauty he pursues always retains a childlike innocence, a pure heart, and sincere feelings, which is especially valuable. No wonder the German radio station commented that his poems are "full of taste, color, vibration and noise", but I am deeply imprinted in my heart for his unique way of thinking and multi-layered artistic expression. The German poet Rainer Maria Rilke (1875-1926) once said: "Genius always brings

駭」。（註 2）川斯綽莫不僅將詩歌在心理孕育結成了各有
其妙的真珠，且不隨時間改變，又在二十一世紀的今日閃出
了奪目的光彩！

註 1.本文譯詩選自美國詩人非馬的部落格《川斯綽莫詩選 21 首》。

註 2.摘自《慢讀里爾克》，里爾克著，商周出版，臺北市，2015
年 9 月初版，頁 202。

— 2021.06.18 完稿

—臺灣《大海洋》詩雜誌，第 104 期，2022.01，
頁 106-108.

horror to his age." (Note 2) Chuansi Tramo not only nurtured poetry psychologically into pearls with their own uniqueness, and did not change with time, but also shone dazzlingly in the 21st century today!

Note 1. The translated poems in this article are selected from the blog 21 Selected Poems of Chuansqiemo by Chinese-American poet William Marr.

Note 2. Excerpted from Slow Reading of Rilke, written by Rilke, published by Shang Zhou, Taipei, first edition in September 2015, page 202.

－Completed on June 18, 2021

13. 試析巴爾蒙特詩二首

一、其人其詩

追溯俄羅斯詩人康斯坦丁•巴爾蒙特（Бальмонт Константин Дмитриевич，1867-1942）詩歌的美感所自，很容易發現的一點就是都有一個樂感（musicality）和節奏在裡面。諸如象徵主義（Symbolism）詩人普遍認同「藝術乃充滿著神秘氣氛」或側重暗示、朦朧之美等說法，都可以在巴爾蒙特的詩作中找到他成為象徵主義領袖人物之一的主要思想；而此一思想也體現了其個人主義並執著於太陽的崇拜。他自稱為「太陽的歌手」，詩風清麗典雅、意境深遠，追求「由音樂性中表現情感」。

出身於貴族家庭的巴爾蒙特，十九歲入莫斯科大學法律系就讀，但轉學至另一個俄羅斯城市雅羅斯拉夫爾（Yaroslavl）大學並順利畢業。他在二十三歲起開始陸續出版詩集；著有《在北方的天空下》(Под северным небом，1894)、《寂靜》(Тишина，1898)、《在無窮之中》（В безбрежности，1895)等多部，三十五至四十八歲間在國外

13. Analysis of Two Balmont Poems

1. His People and His Poems

Tracing back to the origin of the beauty of Russian poet Konstantin Balmont (Бальмонт Константин Дмитриевич, 1867-1942), it is easy to find that there is a musicality and rhythm in it. As symbolism poets generally agree that "art is full of mystery" or focus on hints, hazy beauty, etc., you can find the main ideas of Balmont as one of the leaders of symbolism in his poems; and this thought also reflects its individualism and obsession with the worship of the sun. He calls himself the "singer of the sun", with a beautiful and elegant poetic style, profound artistic conception, and the pursuit of "expressing emotions through musicality".

Balmont, who was born in an aristocratic family, entered the Law Department of Moscow University at the age of nineteen, but transferred to Yaroslavl University in another Russian city and graduated successfully. He began to publish poetry collections at the age of twenty-three;

廣覽文學，五十三歲時移居法國，直到七十五歲時懷著苦悶、
淒涼地在巴黎逝世。

　　儘管其一生得到過許多名家的讚譽或零星的非議，但我
發現他不僅以其一生不凡的創作印證對生活真諦的思考，而
且契合其本身曾表述「我來到這個世界，為的是看太陽」的
精神實質；而探究其詩，最能進一步瞭解其詩歌充滿了複雜
而又神秘的心靈活動。本文試就其中兩首詩歌，略抒己見。

二、詩歌賞析

　　《雨》是巴爾蒙特在三十四歲（1901）時發表的詩作，
詩人採用的喻體，或許是生活中的體驗蘊含想像而成。如這
首詩開頭就十分引人注目：

　　　牆角鼠輩吱吱唧唧，
　　　小屋靜滯睡夢裡。
　　　雨下著──屋簷水珠
　　　沿著壁緣流滴。

　　　雨下著，遲鈍、乏力，
　　　鐘擺叩敲。
　　　我不能分辨鐘聲
　　　和疲憊心靈的撞擊。

authored *Under* thirty-five and forty-eight, immigrated to France at the age of fifty-three, and died in Paris with depression and desolation at the age of seventy-five.

Although he has received praise or sporadic criticism from many famous artists in his life, it is found that he not only confirmed his thinking on the true meaning of life with his extraordinary creations throughout his life, but also fit his own expression "I came to this world to see the sun". The spiritual essence through exploring his poems, the best way to understand his poems is full of complex and mysterious spiritual activities. This article tries to express my views on two of the poems.

2. Poetry Appreciation

Rain is a poem published by Balmont when he was thirty-four years old (1901). The metaphors used by the poet may be imagined from the experiences in life. The opening of this poem is quite striking:

The rats in the corner squeak and chirp,

The hut is still in sleep.

It's raining — drops from the eaves

Drips along the edge of the wall.

It rains, dull and weak,

The pendulum knocked.

I can't tell the bell

And the impact of the tired mind.

融入睡意朦朧的
沉重寂靜，
我失憶失覺
落入夜的昏黑。

黑，如掘墓人，
在我體內翻攪，
壁中蛀蟲
反覆：「吱咯，吱咯」。

彷若句點，
如一切發端的起源，
以小小榔錘
敲擊、敲擊、敲擊。

曲調的原素
在寂靜中交織，
平靜無慍不斷對我
重複：「去死啊！」

而我嚥住氣，
如捻熄之燭的殘肢，

into the sleepy
heavy silence,
I am amnesiac
into the darkness of night.

Black, like a gravedigger,
churning inside me,
wall borers
Repeat: "squeak, squeak".

Like a period,
Like the origin of all beginnings,
with a small hammer
Tap, tap, tap.

elements of tune
Weaving in silence,
calm and non-stop to me
Repeat: "Go to hell!"

And I hold my breath,
Like the stump of a extinguished candle,

奇異的悲傷中
聆聽預言之音。

輕輕，輕輕
有人向我低語。
水珠從漆黑的屋簷
沿著壁緣流滴。

　　此詩巧妙地將詩的起承轉合安排了輔音同音，也有運用復沓，保持著一種渾然天成的優美，且營造出一詠三嘆的氛圍。據俄羅斯民間迷信，如果聽到蛀蟲嚼木的聲音，即預言死亡將至；我們雖然無法洞察詩人創作的靈思，但就其節奏的快感至少有一部分是像他自己在《詩即魔法》一書中寫道，「詩即有節奏的語言表達出來的內在音樂。」而由形象大於思想的眼光來看，此詩每字音的長短高低都恰到好處，而詩人以詩撫慰其精神寂寞或抒寫生活中的傷感，應已交代得十分生動了。

　　類似這樣優秀的詩作是舉不勝舉的。當一九一七年十一月俄國發生十月革命事起，巴爾蒙特對布爾雪維克黨（Bolsheviks）人於十月革命中奪權的作風不以為然，遂而移民法國，從此不歸。接著這首是他在六十二歲（1929）寫出的詩作《此地和彼處》，心境與早期詩歌創作時截然不同。他在詩裡寫道：

in strange sadness
Hear the voice of prophecy.

gently, gently
Someone whispered to me.

Drops of water fall from the black eaves
Drips along the edge of the wall.

This poem cleverly arranges the consonant homophony in the beginning, succession and transition of the poem, and also uses repetition, which maintains a natural beauty and creates an atmosphere of one chanting and three sighs. According to Russian folk superstition, if you hear the sound of maggots chewing wood, it is a prophecy that death is coming; although we cannot penetrate the poet's creative thinking, at least part of the pleasure of its rhythm is like his own in the book *Poetry Is Magic*. It is written in "poetry is the inner music expressed by rhythmic language". From the perspective of image greater than thought, the length of each word in this poem is just right, and the poet uses poetry to soothe his spiritual loneliness or express his life. His sadness should have been explained very vividly.

Such excellent poems are too numerous to list. When the October Revolution broke out in Russia in November 1917, Balmont was disapproving of the style of the Bolsheviks who seized power in the October Revolution, so he emigrated to France and never returned. Then this is the poem *Here and There* written by him at the age of sixty-two (1929), and his state of mind is completely different from that of his early poetry creation. In his poem he wrote:

此地是喧囂的巴黎，反覆的琴
奏鳴著似新卻眾人皆知的老調。

　　而彼處江河之緣是勿忘草，
　　密林中有久久渴望的珍寶。

此地是話語和榮光的漩渦與聲譽，
駕御靈魂的卻是一隻蝙蝠。

　　彼處芬芳花蕾間有沼澤草，
　　無邊的田野，深沉的寂靜。

此地是錙銖必較的理性，
才見深谷，他便低語：「填平它」。

　　彼處是曼陀羅之毒與蠱惑；
　　沼澤裡嗚咽不祥的大麻鳥。

此地對撒旦與上帝恭謹冷漠，
人們導引通向塵世星辰之路。

　　懇求你，至上者，為我開路，
　　好讓我至少死後到達渴望的彼處。

Here is noisy Paris, repeated violins
It plays an old tune that seems new but well-known.

And the edge of the river there is the forget-me-not,
In the dense forest lies a long-desired treasure.

Here is the vortex and reputation of words and glory,
It is a bat that controls the soul.

There is swamp grass among the fragrant buds,
Boundless fields, deep silence.

Here is the rationality of pennies and pennies,
When he saw the deep valley, he whispered, "fill it up."

There is the poison and bewitchment of the mandala;
A hemp bird whimpering ominously in the swamp.

Here reverence and indifference to Satan and God,
People guide the way to the earth and stars.

I implore you, Most High, make a way for me,
So that at least I can reach the desired place after death.

　　詩人像是遊走在真實與虛幻之間，隔著時空距離將現實
生活中的困頓看透，他在一個佛教式的冥想中，以彼處是一
株勿忘草的小比喻道出了他離鄉背井到巴黎卻對俄羅斯懷念
的深情，又表彰了他身為詩人承擔世界所賦予的重擔，卻仍
在與世無爭的孤獨中堅持安享平靜的生活，直到生命的終點。
這種感傷與渴望到達彼岸的願望是真摯的和感性的。因此，
《此地和彼處》所表現的絕不是一般人所想像的「詩人寂寥
的悲嘆」，也不是像北宋文學家范仲淹《蘇幕遮》裡寫的：
「山映斜陽天接水。芳草無情，更在斜陽外。」那種借酒澆
愁、懷念家園的深情；而是自喻為「太陽的歌手」的巴爾蒙
特奇特、敏銳而新穎的靈感，又再次書寫出一首以奇致勝的
好詩。其絕妙的比喻之中，雖有凝聚著憂傷，卻沒有婉轉的
絕望，反而恰似空山的野百合，孤傲挺立且隱隱地發出聖潔
的光芒。

三、結　語

　　無論是巴爾蒙特以時空距離審美生命的本質或於生活的
寂寞中，他始終讓心之所向保持純粹。就詩歌的本質而言，
這是極為珍貴，而非昂貴的。因為，再沒有比能真正欣賞一
首好詩，更幸福的事了。而我在探索的過程中最美好的，莫
過於閱讀到巴爾蒙特詩歌中帶有深情的回憶以及打動人心的

The poet seems to be wandering between the real and the unreal, seeing through the difficulties in real life through the distance of time and space. In a Buddhist meditation, he used the small metaphor of a forget-me-not plant to express the fact that he left his hometown and went to Paris. The deep affection for Russia's nostalgia also commends him as a poet who bears the burden given by the world, but still insists on enjoying a peaceful life in the loneliness of indifference to the world until the end of his life. This sentimentality and desire to reach the other side is sincere and emotional. Therefore, what is expressed in *Here and There* is by no means the "poet's lonely lament" as imagined by ordinary people, nor is it written in *Su Muzhe* by Fan Zhongyan, a writer of the Northern Song Dynasty: "The mountain reflects the setting sun and the sky catches the water. The fragrant grass ruthless, even outside the setting sun." The affectionate feeling of drinking away sorrow and missing home; but the unique, sharp and novel inspiration of Balmont, who calls himself "the singer of the sun", once again wrote a song that wins by surprise good poem. In the wonderful metaphor, although there is sadness, there is no tactful despair. Instead, it is like the wild lily in the empty mountain, standing proudly and faintly emitting holy light.

3. Conclusion

Whether Balmont appreciates the essence of life with the distance of time and space or in the loneliness of life, he always keeps his heart pure. In the nature of poetry, this is extremely precious, not expensive. Because there is nothing happier than being able to truly appreciate a good poem. And the most beautiful thing in the process of my exploration is to read Balmont's poems with affectionate memories and a free spirit that touches people's hearts. It

一種自由的精神，深深地根植於詩歌之中，樂趣與敬慕之情由此生成。

德國詩人里爾克（1875-1926）曾寫下這樣的一段文字：「天才總為他的時代帶來驚駭。」（註 2）我深信，巴爾蒙特的詩歌流傳到二十一世紀的今日 終於在後世得到了復活，如星輝耀。他的精神也必然永遠追隨太陽的光華而亙古永存！這樣一種分析，有助於以其他研究的方式去探析巴爾蒙特詩歌的深層結構，期能接近詩歌的本來面貌。

本文詩作兩首源於普希金等著，歐茵西譯注，《浪漫與沉思 俄國詩歌欣賞》，臺北，聯經出版，2001 年 9 月初版，頁 177-181。

里爾克 Rainer Maria Rilke 著，唐際明譯，《慢讀里爾克》 臺北，商周出版，2015 年 9 月初版，頁 202。

—臺灣《笠》詩刊，第 345 期，2021.10，頁 145-148。

is deeply rooted in the poems, and the joy and admiration are generated from it.

The German poet Rilke (1875-1926) once wrote such a passage: "Genius always brings horror to his era." (Note 2) I firmly believe that Balmont's poems have been handed down to the 21st century today, Finally, he was resurrected in later generations, shining like a star. His spirit must follow the brilliance of the sun forever and last forever! Such an analysis will help to explore the deep structure of Balmont's poems in other research ways, hoping to get close to the original appearance of　the poem.

The two poems in this article are from Romance andMeditation: Appreciation of Russian Poetry, by Pushkin et al.,translated and annotated by Eugene, Taipei, Lianjing Publishing,first edition in September 2001, pages 177-181.

Slow Reading of Rilke, by Rainer Maria Rilke, translated by Tang Jiming, Taipei, Shang Zhou Publishing, first edition inSeptember, 2015, page 202.

14. 淺析約瑟夫·布羅茨基的詩

一、傳　略

　　出生於俄羅斯列寧格勒（聖彼德堡）的約瑟夫·布羅茨基（Joseph Brodsky，1940—1996）是美籍猶太裔詩人；年輕時，命運多舛，被判流放，俄羅斯當局把他驅逐出境，視為異端。後定居美國，曾任教於耶魯大學、劍橋大學等名校，1987 年榮獲諾貝爾文學獎，是第五位獲得此項殊榮、生於俄羅斯的作家。他也是散文家、美國桂冠詩人，其英文散文集《小於一》獲得美國國家書評人協會獎的批評獎，並被授予牛津大學榮譽文學博士；終其一生，均用俄語和英語寫作及翻譯，出版過詩集《長短詩集》、《在曠野紮營》、《演講的一部分》、《 致烏喇尼亞》等多種。

　　當二十歲的布羅茨基遇見了俄羅斯女詩人安娜·阿赫瑪托娃（1889-1966），立即深受影響，除了繼承俄羅斯古典主義詩歌傳統，並成為他的導師；後來又深受現代主義詩歌的薰陶，最終形成了其「沉鬱與抒情」的藝術風格，詩作充滿真摯的思想情感、音韻優美，因而留下許多重要的傳世之作。

14. A Brief Analysis of Joseph Brodsky's Poems

1. Brief Introduction

Joseph Brodsky (1940-1996), born in Leningrad (St. Petersburg), Russia, was a Jewish-American poet. When he was young, he was ill-fated and sentenced to exile, and the Russian authorities expelled him; exiting the country is regarded as heresy. After settling in the United States, he taught at prestigious universities such as Yale University and Cambridge University. He was awarded the Nobel Prize in Literature in 1987, becoming the 5th Russian-born writer to win this award. He is also an essayist and poet laureate of the United States. His collection of English essays *Less Than One* won the National Book Critics Association Award for Criticism and was awarded an Honorary Doctor of Letters by Oxford University. He wrote and translated in Russian and English throughout his life. He has published a collection of poems such as *Long and Short Poems*, *Camping in the Wilderness*, *Part of a Speech*, and *To Urania*.

When the 20-year-old Brodsky met the Russian poetess Anna Akhmatova (1889-1966), he was deeply affected immediately. In addition to inheriting the tradition of Russian classical poetry, he became his mentor; later, he was deeply influenced by modernist poetry. Influenced by him, he finally formed his artistic "depressed and lyrical" style. His poems are full of sincere thoughts and emotions, and have beautiful phonology, thus leaving behind many important works handed down from generation to generation.

值得一提的是，他也喜歡中國文學和古典詩歌，學過漢語，翻譯過唐詩。在他五十五歲時，病死於紐約的一棟社區公寓；1991 年蘇聯解體，轉年，俄羅斯宣佈為他恢復國藉。作為詩人，布羅茨基善感多愁，對感情執著，詩歌音樂性強烈，尤以對生命的脆弱和堅強、愛情的浪漫與沉思，感受深刻。他以深情和哲人般的思辨力與回憶為歷史留下的詩篇，其細膩的感情躍然紙上，亦豐足地保存其純真質樸的心性，最受讀者稱道。

二、詩作賞析

在翻譯家谷羽教授的最新書稿《俄語詩行裡的中國形象》裡，我特別對布羅茨基的詩作持有音樂性的語境感到驚喜，並關注他以身歷其境與想像等方式直探詩歌的藝術手法。如1989 年寫下的《給瑪巴》這首詩，詩人除了抒發情感真實，形象鮮明外，仍有意識地堅持詩人高尚的社會人格理想：

> 親愛的，今天很晚我才走出家門，
> 想呼吸從海洋吹來的新鮮空氣。
> 從公園裡看晚霞形狀似中國摺扇，
> 雲團滾動彷彿一架鋼琴的蓋子。
>
> 二十五年前你喜歡讚美和紅棗，
> 在畫冊上畫水墨畫，偶爾歌唱，
> 陪我玩兒；後來欣賞化學工程師，
> 從信件判斷，頭腦遲鈍不太正常。

It is worth mentioning that he also likes Chinese literature and classical poetry, has studied Chinese and translated Tang poetry. At the age of fifty-five, he died of illness in a community apartment in New York; in 1991, the Soviet Union disintegrated, and the following year, Russia announced the restoration of his citizenship. As a poet, Brodsky is sentimental and persistent, and his poems are musical, especially the fragility and strength of life, and the romance and contemplation of love. He left poems for history with his affectionate and philosopher-like speculative ability and memory. His delicate emotions are vivid on paper, and he also fully preserves his pure and simple heart, which is most praised by readers.

2. Poetry Appreciation

In the latest book *The Image of China in Russian Poetry* by the translator-professor Gu Yu, I was particularly surprised by the musical context of Brodsky's poems, and paid attention to his way of experience and imagination. Exploring the artistic technique of poetry directly. For example, in the poem *To Maba* written in 1989, in addition to expressing true emotions and vivid images, the poet still consciously adheres to the poet's noble ideal of social personality:

Darling, I didn't come out of the house until late today,
Want to breathe the fresh air blowing from the ocean.
Seen from the park, the sunset looks like a Chinese folding fan.
The cloud rolls like the lid of a piano.

Twenty-five years ago you liked praise and red dates,
Draw ink paintings on albums, sing occasionally,
play with me; later appreciate the chemical engineer,
Judging from the letters, dullness of mind was not quite normal.

如今在外省或都市的教堂，在追悼會
連續不斷悼念朋友的場合都能見到你，
我很慶倖，我跟你之間存在著
相隔萬里不可思議的遙遠距離。

別誤解我的意思。跟你的聲音、身體
名字，再沒有任何關係，毫無損害，
但不得不忘卻那段痛徹心扉的經歷，
換一種活法。我體驗過這樣的失敗。

你很幸運：除了照片，哪裡能讓你
沒有皺紋，永葆青春、開朗、微笑？
時間與記憶碰撞，深知個人無能為力。
我在昏暗中抽煙，伴隨海洋落潮呼吸。

詩人筆下所說的瑪巴，是他的初戀女友瑪麗安娜·
巴斯曼諾娃的簡稱，兩人曾同居，並育有一子；因瑪
巴的背叛，愛上一位化學工程師而與之分手，這段經
歷也帶給布羅茨基難以言喻的傷痛。因而，此詩創作
更明確地體現了詩人在回憶與愛情的背叛關係中超越
痛苦的努力，也構成了詩歌的抒情性主題和開啟詩人
內心最深處世界與匯積呈現詩美的萬千風貌。

Now in provincial or metropolitan churches, at memorial services
Seeing you on successive occasions of mourning friends,
I am very glad that there exists between me and you
An incredible distance of thousands of miles.

Don't get me wrong. with your voice, your body
name, nothing more, no harm,
But I had to forget that heart-wrenching experience,
Change your way of life. I have experienced such failures.

You're in luck; where else but photos will get you
Wrinkle-free, youthful, cheerful and smiling forever?
Time collides with memory, knowing that there is nothing
　the individual can do.
I smoke in the dark and breathe with the ebb of the ocean.

The Maba mentioned by the poet is the abbreviation of his first girlfriend Marianna Basmanova. The two lived together and had a son. Because of Maba's betrayal, she fell in love with a chemical engineer and broke up with him. This experience also brought Brodsky unspeakable pain. Therefore, the creation of this poem more clearly embodies the poet's efforts to transcend pain in the betrayal relationship between memory and love, and also constitutes the lyrical theme of the poem and opens up the poet's innermost world and accumulates the myriad styles of poetic beauty.

又如《蝴蝶》組詩，是詩人在三十二歲左右開始轉向玄學思想有密切關係的主要內涵，也是詩人詩學思想的重要時期；摘錄其中四首詩句，如下所述：

I

能否説：你已死亡？
只活了一個晝夜。
造物主嗜好戲謔，
隱含著無限的悲傷！
未必能説"你活過"；
從你降生於塵世
到落進我手心裡
只有短暫一天存活，
你讓我陷入了困惑，
伸出手指數一數，
性命竟那麼短促
未超出一天的邊界。

VII

這些花紋，你説，
如此色彩斑斕，
可惜你在湖畔，
只能有一天存活，

水銀般的明鏡
豈能把空間保存？

Another example is the "Butterfly" series of poems, which is the main connotation closely related to the poet's turning to metaphysics at the age of thirty-two.

I

Can you say: You are dead?
Lived only one day and night.
The Creator is fond of banter,
Contains infinite sadness!
It may not be possible to say "you have lived";
From your birth
To fall into my hand
Only survived for a short day,
You got me confused,
Stretch out your fingers and count,
Life is so short
Day boundaries are not exceeded.

VII

These patterns, you say,
So colorful,
It's a pity you're by the lake,
Only one day to live,

Mirror of mercury
How can space be preserved?

XII

蝴蝶竟如此美麗，
生存這般短暫，
説來有些荒誕，
幻化成一個啞謎：
造物主創造世界，
其實沒有目的，
假如真有目的，
並非為我們而設。
人類不是蝴蝶，
有人把蝴蝶收藏
沒有針刺透陽光，
也難把黑暗探測。

XIV

你畢竟勝過虛無。
確切説，離得近，
形象更清晰更真。
你跟虛無是親屬。
你畢竟接近虛幻。
你曾飛舞遷徙
並獲得了形體；
構成了一段因緣——
你在喧囂的白天，

XII

Butterflies are so beautiful,
Life is so short,
It's absurd to say,
Turned into a charade:
The Creator created the world,
In fact, there is no purpose,
If there is a purpose,
Not for us.
Humans are not butterflies,
Someone collects butterflies
No needles pierce the sun,
It is also difficult to detect the darkness.

XIV

You are better than nothing after all.
To be exact, close
The image is clearer and more real.
You are kin to nothingness.
You are close to unreal after all.
You flew and migrated
And gained form;
Formed a karmic relationship —
You in the hustle and bustle of the day,

　　像輕柔的簾幕
　　引起視線關注
　　處在我和虛無之間。

　　眾所周知，莊子出生於苦難而能超越苦難，故而其思想更適合於當年身處逆境的布羅茨基，也成為他面對苦難的最佳心靈導師。從觀察蝶的生與死，進而延伸出一連串詩意的想像，不難看出，布羅茨基似乎深受莊子思想中的蝶意象以及對「忘我」與「物化」美學的影響。詩裡存在著對莊子主張「以虛無為本」的各種想像力的詩意描述，似乎開啟了布羅茨基對自我存在與虛無之間的思索，也彰顯了最深層的莊子思想與之內在有了聯結的呼應，並期待自己能打開心靈的桎梏，開闢出一種新生的生活方式。

　　能忘我、物化，則能自然、能齊物、能消遙，也就能消解現實苦難於無形，而得人生之消遙自適。（注）詩人在蝴蝶觀賞與莊子美學的關係中發明的奇趣與中國玄理的領悟中獲得了一種人生境界，這是超脫痛苦之後獲得的和諧，也是接近莊子的物化的美學思維。

　　詩人雖未對自己生命中的苦難有具體的描述，但在夢與醒之間，詩人深知，蝴蝶在翩翩飛舞之前，亦必須經歷結繭自縛的階段，始得蛹化為蝶；其蛻變後美麗的

Like a soft curtain
Draw attention
Between me and nothingness.

As we all know, Zhuangzi was born in suffering and was able to transcend suffering, so his thoughts are more suitable for Brodsky who was in adversity at that time, and he became the best spiritual teacher for him to face suffering. From observing the life and death of butterflies, and extending a series of poetic imaginations, it is not difficult to see that Brodsky seems to be deeply influenced by the butterfly imagery in Zhuangzi's thought and the aesthetics of "selflessness" and "materialization". There are poetic descriptions of Zhuangzi's various imaginative powers in the poem, which seems to have opened up Brodsky's thinking about the relationship between self-existence and nothingness, and also revealed the deepest Zhuangzi's thought and inner existence. The echo of the connection, and expecting to open the shackles of the soul and open up a new way of life.

If you can forget yourself and materialize, you will be able to be natural, equal to things, and disappear, and you will be able to eliminate the suffering of reality invisibly, and get the ease of life. (Note) The poet has obtained a realm of life through the novelty invented in the relationship between butterfly viewing and Zhuangzi's aesthetics and the comprehension of Chinese metaphysics. This is the harmony obtained after transcending pain, and it is also close to Zhuangzi's materialized aesthetic thinking.

Although the poet did not describe the sufferings in his own life in detail, between dreaming and waking, the poet knows that before the butterfly dances lightly, it must also go through the stage of cocooning and self-binding before it turns into a butterfly. The beautiful figure and the short life of the butterfly, such awakening and open-mindedness towards life and death, seem to trigger the poet's association with Zhuangzi's transformation from

姿影與蝴蝶生達，似乎觸發詩人跟莊周由人變蝶的聯想，有某種程度的相似。或者，這也與布羅茨基年輕時對監獄牢籠的苦悶與坎坷不斷的命運，有所觸連；

三、結　語

從美學思想來看，布羅茨基的詩的產生除了深受俄羅斯古典優美詩歌傳統及博覽西方現代主義詩歌相關以外，可以確定的是，他的《蝴蝶》組詩等作品，恰恰也與中國詩美學及莊子思想有密切關係。因此，在探討布羅茨基詩歌變革前，對於他長期學習漢語，翻譯過李白、王維、孟浩然的詩，以及曾嘗試翻譯《道德經》的這一部分，目前學界還缺少清楚的認識及深入性的研究。筆者以為，其詩歌、翻譯並存的表現範疇及其辭采豐富的藝術風格，皆與中國道家崇尚「無為而治，與自然和諧相處」有內在關係，以及他最終想體現莊子「物化」的心理機制，而審美移情，就是他在詩歌裡最重要的表現特徵。

布羅茨基以詩歌及散文、文學翻譯等創作實踐，深刻影響於世界文學的結果，尤其是在同輩諾貝爾文學獎得獎人的對比中，他的生命雖然短促，但其詩歌不以「歷劫受難」的苦吟描繪為其情感基調，反而展現出如蛹之生的強韌生命力和以詩美為主的情感基調，讓人感受更加強烈；終其一生，

a human to a butterfly, which is somewhat similar. Or, this is also related to Brodsky's anguish and ups and downs in the prison cage when he was young; therefore, the poetic butterfly image itself is full of philosophical hints, as well as the butterfly image in Zhuangzi's *Qiwulun*. The many meanings of extension, and the joy of longing for spiritual freedom and new life.

3. Conclusion

From the perspective of aesthetics, Brodsky's poems are not only deeply related to the tradition of Russian classical and beautiful poetry, but also related to Western modernist poetry. Aesthetics and Zhuangzi thought are closely related. Therefore, before discussing the changes in Brodsky's poetry, there is still a lack of clear understanding and in-depth understanding of Brodsky's long-term study of Chinese, his translation of poems by Li Bai, Wang Wei, and Meng Haoran, and his attempt to translate the part of *Tao Te Ching*. The author believes that his poems and translations coexist in the expressive category and his artistic style with rich diction, which are all internally related to the Chinese Taoist advocacy of "governing by doing nothing, living in harmony with nature", and his ultimate desire to embody Zhuangzi's "materialization" psychology, mechanism, and aesthetic empathy, is the most important expressive feature in his poetry.

Brodsky's creative practice of poetry, prose, and literary translation has profoundly influenced the results of world literature, especially in the comparison with his peers who won the Nobel Prize in Literature. Although his life was short, his poetry did not use the bitter chanting of suffering, and suffering is described as its emotional tone, but it shows the tenacious vitality of the pupae and the emotional tone based on poetic beauty, which makes people feel more intense; throughout his life, he also

也完成其自我價值的實現，因而成就斐然，獲得諾貝爾文學獎等莫大榮耀。

註：摘自丁旭輝著，《台灣現代詩中的老莊身影與道家美學實踐》，高雄，春暉出版，2010 年初版，頁 306。

—2021.11.10 寫於臺東

—臺灣《大海洋》詩雜誌，第 104 期，2022.01，頁 10

completes the realization of his self-worth. As a result, he has made great achievements and won great honors such as the Nobel Prize in Literature.

> **Note.** Excerpted from Ding Xuhui, *Lao Zhuang and Zhuangzi in Taiwan's Modern Poetry and Taoist Aesthetic Practice*, Kaohsiung, Chunhui Publishing, 2010, 1st edition, page 306.

15. 讀 Prof. Ernesto Kahan 的 一首詩〈Mnemosyne And My Trip〉

Prof. Ernesto Kahan（1940 -）恩涅斯托•可罕，是當代以色列傑出的詩人、1985 年諾貝爾和平獎得主。求學時代的 Ernesto，喜歡研究人類學，古生物學，哲學，音樂，詩歌。自醫學系畢業後，又在 1964 年相繼完成了布宜諾賽勒斯大學公共衛生碩士及 1968 年醫學博士學位。此後的三十多年，擔任過阿根廷及以色列醫師，也教授於阿根廷、以色列、西雅圖、多明尼加共和國等大學，還擔任國際防止核戰爭醫生組織的副總裁，和平醫師和保護環境的主席，地中海社會公眾衛生副總裁，以色列研究顧問，獲史懷哲和平成就獎等殊榮。2016 年六月間，接受了巴塞羅那 Barcelona 標題和皇家歐洲科學院醫生的院士（the title and responsibility of being Academician of the Royal European Academy of Doctors）的新職務。

Ernesto 的詩歌在他一生中也占有較重要的地位，尤以晚年也多次參與世界詩人大會及重要演講中擔任評審及主席。他的詩歌大多是深植於個人生活、內心與經歷，以自己的人文主義世界觀和創作方法，構築著世界和平的理想願景。他

15. Read a Poem Mnemosyne And My Trip by Prof. Ernesto Kahan

Prof. Ernesto Kahan (1940-) is an outstanding contemporary Israeli poet, Nobel Peace Prize winner in 1985. At school age, Ernesto likes the study of anthropology, paleontology, philosophy, music, and poetry, after graduating from the Department of Medicine, and in 1964, he has completed a Master of Public Health from the University of Buenos Aires in 1968 and a doctorate in medicine. In the following thirty years, he served in Argentina and Israel, MD, also a professor at the University of Argentina, Israel, Seattle, Dominican Republic, also served as Vice President, President of the International Physicians for the nuclear war, peace and the protection of the environment to prevent physicians, vice president of public health of the Mediterranean, Israeli research consultant, Albert Schweitzer peace Award and other awards. In June 2016, he accepted the doctor's Academy (the title and responsibility of being Academician of the Royal European Academy of Doctors) new job title in Barcelona and the Royal Academy of Europe.

Ernesto's poetry in his life also plays the more important role, especially in old age, he has also participated in the World Congress of Poets, and made important speech to act as judges and chairman. His poetry is mostly rooted in personal life, heart and experience, with their humanistic worldview and creative methods to build a vision of the ideal of world peace. He was opposed

反對種族衝突，反對戰爭——即便一些帶有玄思色彩的詩歌裡，仍能感覺到語言的真誠質感，以張揚自己的人道主義精神。不妨以〈Mnemosyne and my trip〉一詩為例，最能反映 Ernesto 人文主義理想。在這裡，他塑造了一個記憶女神形象揭露出戰爭所造成的種種社會災難，表現更廣闊、更深刻、更複雜的社會內容。他對戰爭的本質認識是深刻的，他的揭示是有力的，也成為國際詩林中不朽之作：

記憶女神與我的旅程

你激起我的亢奮，記憶女神！
繆司的母親，
極為神秘地
在冥想境界的學習中
你觸到了，是的！文本裡的血漿
你將我的死帶向生
把我放棄的開始重新開始
你碰觸這樣我才能碰觸！
才能聽到沉默之聲
才能看見不能見的
才能識破魔法的騙術
以昭示罪惡之源
你如織夢者的夢想
無意識地夢著
遭風吹散的文字激情

to ethnic conflicts, even if some of the opposition to the war—think poetry with mysterious colors, the language can still feel the texture of good faith, in order to publicize their humanitarian spirit. A poem, for example, *Mnemosyne And My Trip*, the best indicator of Ernesto humanist ideals. Here he created a memory image of the Goddess revealed various social disaster caused by the war, the performance of a broader, deeper, more complex social content. His understanding of the nature of war is profound, and his revelation is a powerful, which has become an international forest immortal poem:

Mnemosyne And My Trip

You touched my orgasm Mnemosyne!
Mother of muses,
In contemplative secret
You touched, yes! The plasma in texts
You took my death towards life
Doing my resigns of the beginning to begin
You touched so that I can touch!
And listen the silence
And see the invisible
And penetrate with the magic that deceives
Into the apocalypse of social crime.
You are dreams of a dreamer
Unconsciously dreamed
Orgasm of words erased by the wind

在無夢的早晨
沒有高潮
沒有光亮
沒有開始
生命接著誕生
然後呢?命運重複?
碼頭的保衛戰,
大屠殺事件-猶太人的浩劫,
種族主義
另一個明天
同樣的戰爭
同樣的暴力
同樣的死亡列車
同樣的自己,

Ernesto Kahan,往下一站的旅途中
(非馬博士中譯)

　　Ernesto 也可以說是名激情型詩人。整首詩要傳達的是一種孤獨的情緒,這種孤獨不完全是通過內省而獲得,反而是外在世界成了 Ernesto 內心的圖景,成了衡量孤獨的基石。那一連串的問號?短促莊嚴有力,不僅勾描出了戰爭與暴力的沉痛、生命誕生與死亡的無常,更成倍地加強了詩人孤寂與無奈的情緒。雖然他堅持著人文主義理想,但在現實中卻

Of the morning without dreams

Without orgasms

Without light

Without beginning

After the childbirths,

AFTER? AGAIN?

The protection of the wharves,

The holocaust - SHOAH,

Racism

Another tomorrow

Same war

Same violation

Same train of death

Same myself,

Ernesto Kahan, in trip to the next station
(translated by Dr. William Marr)

Ernesto can also be said to be a passionate Poet. The whole poem to convey a feeling of loneliness, which is not entirely obtained through introspection, but the outside world has become Ernesto heart picture became cornerstone measure alone. The series of questions? Short solemn and powerful, not only hook delineate a painful war and violence, the birth of life and the impermanence of death, but exponentially strengthened poet lonely and helpless feeling. Although he insisted humanist ideal, but

不易尋覓出路，他不得不借由詩歌的聯想力來反映了某些社會現實，也起了社會省思作用。

　　在最純粹的形式中，他依循著一個單純的理念或性質而塑造了記憶女神，衪是具有豐富思想和性格特徵的「繆斯的母親」。這正是基於 Ernesto 本身也具有豐富的性格和深厚的思想內蘊而說的。一方面，他有磊落的胸懷，另一方面，他又善於思考、敏感與賦予機智、敏捷的特點。他的性格也是因猶太人被屠殺的浩劫跟國際間種族問題難解等等環境使然，因而在一定程度上具有仁愛和同情戰爭下苦難人民疾苦的思維。

　　我選擇閱讀此詩的目的之一，就是為了學習 Ernesto 詩裡不可言傳的神韻。但是 Ernesto 與其他許多哲人不同，能瞭解或記載其思想的文字極少，而他的思想主要反映在他的詩歌及感性的朗誦或演說中。我認為，此詩每一個音節都打動著我，也賦予了當代詩歌一種「重」的品質。而 Ernesto，我尊敬的詩友，在國際上為醫學研究、和平與維護地球環境所做的努力顯然一直未曾停止過。

　　他，是和平的使者，以色列之光耀！

　　— 2016.06.02 作

in reality it is not easy to find a way out, he had to borrow from the imaginative poetry to reflect some of the social. reality, but also played a role in social reflection

In its purest form, he followed with a mere concept or shape memory nature goddess, who is having a wealth of ideas and character of the "mother of the Muses". This is based on Ernesto himself, who also has a wealth of character and deep ideological connotation. On the one hand, he has a candid mind; on the other hand, he was thoughtful, sensitive and gives witty, agile characteristics. His personality is a result of the massacre of the Jews with the Holocaust and so intractable problems of international inter-ethnic environment dictates, thereby having the love and compassion, the sufferings of war, and of the people to some extent.

I choose to read one poem with the purpose to learn the unspeakable charm of Ernesto's poems. But Ernesto is different from many other philosophers, according to their ideology, or understand very little text, and his thought is mainly reflected in his poetry and recitation or emotional speech. I think, each and every poem touched me, but also gives the contemporary poetry in a kind of "heavy" quality. And Ernesto, my esteemed poet-friend, apparently had not been stopped in international medical research, efforts to maintain peace and global environment.

He is a messenger of peace, Israel's glory!

— Written on June 2, 2016

－美國.《Atlanta Chinese News》亞特蘭大新聞，2016. 07. 01，亞城園地，刊詩評〈My friend Prof. Ernesto Kahan〉及與作者攝影合照、贈書。

PS. 2013. 10. 23 於馬來西亞舉辦世詩會，Ernesto 親自簽名，並贈此詩集給 Dr. Lin Ming-Li。

15. 讀 Prof.Ernesto Kahan 的一首詩《Mnemosyne And My Trip》 303

16. 論費特詩歌的藝術美

摘要：費特（1820—1892），是 19 世紀俄羅斯純藝術詩派的領袖。他的詩主要歌詠愛情、大自然、藝術，音調輕柔，清新雋永。本文將著重對其抒情詩進行探討，進而回頭思考費特詩評不只在於正確地詮釋作品及判斷其美學品質，它的功能更多的是襯顯藝術對感性的醞釀及價值，以期能為讀者打開最廣闊的視野。

關鍵字：費特 純藝術 詩人 浪漫主義

1820 年，費特·阿法納西·阿法納西耶維奇（1820—1892）出生於俄羅斯奧廖爾省姆岑斯克縣諾沃肖爾卡村，是 19 世紀俄羅斯純藝術詩派的領袖。其父親原是貴族地主，不料，由於奧廖爾宗教事務所出面干預，費特突然由一個貴族的後代淪為平民，因而，如何討回貴族身份，遂成了費特生活中最強烈的冀望。

費特上中學期間就開始寫詩，他在愛沙尼亞的一所德語寄宿學校學習。1838—1844 年就讀於莫斯科大學語文系期間，費特幾乎每天都沉迷於寫詩；還把德國著名詩人歌德

16. Title: On the Artistic Beauty of Fet's Poetry

Abstract: Afanasy Afanasyevich Fet (1820-1892) was a Russian poet regarded as one of the finest lyricists in Russian literature. He mainly praised love, nature and art in his poetry. His tone was soft and gentle, fresh and thought-provoking. This article probes into his lyrical poetry, not only tries to interpret correctly his poetry and to judge its aesthetic quality, but also to uncover the value of art and to cultivate the sense of perception, thus broaden the artistic vision for the readers.

Key words: Afanasy Fet　pure art　poet　romanticism

Fet Afanasy Afanasyevich (1820-1892) was born in Novosholka Village, Mtsensk County, Orel Province, Russia in 1820. He was the leader of the Russian School of Pure Art in the 19th century. His father was originally a noble landowner. Unexpectedly, due to the intervention of the Orel Religious Office, Fet suddenly became a commoner from a descendant of a nobleman. Therefore, how to recover his noble status became the strongest hope in Fet's life.

Fet began writing poetry while in secondary school, where he studied at a German-language boarding school in Estonia. While studying at the Department of Philology of Moscow University from 1838 to 1844, Fet was obsessed with writing poetry almost every day; he also

（Goethe，1749—1832）及海涅（Heinrich Heine，1797—1856）
的抒情詩翻譯成俄語，得到了好友波隆斯基等詩人的讚美。
1840 年，20 歲的費特以阿·費為筆名出版了第一本詩集《抒
情詩的萬神殿》，其中，《黎明前你不要叫醒他⋯⋯》、《含
愁的白樺》、《求你不要離開我⋯⋯》等詩，雖有著俄羅斯
古典浪漫主義風格，在詩壇也嶄露頭角，可惜並未獲得許多
迴響。但是，到了 1842 年，費特在《祖國紀事》、《莫斯科
人》等開始發表詩作後，便引起了詩壇的認真關注。文學批
評家別林斯基（1811—1848）在《1843 年俄羅斯文學》中讚
賞地指出，「莫斯科健在的詩人當中最有才華的當數費特先
生」，就連大文豪列夫·托爾斯泰也在給一位朋友的信中由
衷地讚賞費特。然而，這些成就並未減輕費特內心深處的痛
苦，其中，失去了貴族身份依然是令他苦悶的主因。

　　於是，費特選擇離開莫斯科，下決心投筆從戎，於 1845
開始參軍服役，其目的就是想在軍中得到升遷，贏得貴族稱
號。起初，他以下士身份被分發到偏遠地區的一個騎兵團；
後來，又輾轉在部隊駐防的赫爾松省的小鎮度過了將近十年
的軍旅生涯。就在費特即將得到中尉軍銜前，軍隊突然頒佈
了新令，規定只有少校軍銜才得以獲得貴族身份，這讓費特
感到十分沮喪，因為繼續升遷已沒有指望。此時，不僅沒能
贏得貴族名銜，反而遭遇了另一次重大挫折。那就是，他喜
歡上了一位清秀少女瑪麗婭·拉季綺。她是小地主的女兒，喜
歡文學詩歌，費特最愛聽她彈奏鋼琴；但她竟意外葬身火海，
讓這場戀情釀成了無可挽回的悲劇，也給費特留下了終身的

translated the lyric poems of the famous German poets Goethe (1749-1832) and Heinrich Heine (1797-1856) into Russian, praised by poets such as his friend Polonsky. In 1840, 20-year-old Fet published his first collection of poems *The Pantheon of Lyric Poems* under the pseudonym of A Fei, among which, *Don't Wake Him Up Before Dawn...*, *Sorrowful Birch, Pray, Don't Leave Me...*, and other poems, although they have the style of Russian classical romanticism, have also emerged in the poetry world, but unfortunately they have not received many echoes. However, by 1842, Fet had attracted serious poetic attention after he began to publish his poems in *Fatherland Chronicle, Muscovites* and others. Literary critic Belinsky (1811-1848) pointed out with appreciation in *Russian Literature in 1843* that "Mr. Fet is the most talented poet among Moscow's surviving poets." Even the great writer Leo Thor Stey also wrote a letter of heartfelt admiration to Fet to a friend. These accomplishments, however, did little to assuage Fet's inner anguish, of which the loss of his nobility remained a major cause of his anguish.

Therefore, Fet chose to leave Moscow and made up his mind to join the army. He began to serve in the army in 1845. His purpose was to get promoted in the army and win the title of nobility. At first, he was assigned to a cavalry regiment in a remote area as a corporal; later, he spent nearly ten years of military career in a small town in Kherson Province where the army was stationed. Just before Fet was about to get the rank of lieutenant, the army suddenly issued a new order, stipulating that only the rank of major can be granted noble status, which made Fet very frustrated, because there was no hope of further promotion. At this time, not only failed to win the title of nobility, but suffered another major setback. That is, he fell in love with a delicate girl, Maria Radiki. She is the daughter of a small landlord, and she likes literature and poetry. Fet loves to listen to her playing the piano the most; but she was accidentally buried in the sea of fire, which made this love affair an irreparable tragedy, and

懊悔與愧疚。於是，費特的心靈又再次被陰影籠罩，《另一個我》、《你身陷火海……》、《當你默默誦讀……》等詩篇，都是費特懷念戀人拉季綺的傷心之作。在他的第二本詩集（1850 年）中更出現許多優美詩篇，如《別睡了……》、《燕子消失了蹤影》等，它們以其獨特的魅力征服了多位俄羅斯名家的目光；《給唱歌的少女》一詩更採用了通感手法，把聽覺形象轉化為視覺形象，亦受到知名作曲家柴可夫斯基（1840—1893）的高度稱許。場戀情釀成了無可挽回的悲劇，也給費特留下了終身的懊悔與愧疚。於是，費特的心靈又再次被陰影籠罩，《另一個我》、《你身陷火海……》、《當你默默誦讀……》等詩篇，都是費特懷念戀人拉季綺的傷心之作。在他的第二本詩集（1850 年）中更出現許多優美詩篇，如《別睡了……》、《燕子消失了蹤影》等，它們以其獨特的魅力征服了多位俄羅斯名家的目光；《給唱歌的少女》一詩更採用了通感手法，把聽覺形象轉化為視覺形象，亦受到知名作曲家柴可夫斯基（1840—1893）的高度稱許。

　　費特 33 歲時，由於部隊換防，來到了彼得堡附近，又恢復跟俄羅斯名士接近，詩人屠格涅夫（1818—1883）和岡察洛夫（1812—1891）、作家列夫·托爾斯泰（1828—1910）、評論家鮑特金等人遂成了他的好友，而柴可夫斯基、格林卡（1804—1857）等名家也紛紛為他的抒情詩譜曲。這期間，費特詩集問世，批評界都給予一致的好評。借薩爾蒂科夫·謝德林（1826—1889）的一句話說：「整個俄羅斯都在傳唱費特的浪漫曲。」尤其 19 世紀 40 年代後期到 50 年代，是純藝

left Fet with lifelong remorse and love. As a result, Fet's mind was once again shrouded in shadows. Poems such as *Another Me, You Are Trapped in Fire...* and *When You Read Silently...* are all sad memories of Fet's lover Rajchi. In his second collection of poems (1850), many beautiful poems appeared, such as *Don't Sleep...* and *The Swallow Disappeared*, etc., which conquered the eyes of many famous Russian writers with their unique charm; The poem *The Girl Who Sings* even used synaesthesia to transform the auditory image into a visual image, which was also highly praised by the famous composer Tchaikovsky (1840-1893).

　　When Fet was 33 years old, due to the change of troops, he came to the vicinity of Petersburg and resumed being close to Russian celebrities, poets Turgenev (1818-1883) and Goncharov (1812-1891), writer Leo Tolstoy (1828-1910), the critic Botkin and others became his good friends, and famous artists such as Tchaikovsky and Glinka (1804-1857) also composed music for his lyric poems. During this period, Fet's collection of poems came out, and the critics gave unanimous praise. Borrowing a sentence from Saltykov Shchedrin (1826-1889): "Fet's romantic songs are being sung throughout Russia." Especially from the late 1840s to the 1850s, it was the

術派最風光的一個階段。費特曾說：「藝術創作的目的就是追求美！」因此，被冠以「唯美主義」的頭銜，又稱為「純藝術派」。費特申請退役後，先在莫斯科定居。37 歲時的費特，娶了批評家鮑特金的妹妹瑪利婭為妻，雖然她相貌平庸，還是再婚，可她的父親是經營茶葉生意的富商，給女兒的嫁妝也十分豐厚，從而大大改善了費特的經濟狀況。

從 19 世紀 60 年代開始，費特意識到文學創作難以維持一家的生計。於是，他在老家姆岑斯克縣的斯捷潘諾夫卡村購置了田莊、土地；他的創作激情衰退，專事農莊經營。此時，俄羅斯實施廢除農奴制，社會進入了一個動盪變革的時期；而費特的純藝術詩歌逐漸被邊緣化，並遭受非議與冷落，著名批評家皮薩列夫在《無害幽默之花》雜誌上甚至對 1863 年出版的費特詩歌極盡嘲諷挖苦，說只配做糊牆壁下邊的襯紙使用。創作連續遭遇打擊後的費特，把心思都集中在種燕麥、修磨房及創建一個大型養馬場上，並擔任鄉間民事調解法官將近 10 年，幾乎與詩界的友人斷絕了來往，只跟列夫·托爾斯泰保持聯繫。托爾斯泰也把費特看成摯友，有一年還親手做了一雙高筒皮靴子送給他，這讓費特感動不已。這樣經營農莊的日子大約持續了 20 年之久，閒暇之際，費特多用來閱讀哲學書籍解悶，尤其喜讀叔本華的著作。

到了 1873 年，53 歲的費特平生期待的一件事終於得以實現：經過沙皇恩准，費特獲得了貴族身份，成了有 300 年歷史的申欣家族的後代。他在得知這一喜訊的當天就給妻子寫了信，要求她立刻更換莊園裏的所有徽章標誌，並在信中

most beautiful stage of pure art. Fet once said: "The purpose of artistic creation is to pursue beauty!" Therefore, he was dubbed the title of "Astheticism", also known as "Pure Art School". After Fet applied for retirement, he first settled in Moscow. At the age of 37, Fet married Maria, the sister of the critic Botkin. Although she was mediocre, she remarried, but her father was a wealthy businessman in the tea business and gave his daughter a very generous dowry. Greatly improved Fet's economy.

Beginning in the 1860s, Fet realized that literary creation was difficult to support his family. Therefore, he bought a farm and land in Stepanovka village in his hometown of Mtsensk County; his creative passion declined and he specialized in farm management. At this time, Russia implemented the abolition of serfdom, and the society entered a period of turmoil and change; Fet's pure art poetry was gradually marginalized, and suffered criticism and neglect. The famous critic Pisarev wrote in "Flowers of Harmless Humor" The magazines even sneered at Fet's poems, published in 1863, as being good enough only for the underside of a wall. Fet, who suffered successive blows to his creation, concentrated his thoughts on planting oats, repairing the mill, and building a large horse farm. He also served as a civil mediation judge in the countryside for nearly 10 years. Leo Tolstoy kepIn his spare time, Fet spent most of his time reading philosophy books to relieve boredom, especially Schopenhauer's works.

In 1873, one thing that the 53-year-old Fet had been looking forward to in his life finally came true: with the permission of the Tsar, Fet obtained the status of a nobleman and became a descendant of the 300-year-old Shenxin family. On the day he heard the good news, he wrote a letter to his wife, asking her to immediately

寫道：「要是你問我：怎麼描述所有的磨難與痛苦，我會回答：所有磨難與痛苦的名字——叫費特。」儘管有的朋友不明白費特為什麼非要改換貴族姓氏不可而肆意調侃，但費特對所有批評的言論置之不理；追究其因，是他從十幾歲就一直期待的夢想，不可能放棄，且以實際的行動繼續追求榮譽。為了報答沙皇的恩寵，費特不顧年事已高，居然申請了當宮廷侍從，也引起了當時許多文人志士的嘲笑。

　　19 世紀 80 年代以後，費特又重提詩筆，但依然保持了旺盛的創作熱情與活力。他晚年出版的三本詩集均以《黃昏燈火》為標題。詩裡仍有許多作品是抒發初戀時期痛愛交織的複雜心情，如《我心裏多麼想……》、《當你默默誦讀……》所有批評的言論置之不理；追究其因，是他從十幾歲就一直期待的夢想，不可能放棄，且以實際的行動繼續追求榮譽。為了報答沙皇的恩寵，費特不顧年事已高，居然申請了當宮廷侍從，也引起了當時許多文人志士的嘲笑。等緬懷之作。詩人主要是對一生所經歷的不幸進行追憶和思索，表現出愛情的滄桑與凝重。費特 19 世紀 90 年代所作的《春天的日子……》、《明天的事……》等作品中透出一股對世道的無奈，深深撥動我們的心弦。十月革命後，費特詩歌再次被打入冷宮，直到 20 世紀 50 年代後期，才重新恢復費特的聲譽。雖然，歷來評家對於費特詩歌褒貶不一，有些人抨擊他題材狹窄或逃避社會鬥爭，但 20 世紀 80 年代俄羅斯人早已把費特視為俄羅斯詩壇十傑之一。

　　費特在他長達半個世紀的創作生涯中，留下的抒情詩共

replace all the emblems in the manor, and wrote in the letter: "If you ask me: how to describe all the suffering and pain, I will Answer: the name of all suffering and pain is Fet." Although some friends did not understand why Fet had to change the noble surname and ridiculed wantonly, Fet ignored all criticisms; It is impossible to give up the dream I have been looking forward to since I was a teenager, and I will continue to pursue honor with practical actions. In order to repay the Tsar's favor, Fet applied to be a court servant regardless of his advanced age, which also aroused the ridicule of many literati at that time.

After the 1880s, Fet returned to poetry, but still maintained a strong creative enthusiasm and vitality. The three collections of poems he published in his later years are all titled "Lights at Evening". There are still many works in the poem expressing the complex feelings of love and pain during the first love period, such as "how much I miss...", "when you read silently..." and other memorial works. The poet mainly reminisces and thinks about the misfortunes experienced in his life, showing the vicissitudes and dignity of love. Fet's works such as *Spring Days...* and *Tomorrow's Things...* written in the 1890s reveal a sense of helplessness towards the world, which deeply touches our hearts. After the October Revolution, Fet's poetry was relegated to the sidelines again, and it was not until the late 1950s that Fet's reputation was restored. Although critics have always criticized Fet's poems in different ways, and some people criticized him for his narrow themes or avoiding social struggles, but in the 1980s Russians had already regarded Fet as one of the ten outstanding Russian poets.

During his half-century-long creative career, Fet left

800 餘首。儘管終其一生詩人的痛苦與快樂是渾成的一片，然而，其才情洋溢，迄今仍受到廣大讀者的喜愛之因，首要一點，正是他詩歌中所抒發的細膩感人的真實情懷和對自然、愛情與美好理想的追求，激起了人們感情的共鳴。曾在軍隊服役多年的費特，滿面絡腮鬍鬚，看起來似乎不像是個俊俏瀟灑的詩人，事實上卻是一位情感特別深厚的詩人。除了繼承俄國抒情詩的浪漫主義傳統外，他還主張詩歌的唯一目的就是描寫美。此外，詩歌不應有社會倫理教育等任何其他目的，也等於是費特的精神宗旨。他也宣揚「藝術思想的無意識性」，並認為，藝術首先必須是藝術，必須是與政治性、公民性無關的「純藝術」。他的詩裡有自己獨自知道的別一世界的愉快，也有著自己獨自知道的鮮明的悲哀與傷痛。雖然，當年俄羅斯文壇曾把「純藝術派」詩歌看成是地主階級知識份子逃避現實的表現，以致費特詩歌曾一度受到不公的評價。但費特詩歌終以其噴薄的熱烈的感情及藝術風格的絢麗多姿，給人一種撼動心神的力感，從而被越來越多的人所喜愛、推崇。他尤其擅長形象的描繪與音樂性的巧妙組合，能把握住世間愛情稍縱即逝的瞬間感受。

一、優雅雋永的抒情美

　　且看詩人在 1840 年寫下的早期之作《燕子》，調子舒緩而幽雅：

　　　　我喜歡駐足觀望，

more than 800 lyric poems. Although the pain and happiness of the poet were integrated throughout his life, the reason why he is full of talent and affection is still loved by readers. The pursuit of love, love and beautiful ideals has aroused people's emotional resonance. Fet, who had served in the army for many years, was full of beards. He didn't seem like a handsome poet, but in fact he was a very emotional poet. In addition to inheriting the Romantic tradition of Russian lyric poetry, he also maintained that the only purpose of poetry is to describe beauty. In addition, poetry should not have any other purpose such as social and ethical education, which is tantamount to Fet's spiritual purpose. He also advocated "the unconsciousness of artistic thinking", and believed that art must first be art, and must be "pure art" that has nothing to do with politics and citizenship. In his poems, there are joys in another world that he knows alone, and there are also distinct sorrows and pains that he knows alone. Although, the Russian literary world once regarded "pure art" poetry as a manifestation of landlord class intellectuals escaping from reality, so Fet's poetry was once unfairly evaluated. However, Fet's poems end up being loved and admired by more and more people because of their gushing passion and colorful artistic style, which give people a sense of power that shakes people's minds. He is especially good at the ingenious combination of image description and music, and can grasp the fleeting moment of love in the world.

1. Elegant and Timeless Lyrical Beauty

Let's look at the early work *Swallow* written by the poet in 1840. The tone is soothing and elegant:

I like to stand and watch,

看燕子展翅飛翔，
忽然間疾速向上，
或像箭掠過池塘。

這恰似青春年少！
總渴望飛上九霄，
千萬別離開土地，——
這大地無限美好！

　　詩中所描繪的在空中飛翔的這一燕子的探求及詩人的設問，體現出一種美妙、俊逸的抒情美。再如 1842 年所寫的《含愁的白樺》，似乎看見詩人在霞光下，向他所愛戀的白樺傾訴心曲：

一棵含愁的白樺，
佇立我的窗前，
脾氣古怪的嚴寒，
為它梳妝打扮。

宛若一串串葡萄，
樹枝梢頭高懸；
披一身銀色素袍，
入目端莊美觀。

我愛這霞光輝耀，

Watch the swallows fly,
Suddenly rushing upwards,
Or like an arrow across a pond.

This is just like youth!
Always longing to fly to the sky,
Never leave the land, —
This earth is infinitely beautiful!

The exploration of the swallow flying in the air and the poet's questioning described in the poem reflect a wonderful and elegant lyrical beauty. Another example is the *Sorrowful Birch* written in 1842. It seems that the poet confides his heart to the white birch he loves under the sun:

A sad birch,
stand at my window,
The queer cold,
Dress it up.

Like bunches of grapes,
tree branches hang high;
Dressed in a silver robe,
It looks dignified and beautiful.

I love this radiance,

將這白樺暈染，
真不忍飛來雀鳥，
搖落一樹明艷。

　　詩人創造出白樺的形象美的方法是，在情的激發下，通過豐富奇特的想像力，來寄託自己的情懷。然而，這含愁的白樺又是詩人人格的化身和自我形象的塑造；在這裡，使情和形象得到了完美的結合，給人一種昂奮向上、悲涼與壯懷盡展的美感力。接著，同樣是在 1842 年寫下的《相信我吧……》，以象達情，是真正發自詩人內心的強烈情感：

相信我吧：隱秘的希望，
激勵我譜寫詩篇；
或許，突發的奇思妙想，
會賦予詩行美好內涵。

這正像秋天烏雲翻捲，
暴風把樹木搖晃，
褪色的葉子飄零悲歎，
偶而吸引你的目光。

　　詩人那種要求自我提升的情緒，是誠摯的；而這種情緒的產生，恰是費特渴望美好的理想時萌發的。

Smudge this birch,
I really can't bear the birds flying around,
Shaking down a tree is bright.

The way for the poet to create the image beauty of birch is to entrust his own feelings through rich and unique imagination under the inspiration of emotion. However, this sad birch is also the incarnation of the poet's personality and the shaping of his self-image; here, the emotion and image are perfectly combined, giving people a sense of beauty that is full of vigor, sadness and grandeur. Then, *Trust Me...*, also written in 1842, uses images to express feelings, which are really strong emotions from the poet's heart:

Trust me: the secret hope,

inspire me to write psalms;

Perhaps, a sudden whimsy,

It will give beautiful connotation to the lines of poetry.

It's like autumn clouds rolling in,

The storm shakes the trees,

The faded leaves lament,

Occasionally catches your eye.

The poet's emotion of asking for self-improvement is sincere; and the emergence of this emotion is exactly the germination of Fet's longing for a beautiful ideal.

二、感情注入物象的音樂美

　　一般而言，象徵主義詩歌的特徵，除了整體的象徵性外，還特別講求音律的美。很顯然地，費特從翻譯德國歌德及海涅詩歌入手中，也學習了這一點。詩人在藝術上的感人之處，還在於常以優美的畫面創造出動人的意境，如他在 1854 年寫下的《森林》。此詩如從內在節律上分析，可看出詩人感情的抑揚起伏：

> 無論我走向哪裡張望，
> 四周的松林鬱鬱蒼蒼，
> 簡直就看不到天空。
> 遠方有板斧伐木的聲響，
> 近處啄木鳥啄木聲聲。
>
> 腳下的枯枝陳腐百年，
> 花崗岩烏黑，樹墩後面
> 藏著銀灰色的野兔，
> 而松樹樹幹長滿了苔蘚，
> 不時閃現長尾巴松鼠。
>
> 一條荒僻的路罕見人跡，
> 有座橋已倒塌圓木發綠，

2. The Beauty of Music Infused with Emotions

Generally speaking, the characteristics of symbolist poetry, in addition to the overall symbolism, also pay special attention to the beauty of rhythm. Apparently Fet learned this from his translations of the German poems of Goethe and Heine. The touching part of the poet's art is that he often creates a moving artistic conception with beautiful pictures, such as *The Forest* he wrote in 1854. If this poem is analyzed from the internal rhythm, we can see the ups and downs of the poet's emotions:

Wherever I look,

The surrounding pine forests are lush and green,

The sky could hardly be seen.

In the distance there is the sound of ax chopping wood,

The sound of woodpeckers pecking nearby.

The dead branches under my feet are old for a hundred years,

The granite is sooty, behind the stumps

hides the silver-gray hare,

And the trunks of the pine trees are covered with moss,

From time to time, long-tailed squirrels flashed.

A deserted road untouched,

A bridge has collapsed and the logs turn green,

　　歪斜著陷入了泥塘，
　　這裡早就再也沒有馬匹
　　沿路賓士蹄聲響亮。

　　這首詩是寫一座森林的寂寞，雖然松林蒼綠，但卻靜無鳥喧，樹幹長滿苔蘚，連橋也倒塌。內裡含著詩人對森林寂靜的感歎與同情，蘊聚著深深的詩情，這讓我們不得不承認他也是用語言描繪出動人畫面的高級畫師。

　　1857 年，詩人又寫下了《又一個五月之夜》，他從五月的夜色 夜鶯的歌唱到白樺的期待與顫動三組意象觸發情思，表現出自己的傷悲與惆悵：

　　多美的夜色！溫馨籠罩了一切！
　　午夜時分親愛的家鄉啊，謝謝！
　　掙脫冰封疆界，飛離風雪之國，
　　你的五月多麼清新，多麼純潔！

　　多美的夜色！繁星中的每顆星，
　　重新又溫暖、柔和地注視心靈，
　　空中，尾隨著夜鶯婉轉的歌聲，
　　到處傳播著焦灼，洋溢著愛情。

　　白樺期待著。那半透明的葉子，
　　靦腆地招手，撫慰人們的目光。

Slanted in the mud,
There are no more horses here
The sound of Mercedes-Benz hooves along the road.

This poem is about the loneliness of a forest. Although the pine forest is green, there are no birds, the trunks are covered with moss, and even the bridges have collapsed. It contains the poet's exclamation and sympathy for the silence of the forest, and contains deep poetic sentiments, which makes us have to admit that he is also a senior painter who uses language to describe moving pictures.

In 1857, the poet wrote *Another May Night*. From the May night, the singing of the nightingale to the anticipation and trembling of the birch, he triggered his emotions and expressed his sadness and melancholy:

what a night! Warmth enveloped everything!
Dear hometown at midnight, thank you!
Break free from the frozen frontier, fly away from the
*   country of wind and snow,*
How fresh and pure your May!

what a night! each of the stars,
Looking again at the heart warmly and softly,
In the air, followed by the melodious song of the
*   nightingale,*
Anxiety spreads everywhere, overflowing with love.

Bai Hua looked forward to it. the translucent leaves,
Waving shyly, soothing people's eyes.

白樺顫動著，像婚禮中的新娘，
既欣喜又羞於穿戴她的盛裝。

啊，夜色，你溫柔無形的容顏，
到什麼時候都不會讓我厭倦！
我情不自禁吟唱著最新的歌曲，
再一次信步來到了你的身邊。

這的確是一首很有韻味的詩，費特在詩的音樂美方面也
是下了大功夫的。有時為了造成一種音樂氣氛，還常以畫體
情，從飛動淒惋的畫面中，使人看到了詩人悲苦的心，以增
添詩的獨特表現力。如他在 1862 年寫下的《不要躲避……》：

不要躲避；聽我表白，
不求淚水，不求心靈痛苦，
我只想對自己的憂傷傾訴，
只想對你重複：‘我愛！’

我想向你奔跑、飛翔，
恰似那茫茫春汛漫過平原，
我只想親吻冰冷的花崗岩，
吻一吻，隨後就死亡！

看，詩人又描繪了一幅多麼淒冷的畫面！可以看出，詩
的節奏是音樂的；他以沉痛的心情悼念戀人拉季綺之死，感
情自然也是真摯而深沉的。

The birch trembled like a bride at a wedding,
Both delighted and ashamed to wear her finery.

O night, your gentle and formless face,
I never get tired of it!
I can't help singing the newest song,
Walking to your side again.

This is indeed a very charming poem, and Fet has also put a lot of effort into the musical beauty of the poem. Sometimes, in order to create a musical atmosphere, the body is often painted. From the flying and mournful picture, people can see the poet's sad heart, so as to add the unique expressive force of the poem. As he wrote in 1862, *Do Not Hide From...*:

Do not hide; hear my confession,
Ask not for tears, nor for pain of heart,
I just want to tell my sorrow,
Just want to repeat to you: "I love!"

I want to run and fly to you,
Just like the vast spring flood flooding the plain,
I just want to kiss the cold granite,
Kiss and die!

Look, what a bleak picture the poet has painted! It can be seen that the rhythm of the poem is musical; he mourns the death of his lover Rajqi with a heavy heart, and his feelings are naturally sincere and deep.

三、以情入境的純粹美

由於愛情的幻變，費特常借助於激蕩的感情，捕捉多姿多色的客體物象和月光、星空、霞光、雪夜、夜鶯、白樺等優美的畫面創造出高遠深邃的意境。如 1878 年所寫的《你不再痛苦……》一詩：

> 你不再痛苦，我卻依然痛心，
> 命中註定我會終生憂慮，
> 魂身顫抖，我不想去追尋——
> 那心靈永遠猜不透的謎。
>
> 有過黎明！我記得，我回憶——
> 月光、鮮花和充滿愛的話語，
> 沐浴在明眸親切的光波裏，
> 敏感的五月怎能不勃發生機！
>
> 明眸已消逝，墳墓何足懼？
> 我羨慕，羨慕你寂靜無聲，
> 何苦去評論善惡，分辨聖愚，
> 快呀，快進入你的虛無之境！

詩歌雖是時間藝術與空間藝術的綜合體，但作為時間藝術的特徵在費特詩歌裡更突出。可以說，此詩是詩人情緒的

3. The Pure Beauty of Entering with Emotion

Due to the changes of love, Fet often uses the turbulent emotions to capture colorful objects and beautiful pictures such as moonlight, starry sky, sunset, snowy night, nightingale, and white birch to create a lofty and profound artistic conception. As in the poem *Thou Shalt Suffer No More...* written in 1878:

You no longer suffer, but I still suffer,
I am fated to spend my life worrying,
My soul trembles, I don't want to pursue —
A riddle that the mind can never understand.

There was dawn! I remember, I recall —
Moonlight, flowers and loving words,
Bathed in the gentle waves of bright eyes,
How can the sensitive May not be alive!

The bright eyes are gone, why fear the grave?
I envy, I envy your silence,
Why bother to comment on good and evil, distinguish
between the holy and the foolish,
Come on, come on into your void!

Although poetry is a synthesis of time art and space art, the characteristics of time art are more prominent in Fet's poetry. It can be said that this poem is a direct

直寫，每段也都押韻，以情入境，思情之深，從而造成了一種淒美苦楚的音樂感。詩人對自然的微妙變化感覺也十分敏銳，從藝術構思來講，正由於費特面對外界的批評與嘲諷不予理會，一心追求詩藝臻於純潔無瑕之美。詩人這一熱切的願望，化為濃烈的詩情。以情為動力，用想像之花，終能結出形象之果。

再如 1885 年寫下的《冬夜閃閃發光……》，寄託著詩人的各種情思，有的幽靜而蕭穆，有的古樸而典型。這是質感多麼強的畫面！或許恰好為詩人長夜難眠、寂寞空寥的內心做了襯托，更表現出詩人以筆燃燒自己、為世界創造花果的欣慰：

　　　當草原、村舍和大森林
　　　都在白雪覆蓋下沉睡，
　　　冬夜閃閃發光顯示威力，
　　　這是一種純潔無瑕之美。

　　　夏季夜晚的濃陰已消失，
　　　樹木也不再喧嘩抱怨，
　　　夜空萬里無雲星光熠熠，
　　　愈發明晰，愈發燦爛

　　　彷彿是遵造神明的指點，
　　　此時此刻你沉靜虔誠，

writing of the poet's emotions, and each paragraph also rhymes, entering the scene with emotion and deep thinking, thus creating a poignant and painful sense of music. The poet is also very sensitive to the subtle changes of nature. From the perspective of artistic conception, it is precisely because Fet ignores criticism and ridicule from the outside world, and pursues pure and flawless beauty in poetry. The poet's ardent desire turned into a strong poetic emotion. With emotion as the driving force and the flower of imagination, the fruit of image can finally be produced.

Another example is *Glittering on a Winter Night...* written in 1885, which entrusts the poet's various emotions, some are quiet and solemn, and some are simple and typical. This is such a strong image! Perhaps it just sets off the poet's sleepless, lonely and empty heart, and also shows the poet's joy of burning himself with a pen and creating flowers and fruits for the world:

When grasslands, cottages, and great forests
All sleeping under the snow cover,
Winter's night sparkles and shows its might,
It is a kind of pure and flawless beauty.

The shadows of the summer evenings are gone,
The trees no longer complain,
The night sky is cloudless and star-studded,
become clearer and brighter

As if following the instructions of the gods,
You are quiet and pious at this moment,

獨自觀賞大自然的安眠，
領悟宇宙祥和的夢境。

　　詩中描繪的是在冬夜冰冷中，萬物祥和而給人帶來希望的景象。從藝術上看，詩人的風格日臻成熟，呈現了區別於其他純藝術派詩人的獨具風貌，也是其詩美藝術主張的具體實現。

四、追求愛與光明的意境美

　　當戀人拉季綺意外喪生火海後，年逾 70 多歲的費特，每一憶及，仍感心傷。於是，在 1886 年寫下了《你身陷火海……》，其中，感情炙人的句子，也寫盡了人物俱非的傷感：

你身陷火海，你的閃光
把我映照得也很明亮；
有你溫柔的秋波庇護，
我不因漫天大火而驚慌。

但是我害怕凌空飛翔，
我難以平衡搖搖晃晃，
你的形象乃心靈所賜，
我該怎麼樣把它珍藏？

Alone watching the peaceful sleep of nature,
Comprehend the peaceful dream of the universe.

The poem depicts a peaceful and hopeful scene in the cold winter night. From an artistic point of view, the poet's style is becoming more and more mature, presenting a unique style that is different from other pure art poets, and it is also the concrete realization of his poetic beauty and artistic proposition.

4. Pursue the Beauty of Artistic Conception of Love and Light

When his lover La Jiqi was accidentally killed in the fire, Fet, who was over 70 years old, still feels sad every time he recalls it. So, in 1886, he wrote *You Are Trapped in the Sea of Fire...*, in which, the emotional sentences are filled with the sadness of none of the characters:

You're in flames, your flash
It shines brightly on me too;
Protected by your gentle glances,
I am not alarmed by the blaze.

But I'm afraid to fly,
I wobble with difficulty balancing,
Your image is given by the heart,
How should I treasure it?

> 我擔心自己面色蒼白，
> 會讓你厭倦垂下目光，
> 在你面前我剛剛清醒，
> 熄滅的火又燒灼胸膛。

　　詩中浸透了詩人對拉季綺由衷的眷戀，而對她淒慘的悲苦命運，又寄予了無限的哀思。當費特已在詩壇嶄露頭角之際，年齡小於費特 20 歲的俄羅斯作曲家柴可夫斯基才剛剛出生；然而，命運的牽繫，讓他們彼此接近。由於費特的不同流俗，柴可夫斯基將其特別推崇為「詩人音樂家」，並為他的抒情詩譜曲，兩人終成了忘年之交。1891 年，費特 70 周歲時，遂而寫下了《致柴可夫斯基》，詩裡熱烈地謳歌兩人之間的相知相惜以及對音樂與詩歌共鳴的感慰，也寫出了詩人對愛與光明的渴求：

> 我們的頌詩，親切的詩句，
> 本不想把他奉承；
> 豈料音樂轟鳴，詩人讚譽，
> 竟然違背了初衷。
>
> 由表及裏被他的琴聲感染，
> 深深震撼心靈，
> 興奮得無力分辨詩樂界限，
> 心情彼此相通。

I'm afraid I'm pale,

Will make you tired of lowering your eyes,

I just woke up before you,

The extinguished fire burned the chest again.

The poem is filled with the poet's sincere nostalgia for Lajiqi, and he expresses infinite sorrow for her miserable fate. When Fet was already emerging in the poetry world, the Russian composer Tchaikovsky, who was 20 years younger than Fet, had just been born; however, the bond of fate brought them close to each other. Due to Fet's different customs, Tchaikovsky especially praised him as a "poet-musician" and composed music for his lyric poems. The two eventually became close friends. In 1891, when Fet was 70 years old, he wrote *To Tchaikovsky*. The poet's longing for love and light:

Our hymn, dear verse,

I didn't want to flatter him;

Unexpectedly, the music roars, the poet praises,

It went against the original intention.

Infected by his piano sound from the outside to the inside,

deeply shocked the soul,

Too excited to distinguish the boundaries of poetry and music,

Moods connect with each other.

　　既然如此，就讓我們的詩神
　　把樂師高聲讚頌，
　　讓他振奮，如酒杯泡沫翻滾，
　　像心臟歡快跳動！

　　是的，音樂雖很難用文字給予把握和傳達，可是詩可以明白表現。費特的許多抒情詩源於歌，語言的節奏全是自然的。詩人理解世界的深度，而致力於將詩美的形象在心裡孕育，結成粒粒真珠，進而使讀者更親近詩歌與音樂。其詩常可歌，歌與詩互相輝映，往往能娓娓動聽。這種為詩歌傳播光明貢獻一切的詩思是何等高尚啊！較之費特過去的作品，此詩更為深邃，追求愛與光明的精神境界更為宏闊。

　　誠然，詩的姐妹藝術，是音樂與繪畫；詩求人能"感"【1】。進入 21 世紀的今天，在俄羅斯各國乃至世界詩歌史上，費特的詩都是直接打動情感的。其抒情詩仍被視為不可多得的瑰寶之因，主要是具有音樂與圖畫的雙重藝術性。費特詩語的特徵是格調高雅，色彩繁盛而不龐雜，飄逸而蘊味悠長、精緻奇巧；時間、空間常能融為一體，凝聚成一種純粹的美、集中的美。而詩裡對愛情的銘感與大自然的哲理意蘊等情趣則是纏綿不盡、往而復返的，尤以優美的韻律贏得了柴可夫斯基、拉赫瑪尼諾夫（1873—1943）等許多作曲家的喜愛。過去，俄羅斯詩歌有過黃金時代，它是由普希金（1799—1837）、丘特切夫（1803—1873）、萊蒙托夫（1814—1841）、涅克拉索夫（1821—1877）、費特等著名

That being the case, let our poet
Praise the musician aloud,
cheer him up like a cup of foam,
Beat like a heart!

Yes, although music is difficult to grasp and convey in words, poetry can clearly express it. Many of Fet's lyric poems are derived from songs, and the rhythm of the language is all natural. The poet understands the depth of the world, and is committed to nurturing the image of poetic beauty in his heart, forming pearls, and making readers closer to poetry and music. His poems can often be sung, and the songs and poems reflect each other, and they can often be eloquent. How noble is this kind of poetic thinking that contributes everything to the spread of poetry! Compared with Fet's previous works, this poem is deeper, and the spiritual realm of pursuing love and light is more magnificent.

It is true that the sister arts of poetry are music and painting; poetry asks people to "feel" [1]. Entering the 21st century today, in the history of poetry in Russia and even in the world, Fet's poems directly touch emotions. The reason why his lyric poems are still regarded as rare treasures is mainly due to the dual artistry of music and pictures. Fet's poetry is characterized by elegant style, rich but not complicated colors, elegant and long-lasting, delicate and ingenious; time and space can often be integrated into one, condensed into a pure and concentrated beauty. However, in the poems, the inscription on love and the philosophical meaning of nature are lingering and back and forth, especially won the praises of Tchaikovsky and Rachmaninov (1873-1943) with their beautiful rhythm.) and many other composers. In the past, Russian poetry had a golden age, it was composed of Pushkin (1799-1837), Tyutchev (1803-1873), Lermontov (1814-1841), Nekrasov (1821-1877), Fei It is

詩人來標誌的。筆者作為詩歌愛好者，對費特的認知是，其詩世界是豐富多彩的。正如《呂進詩學雋語》中所言：「詩來源於生活。詩是生活大海的閃光。把詩與生活隔開，就無法認識詩的內容本質。」【2】研讀谷羽教授所著的《在星空之間──費特詩選》，筆者有以下幾點深刻的體會：其一，費特是以生命為詩的痛苦歌者，而詩歌正是他痛苦又豐富的人生寫照。其詩歌是唯美的藝術，風味雋永，也表達出俄羅斯文學中特有的悲情詩性。從早期的詩歌，直到晚年的創作，費特從不掩飾自己強烈的愛與對美的追求。費特認為，藝術的目的，是追求美、發現美進而再現美。其二，詩人觀察之細、聯想之巧，常創造了他人難以代替的唯美的意象世界。其詩歌的美麗就在於，他能捕捉大自然中的瞬息變化，讓各種生物的形象變得新奇靈活，並賦予愛情不尋常的哲思，讓人體悟到其中的幸福與痛苦，內裡都滲透著費特的靈魂之光。其三，費特的愛情是其創作思想的總匯，愛情可以看作是詩人生命、血液、靈魂的全部傾入。他不尚雕琢，仍然是在藝術返照自然的敘述與畫面中用生動的形象去創造詩美。

總之，對費特而言，詩與音樂是同類藝術，因為它們都以節奏語言與「和諧」為藝術表現的媒介。由於費特有深厚的藝術功底和長期寫抒情詩的創作經驗，因而，他的詩歌寫得很清純，能「從心所欲，不逾矩」，給人以視覺上的美感，而且節奏感也很強，誦讀起來又給人以聽覺上美的感受。

marked by a famous poet. As a poetry lover, the author's perception of Fet is that his poetic world is rich and colorful. As it is said in *Lu Jin's Poetics*: "Poetry comes from life. Poetry is the flash of the ocean of life. If you separate poetry from life, you will not be able to understand the essence of poetry." [2] Studying Professor Gu Yu's *In Between the Starry Sky—Selected Poems of Fet*, the author has the following profound experiences: first, Fet is a painful singer whose life is poetry, and his poetry is a portrayal of his painful and rich life. His poetry is a beautiful art with a meaningful flavor, and also expresses the unique tragic poetry in Russian literature. From his early poetry to his creation in his later years, Fet never concealed his strong love and pursuit of beauty. Fet believes that the purpose of art is to pursue beauty, discover beauty and then reproduce beauty. Second, the poet's meticulous observation and ingenious association often create a beautiful image world that cannot be replaced by others. The beauty of his poetry is that he can capture the instantaneous changes in nature, make the images of various creatures novel and flexible, and endow love with unusual philosophical thinking, so that the human body can realize the happiness and pain in it. Fet's soul light. Thirdly, Fet's love is the summation of his creative thoughts, and love can be regarded as the poet's life, blood, and soul. He is not yet refined, but still uses vivid images to create poetic beauty in narratives and pictures that reflect nature in art.

In short, for Fet, poetry and music are the same kind of art, because they both use rhythmic language and "armony"as the medium of artistic expression. Due to Fet's rofound artistic background and long-term experience in writing lyric poems, his poems are written very purely, "following one's heart's desire, without transgressing the rules", giving people a visual sense of beauty, and also has a strong sense of rhythm. When it rises, it gives people the feeling of auditory beauty. In the

在筆者看來，費特是一位天才而苦悶的詩人，其竭力表現人在苦難中勇於追逐夢想的情感歷程，無疑具有研究的詩學價值，也理當在世界詩史上佔有一席重要地位。費特猶如冬夜裡的一顆燦星，其詩心已然在和大自然的融合中獲得了永恆的平靜。

注解【Notes】

【1】朱光潛：《詩論》，頂淵文化事業有限公司 2004 年版，第 103 頁。

【2】呂進：《呂進文存·第一卷》，西南師範大學出版社 2009 年版，第 61 頁。

—湖北省武漢市《世界文學評論》，第 15 輯，2013 年 05 月，第 1 版，頁 42-46。

author's opinion, Fet is a talented but depressing poet. He tried his best to express the poet's emotional journey of chasing his dream in the midst of suffering, which undoubtedly has poetic value for research and should occupy an important place in the history of world poetry. Fet is like a shining star in the winter night, his poetic heart has obtained eternal peace in the integration with nature.

Notes

[1] Zhu Guangqian: On Poetry, Dingyuan Culture Enterprise Co., Ltd., 2004, p. 103.

[2] LÜ Jin: The Collected Works of LÜ Jin, Volume 1,

Southwest Normal University Press, 2009, p. 61.

17. 論丘特切夫詩歌的藝術美

內容摘要：丘特切夫是十九世紀俄國著名抒情詩人、象徵派的先驅。關於他的詩作的卓絕成就及其思想意義，對後世的影響，幾十年來已有不少專著，分別從美學、哲學等視角進行了比較深入的研究，但從詩美的角度探討其美學意義與藝術特徵，卻不多見，本文試圖在這方面做一嘗試。

關鍵字：費多爾·伊凡諾維奇·丘特切夫 Fedor Ivanovich Tyutchev，詩人，象徵派

傳　略

　　費多爾·伊凡諾維奇·丘特切夫〈Fedor Ivanovich Tyutchev，1803- 1873〉和普希金〈Alexander Pushkin，1799-1837〉、萊蒙托夫〈Mikhail Lermontov，1814-1841〉是俄國浪漫主義時期的三大詩人。一生的詩作約有四百首，多為愛情、風景及哲理詩。然而，不同於普希金的理性、敦厚與萊蒙托夫叛逆、孤獨的文學氣質，丘特切夫的詩，蘊含深邃、優美而沉鬱；其刻意追求藝術美的主體個性，應源自家庭的先天因素和後天環境的影響。他曾說：「為使詩歌繁榮，它應紮根於土壤中。」

17. On the Artistic Beauty of Tyutchev's Poetry

Abstract: Tyutchev was a famous 19th century Russian lyric poet and a pioneer of Symbolism. During the last several decades, there were numerous extensive studies on the outstanding achievement of his poetry, its ideological significance as well as its impacts on future generations. However, most of these studies were done from the aesthetic or philosophic point of view. In this article, we attempt to analyze the aesthetic significance and artistic characteristics from the point of view of its poetic beauty.

Key words: Fedor Ivanovich Tyutchev, poet, symbolism

Biography

Fedor Ivanovich Tyutchev (1803-1873), Alexander Pushkin (1799-1837), and Mikhail Lermontov (1814-1841) were the three major Russian poets in the romantic period. There are about 400 poems in his life, mostly love, landscape and philosophy Poetry. However, unlike Pushkin's rationality and honesty and Lermontov's rebellious and lonely literary temperament, Tyutchev's poems contain profound, beautiful and melancholic; Influence. He once said: "In order for poetry to prosper, it should take root in the soil." He also emphasized that

且強調「詩是心靈的表現」。其藝術風格是把哲理思考與審美感悟變成個性化的詩語,感情豐沛;善於對自然季節的變化作了生動、雅致和形象逼真的描繪,被視為「純藝術派」,而其深刻的思想與高度的美學價值在世界詩史中也佔有獨特地位。

　　他出生於一個古老的貴族家庭,自幼熱愛詩歌,十四歲就開始寫詩;少年時代的家庭教師是詩人兼翻譯家拉伊奇。1819 年進莫斯科大學語文系直至畢業。1822 年起,在德國慕尼克等地的外交機關任職了二十二年,由於懂得拉丁語和其他新語系,開闢出一條掌握古代文學和現代歐洲文學的通路。博學多才又擅於辭令的他,也是貴族社交場上的常客。1858 年起任外國書刊檢查辦公室主任,直到晚年。當時,慕尼克是歐洲文化中心之一,在這裡,他與德國詩人海因裡希‧海涅〈1797-1856〉和唯心主義哲學家弗裡德里希‧謝林〈1775-1854〉交往密切,其哲學觀點受謝林唯心主義影響,對精神和自然的同一性、無差別性的思考,發展成同一哲學,理念相近;而政治觀點上,則肯定重大社會變革的必要,期望帶來新視野的可能性,但又顧忌於革命,因而反映出對革命風暴的預感和心靈的不安於詩中,遭致一時的爭議。

　　30 年代前後,丘特切夫在莫斯科刊物寫了幾十首抒情詩,其中不少極為出色,例如:《春雷》、《不眠夜》、《海

"poetry is the expression of the soul". His artistic style is to turn philosophical thinking and aesthetic perception into personalized poetry, full of emotion; good at the vivid, elegant and lifelike depiction of the changes of natural seasons is regarded as a "pure art school", and its profound thoughts and high aesthetic value also occupy a unique position in the history of world poetry.

Born in an old aristocratic family, he loved poetry since he was a child, and began to write poetry at the age of fourteen; his tutor in his youth was the poet and translator Rajic. In 1819, he entered the Department of Philology of Moscow University until graduation. Since 1822, he has served in diplomatic agencies in Munich and other places in Germany for 22 years. Because of his knowledge of Latin and other new languages, he opened up a channel to master ancient literature and modern European literature. He is knowledgeable and eloquent, and he is also a frequent visitor in the social arena of nobles. From 1858, he served as the director of the Office of Inspection of Foreign Books and Periodicals until his later years. At that time, Munich was one of the cultural centers of Europe. Here, he had close contacts with German poet Heinrich Heine (1797-1856) and idealist philosopher Friedrich Schelling (1775-1854). Influenced by Schelling's idealism, his philosophical views have developed into a philosophy of unity and indifference between spirit and nature, with similar concepts; while in terms of political views, he affirms the necessity of major social changes and expects to bring new horizons to possibility, but scruples about revolution, thus reflecting the foreboding of the revolutionary storm and the uneasiness of the soul in the poem, which caused momentary controversy.

Around the 1930s, Tyutchev wrote dozens of lyric poems in Moscow publications, many of which were

上的夢》、《西塞羅》、《沉默吧！》、《不，大地母親啊》、
《我記得那黃金的時刻》等等，可惜未引起注目。直到 1836
年，邱特切夫把他的一組詩稿寄給彼得堡的友人，當詩人維
亞澤姆斯基和茹科夫斯基〈1783-1852〉將詩稿轉交到普希金
手裡，普希金欣喜地從中選出二十四首詩作刊登在他主辦的
《現代人》雜誌，題名為《寄自德國的詩》，署名〈ф.т.（即
丘特切夫名和姓的第一個字母）。這兩位靈魂知己雖未曾謀
面，但丘特切夫後來得知普希金欣賞他的詩才，非常感動。
1837 年，普希金逝世，丘特切夫立即為他寫詩悼念；同年，
他被任命為俄國撒丁王國的使館一秘。

　　丘特切夫的第一任妻子愛琳娜是伯爵小姐，于 1838 年病
故。次年，在都靈與厄爾芮斯金娜·喬恩別爾結婚，第二個
妻子也是名門望族。1839 年，他被召回俄國，不久，他申請
再度出國，未獲批准。由於他擅自離開俄國到都靈，因而被
解除了公職。1839 至 1844 年間閒居慕尼克。1844 年，丘特
切夫攜眷回到俄國，又在外交部復職。1850 年，丘特切夫認
識了他兩個女兒的同學，斯莫爾學院院長的侄女二十四歲的
葉連娜·傑尼西耶娃。這一年，丘特切夫 47 歲，傑尼西耶娃
才 24 歲，沒想到兩人竟一見鍾情，終於不顧輿論，覓地同居。
傑尼西耶娃也出身上層貴族，她與丘特切夫的關係引起俄國
貴族社會的不滿。當所有的譏諷落在傑尼西耶娃身上時，真

excellent, such as: *Spring Thunder, Sleepless Night, Dreams at Sea, Cicero, Silence!, No, Mother Earth, I Remember That Golden Moment*, etc., unfortunately, they did not attract attention. Until 1836, Tyutchev sent a group of his poems to friends in Petersburg. When the poets Vyazemsky and Zhukovsky (1783-1852) handed over the poems to Pushkin, Pushkin was delighted to learn from them. Twenty-four poems were selected and published in the magazine *Modern People* hosted by him, titled *Poems from Germany*, signed <ф.т. (that is, the first letter of Tyutchev's name and surname). Although the two soul confidants had never met, Tyutchev was very moved when he learned that Pushkin appreciated his poetic talent. When Pushkin died in 1837, Tyutchev immediately wrote poems to mourn him; in the same year, he was appointed First Secretary of the Embassy of the Kingdom of Sardinia in Russia.

Tyutchev's first wife, Elena, a countess, died of illness in 1838. In the following year, he married Erriskina Jonber in Turin, and his second wife was also from a famous family. In 1839, he was recalled to Russia, and soon after, he applied to go abroad again, but was not approved. He was dismissed from public office because he had left Russia for Turin without permission. From 1839 to 1844, he lived in Munich. In 1844, Tyutchev returned to Russia with his family and was reinstated in the Ministry of Foreign Affairs. In 1850, Tyutchev met the twenty-four-year-old Yelena Denisieva, a classmate of his two daughters and the niece of the rector of the Small Academy. This year, Tyutchev was 47 years old and Denisieva was only 24 years old. Unexpectedly, the two fell in love at first sight, and finally found a place to live together regardless of public opinion. Denisieva was also born in the upper class, and her relationship with Tyutchev caused dissatisfaction in Russian aristocratic society. When all the ridicule fell on Denisieva, the sincere grief also carved scars on his heart. This scorned love made it

摯的悲痛也在他心上刻下了創痕，這段被輕蔑的愛情讓他們
相愛變得十分艱辛。但傑尼西耶娃仍為他生了一女二子，關
係維持十四年之久，於 1864 年肺病去世。丘特切夫為此痛徹
心肺，並為她寫出許多詩作，一般習稱「傑尼西耶娃組詩」。

40 年代的丘特切夫幾乎沒有發表什麼力作。50、60 年代
寫的「傑尼西耶娃組詩」是丘特切夫最感人的作品；但傑尼
西耶娃的死，是詩人最悲痛的事件。他一生不追求高官厚祿
或文學聲譽，但在 1854 年第一次詩集問世，就博得一致的好
評。同年，屠格涅夫〈1818-1883〉編輯出版了《丘特切夫詩
集》，並在《現代人》雜誌上撰文評論：《談談丘特切夫詩
歌》。他和作家涅克拉索夫〈1821-1878〉都認為丘特切夫是
位優秀的抒情詩人，並讚譽他的詩既有鮮明的思想又有生動
的形象；同時也肯定詩人在語言上勇於創新，具有普希金式
的美。屠格涅夫又說：「他創造的語言是不朽的，這對一個
真正藝術家來說是至高無上的褒獎了。」在涅克拉索夫和屠
格涅夫的宣傳下，丘特切夫也受到了俄國大作家托爾斯泰、
陀思妥耶夫斯基以及詩人費特〈1820-1892〉的稱頌。從 50
年代起，丘特切夫作為詩人才有了名氣。丘特切夫第二次出
版詩集於 1868 年，其生命的最後十年，經常生病，1873 年
長逝於皇村。

在以往的一些評論文章中，論述了丘詩與俄國、西歐宗
教、哲學與文學等多方面分析了丘特切夫對現當代俄國文學

very difficult for them to love each other. But Denisieva still bore him a daughter and two sons, the relationship lasted for 14 years, and died of lung disease in 1864. Tyutchev suffered a lot from this, and wrote many poems for her, commonly known as "Denisieva's Poems".

In the 1940s, Tyutchev published almost no masterpieces. The "Denisieva Poems" written in the 1950s and 1960s are the most touching works of Yutchev; but the death of Denisieva is the poet's saddest event. He did not pursue high official position or literary reputation in his life, but he won unanimous praise when his first collection of poems came out in 1854. In the same year, Turgenev (1818-1883) edited and published *Tutchev Poetry Collection*, and wrote an article review in *Modern Man* magazine: "Talking about Tyutchev's Poems". Both he and the writer Nekrasov (1821-1878) believed that Yutchev was an excellent lyric poet, and praised his poems for having both vivid thoughts and vivid images; at the same time, he also affirmed that the poet had the courage to innovate in language , with the beauty of Pushkin. Turgenev also said: "The language he created is immortal, which is the highest praise for a true artist." Under the propaganda of Nekrasov and Turgenev, Turgenev was also received. It has been praised by the great Russian writers Tolstoy, Dostoevsky and the poet Fet (1820-1892). From the 1950s, Tyutchev gained fame as a poet. The second collection of poems of Tyutchev was published in 1868. In the last ten years of his life, he often fell ill and died in Tsarskoye in 1873.

In some previous review articles, it discussed the relationship between Qiu's poems and Russia, Western European religion, philosophy and literature, etc., analyzed

的影響與獨特貢獻，也有從文化角度挖掘了丘詩與王維詩歌
的異同，但卻忽略了其在藝術上執著的追求。本文於從實事
求是的分析中，試圖找出正確的答案。

譯詩選讀

　　丘特切夫一生創作的主體是詩歌，他把俄語視為最珍貴
的語言，不願把它浪費在日常瑣事上，而把它為自己的詩純
真地保存起來。其早期詩作，不但有運用奇特的想像與象徵
手法，表達出熱情謳歌美好的人生與青春、赤誠的愛情，從
而形成一種幽雅雋永的風格美。譬如 1828 年寫下的詩歌《春
雷》，用「隆隆」迭字詞摹聲創造出春雷敲擊大地的聽象；
而輕重疾徐相錯雜的雨聲更加具象化，使人如聞其聲，甚至
如見其形。接下去用雷神宙斯之女赫巴，這一青春女神給眾
神斟酒的畫面，渲染出春雷的具象美感，再現了詩人高超的
藝術想像，象徵意蘊自然十分豐富：

　　　　五月初的春雷是可愛的：
　　　　那春季的第一聲轟隆
　　　　好像一群小孩在嬉戲，
　　　　鬧聲滾過碧藍的天空。

　　　　青春的雷一連串響過，
　　　　陣雨打下來，飛起灰塵，

the influence and unique contribution of Qiutchev to modern and contemporary Russian literature, and also excavated the relationship between Qiu's poems and The similarities and differences of Wang Wei's poems, but it ignores his persistent pursuit of art. This article attempts to find out the correct answer from the analysis of seeking truth from facts.

Selected Readings of Translated Poems

The main body of Tyutchev's life creation is poetry. He regards Russian as the most precious language, and he does not want to waste it on daily trivial matters, but preserves it purely for his poems. His early poems not only used unique imagination and symbolic techniques, but expressed enthusiastic praises of beautiful life, youth, and sincere love, thus forming an elegant and timeless style beauty. For example, the poem *Spring Thunder* written in 1828 uses the repeated words "rumbling" to imitate the sound of spring thunder hitting the earth; and the sound of rain, which is mixed with light, heavy, sick and slow, is more concrete, making people feel like hearing the sound. Even as seen in its shape. Next, Heba, the daughter of Thunder God Zeus, the goddess of youth pouring wine to the gods, renders the concrete beauty of Chunlei, reproduces the poet's superb artistic imagination, and the symbolic meaning is naturally very rich:

The spring thunder in early May is lovely:
The first rumble of spring
Like a group of children playing,
The noise rolled across the blue sky.

The thunder of youth sounded in succession,
The showers come down and the dust flies up,

雨點像珍珠似的懸著，
陽光把雨絲鍍成了黃金。

從山間奔下湍急的小溪，
林中的小鳥叫個不停，
山林的喧嘩都歡樂地
回蕩著天空的隆隆雷聲。

你以為這是輕浮的赫巴
一面餵雷神的蒼鷹，
一面笑著自天空灑下
滿杯的沸騰的雷霆。

不難看出，丘特切夫在詩歌中將詩中各種意象混合在一起，也有意徵和比喻的意味，這種混合交叉反而使詩歌意象的內涵更有品味的空間。

事實上，其他歐洲作家對於丘特切夫有著間接性的影響；他汲取了英國詩人拜倫〈1788-1824〉的詩歌中的浪漫且不倦地轉向莎士比亞〈1564-1616〉，認真地瞭解浪漫主義及現實主義長篇小說、法國的歷史科學等等知識，這正是其藝文思考著力之處。俄國文學批評家杜勃羅留波夫曾認為，費特〈Afanasy Afanasyevich Fet, 1820-1892〉的詩只能捕捉自然的瞬息印象，而丘特切夫的詩則除描寫自然外，還有熱烈的

The raindrops hang like pearls,
The sun gilded the raindrops into gold.

Running down the swift brook from the mountains,
The birds in the forest chirped,
The noise of the forest is joyful
The rumbling thunder echoed across the sky.

You thought it was frivolous heba
While feeding Thor's goshawk,
Falling down from the sky with a smile
A cup full of boiling thunder.

It is not difficult to see that Tyutchev mixed various images in the poems together, which also has symbolic and metaphorical meanings. This kind of mixing and crossing makes the connotation of poetic images more tasteful.

In fact, other European writers had an indirect influence on Tyutchev; he drew on the romance of the poetry of the English poet Byron (1788-1824) and turned tirelessly to Shakespeare (1564-1616) for a serious understanding of romance. Novel novels of socialism and realism, French history and science, etc., are the focus of his artistic and literary thinking. The Russian literary critic Dobrolyubov once believed that the poems of Fet's *Afanasy Afanasyevich Fet, 1820-1892* could only capture the fleeting impression of nature, while Tyutchev's poems

感情和深沉的思考。這段論述恰恰給他早期詩作的不同風格
美作出了註腳。丘特切夫詩作的本質在於抒情，但他總離不
開形象思維的規律；而其動人之處，在於以情為統禦，去調
遣、選擇、分割、組合各種具體物象，而創造出鮮明的形象
感。

　　如 1829 年寫下的《不眠夜》，這恰好為詩人寂寞空寥的
內心作了襯托，同時也暗含著對文學運動的興起帶給年輕的
族類的不同感受：

> 詩鐘敲著單調的滴答聲，
> 你午夜的故事令人厭倦！
> 那語言對誰都一樣陌生，
> 卻又似心聲人人能聽見！
>
> 一天的喧騰已逝，整個世界
> 都歸於沉寂；這時候誰聽到
> 時間的悄悄的歎息和告別，
> 而不悲哀地感於它的預兆？
>
> 我們會想到：這孤淒的世間
> 將受到那不可抗拒的命運
> 準時的襲擊：掙扎也是枉然：
> 整個自然都將遺棄下我們。

not only described nature, but also had warm feelings and deep emotions. think. This discussion just makes a footnote to the beauty of different styles in his early poems. The essence of Tyutchev's poems is lyrical, but he can't do without the law of image thinking; and his moving point is that he uses emotion as the rule to mobilize, select, divide, and combine various specific images to create a vivid sense of image.

For example, *Sleepless Night* written in 1829, which just set off the lonely and empty heart of the poet, also implies different feelings about the rise of the literary movement brought to the young people:

The monotonous ticking of the poetry clock,

Your midnight stories are tiresome!

The language is as foreign to everyone,

But it seems that everyone can hear the voice of the heart!

The tumult of the day is gone, the whole world

All fell silent; who then hears

The silent sigh and farewell of time,

Feeling not sadly its portent?

We will think; this lonely world

Will suffer that irresistible fate

The punctual strike: the struggle is in vain:

The whole of nature will abandon us.

我們看見自己的生活站在
對面，像幻影，在大地的邊沿，
而我們的朋友，我們的世代，
都要遠遠隱沒，逐漸暗淡；

但同時，新生的、年輕的族類
卻在陽光下生長和繁榮，
而我們的時代和我們同輩
早已被他們忘得乾乾淨淨！
只偶爾有時候，在午夜時光，
可以聽到對死者的祭禮，
由金屬撞擊所發的音響
有時由於悼念我們而哭泣。

在有意識的自我反思下，詩人如一匹雄邁不羈的靈魂，
儘管年輕的詩心，步履有些彷徨，但他在時間的血液中，仍
不息地飛奔……每一句，都是靈魂的力量。

再如 1836 年寫下的《不，大地母親啊》：

不，大地母親啊，我不能夠
掩飾我對你的深深愛情！
你忠實的兒子並不渴求
那種空靈的、精神的仙境。
比起你，天國算得了什麼？
還有春天和愛情的時刻，

We see our lives standing
Opposite, like phantoms, at the edge of the earth,
And our friends, our generations,
will fade far away and fade away;

But at the same time, the newborn, young race
Yet grow and flourish in the sun,
And our time and our contemporaries
They have long since forgotten about it!
Only occasionally, at midnight,
The rites to the dead can be heard,
Sound made by metal impact
Weep at times in mourning for us.

Under conscious self-reflection, the poet is like a majestic and unruly soul. Although the young poetic heart is a little hesitant, he is still running in the blood of time... Every sentence is the soul and strength.

Another example is *No, Mother Earth* written in 1836:

No, Mother Earth, I cannot
To hide my deep love for you!
Your faithful son does not desire
That ethereal, spiritual wonderland.
What is the kingdom of heaven compared to you?
And the hour of spring and love,

鮮紅的面頰，金色的夢，
和五月的幸福算得了什麼？……

我只求一整天，閒散地，
啜飲著春日溫暖的空氣；
有時朝著那碧潔的高空
追索著白雲悠悠的蹤跡，
有時漫無目的地遊蕩，
一路上，也許會偶爾遇見
紫丁香的清新的芬芳
或是燦爛輝煌的夢幻……

　　詩句如風吹拂過樂器那般自然！在其中，可以感受到丘特切夫詩歌創作及詩的定義 都與自然處於平衡和諧的關係，以及對希望的殷切期盼，是如此的純粹、堅持。特別是他所言所寫，具有滲透人文、擴大藝術視野與清新的特質，構成畫面中不可或缺的元素，讓人重新感知這個世界的美好，也是對祖國大地日益熱愛的美麗象徵。

　　讀者可能會發現，十九世紀俄國文學的重要人物包括寓言作家克雷洛夫、文學評論家別林斯基、劇作家格波多夫、詩人巴拉丁斯基和丘特切夫等。而普希金是俄國文學的奠基人，也是世界偉大的詩人。1837 年 1 月 27 日，普希金因妻子緋聞與流亡到俄國的法國保王黨人丹特士決鬥，兩天后，

Red cheeks, golden dreams,
What is the happiness with May? ...

All I want is a day, idle,
Drinking the warm spring air;
Sometimes towards the clear sky
Chasing the traces of the white clouds,
Sometimes wandering aimlessly,
Along the way, we may occasionally meet
The fresh fragrance of lilacs
Or a glorious dream...

The verses are as natural as the wind blowing over an instrument! In it, one can feel that the creation and definition of Tyutchev's poetry are in a balanced and harmonious relationship with nature, as well as his ardent expectation for hope, which is so pure and persistent. In particular, what he said and wrote has the characteristics of penetrating humanities, expanding artistic vision and freshness, forming an indispensable element in the picture, making people perceive the beauty of the world again, and also a beautiful symbol of the growing love for the motherland.

Readers may find that important figures in Russian literature in the nineteenth century include fable writer Krylov, literary critic Belinsky, playwright Gepodov, poets Baladinsky and Tyutchev, etc. Pushkin is the founder of Russian literature and a great poet in the world. On January 27, 1837, Pushkin had a duel with Dantes, a French royalist in exile in Russia, due to his wife's scandal.

因傷重去世，年僅 38 歲，據說這是沙皇精心策劃的一個陰謀，為此，使全體俄羅斯人哀痛萬分，憤懣之士紛紛抗議，為之沸騰。而丘特切夫的詩歌大多是他經歷了 1816 至 1825 年俄國的文學運動，1820 年他讀了普希金的政治自由詩後，寫了《和普希金的自由頌》，並稱讚普希金「點燃起自由之火」，肯定他勇於「向暴君預言神聖的真理」。由此可見，他對當時極權制度下的俄皇是不滿意的。

之後，丘特切夫不只一次地以口頭和書面的形式，甚至用抨擊的語言來批評俄羅斯共和國政府，也書面的表現於詩中。譬如普希金一死，丘特切夫滿懷激情地寫下了此詩《一八三七年一月二十九日》，並為普希金的不幸而表示沉重哀悼，因為這一天也是普希金決鬥被殺死亡之日：

> 是誰的手射出致命的一擊
> 把詩人的高貴的心擊中？
> 是誰把這天庭的金觥
> 摧毀了，好似易碎的杯盤？
> 讓世俗的法理去判斷吧，
> 不管說他是有罪，是無辜，
> 那天庭的手將永遠把他
> 烙為『弒殺王者』的凶徒。

Two days later, Pushkin died of serious injuries at the age of 38. It is said that this was a conspiracy carefully planned by the tsar. For this reason, all Russians were deeply saddened, and resentful people protested and boiled over it. Most of Tyutchev's poems are his experience of the Russian literary movement from 1816 to 1825. After reading Pushkin's political freedom poems in 1820, he wrote *Ode to Freedom with Pushkin* and praised Pushkin for "igniting freedom", affirming his courage "to prophesy divine truths to tyrants". It can be seen that he was dissatisfied with the Russian emperor under the totalitarian system at that time.

Afterwards, Yutchev criticized the government of the Russian Republic more than once in oral and written form, and even criticized the government of the Russian Republic, which was also expressed in writing in poems. For example, when Pushkin died, Tyutchev wrote the poem *January 29, 1837* with passion, and expressed his deep condolences for Pushkin's misfortune, because this day was also the day when Pushkin was killed in a duel. day:

Whose hand shot the fatal blow

Hitting the poet's noble heart?

Who brought the golden cup of heaven

Destroyed, like fragile cups and plates?

Let the secular jurisprudence decide.

Whether he is guilty or innocent,

The hand of heaven shall forever

The murderer branded as the King of Second Killers.

詩人啊，過早落下的夜幕
將你在塵世的生命奪去，
然而，你的靈魂得享安息，
在一個光明的國度！……！
不管世人怎樣流言誹謗，
你的一生偉大而神聖！……
你是眾神的風琴，卻不乏
熱熾的血在血管裡……沸騰。

你就以這高貴的血漿
解除了榮譽的饑渴——
你靜靜地安息了，蓋著
民眾悲痛的大旗在身上。
讓至高者評判你的憎恨吧，
你流的血會在他耳邊激蕩：
但俄羅斯的心將把你
當作她的初戀，永難相忘！……

　　這種悲痛的感情雖沒有爆發式地噴湧出來，而是緩慢地一點一滴流出來，但給人的心靈的搖撼卻是難禁的。

　　看，詩人不僅向陽光、春水、夏晚、大河、秋天的黃昏或山谷、北風問候，而且擴而遠之，又去關懷他所敬仰的人物。詩人那種要求改造舊世界因襲習慣，化為新我，從而改造出新的社會的心是與普希金相同的。那光明的國度，應和

O poet, night falls prematurely
Take away your earthly life,
Yet your soul rests in peace,
In a kingdom of light! ...
No matter how the world slanders and slanders,
Your life is great and sacred! ...
Thou art the organ of the gods, yet lacking
Hot blood in the veins...boiling.

With this noble plasma
Quenched the hunger for honor——
You rest quietly, covered
The banner of people's grief is on their bodies.
Let the Most High judge your hatred,
Your blood will ring in his ears:
But the heart of russia will take you
As her first love, never forget! ...

Although this kind of grief did not spew out explosively, but slowly flowed out bit by bit, the shaking of people's hearts was unstoppable.

Look, the poet not only greets the sunshine, spring water, summer evening, big river, autumn dusk or valley, and north wind, but also extends far and wide to care for the characters he admires. The poet's desire to transform the traditional habits of the old world into a new self, thereby transforming a new society is the same as

著新時代來臨的感應，激發了詩人的聯想，從而形成了這熱烈而赤誠的詩句。除了表達了心底的傷悲，也毫不保留地表達他對民族的熱情。詩人情感的昇華，同無數個俄羅斯人民的心，又緊聯在一起，感情的抒發和形象得到了完美的結合，進而提升為對民族的大愛；一如魯迅，丘特切夫也是個愛國的詩人，自然他的詩歌是不會沉默無聲的。

　　正因為形象是伴隨著感情而生的 詩人的感情除了澎湃、激越地攫取與之相適應的那些自然界的宏大形象或偉大的哲人、英雄以外，其實也有比較溫柔、靜謐的一面。他善於攫取一些富有真情、雅致的物象，從而創造出一種意境美。如這首《你不只一次聽我承認》，詩句是那樣真摯，體現了詩人細膩婉轉的藝術風格美：

　　　　你不只一次聽我承認：
　　　　「我不配承受你的愛情。」
　　　　即使她已變成了我的，
　　　　但我比她是多麼貧窮……

　　　　面對你的豐富的愛情
　　　　我痛楚地想到自己——
　　　　我默默地站著，只有
　　　　一面崇拜，一面祝福你……

Pushkin's. The bright kingdom responds to the feeling of the coming of the new era and inspires the poet's association, thus forming this warm and sincere verse. In addition to expressing the sadness in his heart, he also unreservedly expressed his enthusiasm for the nation. The sublimation of the poet's emotions is closely connected with the hearts of countless Russian people. The expression of emotions and images are perfectly combined, and then promoted to great love for the nation; just like Lu Xun, Tyutchev is also a patriotic A poet, naturally his poems will not be silent.

Just because the image is born with emotion, the poet's emotion has a softer and quieter side besides the surging and violent grabbing of the grand images of nature or the great philosophers and heroes that are suitable for it. He is good at capturing some real and elegant objects, thus creating a kind of artistic conception. For example, in this song *You Heard Me to Admit More Than Once*, the verses are so sincere, reflecting the beauty of the poet's delicate and graceful artistic style:

> *More than once you have heard me confess:*
> *"I don't deserve your love."*
> *Even if she has become mine,*
> *But how poorer I am than she is...*
>
> *Facing your rich love*
> *I thought painfu*
> *I stood silently, only*
> *Wor*
> *lly to myself—*
> *ship and bless you...*

　　正像有時你如此情深，
　　充滿著信心和祝願，
　　不自覺地屈下一膝
　　對著那珍貴的搖籃；

　　那兒睡著你親生的
　　她，你的無名的天使，——
　　對著你的摯愛的心靈，
　　請看我也正是如此。

　　這是 1851 年丘特切夫寫給傑尼西耶娃的詩。「無名的天使」指詩人和她所生的第一個女兒。丘特切夫對著愛情的結晶「屈下一膝」，充滿了深情，而他深知傑尼西耶娃為這婚姻承受了多少恥辱而感到慚愧，不覺也對愛人「屈下一膝」和「我也正是如此」，展現了詩人優美的情感世界，同時，也是一種昇華。

　　我們再舉一首詩人於 1868 年寫下的感人詩作《我又站在涅瓦河上了》：

　　我又站在涅瓦河上了，
　　而且又像多年前那樣，
　　還像活著似的，凝視著
　　河水的夢寐般的蕩漾。

As sometimes you are so affectionate,
With confidence and best wishes,
Involuntarily bend one knee
To the precious cradle;

There sleep your own
She, thy nameless angel, —
To your beloved heart,
Please see me too.

This is a poem written by Yutchev to Denisieva in 1851. The "unnamed angel" refers to the poet and her first daughter. Yutchev "knelt down" to the crystallization of love, full of affection, and he knew how much shame Denisieva had endured for this marriage, so he also "knelt down" to his lover, and "I am exactly the same", showing the poet's beautiful emotional world. At the same time, it is also a kind of sublimation.

Let's take another touching poem *I'm Standing on the Neva River Again* written by the poet in 1868:

I'm standing on the Neva again,
And like many years ago,
Still alive, staring
The dreamlike rippling of the river.

藍天上沒有一星火花，
城市在朦朧中倍增嫵媚；
一切靜悄悄，只有在水上
才能看到月光的流輝。

我是否在作夢？還是真的
看見了這月下的景色？
啊，在這月下，我們豈不曾
一起活著眺望這水波？

　　這是詩人對傑尼西耶娃永恆的懷思，也可以視為一首安魂曲。從月光的流輝在涅瓦河上波蕩的視覺美轉化為詩人的設問「我是否在作夢？」的情緒變異，不都給人以幽深和雅致的審美感受嗎！這正是其多姿的風格美的一個側面。

　　當然，他絕對不只是一個描寫絕望愛情的詩人，而是表現出深具社會內涵的愛情悲劇。傑尼西耶娃臨終前曾經過長久的昏迷，僅管他們長達十四年婚姻倍受折磨，但傑尼西耶娃直至臨終時，仍深愛著丘特切夫。讀「傑尼西耶娃組詩」的感覺，像是閱讀了一部托爾斯泰式的小說，調子舒緩而幽雅。然而，同那些狂呼吶喊的詩歌截然不同的是，丘特切夫對新舊制度的衝突和民生疾苦的揭示比其他更多側面，是以自己的反思觀照一個時代的反思。我們再來看他的這首在1851年寫下的《波浪與思想》，意在表達出自己對生活的感悟和思考：

Not a single spark in the blue sky,
The city doubles its charm in the haze;
Everything is quiet, only on the water
In order to see the stream of moonlight.

Am I dreaming? still true
See the scenery under this month?
Ah, under this month, have we not
Let's live together to look at the waves?

This is the poet's eternal nostalgia for Denisieva, and it can also be regarded as a requiem. From the visual beauty of the moonlight flowing on the Neva River to the emotional variation of the poet's question "Am I dreaming?" Doesn't it all give people a deep and elegant aesthetic feeling! This is just one side of its colorful style.

Of course, he is definitely not just a poet describing desperate love, but a love tragedy with deep social connotation. Denisieva had been in a coma for a long time before her death. Although their 14-year marriage was tortured, Denisieva still loved Yutchev until her deathbed. Reading *Denisieva's Poems* feels like reading a Tolstoy-style novel, with a soothing and elegant tone. However, quite different from those yelling poems, Tyutchev reveals more aspects of the conflict between the old and new systems and the suffer of people's livelihood than others, and uses his own reflection to observe the reflection of an era. Let's look at his *Wave and Thought* written in 1851, which is intended to express his perception and thinking about life:

> 思想追隨著思想，波浪逐著波浪，——
> 這是同一元素形成的兩種現象：
> 無論是閉塞在狹小的心胸裡，
> 或是在無邊的海上自由無羈，
> 它們都是永恆的水花反復翻騰，
> 也總是令人憂慮的空洞的幻影。

丘特切夫也是個哲人，這裡面有意味著，做大事、成大學問的人必是大求索者。在「求索」這一精神層面上，他更在意俄國民族不斷從劫難中奮起，使斯拉夫民族踏上光明的新生之路。

丘特切夫：詩人的詩人

綜觀丘特切夫一生的創作，可以看出，友誼、愛情與婚姻是其重要主題。他不同於普希金詩風洋溢著浪漫主義的繽紛色彩，也反映了對自由的熱烈；也不同于法國卓著的詩人傑克‧斐外〈1900-1977〉能創造出一種超現實的景觀與寫實並濟的風格。正如俄羅斯文學評論家別林斯基〈1811-1848〉所說：「在真正的藝術作品裡，一切形象都是新鮮的，具有獨創性的，其中沒有哪一個形象重複著另一個形象，每一個形象都憑它所持有的生命而生活著。」〈注 3〉丘特切夫詩歌雖在意象創造上吸納西方文化精神，也講求感情的藏匿，重視意象的選擇和組合；但又不同于現實主義的如實描寫、

Thought after thought, wave after wave, —
Here are two phenomena formed by the same element:
Whether closed in a small heart,
Or free on the boundless sea,
They are eternal splashes tossing and turning,
Also always worryingly empty phantoms.

Tyutchev is also a philosopher, which means that those who do great things and acquire great knowledge must be great seekers. On the spiritual level of "seeking", he cared more about the continuous rise of the Russian nation from the catastrophe, enabling the Slavic nation to embark on a bright road to new life.

Tyutchev: Poet's Poet

Looking at the creations of Tyutchev's life, it can be seen that friendship, love and marriage are important themes. He is different from Pushkin's poetic style, which is full of colorful colors of romanticism, and also reflects his enthusiasm for freedom; different from the outstanding French poet Jack Waiwai (1900-1977) who can create a surreal landscape and a combination of realism. style. As the Russian literary critic Belinsky (1811-1848) said: "In a real work of art, all images are fresh and original, and none of them repeats another. Images live by the life they hold." <Note 3> Although Tyutchev's poems absorb the spirit of Western culture in the creation of images, they also emphasize the hiding of emotions and the selection and combination of images; but they are different from The truthful description of realism and the direct expression of

浪漫主義的直抒胸臆，也不同於朦朧詩派的重意象和象徵，而是為了單純追求在詩中創造美的藝術境界，因而被稱為「詩人的詩人」。

其詩藝的成就是多方面的，除了社會的變遷給了詩人思想的震動，並提供了豐富的表現內容外，他也寫出了一種沉重的歷史感中透出哲理的思索。而人們總是欣賞他的聰明又機智的演說，這樣，他把畢生大部份時間消磨在這些活動中，直到暮年。但我以為最值得稱道的，還是他具有豐富的性格和深厚的思想內蘊而成的詩作。他是偉大、單純、坦率、浪漫的結合體。比如和他同時代的詩人費特在評論丘特切夫時，說了一句看似平常實則極不平常的話：「俄國詩歌在丘特切夫的詩中達到了空前的「精微」和「空靈的高度」。屠格涅夫在寫給費特的信中說：「關於丘特切夫，毫無疑問：「誰若是欣賞不了他，那就欣賞不了詩。」又說：「他(丘特切夫)的每篇詩都發自一個思想，但這個思想好像是一個星火，在深摯的情感或強烈印象的影響下燃燒起來。」而陀斯妥也夫斯基也讚賞說過：「第一個哲理詩人，除了普希金之外，沒有人能和他並列。」就連小說家列夫·托爾斯泰〈1828-1910〉對詩人也十分推崇。

然而，丘特切夫生前曾表示，十二月黨〈注 1〉的起義是「喪失理智的行動」。這席話就不免落入當時文字游戰的泥潭，引起小說家屠格涅夫〈1818-1883〉的不滿且批評的說：「我深為丘特切夫感到惋惜：他是一個斯拉夫派〈注 2〉，但這不表現在詩歌中；而那些表現他這方面觀點的詩都很

the heart of romanticism are also different from the emphasis on images and symbols of the Misty Poetry School, but for the pure pursuit of the artistic realm of creating beauty in poetry, so they are called "poets of poets".

His poetic achievements are multifaceted. In addition to the social changes that shook the poet's thoughts and provided rich content for expression, he also wrote philosophical thinking with a heavy sense of history. And people always appreciated his cleverness and witticism, of his life in these activities until his old age. But I think the most praiseworthy are his poems with rich character and profound thoughts. He was great, simple, frank, romantic all rolled into one. For example, when his contemporary poet Fet commented on Tyutchev, he said something that seemed ordinary but was actually very unusual: "Russian poetry has reached an unprecedented 'delicacy' and 'emptiness' in the poems of Tyutchev at the height". In his letter to Fet, Turgenev said: "With regard to Yutchev, there is no doubt; whoever cannot appreciate him cannot appreciate poetry." He also said: "His (Tutchev's) every poem springs from a thought, but this thought is like a spark that burns under the influence of a deep emotion or a strong impression." And Dostoevsky also praised: "The first philosophical poet, no one can stand beside him except Pushkin." Even the novelist Leo Tolstoy (1828-1910) admired the poet very much.

However, Yutchev said during his lifetime that the Decembrist uprising was "an act of insanity". This remark inevitably fell into the quagmire of literary wars at the time, which aroused the dissatisfaction of the novelist Turgenev (1818-1883) and criticized: "I feel sorry for Tyutchev: he is a Slavophile <Note 2>, but this is not expressed in poetry; and the poems that express his point

糟。」，從總體來看，顯然，丘特切夫的性格中除了善於思考、善良、熱忱的特質外，又有易於敏感、彷徨、苦悶的一面，正是這多種性格的綜合，才使得丘詩具有更高的審美價值。晚年多病的他，於 1865 年仍寫下了這首《東方在遲疑》：

　　東方在遲疑，沉默，毫無動靜；
　　到處屏息著，等待它的信號……
　　怎麼？它是睡了，還是要等等？
　　曙光是臨近了，還是迢遙？
　　當群山的頂峰才微微發亮，
　　樹林和山谷還霧氣彌漫，
　　啊，這時候，請舉目望望天……

　　你會看到：東方的一角天空
　　好像有秘密的熱情在燃燒，
　　越來越紅，越鮮明，越生動，
　　終至蔓延到整個的碧霄——
　　只不過一分鐘，你就能聽到
　　從那廣闊無垠的太空中，
　　太陽的光線對普世敲起了
　　勝利的、洪亮的鐘聲……

　　這是以象徵的手法，寫出東方斯拉夫民族〈注 4〉的政治覺醒；意象警策，令人過目難忘。它唱出了詩人對國家邁向光明這一熱切的願望，也展現了身為詩人燃燒自己，照亮世界，而又給人帶來希望的景象。

of view in this regard are very bad." From the overall point of view, it is obvious that in addition to the qualities of good thinking, kindness, and enthusiasm in Tyutchev's character. In addition, there is a side that is prone to sensitivity, hesitation, and depression. It is the combination of these various personalities that makes Qiu's poems have higher aesthetic value. In his later years, he was sickly, and in 1865 he still wrote the song *The East Is Hesitating*:

> *The East is hesitating, silent, motionless;*
> *Hold your breath everywhere, waiting for its signal...*
> *How? Is it asleep, or should it wait?*
> *Is the dawn near, or far away?*
> *When the peaks of the mountains are only a little bright,*
> *The woods and valleys are still foggy,*
> *Ah, at this time, please raise your eyes to the sky...*
>
> *You will see: a corner of the eastern sky*
> *As if with a secret passion burning,*
> *Redder, brighter, more vivid,*
> *Finally spread to the whole Bixiao —*
> *In just a minute, you can hear*
> *From the vastness of space,*
> *The sun's rays struck the world*
> *Triumphant, resounding bells...*

This is a symbolic way to write about the political awakening of the Eastern Slavic nation <Note 4>; the imagery is a warning, which is unforgettable. It sang the poet's earnest desire for the country to move towards light, and also showed the scene of a poet burning himself, illuminating the world and bringing hope to people.

　　古今中外，文學上一種思潮的興起，總是和社會的變革分不開的。中國詩人艾青有句名言：「人民的心是試金石。」他終其一生的創作都在為揭示生活現實的典型意義，為世界的光明而奉獻一切的思想感情。反觀丘特切夫的詩歌是對一種美好理想的更廣闊的追求。在筆者看來，他們都是追求光明的歌者，晚年的丘特切夫詩作更可看出這一鮮明的思想傾向。1868 年，當他寫下《白雲在天際慢慢消融》，五年後便病逝了：

　　　　白雲在天際慢慢消融；
　　　　在炎熱的日光下，小河帶著炯炯的火星流動，
　　　　又像一面銅鏡幽幽閃爍……

　　　　炎熱一刻比一刻更烈，
　　　　陰影都到樹林中躲藏；
　　　　偶爾從那白亮的田野
　　　　飄來陣陣甜蜜的芬芳。

　　　　奇異的日子！多年以後，這永恆的秩序常青，
　　　　河水還是閃爍地流，
　　　　田野依舊呼吸在炎熱中。

In ancient and modern China and abroad, the rise of a trend of thought in literature is always inseparable from social changes. Ai Qing, a Chinese poet, has a famous saying: "The heart of the people is the touchstone." His creations throughout his life are dedicated to revealing the typical meaning of the reality of life and dedicating all his thoughts and feelings to the light of the world. In contrast, Tyutchev's poetry is a broader pursuit of a beautiful ideal. In the author's opinion, they are all singers pursuing light, and this distinct ideological tendency can be seen in the poems of Yutchev in his later years. In 1868, when he wrote *White Clouds Slowly Dissolving in the Sky*, he died of illness five years later:

The white clouds are slowly melting in the sky;
In the hot sun, the river flows with bright sparks,
And like a bronze mirror flickering faintly...

The heat grows stronger every moment,
The shadows hide in the woods;
Occasionally from the bright white fields
There are bursts of sweet fragrance.

Strange days! Years later, this eternal order evergreen,
The river still glistens,
The fields still breathe in the heat.

　　此詩同樣有著熱烈而真摯的感情，且畫面絢麗多彩，能與具體可感的藝術形象融為一體。看到這樣一幅生動形象的圖畫，人們不能不為他對周遭自然風光和熱愛生活而深受感動，也不得不嘆服他那多彩的藝術畫筆。毫無疑問，丘特切夫的詩歌在思想內容和藝術形式上都取得了很高的成就。詩人對光明新制度的熱烈嚮往之情，經過世代風雨的沖刷，終於得到了應有的歷史評價。也可以毫不誇張地說，由查良錚所譯的《海浪與思想—丘特切夫詩選》是一部值得閱讀的奇書，讓我有很強的共鳴，同時沐浴在藝術的美感之中。

注解（1）《評〈瑪林斯基全集〉》，載自《別林斯基選集》第二卷，上海譯文出版社，1980年版，第165頁。

注解（2）這是發生在1825年12月26日由俄國軍官率領三千名士兵針對沙皇專制的武裝起義，地點在聖彼德堡的元老院廣場；由於這場革命發生於十二月，因此有關的起義者都被稱為「十二月黨人」，即Decembrist。

注解（3）出於人道主義精神站出來反對沙皇瘋狂的行徑，並寧死不從，不肯拋棄尊嚴，淪為奴隸的俄國人，就是斯拉夫派。他們強調要從俄羅斯的歷史中尋找俄國發展的動力，而不是追隨西方的道路；而在貴族資產階級和自由主義知識份子中也形成了肯定俄國歷史特性的斯拉夫派和肯定西歐文明成果的西化派。

This poem also has warm and sincere feelings, and the pictures are colorful, which can be integrated with specific and sensible artistic images. Seeing such a vivid picture, people cannot help but be deeply moved by his love for the surrounding natural scenery and life, and also have to admire his colorful artistic brushes. There is no doubt that Tyutchev's poems have achieved high achievements in both ideological content and artistic form. The poet's ardent yearning for the bright new system, after generations of wind and rain, finally got the due historical evaluation. It is no exaggeration to say that *Sea Waves and Thoughts-Selected Poems of Yutchev* translated by Zha Liangzheng is a wonderful book worth reading.

Notes:

(1) *Comment on the Complete Works of Mariinsky*, contained in the second volume of *Selected Works of Belinsky*, Shanghai Translation Publishing House, 1980 edition, p. 165.

Note (2) This took place on December 26, 1825, when 3,000 soldiers led by Russian officers led an armed uprising against the tsarist dictatorship, at the Senate Square in St. Petersburg; since the revolution took place in December, and the relevant insurgents are called "Decembrists", that is, Decembrist.

Note (3) The Russians who stood up against the crazy behavior of the Tsar out of humanitarian spirit, and would rather die than obey, refused to abandon their dignity, and became slaves, were the Slavophiles. They emphasized the need to find the driving force for Russia's development from Russia's history, rather than following the Western road; and among the aristocratic bourgeoisie and liberal intellectuals, there also formed a Slavophile faction who affirmed Russia's historical characteristics and a Westernization faction who affirmed the achievements of Western European civilization.

注解（4）「俄羅斯族」就是俄羅斯的主體民族的族稱。「斯拉夫」實際是語言的語族，即「斯拉夫語族」；延伸為超越國界的泛民族，即「斯拉夫民族」，不僅有俄羅斯族，還包括塞爾維亞族、波蘭族、捷克族、烏克蘭族、白俄羅斯族、馬其頓族、保加利亞族等等。

—2016.1.7 作

—湖北省武漢市華中師範大學文學院主辦《世界文學評論》（高教版），2016 年 04 月第 1 版，第 7 輯，頁 62-67，中國出版集團，世界圖書出版公司出版。

Note (4) "Russian" is the ethnic name of the main ethnic group in Russia. "Slavic" is actually a language family of languages, that is, "Slavic language family"; it extends to a pan-ethnic group that transcends national boundaries, that is, "Slavic peoples", including not only Russians, but also Serbians, Polishes, Czechs, Ukrainians, and Belarusians, Macedonian, Bulgarian, etc.

18. 簡論米蘭・裏赫特
《湖底活石》的自然美學思想

摘要：米蘭・裏赫特（Milan Richter）是斯洛伐克（Slovensko）的重要作家，本文嘗試以其詩為路標，勘探米蘭・裏赫特新詩創作裡的自然美學思想。

關鍵字：詩人，斯洛伐克，美學思想，猶太人，救贖

米蘭・裏赫特：飛升天堂羽翼的詩才

米蘭・裏赫特〈1948-〉，生於斯洛伐克共和國布拉提斯拉瓦市。性溫儒磊落，思想豐富；熱愛寧靜與自由，是個以詩歌救贖人生的詩人，具有藝術的靈魂。2010年世詩會中吟誦時，那份憂鬱、那份無言的悲慟、自然的肢體語言，都深深地打動了我。由於其文學創作上的卓越表現，於以色列的海法榮獲世界詩人大會授予名譽博士學位、瑞典科學院翻譯獎及奧地利共和國貢獻勳章和挪威王國一級勳章。目前是《斯洛伐克文學評論》總編輯、世界藝術和文化學院第一副院長。2000年建立了楊・斯莫雷克國際文學節，出版過《晚上的鏡子》等八本詩集、還寫了兩個話劇，翻譯了七十本書。

18. On the Aesthetic Thoughts of ature Milan Richter's Living Stones in the Bottom of the Lake

Abstract: Milan Richter is an important Slovakian writer. This essay tries to use one of his poetry collections as a main text to explore the aesthetic thoughts of nature in his writing.

Key words: poet, Slovakia, acsthetic thoughts, Jew, salvation

Milan Richter: a Genius in Poetry, with Wings Ascending into Heaven

Milan Richter (1948-) was born in Bratislava, Slovak Republic. He has gentle, open and upright manner and is rich in thoughts. Preferring to live in tranquil environments and loving freedom, he is a poet with soul of aesthetics regarding poetry as salvation in life. In 2010, in the World Congresses of Poets, when he read his poems, his melancholia, silent sorrow, and natural body language affected me deeply. Owing to his excellent achievement in creative writing, he was awarded an Honorary Doctoral Degree at the World Congress of Poets taking place in Haifa, Israel; Translation Prize in the Royal Swedish Academy of Sciences; Décoration de contribution in the Republic of Austria; and the First Order in the Kingdom of Norway. Currently, he is the chief-editor for Slovak Literature Review and the First Deputy Director of the World Academy of Arts and Literature. In 2000, he set up Yang Simoleike International Literary Festival. He has had eight poetry collections, including Mirror at Night, two stage plays, and seventy translated books published.

　　米蘭在臺灣普普出版的《湖底活石》書裡自述,「對於我
關於猶太人命運和大屠殺的詩歌,我把他理解成通過基因遺
傳下來的對不幸的命運、不利的環境和粗魯的社會多數人的
力量的平衡調節。我想,這個平衡調節從來不是什麼英雄式
的,然而,大多數卻是深刻的,生存本質上的,家族中世代
相傳的。深陷於恐懼和焦慮中。……」

　　由此可以看到他對自然人生的深刻體驗以及他身為猶太
後裔詩人的生存哲學,使他的詩呈現一種遺世獨立、純淨無
塵的情懷,如水的月色。這或許也是他對世事洞明的心魂書
寫,從而映現出一種自然、具思辯深度的氣圍。他以自由的
意志去面對族親遭遇的困境,以詩豐富了命途的無窮;時而
壯懷激越,氣宇雄渾;時而抒寫個人情懷、柔曼憂思。可以
說,米蘭‧裏赫特靈魂裡有某種飄逸與靈動的品格,詩本身
的純粹確立了其在國際詩壇重要的地位。身為猶太人,他也
常在詩中調適自己的心境,以救贖祖先苦難的心靈,以睿智
的思考涵養身心,在大自然的運行中求得安逸舒坦地生存,
表現猶太民族不屈不撓的韌性及哲人般的精神。

In Richter's Živé kamene z jazerného dna published in Pop Publisher, Taiwan, there is a self-account: For me, about poems of Jewish people's destiny and holocaust, with carrying genetic inheritance, I regard them as a balanced adjustment of power combining unfortunate fate, unfavorable environment, and majority of rough people in society. In my view, such a balanced adjustment is never heroic. Instead, most of time, it is profound and has, in surviving nature, been carried on from generation to another in family. It deeply falls into fear and anxiety......

From the above, what we can see is his in-depth realization toward nature and life and his survival philosophy of being as a Jewish poet — the elements make his poems demonstrate a sense of loneliness and spotlessness, just like the moon reflected upon water. This heart-and-soul writing resulted from clear insight toward the world thus leads to illuminating a kind of natural aura with depth of speculative thinking. He employs free will to face difficulties that his ethnicity has encountered and enrich the future's infiniteness by using poems. Sometimes, his poems are full of intensive and excessive passion and heroic forceful bearings; sometimes they are personal feelings and soft and gentle sorrow. It can be said that Richter's soul has some kind of elegant and intelligent characteristics. The degree of purity in his poems has made sure of an international important status. As a Jew, he often adjusts his own state of mind in poems. He searches for a tranquil and comfortable way of survival in law of nature with heart and soul of redemption of forefathers' suffering and by using sagacious thinking to nurture body and mind. Such an attitude indeed shows Jewish people's unyielding endurance and philosopher-like spirit.

救贖：靈魂深處的吶喊與憧憬

德國古典浪漫詩人的先驅荷爾德林(Holderlin)曾高聲唱道："人生充滿了勞績，但仍可以詩意地棲居在大地上。..."由此而知，詩性心靈的胚育，也是關係到自我生命品質的問題。米蘭·裏赫特的作品本身就充滿詩意，他積極參與世詩會等活動，深入了生活、思考了人生，也揉入了靈魂深處的吶喊與憧憬。誠然，在第二次世界大戰期間，猶太人曾被納粹黨有計畫地毀滅，所以作者對德國人有種難以言喻的情結，雖然年輕一代對於過去也稱不上仇視，只是米蘭·裏赫特還是很難像對其他國家般親近。這種內心苦處反而激活了作者勇敢的創作衝動，比如這首〈空氣中的根〉，是對 1942 年猶太人在波蘭距克拉科夫(Krakow)西南 60 公里的小城奧斯威辛(Oświęcim)慘遭滅頂約百萬人的集體大屠殺行動的一種痛絕的吶喊聲。其塑造的猶太人遭劫形象中所蘊含的歷史背景及被不人道的毒殺等迫害，殃及子孫命運的浮沉與生者的恐懼，仍時時懸宕作者心中：

— 您去哪兒，工程師先生？去哪兒？您去掃墓嗎？
— 是的，鄰居先生。我的母親、哥哥還有
妻子的姪女在那裡安眠—去年我們和告別了，
據說是白血病，才十七歲。您呢，鄰居先生？

Salvation: Screaming and Longing of Soul-Depths

Friedrich Hölderlin, who was a German lyric poem pioneer associated with the artistic movement known as Romanticism, once sang loudly: "Full of merit, yet poetically, man. Dwells on this earth...." Therefore, cultivation of poetical heart and mind is also connected to a question of quality of life. Milan Richter's work is brimming with poetic rhythms. Having positively attended events of the World Congress of Poets, he digs out the deeper side of life and thinks about life philosophically by being integrated with scream and longing of soul-depths. During the Second World War, the Nazi regime planned to destroy Jewish people. Naturally, Richter has psychologically developed an unspeakable complex. Although the younger generation don't see the past history as hatred, it is still hard for him to be close to any other countries. Such an inner pain has triggered and activated him a motivation for making a creative writing with courage. For example, this poem "Root in the Air" deals with a kind of painful scream because of the massacre in which in 1942 around one million Jewish people were murdered in a small city Oświęcim in Poland, which is sixty kilometers south-east of Krakow. The catastrophic image of Jewish people, its historical background, inhuman killing and persecution, fate of bringing disasters to descendants and constant fears of survivals al

— *Where are you going, Mr. engineer? Where are you going?*

Are you going to graveside?

— *Yes, Mr neighbour? My mother, brother and*

Wife's niece rest there — who last year made farewell to us.

It is said that it was leukemia. Only seventeen years

old. And you? Mr neighbor?

ways remains in his heart:

— 您去掃墓了嗎？
— 我回家去。天馬上就要黑了。
這個時候我最想待在家裡……
— 我沒有墓。妻子跑了，已經很久了，
　兒子們，您知道，雖然還活著，
　卻是在遙遠的加拿大，正是，在加拿大……
　我沒有墳墓……
— 那麼您的媽媽、爸爸、兄弟還有
　祖父母，他們葬在哪裡呢？
— 在奧斯威辛的空氣中，在那裡，
　在空氣中沉睡。

　　米蘭從故事的真實角度揭示當年納粹黨冷酷本質，更多強調的是猶太民族意識的覺醒與團結意識的萌動再現。他毫不掩飾這種深沉地控訴的情感，幾度跨越時空的隔閡，尋求對祖靈的庇護與哀悼之音。

　　米蘭・裏赫特也是個思想深邃、學識淵博的翻譯家。他一面熱心於詩文和話劇創作，另一方面他也同時擔任過駐挪威大使館〈同時兼顧冰島〉的參贊和臨時負責人。自 1995年起大部份時間負責於總編輯及自己出版社等工作。他的詩藝實踐和人文精神對斯洛伐克產生了深遠的影響。他可以讓讀者在一瞥間，同時見到一幅逼真的景象，如同自然本身一般。這應起源於作者與生俱來的美學思想相關，亦即將詩人心靈變得和天使的心相彷彿。正由於此，他追隨自然，並強調自然和諧對於人類有不可忽缺的重要作用。

— I am going home. The sky is turning dark soon.
At this moment, what I want to do the most is to stay
at home....
— Have you gone to graveside?
— I have no tomb I need to see. My wife has run away
for a long time.
My sons, you know, although being still alive,
Are in Canada far away from here. That's right, in
Canada....
I don't have any tomb I need to see....
— Then your mother, father, brothers and
Grandparents. Where are they buried?
— In the air of Auschwitz, there,
Sleeping in the air.

From the story's true angle, Richter reveals the Nazi party's cool and crude nature and emphasizes Jewish people's ethnic consciousness and awakening and triggering and reappearance of a sense of unity. He never conceals such deep feeling of accusation. He also crosses time and space several times to pursue ancestors' protection and mourning voice.

Richter is also a learned and knowledgeable translator with in-depth thinking. On the one hand, he is enthusiastic on creative writing of poems and stage plays; on the other hand, he also worked as a counselor to the Norway Embassy (also Iceland Embassy) and its temporary director. Since 1995, he spent most of his time on being a chief-editor and working in his own publisher. His practices on poems and humanistic spirit have a profound impact on Slovakia. He can let his readers see a vivid and true-to-life scene at a glimpse, just like nature itself. This originates from his inherent aesthetic thinking. His heart becomes like an angel's. For this reason, he pursues nature and emphasizes the indispensable significance of nature's harmony toward humans.

　　米蘭‧裏赫特既是作家詩人、也是思想家。他的藝術創造和美學思想都具有一種純潔的靈魂。在我看來，他的自然美學思想是一個新的、富有生機的、與人類歷史及生活相關的獨立的思維。詩的美感是超越現實利害又遺世獨立的意象世界，詩境的形成有賴於意象的創造且須感動於他人為先，否則，不能算是好詩。因此，他的詩往往是情景相生、是有情有性的生命主體所創造出的語言藝術。比如他 47 歲寫下〈從你母親的墳墓邊走過〉，就是首感人肺腑的力作：

　　　　午夜前片刻，
　　　　當地女歌手的慶祝結束以後，
　　　　傾盆大雨過後墓地極其的悶熱……

　　　　新墳上的燭光輕搖，
　　　　像嬰兒的靈魂，
　　　　你心裡面母親弱啞的嗓音，
　　　　耐心地撫平
　　　　被未知世界的流行曲和
　　　　瞌睡孩子的哭泣聲弄皺的
　　　　回憶的天鵝絨。

　　　　從你母親的墳墓邊走過，
　　　　不打擾
　　　　自然和瘦弱的自然之手堅持不懈的工作，
　　　　那雙手像天使的翅膀一樣

He is both a poet writer and a thinker. His artistic creation and aesthetic thinking have a kind of pure soul. In my view, his aesthetic thinking of nature is a fresh and vital independent way of thinking related to human history and life. His aesthetic feeling of poems is an aloof imagery world which exceeds gain-or-lose situation of reality. For him, how to form a poetic artistic conception relies on creating imagery and making people feel moved first. Otherwise, a poem cannot be called "distinctive". Therefore, his poems are a kind of art of language because of blending of feeling and setting and life entity of emotion and spirituality. For example, when being 47, he wrote *Walking by Your Mother's Tomb*, a powerful piece which touches the chords of our heart:

Moment before midnight,
After local female singers' celebration ends,
After pouring rain, the graveside is extremely hot....

Candlelight above new tombs is gently weaving,
Like a baby's soul,
Mother of your heart has slightly mute voice,
Patiently smoothened
By unknown world's popular music and
Dozing-off children's crying sound crumples
Recollected velvet.

Walking by your mother's tomb,
Not interfere
Natural and fragile hands of nature insists on
*   indefatigable working*
That pair of hands are like an angel's wings

　　在給你超越生死的擁抱中
　　一刻也不離開你。

　　此詩的背景有段史實，1993 年 1 月 1 日斯洛伐克宣佈脫離捷克斯洛伐克社會主義共和國，成為一個獨立的國家，史稱「天鵝絨分離」(Velvet Divorce) 。這裡包含著作者幽深的審美思想，大量與歷史的滄桑緊密相連的；它包含了斯洛伐克人根深蒂固的精神追求、自由理想與親情關懷。米蘭・裏赫特從回憶中的哲思出發，以其兼具倫理的單純人性為基點，在憶母思鄉情結的回眸中可以看到，作者自然美學思想的樸真方向，而這一方向是始終在此詩集中被作者所堅持著的。每個人生命中都有一段歷史，觀察米蘭・裏赫特的詩，便可以用近距離的猜測，那詩的萌芽早已潛伏在他靈魂的胚胎之中。比如他在 48 歲寫下〈消失的世界〉，是首歌頌自然與親情的詩歌，有著解放了身心的詩人的必然的坦率情懷：

　　在深深的新雪中你沉重地
　　走到了林中的空地。被砍斷的橡樹椿邊，
　　在闊葉和黑莓樹的陰影下
　　八月那是蘑菇生長最好的季節。

　　雪原上印上了上百的腳印，
　　一層層依次堆積的腳印就像是
　　遠古動物的墳墓。好像一會兒前
　　那些應該生存下去的生物剛登上了諾亞方舟。

In embrace of exceeding life and death,
Do not ever leave you at a moment.

This poem has a historical background. On January 1, 1993, Czechoslovakia was broken up and Slovakia became an independent country. It is historically called "Velvet Divorce." With Richter's deep and serene aesthetic thinking, the poem is largely connected with ups and downs of history in an intimate way. It includes Slovakian people's in-rooted spiritual pursuit and concern for freedom and familial affection. Here, Richter's philosophical thinking starts from his memory and combines ethical and pure human nature as a foundation. What can be seen in recollection of mother is straightforwardness and truthfulness — the orientation of his aesthetical thinking of nature which is insisted in the poem collection. Everyone has history in his or her life. Observing Richter's poems, we can in a short distance make an assumption — the poem's source has been hidden in embryo of soul long time ago. For example, at 48, he wrote a poem "Disappearing World." It is a song for praising nature and familial affection. Such frank revelation is an inevitable result of a poet with emancipated body and mind.

In deep new snow, you heavily
Walk into an empty space of forest. By chopped oak trees,
Under shadow of broad-leave and blackberry trees,
August, that is the best season for growing mushrooms.

Snow land has over hundreds of footprints printed.
One layer after another footprints are accumulated in order, just like
Tombs of animals in the ancient world. It seems that a while ago,
Those species which should survive just now mounted Noah's Ark.

這裡有雙足和四足的動物，它們
微小的掌窩留下的痕跡，好像這些動物觸到了
大地如同觸到了天空。在淺淺的火山口中，
神秘地冒著煙霧。

這裡一個人也沒有。輕輕地哨聲，彷彿
遙遠的世界飛過了這塊土地。樹椿上的唱片
自己開始播放被遺棄的寂靜。

慢慢地你回來了，回到了森林的邊緣，
那裡等候著你的女兒。身後，
你沒有留下一絲痕跡。

　　詩裡提到的「諾亞方舟」，喻旨《希伯來聖經·創世紀》中的故事，傳說一艘根據上帝的指示而建造的大船，其建造的目的是為了讓諾亞與他的家人，以及世界上的各種陸上生物能夠躲避一場上帝因故而造的大洪水災難。在一個彷若與世無爭的世界、一片荒涼的雪原上，作者認為只要有家人等待歸來的溫暖、即使被砍斷生柴的橡樹椿邊，那怕只有上百個大大小小動物的足跡一路相伴，在作者看來，只要有自由的新鮮空氣，都是安身立命的樂土。世間的任何事物如過眼雲煙，在此地已沒有了羈絆。米蘭·裏赫特的想像鳴鳥正為他奏著音樂，離家已近的行步中都是愉快的舞蹈；這靜謐的雪景，也讓他感到心靈的平和，這是自然包容人類痛楚的關

Here are animals with two or four feet. Their
Minute heart of palm has traces left. It seem these
animals touch
Earth as much as they do sky. In shallow volcano mouth,
Smoke is mysteriously emitted.

Here is no one. Sound of a whistle is gently blown. It
seems as if
Remote world has flied over this piece of land.
Gramophone records over threes
Start playing in deserted silence.

Slowly you come back, come to the edge of forest,
There, wait for your daughter. Behind,
You don't leave any trace.

This poem mentions "Noah's Ark" whose story is from "Genesis" of the Bible. It is said that according to God's instruction, a large boat was built. Its purpose was to let Noah and his family and all kinds of species of the land stay and help them escape gigantic floods — the disaster which God created. In a tranquil world, in a desolate snow land, Richter thinks as long as there is warmth from family waiting for members' returning and also free fresh air, a paradise for settling down and getting on with our own pursuits is formed, although accompanying all along are hundreds of animals' footprints by chopped oak trees. Things in this world are ephemeral and no longer cause any fetter. Richter imagines birds' singing is just like playing music for him. Footsteps near home make a delightful dance. The tranquil snow scene also makes him feel peaceful, but this is a painful concern: how nature tolerates humans. This

注，從而使詩人筆端彈撥出一首動人的生命之弦。詩人的達觀、超脫與怡然自得也就盡入眼底了。

結語：尊重自然原生態的美學思想

雖然達·芬奇〈Leonardo da Vinci〉曾述及，繪畫藝術是一切藝術中最高尚的藝術。他認為，"在表現言詞上，詩勝畫；在表現事實上，畫勝詩。"但我以為，詩歌才是靈魂契合的知音，它需依靠馳騁的想像外，詩人還必須在心靈上回歸、融入自然、感受它的靈氣、喚起自己的善根和性情，也喚醒人類愛好和諧、自然生態的心性。

而米蘭·裏赫特認為詩是自己靈魂的救贖，他從生活中發現生命的真義與詩意，在於與自然的情感互動中實現經久不變的真理迴圈；他生動地將所思所見保存了歷史片斷中曇花一現的美。法國思想家盧梭（Jean-Jacques Rousseau）曾說，"在人做的東西中所表現的美完全是摹仿的。一切真正的美的典型是存在大自然中的"。米蘭·裏赫特童年生活是清苦的，卻於大學畢業後全心投入詩文創作。他用直率反應的心去觀察自然和感受生活的真諦，最後發現，擁有淡泊的心，是幸

affecting string of life is subtly plucked from the poet's literary quill-pen. His broad perspective, detachment and contentment are all disclosed.

Conclusion: Aesthetic Thinking Respecting Primitive Ecology of Nature

Leonardo da Vinci once wrote that painting is the noblest among all arts. In his view, in expression of languages, poetry exceeds painting; and in expression of facts, painting does poetry. In spite of this, for me, poetry plays a role as a soul-mate or confidante. Not only does It rely on wild imagination, but also a poet needs to return soul and be integrated with nature and to receive its spirit and evoke his or her goodness and character and also to awaken humans' nature of loving for harmony and the ecology of nature.

Milan Richter thinks poetry is a salvation for his own soul. From everyday life, he discovers that true meaning and poetic quality of life lie in realizing everlasting truth loop in a state of emotionally interacting with nature. He vividly preserves what he has thought and seen in fragments of history which come along and disappear quickly. The French thinker Jean-Jacques Rousseau once said that the beauty that man-made things represent is entirely imitative. The model of all real beauty exists in nature. Richter in his childhood led to a simple and austere life. Since graduating from university, he has devoted to creative writing in poems. He uses frank response to observe nature and sense essence of life. Finally, he realizes having a mind of simplicity is the way to happiness. In this collection, some of poems have ridicules with a strong and bitter manner. He doesn't deny that he is still afraid to witness reappearance of such an ethnic massacre before he dies. He interprets his own nature of life affectionately and straightforwardly —

福的。雖然此書裡的詩，有的具有強烈而苦澀的嘲諷，但，他語意深重地認為自己到死都會害怕類似的種族大屠殺還會重演。他深情而灑脫地詮釋自己生命的本質關係，原是尊重自然原生態的一份純真。他以自然為本，以悲憫之情對待世界萬物的興衰與榮枯，其充滿想像的作品，獲得了詩人的讚賞及國際所推崇。

綜觀米蘭的全部詩歌，可以看出，親情與民族情感及社會批評是其重要主題。他以周邊的人為中心，構築著自己靈魂的想望圖景，張揚沉潛的人道主義精神。在一定程度上，《湖底活石》裡的 58 首詩與作者精神上是一致的，深具有民族意識的批判思想。在行為上，他整潔的髭鬚，深邃的眼睛，多似純真又誠摯的天使！他的生存不是為照亮自己，而是普造詩壇；他的智慮與勇氣，憑著詩保全了猶太祖靈遺留下來的血證。雖然在陽光底下，各種自然生態依舊輪轉不停，可是，在那遙遠的奧斯威辛的空氣中，曾帶給所有猶太人深陷的恐懼，在時間的審判之後，依然痛楚於詩人的緬懷之中。而天空偶有片刻的寧寂，是否也跟作者一樣的思緒，期待世人有一顆美好的靈魂，讓其祖靈在死亡的恥辱中能獲得永恒的寧靜，讓人類明瞭：唯尊嚴與自由是世間最純粹的珍寶！

which is a sense of innocence of respecting primitive ecology of nature. Regarding nature as a basis, he looks at the rise and fall and prosperity and decline of all beings with sympathy. His work is full of imagination has won international praise and esteem.

In an all-round view on Richter's poems, we can see familial and ethnic affection and criticisms on society are the main theme. He uses people surrounding him as the center to construct a landscape of his own soul-searching aspiration and to spread hidden humanitarian spirit. The 58 poems in Zive Kamene z jazerneho dna are consistent with the poet's spiritual level — having a critical mind of ethnic consciousness. In his appearance, he has tidy beard and profound eyes and looks like an innocent and sincere angel. His existence is not for promoting himself, but for a wider world of poetry. His wisdom and courage entirely comes from evidences of murdered Jewish ancestors. Although under the sun, all kinds of ecology of nature still carry on its function without stop, in the air of remote Auschwitz, terror and fear have been fallen into all Jews. After trials through time, it is still in the poet's recollection. Is there same emotion in him as nature's tranquil and silent moments? He hopes that the world can hold a good and beautiful soul that ancestors can gain everlasting peace in disgrace of death and that humans can understand: only dignity and freedom are the purest treasure

這或許是米蘭・裏赫特的自然美學思想的初衷。

　一原譯者：方秀雲〈1969-〉，英國愛丁堡博士。

　一2011.1.12 作

　一中國重慶市《世界詩人》季刊（混語版）總第 68 期，2012
年 11 月 8 日，頁 50 - 53。

of the world. This is perhaps Milan Richter's initial aesthetic thinking about nature.

May 7, 2012

Author: Lin Ming-li (1961-) is from Yunlin County, Taiwan, was awarded Master's Degree in Law and once worked as a lecture at National Pingtung Normal University. She is now a poet and writer.

19. 論阿赫馬托娃的詩歌藝術

摘要：近年來，阿赫馬托娃詩歌研究逐漸引起學者的注意，但研究集中於其一生的傳奇與安列坡的情史，對其詩歌藝術少有論及。本文以其詩歌獨具的藝術風貌，著重從詩藝的角度，探索一下她所取得的成就。

關鍵詞：阿赫馬托娃（Akhmatova），俄國，美學，詩歌，詩人

阿赫馬托娃（Akhmatova）（1889-1966）是俄國詩史上永遠的豐碑，她博覽群書，被百姓稱譽「俄羅斯詩歌的月亮」。早期作品探索的主體是愛情，貧窮和流浪。在喪失家園，離別情人，喪夫等各種孤寂的痛苦中，那悲慘的經歷反而成就了她的靈感的源泉。30 年代，她與古米廖夫生的唯一兒子列夫也多次被捕，原因是因為他不承認自己父親有所謂的「歷史問題」。當她兒子被捕，判刑勞改期間，她不斷奔波，直到六十七歲，她兒子才從勞動營獲得釋放。這一連串無盡的迫害與磨難下，驅使她在四十六歲開始創作重要的長詩《安魂曲》。

19. On the Poetic Art of Akhmatova

Abstract: In recent years, the research of Akhmatova's poetic art has attracted more scholarly attention. Yet most of the research has concentrated on her life story as well as her love affair with Anrepo, and very little on her poetic art. This article investigates, from the angle of poetic art, her accomplishment based on the unique quality of her poetry.
Key words: Akhmatova, Russia, Aesthetics, poetry, poet

Akhmatova (1889-1966) is an eternal monument in the history of Russian poetry. She has read extensively and is praised by the people as "the moon of Russian poetry". The themes explored in the early works are love, poverty and vagrancy. In all kinds of lonely pains such as losing her home, parting from her lover, and losing her husband, that tragic experience became the source of her inspiration. In the 1930s, Lev, her only son born to Gumilev, was also arrested many times because he did not admit that his father had so-called "historical problems". When her son was arrested and sentenced to labor reform, she kept running around, and her son was not released from the labor camp until he was sixty-seven years old. This series of endless persecution and tribulations drove her to compose the important long poem *Requiem* at the age of forty-six.

一九六五年，在英國，為七十六歲的阿赫馬托娃舉行隆重儀式，頒發了牛津大學文學博士榮譽學位。不久，她生前最後一本詩集《時間的飛馳》問世。一九六六年三月，阿赫瑪托娃因心臟病逝世，享年七十七歲。直到一九八七年，她的《安魂曲》才得以全文發表。一九八八年，阿赫馬托娃誕辰一百周年，蘇聯為她舉行了盛大的慶典。當年她在聖彼得堡住過的噴泉樓裡的幾個房間改建成故居紀念館，俄國歷史自此洗淨了加諸在她身上的所有羞辱。

一、早期詩歌創造詩美的實踐

英國形式主義美學家克萊夫·貝爾（Clive Bell，1881-1966）最著名的美學命題是認為美是一種「有意味的形式」，也就是說它是能激起審美情感的純粹形式。正如他自己所說：「在各個不同作品中，線條、色彩以某種特殊方式組成某種形式或形式間的關係，激起我們的審美感情。這種線、色的關係和組合，這些審美地感人的形式，我稱之為有意味的形式。」（註 1）同樣，阿赫馬托娃最早的情詩極為迷人，也帶有明顯的視覺藝術的共同形式。她有過愛情的熱烈追求和徬徨、悲哀的親切記憶，對抒情詩也情有獨鍾。當阿赫馬托娃二十三歲出版第一本詩集《黃昏集》時，它的問世引起詩壇及文藝界的矚目及討論。如她寫的〈愛〉，就已描寫出愛情的喜悅與愁思：

In 1965, in the United Kingdom, a grand ceremony was held for the seventy-six-year-old Akhmatova, and an honorary degree of Doctor of Letters from Oxford University was awarded. Soon, her last poetry collection *The Speed of Time* came out. In March 1966, Akhmatova died of a heart attack at the age of seventy-seven. It was not until 1987 that her *Requiem* was published in full. In 1988, the centenary of Akhmatova's birth, the Soviet Union held a grand celebration for her. Several rooms in the fountain building where she lived in St. Petersburg were converted into a memorial hall of her former residence, and Russian history has since washed away all the humiliation imposed on her.

1. The Practice of Creating Poetic Beauty in Early Poetry

The most famous aesthetic proposition of British formalist esthetician Clive Bell (1881-1966) is that beauty is a "significant form", that is to say, it is a pure form that can arouse aesthetic emotion. As he himself said: "In various works, lines and colors form a certain form or relationship between forms in a special way, which arouses our aesthetic feelings. This relationship and combination of lines and colors, these aesthetic Emotional form, I call meaningful form." (Note 1) Similarly, Akhmatova's earliest love poems are extremely charming, and they also have obvious common forms of visual art. She has had the passionate pursuit of love and the intimate memories of hesitation and sadness, and she also has a special liking for lyric poetry. When Akhmatova published her first poetry collection *Twilight Collection* at the age of 23, its publication attracted the attention and discussion of the poetry and literary circles. As she wrote *Love*, she has already described the joy and sorrow of love:

　　有時像條小蛇卷成一團，
　　偎在心田施展法術，
　　有時像隻小鴿子
　　整天在白色窗臺上嘰嘰咕咕，

　　有時在晶瑩的霜花裡一閃，
　　有時在紫羅蘭的夢中浮出……
　　它來自喜悅，來自寧靜，
　　準確而又神秘。

　　只有哀怨的琴聲的祈禱
　　才善於如此甜蜜地哭訴，
　　在陌生的淺笑中
　　還難把它認出。

　　我們以此來考察阿赫馬托娃的抒情詩，就會發現，它既具有清新、亮麗的音色，又有悲情主義的色彩。具體說，就是詩人善於把自己柔美的情感，由她詩歌自己來逐漸揭開，並注入到鮮明具體的物象中，形成一種意象細微，略感悲愴的情懷。這是她作品深受推崇的重要原因。另一首（我的生活恰似掛鐘裡的布穀）也在同年皇村所寫：

　　我的生活恰似掛鐘裡的布穀，
　　對林中的飛鳥並不羨慕。

Sometimes curled up like a little snake,
Nestled in the heart to cast spells,
Like a little dove sometimes
On the white window sill all day chattering,

Sometimes flashes in the crystal frost,
Floating sometimes in Violet's dreams...
It comes from joy, from peace,
Accurate and mysterious.

Only the prayers of the mournful harp
Know how to cry so sweetly,
In a strange smile
It's still hard to recognize it.

If we examine Akhmatova's lyric poems in this way, we will find that it has both fresh and bright timbre and the color of pathos. Specifically, the poet is good at gradually revealing her soft emotions through her poems, and injecting them into vivid and specific images, forming a subtle and slightly sad feeling. This is an important reason why her works are highly regarded. Another song *My Life Is Just Like the Cloth in the Wall Clock* was also written in Huangcun in the same year:

My life is like a corn in a clock,
I don't envy the birds in the forest.

給我上弦──我就叫。
這種命，你要知道，
我真想把它讓給
仇敵才好。

詩中的人兒憂鬱詩意的形象極富感染力。才華出眾的她，志向越受挫折，卻越堅強；越受阻擾，卻越奮發。其柔婉的詩風及作品中所表達的情感又細緻地多層次地描寫了與古米廖夫婚後不平靜的感情生活。作為抒情詩詩人的阿赫馬托娃，其風格不同於其他浪漫詩人的熱情、豪放，而是憂傷、婉麗而清柔。因而她的詩的基調，更具有一種形式上的美感。且看這首〈吟唱最後一次會晤〉：

我的腳步仍然輕盈，
可心兒在絕望中變得冰涼，
我竟把左手的手套
戴在右手上。

臺階好像走不完了，
我明知──它只有三級！
「和我同歸於盡吧！」楓葉間
傳遞著秋天乞求的細語。

「我被那變化無常的
淒涼的惡運所蒙蔽。」

Wind me up — I will.
This kind of life, you have to know,
I really want to give it to
Enemies are good.

The melancholic and poetic image of the people in the poem is very appealing. With outstanding talent, the more she suffers setbacks in her ambition, the stronger she becomes; the more she is hindered, the more she works hard. His gentle poetic style and the emotions expressed in his works describe in detail and at multiple levels the restless emotional life after his marriage with Gumilev. As a lyric poet, Akhmatova's style is different from the enthusiasm and boldness of other romantic poets, but sad, graceful and gentle. Therefore, the tone of her poems has a formal beauty. And look at this (singing the last meeting):

My steps are still light,
Ke Xin'er became cold in despair,
I put the glove of my left hand on my right hand.

There seems to be no end to the stairs.
I know it well - it only has three levels!
"Come with me!" said Maple Leaf
Conveying whispers of autumn begging.

"I have been overwhelmed by the fickle
Blinded by bleak doom."

我回答：「親愛的，親愛的！
我也如此。我死，和你在一起……」

這是最後一次會晤的歌。
我瞥了一眼昏暗的房。
只有寢室裡的蠟燭
漠漠地閃著黃色的光。

　　詩人將初戀的少女等待的焦慮與慌張的維妙維肖的描寫躍然紙上，在情緒上是一環扣一環的。看來，她不但注重詩的戲劇張力，也注意詩的音節美。詩人確如一個無聲畫家繪出心底畫，她用心探索寧靜而多姿多采的大千世界。如她所寫的（我有一個淺笑）：

我有一個淺笑：
就這樣，嘴唇微微翕動，
我為你保留著它——
要知道，這是愛的表徵。
即使你卑鄙狠毒，即使你
招花惹草，我也決不躊躇。
我眼前是閃著金光的誦經台，
我身旁是灰眼睛的未婚夫。

　　詩人通過這少女的神情和動作展示了她心裡另有所屬的內心世界，明明已經與未婚夫站上誦經台前要舉行婚禮了，

I replied, "Honey, honey!
So do I. I die, with you..."

This is the song of the last meeting.
I glanced at the dimly lit room.
Only the candles in the bedroom
Indifferently flashing yellow light.

The poet's vivid description of the anxiety and panic of the girl's first love waiting is vividly described on the paper, which is linked emotionally. It seems that she not only pays attention to the dramatic tension of poems, but also pays attention to the beauty of syllables in poems. The poet is indeed like a silent painter who draws a picture from the bottom of her heart. She explores the peaceful and colorful world with her heart. As she wrote *I Have a Little Smile*:

I have a small smile:
In this way, the lips moved slightly,
I keep it for you —
You know, it's a sign of love.
Even if you're vicious, even if you
I will never hesitate to play tricks.
Before me is the golden lectern,
Beside me is the gray-eyed fiancé.

Through the girl's expression and actions, the poet shows that she has another inner world in her heart. She is already standing in front of the chanting platform with her

少女卻心有旁騖，還在想念那個「卑鄙狠毒」的舊情人。不僅體現在對多種畫面的描繪上，而且也從人物肖像的描繪上表現出來，這就使人看到了阿赫馬托娃富有特色的記敘抒情方式。於此，當二十八歲阿赫馬托娃的第三本詩集《群飛的白鳥》於一九一七年俄國二月革命後出版時，她已擁有廣大的讀者，然而與古米廖夫的八年婚姻也即將於一年後結束。其實他們兩人的個性差異很大，古米廖夫執著地追求阿赫馬托娃七年並因而幾次企圖自殺。婚後，阿赫馬托娃也很少享受到愛情的喜悅，這也是她早期詩歌往往帶有較濃重的悲哀情緒與痛苦的原因。離婚四個月，她再度與一學者希列伊科結婚，但這段婚姻維持不了三年就分居，幾年後亦正式離婚。

再看另一個例子，這首詩寫阿赫馬托娃和鮑•安列坡（1883-1969）最後的離別。也是阿赫馬托娃二十八歲發表的（我們倆不會道別）：

> 我們倆不會道別，——
> 肩並肩走個沒完。
> 已經到了黃昏時分，
> 你沉思，我默默不言。
>
> 我們倆走進教堂，看見
> 祈禱、洗禮、婚娶，
> 我們倆互不相望，走了出來……
> 為什麼我們倆沒有此舉？

fiancé and is about to hold a wedding, but the girl has other distractions and is still thinking about that "despicable and vicious" old man. lover. It is not only reflected in the depiction of various pictures, but also in the depiction of portraits, which makes people see Akhmatova's characteristic narrative and lyrical way. Here, when the 28-year-old Akhmatova's third poetry collection *White Birds Flying in Flocks* was published after the February Revolution in Russia in 1917, she already had a wide readership, but her eight-year marriage with Gumilev. It will also end in a year. In fact, the personalities of the two of them are very different. Gumilev persistently pursued Akhmatova for seven years and attempted suicide several times as a result. After marriage, Akhmatova seldom enjoyed love, which is why her early poems often contained strong sadness and pain. After four months of divorce, she married a scholar Shireiko again, but the marriage could not last for three years and they separated, and they were officially divorced a few years later.

Let's look at another example. This poem is about the final parting of Akhmatova and Paul Anliepo (1883-1969). Also published by Akhmatova at twenty-eight *We Will Not Say Goodbye*:

We won't say goodbye, —
Walk side by side endlessly.
It's dusk,
You ponder, I remain silent.

We both went into the church and saw
Prayers, baptisms, marriages,
We walked out without looking at each other...
Why didn't the two of us make the move?

> 我們倆來到墳地，
> 坐在雪地上輕輕歎息，
> 你用木棍畫著宮殿，
> 將來我們倆永遠住在那裡。

　　安列坡是位鑲崁畫家、美術批評家，早年寫過詩，也是阿赫馬托娃傾心的戀人。當阿赫馬托娃二十五歲認識了正在軍中服役的安列坡時，就種下了愛苗。兩年後，他們二度見面，阿赫馬托娃主動把一枚黑戒指送給安列坡當定情之物，就此展開熱戀。但俄國革命一觸即發，面對混亂的局勢，安列坡希望能一起移居到他曾居住多年的英國，但遭阿赫馬托娃拒絕，為此而多次爭論，因為她不願離開她所熟悉的土地和俄羅斯傳統文化。二月革命爆發後，安列坡獨自離開俄國，兩人的戀情像斷線的風箏，愛情最終走向了幻滅。當他們倆定情前後，阿赫馬托娃在二十七歲為安列坡寫了這首（我知道，你對於我就是一種獎賞）：

> 我知道，你對於我就是一種獎賞，
> 獎賞我多年的勞動和憂傷，
> 獎賞我從未嘗試過
> 人世間的喜悅歡暢，
> 獎賞我從未對情人說：
> 「你真可愛。」
> 獎賞我寬恕所有人的一切，
> 而你——將成為我的天使。

We both came to the cemetery,

Sitting on the snow and sighing softly,

You paint palaces with sticks,

The two of us will live there forever in the future.

Anrepo was a masonry painter, art critic, wrote poems in his early years, and was also Akhmatova's enamored lover. When Akhmatova met Anrepo, who was serving in the army, at the age of twenty-five, she planted a love seedling. Two years later, they met for the second time, and Akhmatova took the initiative to give Anrepo a black ring as a token of love, and they began a passionate love affair. But the Russian Revolution was about to break out. Faced with the chaotic situation, Anrepo hoped to move to the UK where he had lived for many years, but was rejected by Akhmatova. She argued many times because she did not want to leave the land she was familiar with and Russia. Traditional Culture. After the outbreak of the February Revolution, Anrepo left Russia alone. The love between the two was like a kite with a broken string, and their love eventually went to disillusionment. When the two of them fell in love, Akhmatova wrote this song for Anrepo at the age of twenty-seven *I Know, You Are a Reward for Me*:

I know you are a reward to me,

Reward me for years of labor and sorrow,

reward I never tried

The joys and joys of the world,

Reward I never said to my lover:

"You're so cute."

Reward me for all that forgives all,

And you — will be my angel.

　　全詩節奏明快，旋律強烈，這裡就更典型地體現了詩人對愛情的渴求和真摯情感；而這一理想的展現，又象徵詩人開始振醒又變得多情的靈魂。誰能預料得到，這段感情卻好事多磨，當離別在即，詩人感到十分茫然，正如她在另一首詩（家中立刻靜了下來），這可以說是詩人在安列坡離開俄國到英國之後，她在斯列坡涅沃懷著一種悲傷心情的寫照：

> 家中立刻靜了下來，最後一朵
> 罌粟花也已飄落，
> 我在昏昏沉沉中迎來
> 早早降臨的夜色。
>
> 大門已經緊緊的關閉，
> 黑夜漫漫風習習。
> 歡樂在哪兒，憂慮在哪兒，
> 溫存的未婚夫你又在何地？
>
> 我白等了多日，也沒有得到
> 神秘戒指去向的信息，
> 歌兒像嬌嫩的女俘虜
> 在我胸房中斷了氣。

　　阿赫馬托娃一生時時在追求理想，追求愛情，也追求詩藝的創新，但時時遇到感情的挫折，使她感到苦悶與失望，

The whole poem has a bright rhythm and a strong melody, which more typically reflects the poet's longing for love and sincere emotion; and the display of this ideal symbolizes the poet's soul that has begun to wake up and become passionate. Who could have expected that this relationship was smooth sailing, and when the parting was imminent, the poet felt very at a loss, just as she said in another poem *The House Immediately Fell Silent*, which can be said to be the poet after Anrepo left Russia for England. Her portrayal in *Sleponevo* with a sad mood:

The house immediately fell silent, and the last flower
The poppies have also fallen,
I welcome in the groggy
Night fell early.

The door is tightly closed,
The night is long and windy.
Where is the joy, where is the worry,
Where are you, gentle fiancé?

I waited for many days in vain, but I didn't get it
Information about the whereabouts of the mysterious
     ring,
Geer is like a delicate female captive
Breathing out in my chest.

Akhmatova has been pursuing ideals, love, and innovation in poetic art all her life, but she often encounters emotional setbacks, which make her feel depressed

因而更具濃重的感情色彩。如這首詩也是她在二十八歲為畫家安列坡在一九一七年流亡英國後寫的（你背信棄義：為了綠色的島嶼）：

> 你背信棄義：為了綠色的島嶼
> 拋棄了，拋棄了自己的祖國，
> 拋棄了我們的聖像、我們的歌，
> 還有靜靜湖畔的松柏。
>
> 你這個剽悍的雅羅斯拉夫人
> 既然你的理智還沒有泯沒，
> 為什麼要死盯住紅髮美女，
> 還有那些豪華的樓舍？
>
> 如今你就褻瀆神靈吧，妄自尊大吧，
> 你就踐踏東正教徒的靈魂吧，
> 你就留在英國皇家的首府吧，
> 你就愛你的自由吧！

看，詩人又細緻生動地描繪了一幅多麼悲苦的圖畫！可見詩的基調、氛圍，是隨著詩人愛恨交織的心緒而變化的。但即使這樣，她仍不願為了情人而遠離家鄉。三十二歲的阿赫馬托娃一九二一年出版的《車前草》，著名的老革命家尼‧奧辛斯基談到這本詩集，寫道：「阿赫馬托娃沒有辱罵革命，而是歌頌了革命，她歌頌了在戰火中誕生的美好事物，她越來越接近了我們從饑荒和貧困的枷鎖中爭來的東西。」

and disappointed, which makes her more emotionally charged. For example, this poem was also written by her at the age of twenty-eight for the painter Anrepo after he went into exile in England in 1917, *You Betrayed: for the Green Island*:

> *You perfidious: for the green island*
> *Abandoned, abandoned his country,*
> *Abandoned our icons, our songs,*
> *There are also pines and cypresses by the quiet lake.*

> *You fierce lady yaroslav*
> *Since your reason is not yet dead,*
> *Why stare at the red-haired beauty,*
> *And those luxurious buildings?*

> *Now blaspheme and be arrogant,*
> *You trample on the souls of Orthodox Christians,*
> *You stay in the royal capital of England,*
> *You just love your freedom!*

Look, what a sad picture the poet has painted in detail and vividly! It can be seen that the tone and atmosphere of the poem change with the poet's love-hate mood. But even so, she is still reluctant to leave home for her lover. Thirty-two-year-old Akhmatova published *Plantago* in 1921. The famous old revolutionary Ni Osinsky talked about this collection of poems and wrote: "Akhmatova did not insult the revolution, but praised the revolution. She praised for the good things born in the flames of war, she comes closer and closer to what we won from the chains of famine and poverty."

　　與安列波分手後 阿赫馬托娃與古米廖夫也結束了婚姻，
不久，她就嫁給亞述學學者希列依科，阿赫馬托娃可能因欽
佩其人而跟他結婚，熟料，希列依科完全不懂得珍惜阿赫馬
托娃的詩才，他們婚姻實際只維持了三年便分居。當他們倆
的關係陷於僵局時，她和作曲家盧里耶的交往逐漸密切。盧
里耶邀請她把勃洛克的名詩《白雪假面》寫成芭蕾舞腳本，
由他譜曲，準備在巴黎上演。他雖鍾愛於阿赫馬托娃，並希
望她跟他去巴黎，然而，阿赫馬托娃如同拒絕安列坡的理由
一般，也斷然拒絕了盧里耶。於是一九二二年七月，心力交
瘁的她，在彼得堡寫下了這首名詩（拋棄國土，任敵人蹂躪），
這是為了熱愛的祖國，她寧可選擇不要這個難以忘懷的情人
的心跡：

　　　　拋棄國土，任敵人蹂躪，
　　　　我不能和那種人在一起。
　　　　我厭惡他們粗俗的奉承，
　　　　我不會為他們獻出歌曲。

　　　　我永遠憐憫淪落他鄉的遊子，
　　　　他像囚徒，像病夫。
　　　　旅人啊，你的路途黑暗茫茫，
　　　　異鄉的糧食含著艾蒿的苦楚。

　　　　我剩餘的青春在這兒，
　　　　在大火的煙霧中耗去，

After breaking up with Anlebo, Akhmatova and Gumilyov also ended their marriage. Soon, she married the Assyrian scholar Shireiko. Akhmatova probably married him because of his admiration. Clinker, Shireiko They didn't know how to cherish Akhmatova's poetic talent at all, and their marriage actually lasted only three years before they separated. While their relationship was at an impasse, she grew closer to the composer Lourier. Lourier invited her to write Blok's famous poem *Snow Mask* into a ballet libretto, and he composed the music for it to be staged in Paris. Although he loves Akhmatova and wants her to go to Paris with him, Akhmatova categorically rejects Lurier just like the reason for rejecting Anlepo. So in July 1922, exhausted physically and mentally, she wrote this famous poem in Petersburg: *Abandoning the Country and Letting the Enemy Ravage It*, which is for the motherland she loves, and she would rather not have this unforgettable lover:

Abandoning the land to be ravaged by the enemy,
I can't be with that kind of person.
I loathe their vulgar flattery,
I don't dedicate songs to them.

I will always pity the wanderer who is lost in a foreign land,
He is like a prisoner, like a sick man.
Traveler, your way is dark and dark,
The food in a foreign land contains the bitterness of
    mugwort.

The rest of my youth is here,
Consumed in the smoke of the fire,

我們從來沒有回避過
對自己的任何一次打擊。

我們知道，在將來進行審判時，
每個小時都將證明自己無罪……
然而世上不流淚的人中間，
沒人比我們更高傲、更純粹。

　　此詩開頭的微妙的反語，可以在作者和讀者之間構成一
種特殊的諒解，從而增加作品的魅力。阿赫馬托娃並不了解
革命，但她寧願選擇留下來面對自己祖國的一切困厄。雖然
內戰後的俄羅斯一片殘破，但她仍然相信奇蹟正在走近。這
時候的阿赫馬托娃已是一個能禁得起苦難、堅定不屈的詩人
了。之後，她和尼古拉•普寧相處了十五年，最後也分手。

二、《安魂曲》情象的流動與展現

　　情象的流動，或稱意象的變幻，是在詩人感情的催動下
展現的。《安魂曲》（Реквием）是阿赫瑪托娃正義的聲音，
也是代表作，寫於一九三五至一九四０年間，也就是令俄羅
斯人不堪回首的大清洗時代。她敢於在史達林大整肅的恐怖
時期寫下了這首歷史抒情詩巨作，這是為俄羅斯所有苦難者
哀悼而作。故而，《安魂曲》不單依靠詩人的馳騁想像，而
是通過全心靈的觀照創造出詩的形象美來。全詩由烏蘭汗翻
譯，僅將尾聲摘釋如下：

We never shy away
Any blow to yourself.

We know that in future judgments,
Each hour will prove his innocence...
But among those who do not shed tears in the world,
No one is more proud and pure than us.

The subtle irony at the beginning of this poem can form a special understanding between the author and the reader, thus adding to the charm of the work. Akhmatova didn't understand the revolution, but she chose to stay and face all the difficulties in her homeland. Although post-civil war Russia is in shambles, she still believes that a miracle is approaching. At this time, Akhmatova was already a poet who could withstand suffering and was unyielding. After that, she got along with Nikolai Pnin for fifteen years, and finally broke up.

2. The Flow and Display of Emotional Images in "Requiem"

The flow of emotional images, or the change of images, is displayed under the urging of the poet's emotions. *Requiem* (Реквием) is the voice of Akhmatova's justice and is also a representative work. It was written between 1935 and 1940, that is, the era of great purges that Russians can't bear to look back on. She dared to write this monumental historical lyric during the horrors of the Stalinist purges, a tribute to all suffering in Russia. Therefore, *Requiem* does not rely solely on the poet's galloping imagination, but creates the image beauty of the poem through the observation of the whole soul. The whole poem was translated by Ulan Khan, and only the epilogue is excerpted as follows:

《安魂曲》（1935-1940）：

1.

我知道一張張臉怎樣憔悴，
眼瞼下怎樣流露驚恐的神色，
痛苦如同遠古的楔形文字，
在臉頰上烙刻粗礪的內容，
一綹綹卷髮怎樣從灰黑
驟然間變成一片銀白，
微笑怎樣在謙遜的唇間凋落，
驚恐怎樣在乾笑中顫慄。
我也並非是為自個兒祈禱，
而是為一起站立的所有人祈禱，
無論是嚴寒，還是七月的流火，
在令人目眩的紅牆之下。

2

祭奠的時刻再一次臨近，
我看見，我聽見，我感到了你們：
那一位，好不容易被帶到窗前，
那一位，再也無法踏上故土一步，
那一位，甩了一下美麗的腦袋，
說道："我來到這裡，如同回家！"
我多麼希望——報上她們的姓名，
但名單已被奪走，更無從探詢。

Requiem (1935-1940)：

1

I know how haggard every face is,
How the frightened look under the eyelids,
Pain is like ancient cuneiform writing,
Burned rough content on the cheek,
How locks of curly hair turn from gray to black,
Suddenly turned silvery white,
How smiles wither on humble lips,
How panic trembled in dry laughter.
Nor am I praying for myself,
But pray for all who stand together,
Whether it's severe cold or July fire,
Beneath the blinding red walls.

2

Once again the time of funeral draws near,
I see, I hear, I feel you:
That one, who was finally brought to the window,
That one, who can no longer set foot on his homeland,
That one, tossing her beautiful head,
Said: "When I come here, it's like going home!"
How I wish to report their names one by one,
But the list has been taken away, and there is no way to
inquire.

我用偷聽到的那些不幸的話語，
為她們編織一幅巨大的幕布。
無論何時何地，我都會追憶她們，
哪怕陷入新的災難，也決不忘記，
倘若有人要封堵我備受磨難的雙唇，
它們曾經為數百萬人民而呼喊，
那麼，就在我忌辰的前一天，
讓她們也以同樣的方式來祭奠我。
而未來的某一天，在這個國家，
倘若要為我豎起一座紀念碑，
我可以答應這樣隆重的儀典，
但必須恪守一個條件——
不要建造在我出生的海濱：
我和大海最後的紐帶已經中斷，
也不要在皇家花園隱秘的樹墩旁，
那裡絕望的影子正在尋找我，
而要在這裡，我站立過三百小時的地方，
大門始終向我緊閉的地方。
因為，我懼怕安詳的死亡，
那樣會忘卻黑色瑪魯斯的轟鳴，
那樣會忘卻可厭的房門的抽泣，
老婦人像受傷的野獸似地悲嗥。
讓青銅塑像那僵凝的眼瞼
流出眼淚，如同消融的雪水，
讓監獄的鴿子在遠處咕咕叫，
讓海船沿著涅瓦河平靜地行駛

　　　　　－1940 年 3 月 噴泉屋

With those unfortunate words I overheard,
Weave a great curtain for them.
Whenever and wherever, I will recall them,
Even if caught in a new disaster, never forget,
If anyone should seal my tortured lips,
They have cried out for millions of people,
Then, on the day before my death day,
Let them honor me in the same way.
And someday in the future, in this country,
If a monument were to be erected for me,
I can promise such a solemn ceremony,
But one condition must be abided by —
Don't build on the shore where I was born:
My last bond with the sea is broken,
Nor by the hidden stumps of royal gardens,
There the shadow of despair seeks me,
And to be here, where I stood three hundred hours,
The door is always closed to me.
For, I dread a peaceful death,
That would forget the roar of the black Malus,
That would forget the loathsome sobs of the door,
The old woman howled like a wounded animal.
Let the frozen eyelids of bronze statues
Shed tears like melted snow,
Let the prison pigeons coo in the distance,
Let the sea boat sail peacefully along the Neva.
　　　　— March 1940 Fountain House

　　《安魂曲》是誕生於俄羅斯民族苦難時代的長詩，而阿赫馬托娃的深情低吟就是朗誦詩的熱烈提倡者。這悲壯的詩句，幾乎把阿赫馬托娃整個生活的時代記錄下來，也是她昂揚的愛國主義思想感情的真實寫照。全詩的主題是以阿赫馬托娃的苦難來折射俄羅斯民族適逢二月革命的災難和不幸，內裡有血淚，有生死，也有光榮的創傷；同時，用詩的號角，毅然為民請命，歌頌了受難者的崇高與尊嚴。詩中密密麻麻地容納了那個時代的各種生活苦楚，就像一部歷史的序曲。在尾聲，用「微笑怎樣在謙遜的唇間凋落」同「驚恐怎樣在乾笑中顫慄」做對比，就一針見血地揭露了劊子手的卑鄙和殘暴的行逕，而且在藝術形象上阿赫馬托娃的諷刺才能，使讀者從中獲得更大的美感。

　　從內容上看，這首詩反映的是阿赫瑪托娃悲苦愁悶的心境，格調是低沉的。但從藝術方面來看，通感手法運用得十分巧妙。詩人對著大地發抒感慨，設想自己流下自己滾燙的淚水，去燒穿那新年的堅冰，這裡就有通感的作用。而「讓青銅塑像那僵凝的眼瞼／流出眼淚，如同消融的雪水，」不但把視覺變為觸覺，而且把記憶、沉痛等抽象概念變為有形之物，比之通感又進了一步，這就使情象的流動，更具有可感性了。她懷著苦澀的同情寫的「我要效仿火槍手們的妻子，／到克里姆林宮的塔樓下悲號。」更加重了此詩的悲涼的音階。此外，她也特別講求音律的美。如「天使們合唱同聲讚美偉大的時刻，／天穹在烈火中逐漸熔化。」不僅節奏對稱，

Requiem is a long poem born in the era of Russian national suffering, and Akhmatova's affectionate crooning is an enthusiastic advocate of reciting poetry. This tragic verse almost records Akhmatova's entire life, and it is also a true portrayal of her high-spirited patriotic thoughts and feelings. The theme of the whole poem is that Akhmatova's suffering reflects the disaster and misfortune of the Russian nation in the February Revolution. There are blood and tears, life and death, and glorious wounds in it; nobility and dignity. The poem densely contains all kinds of sufferings of life in that era, just like a prelude to history. In the epilogue, the contrast between "how the smile faded on the humble lips" and "how the horror trembled in the dry laugh" pointedly exposed the despicable and brutal behavior of the executioner, and Akhmatova's satirical talent in artistic image made the Readers get a greater sense of beauty from it.

Judging from the content, this poem reflects Akhmatova's sad and depressed state of mind, and the style is low. But from an artistic point of view, synaesthesia is very skillfully used. The poet expresses his emotions towards the earth, imagining that he shed his hot tears to burn through the ice of the New Year, and here there is the effect of synaesthesia. And "let the frozen eyelids of the bronze statue shed tears like melted snow," not only turning vision into touch, but also turning abstract concepts such as memory and pain into tangible things, which is a step further than synaesthesia , which makes the flow of emotions more perceptible. She wrote with bitter sympathy, "I will imitate the wives of the musketeers, / To wail under the towers of the Kremlin." In addition, she also pays special attention to the beauty of rhythm. For example, "The angels sang together to praise the great moment, / The sky gradually melted in the fire." Not only the rhythm is symmetrical, but the rhythm is also very neat

韻律也很整齊和諧。又如「你遲早都要來——何必不趁現在？
／我一直在等你——過得很艱難。」在這裡，詩人詛咒死神的
遲來，哀悼美好光明的事物的沉落，象徵性強，也表達出痛
苦煎熬的心緒。結尾處，更趨向寂寞：「讓監獄的鴿子在遠處
咕咕叫，／讓海船沿著涅瓦河平靜地行駛。」內裡含著詩人對
受刑人的感嘆與同情，以鴿子沉沉而淒涼的喧嘩，而海船靜
靜地駛過……巧妙地摹狀出靜裡活躍的動態，可看出詩人感
情的抑揚起伏。

　　《安魂曲》的誕生也顯示詩人已走出個人情愛的小天地，
以穿越新生界，像鳳凰一樣再生的有力聲調，獻出了畢生的
心血之作，或者說是美的詩篇之永存。這首長詩寫得很具有
史詩的氣度，能點燃溫暖和照亮人心，完全不同於早期抒情
詩寫作的典雅、纖柔而呈現了悲壯、肅穆的風格。而文本體
現出這一個勇敢而英武的生命，她受傷的但又不屈的靈魂雖
進入一個充滿歷史感的苦難時代，但這是她以生命的體驗和
人生感情構思的。也就是說，她把對俄國二次革命的憎惡和
潛伏的深刻的愛，都交織在這詩裡了。為了保存這部作品，
她每次寫完一些片段，便由幾位可靠的朋友朗誦，然後由後
者背誦，在腦子裡「存檔」，再毀棄手稿。因此，《安魂曲》
在很長一個時間裡，成了俄國一部口口相傳的詩歌。而阿赫
馬托娃憑藉這首長詩豐富了俄羅斯詩歌傳統，她所追求的是
具體而富於形象的詞語，而不是抽象或浮泛的詞語。因而，
也為自己躋身於國際詩歌大師之林。她的詩品和人品都為詩
界、乃至整個文藝界做出了典範。雖然，直到一九八七年，
這部長詩才得以全文發表在《十月》雜誌上。

arrival of death, mourns the sinking of beautiful and bright things, symbolic strong, but also expresses the mood of pain and suffering. At the end, it tends to be more lonely: "Let the prison pigeons coo in the distance, / Let the sea boats sail peacefully along the Neva River." It contains the poet's exclamation and sympathy for the prisoners, and the pigeons are heavy and desolate. The hustle and bustle of the sea, while the sea boat sails quietly... subtly depicts the active dynamics in the silence, and we can see the ups and downs of the poet's emotions.

The birth of *Requiem* also shows that the poet has stepped out of the small world of personal love, and dedicated his life's painstaking work with the powerful voice of passing through the new world and reborn like a phoenix, or it is the eternity of beautiful poems. This long poem is written with an epic bearing, which can ignite warmth and illuminate people's hearts. It is completely different from the elegance and tenderness of early lyric poetry, but presents a tragic and solemn style. The text reflects this brave and heroic life. Although her wounded but unyielding soul has entered an era of suffering full of historical sense, this is conceived by her life experience and emotions. In other words, she interweaves her hatred of the Second Russian Revolution and her latent deep love in this poem. In order to preserve this work, every time she finished writing some fragments, she would read aloud by several reliable friends, and then the latter would recite, "archive" in her mind, and then destroy the manuscript. Therefore, *Requiem* has become an oral poem in Russia for a long time. And Akhmatova enriches the Russian poetic tradition with this long poem, which seeks concrete and figurative words rather than abstract or general ones. Therefore, he also ranks himself among the forests of international poetry masters. Her poetry and character have set an example for the poetry world, and even the entire literary and art circle. Although, it was not until 1987 that this long poem was published in full in the magazine of *October*.

　　至此，我們才充分體會，阿赫馬托娃不論在人格上，或對愛情的純真，還是在文學的成就，都是偉大的。她是俄羅斯堅強女性的代表與體現，這是當今文學史上客觀的定評，也永遠銘記在俄羅斯人民的心中。

三、阿赫馬托娃：神韻盡出的肖像

　　當七十六歲的阿赫馬托娃和往日情人安列坡終於在一九六五年初在巴黎會面後，她在七十七歲去世前寫下（我們倆低垂下眼瞼），二人在相對默默無語之後是，

> 我們倆低垂下眼瞼，
> 鮮花拋在床頭，
> 彼此不知如何稱呼
> 一直熬到最後
> 我們倆終究都沒敢
> 把對方的名字招呼，
> 在神奇路途的終點前
> 彷彿放慢了腳步。

　　詩人寫得細膩生動，通過意象的組合、跳躍和轉化，從而造成一種意象美。這段愛情雖令詩人心碎，但讀後使人有一種蒼茫和悵然若失之感，這正是詩的魅力所在。正如艾青所說：「什麼感情都可以寫成詩。但是，高尚的感情出高尚的詩，卑鄙的感情出卑鄙的詩。」（註2）在阿赫馬托娃詩

So far, we have fully realized that Akhmatova is great no matter in her personality, her innocence in love, or her achievements in literature. She is the representative and embodiment of strong women in Russia. This is an objective evaluation in the history of today's literature and will always be engraved in the hearts of the Russian people.

3. Akhmatova: A Portrait with Full Charm

When the seventy-six-year-old Akhmatova and her former lover Anliepo finally met in Paris in early 1965, she wrote before she died at the age of seventy-seven *We Both Lowered Our Eyelids*, after a period of relative silence yes,

> *We both lowered our eyelids,*
>
> *Flowers on the bed,*
>
> *Don't know how to call each other*
>
> *Stay till the end*
>
> *Neither of us dared after all*
>
> *Say hello to someone by name,*
>
> *Before the end of the magical journey*
>
> *It seems to slow down.*

The poet writes delicately and vividly, creating a kind of image beauty through the combination, jump and transformation of images. Although this love story broke the poet's heart, after reading it, it makes people feel lost and lost, which is exactly the charm of poetry. As Ai Qing said: "Any emotion can be written into poetry. However, noble emotions produce noble poems, and base emotions produce low-level poems." (Note 2) In Akhmatova's

中，詩人以其鮮明的比喻、生動的意象、強烈的節奏和真摯的情感永遠吸引著讀者；除了對愛情、歷史、戰爭、現實抒懷外，從中又可使人生發一種不可名狀的美感力量，而其赤誠的愛，正如一隻歌唱著星月的光輝與祖國的希望的癡鳥，聽來感人，又形象生動。她生平最後一次公開發表演講，是在七十七歲參加莫斯科大劇院隆重舉行義大利詩人但丁誕辰七百周年晚會；四個多月後，因心肌梗塞逝世，安葬於列寧格勒郊區科馬羅沃村。離世三年後，她的愛人安列坡也告別人世。

　　通過上述的分析，可以得出，阿赫馬托娃的性格是可貴的。她的宿命是注定要孤寂的，痛苦是她的生存環境，在詩的殿堂裡是她全部的存在實質。也就是說，整個半世紀以來，阿赫馬托娃所創作的詩語言如神話般豐富多彩，在抒情和敘事的結合上達到了融合為一的境地。她是一個真正的歌者，無論是描寫愛情的痛苦折磨或瘋狂歡樂，或是銘人肺腑的控訴，都是她發自內心深處的聲音。我們已經看到了她的激情與驚惶，也看到她的孤獨與倔強不屈的心志。她的所有抒情詩，幾乎內裡都藏有情節，對於建築物與雕像，也有生動的藝術形象。她的許多詩，都記錄了「皇村雕像」、「斯莫爾尼教堂的穹窿」、「涅瓦河畔的圓柱」等建築物及青銅和石頭、大理石的美。然而我們也不應該忘記，在那民族受難的歷史關頭，她追求那不平凡的平凡。在那俄國革命之後，她仍繼續探索詩歌的音樂曲調。正因為俄國有這樣一個豪傑的女詩人，不但不能被輿論的激諷所屈服，相反，卻最終能獲

poems, the poet uses his vivid metaphors. The imgery, strong rhythm and sincere emotion will always attract readers; apart from expressing feelings about love, history, war and reality, it can also inspire an indescribable aesthetic power in life, and its sincere love is like a singing bird. The silly bird watching the brilliance of the stars and the moon and the hope of the motherland sounds touching and vivid. The last time she gave a public speech in her life was at the age of seventy-seven when she participated in a gala celebrating the 700th anniversary of the birth of the Italian poet Dante at the Bolshoi Theater; more than four months later, she died of myocardial infarction and was buried in Koma, a suburb of Leningrad Rovo village. Three years after her death, her lover Anrepo also passed away.

Through the above analysis, it can be concluded that Akhmatova's character is valuable. Her fate is doomed to be lonely, pain is her living environment, and it is her whole existence essence in the palace of poetry. That is to say, throughout the half century, the poetic language created by Akhmatova is as rich and colorful as mythology, and the combination of lyricism and narrative has reached a state of fusion. She is a true singer, and whether she is describing the pain and suffering of love or the crazy joy, or the indictment that is deeply rooted, it is her voice from the bottom of her heart. We have seen her passion and panic, as well as her loneliness and unyielding determination. Almost all her lyric poems have plots hidden in them, and there are vivid artistic images for buildings and statues. Many of her poems record the beauty of buildings such as *The Statue of Huangcun, The Dome of the Smolny Church, Columns on the Bank of the Neva River* and bronze, stone and marble. However, we should not forget that at the historical juncture of the suffering of the nation, she pursued the extraordinary ordinary. After the Russian Revolution, she continued to

得廣大群眾的尊敬。她精湛的詩歌藝術,最終獲得了長久的生命。因為她那富於強烈情感的抒情詩,她的名字成為整個東歐理想的象徵。我想,對廣大的詩歌愛好者來說,無疑是最有益的啟示。

註 1.克萊夫•貝爾,《藝術》,中國文聯出版公司,1984 年版。

註 2.《艾青研究專輯》,《就當前詩歌問題訪艾青》,第 402 頁。

林明理(1961-),雲林縣人,曾任屏東師院講師,詩人,詩評家,美國世界文化藝術學院文學博士。

—浙江《語言與文化研究》,浙江越秀外國語學院主辦,光明日報出版社出版,總第 11 輯,2018 年。

explore the musical tune of poetry. It is precisely because Russia has such a heroic poetess that not only cannot be succumbed to the irony of public opinion, on the contrary, she can eventually win the respect of the masses. Her superb poetic art finally won a long life. Because of her powerful lyric poems, her name became a symbol of ideals throughout Eastern Europe. I believe it is undoubtedly the most beneficial enlightenment for the majority of poetry lovers.

Note 1. Clive Bell, *Art*, China Federation of Literary and Art Circles Publishing Company, 1984 edition.

Note 2. *Ai Qing Research Album, Interview with Ai Qing on Current Poetry Issues*, p. 402.

Dr. Lin Ming-Li was born in 1961 in Yunlin, Taiwan. She holds a Master's Degree in Law and lectured at Pingtung Normal College. A poetry critic, on the 21st of October, 2013, she received a Doctor of Literature degree from America's World Culture and Art Institute.

20. 布邁恪抒情詩印象

　　日前，美國華裔詩人非馬寄來一些漢譯的佳篇，一氣讀完，特別對布邁恪（1918-2008）的詩歌倍感親切。這位傑出的英國詩人學者，曾任教於加拿大英屬哥倫比亞大學，著有二十多本詩集、小說及劇本，其詩作也被翻譯成多種東方的語言。

　　布邁恪的詩，有一種對純真美的追求，多通過意象組合和象徵、隱喻，創造出優美的詩境。如這首：

　　在夏天的花園裡
　　嗡嗡的蜂鳴
　　淹蓋了一架過境飛機的隆隆聲

　　在某個神秘的角落
　　蜂蜜
　　滲出了琥珀色調甜汁

　　當花園張開手臂
　　迎接太陽的長矛

20. Impressions of Michael Bullock's Lyric Poetry

A few days ago, Chinese-American poet William Marr sent me some of his excellent articles of Chinese translation, and I read them all at once. He was especially fond of the poems of Michael Bullock (1918-2008). This outstanding British poet-scholar once taught at the University of British Columbia in Canada. He has written more than 20 poetry collections, novels and plays, and his poems have also been translated into many oriental languages.

There is a kind of pursuit of pure beauty in Michael Bullock's poems, which create a beautiful poetic environment through the combination of images, symbols, and metaphors. Such as this one:

In the summer garden
the buzzing of a bee
drowns the hum of a passing plane

In some secret corner
honey
distils its amber sweetness

as the garden opens its arms
to welcome the sun's long lances

　　這是其中的一節,詩人把神秘的花園象徵化,賦予很大的感情容量,通過嗡嗡的蜂鳴,撥動他情感的絲弦,將情、象的有機組合後,又滲進其思想和某些哲思,讓感動流出了詩篇。且看在下一節中,也體現了詩人對詩歌冥想的熱愛:

　　　　花園在等待
　　　　用半閉的眼睛注視
　　　　一些未可預知的事情

　　　　一朵鮮花
　　　　在一個空壇上綻開

　　　　一股泉水
　　　　從一個牆角噴出

　　　　高大的栗樹俯下身去
　　　　用樹枝掃地

　　　　坐在紫丁香花下
　　　　我也半閉著眼等待
　　　　注視著花園

　　在這裡,情景齊到,詩人不熱衷於玄奧或晦澀的語言,反而借用夢幻、通感之妙,在欣賞一草一木的美好光明的事物之際,也讓讀者感受到花園具有生命感的活靈活現。

This is a part of the poem. The poet symbolizes the mysterious garden and endows him with a great emotional capacity. Through the buzzing and beeping, he plucks his emotional strings, and after the organic combination of emotion and imagery, it penetrates into his thoughts and feelings. Some philosophical thinking makes the emotion flow out of the poem. Let's look at the next section, which also reflects the poet's love for poetic meditation:

The garden waits
watching through half-closed eyes
for some unforeseen event

a new flower springing up
in an empty bed

a fountain bursting forth
from a corner of the wall

the tall chestnut bending down
and sweeping the earth with its branches

Sitting beneath the lilacs
I too wait with half-closed eyes
watching the garden

Here, the scenes are complete, the poet is not keen on mysterious or obscure language but borrows the magic of dreams and synaesthesia to let readers feel the vitality of the garden while appreciating the beautiful and bright things of every plant and tree, vividly

　　我特別喜歡布邁恪詩歌之因，是他擅於運用聲調、抒情
的語氣和節奏的變化，把各種情景比喻得惟妙惟肖，且鄉土
生活氣息很濃厚，震撼讀者心靈。如其中一節：

　　　　沙礫嘰哩咕嚕
　　　　在我腳底下
　　　　是被埋者在泥土深處
　　　　所發出的聲音

　　　　他們喁喁低語著
　　　　失落的遙遠的過去
　　　　喚起了
　　　　前世的幻影

　　　　自閉起的眼瞼後面
　　　　我見到了一幕幕恐怖的場面
　　　　人與獸間的
　　　　強掠與爭鬥

　　　　勉強地
　　　　我走進這世界
　　　　有如走進一面鏡子
　　　　在我身後

　　　　無路可遁

The reason why I especially like Michael Bullock's poems is that he is good at using tone, lyrical tone and rhythm changes to describe various situations vividly, and the strong flavor of rural life shocks readers' hearts. As one of the sections:

The crunching of the gravel
beneath my feet
is the voice of the buried
deep in the earth

They whisper of the distant
lost and vanished past
calling up visions
of an earlier world

Behind closed lids
I see hideous scenes
of rapine and conflict
between men and beasts

Unwillingly
I walk into this world
as though into a mirror
leaving behind me

no way of escape

中國自唐宋以來就有許多精彩的詩作,有的詩人以悲憫之情書寫鄉土和農村,有的詩人注重藝術上的昇華,寫得靈動而真切感人。但更令人欣慰的是,布邁恪透過一顆敏感的心,以獨具的意象打開了想像的空間,讓詩作延伸到對輪迴的思想與人類生存的哲思。內裡通過聯想確切地表達出了詩人內心悲傷的情緒,尾句說得特別深刻。

一首短詩,如能寫得優美而空闊,實屬不易。我記得非馬寫過一首《花開》:

> 天空
> 竟是這般遼闊
>
> 驚喜的小花們
> 爭著
> 把每一片花瓣
> 都伸展到
> 極
> 限

畫面是如此清麗,充滿生機及喜悅之情。而布邁恪的這首短詩:

> 棲息枝上
> 最後的一朵玫瑰
> 一隻鳥
> 擺出飛向秋天的
> 姿勢

Since the Tang and Song dynasties, there have been many wonderful poems in China. Some poets wrote about the countryside with compassion, and some poets paid attention to the sublimation of art, writing vividly and touchingly. But what is even more gratifying is that, with a sensitive heart, he opened up the space of imagination with his unique imagery, allowing his poems to extend to thoughts about reincarnation and philosophical thinking about human existence. Neil expresses the poet's inner sadness through association, and the last sentence is particularly profound.

It is not easy for a short poem to be beautifully and spaciously written. I remember William Marr has written a poem *Flowers Blooming*:

What a vast sky

The inspired little flowers
joyfully stretch each and every petal
to the fullest

e
x
t
e
n
t

The picture is so clear and beautiful, full of vitality and joy. And this short poem by Michael Bullock:

Perched on a branch
the last rose
a bird
poised for flight
into fall

　　詩人不但把感情注入景物，而且也注入了秋天的詩意。這都是動態美的佳句。他在捕捉生活，也樂於在繁忙的教學研究之餘，讓自己的想像力飛動起來。

　　看，布邁恪又描繪了一幅構思新穎的畫面！詩句給人以清奇之感，又不失簡約含蓄，也是我最欣賞布邁恪借物抒情的短詩之作：

> 冬天的黑枝
> 戳刺鴿灰的天空
>
> 一陣羽毛降落
> 把大地罩白
>
> 花園在它的柩蓋下
> 沉沉睡去

　　……詩人對美有深刻的理解，因而看世界的眼光特別精細。他靜默孤獨地站在花園，看著冬雪覆蓋大地的蕭條，也感嘆生命的河流流逝。我認為，善感的布邁恪，應該不是個做作、自負的學者；相反的，他情感豐富細膩，又有一顆赤誠的心，尤其重視優雅。

　　The poet not only injects emotion into the scenery, but also injects the poetry of autumn. These are all dynamic and beautiful sentences. He is capturing life, and he is also willing to let his imagination fly when he is busy with teaching and research.

　　Look, Michael Bullock has painted a new picture! The verses give people a sense of freshness and wonder yet are simple and implicit. They are also short poems that I admire the most about Michael Bullock's lyricism:

> *Black winter branches*
> *pierce the dove-grey sky*
>
> *A shower of feathers falls*
> *blankets the world in white*
>
> *The garden falls asleep*
> *beneath its glistening pall*

　　Poets have a deep understanding of beauty, so they have a particularly fine eye for seeing the world. He stood silently and alone in the garden, watching the depression covered by winter snow, and lamenting the flow of the river of life. In my opinion, the sensitive Michael Bullock should not be an artificial and conceited scholar; on the contrary, he is rich in emotion and has a sincere heart, with a special emphasis on elegance.

　　德國詩人里爾克說：「無一物逝去，萬物皆繼續存在。」
又說：「一切藝術皆是：愛」是的，雖然布邁恪已去世，但能
拜讀非馬翻譯其詩，是幸運的。因為，非馬始終被詩界作為
詩藝家而加以推崇；同樣的，在非馬翻譯布邁恪詩歌的進程
中，在他眼裡，並不在於其詩人學者的身份，更重要的是欣
賞布邁恪那獨特抒寫的視角及語言具有「精彩絕倫」的質感。
我熱切地希望非馬在晚年翻譯更多的佳詩，讓優秀的英詩助
漢詩繁榮發展。

　　　　註：文中詩作源自非馬於 1999 年編譯出版的《讓
　　　　　　盛宴開始 --我喜愛的英文詩》書中選錄。

　　　── 2021.02.26.

　　　── 臺灣《秋水》詩刊，第 189 期，2021.10，頁 76-77。

The German poet Rilke once said: "Nothing dies, everything continues to exist." He also said: "All art is: love." Yes, although Michael Bullock has passed away, but it is great to be able to read and translate his poems by William Marr luckily. Because, William Marr has always been respected by the poetic circles as a poetic artist; similarly, in the process of William Marr's translation of Michael Bullock's poems, in his eyes, it is not his identity as a poet and scholar, but more importantly, his appreciating Michael Bullock from a unique perspective and language have a "wonderful" texture. I earnestly hope that William Marr could translate more good poems in his later years, so that excellent English poems can help Chinese poetry flourish.

> Note. The poems in this article are selected from the book *Let the Feast Begin — My Favorite English Poems* compiled and published by William Marr in 1999.

21. 試析康拉德·艾肯的詩
〈先林的晨歌〉

摘要：本文對美國詩人康拉德·艾肯在詩歌創作上的文學成就及其詩作〈先林的晨歌〉進行了研究，試析其中的內涵與以真情為詩美的審美趣味。

關鍵詞：康拉德·艾肯 托馬斯·艾略特 象徵主義

一、其人其詩

曾獲普立茲獎的美國詩人康拉德·艾肯（Conrad Potter Aiken，1889-1973），一生出版過詩歌、小說、戲劇等，主要以詩歌聞名。他與曾獲諾貝爾文學獎的美國詩人托馬斯·艾略特（Thomas Stearns Eliot，1888-1965）交情甚篤，同為哈佛大學校友及文學史上具有崇高地位、象徵主義詩歌的代表人物之一。

眾所周知，象徵主義者最重視感覺與想像，並強調詩歌應具有音樂性、暗示性及有質感的形象美。而他們兩人的詩歌

21. Analysis of Conrad Aiken's Poem Morning Song of Senlin

Abstract: This article studies the American poet Conrad Aiken's literary achievements in poetry creation and his poem *Morning Song of Senlin*, and tries to analyze the connotation and aesthetic taste of poetry beauty based on true feelings.

Key words: Conrad Aiken, Thomas Eliot, symbolism

1. His People and His Poems

The American poet Conrad Aiken (1889-1973), who won the Pulitzer Prize, published poems, novels and plays in his lifetime, and is mainly famous for his poems. He has close friendship with Thomas Stearns Eliot (1888-1965), an American poet who won the Nobel Prize in Literature. He is also an alumnus of Harvard University and one of the representatives of symbolist poetry with a high status in the history of literature.

As we all know, symbolists attach the most importance to feeling and imagination, and emphasize that poetry should be musical, suggestive and textured. And the poetic charm of the two

魅力有著某種共同的特徵,那就是艾略特主張詩歌要靠「直覺」(intuition)來表現內心,而不應直接抒發和表現個人的情緒及個性;他的詩歌理論在文學史上,迄今依然保有其價值性。同樣的,艾肯詩歌也表現在象徵的廣泛運用與擅用比喻的特質上,且強調色彩及音樂性,因而開拓詩藝更廣闊的空間。也正因為他們兩人在象徵主義和衍變而來的當代詩歌藝術之間有一種連結,形成了一座溝通思想與經典文學的橋梁,才能夠使我們進而認識到現代詩藝傳承的某種規律,也得以去探討艾肯詩歌的藝術美以及其可貴的詩作。

二、詩歌賞析

這首詩〈先林的晨歌〉是艾肯在其著作《先林傳記》裡的一部分,由美國詩人非馬翻譯而成(注1)。在《先林傳記》中,非馬認為,艾肯也同艾略特一樣,喜歡用一連串物件來營造氣氛。本文則嘗試用心靈去感悟艾肯如何以心靈進行詩美的創造,去編織綺麗的意象。詩人寫道:

> 這是清晨,先林說,而在清晨
> 當光從百葉窗隙露水般滴入,
> 我起身,面向朝陽,
> 做我祖先們學著做的事。
> 屋頂上紫靄裡的星星
> 在鬱金色的迷霧中蒼白欲絕,
> 而我自己在一個疾傾的星球上
> 站在鏡前打我的領結。

of them has a certain common feature, that is, Eliot advocated that poetry should rely on intuition to express the heart, rather than directly express personal emotions and personality; his poetic theory in the history of literature still retains its value. Similarly, Aiken's poetry is also manifested in the extensive use of symbols and the characteristics of using metaphors, and emphasizes color and music, thus opening up a broader space for poetic art. It is precisely because the two of them have a connection between symbolism and the evolved contemporary poetic art, forming a bridge to communicate ideas and classic literature, so that we can further understand a certain law of modern poetic art inheritance. It is also possible to explore the artistic beauty of Aiken's poems and his precious poems.

2. Poetry Appreciation

This poem *Morning Song of Senlin* is part of Aiken's *Senlin: A Biography*, which was translated by American poet William Marr (Note 1). In *The Biography of Senlin*, William Marr believes that Aiken, like Eliot, likes to use a series of objects to create an atmosphere. This article tries to understand how Aiken uses his soul to create poetic beauty and weave beautiful images. The poet wrote:

> *It is morning, Senlin says, and in the morning*
> *When the light drips through the shutters like the dew,*
> *I arise, I face the sunrise,*
> *And do the things my fathers learned to do.*
> *Stars in the purple dusk above the rooftops*
> *Pale in a saffron mist and seem to die,*
> *And I myself on a swiftly tilting planet*
> *Stand before a glass and tie my tie.*

藤葉輕叩我窗，
露滴對著園石歌唱，
知更鳥在櫻桃樹上啁啾
重複著三個清晰的音調。

這是清晨。我站在鏡前
再一次打我的領結。
當遠處波浪在淺玫瑰色的微曦裡
沖擊著白沙的岸灘。
我站在鏡前梳我的頭髮：
好小好白呀我的臉！——
綠色的地球穿刺氣團
沐浴於太空的烈焰。
有屋懸在星上
有星懸在海底……
而遠處一個寂殼裡的太陽
為我斑飾四壁……

這是清晨，先林說，而在清晨
我不該在光中稍息以懷神祇？
我屹立於一個不穩的星球上
他廣漠且孤獨如雲
我將獻這一刻於我鏡前
給他一人，為他我將梳我的頭髮
接受這卑微的奉獻，靜默的雲！
我將想起你當我步下階梯。

Vine leaves tap my window,
Dew-drops sing to the garden stones,
The robin chirps in the chinaberry tree
Repeating three clear tones.

It is morning. I stand by the mirror
And tie my tie once more.
While waves far off in a pale rose twilight
Crash on a white sand shore.
I stand by a mirror and comb my hair:
How small and white my face! —
The green earth tilts through a sphere of air
And bathes in a flame of space.
There are houses hanging above the stars
And stars hung under a sea......
And a sun far off in a shell of silence
Dapples my walls for me......

It is morning, Senlin says, and in the morning
Should I not pause in the light to remember god?
Upright and firm I stand on a star unstable,
He is immense and lonely as a cloud.
I will dedicate this moment before my mirror
To him alone, for him I will comb my hair.
Accept these humble offerings, cloud of silence!
I will think of you as I descend the stair.

藤葉輕叩我窗，
蝸跡在石上閃耀，
露滴自櫻桃樹上墜降
重複著兩個清晰的音調。

這是清晨，我從寂靜的床上醒來，
光輝地我自無星的睡海裡起身。
四壁依然包圍著我一如黃昏，
我還是我，依然保有同樣的姓名。

地球同我旋轉，但不曾移動分毫，
星星在珊瑚色的空中懨懨欲滅。
在嘯鳴的虛空裡我站立鏡前，
漠然地，打我的領結。

有馬在遠處的山崗嘶叫
抖索著長而白的馬鬃，
而山在玫瑰白的迷濛中閃動，
它們的肩被雨淋黑……

這是清晨。我站在鏡前
再一次讓我的靈魂驚奇；
藍色的空氣在我天花板上馳過，
眾多的太陽在我地板底下……

Vine leaves tap my window,
The snail-track shines on the stones,
Dew-drops flash from the chinaberry tree
Repeating two clear tones.

It is morning.　I awake from a bed of silence,
Shining I rise from the starless waters of sleep.
The walls are about me still as in the evening,
I am the same, and the same name still I keep.

The earth revolves with me, yet makes no motion,
The stars pale silently in a coral sky.
In a whistling void I stand before my mirror,
Unconcerned, and tie my tie.

There are horses neighing on far-off hills
Tossing their long white manes,
And mountains flash in the rose-white dusk,
Their shoulders black with rains ...

It is morning.　I stand by the mirror
And surprise my soul once more;
The blue air rushes above my ceiling,
There are suns beneath my floor ...

……這是清晨，先林說，我從黑暗中起身
乘長風離去向我不知的何處，
我的錶已上好發條，鑰匙在我口袋裡，
而天空陰暗當我步下階梯。
陰影在窗間，雲在天上，
神在星際：而我將離去

想他正如我可能想起破曉
且哼我知道的一個曲調……

藤葉輕叩我窗，
露滴對著園石歌唱，
知更鳥在櫻桃樹上啁啾
重複著三個清晰的音調。

　　此詩塑造了一些突破傳統審美觀念的形象，詩裡的「先林」，其精神意義常被人加以臆想，也指望能從他的作品中找出其神秘的意涵。其實，「先林」並非一個人，而是艾肯追求「絕對音樂」(Absolute music)，又稱為「抽象音樂」的一種純粹的喜悅。它也泛指一群喜愛觀察大自然的性格總和，並將物象特徵以一種精練的語言呈現出。或許艾肯也相信詩歌的本質在於透過創作與精神世界進行直接溝通，所以他持之超脫物外，拋棄空間的限制，像所有偉大的詩人那樣，以直接想像加入比喻新奇的方式創作而得此詩。

It is morning, Senlin says, I ascend from darkness
And depart on the winds of space for I know not where,
My watch is wound, a key is in my pocket,
And the sky is darkened as I descend the stair.
There are shadows across the windows, clouds in heaven,
And a god among the stars; and I will go

Thinking of him as I might think of daybreak
And humming a tune I know ...

Vine-leaves rap at the window,
Dew-drops sing to the garden stones,
The robin chirps in the chinaberry tree
Repeating three clear tones.

This poem creates some images that break through the traditional aesthetic concept. The spiritual meaning of "Senlin" in the poem is often imagined by people, and it is expected to find out its mysterious meaning from his works. In fact, "Senlin" is not a person, but Aiken's pursuit of "absolute music", also known as "abstract music", is a kind of pure joy. It also generally refers to the sum of a group of characters who like to observe nature, and present the characteristics of objects in a refined language. Perhaps Aiken also believes that the essence of poetry lies in direct communication with the spiritual world through creation, so he detaches himself from the outside world, abandons the limitation of space, and, like all great poets, creates this through direct imagination and metaphorical novelty.

首先，詩裡細緻而不加絲毫矯情地描繪了一個清晨的景像，並典型地反映了艾肯美學觀念的一個特徵，它包含的是一種跳脫的現實，讓詩歌化為品味與美學的化身。更重要的顛覆性則是，他在構思作品時，會注入個人的某種特殊意義，讓他的作品看來更為靈巧、音韻優美又帶有冷漠超然的書卷氣質。

此詩雖然繼承了象徵主義多注重詩歌的音樂性，在創作中不僅透過抽象的思維來表現，也運用飽含情感和詩意的方式去描述，因此根本不必去刻意揣摩領略外界的詩歌世界，就已獲得國際間廣泛迴響。

三、結　語

康拉德•艾肯一生留下許多部詩集，他在詩歌藝術上的探索和貢獻，已被譽為美國當代最重要的文學家之一，其詩作中所抒發的細膩情感和對美好理想的追求，激起了無數讀者感情的共鳴；透過此詩的翻譯，不但把艾肯的詩描繪得飛動起來，而且朗讀的音樂性更具濃厚的感情色彩。誠如學者呂進所述：「詩的節奏是宇宙中的自然節奏的詩化。」（註 2）此詩音韻輕巧，富濃厚鄉村風情，反映詩人豐富的想像，有喜悅，也有傷感，神秘而浪漫；聚散之美，在於隨緣自在，淡泊優雅。

First of all, the poem depicts a scene in the early morning in a meticulous and unaffected manner, which typically reflects a characteristic of Aiken's aesthetic concept. What is more subversive is that when he conceives his works, he injects some special personal meaning, which makes his works look more ingenious, beautiful in rhythm and with a cold and detached bookish temperament.

Although this poem inherits symbolism and pays more attention to the musicality of poetry, it is not only expressed through abstract thinking, but also described in an emotional and poetic way in its creation. He has received widespread international response.

3. Conclusion

Conrad Aiken left many collections of poems in his life. His exploration and contribution to the art of poetry has been hailed as one of the most important contemporary American writers. The delicate emotions expressed in his poems and his desire for beautiful ideals The pursuit has aroused the emotional resonance of countless readers; through the translation of this poem, not only Aiken's poems are depicted in flight, but also the musicality of the reading is more emotional. As the scholar Lü Jin said: "The rhythm of poetry is the poeticization of the natural rhythm in the universe." (Note 2) This poem has a light rhyme and a strong rural style, reflecting the poet's rich imagination. There are joy, sadness, mystery, and romance; the beauty of gathering and parting lies in being free and elegant.

　　由上所述，可見艾肯詩歌的基調與音韻、色彩，都是隨
著詩人的想像與心緒的變化而變化的。而通過超感官知覺
（extrasensory perception）的出現，不論是充滿淡雅清麗的
境界也好，還是動中孕靜的想像也好，恰是一幅流動的山水
畫，都能牽動著我們的心，讓靈魂驚奇。這也鮮明地體現了
詩人艾肯的審美趣味及注重表達詩人自我個性和真情的藝術
特徵。

　　　　註 1.本文譯作《先林的晨歌》出自非馬編譯的《讓盛
　　　　　　宴開始──我喜爱的英文詩》（英漢對照），書林，
　　　　　　臺北，1999 年 6 月。
　　　　註 2.呂進著，《呂進詩學雋語》，秀威，臺北，2012
　　　　　　年 11 月初版，頁 69。

　　　─　2021.07.04.完稿

　　　─　臺灣《笠》詩刊，第 344 期，2021.08，頁 164-167。

From the above, it can be seen that the tone, rhyme, and color of Aiken's poems all change with the poet's imagination and mood. And through the emergence of extrasensory perception, whether it is full of elegant and beautiful realms, or imaginings that are moving and pregnant, it is just a flowing landscape painting that can affect our hearts and make our souls feel better surprisingly. This also clearly reflects the aesthetic taste of the poet Aiken and the artistic characteristics of focusing on expressing the poet's personality and true feelings.

Note 1. The translation of *Morning Song of Senlin* is from *Let the Feast Begin — My Favorite English Poems* compiled by William Marr, Shulin, Taipei, June 1999.

Note 2. Lü Jin, *Lü Jin's Poetics*, Xiuwei, Taipei, first edition in November, 2012, p. 69.

22. 一座沉思的雕像——讀若澤・薩拉馬戈的詩

美德在通往完美的艱辛道路上總是遇到困難，而罪孽和惡習非常受好運垂青。

——José Saramago 名言

　　若澤·薩拉馬戈(José Saramago1922–2010)一生創作了小說、戲劇寫作、詩集等多種文學著作，是葡萄牙史上極負盛譽的卓越作家、詩人，也是 1998 年諾貝爾文學獎得主。他生於里斯本北部的務農家庭，兩歲即隨父母到首都里斯本。因家境清貧，小學畢業後就進了職業學校學修車，並利用時間於圖書館自修。十七歲時，這位年輕的技工接觸到里卡多·雷耶斯（Ricardo Reyes）的詩，當時他並不知道里卡多是葡萄牙詩人佩索阿（Fernando Pessoa，1888－1935）的化名。多年後他寫了小說《里卡多·雷耶斯辭世的那一年》來紀念這位偉大的詩人。

　　1974 年 4 月 25 日葡萄牙爆發左翼革命，又稱四•二五革命，指葡萄牙首都里斯本發生的一次軍事政變，期間並有很多平民自發參與。此革命推翻了 20 世紀西歐為期四十多年的獨裁政權，之後引發了兩年混亂的「過渡時期」，政府更替頻繁。當

22. A Contemplative Statue — Reading José Saramago's Poems

> Virtue always encounters difficulties on the arduous path to perfection, while vice and vice are very much favored by good fortune.
>
> — José Saramago famous quote

José Saramago (1922–2010) has created novels, drama writing, poetry collections and other literary works throughout his life. He is an outstanding writer and poet with a high reputation in Portuguese history, and he is also the winner of the 1998 Nobel Prize in Literature. He was born in a farming family in the north of Lisbon, and moved to the capital Lisbon with his parents when he was two years old. Owing to his poor family, he entered a vocational school to learn car repair after graduating from elementary school, and spent time in the library for self-study. At the age of seventeen, the young mechanic came into contact with the poems of Ricardo Reyes, at the time he did not know that Ricardo was the pseudonym of the Portuguese poet Fernando Pessoa (1888-1935). Many years later he wrote the novel *The Year Ricardo Reyes Died* to commemorate this great poet.

The left-wing revolution broke out in Portugal on April 25, 1974, also known as the April 25th Revolution. It refers to a military coup in Lisbon, the capital of Portugal, during which many civilians participated spontaneously. The revolution toppled dictatorships that had lasted for more than four decades in Western Europe in the 20th century, followed by

時，若澤擔任左翼報社副主編，白色恐怖和暴力衝突不斷，有許多的同志被捕或流放，所幸，他沒有遭受被出賣的厄運。就在他被解除報社副主編的職務後，這一年，是若澤最重要的一年，他已五十二歲，又重新執筆寫作。之前他陸續做過汽車修理工、鉗工、公益機關辦事員、出版社經理、報社記者、編輯等。六十歲那年，他寫出了《修道院紀事》這部小說，獲得巨大成功，人們就將其與 1982 那年的諾貝爾文學獎得主哥倫比亞籍作家加夫列爾·加西亞·馬爾克斯（Gabriel García Márquez）的作品相提並論，他奇幻的想像終於引起文壇高度的矚目。讚美的呼聲迎接著他的一本本著作，一直到 1995 年他出版了《失明症漫記》，1998 年在他獲頒諾貝爾文學獎受獎演說中，這呼聲不變。

若澤生前曾說，自己是一個文字工匠，作品真實反映了葡萄牙現實，屬於所有人，屬於葡萄牙語文學。他把外祖父稱為「有生以來認識的最有智慧的人」。原因是他的幻想力要歸功於在炎熱的夏夜招呼他在樹下聽講故事的外祖父，而這位不識字的老農民說的故事充實了若澤無數個童年之夢。其諾貝爾獎成名的小說《失明症漫記》，評審頒給若澤的讚許裡寫道：「由於他那極富想像力、同情心和頗具反諷意味的作品，我們得以反覆重溫那一段難以捉摸的歷史。」這部作品被譯成多種語言，享譽國際。若澤於 2010 年在西班牙加那利群島的家中去世，享年八十七歲。葡萄牙政府決定派

a chaotic two-year "transition period" with frequent changes in the government. At that time, Jose was the deputy editor-in-chief of a left-wing newspaper. White terror and violent conflicts continued. Many comrades were arrested or exiled. Fortunately, he did not suffer the bad luck of being betrayed. Just after he was dismissed from the position of deputy editor of the newspaper, this year was the most important year for Jose. He was fifty-two years old and started writing again. Before that, he successively worked as a car mechanic, fitter, clerk of a public welfare organization, manager of a publishing house, newspaper reporter, editor, etc. At the age of sixty, he wrote the novel *The Chronicle of the Monastery*, which was a great success. Gabriel García Márquez's works, his fantastic imagination has finally attracted the attention of the literary world. The voice of admiration greeted his books one by one, until he published *Blindness Essays* in 1995, and in his acceptance speech for the Nobel Prize in Literature in 1998, the voice remained unchanged.

José Saramago once said before his death that he was a word craftsman, and his works truly reflected the reality of Portugal, belonged to everyone, and belonged to Portuguese literature. He called his grandfather "the wisest man I've ever known". The reason is that he owes his imagination to his grandfather who greeted him on hot summer nights and listened to stories under the tree, and the stories told by this illiterate old farmer enriched José's countless childhood dreams. In his Nobel Prize-winning novel *An Essay on Blindness*, the judges awarded Jose: "Thanks to his imaginative, sympathetic and ironic works, we can revisit that difficult period again and again. An elusive history." This work has been translated into many languages and is internationally acclaimed. José Saramago died in 2010 at his home in the Canary Islands, Spain, at the age of eighty-seven. The Portuguese government decided

飛機前往加那利群島，將他的遺體接回首都，並於里斯本舉
行葬禮。之後，他的骨灰一半在老家入土，另一半運回蘭索
羅特島，埋在自家花園他喜愛的橄欖樹下。人們不會忘記他
飛機前往加那利群島，將他的遺體接回首都，並於里斯本舉
行葬禮。之後，他的骨灰一半在老家入土，另一半運回蘭索
羅特島，埋在自家花園他喜愛的橄欖樹下。人們不會忘記他
對文學創作的貢獻，更不會忽略他用藝術之筆對詩界的影響。
具體說來，他的詩歌有以下突出的特點：

　　首先是對他獨特的生活風貌和藝術個性。比如他在年少時
代雖然貧困仍力爭上游和嚮往寫作的敘述。在這首（憂傷的小
提琴），就可捕捉到許多生動的生活畫面：

　　　　我將雙手放在你的音樂軀體上
　　　　昏昏欲睡的聲音正在那裡等候。
　　　　我在沉寂中開始，於是
　　　　真實的音調突然響起。
　　　　當心靈沿著感情的階梯
　　　　放開歌喉拾級而上時，
　　　　心靈不會撒謊，軀體不會撒謊。
　　　　假如在生硬的刺耳聲中，
　　　　在一個錯誤的諧音咯咯吱吱的響聲中，
　　　　喉嚨嘶啞和突然沉默，
　　　　那絕不是因為我們的過錯。

to send a plane to the Canary Islands to bring his body back to the capital and hold his funeral in Lisbon. After that, half of his ashes were buried in his hometown, and the other half was transported back to Lanzarote and buried under his favorite olive tree in his garden. People will never forget his contribution to literary creation, let alone ignore his influence on the world of poetry with his artistic pen. Specifically, his poems have the following outstanding features:

The first is his unique life style and artistic personality. For example, in his youth, although he was poor, he still strived for the top and yearned for writing. In this song *Sad Violin*, many vivid pictures of life can be captured:

I put my hands on your musical body
Sleepy voices are waiting there.
I started in silence, so
The real tone suddenly sounded.
When the heart goes down the emotional ladder
When you let go of your singing voice and climb up the
　　stairs,
The mind does not lie, the body does not lie.
If in harsh harshness,
In the creak of a false homophony,
Hoarse throat and sudden silence,
It was never our fault.

假如在沉寂中歌聲減弱
另一個聲音巧妙闖入並被記憶，
無需許久便會消失，緘默不語，
因為它不贊同憂傷的小提琴。

　　這裡有許多鮮為人知的心事 他觀察生活比較細緻敏感，
並善於思考，詩人的目光直擊民生的艱辛。其次是由詩作中
折射出他的隱忍的個性及正氣的氣質。由於直接寫他自己最
熟悉的生活，挖掘得深，就昇華得高。這首（軀體），是詩
人經過痛苦的蛻變，渴望進入到深層次的吸收與改造，也可
以說是對民族命運的關注，反思人類的盲目的根源，表現出
一種大無畏的批判精神：

眼睛睜開時，也許在它的背後
映出一束清晨的灰色光線
或是隱蔽在濃霧中朦朧的太陽。

其餘則是一片黑暗，
在柱形和弓形的骨骼之間，
彷彿黏性的動物抽動，
躲藏著內臟的茫然憂傷。
其餘皆由深深的洞穴構成，
伴隨著血液和記憶的節拍，
來自深淵的眩暈證明著
不可否認的時間計量。

If the singing fades in the silence
Another voice subtly breaks in and is remembered,
Will not be long to disappear, silent,
Because it disapproves of the sad violin.

There are many little-known things here. He observes life meticulously and sensitively, and is good at thinking. The poet's eyes directly touch the hardships of people's livelihood. Secondly, his forbearing personality and righteous temperament are reflected in his poems. Since he directly wrote about the life he was most familiar with, he dug deeper and became more sublimated. This poem *Body* is the poet's painful transformation, eager to enter into deep absorption and transformation, it can also be said to be concerned about the fate of the nation, reflect on the root of human blindness, and show a fearless critical spirit:

Maybe behind it when the eyes are open
Reflecting a ray of gray morning light
Or the dim sun hidden in the thick fog.

The rest is darkness,
Between the cylindrical and arched bones,
Like a viscous animal twitching,
A dazed sadness that hides viscera.
The rest are made of deep caves,
To the beat of blood and memory,
Vertigo from the abyss proves
Undeniable tim
e measurement.

> 一切都如此微妙且行動遲緩，
> 在眼睛明暗交接處迎出了
> 對一個被遺棄的軀體的記憶。

更值得一提的是，他深刻地隱喻了人類的生存環境和人性的回歸，將人類自以為掌握一切的盲目，提供了另類思維，也體現了對命運抗爭的精神。正如他所說：「《失明症漫記》這部作品裡發生的任何事情都能在現實生活中遇到。」由此看來，他對現實的隱喻在詩裡則表現出生命的無限珍惜。再次，他還善於把哲理融於形象。詩，是可以把觀念進入其中的。正如他的這首（乾枯的詩），使讀者對若澤有一個多側面的立體的了解：

> 我願這首詩無用且乾枯，
> 彷彿被反覆啃咬的樹幹短促的爆裂，
> 或是上面有人跳舞的地板咯吱吱作響。
> 我願繼續向前，
> 低下糅和著憤怒與沉默的雙眼，
> 因為一切全已表明，我已厭倦。

若澤把生命體驗與感情融入此詩，他面對現實中人性的善與惡，人類狂妄的盲目、蒙蔽的盲目，這一切都促使他發出生命的呼喊。他更著力於對人類未來命運的關注，似更多一些渴望著人生境遇的改變。詩人也在這首（放在你的肩上）

Everything is so delicate and slow-moving,
Greeted at the intersection of light and shade in the eyes
The memory of an abandoned body.

What is more worth mentioning is that he profoundly metaphors the living environment of human beings and the return of human nature, provides alternative thinking to the blindness of human beings who think they have everything under control, and also embodies the spirit of fighting against fate. As he said: "Anything that happens in the work *Blindness* can be encountered in real life." From this point of view, his metaphors for reality in his poems show his infinite cherishment of life. Again, he is also good at integrating philosophy into images. Poetry can incorporate concepts into it. Just like his *Dry Poem*, readers have a multi-faceted three-dimensional understanding of José Saramago:

I wish this poem was useless and dry,
Like a short burst of a repeatedly bitten tree trunk,
Or the creaking of the floor on which someone is dancing.
I would like to move on,
Downcast eyes blending anger and silence,
For all that has been said, I am weary.

José Saramago integrates life experience and emotion into this poem. He faces the good and evil of human nature in reality, the blindness of human arrogance and blindness, all of which prompt him to give out the cry of life. He pays more attention to the future destiny of mankind, and seems to be more eager to change the life situation. The poet also

深刻指出一種積極向上的生命感,然而,它深深觸動我的是,
它對崇高美的藝術美學追求:

> 放在你的肩上,我的手
> 便佔有了世界,我不打算
> 改換成另外的動作:
> 在這個手勢所廢除的空間
> 命運的形式得以顯現。

　　這段詩,不但較詳細地敍說了在那獨特年代若澤的苦悶
心情,和不趨炎附勢的高尚品格,而採用了象徵和隱喻等藝
術手法,表現出詩人與時代同步的自覺追求,達到了一種「言
近旨遠」的藝術境界。現在看一下這首〈在心中,也許〉,
更是一篇淋漓盡致的嘲諷現實的詩篇:

> 在心中,也許,或最好由我講明:
> 一處深深的刀傷,
> 自覺地將我們撕碎,
> 耗盡的生命從那裡跳出,
> 渴求、欲望、不知滿足,
> 徒勞地尋找著理由,
> 讓偶然為之替我們辯解,
> 也許這正是心中的痛苦。

　　在無奈和調侃的語氣中深藏著詩人嚴峻的批評,詩人把
悲痛之情進一步昇華並詩化了。在詩的內容中也以自我坦蕩
的形象與醜惡現實及人類無止的渴求、欲望與不知滿足作為

pointed out a positive sense of life in this poem *On Your Shoulders*. However, what deeply touched me was its artistic aesthetic pursuit of sublime beauty:

> *On your shoulders my hand*
> *Take over the world, I don't intend*
> *Change to another action:*
> *In the space abolished by this gesture*
> *The form of destiny is manifested.*

This poem not only describes in detail José's depressed mood in that unique era and his noble character of not following others, but also uses artistic techniques such as symbols and metaphors to show the poet's conscious pursuit of keeping pace with the times, achieving the artistic realm of "speaking is close and purpose is far". Now look at this poem *In My Heart, Maybe*, which is a poem that satirizes reality vividly and vividly:

> *In my mind, maybe, or better I spell it out:*
> *A deep knife wound,*
> *Consciously tore us apart,*
> *Spent life leaps from there,*
> *Craving, desire, insatiable,*
> *Searching in vain for a reason,*
> *Let chance justify it for us,*
> *Maybe this is the pain in my heart.*

The poet's severe criticism is hidden deep in the helpless and mocking tone, and the poet further sublimates and poetizes the grief. In the content of the poem, the image of self-effacement is compared with the ugly reality

對比，令人深思。他曾說：「希望就像鹽巴一樣，沒有營養，
但它給麵包增添了味道。」有人問他，為何寫出這部小說《失
明症漫記》時，若澤坦言：「我活得很好，可是世界卻不是
很好。我的小說不過是這個世界的一個縮影罷了。作為一個
人和一名作家，我不願不留下這個印記而離開人世。」詩人
為生命的被壓抑而呼吁，馱起現實生活的責任，渴求心靈的
撞擊與共鳴。

　　英國詩人雪萊（Percy Bysshe Shelley，1792－1822）說：
「一首詩則是生命的真正的形象，用永恆的真理發現出來。」
若澤在那特殊的年代與社會環境，不但養成了他那堅毅的個
性，而且潛移默化地滲透到他的文學創作中。他經歷過各種
生命的艱辛和苦難，非但沒有擊垮他的心智，反而在作品中
呈現出一種獨有的美。這也許是他在惡劣生活環境下的一種
自我解脫，從而又深含著對腐朽意識的批判與其生命力的體
現，是具有撼人心魄力量的。他的小說是現代文學區裡最具
價值的一部經典，而他的詩歌，是心靈的博動之聲，美得像
一座沉思的雕像，同樣讓詩神為他而驕傲。也因此，他的文
學價值便不言而喻了。

　　　　－2016.6.22 台湾

　　　　－臺灣《新文壇》季刊，第 45 期，2016.10，頁 67-74。

and the endless longing, desire and dissatisfaction of human beings, which is thought-provoking. He once said: "Hope is like salt, without nutrition, but it adds flavor to bread." When someone asked him why he wrote this novel *Blindness*, Jose said frankly: "I live very well, but the world is not very good. My novel is just a microcosm of this world. As a person and a writer, I don't want to leave this world without leaving this mark." The poet appealed for the oppression of life; take up the responsibility of real life, longing for the impact and resonance of the soul.

British poet Percy Bysshe Shelley (1792-1822) said: "A poem is the true image of life, discovered with eternal truth." José Saramago not only cultivated him in that special age and social environment. That resolute personality subtly infiltrated into his literary creation. He has experienced all kinds of hardships and sufferings in life, but instead of breaking his mind, he presents a unique beauty in his works. This may be a kind of self-liberation for him in the harsh living environment, and thus contains a deep critique of decadent consciousness and a manifestation of vitality, which has a shocking power. His novels are the most valuable classics in the modern literature area, and his poems are the pulsating voice of the soul, as beautiful as a contemplative statue, which also makes the god of poetry proud of him. Therefore, his literary value is self-evident.

23. 讀秦立彥譯
《華茲華斯抒情詩選》

畢業於劍橋大學的英國浪漫主義詩人威廉‧華茲華斯（William Wordsworth，1770-1850）一生有許多優美的抒情詩，流傳一百七十餘年而不衰。他的詩激盪著時代的旋律，與雪萊、拜倫等齊名，也是湖畔詩人的代表，在英國文學史上占據了顯赫的地位。詩，是他生活的藝術折射，也飽含著最純真的感情；基調儒雅而細膩，節奏輕盈，能開啟心胸與思想，讓人重新獲得心靈力量。

而秦立彥將其抒情佳篇集中出版，這無疑是對華茲華斯詩創作的新貢獻。此書最突出之點，是譯者本身也是學者、詩人，因此，她在翻譯上特別注重韻腳，以體現原作詩美的意象和意境，能做到這一點是難能可貴的。比如書裡的（一篇少作）一首：

> 整個大自然如靜止的車輪般平和，
> 幾頭母牛俯臥於沾滿露珠的青草；
> 我在經過的時候，只隱約看到
> 一匹馬站立著，將傍晚的牧草嚼嚙；

23. Reading Selected Lyric Poems of William Wordsworth Translated by Qin Liyan

The British romantic poet William Wordsworth (1770-1850), graduated from Cambridge University, has written many beautiful lyric poems in his life, which have been circulating for more than 170 years. His poems agitate the melody of the times. He is as famous as Shelley and Byron. As a representative of lakeside poets, he occupies a prominent position in the history of English literature. Poetry is the artistic reflection of his life, and it is also full of the purest feelings; the tone is elegant and delicate, and the rhythm is light, which can open the heart and mind and let people regain spiritual strength.

Qin Liyan published his best lyric poems together, which is undoubtedly a new contribution to Wordsworth's poetry creation. The most outstanding point of this book is that the translator is a scholar-poet; therefore, she pays special attention to rhyme in translation to reflect the beautiful imagery and artistic conception of the original poem. It is commendable that she can do this. For example, a poem in the book:

All nature is as peaceful as a stationary wheel,
A few cows lie prostrate in the dew-stained grass;
When I passed by, I only vaguely saw
A horse stands and chews the evening pasture;

地面黑沉沉的；彷彿睡眠悄悄漫過
谷地，山巒，沒有星星的高天。
現在，在這萬物的一片空白裡，
一種家中感到的，家所創造的和諧，
彷彿治癒了悲傷，而它一直從感官
獲得新的養料；只有此時，當回憶
寂然無聲，我才得到安寧。朋友們，
請你們克制試圖減輕我痛苦的焦心：
就由我一個人吧；不要讓我感覺
那多事的觸碰，那會讓我再度消沉。

　　讀後頗感有滋味，內裡包含了詩人藝術思維的多向化和愁思。由於他的母親在他八歲時去世，之後他那當律師的父親就把他送到附近的小鎮霍克斯黑德（Hawkshead）讀書，所以他的詩裡時常蘊聚著對霍克斯黑德鄉景的愛，甚至在劍橋唸書期間還會在夏季返回這鄉間漫步、遐思。

　　再如〈歌〉，最能代表詩人以情為動力，借物抒懷的特點，也證實了詩的永恆力量：

她住在人跡罕至的幽徑間，
鴿泉邊的去處，
沒有人為這位少女讚歎，
愛她的人屈指可數。

The ground is dark; as if sleep creeps over
Valleys, mountains, high heavens without stars.
Now, in the emptiness of all things,
A harmony felt at home, created by home,
As if cured of sorrow, which has been from the senses
Gain new nourishment; only then, when memories
In silence, I find peace. friends,
Please refrain from trying to assuage my pain:
Just leave me alone; don't make me feel
That troublesome touch, that would bring me down again.

After reading it, I feel very interested, and it contains the multi-directional and melancholy of the poet's artistic thinking. Because his mother died when he was eight years old, his father, a lawyer, sent him to study in the nearby town of Hawkshead, so his poems often contain references to Hawks. I love the rural scenery of Head, and even return to this countryside in summer to stroll and think about it while studying in Cambridge.

Another example is *Song*, which best represents the characteristics of poets who use emotion as the driving force and express their feelings through objects, and also confirms the eternal power of poetry:

She dwelt in the deserted lanes,
A place by the Dove Fountain,
No one admired the maiden,
There are only a handful of people who love her.

一朵紫羅蘭，在生滿蒼苔的石旁，
半被遮住了容色，
——星一般美麗，當天上
只有一顆明星閃爍。
她一生無聞，也少有人知，
露西的生命何時走盡；
但是，啊，她如今在墳墓裡，
這於我是多麼不同。

　　此詩唱出了年輕詩人對露西熾熱的思念之情，也寫出了
在視覺和含蓄的藝術表達中所造成的形式美。華茲華斯的詩，
有別於法國象徵派詩歌的先驅波特萊爾（1821-1867）重視音
樂性和韻律感，他擅於把具體景物概括昇華為一種不同尋常
的藝術境界。他是個心思細膩、對大自然及親友都充滿憐惜
與溫柔的人。如人們稱讚的這首〈麻雀的巢〉：

看，五枚泛青的鳥蛋閃著光！
我很少見過比這更美的景象；
這單純的場景，比它更歡樂，
更令人愉快的，不會很多。
我吃了一驚，彷彿看見
那家和隱蔽的床榻，
是麻雀居住在裡面，
就在我父親的房子旁邊；
妹妹埃米琳和我，晴天雨天，
都一起去看它。

A violet, by a mossy stone,
Half-hidden face,
— Beautiful as a star, in the sky
Only one star twinkles.
She was unknown all her life, and few people knew her,
When will Lucy's life end;
But, ah, she is now in the grave,
How different it is to me.

This poem expresses the young poet's ardent yearning for Lucy, and also expresses the beauty of form in the visual and implicit artistic expression. Wordsworth's poems are different from Baudelaire (1821-1867), the pioneer of French symbolist poetry, who emphasized music and rhythm. He is good at summarizing specific scenes into an unusual artistic realm. He is a delicate person who is full of compassion and tenderness towards nature and relatives and friends. Such as this song *Sparrow's Nest* praised by people:

Look, five bluish eggs are shining!
I have seldom seen a more beautiful sight;
This simple scene, more joyous than it,
More pleasant, not by much.
I was startled, as if seeing
The house and the hidden bed,
It is the sparrow that dwells in it,
Next to my father's house;
Sister Emmeline and I, rain or shine,
All go see it together.

她看著那鳥巢，彷彿害怕它，
滿心期待，又不敢靠近它；
她有如此的心，當時她只是
人們中一個言語絮絮的孩子。
我後來歲月中的福澤，
在我童年時就與我同在，
她給了我眼睛，給了我耳朵，
謙卑的關懷，細膩的畏怯，
一顆心，從中湧出甜蜜的淚波，
還有愛，沉思，歡快。

從中可看出，華茲華斯也是個情感充沛的詩人，善感而擁有寧靜樸素的心。詩裡讓我覺著大自然一切活潑生靈，都是鮮明的。詩中浸透了詩人對他的家鄉親友的由衷讚美，而這份浪漫的愛與沉思恰恰是詩人在未來歲月中要為幸福而前進的決心所帶給讀者的感動。

閱讀友人寄來這本譯書，已是遠方大雪紛飛的十二月，卻給人一種值得回味的親切感受。她在另寄的一本今年出版的書裡寫下這樣的一段詩句：

如果打開一本新書
發現它是自己喜愛的
那有多麼幸福

She looked at the nest as if afraid of it,
Full of anticipation, but dare not approach it;
She had such a heart when she was just
A chattering child among people.
Fuze in my later years,
Was with me in my childhood,
She gave me eyes, she gave me ears,
Humble care, delicate timidity,
A heart from which sweet tears flow,
And love, contemplation, and cheerfulness.

It can be seen from this that Wordsworth is also a poet full of emotions, with good feelings and a quiet and simple heart. The poem makes me feel that all the lively creatures in nature are vivid. The poem is permeated with the poet's heartfelt admiration for his relatives and friends in his hometown, and this romantic love and contemplation is exactly what the poet's determination to move forward for happiness in the years to come moves the readers.

Reading this translated book sent by a friend, it is already December when there is heavy snow in the distance, but it gives people a kind feeling which is worthy of an aftertaste. In a separate book published this year, she wrote the following verse:

If you open a new book
Found it to be my favorite
How happy that is

> 彷彿忽然認識了一個新的人
> 越過幾個世界的距離
> 來到他的靈魂旁邊
> 聽見那裡發出的低語

這裡有著詩人內心的獨白，而我正為她除了翻譯研究以外，仍執著地追求詩美的新探索，而感到欣喜，也祝願她在今後的創作與教學中取得更大豐收！

－2021.12.01 寫於臺東

－臺灣《金門日報》副刊，2021.12.19。

It's like meeting someone new all of a sudden
Across the distance of several worlds
Come to his soul
Hear the whispers from there

There is a poet's inner monologue here, and I am delighted that she is still persistently pursuing new explorations of poetic beauty in addition to translation studies, and I wish her greater harvest in her future creation and teaching.

24. 庫爾特·F·斯瓦泰克的詩歌藝術

在當今國際新詩潮成為一股澎湃的詩歌浪潮之中，體現了詩人們思維的藝術表現是最為明顯的，其中，有一位投身於文學創作裡耕耘最耀眼的詩人之一，是庫爾特·F·斯瓦泰克（Kurt F. Svatek，1949-）。

他的一生是傳奇的，許多文評家曾稱他的文學成就豐富了審美詩歌的內涵，並在促進國際和平之間形成了一個長久推展的橋樑。而我卻明白地認為，Svatek 詩歌的勝境與其至性深情的關聯無法忽略，也正是因為藝術灌注了生命給他，才能夠使我從欣賞的角度去探討 Svatek 對於自己詩歌的藝術創新。

出生於維也納的 Svatek，憑藉著一股過人的志氣，苦學有成。他從年輕時就開始嶄露頭角，進而贏得了國際間無數獎項，而其詩歌被翻譯成多種語言，在他浩瀚的書籍之中，有許多首詩歌則成了當代文學的經典之作。比如在今年新春義大利出版的《詩選》中，他歌詠了窮苦的、無家棲身的人，也把現實人生中悲傷的一面與創作詩歌的美好境界勾勒出來。身為詩人，他為追求詩歌的審美趣味的直抒胸臆，既有感性，又有其真切同情弱者的儒者情懷。

24. The Art of Poetry by Kurt F. Svatek

In today's international tide of new poetry, which has become a surging wave of poetry, the artistic expression of poets' thinking is the most obvious. Among them, one of the most dazzling poets devoted to literary creation is Kurt F. Svatek (1949—).

His life is legendary, and many literary critics have said that his literary achievements have enriched the connotation of aesthetic poetry and formed a long-lasting bridge between promoting international peace. However, I clearly believe that the relationship between the beauty of Svatek's poetry and his deep affection cannot be ignored, and it is precisely because art has instilled life into him that I can explore Svatek's artistic innovation of his own poetry from the perspective of appreciation.

Svatek, born in Vienna, succeeded in studying hard with his extraordinary ambition. He emerged from a young age, and has won numerous international awards, and his poems have been translated into many languages. Among his vast books, many poems have become classics of contemporary literature. For example, in *Selected Poems* published in Italy in the Spring Festival this year, he sang about the poor and homeless people, and also outlined the sad side of real life and the beautiful realm of poetry creation. As a poet, he expresses his heart directly in pursuit of the aesthetic taste of poetry. He has both sensibility and Confucian feelings of genuine sympathy for the weak.

〈為我歌唱這一天〉一首，是詩人放在這本詩選的第一首，描寫愛情的憂鬱與剎那間心的搏動，抒發了愛情的美麗與憂傷、夢想與渴望之間的反思：

> 過去的，消失了。
> 不要為我歌唱明天，
> 夢想的
> 可能永遠不會實現
> 只會讓心痛
> 或使心煩躁不安。
> 為我歌唱那剛開始綻放的玫瑰，
> 被柔和的風親吻
> 為我翻譯漸漸融入沙灘的
> 海浪之歌，
> 鳥兒的歌聲
> 或不知疲倦的蟬鳴。
> 為我唱這首
> 對這一天的愛的歌，
> 而不是遙遠的嚮往。只給我唱這首
> 現在，
> 獨一無二的時刻，
> 因為只有在這裡，生命才會搏動。

Sing to Me of This Very Day is the first poem that the poet put in this anthology. It describes the melancholy of love and the pulsation of the heart in an instant, and expresses the beauty and sadness of love, the gap between dreams and longing reflection:

Do not sing to me of yesterday.
What was, is gone.
Do not sing to me of tomorrow,
Of dreams
That may never come true
And only make the heart ache
Or cause the mind to flutter restlessly.
Sing to me of the rose
That is just starting to bloom,
Kissed by a soft wind.
Translate for me the song of the waves
Gradually melting into the beach,
The song of the birds
Or the chirping of the tireless cicadas.
Sing to me the song
Of love for this very day,
Not of faraway yearning.
Sing to me the song only
Of this present,
Unique moment,
For it is only here that life is throbbing.

　　這首詩對愛情的痛苦與悸動的幸福的率性揭示中體現了對愛情虛偽和嚮往的反思，也是一種浪漫主義的美麗的想像。再如（瓶子裡給你自己的信息），這首詩中描寫了從回憶的沙漏中的審美感受，以達到一種唯美的寧靜詩意：

> 就連最美麗時刻的
> 記憶
> 都會隨著歲月的流逝而褪色，
> 因為記憶
> 有時會遺漏細節。
> 你該用瓶子
> 裝滿當時的氣氛
> 然後你該為特別的時節
> 打開它
> 有如打開一瓶陳年的老酒。

　　若引用後期印象派名家文生•梵谷的名言是：「痛苦即是人生」。在這首詩裡，我所看到的是，詩人所回憶中的一切都是寧靜與感性。或許，對 Svatek 來說，故鄉城鎮的景物培育了他的靈感，奧地利文化藝術的南部環境也為其詩歌創作注入了強烈的鄉土情懷。他在（片刻）這首詩中描寫了熱愛鄉土這種精神狀態，這是他嚮往從大自然中尋找靈思的具體形象，又象徵詩人開始振醒，並顯示其鮮明而純淨的靈魂之光：

The poem reveals the pain and throbbing happiness of love embody the reflection on the hypocrisy and yearning of love, and it is also a kind of romantic and beautiful imagination. Another example *Time Is a Princess with Many Garments*, this poem describes the aesthetic feeling from the hourglass of memories, in order to achieve a beautiful and peaceful poetry:

> *Despite the stillness, you sense time going by,*
> *You see how the light*
> *Changes in the course of a day,*
> *Or how the rocks*
> *Change color to the rhythm of the hours.*
> *Towards sunset time, drive to the reservoir*
> *And scream until all the sadness has been expelled from*
> *your being.*
> *The evening breeze*
> *Will spread it across the surface*
> *And, ultimately, let it sink down,*
> *Yet after a few minutes,*
> *It will return with the frogs' croaking.*
> *The moon will never come to you,*
> *But maybe one time you will be able*
> *To visit her.*

If I quote the famous post-impressionist Vincent van Gogh's famous saying: "Pain is life". But in this poem, what I see is that everything the poet recalls in his memory is tranquility and sensuality. Perhaps, for Svatek, the scenery of his hometown town cultivated his inspiration, and the southern environment of Austrian culture and art also injected strong local feelings into his poetry creation. He described the spiritual state of loving the country in *For a Moment*; this poem, a concrete image of his longing to find spiritual thoughts from nature, also symbolizes that the poet is awakening and showing the light of his pure soul:

一朵小白雲
正帶著你的夢想飛走。
飛鳥抓不到它，
蝴蝶更別夢想，
最重要的是
蒲公英的小降落傘，
——某時，某地——，
遵從風的低語指示，會飄到地上：
也許在高草上，
也許
飄進季節性乾燥的小溪河床，
那裡有一顆小鵝卵石
在陽光下向他們閃閃發光
如翡翠。

　　類似這種以真情為美的情感表現，已在 Svatek 諸多以多
種藝術形式所創造的詩美之中。其中，我最喜歡的一首，是
他在長期寫詩的創作中，以這首（詩）寫道：

詩懸掛在絲線上
在樹上
以及風聲裡。
他們打開到房間的
百葉窗
在我們自己身上。

A small, white cloud
Is flying away with your dreams.
The birds cannot reach it,
The butterflies even less so,
And least of all
The little parachutes of dandelion,
Which — sometime, somewhere —,
Following the whispered instructions of the wind,
Will float to the ground:
Perhaps onto the high grass,
And perhaps
Into a seasonally dry bed of the brook,
Where a tiny pebble
Is glittering at them in the sun
Like an emerald.

This kind of emotional expression with true feelings as beauty has been included in many poetic beauty created by Svatek in various art forms. Among them, my favorite one is that he wrote this poem in his long-term creation of poetry:

Poems hang on silk threads
In the trees
And sound in the wind.
They open the window shutters
To rooms
Which are in ourselves.

用文字建造一座大教堂。
這樣黑度
失去它的重量。
它們是生命洪流中
閃爍的蠟燭
他們是人生的夢想。

在過去的文評界，大多認為 Svatek 是最講究詩的想像力
和真情的美感的，因為，他自己就是一位對詩歌藝術進行過
專門探討的大家，而且他也對翻譯的要求是很嚴謹的。他有
時確實像一位多采詩歌形式的建築大師，逐一細心建構他的
詩歌堡壘，從而創造出別具一格的美感，也體現了他以真情
為美的詩歌藝術特徵，故而廣為國際文壇敬佩。

－2023.01.04 作

－臺灣《金門日報》副刊，2023.01.16。

Building a cathedral from words.
So the blackness
Loses its weight.

They are in the stream of life
The flickering candle.
They are dreams of life.

In the past literary critics, most people thought that Svatek was the one who paid the most attention to the poetic imagination and the beauty of true feelings, because he himself is a master who has specially discussed the art of poetry, and he also has very strict requirements for translation. Sometimes he is indeed like a master architect with various poetic forms, carefully constructing his poetic fortresses one by one, thus creating a unique aesthetic feeling, which also reflects his poetic artistic characteristics of taking true feelings as beauty, so he is widely admired.

— January 4, 2023.

Dr. Lin Mingli (1961-), Taiwanese scholar and poetry critic

25. 試析喬凡尼·坎皮西抒情詩三首

喬凡尼·坎皮西（Giovanni Campisi）是 21 世紀活躍於國際的意大利詩人，應該說，他是通曉多種語言，並被世界各地推薦給諾貝爾獎委員會的著名人物。他對新詩的編輯、創作與評論始終不懈怠，是位熱愛祖國鄉土、大自然及關懷社會的悲憫詩人。

居住在西西里島北部墨西拿和巴勒莫之間的內布羅迪山脈中俯瞰第勒尼安海的一個小鎮的喬凡尼，是一位獨特的詩人。多年來，有許多評論家曾把他歸列為國際詩人之列；原因是，他與來自世界各地的知名作家一起出版了許多書籍，其中，以柔美、精短的抒情詩最為許多人所稱頌。

他的孤獨與快樂是渾成的一片，其詩充滿了浪漫主義的思想感情和強烈的鄉土情懷，總能喚起讀者感情上的共鳴。如（冬天的晚上）中寫道：

　　無聲地
　　雪降落
　　在一個寂靜
　　村莊
　　坦露的白色

25. Analysis of Three Lyrical Poems by Giovanni Campisi

Giovanni Campisi is an Italian poet active internationally in the 21st century. It should be said that he is proficient in multiple languages and has been recommended to the Nobel Prize Committee from all over the world. He has never slackened in editing, creating and commenting on new poems. He is a compassionate poet who loves his motherland, nature and society.

Giovanni, who lived in a small town overlooking the Tyrrhenian Sea in the Nebrodi Mountains between Messina and Palermo, in the northern part of Sicily, was a unique poet. Over the years, many critics have ranked him among the international poets; the reason is that he has published many books with well-known authors from all over the world, and among them, he is most praised by many for his soft and short lyric poems.

His loneliness and happiness are integrated, and his poems are full of romantic thoughts and feelings and strong local feelings, which can always arouse the emotional resonance of readers. As written in *Winter Evening*:

Silent

Snow falls

On the village hushed

And candidly white

從窗口
你只看到
柔和的光線
還有路燈
沿著空無一人的街道
晶亮的雪花
輕柔地在地面上
歇息。

　　這首詩作中隱隱有一種孤獨之感，有很大程度上體現了喬凡尼「精於煉句」的詩意，語言自然貼切，甚有詩家氣魄。

　　此外，還有另一首（孤單），這同樣是詩人在詩的審美特徵上的折光反映，還造就了「清新淡雅」、「翻新出奇」的語言風格：

你似乎對照亮
我疲憊的
被刺骨
碰撞靈魂的
悲傷掏空的
臉上
那片陽光
感興趣。
雙手

From windows
You just see
The soft lighting
And the street lights
Along the deserted streets
Enlighten snowflakes
That rest gently
On the ground.

There is a faint sense of loneliness in this poem, which to a large extent embodies Giovanni's poetic flavor of "good at refining sentences", the language is natural and appropriate, and it is very poetic.

In addition, there is another poem *Alone*, which is also a refraction of the poet's aesthetic characteristics of the poem, and also created a "fresh and elegant" and "surprisingly refurbished" language style:

You looked
Interested
In my slice of sun
That illuminated
My tired face
Hollowed out by gri
My poor hands
Still trembling
Caress your face

我可憐的雙手
還在抖索著
撫摸你
被淚水犁出溝渠的
臉。
我們之間的沉默
很重
似乎即將
指出
一條未知的途徑，
然而太陽在那裡
溫暖我們的心
像有一次
當你和我
單獨
在世上
如現在。

　　儘管喬凡尼三十多年來編輯出版許多具有創新意識的詩
集、詩學著作，閱歷增多，思考也更深遠遼闊了，但他始終
是一個抒情詩人，也喜歡以抒情筆法來敘事的。如這首（陽
光），又蘊聚著他起伏迭宕的抒情，語言真摯而新穎：

讓我看你的眼睛
閃耀著愛

Furrowed by
Copious tears.
The silence between us
Is heavy
It seems almost ready
To indicate a path
With unknown implications,
Yet the sun is there
To warm our hearts
Like a time
When you and me
Were in the world
Alone
Like now.

Although Giovanni has edited and published many innovative collections of poetry and poetics over the past 30 years, his experience has increased and his thinking has become more profound and broad, but he has always been a lyric poet, and he also likes to use lyrical brushwork to narrate. For example, this song *A Ray of Sun* also contains his ups and downs of lyricism, with sincere and novel language:

Show me your eyes
Sparkling with love

我會永遠給你
我的心。

給我看你所有的
輝煌
我會讚美你
好幾個鐘頭。

讓我看你的好心情
每天
我會給你看
白天的太陽。

給我看
你最壞的一面
我會把你
暗淡的生活
轉變成一縷陽光。

喬凡尼的抒情詩是多彩的，往往也正是由自己的孤獨感受了社會生活中普遍存在的痛苦、願望及愛的力量的存在，才生成了這些詩作的無與倫比。

他的詩歌風格的形成與他大量閱讀與翻譯詩歌不無關係，對此，歷來的詩歌評論家往往較多地注意到喬凡尼身為詩人、

And I will always give you
My heart.

Show me all
Your splendor
And I'll be admiring you
For hours.

Show me your good mood
Every day
And I will show you
The sun of the day.

Show me
The worst side of you
And I'll turn
Your colorless life
Into a ray of sunshine.

　　Giovanni's lyric poems are colorful, and it is often because of his own loneliness that he feels the pain, desire and the power of love that are common in social life, which makes these poems unparalleled.

　　The formation of his poetic style is not unrelated to his extensive reading and translation of poems. For this, poetry critics have often paid more attention to Giovanni's origin as a poet and

出版家的淵源；然而，我認為，喬凡尼的詩，妙在描寫情境
上，詩意高遠，有著非常鮮明的抒情傾向性。在他溫和謙虛
的外表下，其實深藏的是他始終不忘家鄉及關懷世界的儒者
之心。

　　一直以來，他通過詩歌的創作與出版的實踐，以果敢與魄
力，不斷地努力以赴；因而，在國際文壇上給予他一個極高
的評價。

　　　　－2022.1.03 寫於台灣

　　　　－義大利《國際詩新聞》〈INTERNATIONAL POETRY
　　　　NEWS〉，2022.12.31，中英文版。
　　　　（林明理博士（1961-），出生於台灣，學者，詩歌評
　　　　論家）

publisher; however, I think that Giovanni's poems are wonderful in describing the situation, with a lofty poetic flavor and a very distinct lyrical tendency. Beneath his gentle and modest appearance, there is actually a Confucian heart that never forgets his hometown and cares about the world.

For a long time, through the practice of poetry creation and publication, he has been working hard with courage; therefore, he has been given a very high evaluation in the international literary world.

— 2022.12.31. Written in Taiwan

Dr. Lin Mingli (1961-), born in Taiwan, scholar, poetr

26.米拉‧洛赫維茨卡婭抒情詩印象

一、其人其詩

米拉‧洛赫維茨卡婭（1869-1905）是俄羅斯白銀時代對新詩發展做出重大貢獻的女詩人。她生於聖彼得堡的貴族家庭，父親是法學教授，母親是法國人，熱愛詩歌。米拉自幼聰慧，就讀於莫斯科亞歷山大學院，二十三歲與一名英俊的建築師結婚，原本幸福美滿；二十七歲就獲得俄羅斯科學院頒發的普希金獎。她的詩歌給人以浪漫、輕柔明麗和雅緻的審美感受，是顯而易見的。

在一次偶然機會，米拉與俄羅斯象徵主義詩歌的領袖之一康斯坦丁‧巴爾蒙特（1867-1942）一見鍾情；然而這段悽美的戀情，導致其婚姻破裂。之後，米拉因罹患肺結核，抑鬱咽氣於三十六歲，身後遺留下五名年幼子女。去世的同年，她仍再度獲得了普希金文學獎的讚譽；而遷移至國外的情人巴爾蒙特，為昭顯對米拉‧洛赫維茨卡婭的思念，亦將自己的女兒取名為「米拉」。

米拉的愛情詩，不僅象徵意味濃厚，給人一種多層次的美感，還不時流露出其坦率的個性，促使情象的流動可感、可聞。她像一匹酷愛自由而不羈的白馬，不顧世人的眼光，

26. Impressions of Mila Lokhvitskaya's Lyrical Poems

1. Her People and His Poems

Mira Lokhvitskaya (1869-1905) was a female poet who made great contributions to the development of new poetry in the Silver Age of Russia. She was born in an aristocratic family in St. Petersburg. Her father was a law professor and her mother was French. She loved poetry. Mila was smart since she was a child, and studied at the Alexander Academy in Moscow. She married a handsome architect at the age of 23 and was originally happy; she was awarded the Pushkin Prize by the Russian Academy of Sciences at the age of 27. It is obvious that her poems give people a romantic, soft, bright and elegant aesthetic feeling.

By chance, Mira fell in love with Konstantin Balmont (1867-1942), one of the leaders of Russian symbolist poetry; however, this poignant love affair led to the breakdown of his marriage. Afterwards, Mira suffered from tuberculosis and died of depression at the age of 36, leaving behind five young children. In the same year of her death, she still won the praise of the Pushkin Literature Prize again; and her lover Balmont, who moved abroad, also named his daughter "Mila".

Mira's love poems are not only rich in symbolic meaning, giving people a multi-layered aesthetic feeling, but also revealing her frank personality from time to time, making the flow of emotions perceptible and audible. She

奮力往前衝，甚而讓這段戀情成為促動創作前進的動力。而本文透過谷羽教授翻譯米拉最具動態美的佳句，恰好地表現了她的奇特想像，並通過有韻律的詩來抒發其感性的一面，生動地展現在讀者面前，為俄羅斯詩史上放出奪目的光彩。

二、詩作賞讀

印度詩人、思想家泰戈爾（1861-1941）在其詩集裡曾說：「愛就是充實的生命，一如盛滿了酒的酒杯。」（註）而年輕的米拉往往是把愛情的理想上升到完美的程度，是很少在結句時突然把對愛情的想像之門關閉的。如（假如我的幸福…）一首，最能代表她的少女情懷：

> 假如我的幸福是自由的鷹，
> 假如它翱翔在碧藍的天空，
> 我願搭弓射箭讓箭鏃唱歌，
> 一定射中它不管是死是活！
>
> 假如我的幸福是奇異的花，
> 假如它盛開在陡峭的懸崖，
> 我發誓攀上絕壁無所畏懼，
> 摘來鮮花並暢飲它的香氣！
>
> 假如我的幸福是貴重指環，
> 假如這指環埋在河泥下面，

is like a free and unrestrained white horse, regardless of the eyes of the world, and strives to move forward, and even makes this relationship a driving force for the creation. This article, through Professor Gu Yu's translation of Mira's most dynamic and beautiful lines, just expresses her peculiar imagination, and expresses her emotional side through rhythmic poems, vividly displayed in front of readers, and set a new record for the history of Russian poetry with dazzling brilliance.

2. Appreciation and Reading of Poems

Indian poet and thinker Rabindranath Tagore (1861-1941) once said in his poetry collection *Love Is a Full Life, Just Like a Wine Glass Full of Wine.* (Note) The young Mira often raised the ideal of love to the degree of perfection rarely closes the door to the imagination of love suddenly at the conclusion of a sentence. For example, *If My Happiness...* is a song that best represents her girlish feelings:

> *If my happiness were a free eagle,*
> *If it soars in the blue sky,*
> *I would like to shoot the bow and let the arrows spin and sing,*
> *Make sure to shoot it dead or alive!*
>
> *If my happiness were a strange flower,*
> *If it blooms on a steep cliff,*
> *I swear to climb the cliff without fear,*
> *Pick a flower and drink its fragrance!*
>
> *If my happiness were a precious ring,*
> *If this ring were buried under the river mud,*

我必化作美人魚潛入河底，
戴上這指環讓它光彩熠熠！

假如我的幸福藏在你心中，
我讓神火燒灼它晝夜不停，
讓這顆心獻給我忠貞不渝，
只要一想到我就跳蕩不已！

正因為米拉是這樣一位多情的豪傑詩人，不但嚮往被愛情征服，最終也選擇保衛住自己的愛情並昭示了自己對愛執著的決心。當她義無反顧，意識到愛情的強大力量，二十七歲的米拉寫下了這首（這韻律屬於你，無人可比…），她與巴爾蒙特之間的苦戀，就更震動整個俄羅斯文壇了：

這韻律屬於你，無人可比，
我能辨認出這流暢的話語，
你的歌曲如溪水淙淙流淌，
發出水晶一般悅耳的音響。

我一眼認出你透明的詩句，
形象豐富蘊含朦朧的甜蜜，
交織著出人意料的荒誕，
還有新奇的花邊與圖案，

細細聆聽，卻聽不太清，
難以如願叫我心情沉重。
我多麼渴望成為你的韻律，
屬於你的韻律，無人可比。

I will turn into a mermaid and dive to the bottom of the river,
Make it sparkle with this ring!

If my happiness is hidden in your heart,
I let the divine fire burn it day and night,
Give this heart to me faithfully,
Just thinking about it makes me jump!

Just because Mira is such a passionate and heroic poet, she not only yearns to be conquered by love, but also chooses to defend her love in the end and shows her determination to love persistently. When she realized the power of love without hesitation, twenty-seven-year-old Mira wrote this song *This Rhythm Belongs to You, No One Else Can Compare...*, her bitter love with Balmont shocked the entire Russian literary world even more:

This rhythm belongs to you, like no other,
I can recognize the smooth words,
Your song flows like a brook,
It emits a crystal-like pleasant sound.

I recognize your transparent verse at a glance,
The image is rich and contains hazy sweetness,
intertwined with unexpected absurdity,
There are also novel lace and patterns,

Listen carefully, but can't hear clearly,
The difficulty of getting what I want makes me feel heavy.
How I long to be your rhythm, The rhythm that belongs to
*   you is unmatched.*

　　然而，理想中的愛情終究與現實相違，婚姻的危機與外界的批評，迫使米拉詩裡的的筆調由輕快、高尚開始蒙上一種淡淡的愁緒。因為米拉擁有一顆不羈的靈魂，所以二十八歲的米拉仍在多重外界的壓力下寫下了這首（我的靈魂像清純的白蓮...）：

　　　　我的靈魂像清純的白蓮，
　　　　困居在這幽靜的水塘，
　　　　綻放出閃爍銀輝的花瓣，
　　　　籠罩柔和神秘的月光。

　　　　你的愛情似光線朦朧，
　　　　施展著神奇悄然無聲。
　　　　我的白蓮釋放縷縷清香，
　　　　感受莫名其妙的愁情，
　　　　而一股寒氣浸透了心腸。

　　這首從詩人心靈中迸發憂愁意象的詩，就像她的情人巴爾蒙特曾在詩裡寫過的一段詩句：

　　　　我的理想來自痛苦，
　　　　所以我擁有世人之愛。

　　他與米拉之間的愛情是命中注定、不可避免的。雖然兩人都過於追求「理想」，不免失之於現實冷酷的無情，最終以悲劇收場。

However, the ideal love is contrary to the reality after all. The crisis of marriage and criticism from the outside force the tone of Mira's poems to change from brisk and noble to a kind of melancholy. Because Mira has an unruly soul, the 28-year-old Mira still wrote this song under multiple external pressures *My Soul Is Like a Pure White Lotus...*:

My soul is like a pure white lotus,
Trapped in this secluded pond,
Blooming silvery petals,
Soft and mysterious moonlight envelops.

Your love is like a dim light,
Performing magic quietly.
My white lotus releases strands of fragrance,
Feeling unexplainable sadness,
And a cold air permeated the heart.

This poem, bursting with melancholy images from the poet's heart, is like a line once written by her lover Balmont:

My ideals come from pain,
So I have the love of the world.

The love between him and Mira is predestined and inevitable. Although both of them pursue "ideals" too much, they inevitably lose the cold and ruthless reality, and finally end in tragedy.

在米拉三十六歲去世的前一年，重病之際，猶不能抹去她對巴爾蒙特的這段戀情記憶，遂而寫下（我願成為你心愛的人…），詩人以深入自我靈魂的反思後，在前段裡寫道：

> 我願成為你心愛的人，
> 並非為了熾熱甜美的夢，
> 而是想讓永恆的命運
> 長久聯結起我們的姓名。

是的，這些詩作，在在昭示了她的真誠與強烈的愛，至死不渝，真切感人。米拉一生的成就，在俄羅斯文壇曾進行了多種探索，但國際間對其抒情詩深入研究者卻仍欠缺。她以詩歌詠青春和愛情，終將在中西文化的翻譯成果下，讓詩神為米位的傑出作品而驕傲。

三、結　語

我認為，米拉•洛赫維茨卡婭在那樣一個時代中，能勇於為愛，袒露自己的心靈，這點是不易的。可貴的是，即使在病危之際，仍要做一名蓬勃向前的詩人，這或許是米拉最純真的嚮往，卻也張揚了一種崇高的寫作精神。

也許，對米拉來說，沒有比愛情，在她的理想之中更重要了。但愛情在現實環境中多幻變，往往難在歲月中常存。

One year before Mira died at the age of thirty-six, when she was seriously ill, she still could not erase the memory of her love affair with Balmont, so she wrote *I Would Like to Be Your Beloved...*, the poet penetrated into himself after reflection of the soul, I wrote in the preceding paragraph:

I would like to be your beloved,
Not for hot sweet dreams,
but want eternal destiny
Connected our names for a long time.

Yes, these poems show her sincerity and strong love, which will last until death, which is really touching. The achievements of Mira's life have been explored in many ways in the Russian literary world, but there is still a lack of in-depth research on her lyric poetry in the world. She eulogizes youth and love with poetry, and will eventually make the god of poetry proud of Mi Wei's outstanding works under the translation results of Chinese and Western cultures.

3. Conclusion

I think it is not easy for Mira Lokhvitskaya to have the courage to expose her heart for love in such an era. What is valuable is that, even when she is dying, she still wants to be a vigorous poet. This may be Mira's purest yearning, but it also promotes a noble writing spirit.

Perhaps, for Mira, nothing is more important than love in her ideal. But love is often changing in the real environment, and it is often difficult to survive in the

只有從她對詩歌寫作過程中艱辛的跋涉，才能更理解米拉的抒情詩內涵。

　　她短暫而耀眼的一生，確實令人矚目。但倘若抹煞了她對愛情的顧盼，活著對她來說，或許更像是一種煎熬。細讀其詩，我終於能理解生命因為有了愛而獲得更完整的重要性。雖然後世仍有文學批評的詞滙裡對米拉的婚外戀情說了重話，但在她百年後的今日看來，這些是無關緊要的。因為這段戀情，確實使她付出了生命的代價。但如果理智真能夠控制愛情的話，又怎能讓她對愛情的想像的火花燃燒起來？

　　又或許她勇於坦誠地面對愛情的精神已在星辰間飄蕩，而她的愛情長眠於故鄉。但多少年過去了，米拉，這名字仍留在俄國文學史上占有一席之地，並被廣泛稱為「頹廢派的先驅者」，甚至影響俄羅斯詩歌的發展超過一世紀。

　　是啊，任何世間萬物都不可能改變愛情的際遇。米拉像一顆永不殞落的金星，哪怕再過千年之後，世人一樣會喜歡她毫不掩飾自己對愛情的歌詠與勇於付出的執著。她的詩歌，仍是美麗、動人的，沉浸在神秘、靜謐的星空與神的愛之中。

years. Only from her arduous trek in the process of writing poetry can one better understand the connotation of Mira's lyric poetry.

Her short and dazzling life is indeed eye-catching. But if her longing for love is wiped out, living may be more like a torment for her. After reading his poems carefully, I can finally understand the importance of life being more complete because of love. Although there are still serious words about Mira's extramarital affairs in the vocabulary of literary criticism in later generations, in her eyes a hundred years later, these are irrelevant. Because of this relationship, she did pay the price of her life. But if reason can really control love, how can it ignite the spark of her imagination about love?

Or maybe her spirit of facing love bravely and honestly has drifted among the stars, and her love is buried in her hometown forever. But how many years have passed, Mira, this name still occupies a place in the history of Russian literature, and is widely known as the "pioneer of the decadent school", even affecting the development of Russian poetry for more than a century.

Yes, nothing in the world can change the fate of love. Mira is like a golden star that will never fall. Even after a thousand years, the world will still like her, making no secret of her dedication to singing love and giving courageously. Her poems are still beautiful and moving, immersed in the mysterious, quiet starry sky and God's love.

　　恍惚中，我也聽見米拉獨處一隅的吟咏，字字情真意切。世間的喧嘩、虛偽的快樂，或塵世的空虛，已離得遠遠的。她也獲得一種最終的安慰。透過這些譯作，也讓我感到米拉燃燒著的青春熱情，從而揭示其多情而睿智的本質。毫無疑問，這也為俄羅斯詩歌研究提供了很好的範本。

　　　　　　註.羅賓德拉納德•泰戈爾著，徐翰林譯，《泰戈爾的
　　　　　　詩》，臺北，海鴿文化，2016 年增版，頁 42。

　　—2022.02.18 寫於臺東

　　—臺灣《秋水》詩刊 192 期，2022.07，頁 71-73。

In a trance, I also heard Mira chanting alone in a corner, every word was sincere. The noise of the world, the false happiness, or the emptiness of the world are far away. She also finds a final consolation. Through these translations, I also feel Mira's burning youthful enthusiasm, thus revealing her passionate and wise nature. Undoubtedly, this also provides a good model for the study of Russian poetry.

Note. Written by Robin Delanad Tagore, translated by Xu Hanlin, *Tagore's Poems*, Taipei, Haige Culture, 2016 edition, p. 42.

27. 真摯的詩情與崇高美的融合

—讀倫扎・阿涅利（Renza Agnelli）的詩

　　生長於義大利北部的一個小鎮特倫托的倫扎・阿涅利（Renza Agnelli），自幼感受著阿爾卑斯山遼闊的雪地之美與文學的薰陶，她最喜歡的自然是大自然、閱讀與創作。長大後，她遠嫁到意大利南部，成為一名奉獻教學三十餘年的教師，也獲得了來自國際的諸多文學獎項，成為詩苑備受尊榮的奇葩。

　　在她歌詠下的家鄉，詩歌語言獲具一種獨特的質感，且帶有濃郁的思辨色彩，詞匯也充滿力度。如（在卡普里昂的羅卡等待黎明）這部長詩中的第一首（卡普里昂的羅卡）：

> 美麗，為你驕傲，
> 依偎在高地上
> 你像女王一樣觀看，
> 意識到她的價值，
> 你可愛的四肢
> 帶著愛，在山谷中伸展。

27. A Fusion of Sincere Poetry and Sublime Beauty
— Reading the Poems by Renza Agnelli

Renza Agnelli grew up in Trento, a small town in northern Italy. She felt the beauty of the vast snowfields of the Alps and the influence of literature since her childhood. Her favorites from nature is the great nature, reading and writing. When she grew up, she married far away from her home, to the south of Italy, and became a teacher dedicated to teaching for over 30 years. She also won many international literary awards and became a highly respected and wonderful flower in the garden of poetry.

When she praises her hometown, her poetic language has a unique texture, with a strong speculative color, and the vocabulary is also full of strength, as in *Waiting for Dawn at Rocca of Caprion*, the first of this long poem *Rocca of Caprion*:

> *Beautiful, proud of you,*
> *Nestled on the high ground*
> *You watch like a queen,*
> *Aware of her own worth,*
> *Your sweet extremities*
> *Stretch out in the valley with love.*

在那裡，你有很好的陪伴
與廷達里的麥當娜
和聖父皮奧。
來自天堂的一根手指
和上帝如此親近，
你欣喜若狂地欣賞平原
點綴著青山、樹籬、村舍
和平靜流淌的金色菲塔利亞河
和平靜的和諧鄉村。
這不會打擾你
想想你過得怎麼樣
你有一天會成為什麼樣的人。
你看著時間慢慢流逝
永遠不一樣。
微笑著面對
那折磨我們的問題
讓世界任其作惡

　　全詩以家鄉的羅卡（Rocca）為中心，同時又站在一個美麗的地方，抒寫了生活當中對社會人生的觀察與親友相伴的體悟，最後融入了她心靈的冀望與喜悅之情。閱讀阿涅利的詩，也可以說是一部情感史，她擅長從生活細節中展開抒情，並賦予崇高性的語言以臻於更大的詩性能量。如（在教堂「廷達里的聖母」）：

Up there you are in good company
With the Madonna of Tindari
And the Holy Father Pio.
One finger from heaven
And so close to God,
You admire in ecstasy the plain
Dotted with green hills, hedges, cottages
And the blond Fitalia river flowing placidly
And serenely in rural harmony.
And it doesn't bother you
To think how you were
And what you will one day be.
You watch time go by slowly
And never the same.
Smile at the problems
That torment us
And leave the world to its vices.

The whole poem centers on Rocca, her hometown, while standing in a beautiful place, to give her observation of social life and her understanding of being with relatives and friends, and finally to integrate the hope and joy from the bottom of her heart. Reading Agnelli's poems, it can be said to be reading a history of human emotions. She is good at expressing emotions from the details of life, and endowing sublime language with greater poetic energy. Such as *At the Church "Holy Madonna of Tindari"*:

羅卡有個小教堂
我真心喜歡。
最初是簡單構造，但後來
越來越漂亮，越來越有人氣，
它現在可以容納
市中心所有的人。
在神聖的穹頂之下
你可以親密呼吸，
淡定，有家庭氛圍
給精神注入和平
這會把你帶入靈魂。
在人性之上，
忠於主的話，
廷達里聖母守望著
帶著無限的憐憫和愛意。

　　這首詩使用的是一種帶有虔誠的宗教信仰的口語，來摹寫自我的心靈感悟。正因詩人有一顆白雪般澄淨的心，從她身上所體現出來的那種純真的喜悅，也就具有了神性寫作的尊榮和光采。她對世人的關愛，對故鄉的思念與頌揚，這正是她的詩給人以心靈的愉悅所在。

　　德國詩人里爾克（Rainer Maria Rilke，1875-1926）曾說：「一顆愛戀著的心促使我們歌詠世界。」事實上，在 Agnelli

There is a little church in Rocca
That I really like.
Initially built with little means, but then
More and more beautiful and welcoming,
It can now contain all the people
Of the upper part of the town.
Under the holy vault
You can breathe an intimate,
Collected and family atmosphere
That infuses peace to the spirit
And that takes you right into your soul.
Over that humanity,
Faithful to the word of the Lord,
The Virgin of Tindari watches over
With infinite mercy and love.

This poem uses a kind of oral language tinctured with pious religious beliefs to describe her spiritual enlightenment. Just because the poet has a heart as clear as snow, the pure joy embodied in her has the honor and brilliance of divine writing. Her love for the world, and her yearning for and praise of for her hometown are exactly where her poems bring joy to the soul.

The German poet Rilke (Rainer Maria Rilke, 1875-1926) once said: "A loving heart prompts us to sing about the world." In fact, in Agnelli's writing, the thought of every poem seems

的寫作之中，每一首詩的思想，都彷若是自己的生命情愫在躍動。從美學角度講，這種抒情的韻律，恰好表達了詩人源源不絕的詩思。再如〈等待黎明〉，詩人的想像力是豐富的，意在抒發她的日常生活的所見所思，不但把詩裡的畫面描繪得飛動起來，而且具有濃重的感情色彩：

> 在這奇怪的照片匯總中
> 我想獻上我短暫的一瞥
> 看看定居在我日子裡的人們。
> 我一大早醒來
> 暖暖的南方太陽
> 窗含全景
> 在我眼裡始終如一。
> 目光被我的鄰居俘獲
> 總是忙於家務，開朗、
> 勤勞、健談、大方。
> 瑪律齊亞很忙
> 洗衣，清潔，擦洗
> 美麗的欽齊亞與其呼應，
> 忙著照顧孩子，事情沒完沒了。
> 街上，商店的百葉窗捲起
> 準備接待客戶，
> 男孩上學，男人上班，
> 像那勤勞的蜘蛛
> 忙著織網再織網。
> 我環顧四周，終於找到自己。

to be her life in throbbing. From an aesthetic point of view, this lyrical rhythm just expresses the poet's endless poetic thoughts. Another example is *Waiting for Dawn*, the poet's imagination is rich, and she intends to express what she sees and thinks in her daily life, not only depicting the pictures in the poem, but also with a strong emotional color:

> *In this strange roundup of photographs*
> *I want to dedicate a small glimpse*
> *To the people who populate my days too.*
> *I wake up early in the morning*
> *To the warm southern sun and*
> *From the windows I look at the panorama*
> *Which is always the same to my eyes.*
> *The gaze is captured by my neighbors*
> *Always busy with chores, cheerful and*
> *Industrious, talkative and generous.*
> *There is Marzia busy*
> *Washing the laundry, cleaning, scrubbing*
> *And she is echoed by the beautiful Cinzia,*
> *Busy with the baby, with a thousand things to do.*
> *In the street the shutters of the shops are raised*
> *And are preparing to receive customers,*
> *The boys go to school, the men at work,*
> *Like so many industrious spiders*
> *Who are busy weaving the web.*
> *I look around and, finally, I find my*

我花了很長時間，才找到自己的路；
夜裡，我數到一千顆星星，
直到黎明終於破曉，
我意識到
我不想在別的地方，
因為黎明在我心中……

從中可看出，Agnelli 從文學、史學和神學等知識中汲取了不少有價值的思想，融入她的詩篇，也為她創造詩美提供了別具一格的風格美。其真摯的詩情，深深地印在我的心田裡。令人高興的是，同為詩人的丈夫 Giovanni G.Campisi 喬凡尼·坎皮西將親手為她製作這本新詩集，更體現了這一對詩人對家鄉的忠貞之愛，詩中自然也蘊含著 Agnelli 對明日的期許及其崇高的情懷。義大利詩人夸西莫多（Salvatore Quasimodo，1901-1968）曾說：「人的千情百感，對自由的嚮往，擺脫孤獨的渴求，這就是詩歌的嶄新內容。」而我覺得 Agnelli 的詩，不論是描景記事，已構成了一個恬靜又美好的藝術境界，這是她對生活中的回顧與展望，也是由她心靈綻放出來潔淨的花朵，從而完成了詩美的創造。

—寫於 2023.01.11.

I've spent a long time finding my way;

In the night I counted a thousand stars,

When dawn finally broke,

I realized that

I wouldn't want to be anywhere else,

Because dawn is already inside me...

From this, it can be seen that Agnelli has absorbed a lot of valuable ideas from literature, history and theology, to integrate them into her poems, which guarantee a unique style of beauty in creation of poetic beauty. Her poetry of sincerity is deeply rooted in my heart. Happily, her husband Giovanni G. Campisi, also a poet, personally produces this new poetry collection for her, which reflects the poets' loyalty in love for their hometown, and the poems naturally contain Agnelli's great expectations and lofty sentiments for tomorrow. Salvatore Quasimodo (1901-1968), an Italian poet, once said: "Man's emotions and yearning for freedom, as well as the desire to get rid of loneliness, these are the new content of poetry." It is my belief that in Agnelli's poems, whether describing scenes or recording events, a quiet and beautiful artistic realm has been formed. This is her review and prospect of life, as well as a fair and pure flower blooming out of her heart, thus to complete the creation of poetic beauty.

Written on January 11, 2023

作者：林明理（1961-），臺灣學者，詩歌評論家

譯者：張智中，南開大學外國語學院教授、博士研究生
　　　導師）

－臺灣《更生日報》副刊，2023.04.22

By Dr. Lin Mingli, (1961-), a Taiwanese scholar and poetry critic

（Translator：Zhang Zhizhong is professor, doctoral supervisor and dean of the Translation Department of Foreign Languages College, Nankai Universit

28. 追求光明的勇者—Sara Ciampi 的詩世界

在蓬勃發展的國際詩壇中，Sara Ciampi（1976-）的新詩脫穎而出，彷若一顆耀眼的藍星呈現於世界面前。她出生在義大利西北部一個叫熱那亞（Genova）的小鎮裡，度過了自己艱難卻不平凡的童年和少年時代。然而正是那岬角與海浪花輝映，那矗立著藝術的建築和海邊的美景，培育了詩人對自己的家鄉的深情厚意；而生活中所經歷的磨難又鍛鍊了她堅強不屈的傲骨和沉靜而樸實無華的性格。

走過風雨的苦痛歲月，Sara Ciampi 在獲得文學碩士後，她那激情澎湃、用心血釀成的諸多詩集與詩篇，她的深情低吟，正是從熱那亞這裡萌生出來的；最終成為熱那亞大學備受矚目的當代作家之一，且多次獲得諾貝爾文學獎提名等殊榮。

雖然在某一段成長的時間裡，Ciampi 的思想也曾一度苦悶徬徨，但她透過詩歌創作逐步建立了自我生命的體驗與感觸而生的文學意象的同構關係，努力以赴，成為詩思敏捷的著名詩人，因而被譽為「義大利之新星」。她的詩，充滿了

28. The Warrior-Pursuer of Light — The Poetic World of Sara Ciampi

In the flourishing international poetry circle, the new poems of Sara Ciampi (1976-) stand out like a dazzling blue star appearing in the world. She was born in a small town called Genoa in northwest Italy, where she spent her difficult yet extraordinary childhood and adolescence. However, it is the reflection of the headland and the waves, the artistic buildings and the beautiful scenery of the sea that have cultivated the poet's deep affection for her hometown; the hardships experienced in life have tempered her indomitable pride and calmness, as well as her unpretentious character.

After going through the bitter years of winds and rains, and after Sara Ciampi has obtained a master of arts, her passionate collection of poems through painstaking efforts was born in Genoa. Eventually she became one of the high-profile contemporary writers, and has time and again been nominated for the Nobel Prize in Literature.

Although in a certain period of her growing up, Ciampi's thoughts were once depressed and hesitant, through poetry creation, she gradually established the isomorphic relationship between her own life experience and literary images born of feelings, and she worked hard to become a poet of profound thinking, for which she is famed as the "Rising Star of Italy" Her poems are full of compassionate

.悲憫的思想感情和強烈的時代精神，如今更以嶄新的勇者姿態，繼續揮灑著她的詩筆，且深深地烙印在廣大讀者的心田裡。如（流星）中寫道：

> 浩瀚星空，
> 在這個八月的夜晚，我著迷
> 於你的神奇，
> 趁著涼風
> 輕輕搖曳
> 高大的松樹，
> 我看著你，若有所思。
>
> 流星啊，
> 蒼穹的飛逝之淚，
> 多少模糊的目光
> 充滿喜悅和希望
> 等待你的通過！
>
> 多麼甜蜜的夢
> 幸福和愛的幻影
> 你是否有能力給予
> 我們悲慘的靈魂！
>
> 流星啊，
> 小水滴閃爍

thoughts and feelings and a strong spirit of the times, and now she continues to write her poems with a brand-new brave attitude, which is deeply imprinted in the hearts of her readers. As in Falling Stars:

Immense starry universe,
on this August night I am enchanted
by your wonders and,
while a cool breeze
gently bends
the tall pines,
I look thoughtfully at you.

O falling stars,
fleeting tears of the firmament,
how many vague glances
full of joy and hope
await your passage!

What sweet dreams
and what illusions of happiness and love
are you capable of giving
to our miserable souls!

O falling stars,
little drops flickering

在壓抑的夜色中，
但你如何改變
人類命運的進程？

噢，慾望，幻想，
你多像那些
快速的星星，
只是帶來
最為虛榮和轉瞬即逝的幻想
最後消失
被最深的黑暗所吞噬！

她以詩歌詠生命中的快樂或痛苦，熱愛或內心深處的聲音，偶爾也會以理性思辨來表達某種深沉的思索。（沉默的聲音）一詩，便是超越時間和空間的界限，創造出一種純粹詩美的境界，並冀望充滿友善、寧靜、思想自由馳騁的境界的到來：

浸在微弱的光中
我溫暖的房裡，
我獨自在夜裡聆聽
悅耳甜美的聲音：
沉默的聲音。

絕對的平靜中
與白天的噪音一點也不和諧，

in the oppressive darkness of the night,
but how can you change
the course of human destiny?

O desires, o chimeras,
how much you resemble
those rapid stars,
which give only
the most vain and fleeting illusion
and finally disappear
swallowed by the deepest darkness!

She sings the joy or pain in life, love or inner voice in her poems, and occasionally she expresses some deep thinking with rational thinking. The Voice of Silence is a poem which transcends the boundaries of time and space, to create a realm of pure poetic beauty, hopeful for the arrival of a realm filled with friendliness, tranquillity, and freedom of thought:

Dipped in the faint light
of my warm room,
alone I listen in the night
a pleasant and sweet voice:
the voice of silence.

In this absolute calm
so discordant from diurnal noise,

多少淒涼悲傷的回憶錄
多少愉快的回憶，
讓我痛苦，讓我快樂
在我的記憶中，再次醒來！

親愛的，沉默的聲音，多麼重要，
只有你，能夠安撫
我那顆飽受考驗之心的憂慮，
只有你，回憶
鳥兒悅耳的歌聲，
枝葉的沙沙聲，
大海的破裂聲
以及小溪的潺潺聲！

沉默的聲音啊，
只有那些能夠
聽到你的聲音
夢想並召喚你，
安靜的崇高耳語，
在充滿噪音的粗糙世界中，
震耳欲聾的愚蠢
以及嘈雜的髒話！

　　詩裡的筆調雖然是抒情婉約，但隱逸其中的是，對社會
人生的思考，也奔湧在她的血液中；從而給人一種層次清晰、

how many sad and sorrowful memoirs
and how many cheerful remembrances,
that make me suffer and rejoice
wake up again in my memory!

How much are you dear, voice of silence,
just you, able to appease
the worries of mine tried heart,
just you, that recall
the sweet songs of birds,
the rustle of leafy branches,
the break of sea
and the murmur of brooks!

O voice of silence,
only those people
who are able to hearing you
dreaming and invoking you,
o sublime whisper of quiet,
in a rough world full of noises,
deafening stupidities
and noisy obscenities!

Although the tone of the poem is lyrical and graceful, what is hidden in it is that the thinking about social life is interwoven in her blood, thus giving people a feeling of

讀來鏗鏘悅耳的感覺。她總能運用豐富的想像力，使詩作出
現的意象有著眾多面目。比如（蹺蹺板）一詩：

> 沉浸在公園的寧靜中，
> 我記得遙遠的時光
> 我是個快樂的孩子
> 跑在陽光明媚的路上
>
> 像其他孩子一樣
> 在可愛的蹺蹺板上
> 我高興地搖晃：
> 輕鬆省心的蹺蹺板。
>
> 悶熱的午後
> 我追溯那些舊路
> 現在竟如此靜默，
> 如此孤單，
> 如此費勁。
>
> 我累了，但我現在
> 只有一個蹺蹺板：
> 人生的蹺蹺板，
> 命運之風
> 搖擺
> 痛悔之間
> 從未真正活過的日子
> 明天的崇高夢想。

clear layers andsonorous and pleasant reading. She can always use her rich imagination to lend many-faceted images to her poems. Take *The Carousel* for example:

In the gentle quiet of the park
happy voices and laughter
of happy and lively children were heard,
who enjoyed shooting
on bright coloured rides.

How sweet, tender and playful were
those little children with serene glances,
who played so carefree
yet unaware of human evils, tragedies,
misfortunes and tribulations!

What immense nostalgia and great regret
arose strong from the bottom of my heart
at the sight of joyful creatures,
who only savoured the exquisite taste
of childhood on that carousel!

By now it has fled and lost forever
that distant season so dear to me,
source of gaiety and pleasant memories,
and now during my sad run
on the merry-go-round of existence
vague yearnings, sublime hopes
and ephemeral enjoyments alternate
quick to pains, anxieties and suffering,
until the last lap is inevitable
and everything will stop sadly
in the most total, oppressive darkness
and perpetual, absolute silence.

　　這首詩暗示著在夏日公園的景色中一舒懷抱的潛意識，它必然也在整體上包含了 Sara Ciampi 的審美意識和崇高的人格特質。這些都是詩人尋求心靈淨化而寫下富有特色的抒情詩。

　　義大利航海家哥倫布（Cristoforo Colombo）曾說：「世界是屬於勇者的。」細讀 Ciampi 的詩，其實內裡也蘊聚著一種強烈的現代詩人的生命律動。她的身心似能與宇宙融合，也具有深刻的批判精神。她對家鄉的情韻仍是她詩歌創作的一根臍帶，更貼近於對民族的愛國精神，對受苦者的痛感同身受。

　　她已全心投身於義大利詩歌史上勇於追求光明的詩家之林，猶如冬夜的一顆璨星，閃著同等的光芒。顯然地，在 Sara Ciampi 的詩的王國裡，已打開了一座更廣闊的審美天地。

　　　　　　　　　　－2023 年 01 月 13 日，寫於台灣。（作者：林明理，學者詩人，詩歌評論家）

The poem is suggestive of the subconsciousness of embracing the landscape of a summer park, which is sure to contain Sara Ciampi's aesthetic sense and sublime personality as a whole. These are the characteristic lyric poems by poet in seeking spiritual purification.

Cristoforo Columbus, an Italian navigator, once said: "The world belongs to those who are brave." After carefully reading Ciampi's poems, there is actually a strong pulse of life in modern poets. Her body and mind seem to be able to be integrated with the universe, and she boasts a profound critical spirit. Her affection for her hometown is still an umbilical cord of her poetry creation, which is closer to her patriotic spirit, and she empathizes with the painful and suffering people.

She devotes herself wholeheartedly to the forest of poets who have the courage to pursue the light in the history of Italian poetry, like a bright star on a wintry night, shining with the same rays of light. Obviously, in the kingdom of her poems, Sara Ciampi has opened an aesthetic world which is wider.

Author: Dr. Lin Mingli, (1961-), a Taiwanese scholar and poetry critic; written on January 13, 2023

Translator: Zhang Zhizhong, professor, doctoral supervisor and dean of the Translation Department of Foreign Languages College, Nankai University）

——意大利，EDIZIONI UNIVERSUM（埃迪采恩尼大學）《國際詩新聞》（INTERNATIONAL POETRY NEWS），刊林明理詩評（追求光明的勇者——Sara Ciampi 的詩世界），張智中教授譯，及林明理在意大利的合著詩集封面，2023.2.19。

2023.2月日意大利 EDIZONI UNIVERSUM（埃迪米恩尼大學）《国際詩新聞》
《INTERNATIONAL POETRY NEWS》刊林明理詩評〈
追求光明的勇者—Sara Ciampi的詩世界〉,張智中教授翻譯,及林明理在義大利的得獎讚討函.

EDIZONI UNIVERSUM
INTERNATIONAL POETRY
NEWS

SARA CIAMPI ACHIEVES THE DIPLOMA
"Universal Literature Grand Prize for Peace"
for the English-Chinese bilingual authors' trilogy
"IN MEMORY OF DAPHNIS AND CHLOE"

The Warrior-Pursuer of Light
The Poetic World of Sara Ciampi

In the flourishing international poetry circle, the new poems of Sara Ciampi (1976-) stand out like a dazzling blue star appearing in the world. She was born in a small town called Genoa in northwest Italy, where she spent her difficult yet extraordinary childhood and adolescence. However, it is the reflection of the headland and the waves, the artistic buildings and the beautiful scenery of the sea that have cultivated the poet's deep affection for her hometown; the hardships experienced in life have tempered her indomitable pride and calmness, as well as her unpretentious character. After going through the bitter years of winds and rains, and after Sara Ciampi has obtained a master of arts, her passionate collection of poems through painstaking efforts was born in Genoa. Eventually she became one of the high-profile contemporary writers, and has time and again been nominated for the Nobel Prize in Literature.

Although in a certain period of her growing up, Ciampi's thoughts were once depressed and hesitant, through poetry creation, she gradually established the isomorphic relationship between her own life experience and literary images born of feelings, and she worked hard to become a poet of profound thinking, for which she is famed as the "Rising Star of Italy". Her poems are full of compassionate thoughts and feelings and a strong spirit of the times, and now she continues to write her poems with a brand-new brave attitude, which is deeply imprinted in the hearts of her readers. As in *Falling Stars*:

Immense starry universe,
on this August night I am enchanted
by your wonders and,
while a cool breeze
gently bends
the tall pines,

I look thoughtfully at you.

O falling stars,
fleeting tears of the firmament,
how many vague glances
full of joy and hope
await your passage!

What sweet dreams
and what illusions of happiness and love
are you capable of giving
to our miserable souls!

O falling stars,
little drops flickering
in the oppressive darkness of the night,
but how can you change
the course of human destiny?

O desires, o chimeras,
how much you resemble
those rapid stars,
which give only
the most vain and fleeting illusion
and finally disappear
swallowed by the deepest darkness!

She sings the joy or pain in life, love or inner voice in her poems, and occasionally she expresses some deep thinking with rational thinking. *The Voice of Silence* is a poem which transcends the boundaries of time and space, to create a realm of pure poetic beauty, hopeful for the arrival of a realm filled with friendliness, tranquility, and freedom of thought:

Dipped in the faint light
of my warm room,
alone I listen in the night
a pleasant and sweet voice:
the voice of silence.

In this absolute calm
so discordant from diurnal noise,
how many sad and sorrowful memoirs
and how many cheerful remembrances,
that make me suffer and rejoice
wake up again in my memory!

How much are you dear, voice of silence,
just you, able to appease
the worries of mine tried heart,
just you, that recall
the sweet songs of birds,
the rustle of leafy branches,
the break of sea
and the murmur of brooks!

O voice of silence,
only those people
who are able to hearing you
dreaming and invoking you,
o sublime whisper of quiet,
in a rough world full of noises,
deafening stupidities
and noisy obscenities!

Although the tone of the poem is lyrical and graceful, what is hidden in it is that the thinking about social life is interwoven in her blood, thus giving people a feeling of clear layers and sonorous and pleasant reading. She can always use her rich imagination to lend many-faceted images to her poems. Take *The Carousel* for example:

In the gentle quiet of the park
happy voices and laughter
of happy and lively children were heard,
who enjoyed shooting
on bright coloured rides.

How sweet, tender and playful were
those little children with serene glances,
who played so carefree

P. 1

29. 托馬斯·特蘭斯特羅默 《巨大的謎語》賞析

一、其人其詩

閱讀瑞典詩人托馬斯·特蘭斯特羅默（ Tomas Transtromer，1931-2015）詩歌，能夠明顯感受到他對於詩歌的凝鍊簡約性有一種較為自覺的追求。或許他集詩人、音樂家、作家與畫家於一身，著迷於為純粹的詩歌，以臻為藝術理想與美學思想的實踐者。他的詩節奏性強，常以深刻的比喻或諸多聯想來表達其強烈的感情；自覺地進行著思維層面的自問。

詩人曾著有詩集十餘卷，在斯德哥爾摩大學研究後，轉到一個青少年拘留所做心理學家。終其一生閱歷豐富，生性淡泊、生活簡約。五十九歲時，患腦溢血，致語言功能受到阻礙，但仍繼續努力於創作；直到八十歲那年，獲得二〇一一年諾貝爾文學獎的殊榮，四年後，安詳地走完人生。托馬斯的詩歌被翻譯成三十多國的文字，流傳於世。

29. Appreciation of The Great Riddle by Tomas Transtromer

1. His People and His Poems

Reading the poems of the Swedish poet Tomas Transtromer (1931-2015), one can clearly feel that he has a more conscious pursuit of the simplicity of poetry. Perhaps he is a poet, musician, writer and painter all in one, obsessed with pure poetry and a practitioner of artistic ideals and aesthetic thoughts. His poems have a strong rhythm, and he often expresses his strong feelings with profound metaphors or many associations; he consciously asks himself at the level of thinking.

The poet has written more than ten volumes of poetry collections. After studying at Stockholm University, he was transferred to a psychologist in a juvenile detention center. Throughout his life, he has rich experience, indifferent nature and simple life. At fifty-nine, he suffered from a cerebral hemorrhage, which hindered his language function, but he continued to work hard on his creation; until he was eighty years old, he won the 2011 Nobel Prize in Literature. Four years later, he finished his life peacefully. Thomas's poems have been translated into more than 30 languages and spread around the world.

其中，由瑞典漢學家、曾任諾貝爾文學獎評審委員的馬悅然（1924-2019）教授於生前翻譯了這本譯詩集，並在臺北出版。全書難能可貴的主要特點有：一是這種借助文學傳播增強國際詩歌視野的形式，對於研究托馬斯詩歌或賞讀者，將有一定的啟示意義。二是馬悅然教授也在序言裡對托馬斯詩歌的翻譯進行了微觀與宏觀的探討與分析，力圖通過此部譯詩集，體現他對托馬斯詩歌較為扎實的視角研究，實具有重要的譯介意義。三是托馬斯詩集本身的內容豐富，有一種超越純粹的完美主義和提升；也讓讀者視野開闊。

二、詩作賞析

當托馬斯·特蘭斯特羅默因中風而失去說話的能力時，他的愛妻莫妮卡不棄不離地照顧他，也激發他的創作鬥志，這首〈四月和沉默〉，正表達詩人對自己命運的慨歎：

> 荒涼的春日
> 像絲絨暗色的水溝
> 爬在我身旁。沒有反射。
>
> 唯一閃光的
> 是黃花。
>
> 我的影子帶我
> 像一個黑盒裡的小提琴。

Among them, Professor Goran Malmqvist (1924-2019), a Swedish Sinologist and former Nobel Prize jury member, translated this collection of translated poems during his lifetime and published them in Taipei. The main features of the book are as follows: First, this form of enhancing international poetry vision through literary communication will have certain enlightening significance for studying Thomas' poetry or appreciating readers. Second, Professor Goran Malmqvist also discussed and analyzed the translation of Thomas' poems at the micro and macro levels in the preface, trying to reflect his more solid perspective research on Thomas's poems through this collection of translated poems, which is of great translation significance. The third is that the content of Thomas's poetry collection itself is rich, and there is a kind of perfectionism and improvement beyond the pure; it also broadens readers' horizons.

2. Poetry Appreciation

When Thomas Tranströmer lost the ability to speak due to a stroke, his beloved wife Monica took care of him and inspired him to create. This poem *April and Silence* is expressing the poet's love for the lament of one's own destiny:

> *Desolate spring day*
> *Like velvet dark gutters*
> *Crawl beside me. There is no reflection.*
>
> *The only shining*
> *It is a yellow flower.*
>
> *My shadow takes me*
> *Like a violin in a black box.*

　　我唯一要說的
　　在摸不著的地方閃光
　　像當舖中的
　　銀子。

　　從主體上講，此詩是抒情的，強調藝術直覺和幻想。詩人以心靈的想像，把病中複雜微妙的感情與精神之間結合起來，也存在某種契合的關係，來表達他的思想感情，達到虛擬似的精神上的昇華；而詩的基調、色彩、光影的變化，都隨著他起伏的心緒而變化，也形成富有韻味的藝術效果。再如（一八四四年的草圖）：

　　威廉透納的臉是飽經風霜的
　　他的畫架放在遙遠的大海浪中。
　　我們跟從那銀光綠色的纜索沉入水中。

　　他涉水到緩緩傾斜的死亡的國度。
　　一列火車行進。來近一點。
　　雨，雨在我們頭上行走。

　　此詩境界開闊，有無限的深意。威廉・透納（1775-1851）是位英國畫家，也是詩人的好友，詩裡的畫面蘊含著詩人對人生與死亡的叩問和思考，也創造了一個多彩的意象世界，讓人遐思。恍惚中，我看到兩個孤獨卻心靈相依的好友，沙灘上的天空褪為早冬的淺藍，岸旁的纜索泛著微弱的陽光，有列火車急駛而過，又消失無蹤。唯一伴隨著他們倆的，是

The only thing I have to say
Glitter where you can't reach
Like in a pawn shop
Silver.

In terms of subject, this poem is lyrical, emphasizing artistic intuition and fantasy. The poet uses the imagination of the soul to combine the complex and delicate emotions in the illness with the spirit, and there is also a certain fit relationship to express his thoughts and feelings and achieve a virtual spiritual sublimation; while the tone and color of the poem, *The Changing of Light and Shadow*, all change with his ups and downs of mood, and also form an artistic effect full of charm. Another example *Sketch in 1844*:

William Turner's face is weather-beaten
His easel rests in the great distant waves.
We followed the silver-green cable into the water.

He wades into the gently sloping realm of death.
A train moves. come closer.
Rain, rain walks on our heads.

The realm of this poem is broad and has infinite deep meaning. William Turner (1775-1851) was a British painter and a friend of the poet. The pictures in his poems contain the poet's questioning and thinking about life and death, and he also created a colorful world of images that makes people daydream. In a trance, I saw two friends who were lonely but connected with each other. The sky on the beach faded to the light blue of early winter, the cables on the bank were glowing with faint sunlight, and a train passed by in a hurry and then disappeared without a trace. The only thing that accompanied the two of them was the

微雨開始下了……詩人幫忙倉促地收拾畫架的背影是孤寂的，只有蕈狀的北風輕輕呼喚他們的名字。

　　雖然俳句是源於日本的一種古典短詩，但托馬斯在五○年代就已經寫過類似日本的連歌或俳諧的詩歌形式，但是他強調的不是由十七字音組成，而是音節。例如，他的這首（俳句）詩裡有許多美麗的斷句，這是其中的一節：

　　　　思想站住了
　　　　像宮殿廳宇裡的
　　　　彩色的石板。

　　　　陽台上的我
　　　　站在日光的籠裡——
　　　　像雨後的虹。

　　這些帶有邏輯地自問的意象，恰好地體現托馬斯的風格簡單，卻聯想力驚人的表現，因為，經過了歲月的洗禮和疾病的折磨，他的詩沒有不屈服於命運的搏鬥精神，卻有一種處之泰然的恬靜情懷，更具有感人的力量。誠如馬悅然教授在此書裡的序言提及譯者董繼平翻譯托馬斯《特蘭斯特羅默詩選》其中的一首詩（暴雨），就是一例：

　　　　散步者在這裡突然遇見巨大的
　　　　橡樹，像一頭石化的麋鹿，它的冠
　　　　寬大。在九月的海洋那陰沉的
　　　　綠色堡壘前面。

light rain that began to fall... The back of the poet helping to tidy up the easel in a hurry was lonely, only the fungus-shaped north wind gently calling their names.

Although haiku is a kind of classical short poem originated from Japan, Thomas had already written poetic forms similar to Japanese liange or haiku in the 1950s, but what he emphasized was not composed of seventeen-character sounds, but syllables. For example, this haiku poem of his has many beautiful stanzas, and here is one of them:

Thoughts stopped
Like in a palace hall
Colored slate.

Me on the balcony
Standing in a cage of sunlight—
Like a rainbow after rain.

These images with logical self-questioning just embody Thomas's simple style but astonishing performance, because, after years of baptism and illness, his poems do not have a fighting spirit that does not succumb to fate, but there is a calm feeling of tranquility is even more touching. Just as Professor Goran Malmqvist mentioned in the preface of this book that the translator Dong Jiping translated a poem *Rainstorm* in Thomas's *Selected Poems of Tranströmer* as an example:

Here the wanderer suddenly meets the gigantic
Oak, like a petrified elk, its crown
Lenient. In the gloomy sea of September
Green Fort front.

北方的暴雨。花楸果串膨脹的
季節。
醒在黑暗中，傾聽吧：
星座在廊棚裡跺腳走動，在
高高的樹端上面。

托馬斯的詩絕少涉及抽象的哲理思考，大多是其日常生活中接觸的人物，在瞬間捕捉到詩音的感覺，或與大自然相處的反想。他的詩，常能讓人覺得新穎，畫境優美，反映出詩人內心的寧靜與超越，而畫面整體的和諧，宛若一首綺麗的小詩，是一種優美意象的伸展，包含著詩人既深又廣的意蘊，更有色彩、味道和音樂性，融入其中。

三、結　語

從文學史的觀點來看，有評論家認為托馬斯•特蘭斯特羅默和法國象徵主義後期詩人、法蘭西學術院院士保爾•瓦萊裏（Paul Valery，1871—1945）的純粹的詩歌相近。而瓦萊裏著名的一首《海濱墓園》曾被日本導演宮崎駿在其動畫電影作品《起風了》的法文片名中引用了一段詩句：「縱有疾風起，人生不言棄」，這也正是我在上面所談到的托馬斯的一生寫照。

如果他們兩位偉大的詩人之間還有什麼聯結的話，那麼我覺得他們都是為了讓詩歌意象表現藝術化，亦即那種綜合

Heavy rain in the north. Swelled Rowan Bunches
Season.
Wake up in the dark and listen:
Constellations stomp about in the porch, in
Tall tree tops.

Thomas's poems seldom involve abstract philosophical thinking. Most of Thomas's poems are about the people he comes into contact with in his daily life. His poems often make people feel novel, and the painting environment is beautiful, reflecting the poet's inner tranquility and transcendence, and the overall harmony of the picture is like a beautiful little poem, which is an extension of beautiful images, containing the poet's deep and wide connotation, more color, taste and musicality, integrated into it.

3. Conclusion

From the point of view of literary history, some critics believe that Thomas Transtromer is similar to the pure poetry of Paul Valery (1871-1945), a poet of late French symbolism and academician of the French Academy. Valery's famous song *Cemetery by the Sea* was once quoted by Japanese director Hayao Miyazaki in the French title of his animated film *The Wind Rises*: "Even though there is a strong wind, life will never give up". This is exactly the portrayal of Thomas's life I mentioned above.

If there is any connection between these two great poets, it seems to me that both of them are for the artistic expression of poetic imagery, that is, the kind that synthesizes

著想像、藝術直覺、感情,甚或結合和諧的旋律,以達到新奇、純粹的詩美,從而獲得靈魂的自由。我深信,他們都在我心中活著。而托馬斯這些動人的詩篇,也將留存給後人欣賞與瞭解。

　　　　　註.全文詩句摘自《巨大的謎語》,托馬斯•特蘭斯特羅默著,馬悅然譯,臺北市,行人文化實驗室出版,2011 年 11 月。

-2022.01.21 作

-臺灣《中華日報》副刊,2023.02.12。

imagination, artistic intuition, emotion, and even combines harmonious melody to achieve novelty, pure poetic beauty, so as to obtain the freedom of the soul. I am convinced that they are all alive in my heart. These moving poems of Thomas will also be preserved for future generations to appreciate and understand.

Note. The full text of the verses is excerpted from *The Huge Riddle*, written by Thomas Tranströmer, translated by Goran Malmqvist, Taipei, published by Pedestrian Culture Lab, November 2011.

名家抒情詩評賞

二、中國大陸、台灣詩人

2. Poets from Mainland China and Taiwan

1. 一棵冰雪壓不垮的白樺樹──淺釋北島的詩

摘要：北島的詩歌記錄了沉思中的直覺感知、想像，及其幽深的思辨過程，它的藝術魅力源於其感性與理性的完整契合、一種超越生命的追求以及內心深層的憂鬱。

關鍵詞：北島；詩歌，意象

一、朦朧派詩人─北島

　　北島〈1949—〉，原名趙振開，祖籍浙江湖州，生於北京，畢業於北京四中，是當代中國極具影響力的詩人作家，朦朧詩代表人物之一。20 歲時當建築工人，後作過翻譯，並在《新觀察》雜誌作過短期編輯。２１歲即開始創作詩歌和小說，２９歲時與芒克等人創辦《今天》雜誌。其間，是中國文藝界備受矚目的年輕詩人。1989 年移居國外，曾一度旅居瑞典等七個國家，後來任教於加利福尼亞大學戴維斯分校、柏克萊分校、史丹福大學，５２歲時曾回國為父奔喪。５８歲獲聘香港中文大學客座教授，同年，正式移居香港，與親人團聚，結束幾近二十年的漂泊生活。

1. A White Birch Which Can Never Be Bent by Ice or Snow: An Interpretation of Bei Dao's Poetry

Abstract: Bei Dao's poems record the intuitive perception, imagination, and deep speculation process in meditation. Its artistic charm comes from the complete integration of sensibility and rationality, a pursuit beyond life, and deep-seated melancholy.

Key words: Bei Dao; poetry, imagery

1. Misty Poet — Bei Dao

Bei Dao (1949—), formerly known as Zhao Zhenkai, native of Huzhou, Zhejiang, was born in Beijing and graduated from Beijing No. 4 Middle School. He is a very influential poet-writer in contemporary China and one of the representatives of Misty poetry. At the age of 20, he worked as a construction worker, and later worked as a translator, and worked as a short-term editor in the *New Observation* magazine. At the age of 21, he began to write poetry and novels. At the age of 29, he founded the magazine of *Today* with Mang Ke and others. Among them, he is a young poet who has attracted much attention in the Chinese literary and art circles. In 1989, he emigrated abroad and once lived in seven countries including Sweden. He later taught at the University of California, Davis, Berkeley, and Stanford University. At the age of 52, he returned to China to attend his father's funeral. At the age of 58, he was hired as a visiting professor at the Chinese University of Hong Kong. In the same year, he officially moved to Hong Kong to reunite with his relatives, ending nearly two decades of his wandering life.

　　北島是個感情深篤、精神頗為敏感的詩人，他不趨炎附勢、機敏而睿智，彷彿一棵筆直又孤獨的白樺樹。他的詩有某種英雄的氣慨與夢幻的氛圍，音韻中近似冰雪的舞步。中年時，他的想像力更有一種充滿詩意的吶喊…一種朦朧而浩瀚無邊的想像，具有觸動讀者潛在意識的感動力。因此，透過其意象的構圖，也能夠彰顯出北島生命的意義與對外在世界的關懷。

二、北島詩的藝術特色

　　詩，對於北島來說，正體現了劉勰曾提出的「隨物以宛轉」到「與心而徘徊」的的一種深入的開掘。而這種意識活動，並不是將零碎的表像拼湊疏薄的世界；相反地，他通過「格式塔質」〈Gestalt qualities〉的思維模式與意境的審美想像空間的超越性，在現代視覺傳遞設計的詩藝鑒賞中，常能達到傳形又傳神的效果。

　　北島的詩，常能呈現豐富的音色和音質，它象徵著自己靈魂的解放與救贖，也是作者內心非常深切、不可磨滅的印記，而且絕對真誠。早期詩作明顯可見受到文革後的影響，讓他斷然而勇敢拒絕了浪漫主義〈Romanticism〉注重以強烈

Bei Dao is a poet with deep feelings and a sensitive spirit. He does not follow others, but is alert and wise, just like a straight and lonely birch tree. His poems have a certain heroic spirit and dreamy atmosphere, and the rhyme is similar to the dance steps of ice and snow. When he was middle-aged, his imagination had a more poetic cry..., a kind of hazy and boundless imagination, which has the moving power to touch the reader's subconscious. Therefore, through the composition of its images, it can also demonstrate the meaning of Bei Dao's life and concern for the external world.

2. The Artistic Features of Bei Dao's Poems

Poetry, for Bei Dao, embodies a kind of in-depth exploration from "following things to change" to "wandering with the heart" once proposed by Liu Xie. And this kind of consciousness activity is not a patchwork of fragmented images into a sparse world; on the contrary, he conveys in modern visual through the thinking mode of "Gestalt qualities" and the transcendence of aesthetic imagination space of artistic conception. In the poetic art appreciation of design, the effect of conveying form and expressing spirit can often be achieved.

Bei Dao's poems can often present rich timbre and sound quality. It symbolizes the liberation and redemption of one's own soul, and it is also a very deep and indelible mark in the author's heart, and it is absolutely sincere. His early poems were clearly influenced by the Cultural Revolution, which made him decisively and bravely reject Romanticism's idea of focusing on strong emotion as an aesthetic experience,

的情感作為美學經驗的思想，但也接受了對於歷史和自然題
材的強烈訴諸的理念，賦予意象盤旋的空間。代表作中，尤
以 1976 年天安門「四五運動」期間的《回答》，最為讀者所
熟悉：

> 卑鄙是卑鄙者的通行證，
> 高尚是高尚者的墓誌銘，
> 看吧，在那鍍金的天空中，
> 飄滿了死者彎曲的倒影。
> 冰川紀過去了，
> 為什麼到處都是冰凌？
> 好望角發現了，
> 為什麼死海裏千帆相競？
> 我來到這個世界上，
> 只帶著紙、繩索和身影，
> 為了在審判前，
> 宣讀那些被判決的聲音。
> 告訴你吧，世界
> 我——不——相——信！
> 縱使你腳下有一千名挑戰者，
> 那就把我算作第一千零一名。
> 我不相信天是藍的，
> 我不相信雷的回聲，
> 我不相信夢是假的，
> 我不相信死無報應。

but he also accepted the idea of a strong appeal to historical and natural themes, giving the imagery circles the space. Among the masterpieces, *Answer*, written during the "Fourth Five-Year Movement" in Tiananmen Square in 1976 is the most familiar to readers:

Despicableness is the passport of the despicable,

Nobility is the epitaph of a noble man,

Behold, in that gilded sky,

It was filled with the curved reflections of the dead.

The Ice Age has passed,

Why are there icicles everywhere?

The Cape of Good Hope has been discovered,

Why are thousands of sails competing in the Dead Sea?

I came into this world,

With only paper, rope and figure,

In order that before the trial,

Read the voices of those who were judged.

Let me tell you, the world

I do not believe!

Even if there are a thousand challengers under your feet,

Then count me as number one thousand and one.

I don't believe the sky is blue,

I don't believe Ray's echo,

I don't believe that dreams are fake,

I don't believe in death without retribution.

如果海洋註定要決堤，
就讓所有的苦水都注入我心中，
如果陸地註定要上升，
就讓人類重新選擇生存的峰頂。
新的轉機和閃閃星斗，
正在綴滿沒有遮攔的天空。
那是五千年的象形文字，
那是未來人們凝視的眼睛。

　　其實，這首詩是有其歷史背景的複雜性，顯露出一種激憤的抗議聲調；而不像是一首悲傷的輓歌，嚴格來說，顯得詩味淡薄點而過於莊嚴。詩的背景是 1976 年 1 月 8 日，周恩來總理逝世後，「四人幫」一夥的壓制群眾追思活動，導致萬人自發地集合到天安門廣場抗議，它為後來粉碎江青反革命集團奠定了群眾基礎。在筆法中，詩句已呈現出俯瞰似的全景圖象，向讀者解釋自己的創作理念，並要求我們付出強烈的視覺關注，而非在詮釋詩的含蓄之美。

　　離開祖國後，北島的異域作品向著一種獨特而風格高雅簡樸的方向發展。他的詩開始獲得國際詩壇的矚目，內容多半是人生的寫照，巧妙的筆法無抽象表現主義(Abstract Expression)那種反叛的、無秩序的、虛無以及逃避現實的特性。不僅訴諸讀者以視覺的吸引力，同時也在表現詩人的情感。比如這首《日子》，就是首深刻雋永、韻味無窮的小詩：

If the ocean is doomed to break its banks,
Just let all the bitterness pour into my heart,
If the land is destined to rise,
Just let human beings choose the peak of existence again.
A new turning point and twinkling stars,
Is filling the unobstructed sky.
That is five thousand years of hieroglyphs,
Those are the eyes through which people will stare in the future.

In fact, this poem has the complexity of its historical background, revealing a tone of angry protest; it does not look like a sad elegy, strictly speaking, it seems a little poetic and too solemn. The background of the poem is that on January 8, 1976, after the death of Premier Zhou Enlai, the "Gang of Four" suppressed mass memorial activities, which led to tens of thousands of people spontaneously gathering in Tiananmen Square to protest. In the brushwork, the poems have presented a panoramic image like a bird's-eye view, explaining one's own creative ideas to the readers, and requiring us to pay strong visual attention, rather than explaining the implicit beauty of the poem.

After leaving the motherland, Bei Dao's exotic works developed in a unique and elegant and simple direction. His poems began to attract the attention of the international poetry circle. Most of the content was a portrayal of life, and his clever brushwork did not have the rebellious, chaotic, nihilistic and escapist characteristics of Abstract Expressionism. It not only appeals to readers with visual appeal, but also expresses the emotions of poets. For example, this song *Days* is a profound and meaningful poem with endless charm:

用抽屜鎖住自己的秘密
在喜愛的書上留下批語
信投進郵箱　默默地站一會兒
風中打量著行人　毫無顧忌
留意著霓虹燈閃爍的櫥窗
電話間裡投進一枚硬幣
向橋下釣魚的老頭要支香煙
河上的輪船拉響了空曠的汽笛
在劇場門口幽暗的穿衣鏡前
透過煙霧凝視著自己
當窗簾隔絕了星海的喧囂
燈下翻開褪色的照片和字跡

　　《日子》在表現形式上，有生動的影像卻帶有憂鬱的浪漫主義色彩。作者特地將心靈的圖像逐步推展出來，原是細訴對意中人的悵然若失，卻可看出其中思念的意義勝於類似電影蒙太奇畫面的處理。我們不僅看到多層次的畫面轉接輝映，而且也看到異國窗前映照出來的街景與孤單。

　　北島在創作時所期待的，是將作品擺在讀者眼前時，能引發作者對社會人生問題的思考，他的詩裡通常不加矯飾，有清澄的詩泉；也具有不平凡的天賦，能把握直觀景物的剎那間，讓詩的潛在次序進入到深層的領地，去追逐一種終極的、本原的意識聚焦。如這首早期之作《走吧》，極富象徵意味：

Lock your secrets with a drawer
Leave a comment on a favorite book
Put the letter in the mailbox and stand silently for a while
Looking at pedestrians in the wind without any scruples
Keep an eye out for the neon shop windows
Drop a coin in the phone booth
Ask the old man fishing under the bridge for a cigarette
The steamship on the river blows the air whistle
In front of the dark full-length mirror at the entrance of
　　the theater
staring at myself through the smoke
When the curtain cuts off the hustle and bustle of the star sea
Flipping faded photos and handwriting under the light

In terms of form of expression, *Days* has vivid images but has a melancholic romanticism. The author deliberately unfolds the images of the heart step by step, originally to express the loss of the person he loves in detail, but it can be seen that the meaning of missing in it is better than that of a movie montage. We not only see the multi-layered picture transitions, but also the street scenes and loneliness reflected in front of foreign windows.

What Bei Dao expects when he writes is that when the works are placed in front of the readers, they can trigger the author to think about social and life issues. His poems are usually unpretentious and have a clear poetic spring; grasp the moment of intuitive scenery, let the potential sequence of poetry enter the deep territory, and pursue an ultimate and original focus of consciousness. For example, this early work *Let's Go* is very symbolic:

走吧，
落葉吹進深谷，
歌聲卻沒有歸宿。

走吧，
冰上的月光，
已從河面上溢出。

走吧，
眼睛望著同一片天空，
心敲出暮色的鼓。

走吧，
我們沒有失去記憶，
我們去尋找生命的湖。

走吧，
路啊路，
飄滿了紅罌粟。

　　這首詩寫在上世紀 70 年代後期 詩所反映的是北島與好
友分離前心靈折射的痛苦 這些詩句或許是詩人的片刻憂傷。
然而，從創作角度看，詩句深摯動人，誰也不能否認這首詩
純粹的詩意，是多麼獨具一格的創意表現。總的說，就是心
境清明洞徹，方有澹泊的詩思。

Let's go
Fallen leaves blow into the valley,
The singing has no destination.

Let's go
Moonlight on ice,
Has overflowed from the river.

Let's go
Eyes looking at the same sky,
The heart beats the drum of twilight.

Let's go
We have not lost our memory,
We go in search of the lake of life.

Let's go
Road, road,
Full of red poppies.

This poem was written in the late 1970s, and it reflects the pain of Bei Dao's heart before he separated from his friends. These verses may be the poet's momentary sadness. However, from a creative point of view, the lines are profound and moving, and no one can deny the pure poetry of this poem, which is a unique expression of creativity. Generally speaking, it is only when the state of mind is clear and clear that one can have indifferent poetic thoughts.

另一首《明天，不》，可見到北島遊心於天地的詩美的一面：

> 這不是告別
> 因為我們並沒有相見
> 盡管影子和影子
> 曾在路上疊在一起
> 像一個孤零零的逃犯
>
> 明天，不
> 明天不在夜的那邊
> 誰期待，誰就是罪人
> 而夜裡發生的故事
> 就讓它在夜裡結束吧

這首詩起源於平靜中回憶起來的情感，讓人會聯想到，北島在異域裡對祖國的懷思，不但在清醒時念念不忘，即或在夜裡也難於排遣 詩句充滿張力的審視和無意識的統一間，寄意於言外，就好像一切歷史悲劇全都碎裂於大浪。在它平靜地接受與緩緩的逝去前，誰又能預料未來所揭示的理想？彷彿中，我看見詩人站在環繞岩頂的天空下，對每個自然的元素充滿著生命之外的召喚，眼底深 處，潛伏的詩思在暗中閃爍著幽幽的微光。

Another song *Tomorrow, No*, we can see the beautiful side of Bei Dao's poetic wandering in the world:

This is not farewell
Because we didn't meet
Despite shadows and shadows
Stacked together on the road
Like a lone fugitive

Tomorrow, no
Tomorrow is not on the other side of the night
Whoever expects is a sinner
And the story that happened at night
Just let it end at night

This poem originated from the emotions recalled in peace, which reminds people of Bei Dao's nostalgia for the motherland in a foreign land, not only in his waking hours, but also difficult to dispel at night. Between the tense inspection and the unconscious unity of the verses, the implication lies beyond the words, as if all historical tragedies were broken by the big waves. Before it is peacefully accepted and slowly passed away, who can predict the ideal revealed in the future? As if, I saw the poet standing under the sky surrounding the rock top, full of calls beyond life for every natural element, deep in the depths of my eyes, the latent poetic thoughts shone faintly in the dark.

再如《睡吧，山谷》，這首詩的內涵更加含蓄蘊藉，在其詩性時空中，等待著讀者去欣賞和解讀：

睡吧，山谷
快用藍色的雲霧蒙住天空
矇住野百合蒼白的眼睛

睡吧，山谷
快用雨的腳步去追逐風
追逐布穀鳥不安的啼鳴

此詩的思理異彩紛呈，是時間的足印催發了他的詩性，讓讀者反覆地吟遊體味，享受閱讀如沐浴清暉般的愉悅。想像中，那藍霧沒一點雜色，把野百合蒸出了香氣，使山谷薄染了歡愉；我不禁嗅著，帶著一勻微笑，在冰涼的夜風裡，意識之流也開始伸展，我願化為一隻布穀鳥，遺忘在雨中的春之舞。

在人生的奮鬥場上，北島無疑是個有著堅強意志力的行者。但是，在國外流亡歲月中，無論命運對他如何殘酷，他最後選擇以詩呼喚心靈的觸動，詩甚至就是生命最重要的特質，體驗詩也是健康與幸福的開始。所以當他晚年返回香港任教時，心境是平和寧靜的。迄今仍常出現於重要性詩歌研討會上，也致力於國際詩歌開拓的工作。他的詩歌強調意象、

Another example is *Sleep, Valley*. The connotation of this poem is more subtle, and in its poetic time and space, it is waiting for readers to appreciate and interpret:

Sleep, valley
Cover the sky with blue clouds
Blindfolded wild lily's pale eyes

Sleep, valley
Quickly use the footsteps of the rain to chase the wind
Chasing the restless crow of the cuckoo

The thought of this poem is brilliant, and it is the footprint of time that stimulates his poetic quality, allowing readers to linger over and over again, and enjoy the pleasure of reading like bathing in the clear light. In my imagination, the blue mist has no variegated colors, steaming the wild lilies with fragrance, and dyeing the valley with joy; I can't help sniffing, with a smile, in the cold night wind, the stream of consciousness also begins Stretch, I would like to be a cuckoo, forgetting the dance of spring in the rain.

In the struggle field of life, Bei Dao is undoubtedly a walker with strong willpower. However, during the years of exile abroad, no matter how cruel the fate was to him, he finally chose to use poetry to appeal to the soul. Poetry is even the most important quality of life, and experiencing poetry is also the beginning of health and happiness. So when he returned to Hong Kong to teach in his later years, his mind was peaceful and tranquil. So far, it still often appears in important poetry seminars, and is also committed to the development of international poetry. His poems emphasize the beauty of imagery and music,

音樂美，以細膩的筆觸渲染出矇矓的氣氛。晚年吟誦時，語調深沉浪漫，更偏愛大量和聲色彩的詩作。比如這首《紅帆船》，流露出縹緲的藍調意向，通過敏銳的聽覺的辨別，向我們揭示出音韻的美感，呼喚出人性的富貴：

> 到處都是殘垣斷壁
> 路，怎麼從腳下延伸
> 滑進瞳孔的一盞盞路燈
> 滾出來，並不是星星
> 我不想安慰你
> 在顫抖的楓葉上
> 寫滿關於春天的謊言
> 來自熱帶的太陽鳥
> 並沒有落在我們的樹上
> 而背後的森林之火
> 不過是塵土飛揚的黃昏

　　這首詩感染力十足，讀起來節奏分明、起伏有致。音域畫面寬闊，詩歌傳遞出一種滄桑感、時空感、悲涼感，並且在風格形式上具有很高的詩藝傳承價值。詩人晚年更養成自由而高潔的情操，用友善的心靈去看待一切事物。他吟誦詩歌、積極地通過詩歌傳播其藝術理想。西方近代的哲學家斯賓諾莎（Baruch de Spinoza）有句名言是：「自由人最少想到死，他的智慧不是關於死的默念，而是對於生的沉思。」

and render the hazy atmosphere with delicate brushstrokes. When reciting in his later years, the tone was deep and romantic, and he preferred poems with a lot of harmony and color. For example, this song *Red Sailboat* reveals the misty blues intention, reveals to us the beauty of rhythm and calls out the wealth of human nature through keen auditory discrimination:

Ruins everywhere

The road, how to extend from the foot

A street lamp that slides into the pupil

Get out, it's not a star

I don't want to comfort you

On trembling maple leaves

Full of lies about spring

Sunbird from the tropics

Did not fall on our tree

And behind the forest fire

It's just a dusty evening

This poem is full of appeal, and it reads with a clear rhythm and rhythm. The sound range is wide, and the poetry conveys a sense of vicissitudes, time and space, and sadness, and has a high value of poetic art inheritance in terms of style and form. In his later years, the poet cultivated a free and noble sentiment, and looked at everything with a friendly heart. He recites poetry and actively spreads his artistic ideals through poetry. The modern western philosopher Baruch de Spinoza has a famous saying: "A free man thinks of death at least. His wisdom is not meditation on death, but meditation on

在這裡，我們也可以瞭解到詩人在漂流生涯中獨守情操的悲憫精神。北島在異域時以詩抒發了守望的哀傷之情及自己對祖國的綿緲深情。

三、北島詩的時代價值

　　北島的詩歌創作開始於十年文革後期，因處於身不由己的時代，加以時間因素上文革的荒誕現實，影響了詩人早期詩歌有一種叛逆的詩藝風範。或許有些評論家認為其深層的思辨力，對於人性的扭曲和異化有抱持著信賴又猶疑的矛盾的心情。基於此，我以為絕大部份的人對北島的人格道義及其創作的詩歌和散文是讚譽有加的。北島一心一意想通過作品建立一個自己的世界，這是一個真誠而獨特的世界，正直的世界，正義和人性的世界。在這個世界中，北島也希望自己變成一種開拓詩藝美的典範或者是推展行動的標竿。晚年時，他更以渾厚的北京腔，在詩歌吟誦會上闡揚詩藝的真諦與理想。這位浪跡天涯的漂泊吟唱者不是為藝術而藝術，而是以情注入其中。他也以概括性的詩句昭示出某種哲理的思考，這就增加了詩藝的力度及深度。本文嘗試觀照北島的詩風及其時代價值，也可以說，新世紀起，北島以沉著凝心與

life." Here, we can also understand to the compassionate spirit of the poet in his drifting career. When Bei Dao was in a foreign land, he expressed his sadness and deep love for the motherland in poems.

3. The Era Value of Bei Dao's Poetry

Bei Dao's poetry creation began in the late period of the ten-year Cultural Revolution. Due to the time when he was involuntary, and the absurd reality of the Cultural Revolution due to the time factor, the poet's early poetry had a rebellious poetic style. Perhaps some critics believe that its deep speculative ability has a contradictory feeling of trust and hesitation towards the distortion and alienation of human nature. Based on this, I think that most people praise Bei Dao's personality and morality as well as his poems and prose. Bei Dao wholeheartedly wants to build his own world through his works, which is a sincere and unique world, a world of integrity, justice and humanity. In this world, Bei Dao also hopes to become a model of developing poetic beauty or a benchmark for promoting action. In his later years, he used his strong Beijing accent to expound the true meaning and ideal of poetry at poetry recitals. This wandering singer does not make art for art's sake, but injects emotion into it. He also expresses some kind of philosophical thinking with general lines, which increases the strength and depth of poetic art. This article attempts to observe Bei Dao's poetic style and its value of the times. It can also be said that since the new century, Bei Dao has worked hard to develop poetry art with calmness and concentration. He has a stern and tall and thin appearance, his meditation is like a quiet green pool in an empty

專注,更為詩藝的開拓工作而努力。他有冷峻而高瘦的外貌,沉思如同空谷中寧靜的綠淵潭,吟誦時語速如潺潺清溪舒緩而出。他也是全球卓著的詩人作家,曾獲許多國際大獎並被選為美國藝術文學院終身榮譽院士。

北島早期成名的詩著重對事物的表像投注關心,其中有些詩思即是從現代主義的探索中重新粹取的。他擅用單純的語言表達深邃的情感,散發出完整尊嚴的風貌;為了呈現前衛性的藝術語言,主張機巧的處理象徵性或歷史的聯想,用以昇華現實的創傷。我認為,透過他的詩能觀察到自然與許多新生事物的力量 他對詩歌追敘探索的直覺與高度思辨力,有很大的自由度;對悖論的矛盾性也有極大的包容空間,這就造成了北島詩富於「尋求心靈的自由與實現社會和精神的解放」的時代價值。

－2010.10. 4 作

－山東省《青島大學師範學院學報》,第 28 卷,第 2 期,2011 年 6 月,頁 122-124。

valley, and his speech is as slow as a gurgling stream when he recites. He is also an outstanding poet and writer in the world. He has won many international awards and was elected as a lifetime honorary fellow of the American Academy of Arts and Letters.

Bei Dao's early famous poems focused on the appearance of things, and some of the poetic thoughts were re-absorbed from the exploration of modernism. He is good at expressing deep emotions with simple language, exuding a complete and dignified appearance; in order to present an avant-garde artistic language, he advocates skillfully dealing with symbolic or historical associations to sublimate the trauma of reality. I think that the power of nature and many new things can be observed through his poems. He has a great degree of freedom in his intuition and high speculative ability in the exploration of poetry; he also has a great tolerance for the contradictions of paradox. As a result, Bei Dao's poems are rich in the value of the times of "seeking spiritual freedom and realizing social and spiritual liberation".

2. 一棵挺立的孤松──淺釋艾青的詩

摘要：艾青是中國當代詩壇的巨匠，血液裡流淌著熾烈而自然的詩行，表達對靈魂的詩性拷問。作品多伸入人世，充滿了原始、大膽、鮮明、沉雄等各具其態的藝術形象；而時間將證明他存在的價值。

關鍵詞：艾青、詩歌、意象美、象徵美

一、心鏡澄澈、蕩以遠思的歌者

艾青〈1910-1996〉，浙江金華人，是中國詩壇最重要的詩人之一。18 歲入杭州西湖藝術學院，翌年赴法國勤工儉學；習畫期間開始接觸到西方現代派詩歌。22 歲回國，因參加中國左翼美術家聯盟，被打成右派流放到北大荒勞改；25 歲出獄，四處流亡。在重慶，因受到國民黨特務監視，接受周恩來的建議和資助，於 31 歲時奔赴延安；同年 11 月當選爲陝甘寧邊區參議員。1942 年 6 月，參加延安文藝座談會，後到魯迅藝術學院任教，兼《詩刊》主編。抗戰勝利後，曾任華

2. A Lone Pine Standing Erect —
A Brief Analysis of Ai Qing's Poetry

Abstract: Ai Qing is a master of contemporary Chinese poetry. Flowing in his blood, the blazing yet natural lines express the poetic torture of the soul. His works probe deep into the world, and is full of original, bold, bright and profound artistic images. Time will prove the value of his existence.

Key words: Ai Qing, poetry, imagery beauty, symbolic beauty

1. A Singer with a Clear Mind and Thinking Far Away

Ai Qing (1910-1996), born in Jinhua, Zhejiang, is one of the most important poets in the Chinese poetry circle. At the age of 18, he entered Hangzhou West Lake Academy of Arts, and went to France for a work-study program in the following year. During his painting studies, he came into contact with Western modernist poetry. When he returned to China at the age of 22, he was labeled as a rightist and exiled to the Beidahuang Labor Camp for joining the Chinese Left-wing Artists Alliance. He was released from prison at 25 and went into exile. In Chongqing, because of being monitored by the Kuomintangsecret agents, he accepted Zhou Enlai's suggestion and funding, and went to Yan'an at the age of 31; in November of the same year, he was elected as a senator for the Shaanxi-Gansu-Ningxia Border Region. In June 1942,

北聯合大學文藝學院副院長，華北大學副主任。解放後，參加軍事管制委員會，接管中央美術學院。主要作品有《歡呼集》、《新文藝論集》、《寶石的紅星》、《黑鰻》、《春天》、《新詩論》等。不料，47 歲那年，在反右運動中，被錯劃為右派。48 歲時又流放到東北、新疆勞動了近 20 年，直至 69 歲才徹底平反。一生心鏡澄澈，恰如冰痕雪影中，蕩以遠思的歌者。曾任中國作家協會副主席、全國人大常委會委員等職，86 歲病死於北京。出版過詩集、散文、譯詩、論文集等數十多種，呈現了他詩藝的種種面向，也獲得中國作家協會全國優秀新詩獎、法國文學藝術最高勳章等殊榮。

　　艾青最可貴之處，是他悲愴的命運竟激發起鐵一般的意志力，鞭策他在獄中寫下了不少詩；可以說是詩人生命與心靈歷程的總結性觀照。不僅對國家民族的誠摯關心、以悲憫心為人民請命；他控訴罪惡，又能搖起希望之旗幟，為無數被壓迫人民的靈魂所遭受的苦難而謳歌。他嚮往幸福，朝向光明。其中，〈大堰河——我的保姆〉就是在獄中翻譯比利時

he participated in the Yan'an Forum on Literature and Art, and later taught at the Lu Xun Academy of Art, and was also the editor-in-chief of *Poetry Magazine*. After the victory of the Anti-Japanese War, he served as the deputy dean of the College of Literature and Art of North China United University and the deputy director of North China University. After liberation, he participated in the Military Control Committee and took over the Central Academy of Fine Arts. His main works include *Cheering Collection, New Literature and Art Essays, The Red Star of the Gem, Black Eel, Spring, New Poems* and so on. Unexpectedly, at the age of 47, during the anti-rightist movement, he was wrongly classified as a rightist. At 48, he was exiled to Northeast China and Xinjiang to work for nearly 20 years, and he was not completely rehabilitated until he was 69 years old. Throughout his life, his heart is clear, just like a singer who thinks far away in the shadow of ice marks and snow. He served as vice chairman of the Chinese Writers Association, member of the Standing Committee of the National People's Congress, etc., and died of illness in Beijing at the age of 86. He has published more than dozens of collections of poetry, prose, translated poems, and collections of essays, presenting various aspects of his poetic art. He has also won the National Excellent New Poetry Award of the Chinese Writers Association and the highest medal of French literature and art.

The most valuable thing about Ai Qing is that his sad fate inspired his iron willpower, spurring him to write many poems in prison; it can be said to be a conclusive observation of the poet's life and spiritual journey. He not only cared sincerely for the nation, pleaded for the people with compassion; he accused crimes, but also waved the banner of hope and sang praises for the suffering suffered by the souls of countless oppressed people. He yearns for happiness, toward the light. Among them, *Dayanhe—My Nanny* is a long poem written while translating the poems of the Belgian poet Verhaalen in prison, and it

詩人凡爾哈侖的詩時寫下的長詩而聲名遠播。三、四十年代出版的詩集主要有《大堰河》、《北方》、《他死在第二次》、《向太陽》、《獻給鄉村的詩》、《反法西斯》、《曠野》、《黎明的通知》、《雪裏鑽》等。早期作品深受古典詩歌的浪漫主義與現實主義傳統的影響,其特色是「沉鬱而感傷,文筆疏放而流暢」;浩瀚的氣勢,如一棵挺然自立的孤松。抗戰以後,血液裡流淌著更熾烈而自然的詩行,詩風逐漸轉向悲壯、激昂。長詩〈向太陽〉和〈火把〉就是這一時期的代表作,顯示了革命的現實主義的特點;也採用民歌體,其激越的愛國思想,引導他去為廣大的勞動百姓的疾苦而獻身。

五十年代詩作,顯得平淡,詩的表現方法寫實與象徵互滲,仍保有真樸、凝練、想像豐富、意象獨特的格局。70 年代末復出後,文思泉湧。1978 年 4 月,上海《文匯報》發表他沉寂後第一首詩《紅旗》,繼而陸續發表了長詩〈在浪尖上〉、〈光的讚歌〉等詩作。正如他所說一般,「在汽笛的長鳴聲中,我的生命開始了新的航程。」他已從歷史的迷霧中放射出異彩,至此,其風格轉為注重在具體物象中把握超越物象的意蘊,呈現出深沉的哲思。晚年主要作品有:詩集《艾青詩選》、《艾青敘事詩選》、《歸來的歌》、《雪蓮》、《彩色的詩》、《抒情詩一百首》、《艾青短詩選》等。論文集《詩論》、《艾青談詩》。長篇小說《綠洲筆記》。詩人先後出訪了西德、奧地利、意大利、法國、美國、南斯拉夫、日本、新加坡等國,為促進中西文化匯合而努力,其作品被收入各種選本,也被譯成多種文字。

became famous far and wide. The poetry anthologies published in the 1930s and 1940s mainly include *Dayan River*, *North*, *He Died the Second Time*, *To the Sun*, *Poems Dedicated to the Countryside*, *Anti-Fascism*, *The Wilderness*, *Notice of Dawn*, *Drilling in the Snow*, and so on. His early works were deeply influenced by the traditions of romanticism and realism in classical poetry, and are characterized by "depressed and sentimental, loose and smooth writing"; the vast momentum is like a solitary pine standing on its own. After the Anti-Japanese War, more fiery and natural lines of poetry flowed in the blood, and the poetic style gradually turned tragic and passionate. The long poems *Towards the Sun* and *Torch* are representative works of this period, showing the characteristics of revolutionary realism; they also adopt the style of folk songs, and their passionate patriotic thoughts lead him to dedicate himself to the suffering of the vast number of working people.

Poetry in the 1950s seemed plain, and the expression methods of poetry interpenetrated between realism and symbolism, and still maintained a pattern of simplicity, conciseness, rich imagination, and unique imagery. After his comeback in the late 1970s, Wen Si springs up. In April 1978, Shanghai Wen Wei Po published his first poem *Red Flag* after his silence, and then successively published long poems such as *On the Top of the Waves* and *Ode to Light*. As he said, "In the long sound of the siren, my life started a new voyage." He has radiated splendor from the fog of history. So far, his style has turned to focus on grasping the transcendence of objects in specific objects. Connotation, showing deep philosophical thinking. His main works in his later years include poetry collections such as *Selected Poems of Ai Qing*, *Song of Return*, *Snow Lotus*, *Colorful Poems*, *One Hundred Lyric Poems*, *Selected Short Poems of Ai Qing*, etc. Collected essays *On Poetry* and *Ai Qing on Poetry*, and the novel *Oasis Notes*. The poet successively visited West Germany, Austria, Italy, France, the United States, Yugoslavia, Japan, Singapore and other countries, and worked hard to promote the integration of Chinese and Western cultures. His works have been included in various anthologies and translated into many languages.

二、詩美的意象與內涵

艾青的作品充滿了原始、大膽、鮮明、沉雄等各具其態的藝術形象，與他強烈的個人風格相關，這點是無庸置疑的。他詩文創作的根深深地扎在中國文學傳統的沃土之中，在詩藝上，他留法期間也汲取了西方象徵派詩歌的藝術營養。因此，詩歌裡不只是單純而抒情地吟誦，而是融入了一種深沉的思想力，顯得凝碧而有生命力，自成一家的風格。他一生經歷過成名的輝煌，也遭遇過政治的磨難。然而，在命運的顛沛中，更可以看出一個人的氣節。出現在三十年代的他，如閃耀於冬季的燦星，其詩歌情緒的節奏較悲切、感傷，由內斂而奔瀉，試圖敲響讀者的思想回音。異國求學，自然思鄉情切；尤其是當時中國正籠罩在"一‧二八"戰爭的炮火裏。當艾青返國時，目賭了處處瘡痍的山河；他直想用自己的畫筆投入戰鬥。可是不久，他遭到逮捕。也就是在那個時期，他寫下許多力作。其中最著名的一首詩是 1933 年春天，在上海監獄裡，青年詩人蔣海澄初次使用「艾青」這個筆名寫下了〈大堰河──我的保姆〉。詩歌清新雋永，令人憾動，並珍藏在廣大的人民的心田。它以真情形象地把其乳母的慈愛與中國千千萬萬村婦傳統的勤勞美德與犧牲精神相融合，細膩地描摩出大堰河-艾青的乳母勞動的情景；其間浸透出詩人滿腔的愛憐與同情：

2. The Imagery and Connotation of Poetic Beauty

Ai Qing's works are full of original, bold, bright, and solemn artistic images, which are related to his strong personal style, which is beyond doubt. The roots of his poetry creation are deeply rooted in the fertile soil of Chinese literary tradition. In terms of poetic art, he also absorbed the artistic nutrition of Western Symbolism poetry during his stay in France. Therefore, the poems are not just simple and lyrical reciting, but a kind of deep thinking power is integrated into them, which appears solid and vital, and has a style of its own. He has experienced the glory of fame and the tribulation of politics in his life. However, in the ups and downs of fate, one can see a person's integrity. Appearing in the 1930s, he is like a shining star in winter. The emotional rhythm of his poems is more sad and sentimental, from restrained to rushing, trying to echo the readers' thoughts. Studying in a foreign country made me feel homesick; especially at that time when China was under fire from the "January 28th" War. When Ai Qing returned to China, he saw the devastated mountains and rivers everywhere; he always wanted to use his paintbrush to fight. But soon, he was arrested. It was during that period that he wrote many masterpieces. One of the most famous poems is that in the spring of 1933, in the Shanghai Prison, the young poet Jiang Haicheng wrote *Dayanhe — My Nanny* for the first time using the pseudonym "Ai Qing". The poems are fresh and timeless, touching, and treasured in the hearts of the majority of the people. It vividly integrates the love of its wet nurse with the traditional hardworking virtues and sacrifice spirit of thousands of village women in China, and delicately depicts the scene of Dayanhe — Ai Qing's wet nurse working; the poet's full of love and compassion with sympathy:

《大堰河，是我的保姆》

　　她的名字就是生她的村莊的名字，
　　她是童養媳，
　　大堰河，是我的保姆。
　　我是地主的兒子；
　　也是吃了大堰河的奶而長大了的
　　大堰河的兒子。
　　大堰河以養育我而養育她的家，
　　而我，是吃了你的奶而被養育了的，
　　大堰河啊，我的保姆。
　　大堰河，今天我看到雪使我想起了你：
　　你的被雪壓著的草蓋的墳墓，
　　你的關閉了的故居檐頭的枯死的瓦菲，
　　你的被典押了的一丈平方的園地，
　　你的門前的長了青苔的石椅，
　　大堰河，今天我看到雪使我想起了你。
　　你用你厚大的手掌把我抱在懷裏，撫摸我；
　　在你搭好了灶火之後，
　　在你拍去了圍裙上的炭灰之後，
　　在你嘗到飯已煮熟了之後，
　　在你把烏黑的醬碗放到烏黑的桌子上之後，
　　你補好了兒子們的為山腰的荊棘扯破的衣服之後，
　　在你把小兒被柴刀砍傷了的手包好之後，
　　在你把夫兒們的襯衣上的虱子一顆顆的掐死之後，
　　在你拿起了今天的第一顆雞蛋之後，

Dayanhe is my nanny.

Her name is the name of the village where she was born,
She is a child bride,
Dayanhe is my nanny.
I am the son of the landowner;
He also grew up by eating Dayanhe's milk.
The son of Dayanhe.
Dayanhe nurtures her family by nurturing me,
And I, who was nourished by your milk,
Dayanhe, my nanny.
Dayanhe, the snow I saw today reminded me of you:
Your grass-covered grave under the weight of snow,
The dead Wafi of your closed eaves,
Your pledged ten-foot-square garden,
The mossy stone chair in front of your door,
Dayanhe, the snow I saw today reminded me of you.
You take me in your arms with your thick palms and touch me;
After you set up the fire,
After you slapped the charcoal off your apron,
After you taste the rice is cooked,
After you put the sooty bowl of sauce on the sooty table,
After you mend the clothes of your sons that were torn by
　　the thorns of the mountainside,
After you wrapped up the child's hand that was cut with
　　a hatchet,
After you've strangled the lice from the shirts of your
　　husbands one by one,
After you picked up the first egg of the day,

你用你厚大的手掌把我抱在懷裏，撫摸我。
我是地主的兒子，
在我吃光了你大堰河的奶之後，
我被生我的父母領回到自己的家裏。
啊，大堰河，你爲什麼要哭？
我做了生我的父母家裏的新客了！
我摸著紅漆雕花的傢俱，
我摸著父母的睡床上金色的花紋，
我呆呆地看著檐頭的我不認得的"天倫叙樂"的匾，
我摸著新換上的衣服的絲的和貝殼的鈕扣，
我看著母親懷裏的不熟識的妹妹，
我坐著油漆過的安了火鉢的炕凳，
我吃著碾了三番的白米的飯，
但，我是這般怔怔不安！因爲我
我做了生我的父母家裏的新客了。
大堰河，爲了生活，
在她流盡了她的乳液之後，
她就開始用抱過我的兩臂勞動了；
她含著笑，洗著我們的衣服，
她含著笑，提著菜籃到村邊的結冰的池塘去，
她含著笑，切著冰屑悉索的蘿蔔，
她含著笑，用手掏著豬吃的麥糟，
她含著笑，扇著燉肉的爐子的火，
她含著笑，背了團箕到廣場上去
曬好那些大豆和小麥，

You hold me in your arms and touch me with your thick palms.
I am the son of the landowner,
After I ate all the milk of your Dayanhe,
I was taken back to my own home by the parents who
　　gave birth to me.
Ah, Dayanhe, why are you crying?
I'm a new guest in my parents' house!
I touched the red lacquered and carved furniture,
I touched the golden patterns on my parents' bed,
I stared blankly at the "Tian Lun Xu Le" plaque on the
　　eaves that I didn't recognize,
I feel the silk and shell buttons of my new clothes,
I looked at the unfamiliar younger sister in my mother's arms,
I sat on a painted Kang stool with a fire bowl,
I eat white rice that has been milled three times,
But, I am so coy and uneasy! because I
I'm a new guest in the house of my parents.
Dayan River, for life,
After she drained her lotion,
She began to work with the arms that embraced me;
With a smile on her face, she washed our clothes,
With a smile on her face, she carried a vegetable basket to
　　the frozen pond by the village,
With a smile on her face, she sliced the radish with ice crumbs,
With a smile on her face, she took out the wheat grains
　　that pigs ate with her hands,
With a smile on her face, she fanned the fire of the
　　stewing stove,
With a smile on her face, she carried the pan and went to
　　the square
Dry those soybeans and wheat,

大堰河，爲了生活，
在她流盡了她的乳液之後，
她就用抱過我的兩臂，勞動了。
大堰河，深愛著她的乳兒；
在年節裡，爲了他，忙著切那冬米的糖，
爲了他，常悄悄地走到村邊的她的家裏去，
爲了他，走到她的身邊叫一聲"媽"，
大堰河，把他畫的大紅大綠的關雲長
貼在灶邊的墙上，
大堰河，會對她的鄰居誇口贊美她的乳兒；
大堰河曾做了一個不能對人說的夢：
在夢裏，她吃著她的乳兒的婚酒，
坐在輝煌的結彩的堂上，
而她的嬌美的媳婦親切的叫她"婆婆"
…………
大堰河，深愛她的乳兒！
大堰河，在她的夢沒有做醒的時候已死了。
她死時，乳兒不在她的旁側，
她死時，平時打罵她的丈夫也爲她流淚，
五個兒子，個個哭得很悲，
她死時，輕輕地呼著她的乳兒的名字，
大堰河，已死了，
她死時，乳兒不在她的旁側。
大堰河，含淚的去了！
同著四十幾年的人世生活的凌侮，

Dayan River, for life,
After she drained her lotion,
She just used the two arms that hugged me and worked.
Dayanhe loves her baby dearly;
During the New Year's festival, for him, I was busy
　　cutting the sugar of the winter rice,
For him, Chang quietly went to her house on the edge of
　　he village,
For him, go to her side and call "Mom",
Dayanhe, Guan Yunchang who painted him red and green
On the wall next to the stove,
Dayanhe will boast to her neighbors about her baby;
　Dayanhe once had a dream that could not be told to others:
　　　In dreams she drank her baby's wedding wine,
Sitting in the glorious festooned hall,
And her beautiful daughter-in-law affectionately called
　　her "mother-in-law"
. . . .
Dayanhe loves her baby dearly!
Dayanhe died before she woke up from her dream.
When she died, the baby was not by her side,
When she died, her husband who usually beat and scolded
　　her also shed tears for her,
Five sons, all weeping bitterly,
When she died softly calling her baby's name,
Dayan River is dead,
When she died, the baby was not by her side.
Dayanhe, I went there with tears in my eyes!
With more than forty years of humiliation in human life,

同著數不盡的奴隸的悽苦，
同著四塊錢的棺材和幾束稻草，
同著幾尺長方的埋棺材的土地，
同著一手把的紙錢的灰，
大堰河，她含淚的去了。
這是大堰河所不知道的：
她的醉酒的丈夫已死去，
大兒做了土匪，
第二個死在炮火的烟裏，
第三，第四，第五
而我，我是在寫著給予這不公道的世界的咒語。
當我經了長長的飄泊回到故土時，
在山腰裏，田野上，
兄弟們碰見時，是比六七年前更要親密！
這，這是爲你，靜靜的睡著的大堰河
所不知道的啊！
大堰河，今天你的乳兒是在獄裏，
寫著一首呈給你的讚美詩，
呈給你黃土下紫色的靈魂，
呈給你擁抱過我的直伸著的手，
呈給你吻過我的唇，
呈給你泥黑的溫柔的臉顏，
呈給你養育了我的乳房，
呈給你的兒子們，我的兄弟們，
呈給大地上一切的，

With the misery of countless slaves,
With a coffin of four dollars and a few bundles of straw,
With the coffin land a few feet long,
With handfuls of ashes from paper money,
Dayan River, she went there with tears in her eyes.
This is what Dayanhe didn't know:
Her drunken husband is dead,
The eldest son became a bandit,
The second died in the smoke of the gunfire,
third, fourth, fifth
And I, I am writing the spell for this unjust world.
When I returned to my native land after a long wandering,
In the hillsides, in the fields,
When brothers meet, they are closer than six or seven years ago!
This, this is for you, the peacefully sleeping Dayan River
What I don't know!
Dayanhe, your baby is in prison today,
Wrote a hymn to you,
To you purple soul under the loess,
To your outstretched hand that embraced me,
To the lips that you kissed me,
With your muddy, gentle face,
To you the breasts that nourished me,
To your sons, my brothers,
to all that is on earth,

　　我的大堰河般的保姆和她們的兒子，
　　呈給愛我如愛她自己的兒子般的大堰河。
　　大堰河，我是吃了你的奶而長大了的
　　你的兒子
　　我敬你
　　愛你

　　詩語的意象和節奏的掌握功力是一首詩的重要特質，艾青寫這首詩時，大堰河早已離開人世。他以此詩引領讀者進入一個理性與感性交融又帶有悲愴色彩的世界。首行即凸顯了「大堰河」的主角地位，點出大堰河悲苦的身世；詩人因吃了大堰河的奶而長大，所以對她自然充滿了特有的深情，故觸目所及皆是對乳母悲苦的經歷與思念。詩人別出心裁地塑造出舊中國勞動婦女勤奮、健壯、仁厚溫良的大堰河保姆的崇高形象。

　　第二段以下，情思細膩，詩人透過冰冷的鐵窗，在悲泣中，特別想念起他的乳母被雪壓著的草蓋的墳墓；加上畫面上象徵著淒涼的一系列形象，怎能不動人心眼而對大堰河悲慘經歷產生哀傷悼念之思。詩人繼以八個排比句式，描摩出詩人自幼在自己父母家裏的"忸怩不安"與對大堰河情感之彌堅，也鮮明塑造出自己心靈萌發著叛逆思想和反抗精神，無矯飾雕章的痕跡。接著，又連用六個排比句式，描述了大堰河怎樣"含著笑"，透過移覺把視覺印象轉換為聽覺，精確地反映出現實的勞動面，也充分表現了大堰河樸實的美。末節

My Dayanhe-like nurses and their sons,
To Dayanhe who loves me like her own son.
Dayanhe, I grew up by drinking your milk
Your son
I respect you
Love you

The mastery of poetic imagery and rhythm is an important characteristic of a poem. When Ai Qing wrote this poem, Dayanhe had already passed away. With this poem, he leads readers into a world where rationality and sensibility are blended together and also full of sadness. The first line highlights the protagonist status of "Dayanhe" and points out Dayanhe's tragic life experience; the poet grew up on the milk of Dayanhe, so he is naturally full of special affection for her, so everything he sees is about the wet nurse. Sad experiences and thoughts. The poet ingeniously portrays the lofty image of Dayanhe's nanny who is a diligent, robust, benevolent and gentle working woman in old China.

After the second paragraph, the sentiment is delicate. Through the cold iron window, the poet, in weeping, especially misses the grass-covered grave of his nurse under the weight of snow; plus a series of images symbolizing desolation on the screen, how can he not move? People feel sad and mourn for the tragic experience of Dayan River. The poet continued to use eight parallel sentence patterns to describe the poet's "coy and uneasiness" in his parents' home since childhood and his strong feelings for Dayanhe, and also clearly portrayed the rebellious thoughts and rebellious spirit sprouting in his heart, without pretentiousness. Traces of engravings. Then, it uses six parallel sentence patterns to describe how Dayanhe "smiles" and converts visual impressions into auditory senses through telepathy, accurately reflecting the

道出詩人獻給大堰河的輓歌和讚美，令孺慕之情帶來赫然有力的情感。此詩內涵之美，在於詩人對大堰河溫柔且深情，才能打動讀者的心。而艾青善以最真實的影象折射出最現代的敏感，且用語豐富，形象準確，在平凡之中鋪陳出不凡的聯想。這便使此詩的主題的社會意義有二：其一、如實的描繪，都是對現實生活準確的提煉和凝聚；其二、是真情實感的迸發和流淌。詩裡無論是對往事的追懷，對乳母的讚揚，對人生的慨嘆，對世界的憤懑，均能溶和在他思想感情之中，且蕩氣迴腸。或許大堰河的痛苦時代已成為歷史的追憶。但艾青經歷一次次痛苦的磨難，卻始終能堅強地活下來為人民繼續謳歌。

在 1937 年，"七七事變"後，艾青成了逃亡的難民，先是從杭州逃到老家金華，然後帶著妻子，從金華逃往武漢，中華民族確實到了最危急的時刻。詩人於 12 月 28 日，一個嚴冬的夜晚。他悲痛地寫下了〈雪落在中國的土地上〉這首震撼人心的詩歌。搖吶出中國土地被侵略戰爭無情的破壞與為苦難的底層百姓發出哀號：

> 雪落在中國的土地上。
> 寒冷在封鎖著中國呀……
> 風，

reality of labor and fully expressing the simple beauty of Dayanhe. The last section expresses the poet's elegy and praise to Dayanhe, which brings impressive and powerful emotions to the admiration of children. The beauty of the connotation of this poem lies in the poet's tenderness and affection for the Dayan River, which can move the readers' hearts. And Ai Qingshan reflects the most modern sensitivity with the most authentic images, with rich language and accurate images, laying out extraordinary associations in the ordinary. This makes the theme of this poem have two social meanings: first, the truthful description is an accurate refinement and condensation of real life; second, it is the burst and flow of true feelings. No matter in the poem, whether it is the nostalgia for the past, the praise for the nurse, the lament for life, or the resentment for the world, they can all be melted into his thoughts and feelings, and they are soul-stirring. Perhaps Dayanhe's painful era has become a memory of history. But Ai Qing has experienced painful ordeals again and again, but she has always been able to survive firmly and continue to sing for the people.

In 1937, after the "July 7th Incident", Ai Qing became a fugitive refugee. He first fled from Hangzhou to his hometown of Jinhua, and then fled from Jinhua to Wuhan with his wife. The Chinese nation has indeed reached the most critical moment. The poet wrote on December 28, a harsh winter's night. He wrote the shocking poem *Snow Falls on the Land of China* in grief. Shaking out the ruthless destruction of the Chinese land by the war of aggression and wailing for the suffering people at the bottom:

Snow falls on the land of China.
The cold is blocking China ...
Wind,

　　像一個太悲哀了的老婦。
　　緊緊地跟隨著
　　伸出寒冷的指爪
　　拉扯著行人的衣襟。
　　用著像土地一樣古老的
　　一刻也不停地絮聒著……
　　那從林間出現的，
　　趕著馬車的
　　你中國的農夫，
　　戴著皮帽，
　　冒著大雪
　　你要到哪兒去呢？
　　告訴你
　　我也是農人的後裔──
　　由於你們的
　　刻滿了痛苦的皺紋的臉，
　　我能如此深深地
　　知道了
　　生活在草原上的人們的
　　歲月的艱辛。
　　而我
　　也並不比你們快樂啊
　　── 躺在時間的河流上
　　苦難的浪濤
　　曾經幾次把我吞沒而又捲起 ──

Like a very sad old woman.
Follow closely
Stretch out cold fingers
Pulling the skirt of the pedestrian.
With as old as the earth
Non-stop nagging …
That came out of the woods,
Driving a carriage
You Chinese farmer,
Wearing a fur hat,
Braved the snow
Where are you going?
Tell you
I am also a descendant of farmers —
Because of your
A face wrinkled with pain,
I can so deeply
Understood
People who live on the grasslands
The hardships of the years.
But me
I'm not happier than you
Lying on the river of time one by one
Waves of misery
Has engulfed me and rolled me up several times

流浪與監禁
己失去了我的青春的最可貴的日子，
我的生命
也像你們的生命
一樣的憔悴呀。
雪落在中國的土地上，
寒冷在封鎖著中國呀……
沿著雪夜的河流，
一盞小油燈在徐緩地移行，
那破爛的烏篷船裏
映著燈光，垂著頭
坐著的是誰呀？
──啊，你
篷髮垢面的小婦，
是不是
你的家
──那幸福與溫暖的巢穴──
己被暴戾的敵人
燒毀了麼？
是不是
也像這樣的夜間，
失去了男人的保護，
在死亡的恐怖裏
你已經受盡敵人刺刀的戲弄？
咳，就在如此寒冷的今夜，

Vagrancy and imprisonment
I have lost the most precious days of my youth,
My life
Also like your life
Same haggard.
Snow falls on the land of China,
The cold is blocking China ...
Along the snowy night river,
A small oil lamp is moving slowly,
In that tattered bird canopy
With the light on, head down
Who is sitting?
One by one, you
The shaggy little woman,
Yes or no
Your home
— the nest of happiness and warmth —
Violent enemy
Is it burnt?
Yes or no
And nights like this,
Lost the protection of men,
In the terror of death
Have you been teased by the enemy's bayonet?
Cough, on such a cold night,

無數的
我們的年老的母親，
都蜷伏在不是自己的家裏，
就像異邦人
不知明天的車輪
要滾上怎樣的路程？
──而且
中國的路
是如此的崎嶇，
是如此的泥濘呀。
雪落在中國的土地上。
寒冷在封鎖著中國呀……
透過雪夜的草原
那些被烽火所嚙啃著的地域，
無數的，土地的墾植者
失去了他們所飼養的家禽
失去了他們肥沃的田地
擁擠在
生活的絕望的污巷裏；
機遇的大地
朗向陰暗的天
伸出乞援的
顫抖著的兩臂。
中國的痛苦與災難
像這雪夜一樣廣闊而又漫長呀！

Countless

Our old mother,

Crouching in a home that is not their own,

Like a stranger

I don't know the wheels of tomorrow

What kind of journey do you want to roll on?

One by one and

China's road

So rough,

It's so muddy.

Snow falls on the land of China.

The cold is blocking China ...

Through the grassland of the snowy night

Those areas gnawed by the flames of war,

Countless, cultivators of the land

Lost their poultry

Lost their fertile fields

Crowded in

In the hopeless alleys of life;

Land of opportunity

Bright to the dark sky

Outstretched

Trembling arms.

Pain and Disaster in China

As wide and long as this snowy night!

> 雪落在中國的土地上
> 寒冷在封鎖著中國呀……
> 中國，
> 我的在沒有燈光的晚上
> 所寫的無力的詩句
> 能給你些許的溫暖麼？

　　就詩的結構而言，首先從視覺起筆，雪聲、風聲、馬車聲交織成蒼茫的底色，凸出油燈、烏篷船及監獄裡雪夜的心情，最後再以想像之筆蕩開詩意，再次傳達出詩人為人民痛苦生活和對政治的迫害，感到極為失望，其滿腔的憤懣和控訴日本侵略者的蠻橫行徑，在詩人銘人肺腑的筆下，終於發出了時代沉重的強音。全詩的意象生動、明朗又口語化的語言，能喚起人們感情的共鳴；此外，詩的內在節奏加強了，而響亮的音韻與直抒胸臆的形式，也形成此詩具體可感的藝術形象。

　　再看這首 1938 年初寫下的〈手推車〉，艾青就特意的安排了映入眼底的手推車，個別形成「象」，凸顯出中國東北人民在戰事陰影下貧窮的身影，這些由近及遠的景物〈象〉，對詩人來說，每一觸及，就足以增添他的一份愁。寫的是詩人情寓景中，與祖國土地深密不可分割的悲痛：

> 在黃河流過的地域
> 在無數的枯乾了的河底

Snow falls on the land of China
The cold is blocking China ...
China,
Mine at night without lights
Feeble verse written
Can I give you some warmth?

As far as the structure of the poem is concerned, it starts from the visual, and the sound of snow, wind, and carriages interweave into a vast background, highlight the mood of oil lamps, bird canopy boats and the snowy night in the prison, and finally use the pen of imagination to express the poetic flavor, once again conveying the poet's extreme disappointment for the people's painful life and political persecution, his full of resentment and accusation against Japan The barbaric behavior of the invaders, under the poet's heartfelt pen, finally uttered the heavy voice of the times. The vivid imagery of the whole poem and the clear and colloquial language can arouse people's emotional resonance; in addition, the internal rhythm of the poem is strengthened, and the loud rhyme and straight-forward form also form the specific and sensible artistic image of the poem.

Looking at the song *Trolley* written in early 1938, Ai Qing specially arranged the trolleys that catch the eye, each forming an image, highlighting the poverty of the people in Northeast China under the shadow of war. These scenes from near to far Elephant, for the poet, every touch is enough to add to his sorrow. What is written is the grief that is inseparable from the land of the motherland in the poet's love scene:

In the area where the Yellow River flows
At the bottom of countless dry rivers

手推車
以唯一的輪子
發出使陰暗的天穹痙攣的尖音
穿過寒冷與靜寂
從這一個山腳
到那一個山腳
徹響著
北國人民的悲哀

在冰雪凝凍的日子
在貧窮的小村與小村之間
手推車
以單獨的輪子
刻畫在灰黃土層上的深深的轍跡
穿過廣闊與荒漠
從這一條路
到那一條路
交織著
北國人民的悲哀

　　此詩情感沉鬱，語言質樸平白；採用隱喻、象徵的表現手法，似睹其容。藉「手推車」形象來表達抽象事理，以「北國人民的悲哀」形成「意」，由「情」轉化為「理」，以達到象徵的作用，來拈出主旨；是為寄託江河受外敵污染，乃

Trolley
With only wheels
With a shriek that convulses the dark sky
Through the cold and silence
From the foot of this mountain
To the foot of that mountain
Resounding
The sorrow of the people of the north

On a snowy day
Between poor villages and villages
Trolley
With separate wheels
Deep ruts carved on the gray-yellow soil layer
Through the vastness and desert
From this road
To that road
Intertwined
The sorrow of the people of the north

This poem is full of gloomy emotions and simple and plain language; it uses metaphor and symbolic expression techniques, which seems to be betting on its content. Using the image of the "trolley" to express abstract truths, using "the sorrow of the people of the Northland" to form "meaning", and transforming "feeling" into "reason", in order to achieve the role of a symbol,

世之悲哀。意象的轉換，使詩歌節奏極為迅速。由黃河到北國，由山腳到荒漠，時空在急速轉換，傳達出詩人激蕩的心潮。詩句的感人正來源於詩人深刻的感思，當時外侮的侵略，戰火的燎原，彷彿只一瞬間。唯有北國人民因動亂年代所帶來的恐懼，讓詩人真實地表現了對北國人民的憂患和複雜的心態。回顧 1939 年 7 月，為了紀念"七七事變"兩周年，當時中國許多地方掀起了抗日宣傳的高潮。艾青的熱血頓時沸騰起來了，也加入浩大的抗議隊伍中，不久之後，他便寫下了氣魄恢弘的長詩〈火把〉，以自己的反思觀照一個時代的反思。之後，艾青在四十年代初期，由於延安「整風」遭受打擊，直到 1949 年作品創作量並不多，但仍有一些值得注目之作。

如 1941 年 12 月寫下〈時代〉這首力作時，艾青剛抵達延安不久，仍抱著對關懷苦難人民的理想與抨擊黑暗的浪漫情懷。然而，為奔赴延安，他風塵僕僕抵達後，感受的卻是相當地鬱悶，詩裡更痛切地說著：

> 我站立在低矮的屋檐下
> 出神地望著蠻野的山崗
> 和高遠空闊的天空，
> 很久很久心裏像感受了什麼奇蹟，
> 我看見一個閃光的東西
> 它像太陽一樣鼓舞我的心，
> 在天邊帶著沉重的轟響，

to draw out the main idea; it is to sustenance that the rivers are polluted by foreign enemies, is the sorrow of the world. The conversion of images makes the rhythm of poetry extremely fast. From the Yellow River to the Northland, from the foot of the mountain to the desert, time and space are changing rapidly, conveying the poet's agitated heart. The moving verses come from the poet's deep thoughts. At that time, the invasion of foreign aggression and the prairie fire of war seemed to be only a moment. Only the fear brought about by the people of the Northland due to the turbulent years allowed the poet to truly express his worries and complicated mentality towards the people of the Northland. Looking back at July 1939, in order to commemorate the second anniversary of the "July 7th Incident", anti-Japanese propaganda climaxed in many places in China. Ai Qing's blood boiled immediately, and he also joined the huge protest team. Not long after, he wrote a magnificent long poem *Torch*, reflecting the reflection of an era with his own reflection. After that, in the early 1940s, Ai Qing was hit by the "rectification movement" in Yan'an. Until 1949, the number of works produced was not much, but there were still some notable works.

For example, when Ai Qing wrote the masterpiece *Time* in December 1941, not long after he arrived in Yan'an, he still held the ideal of caring for the suffering people and his romantic feelings of attacking darkness. However, in order to go to Yan'an, after he arrived in a long way, he felt quite depressed, and the poem said more painfully:

> *I stand under the low eaves*
> *Gazing raptly at the savage hills*
> *And the high and wide sky,*
> *For a long time, I felt like a miracle in my heart,*
> *I saw a shiny thing*
> *It lifts my heart like the sun,*
> *With a heavy bang on the horizon,*

帶著暴風雨似的狂嘯，
隆隆滾輾而來……

我向它神往而又歡呼！
當我聽見從陰雲壓著的雪山的那面
傳來了不平的道路上巨輪顛簸的軋響
我的心追趕著它，激劇地跳動著
像那些奔赴婚禮的新郎
——縱然我知道由它所帶給我的
並不是節日的狂歡
和什麼雜耍場上的哄笑
卻是比一千個屠場更殘酷的景象，
而我却依然奔向它
帶著一個生命所能發揮的熱情。

我不是弱者——我不會沾沾自喜，
我不是自己能安慰或欺騙自己的人
我不滿足那世界曾經給過我的
——無論是榮譽，無論是恥辱
也無論是陰沉沉的注視和黑夜似的仇恨
以及人們的目光因它而閃耀的幸福
我在你們不知道的地方感到空虛
我要求更多些，更多些呵
給我生活的世界
我永遠伸張著兩臂

命。詩人因為這片土地的脈搏，時時在他的血液裏湧動，
更增強了詩的情味力量；而願意獻身於時代的艾青，說出熱

With howling like a storm,
Rumbling and rolling ...

I am fascinated by it and cheer!
When I hear from the side of the snow-capped mountains
There is the sound of bumpy wheels on the uneven road
My heart chases after it, beating wildly
Like those grooms who go to the wedding
— Even though I know what it brings me
It's not a festive carnival
And what sideshow laughter
But a crueler sight than a thousand slaughterhouses,
And I still run towards it
With the enthusiasm that a life can exert.

I am not weak — I will not be complacent,
I'm not someone I can comfort or lie to myself
I'm not satisfied with what the world has given me
— Neither honor nor disgrace
Whether it is the gloomy gaze and the night-like hatred
And the happiness with which people's eyes shine
I feel empty where you don't know
I want more, more
Give me the world to live in
I always have my arms outstretche

This is obviously to set off the "concern for the country" by means of the sparse scene or image of the turbulent era seen by the mind. The beauty of poetry is always attached to certain

愛祖國「勝過我曾經愛過的一切」時，情韻便格外深長，令
人咀嚼不盡。但總觀全詩，無疑是表現了詩人對動亂時代的
沉痛之聲，也是對一種渴望美好未來的更廣闊的追求。詩裡
跳躍著對國家民族赤誠的心、對政治不平的憤慨，也交織著
詩人的希望、憧憬和迎向永恆的光明。晚年的艾青，詩歌更
為深邃，意境更為宏闊。對祖國深沉的愛與為真理而勇於獻
身的精神終於獲得廣大的禮讚與迴響。如 1979 年年 3 月於上
海寫下〈盼望〉，可以說是艾青重新復出的代表作之一：

> 一個海員說，
> 他最喜歡的是起錨所激起的
> 那一片潔白的浪花……
>
> 一個海員說，
> 最使他高興的是拋錨所發出的
> 那一陣鐵鏈的喧嘩……
>
> 一個盼望出發
> 一個盼望到達

things. As time goes by, after thousands of years, what kind of vision should we use to look at my motherland? Although the land is under our feet, it carries the entire life of the Chinese people. Because of the pulse of this land, the poet always surges in his blood, which strengthens the power of emotion in the poem; and Ai Qing, who is willing to dedicate himself to the times, said that loving the motherland "better than everything I have ever loved", the charm is particularly deep and long, which makes people chew endlessly. But looking at the whole poem in general, it undoubtedly expresses the poet's sorrowful voice for the turbulent era, and also a broader pursuit of a desire for a better future. In the poem, there is a heart of sincerity to the country and the indignation against political injustice, and the poet's hope, longing and facing the eternal light are also intertwined. In his later years, Ai Qing's poems are more profound and his artistic conception is more magnificent. The deep love for the motherland and the spirit of daring to sacrifice for the truth have finally won praise and echo from the masses. For example, *Hope* was written in Shanghai in March 1979, which can be said to be one of the masterpieces of Ai Qing's comeback:

> *Said one sailor,*
> *What he likes most is what is stirred up by the lifting of*
>   *the anchor*
> *That white wave ...*
>
> *Said one sailor,*
> *What pleases him most is the sound of breaking down*
> *The noise of the chains*
>
> *A longing to start*
> *A longing to arrive*

艾青有句名言：「人民的心是試金石。」他終其一生的創作都在為揭示生活現實的典型意義，為世界的光明而貢獻一切的思想感情。此詩具有強烈的內在節奏感，藉以表達一種雀躍、熾熱的情緒。詩人情感的昇華，同浪花、同海、同希望一起出航，情感和形象得到了完美的結合；彷彿中，詩人心靈展開翅膀輕柔地遨遊於時空了。

三、艾青詩歌的藝術美

無疑的，艾青詩歌豐富了中國詩歌藝術的寶庫，但在過去的許多評論文章中，也有對其批評之聲。比如名詩人聞一多在肯定艾青的成就的同時，也曾指出他詩的弱點："用浪漫的幻想 給現實鍍上金 ,但對赤裸裸的現實 ,他還愛得不夠 。"。諸如這些見解，或許忽略了艾青在藝術上多方面的追求，或認為他的詩在表現上，感情的直接宣洩大於詩的形象美。凡此，雖然無法減滅艾青詩歌對文學藝術發展的貢獻，但從詩美的角度探討其美學意蘊及藝術特徵，卻不多見。下面，試圖在這一方面做一嘗試。

(1) 感情注入物象的形象美

從審美心理規律上看，以〈大堰河──我的保姆〉為例，此詩不為詩律所困，它是出於"性靈"的，是從形式上尋求不到的。詩中所表現的由哀而至傷的強烈情感與孤單的思緒，是經過回憶、沉思、再度體驗的情感。對詩人來說，不僅是

Ai Qing has a famous saying: "The heart of the people is the touchstone." All his creations throughout his life are dedicated to revealing the typical meaning of the reality of life and contributing all his thoughts and feelings to the light of the world. This poem has a strong sense of internal rhythm to express a kind of joyful and fiery emotion. The sublimation of the poet's emotions, sailing with the waves, the sea, and the hope, the emotion and image are perfectly combined; it seems that the poet's soul spreads its wings and travels gently in time and space.

3. The Artistic Beauty of Ai Qing's Poetry

Undoubtedly, Ai Qing's poems have enriched the treasury of Chinese poetry art, but there are also criticisms of it in many review articles in the past. For example, while affirming Ai Qing's achievements, the famous poet Wen Yiduo also pointed out the weaknesses of his poems: "Using romantic fantasy to gild reality, but he still doesn't love the naked reality enough." Such opinions may ignore Ai Qing's pursuit of art in many aspects, or think that in his poems, the direct expression of emotion is greater than the beauty of poetry. All these, although the contribution of Ai Qing's poetry to the development of literature and art cannot be reduced, but it is rare to discuss its aesthetic connotation and artistic characteristics from the perspective of poetic beauty. Next, try to make a try in this regard.

(1) The image beauty of emotional infusion

From the perspective of aesthetic psychology, take *Da Yanhe — My Nanny* as an example, this poem is not trapped by the rhythm of poetry, it comes from "spirituality", which cannot be found in form. The strong emotions and lonely thoughts expressed in the poem are

令人蕩氣迴腸的舒洩，往往也是一種刻骨銘心的感受；然而，並不會因情感過分強烈，而被迫走出心中的藝術世界。那麼，艾青又何以情感能控制得當？原因就是他在回憶，而不是在單純的痛哭；其藝術情感的快適度，是符合藝術實際的，既精闢又獨到。再者，詩語的具體含意之外另有寄託，大堰河反映出中國勞動婦女的傳統美德，這是此詩「氣勢開闊、以傳不朽」的特點。

(2) 對現實主義詩作的建樹

一首優秀的詩歌是時代之明鏡，也是鏗然的強音。在體現艾青詩另一種風格美的作品中，從宏觀的角度看，艾青是當代中國詩歌中具現實主義代表性詩人之一。四十年代詩歌大眾化已成為抗戰時期壓倒一切的頭等大事，因此，絕大部份的詩人傾向於詩歌的“運動”。即詩話文體本身應像標語口號那樣富有鼓動力量，使讀者在詩裏能清楚地感到與勞動人民生活的脈搏。然而，當時所朗誦詩和街頭詩也引起了批評家的指責，認為街頭詩過於激進而帶來了“粗糙”感。這時，延安時期的艾青，已拋棄了理想化的浪漫想像，而主張「最偉大的詩人，永遠是他所生活的時代的最忠實的代言人。」，詩裡以對題材的理解與感知、做準確的描述，也包含了東西文化中的許多藝術思潮為特徵。據此，〈雪落在中國的土地上〉、〈手推車〉等力作的確率直地反映了當時的

emotions that have been recalled, contemplated, and re-experienced. For a poet, it is not only a soul-stirring relief, but also an unforgettable feeling; however, it is not forced to leave the artistic world in the heart because of excessive emotion. Then, how can Ai Qing control her emotions properly? The reason is that he is reminiscing, not simply weeping bitterly; the joy and moderateness of his artistic emotion is in line with the reality of art, which is both incisive and unique. Furthermore, there are other sustenances beyond the specific meaning of the poem. The Dayan River reflects the traditional virtues of Chinese working women. This is the characteristic of this poem "open and immortal".

(2) Contributions to realistic poetry

An excellent poem is the mirror of the times, and it is also a sonorous strong voice. In the works embodying the beauty of another style of Ai Qing's poems, from a macro perspective, Ai Qing is one of the representative poets of realism in contemporary Chinese poetry. The popularization of poetry in the 1940s had become the overriding priority during the Anti-Japanese War. Therefore, most poets tended to the "movement" of poetry. That is to say, the poetry style itself should be as inspiring as slogans, so that readers can clearly feel the pulse of the working people's life in the poems. However, the recited poems and street poetry of the time also drew criticism from critics, who felt that street poetry was too aggressive and brought a sense of "roughness". At this time, Ai Qing in the Yan'an period had abandoned idealized romantic imagination, and advocated that "the greatest poet is always the most faithful spokesperson of the era in which he lives." The description also includes many artistic trends in Eastern and Western cultures. Based on this, masterpieces such as *Snow Falls on the Land of China* and *Trolley* truly reflected

時代生活。其詩情如火，人物的典型性、豐富性、情節性等，給人深刻的思想啟迪。此外，艾青也注重把藝術的魅力和智慧的全部尊嚴的結合起來，這種將主觀的圖式加以投射機制的運用，可以說是艾青詩歌創作的奧妙處。

(3) 藝術表現與東方文化精神〈spirit of Oriental culture〉的回歸

艾青詩歌的藝術表現中，早期最主要的特徵是「沉鬱、凝重」，以率真、熾熱的直覺構成了獨特的藝術風格。這是由於詩人富有無與倫比的同情感，並善於把心中的創痕從正面望去，進行高貴的聯想。其面對命運挑戰的生存勇氣能夠使他多次轉危為安，成為當代值得崇敬的詩人。他吸收東方文化中的人文主義理想，並把它同西方現實主義及美學結合起來，以便取長補短，相得益彰。可由〈時代〉到〈盼望〉的詩路歷程，使我們深信，真正勇敢的人，應當能智慧地忍受屈辱，不以身外的榮辱介懷。晚年的艾青，依然以「抒真情、說真話」為詩生命；至死猶對祖國深沉的愛不變。我深信，其勇者的塑像已贏得了歷史對其評價的尊嚴。

—2011.9.12 中秋節作

—西南大學中國新詩研究所主辦《中外詩歌研究》，2012 年第 01 期，頁 17-24。

he life of the time. Its poetic sentiment is like fire, and the typicality, richness and plot of the characters give people profound ideological enlightenment. In addition, Ai Qing also pays attention to the combination of the charm of art and the full dignity of wisdom. This use of subjective schema to project the mechanism can be said to be the mystery of Ai Qing's poetry creation.

(3) Artistic expression and the return of the spirit of Oriental culture

In the artistic expression of Ai Qing's poetry, the most important feature in the early stage is "gloomy and dignified", forming a unique artistic style with frankness and fiery intuition. This is because the poet is full of unparalleled sympathy, and is good at looking at the scars in his heart from the front and making noble associations. His survival courage in the face of the challenges of fate enabled him to turn danger into safety many times and become a contemporary poet worthy of reverence. He absorbed the ideal of humanism in Eastern culture and combined it with Western realism and aesthetics in order to learn from each other and bring out the best in each other. But the poetic journey from "Time" to "Hope" makes us firmly believe that a truly brave person should be able to endure humiliation wisely and not care about honor or disgrace outside of himself. In his later years, Ai Qing still took "expressing true feelings and telling the truth" as his poetic life; his deep love for the motherland remained unchanged until his death. I am convinced that the statue of its brave man has won the dignity as history has judged it.

3. 夜讀張智中的詩

　　與張智中教授相識已多年了，原來只知他是一位勤奮的博士生導師，近日，讀了他的詩，才知他同時還是一位靈感豐沛且又語言質感非常抒情的詩人。用一句話來概括其生活態度：「癡迷於英譯及文學」，在燈下，他專於翻譯與研究，出版編輯、譯著等百餘部，這樣的經歷在這一位詩人型的學者身上令人難以置信的是，他的詩作深深地根植於他的全部思考和熱情之中。

　　走進張智中的詩世界，幾乎都表現著詩人對生活、自然、人生或命運的深刻感悟，不乏對故鄉的緬懷和詩美的追求；可謂都是在那種直透歲月的目光中使其詩歌顯示出對自己人生的思考。也可以說，詩，正是他心靈之聲的交響。如（故鄉春曉）一詩，透射出詩人燃燒的思鄉激情：

文／圖　林明理

3. Reading Zhang Zhizhong's Poems at Night

I have known Professor Zhang Zhizhong for many years, yet I only knew him as a diligent doctoral supervisor. Recently, after reading his poems, I realized that he is also a poet full of inspiration and with a very lyrical language quality. To summarize his attitude towards life in one sentence: "obsessed with English translation and literature". Under the lamp, he specializes in translation and research, and has published, edited, and translated more than one hundred books. Such an experience is in this poet-scholar. Incredibly, his poetry is deeply rooted in all his thoughts and passions.

Walking into the world of Zhang Zhizhong's poems, almost all of them express the poet's deep understanding of life, nature, life or destiny, and there is no lack of nostalgia for his hometown and pursuit of poetic beauty. It can also be said that poetry is just the symphony of his inner voice. For example, the poem *Spring Dawn in My Hometown* reflects the poet's burning passion of homesickness:

這是母親走後
的第四個春天
我成年後第一次
乘春天回到老家
探望身體些微佝僂
卻仍健談的父親
春眠，老家的
春眠，當然
不覺其曉
一夜無風無雨無攪擾
房前屋後
鳥啼清脆
故鄉的春花
永不凋落

　　不但表現了詩人解剖自己心靈，也真實生動地寄予對父
母思念深厚的情懷，讀來讓人覺得熟悉親切。再如（母親的
哲學），內裡蘊聚著詩人對母親深厚的愛與留戀之情：

母親生前常說
人就像割韭菜
一茬一茬的

今日立春
心裡的韭菜
不覺蔥鬱起來

This is the fourth spring
After mother left me and this world
The first time in my adult life
For me to be back home in spring
To see my father who is slightly bent
Yet still talkative
Spring sleep, in my native home
Spring sleep, of course
Unconscious of the dawn
A quiet night without wind or rain or disturbance
Around the house
Liquid birdsongs
Spring flowers in my hometown
Never wither

It expresses not only the poet's anatomy of his own soul, but also the deep feelings for his parents in a real and vivid way, which makes people feel familiar and friendly after reading it. Another example is *Mother's Philosophy*, which contains the poet's deep love and nostalgia for his mother:

Mother used to say
Humans are like cutting leeks
Crop by crop

Today is the Beginning of Spring
And the leek in my heart
Begins to thrive

　　別有意味的是，這首〈好大一棵樹〉，詩句想像奇特，已達到了詩藝更臻於成熟的地步。在他眼中的一草一木，或外在世界的狂風霜雪，都成為了詩人內心的圖景，也發出自己的聲音。此刻詩人以真切感人的詩筆寫道：

　　　　一群群的狂風如同暴徒
　　　　剝光了你的衣衫
　　　　一陣陣的霜雪如同刀片
　　　　在你身上留下
　　　　瘡痍的斑點
　　　　你只是微笑　岸然
　　　　一身的硬骨　不變
　　　　經歷了數十年四季的輪轉
　　　　永不消失的是
　　　　蘊藏在你年輪中心的
　　　　春天

　　在詩中，這棵「大樹」無畏狂風暴雪，但它在瞬間體現了自己的價值，給世界帶來了堅韌的勇氣，給人以精神上的強烈感染和莫大鼓舞；也隱喻了詩人欲把自己的審美理想融入了抒情詩的意象中，從而反映了張智中的詩歌才華和看到他感情深厚、堅強不屈的個性。

Interestingly, the poem entitled *What a Big Tree* has a strange imagination, and has reached the point where the poet's poetic art has become more mature. The plants and trees in his eyes, or the wind, frost and snow in the external world, all become the poet's inner picture, and the poet makes his own voice. At this moment, the poet wrote a poem which is real and touching:

Crowds of wind, like mobs
Strip off your clothes
Blasts of frost and snow, like blades
Leaving wounds
And scars on you
Yet you keep smiling   with pride
Dauntless and unyielding   changeless
Through decades of cycling of the four seasons
What never dies away, hidden
In your annual rings, is the
Spring

In the poem, this "big tree" is fearless of the storm, but it reflects its own value in an instant, brings tenacity and courage to the world, and gives people a strong spiritual infection and great encouragement. The poet's own aesthetic ideals are integrated into the imagery of lyric poems, which reflects his poetic talent and sees his deep feelings and strong and unyielding personality.

張智中在教學與英譯研究之餘，其詩歌創作上的主要傾向，是形式要精煉、抒情，也同樣是其赤子情懷的流露。我很喜歡波蘭現代詩人辛波絲卡寫過的一首（微笑）最後一節：

高興春天到了，所以才動動臉。
然而人類天生憂傷。
就順其自然吧。那也不是什麼壞事。

而張智中教授在詩歌美學和西方文學的翻譯與學術的探索上雖已取得了可喜的成績，但他只有在詩創作中才能更好的認識自我；也可以說，詩，是他內心的一種情感表達。他就像深山一棵峭拔向上的大樹，以嶄新的勇敢的姿態，在發揮著它旺盛的生命力。而他所有的詩作，都是用他自己對生活中切身的感受，因而才能從平凡中寫出不平凡，增添詩作的力度。

——2023.01.21 作

-臺灣《中華日報　》副刊，2023.02.04.及畫作 1 幅。

Apart from teaching and English translation research, Zhang Zhizhong's main tendency in his poetry creation is to refine the form and express emotion, which is also the expression of his innocent feelings. I really like the last stanza of a poem entitled *Smiling* by the modern Polish poet Szymborska:

> *I am glad that spring is here, so I move my face.*
> *Yet human beings are inherently sad.*
> *Just let it be. That's not a bad thing either.*

Although Professor Zhang Zhizhong has made gratifying achievements in poetry aesthetics, translation, and academic exploration of Western literature, he can only better understand himself in poetry creation. It can also be said that poetry is an emotion in his heart. He is like a stalwart and upward tree in a deep mountain, displaying its exuberant vitality with a new and brave attitude. And all his poems are based on his own personal feelings about life, so that he can write extraordinarily from the ordinary, thus adding vitality to his poems.

－臺灣《中華日報》副刊，2023.02.04.及畫作 1 幅。

4. 讀盧惠餘
《聞一多詩歌藝術研究》

摘要：《聞一多詩歌藝術研究》是盧惠餘〈註 1〉十年來對聞一多詩歌的藝術價值進行的研究成果。作者自 1999 年開始研究聞一多，整整 10 年中，主要研究了聞一多〈註 2〉詩歌藝術風格之間的關係及其詩歌與其它先驅詩歌風格的差別。

關鍵詞：盧惠餘；聞一多詩歌；意象；音樂美

一、前　言

　　盧惠餘的學術背景使他能夠駕輕就熟地理解聞一多對詩歌創作過程的高度自覺，因此他不斷嘗試、追索聞一多創作中蘊涵的人生感悟與社會體驗。聞一多是位求真務實的詩學理論家與詩人，他提出了新詩創作要達到音樂美、繪畫美與建築美的「三美」主張。盧惠餘著眼於探索聞一多創作的思想藝術的嬗變歷程，進而研究其詩學理論層面，最後選擇幾位名詩人分別從詩風、格律形式、象徵詩藝等側面作一比較

4. Reading Lu Huiyu's A Study of Wen Yiduo's Poetic Art

Summary: *A Study of Wen Yiduo's Poetic Art* is the research result of Lu Huiyu's "Note 1" on the artistic value of Wen Yiduo's poetry in the past ten years. The author began to study Wen Yiduo in 1999. During the whole 10 years, he mainly studied the relationship between the artistic styles of Wen Yiduo's <Note 2> poetry and the differences between his poetry and other pioneer poetry styles.

Key words: Lu Huiyu; Wen Yiduo's poetry; imagery; musical beauty

I. Introduction

Lu Huiyu's academic background enables him to understand Wen Yiduo's highly conscious process of poetry creation with ease, so he keeps trying to trace the life perception and social experience contained in Wen Yiduo's creation. Wen Yiduo is a poetic theorist and poet who seeks truth and pragmatism. He put forward the idea of "three beauties" that the creation of new poems should achieve the beauty of music, painting and architecture. Lu Huiyu focused on exploring the evolution of Wen Yiduo's ideological and artistic creations, and then studied the theoretical aspects of his poetics. Finally, he selected several famous poets to make a comparative study from the aspects of poetic style, metrical form, and symbolic poetic art, and strived to make the research rise. To the

研究，力求使研究上升到理論層次，藉由突顯出聞一多詩歌藝術的理論貢獻。於是我們看到盧惠餘使命感的召喚，也看到聞一多偉大情操背後的真實純真的情感及其命運的悲壯。

在第一章《創作論》中，盧惠餘認為，《雨夜》是聞一多最早創作的新詩，創作的背景因素應是聯繫聞一多對當年「五四」之後軍閥政府鎮壓學生運動，他對此表明了鮮明的憎惡之情，展現出詩人的良知和清醒。個人以為，在政治上，聞一多早期詩作就很有批判精神的，他厭惡現實，轉而對詩不悔的熱愛與追求；生活中，他又耿介不群，既不沉溺於失望，也沒有癡迷於夢幻，而是以詩表達情感的頓宕停蓄、穿透延伸或回旋蕩漾等各種複雜形態。題材主要表現在對真實人性的理性認識、與賦予生命價值的哲思；藉以追求個體人格的完善。在聞一多短暫的 47 歲生命中，詩歌以苦吟錘煉、浪漫抒情聞名於世，既有現實性內涵，又能傳神地表現出生命的低沉和悲絕。其新詩格律理論更是中西詩學理論相互交融的結晶，也有著深遠的影響，值得細讀、探究。

二、聞一多詩歌的象徵藝術傾向

對聞一多早期詩歌，盧惠餘認為，或許較為少了點豐厚的感性生活為基礎；也有評家指出，或帶有年輕人的夢幻與

theoretical level, by highlighting the theoretical contribution of Wen Yiduo's poetic art. So we see the calling of Lu Huiyu's sense of mission, as well as the true and pure emotion and the tragic fate behind Wen Yiduo's great sentiment.

In the first chapter *On Creation*, Lu Huiyu believes that *Rainy Night* is the earliest new poem written by Wen Yiduo. This shows a clear feeling of hatred, showing the poet's conscience and sobriety. I personally think that in politics, Wen Yiduo's early poems were very critical. He hated reality and turned to love and pursue poetry without regret; He is not obsessed with dreams, but uses poetry to express various complex forms of emotion, such as pauses, pauses, penetrations, extensions, and rippling. The subject matter is mainly manifested in the rational understanding of true human nature and the philosophical thinking of giving life value; in order to pursue the perfection of individual personality. In Wen Yiduo's short 47-year-old life, his poems were famous for their painstaking chanting and romantic lyricism, which not only contained realistic connotations, but also vividly expressed the depression and sadness of life. His theory of new poetry is the crystallization of the integration of Chinese and Western poetics theories, and it also has far-reaching influence, which is worth reading and exploring.

2. The Symbolic Art Tendency of Wen Yiduo's Poems

Regarding Wen Yiduo's early poems, Lu Huiyu believes that they may not be based on a rich emotional life; some critics also pointed out that they may contain

理想等論述。但我以為，年少的聞一多或許帶有涉世未深的
青年人那種內在的無為感，是個思想深邃、不願受束縛的人。
他的新詩坦蕩真誠，不故弄玄虛，能表達出自己愛國的一腔
熱血。如《雨夜》：

> 幾朵浮雲，仗著雷雨底勢力，
> 把一天底星月都掃盡了。
> 一陣狂風還喊來要捉那軟弱的樹枝，
> 樹枝拚命地扭來扭去，
> 但是無法躲避風底爪子。
> 凶狠的風聲，悲酸的雨聲——
> 我一壁聽著，一壁想著；
> 假使夢這時要來找我，
> 我定要永遠拉著他，不放他走；
> 還剜出我的心來送他作贄禮，
> 他要收我做個莫逆的朋友。
> 風聲還在樹裏呻吟著，
> 淚痕滿面的曙天白得可怕，
> 我的夢依然沒有做成。
> 哦！原來真的已被我厭惡了，
> 假的就沒他自身的尊嚴嗎？

這裡，有著詩人明顯的愛國理想及情操，是東方藝術精
神的至境。《雨夜》以「雷雨」為核心意象，把狂風和軟枝
隱喻為五四運動遭受暴戾壓制的景象，這就擁有了一種強烈

young people's dreams and ideals. But I think that the young Wen Yiduo may have the inner sense of inaction of young people who are not deeply involved in the world, and he is a person with deep thoughts and unwilling to be restrained. His new poems are magnanimous and sincere, without any mystification, and can express his patriotic passion. Such as *Rainy Night*:

Swept away all the stars and the moon.
A gust of wind still calls to catch the weak branch,
The branches twisted and twisted desperately,
But there is no way to avoid the wind bottom claws.
The fierce wind, the sad rain —
I listened, and thought;
If the dream should come to me now,
I will hold him forever and never let him go;
And gouged out my heart to give him as a gift,
He wants to accept me as an irresistible friend.
The wind still groans in the trees,
The tear-stained dawn is frightfully white,
My dream is still unfulfilled.
Oh! It turned out that I was really disgusted.
Doesn't the fake have no dignity of his own?

Here, with the poet's obvious patriotic ideals and sentiments, is the pinnacle of oriental artistic spirit. *Rainy Night* takes "thunderstorm" as the core image, and metaphorizes the strong wind and soft branches as the

的張力。接著,「樹枝拚命地扭來扭去,但是無法躲避風底爪子。」使得詩的張力漸次累積,「凶狠的風聲,悲酸的雨聲——」,則營造出聲音交響的效果,更步步牽動讀者的情緒。「淚痕滿面的曙天白得可怕,我的夢依然沒有做成。」這意象暗示出孤立無助的痛苦依然未解,也為最後的吶喊與悲憤預作鋪陳;因任何言語的安慰已失去意義,只剩下接受苦澀現實的感慨。

盧惠餘以為聞一多赴美留學至回國期間〈1922 年 7 月－1925 年 5 月〉,是詩歌創作的高潮;由於身處異域而激起起強烈的思鄉情感,最終凝聚許多浪漫式傾訴的詩篇。如《孤雁》,為出國之後的力作,描寫出詩人在異域為尋求新知,必須自強不息、淋漓盡致表現出思鄉之煎熬。我們不妨看一下全詩:

> 不幸的失群的孤客!
> 誰教你拋棄了舊侶,
> 拆散了陣字,
> 流落到這水國底絕塞,
> 拚若寸磔的愁腸,
> 泣訴那無邊的酸楚?
>
> 啊!從那浮雲底密幕裏,
> 迸出這樣的哀音;
> 這樣的痛苦!這樣的熱情!

scenc of the violent suppression of the May Fourth Movement, which has a strong tension. Then, "the branches twisted and twisted desperately, but they couldn't escape the claws of the wind." The tension of the poem gradually accumulated, and "the fierce wind, the sad rain 一" created a symphonic effect of sound, step by step. Touch the reader's emotions. "The tear-stained dawn is terribly white, and my dream is still unfulfilled." This image implies that the pain of isolation and helplessness is still unresolved, and it also paves the way for the final cry and grief; because any words of comfort have lost their meaning, only the emotion of accepting the bitter reality remains.

Lu Huiyu believed that Wen Yiduo's period from studying in the United States to returning to China (July 1922-May 1925) was the climax of poetry creation; being in a foreign land aroused strong homesickness, and finally condensed many romantic poems . For example, *The Lone Wild Goose*, which is a masterpiece after going abroad, describes the poet's constant self-improvement in order to seek new knowledge in a foreign land, vividly expressing the torment of homesickness. Let's take a look at the whole poem:

> *Poor straying loner!*
> *Who taught you to abandon old lovers,*
> *Dismantled the array of words,*
> *Drifted to the bottom of this watery country,*
> *Fighting like an inch of sorrow,*
> *Weeping about the boundless sorrow?*
>
> *What! From the veil of floating clouds,*
> *Burst forth such mournful voices;*
> *Such pain! Such enthusiasm!*

孤寂的流落者！
不須叫喊得喲！
你那沉細的音波，
在這大海底驚雷裏，
還不值得那濤頭上，
濺落的一粒浮漚呢！

可憐的孤魂啊！
更不須向天回首了。
天是一個無涯的秘密，
一幅藍色的謎語，
太難了，不是你能猜破的。
也不須向海低頭了。
這辱罵高天的惡漢，
他的鹹鹵的唾沫，
不要漬濕了你的翅膀，
粘滯了你的行程！

流落的孤禽啊！
到底飛住哪裡去呢？
那太平洋底彼岸，
可知道究竟有些什麼？

啊！那裏是蒼鷹底領土 ——
那鷙悍的霸王啊！

Lonely wanderer!
No need to shout!
Your deep voice,
In this thunderstorm under the sea,
It's not worth Natao's head,
How about a grain of floating retting that splashed down!

Poor lonely soul!
There is no need to look back to the sky.
Heaven is a boundless secret,
A blue riddle,
It's too difficult, you can't guess it.
There is no need to bow to the sea.
This villain who insulted Gao Tian,
His salty spittle,
Don't wet your wings,
Stick to your itinerary!

Wandering lone bird!
Where are you going to fly to?
On the other side of the Pacific Ocean,
Do you know what is there?

What! There is the territory of Goshawk—
That fierce overlord!

他的銳利的指爪，
已撕破了自然底面目，
建築起財力底窩巢。
那裏只有鋼筋鐵骨的機械，
喝醉了弱者底鮮血，
吐出些罪惡底黑烟，
塗污我太空，閉熄了日月，
教你飛來不知方向，
息去又沒地藏身啊！

流落的失群者啊！
到底要往哪裡去？
隨陽的鳥啊！
光明底追逐者啊！
不信那腥臊的屠場，
黑暗的烟灶，
竟能吸引你的踪迹！

歸來罷，失路的游魂！
歸來參加你的伴侶，
補足他們的陣列！
他們正引著頸望你呢。

歸來僵臥在霜染的蘆林裏，
那裏有校獵的西風，

Has torn the face of nature,
Build a nest of financial resources.
There are only steel and iron machines,
Drunk with the blood of the weak,
Breathing out the black smoke of sin,
Smear my space, shut out the sun and moon,
Teach you to fly without knowing the direction,
There is nowhere to hide!

O wandering outcast!
Where are you going?
Sunny bird!
O Bright Chaser!
Don't believe in the smelly slaughterhouse,
Dark smokehouse,
Can attract your traces!

Come back, lost wandering soul!
Come back to join your mate,
Make up their array!
They are staring at you.

Returned to lie down in the frost-stained reed forest,
There is the west wind of school hunting,

將茸毛似的蘆花，
鋪就了你的的床褥，
來溫暖起你的甜夢。

歸來浮游在溫柔的港澂裏，
那裏方是你的浴盆。
歸來徘徊在浪舐的平沙上
趁著溶銀的月色，
婆婆著戲弄你的幽影。

歸來罷，流落的孤禽！
與其盡在這水國底絕塞，
拼著寸磔的愁腸，
泣訴那無邊的酸楚，
不如擺翅回身歸去罷！

啊！但是這不由分說的狂飆，
挾著我不息地前進；
我腳上又帶著了一封信，
我怎能拋却我的使命，
由著我的心性，
回身擺翅歸去來呢？

　　詩的總體格調不乏愁苦之意，詩人敏銳的心靈裡，為了
生動而曲折地傳情達意，不乏對「思鄉之愁」或對異國種族

The hairy reeds,
Made your mattress,
Come warm up your sweet dreams.

Returning to float in the gentle harbor,
Over there is your bathtub.
Returning and hovering on the flat sand licked by the waves
Taking advantage of the melting silver moonlight,
Mother-in-law teases your shadow.

Come back, wandering lonely bird!
Instead of being stuck at the bottom of this water country,
Struggle with sorrow,
Weeping the boundless sorrow,
It's better to turn around and go back!

What! But this inexplicable frenzy,
Carrying me forward without stopping;
I have another letter on my feet,
How can I abandon my mission,
By my heart,
Turn around and flap your wings and go back?

The overall style of the poem is not lacking in melancholy. In order to express his feelings vividly and with twists and turns, the poet's keen mind is not lacking

岐視社會的深刻感受，也不乏對未來人生理想的憧憬。全詩只有一只緩緩飛行的孤雁，但也造就為一種沉重的節奏，這與孤雁本身著力呈現出蒼涼、博大的詩境，運用空幻回合，並追求內在的氣格和骨力，成就為一種奇崛深折的風貌。我以為，聞一多的苦吟背後內在的精神，仍體現著知識份子不與流俗的高傲氣格和愛國思鄉之心，它承載著時代信息和文化內涵，這是其詩歌藝術內部發展深沉有力的原因。

從 1925 年 6 月回國直至離開詩壇，盧惠餘認為是聞一多詩歌創作的第三階段，其主要作品收集在詩集《死水》之中；此階段能真切而準確地描寫社會人生與心靈世界的本質真實，使得詩歌形成了「厚實、含蓄、深沉、凝重」的藝術風格。比如《死水》，聞一多自認為是「第一次在音節上最滿意的試驗」，堪稱為現代新格律詩的典範。筆者亦嘗試淺釋於下：

這是一溝絕望的死水，
清風吹不起半點漪淪。
不如多扔些破銅爛鐵，
爽性潑你的剩菜殘羹。

in the deep feeling of "homesickness" or the racial discrimination society of a foreign country, as well as his longing for the ideal of future life. There is only one lone goose flying slowly in the whole poem, but it is also made into a heavy rhythm. This is related to the lone goose itself, which focuses on presenting a desolate and broad poetic scene, uses illusory rounds, and pursues the inner temperament and bone strength. Strange and deep fold style. In my opinion, the inner spirit behind Wen Yiduo's bitter chanting still embodies the intellectuals' arrogance and patriotic homesickness, which carries the information of the times and cultural connotation, which is the deep and powerful internal development of his poetic art.

From returning to China in June 1925 to leaving the poetry world, Lu Huiyu considered it the third stage of Wen Yiduo's poetry creation, and his main works were collected in the collection of poems entitled *Still Water*; this stage can truly and accurately describe the essence of social life and the spiritual world reality makes poetry form an artistic style of "thick, implicit, deep, and dignified". For example, *Dead Water*, which Wen Yiduo considers to be "the first and most satisfying experiment in syllables", can be regarded as a model of modern new metrical poetry. The author also tried to explain it briefly as follows:

> *This is a ditch of hopeless stagnant water,*
>
> *The breeze can't blow the slightest ripple.*
>
> *Why don't you throw more scrap metal,*
>
> *Simply splash your leftovers.*

也許銅的要綠成翡翠，
鐵罐上綉出幾瓣桃花；
再讓油膩織一層羅綺，
黴菌給他蒸出些雲霞。

讓死水酵成一溝綠酒，
漂滿了珍珠似的白沫；
小珠們笑聲變成大珠，
又被偷酒的花蚊咬破。

那麼一溝絕望的死水，
也就誇得上幾分鮮明。
如果青蛙耐不住寂寞，
又算死水叫出了歌聲。

這是一溝絕望的死水，
這裏斷不是美的所在，
不如讓給醜惡來開墾，
看他造出個什麼世界。

　　全詩分為五折，每折各以敘述、預示、倒敘、詠歎或嘲諷，讓多股詩意力量相互撞擊；也聳立起自己的精神高度；暗含著底層人民生命被圍剿的痛楚，以及捕捉具有強烈衝突的瞬間，訴說的正是聞一多浸透心靈的人生感慨。詩人嘗試以現代語言傳遞出世事多變與滄桑，那剪不斷理還亂的，是

Maybe copper will turn green into emerald,
A few peach blossoms are embroidered on the tin can;
Then let the greasy weave a layer of Luo Qi,
The mold steamed some clouds for him.

Let dead water ferment into a ditch of green wine,
Floating like pearls of white foam;
Small pearls laugh and become big pearls,
*　It was bitten by the flower mosquito who stole the wine*
*　again.*

So a ditch of hopeless stagnant water,
It can be said to be somewhat clear.
If the frog can't stand the loneliness,
And the dead water called out singing.

This is a ditch of hopeless stagnant water,
This is definitely not a place of beauty,
It's better to let the ugliness do the reclamation,
See what kind of world he creates.

The whole poem is divided into five parts, and each part uses narration, foreshadowing, flashback, chants or sarcasm, allowing multiple poetic forces to collide with each other. The moment of intense conflict tells the story of Wen Yiduo's soul-soaked emotion of life. The poet tries to convey the vicissitudes and vicissitudes of the world in modern language, but what keeps cutting things

他重任在肩的悲憫情懷與對文化沒落的自覺追求。詩裡的聞一多，始終關注著民間疾苦。那前後呼應的意象與酒的意象的反覆再現，讓飛揚的思緒彷彿有了次序感，對句更是精巧有味。

　　在此書第二章《詩學論》，盧惠餘指出，聞一多早期提出的「幻象學說」中明確地說過：「詩有四大原素：幻象、感情、音節、繪藻。」「幻象真摯，則無景不肖，無情不達。」由此可以解讀，聞一多把「幻象」作為詩歌批評的首要依據。究竟「幻象」指的是什麼呢？盧惠餘認為是把真確的形象性、超越現實的虛幻性、富於幻想的奇異性、蘊藏神韻的含蓄性四者相輔相成、相互融合而成為「幻象說」的基本理論。對此，擬以聞一多的一首詩《雪》為例，說明聞一多詩歌善用貼切的比喻、幻象，也是一種痛苦的昇華：

　　　夜散下無數茸毛似的天花，
　　　織成一件大氅，
　　　輕輕地將憔悴的世界，
　　　從頭到腳地包了起來：
　　　又加了死人一層殮衣。
　　　伊將一片魚鱗似的屋頂埋起了，
　　　卻總埋不住那屋頂上的青烟縷。
　　　啊！縷縷蜿蜒的青烟啊！

back into chaos is his compassion and conscious pursuit of cultural decline. Wen Yiduo in the poem always pays attention to the sufferings of the people. The repeated reappearance of the echoing images and the image of wine makes Feiyang's thoughts seem to have a sense of order, and the couplets are more delicate and interesting.

In the second chapter of this book, *On Poetics*, Lu Huiyu pointed out that Wen Yiduo's early "illusion theory" clearly stated: "poetry has four elements: illusion, emotion, syllable, and painting." "Illusion If there is sincerity, there will be no scene, no love, and no emotion." From this, it can be interpreted that Wen Yiduo regards "illusion" as the primary basis for poetry criticism. What exactly does "illusion" refer to? Lu Huiyu believes that it is the basic theory of "illusion theory" that complements each other and integrates the four aspects of authentic imagery, illusion beyond reality, fantasy full of singularity, and implicitness with charm. In this regard, I would like to take Wen Yiduo's poem *Snow* as an example to illustrate that Wen Yiduo's poems use appropriate metaphors and illusions, which is also a sublimation of pain:

Innumerable fluffy smallpox scattered at night,
Woven into a great cloak,
Gently will the haggard world,
Packed from head to toe:
Another layer of mortuary clothing was added.
Yi buried a roof like fish scales,
But it can't always bury the green smoke on the roof.
What! Wisps of winding smoke!

仿佛是詩人向上的靈魂，
穿透自身的軀殼，直向天堂邁往。
高視闊步的風霜踩躪世界，
森林裏抖顫的眾生戰鬥多時，
最末望見伊底白氅，
都歡聲喊道：“和平到了，奮鬥成功了！
這不是冬投降底白旗嗎？

　　這首《雪》的意象本身即含有濃郁的主觀意向，它是昂揚向上的，寫得景壯情豪，也可以激發讀者的視覺想像，讓人仿佛看見那一張張像雪花般蒼白的臉龐，並且能感受到戰爭煙囂下人們渴望飛翔與自由的背景。如果我們注意到，詩的基本立場是生命與自然間無言的泣訴，當詩人面對雪花紛飛如落葉般的淒美，他見象生意，但心境是壓抑且沉鬱的。因為，他深知窗外的世界仍是晦暗不明、破敗憔悴！那冰瀅的雪花反應給人一種痛苦的美，也是一種人生的昇華。

　　而聞一多採用了雪花就是死人的一層殮衣這一比喻意象，試圖以雪的明淨把晦暗蒼茫的世界緊緊地包裹起來。這裡形成的對立面，是崇尚生命的聞一多的泣血謳歌。當詩人的目光投向遠方密林裡的屋頂，心靈立即發生劇烈的變化，一股說不出的欣慰油然而生。因漫天飛雪無法掩蓋那一片屋頂上的「青烟縷」，風中隱隱約約的一縷縷而活躍起來的，竟是人的生命力啊！這裡傳達得很生動。很顯然，「最末望見伊底白氅」是既抽象又具體的，那瘋狂的雪終於展現了白

Like the upward soul of a poet,
Penetrate your body and go straight to heaven.
Strutting winds and frosts ravage the world,
The trembling beings of the forest fought long,
At last I saw the cloak of Idida,
They all shouted happily: "Peace has arrived, and the
struggle has been won!"
Isn't this the white flag of winter surrender?

The imagery of this song *Snow* itself contains strong subjective intentions. It is high-spirited and written with grandeur and emotion. It can also stimulate readers' visual imagination, making people seem to see those pale faces like snowflakes. And you can feel the background of people yearning for flight and freedom under the smog of war. If we notice that the basic standpoint of the poem is the silent weeping between life and nature, when the poet faces the poignant beauty of snowflakes flying like falling leaves, he sees business, but his mood is depressed and gloomy. Because, he knows very well that the world outside the window is still dim, dilapidated and haggard! The icy snowflakes give people a kind of painful beauty, and it is also a kind of sublimation of life.

Wen Yiduo adopted the metaphorical image that snowflakes are a layer of burial clothes for the dead, trying to wrap the dark and boundless world tightly with the clarity of snow. The opposite formed here is Wen Yiduo's weeping eulogy of life. When the poet casts his eyes on the roof in the distant dense forest, his soul immediately undergoes a drastic change, and an indescribable gratification arises spontaneously. Because the flying snow could not cover up the "blue smoke" on the roof, the faint wisps of smoke in the wind made people's vitality come alive! It is vividly conveyed here. Obviously, "I finally saw the white cloak of Ida" is both

旗的象徵，它既有現實性冀望抗戰勝利的內涵，又有形而上想獲得真正和平的神聖意義。當然，這也是聞一多表現出坦蕩開闊的胸襟和寄望，詩句朗朗上口的音樂性及或輕柔、或激昂，或悠揚、或沉鬱的情狀，描繪得很新鮮、很具動感，其藝術的張力再次表現出詩人的妙手神技。

至於聞一多的新詩格律理論，在此書第三章裡多有論述，盧惠餘認為，聞一多的詩歌意象世界也具有「濃麗、繁密、含蓄、典型」的特徵。由於聞一多喜愛杜甫的「沉郁頓挫」與勃朗寧的對戲獨白體的客觀抒情詩以及艾略特的詩歌的獨特詩風，都潛移默化地影響了聞一多的詩歌創作。此外，在第四章"淵源論"裡，盧惠餘除列舉出聞一多受到中西文藝思潮的影響及推崇的詩人外，他也同意胡喬木對聞一多的評觀，一致認為聞一多是「聯結著中國古代詩、西洋詩和中國現代各派詩的人」。對此，盧惠餘在第五章「比較論」裡，以郭沫若詩歌熱情奔放、氣勢磅礡與聞一多的把自己的情感比喻為「沒有爆發的火山」作一比較後，提出了個人見解，大致是，如果郭沫若的詩令人暢快淋漓，那麼，聞一多的詩情是持久的內在震撼力。再者，作者也以徐志摩為例作一比較。認為，徐志摩對詩體外形雖沒有聞一多講究嚴謹，但聞一多自認，比起徐志摩詩歌裡的音樂美及建築美方面，是「比較占次要的位置」。

abstract and concrete. The crazy snow finally showed the symbol of the white flag. sacred meaning. Of course, this is also Wen Yiduo's magnanimity and hope. The catchy musicality of the poems and the soft, passionate, melodious, or melancholic moods are fresh and dynamic. The tension once again shows the poet's skill.

As for Wen Yiduo's theory of new poetry, it is discussed in chapter three of this book. Lu Huiyu believes that Wen Yiduo's poetic image world also has the characteristics of "thick, dense, implicit, and typical". Wen Yiduo's poetic creation was subtly influenced by Wen Yiduo's love of Du Fu's "depressed and frustrated" and Browning's objective lyric poems in antithetical monologue, as well as the unique style of Eliot's poems. In addition, in the fourth chapter *Origin Theory*, Lu Huiyu not only lists the poets Wen Yiduo was influenced by Chinese and Western literary thoughts and admired, he also agrees with Hu Qiaomu's evaluation of Wen Yiduo, and agrees that Wen Yiduo is a poet. "A person who connects ancient Chinese poetry, Western poetry, and modern Chinese poetry." In this regard, in the fifth chapter *Comparison*, Lu Huiyu compared Guo Moruo's passionate and imposing poetry with Wen Yiduo's comparison of his emotions to "a volcano that has not erupted", and then put forward his personal opinion. Yes, if Guo Moruo's poems are refreshing, then Wen Yiduo's poems are enduring inner shock. Furthermore, the author also takes Xu Zhimo as an example for comparison. I think that although Xu Zhimo is not as rigorous as Wen Yiduo in his poems; Wen Yiduo thinks that compared with Xu Zhimo's music and architectural beauty in his poems, they are "relatively secondary".

盧惠餘繼而以李金發為例作一比較，除了肯定李金發的象徵詩對中國現代詩壇的震撼外，他認為，聞一多並的象徵詩並沒有如此強烈的震撼力，而是煥發著強大而持久的藝術活動。書的附錄裡，也對聞一多與美國意象派研究作一述評，大部份資料取之於聞一多的手稿及與其往來的英文書信。盧惠餘由其中陸續地整理出其它研究者對聞一多相關性論文的要評，最後附錄是聞一多新詩創作年表。對盧惠餘而言，完成此書的過程，是因喜愛聞一多詩歌藝術的真義，它驅使著盧惠餘的精神不斷自我發展、自我超越，並邁向那更為恢宏的目標;這可能是盧惠餘這 10 年來始終堅持聞一多研究的內在動因。

三、小　結

收到由鹽城師範學院郭錫健教授寄來同仁新著《聞一多詩歌藝術研究》與其它三本論著時，特為感動。欣喜之餘，當即仔細一一拜讀，除了感佩盧惠餘對這部別開生面的詩歌藝術論著所付出的心血外，尤其感佩他提出許多聞一多的詩歌象徵主張及對其創作的理論總結，深信在今後文學史上將占有不可忽視的地位。

Lu Huiyu then took Li Jinfa as an example for comparison. In addition to affirming the shock of Li Jinfa's symbolic poems to the modern Chinese poetry circle, he believed that Wen Yiduo's symbolic poems did not have such a strong shocking power, but glowed with a powerful and persistent artistic activity. In the appendix of the book, there is also a review of Wen Yiduo and the study of American Imagism. Most of the information is taken from Wen Yiduo's manuscripts and English correspondence with him. From it, Lu Huiyu sorted out the main comments of other researchers on Wen Yiduo's related papers, and the final appendix is the chronology of Wen Yiduo's new poems. For Lu Huiyu, the process of completing this book is because he loves to hear the true meaning of Yiduo's poetic art, which drives Lu Huiyu's spirit to continuously develop and surpass himself, and to move towards a more ambitious goal. Over the past 10 years, I have always adhered to the internal motivation of Wen Yiduo's research.

3. Summary

I was very moved when I received my colleague's new book *Research on the Poetic Art of Wen Yiduo* and three other works from professor Guo Xijian of Yancheng Normal University. When I was delighted, I immediately read them one by one carefully. In addition to thanking Lu Huiyu for his hard work on this unique poetic art treatise, I especially appreciate him for putting forward many symbolic propositions of Wen Yiduo's poetry and theoretical summaries of his creation. It will occupy a place that cannot be ignored in the history of literature.

在詮釋三首聞一多的詩歌意象中，發覺其實聞一多不僅是學者詩人，也應該是批判家。他能把詩思化為意象，一方面積極在堅困中尋求人生的光明、歌頌生命的尊嚴；另一方面也鞭笞假惡醜。其詩歌語言應是「深沉蒼勁、音律動感和諧」，表現出對大時代生存環境的悲憫及五四時期追求光明與新生的時代精神，且富有表現力。畫面的處理也不時地觸痛人們的眼睛，震撼著讀者的心靈。

此外，聞一多詩句包含著「清麗的東方意象」，其實並不那麼地濃麗，而其情詩也寫得超凡脫俗，確有非同尋常的魅力，並非那麼的隱喻「含蓄」，讓人細細回味於奇妙的瞬間。此外，聞一多詩歌意象的視覺刺激的鋒利性，把詩人的主觀情志的那種憂鬱的迷惘很好地表現出來，像樂曲的低音般激蕩，使我們體味到了宇宙的壯美與靜穆的力量。總之，在讚美此書的同時，也欣賞到聞一多意象創造中的智慧。聞一多詩歌意象是豐富又多元的，有時蘊藏著地火運行般的轟隆聲，營造出中華兒女對時代深沉的力量；其大氣魄如匹革命的駿馬，縱橫於廣漠的蒼穹……。有時又頗有融具中西詩詞的美學風致，或表達出對愛情細膩的情思，恰如靜立於清波的一隻秋鷺……。我認為，對於這樣有著偉健人格的詩人的進一步研究，是當代文人的責任。

In interpreting the images of the three poems by Wen Yiduo, I found that Wen Yiduo is not only a scholar and poet, but also a critic. He can turn poetic thoughts into images. On the one hand, he actively seeks the light of life and praises the dignity of life in difficulties. The language of his poems should be "deep and vigorous, with dynamic and harmonious rhythms", showing compassion for the living environment of the great era and the spirit of the times in pursuit of light and new life during the May Fourth Movement, and it is full of expressive force. The handling of the picture also touches people's eyes from time to time and shocks the readers' hearts.

In addition, Wen Yiduo's poems contain "beautiful oriental images", which are actually not so gorgeous, and his love poems are also written in an extraordinary way, and indeed have extraordinary charm, not so "implicit" in metaphor, which makes people feel reminiscing about the wonderful moments. In addition, the sharpness of the visual stimulation of Wen Yiduo's poetic images well expresses the melancholy confusion of the poet's subjective emotions, stirring like the bass of a music, making us appreciate the magnificence and quietness of the universe. strength. In short, while praising this book, I also appreciate the wisdom in Wen Yiduo's image creation. The imagery of Wen Yiduo's poems is rich and diverse, and sometimes contains the roaring sound of earth fire, which creates the profound power of the Chinese sons and daughters to the times; its grandeur is like a revolutionary horse, flying across the vast sky... Sometimes it has an aesthetic style that blends Chinese and Western poetry, or expresses delicate thoughts about love, just like an autumn heron standing quietly in Qingbo... I think it is the responsibility of contemporary literati to further study such a poet with a strong personality.

〈註 1〉：江蘇東台人，1982 年畢業於南京師範大學中文系，現任鹽城師範學院文學院副教授，主要從事中國現當代文學的教學與研究。

〈註 2〉：聞一多（1899－1946），生於湖北黃岡浠水；係學者型愛國詩人，自幼愛好詩藝。1912 年考入北京清華學校，4 年後開始在《清華周刊》上發表系列讀書筆記，總稱《二月盧漫記》。1919 年五四運動時積極參加學生運動，翌年發表首篇白話文《旅客式的學生》，同年 9 月，發表了第一首新詩《西岸》。1921 年 11 月與梁實秋等人發起成立清華文學社，次年 3 月，寫成《律詩底研究》，開始系統地研究新詩格律化理論。1922 年 7 月赴美國芝加哥藝術學院學習，年底出版與梁實秋合著的《冬夜草兒評論》。1923 年 9 月正式出版第一本新詩集《紅燭》，收錄了 103 首新詩。曾任北京藝術專科學校教務長、南京第四中山大學外文系主任、武漢大學文學院長、國立青島大學文學院長等職。1928 年 1 月出版第二部詩集《死水》收錄 28 首新詩，此後致力於古典文學的研究。對《周易》、《詩經》、《莊子》、《楚辭》四大古籍的整理研究，被郭沫若稱為「前無古人，後無來者」。1937 年抗戰開始，他在昆明西南聯大任教。1946 年 7 月 15 日在悼念被國民黨特務暗殺的李公樸的大會上，發表了著名的《最後一次的講演》，當天下午即被國民黨昆明警備司令部下級軍官湯時亮和李文山槍殺。

—2012.5.10 作

—刊登中國內蒙古《集寧師範學院學報》，2013.第 2 期，第 35 卷總第 121 期，頁 1-5 頁。

<Note 1>: Born in Dongtai, Jiangsu, graduated from the Chinese Department of Nanjing Normal University in 1982, and is currently an associate professor at the School of Liberal Arts of Yancheng Normal University, mainly engaged in the teaching and research of modern and contemporary Chinese literature.

<Note 2>: Wen Yiduo (1899-1946), was born in Xishui, Huanggang, Hubei Province; he is a scholar-type patriotic poet who has loved poetry since childhood. In 1912, he was admitted to Tsinghua School in Beijing. Four years later, he began to publish a series of reading notes in *Tsinghua Weekly*, collectively called *Manji in Eryuelu*. In 1919, he actively participated in the student movement during the May 4th Movement. The following year, he published his first vernacular essay "A Passenger-like Student". In September of the same year, he published his first new poem *West Bund*. In November 1921, he initiated the establishment of the Tsinghua Literature Society with Liang Shiqiu and others. In March of the following year, he wrote *Research on the Underlying of Rhythmic Poetry* and began to systematically study the metrical theory of new poetry. In July 1922, he went to the Art Institute of Chicago to study in the United States. At the end of the year, he published *Winter Night Grass Review*, co-authored with Liang Shiqiu. In September 1923, the first collection of new poems *Red Candle* was officially published, which included 103 new poems. He used to be the dean of Beijing Art College, the director of the Foreign Languages Department of Nanjing Fourth Sun Yat-sen University, the dean of literature at Wuhan University, and the dean of literature at National Qingdao University. In January 1928, he published his second collection of poems, *Still Water*, which included 28 new poems, and devoted himself to the study of classical literature thereafter. The collation and research of the four ancient books *Book of Changes*, *Book of Songs*, *Zhuangzi* and *The Southern Songs* were called by Guo Moruo as "there is no one before, and no one to come after". When the Anti-Japanese War began in 1937, he taught at Southwest Associated University in Kunming. On July 15, 1946, at the meeting to commemorate Li Gongpu who was assassinated by Kuomintang agents, he delivered the famous *The Last Lecture*. In the afternoon, he was shot dead by Tang Shiliang and Li Wenshan, lower-level officers of the Kuomintang Kunming Garrison Command.

5. 沉雅與靜穆 — 讀牛漢 〈落雪的夜〉〈根〉〈海上蝴蝶〉

一、前　言

　　牛漢〈1923-〉一生的遭遇是無與倫比的，他生於山西定襄縣一個窮苦的農民家庭，20 歲考入西北大學。23 歲，因參加民主學生運動，被國民黨政府逮捕，判刑 2 年。32 歲時又因胡風案，被關押 2 年，直到 57 歲才得以平反。詩人憑著永不服輸的毅力與膽識，懷著崇高的理想，歷經無數的啟蒙與蛻變，在坎坷的磨練中，卓然聳峙；精神上始終屹立不搖，也刻下了詩歌史上最為神聖的烙痕。

　　如果說牛漢是位紮實的詩人，倒不如說他是比較哀傷的詩人；他掀開了愛好自然悲壯的一面而傳遞給讀者，不斷地揚棄舊我，以完成追求詩歌藝術的超越性，進而新生靈魂空前的自由。

5. Elegance and Serenity — Reading Niu Han's Night of Falling Snow, Root, and Butterfly on the Sea

1. Introduction

Niu Han (1923-) had an incomparable experience in his life. He was born in a poor peasant family in Dingxiang County, Shanxi Province, and was admitted to Northwest University at the age of 20. At 23, he was arrested by the Kuomintang government and sentenced to 2 years in prison for participating in the democratic student movement. At 32, he was imprisoned for 2 years for the "Hu Feng Incident", and he was not rehabilitated until he was 57. With the perseverance and courage of never bowing before defeat, the poet has gone through countless enlightenment and transformation with lofty ideals. He stands tall in the rough temper.

If Niu Han is a solid poet, it is better to say that he is a sad one; he reveals the tragic side of nature and passes it on to the readers, and constantly sublates the old self in order to complete the pursuit of the transcendence of poetic art, and then unprecedented freedom for the newborn soul.

　　牛漢曾如此說：「我的詩不是個人的自傳，而是歷史大傳的一個微小的細節，是歷史結出的一枚果子。」是以，牛漢致力追尋一種藝術精神向度之美，文筆有著簡逸中的聖潔質感；他以真樸的語言，詩風介於浪漫主義與寫實主義之間。就是這種深深愛著自己國家、家鄉的自然，他創出一種令人心碎的寧靜詩意、一種殉難的壯美。這是詩人激動的靈魂與備受折磨的心理的完整反射，總能喚起讀者陷入一種既沉雅又靜穆的「絕美」深淵，而全神貫注投入於其詩中。

　　牛漢的成功絕非偶然。他一生淡泊、謙虛，喜歡追求心靈的深度化。曾擔任《中國文學》執行副主編等，著有《溫泉》、《牛漢詩集》等詩集十餘本，作品除獲文學創作獎外，也被譯成日、英、法、西等國文字出版。牛漢以其旺盛的生命力來寫詩，永不懈怠地敲響希望之鐘，用詩來展現他滿懷的哲思和熱忱的情感，也為國家增添了許多光采。

二、不斷奮鬥的成長軌跡─生命的實感體驗

　　牛漢生涯中，曾因兩度遭遇被關禁的命運，因此，戰爭的拂逆與苦難，所帶來的挫折與打擊，正用來試鍊詩人的勇

Niu Han once said: "My poetry is not a personal autobiography, but a tiny detail of the history biography, a fruit of history." Therefore, Niu Han is committed to pursuing the beauty of an artistic spiritual dimension; his writing has a simple and holy texture. He uses simple language, and his poetic style is between romanticism and realism. It is this kind of deep love for his own country and the nature of his hometown that he created a heartbreaking tranquil poetry and a martyrdom magnificence. This is a complete reflection of the poet's excited soul and tormented psychology, which can always arouse readers to fall into an abyss of "beautiful beauty" that is both elegant and quiet, and concentrate on his poems.

Niu Han's success is no accident. He was indifferent and modest throughout his life, and liked to pursue the depth of the soul. Serving as the executive deputy editor-in-chief of *Chinese Literature*, etc., and authored more than ten volumes of poetry anthologies such as *Hot Spring* and *The Collected Poems of Niu Han*. In addition to winning literary creation awards, his works have also been translated into Japanese, English, French, Spanish and other languages. Niu Han wrote poems with an exuberant vitality, never slacks off ringing the bell of hope, using poems to fully express his philosophical thinking and passionate emotions, while adding a lot of brilliance to the country.

2. The Growth Track of Continuous Struggle — the Real Experience of Life

In his life his career, Niu Han has twice encountered the fate of being imprisoned. Therefore, the setbacks and blows caused by the adversity and suffering of the war

毅耐力；而這段困厄的歲月，亦成為他精神生活層次與藝術
文化素養的經驗。這就是成長—詩人把逆境當成是人生樂章
中的抑揚頓挫，而藉由詩句來觀照自己的靈魂，無懼於外界
的紛紜，昂然挺立於詩文的創作中……我們不禁懷嘆詩人的
灑脫，才能盡情地彈響生命的音符。

　　這首〈落雪的夜〉樸實無華，更有逸緻；我們可以感受
出詩人的純潔來，也有一種無可言喻的美感：

> 北方，
> 落雪的夜裏
> 一個夥伴
> 給我送來一包木炭。
> 他知道我寒冷，我貧窮
> 我沒有火。
>
> 祖國呵，
> 你是不是也寒冷？
>
> 我可以為你的溫暖，
> 將自己當作一束木炭
> 燃燒起來……
> 你溫暖了，
> 我也再沒有寒冷。

were used to test the poet's courage and endurance, and this difficult period also became an experience of his spiritual life as well as artistic and cultural literacy. This is growth—the poet regards adversity as the ups and downs of life, and uses poems to reflect on his own soul. He is not afraid of the chaos of the outside world, standing proudly in the creation of poems.... We cannot help but admire the poet's free and unbounded talent, with which to play the notes of life

This song "Snowy Night" is simple and elegant, and we can feel the poet's purity, not without an ineffable beauty:

In the north
A snowy night
A partner
Send me a bag of charcoal.
He knows I'm cold, I'm poor
I have no heat.

Motherland,
Are you cold too?

For the sake of your warmth,
I can be a bouquet of charcoal
Burn them ...
You are warm
And I also don't feel cold anymore.

　　詩中畫面一開始，夜是落雪的，北方的一個冬天——在
酷寒的氣候下，詩人有個夥伴，特冒寒送來一包木炭——詩
人似乎感覺到真心的安慰，但又驚訝友人關懷他寒冷，貧窮
得連生火取暖都是一種奢侈。吸引我讀下去的主因，是我可
以想像，有誰又能想到這樣嚴寒的時刻，一包木炭卻給了詩
人如夏日般的溫暖；而詩人時時珍惜這份友誼的幸福，就是
知足最深刻的道理了。

　　緊接著詩人深藏他自己對祖國熾熱的情感，在他山窮水
盡之際，仍心繫祖國艱辛的時局，是否也能不怕冬寒？最後，
詩人在勇者不畏艱難之下，有仁者憂國憂民的感懷，更有積
極的人生觀；以燃燒自己，忠貞不變的情操，迎向每天到來
的挑戰。彷彿中，詩人化身為一棵高聳挺拔的巨木，努力向
不可預知的藍天伸展。

　　〈根〉是首意象鮮活、境廣意深的佳作；詩人暗喻自己
的痛苦與不幸，並非全然悲觀絕望的。牛漢以詩寄託其情志，
以接受了師長點滴努力的栽培，就應貢獻自己全部的心血，
創造出更為嶄新的作品，才能回報祖國庇蔭的恩澤，才能回
饋父母「飲水思源」最高的意義；而且熱烈地為生命的美好
而謳歌以及對未來的自我期許：

At the beginning of the picture in the poem, the night is snowing, a winter in the north — in the extremely cold climate, the poet has a partner who sent a pack of charcoal especially in the cold — the poet seems to feel sincere comfort, but he is surprised by his friend caring for him is cold, so poor that even lighting a fire for warmth is a luxury. The main reason that attracts me to read is that I can imagine — who can imagine that a bag of charcoal can give the poet the warmth like summer in such a severe cold moment; and the poet always cherishes the happiness of this friendship. The truth is profound.

Immediately afterwards, the poet hides his own passionate feelings for the motherland. When he is at the end of his life, he still cares about the difficult situation of the motherland. Can he not be afraid of the winter cold? In the end, the poet has the feeling of the benevolent who is concerned about the country and the people, and has a positive outlook on life under the courage of the brave who is not afraid of difficulties. As if, the poet turned into a towering giant tree, striving to stretch towards the unpredictable blue sky.

Root is a masterpiece with vivid imagery and deep meaning; the poet is not completely pessimistic and desperate when he alludes to his own pain and misfortune. Niu Han entrusts his emotions with his poems, and accepts the cultivation of his teacher's efforts. He should devote all his efforts to create more brand-new works in order to repay the blessing of the motherland and the highest meaning of "Drinking Water and Thinking of the Source"; and ardently eulogize for the beauty of life and self-expectation for the future:

我是根，
一生一世在地下
默默地生長，
向下，向下……
我相信地心有一個太陽
聽不見枝頭鳥鳴，
感覺不到柔軟的微風，
但是我坦然
並不覺得委屈煩悶。
開花的季節，
我跟枝葉同樣幸福
沉甸甸的果實，
注滿了我的全部心血。

　　每個人都有根，根紮得越深，樹木長得越是茂盛。但有
幾人曾經加以深思過？甚或漠視自己的本源？然而，牛漢幾
經歷難，仍不停的紮根，默默地向下伸展。因為熱情，因為
關愛，所以表現在詩裡正是堅韌無比的剛毅，正是詩人博大
的胸懷的顯現。他看不見自己的不幸，也明白歷史告訴我們，
從無勁健的小草，來自安逸中成長的道理。唯有悍然接受磨
難的考驗，才能具備捨我其誰的氣慨，成為頂天立地的詩人。

　　牛漢的浩然正氣，是個人的精神圖騰；他的詩，隨著創
作的動力，志節堅定如一。他必須不斷的自我鞭策，以向上
奮發的本能為基礎，同時具備了隱忍和果敢。縱然處在動亂

I am a root,
Spending my entire life underground
Grow silently,
Down, down...
I believe there's a sun in the center of the earth

I can't hear the birds chirping on the branches,
Can't feel the soft breeze,
But I am taking it easy
I don't feel mistreated or bored.

Flowering season,
I am as happy as branches and leaves
Heavy fruits,
Fill my heart and soul.

Everyone has roots, and the deeper the roots, the lusher the tree will grow. But how many people have thought about it? Or even ignore your own origin? However, Niu Han has gone through several hardships, but he still keeps taking root and stretches downward silently. Because of enthusiasm and caring, it is the incomparable fortitude expressed in the poem, which is the manifestation of the poet's broad mind. He can't see his own misfortune, and he also understands the truth that history tells us to grow from a grass that is weak and healthy. Only by brazenly accepting the test of suffering can one have the spirit of giving up to others and become an upright poet.

Niu Han's awe-inspiring righteousness is a personal spiritual totem; his poems are as firm as the momentum of creation. He must constantly spur himself on, based on the instinct of striving upwards, possessing forbearance and

時代，任何荊棘都無法阻擋詩人追求精神自由的渴望；其綻
放出來的花，當然幸福、絢麗；締結出來的果實當然偉大！
而讀者的心靈也一下子就激起深刻又熱烈的共鳴。

　　這首〈海上蝴蝶〉極具藝術的高格與超逸之美，反映詩
人在災難歲月的一種驚詫的審美知覺的體驗；其獨特的意象
與本原的生命相聯，是詩人自我靈魂之光，也能喚起讀者的
感知和想像：

幾十年來，我遇到過不少無法解釋的奇跡

——題記

> 人們都會説：
> 能在海上飛翔的，
> 一定有堅硬的翅膀，
> 敢於跟風暴雷雨搏擊。
>
> 可是，我看見過，
> （千真萬確）
> 幾隻黃色小蝴蝶
> 在渤海灣茫茫的浪濤上
> 不是貼著岸邊飛，
> 是朝遠遠的大海飛去，飛去！
> 它們忽上忽下
> 很像矯健的海鷗（註1）。

courage at the same time. Even in the turbulent era, no thorns can stop the poet's desire to pursue spiritual freedom; the flowers that bloom are of course happy and gorgeous; the fruits that are formed are of course great! And the reader's heart immediately aroused a deep and warm resonance.

This song *Butterfly on the Sea* is highly artistic and elegant, reflecting the poet's astonishing aesthetic perception experience in the disaster years; its unique image relates to the original life, it is the light of the poet's own soul, and it can also arouse the reader's perception and imagination:

Over the decades, I've experienced quite a few unexplained miracles 　　— Inscription

People will say:
To be able to fly in the sea,
Must have strong wings,
Dare to fight against the thunderstorms.

But I have seen,
Definitely
Several yellow butterflies
On the vast waves of Bohai Bay
Instead of flying close to the shore,
They are flying towards the far sea, flying!
They go up and down
Much like the vigorous sea genus <Note 1>.

黃色小蝴蝶，
火苗一般閃爍，
不像迷路，
也顯不出一點兒驚慌；
它們越飛越遠，
海岸漸漸地消失。

小小的蝴蝶
你們為什麼不回頭？

　　一開頭，出現了一個十分引人注目的思考，那就是從不同的視角關切並研究著詩人自身。人們會想，在牛漢生活最悲痛的時候，卻能陸續地完成許多詩篇。是否意味，一定要有極堅硬的翅膀，才能抵擋外在的雷風暴雨的搏擊？

　　詩人有溫和蘊藉的智慧情感，也有虛懷若谷的襟懷；他很巧妙地解開了這謎題。他以為，千萬不要漠視自己的力量，一旦這股力量凝聚起來，創作之泉，也會洶湧澎湃地迴盪。

　　此時，詩人讓讀者看到了這樣一幅真實的圖畫，海上蝴蝶是出奇的靜謐。當火苗一般閃爍的黃蝴蝶出現時，牠的生

The little yellow butterflies,
Like flickering flames,
They don't look like getting lost,
Nor show any sign of panic.
They fly farther and farther,
The coast gradually disappears.

Little butterflies
Why don't you turn back?

At the beginning, there is a very striking thinking, that is, to care about and study the poet himself from different perspectives. People would think that Niu Han was able to finish many poems one after another when he was in the most sorrowful life. Does it mean that there must be extremely hard wings in order to withstand the blows of external thunderstorms?

The poet has gentle and contained wisdom and emotions, but also has a broad-minded mind; he solved this puzzle very skillfully. He thought, don't ignore your own power, once this power is condensed, the fountain of creation will also surge and reverberate.

At this time, the poet let the readers see such a real picture, the butterflies on the sea are surprisingly quiet. When the yellow butterfly, flickering like a flame, and sea

動令人傾心！使讀者瞬間離開現實的重擔而升騰於幻境。牠勇敢地從自己的眼前飛過岸海的另一邊的影像，那逐漸消失的光點，伴隨著詩人的痛感，讓讀者也從這種以動表靜的情景中感悟到一種人生的境界。每當詩人回頭望著，內心又重新燃起了無窮的希望；而我也看到詩人的雙眼，絲毫不經掩飾地在黑暗中透露著光芒……

三、以愛飛翔──跨入無止境的心靈時空

研究牛漢，是由於他擁有一種罕見的崇高品格，勇於向自己挑戰，能成為所有知識分子的一種絕佳典範。他的筆力深澈而真純，有如水彩畫透明的神韻；也有英雄式的大氣魄，沉潛的和諧中，含容著憂傷與悲憫的逸致，這正是牛漢思想的具體表現。讀牛漢的詩，可以感受到他藝術生命的躍動，夾雜著他坎坷的風暴；但潛伏的光采，是近代詩歌史上絕無僅有的，他就是這樣一位難得的奇才。

牛漢的力量，是由於他的藝術一直昇華到足以溝通他的特殊思維的狀態，詩中盎然的生氣，常能激發讀者無窮的信心。他歷經了滄桑，才能擁有開拓曠闊的胸懷；以愛飛翔，才能跨入無止境的心靈時空。世界是可愛的，縱有黑暗，但沒有永遠的黑暗；而所有短暫的黑暗，都將轉成另一面的光明。最後僅以一首詩，致牛漢這位不朽的詩人：

appears, its vividness is fascinating! It makes readers leave the burden of reality in an instant and ascend to the illusion. It bravely flies over the other side of the shore and sea from before my eyes, and the gradually light spot, accompanied by the poet's pain, makes readers feel a kind of realm of life from this scene of static and dynamic. Whenever the poet looks back, endless hope is rekindled in his heart; and I also see the poet's eyes revealing light in the darkness without any concealment...

3. Flying with Love — Stepping into the Endless Spiritual Time and Space

The reason for studying Niu Han is that he possesses a rare noble character, dares to challenge himself, and can become an excellent example for all intellectuals. His brushwork is deep and pure, like the transparent charm of watercolor painting; he also has heroic grandeur, and the submerged harmony contains the ease of sadness and compassion, which is the specific expression of Niu Han's thought. Reading Niu Han's poems, one can feel the dynamism of his artistic life, mixed with his bumpy storms; but the latent brilliance is unique in the history of modern poetry, and he is such a rare genius.

Niu Han's power is due to his art has been sublimated enough to communicate his special state of thinking, and the vitality in his poems often inspires readers' boundless confidence. Only after he has experienced vicissitudes can he have a broad mind; only by flying with love can he enter the endless spiritual time and space. The world is lovely, although there is darkness, but there is no eternal darkness; and all the short-term darkness will turn into light on the other side. In the end, only one poem is dedicated to Niu Han, the immortal poet:

致牛漢

沒有人能像你一樣聳立山中
清絕，靜絕，沉入忘我
在小樓的一方
你的坦蕩是雪林的撼動

不可逼視的冬風
掀起了冰霜
在蒼茫的幽徑上
你，伴著隨階而上的星月
透出了漸次低吟的清音

－2009.9.18 作

－山東省全國中文核心期刊，《時代文學》，2009
年第 12 期，總第 169 期，封面特別推介林明
理於「理論、評論版」，詩評〈讀辛鬱〈豹〉
〈鷗和日出〉〈風〉〉、〈讀牛漢〈落雪的夜〉
〈海上蝴蝶〉〉、〈商禽心理意象與詩化

To Niu Han

Nobody can stand in the mountains like you
Extremely clear, extremely quiet, immersed in selflessness
On the side of the small building
Your magnanimity is the shake of the snow forest

The inviolable winter winds
Set off ice and frost
On the vast path
You, accompanied by the stars and the moon
Utter a clear murmuring voice

6.陳義海詩歌的思想藝術成就

摘　要：陳義海，作為雙語詩人已走過了三十年的創作歷程，現為鹽城師範學院文學院院長。他的詩歌曾經獲得沃里克大學40周年校慶英文詩歌競賽第二名。三十年來，他以浪漫、纖細的詩思為表現出他所理想的美而歌唱，並以清麗多彩的筆墨，描繪出了各具其態的藝術形象，也翻譯出版過世界名著與文學著作等多種，為中國當代詩壇做出了實質的貢獻。本文以其詩集《狄奧尼索斯在中國》為基礎，嘗試對其詩歌的思想藝術做一探討。

關鍵詞：陳義海，詩歌，藝術，唯美主義

在陳義海接受中西合璧的正規教育，並吸收、轉化為自己的現代詩歌書寫之餘，我們可以從這本《狄奧尼索斯在中國》詩集中窺見、感受陳義海身影與豐采的藝術形象，甚至發現被後期象徵主義詩壇的領袖古爾蒙，R.de〈1858-1915〉詩人隔世繼承、並重新發揚了抒情的形式；而意象主義甚或唯美主義的精神情懷，也在作者的創新承續中，鎔鑄為全新詩作與不凡的神采內涵。

6. The Ideological and Artistic Achievements of Chen Yihai's Poems

Abstract: Chen Yihai, as a bilingual poet, has gone through 30 years of creative process, and is now the dean of the School of Liberal Arts of Yancheng Normal University. His poetry once won the second place in the English poetry competition for the 40th anniversary of the University of Warwick. For thirty years, he has sung to express his ideal beauty with romantic and delicate poetic thinking, and has depicted various artistic images with clear and colorful pen and ink. He has also translated and published world famous books and literary works, etc. A variety of works have made substantial contributions to the Chinese contemporary poetry circles. Based on his collection of poems *Dionysus in China*, this article tries to discuss the ideological art of his poems.

Key words: Chen Yihai, poetry, art, aestheticism

After Chen Yihai received a formal education combining Chinese and Western elements, and absorbed and transformed it into his own modern poetry writing, we can glimpse and feel Chen Yihai's figure and rich artistic image from this collection of poems *Dionysus in China*, and even It was discovered that Gourmont, the leader of the symbolist poetry circle in the later period, and the poet R. de (1858-1915) inherited and re-developed the lyrical form; and the spiritual feelings of imagism or even aestheticism are also in the author's innovative inheritance , into a brand-new poem with extraordinary spirit and connotation.

在閱讀此詩集的各種表現手法，由「象」而「意」地凸出主旨、風格的創造的過程中；該如何經由對藝術形象的解剖，以體會隱於詞外之「情」或鑑別其詩歌藝術之美？關於此，作者在自序裡已提及，他始終堅持，詩歌不能少掉兩樣東西：一是美，二是崇高。作者也將此詩集與過去的詩集做了比較，稱這裡的詩歌，似乎多了些許蒼涼，他稱說，這種蒼涼是「跨文化語境中的秋風辭」。其實，陳義海的可貴之處，恰恰在於：他既是「用生命和詩歌結合」的學者詩人，深邃而憂傷，寫實又似幻影，又善以在平凡中鋪陳出不凡的聯想與想像。當然，他的詩篇裡的孤獨與愛情、痛苦與期盼……時而冷凝時而溫馨，忠於生命又追尋詩歌永恆。因而，不論其描寫生活中的感觸或是異域題材的詩，都可看出作者並非只關在象牙塔裡自我吟咏和悲吟，而是其風格能呈現出淨化後靈魂之音這一鮮明的思想傾向。如這首〈希爾頓酒店〉詩中這樣感情炙人的句子：

我數了數
我是第二十七個

我在燈光無力的一角坐下
我看不見鋼琴
所以鋼琴也看不見我

但我聽見她

In the process of reading the various expression techniques in this collection of poems, from "image" to "meaning" to highlight the theme and the creation of style. The beauty of its poetic art? Regarding this, the author has already mentioned in the preface, and he always insists that poetry cannot lack two things: one is beauty, and the other is sublime. The author also compared this collection of poems with previous collections of poems, saying that the poems here seem to be a little more desolate. He called this desolation "Autumn Wind Ci in a cross-cultural context". In fact, Chen Yihai's value lies precisely in that he is a scholar-poet who "combines life and poetry", is profound and sad, realistic and phantom-like, and good at laying out extraordinary associations and imaginations in the ordinary. Of course, the loneliness and love, pain and expectation in his poems are sometimes condensed and sometimes warm, loyal to life and pursuing the eternity of poetry. Therefore, whether it describes the feelings in life or the poems with exotic themes, it can be seen that the author is not just shutting himself in an ivory tower to chant and lament, but his style can present the distinct sound of the purified soul and ideological tendency. Such an emotional line from the poem *Hilton Hotel*:

I counted
I am the twenty-seventh

I sit down in a corner where the light is weak
I can't see the piano
So the piano can't see me

But I heard her

音樂用二十七雙細膩的手
撫摸著二十七顆粗糙的心

當 whiskey 把我的血染成咖啡色
我的血管裡奔騰著多惱河的咖啡因

雖然淚水朦朧了我的雙眼
但我依然看見
隔著窗紗
空中的月光是用一種象形文字寫的

　　全詩在酒店琴聲中寄託深摯的情感，他的預感、思慮和深深的憂愁，不僅是愛情磨難的見證者，而且也是想鏟除這不幸的思想者。也許有人稱呼他為「唯美主義者」，雖不無道理，但畢竟不夠全面。陳義海，還有昂然勤奮的一面。確實如此！他在完成這部詩集的寒假裡，每天埋首於辦公室工作 10 至 12 個小時。他說，我一直在努力，但不知努力的結果如何。從中，可以看出，有不少詩就是寫酒神，也寫出了詩人對未來的憧憬與孤獨的探索。如這首小詩〈酒〉，陳義海在進行詩歌創作的同時，還致力於翻譯詩歌的探究。他在 2009 年出版的第一本個人詩集《被翻譯了的意象》後，沒想到，不到半年，2010 年 8 月又出版了中英雙語詩集《迷失英倫》；接著，又立即出版了這本詩集，並在書後寫下一篇後記，陳述「詩人怎樣翻譯自己的詩歌」。其中研究了詩歌與英譯之間的一些問題，對學術研究是有裨益的。而此詩是詩

Music with twenty-seven delicate hands
Caressing twenty-seven rough hearts

When the whiskey stains my blood brown
A river of caffeine rushes through my veins

Although tears blur my eyes
But I still see
Through the window screen
The moonlight in the sky is written in a hieroglyph

The whole poem expresses his deep emotions in the sound of the piano in the hotel. His premonitions, thoughts and deep sorrows are not only the witnesses of the suffering of love, but also the thinkers who want to eradicate this misfortune. Some people may call him an "aesthete". Although it is not unreasonable, it is not comprehensive enough. Chen Yihai also has a bold and diligent side. Indeed! During the winter vacation when he was finishing this collection of poems, he buried himself in the office and worked 10 to 12 hours a day. He said, I have been working hard, but I don't know the result of my efforts. From it, it can be seen that many poems are about Dionysus, and also about the poet's longing for the future and exploration of loneliness. For example, in this little poem *Wine*, while Chen Yihai was writing poetry, he also devoted himself to the exploration of translation poetry. After his first personal poetry collection *Translated Images* was published in 2009, he did not expect that in less than half a year, in August 2010, he published a Chinese-English bilingual poetry collection *Lost in England.* This collection of poems, and write an epilogue at the end of the book, stating "how poets translate their own poems". Among them, some problems between poetry and English translation are studied, which is beneficial to academic research. In this poem, the poet

人一面形象地理解世界，一面又借助於形象向人解說世界的
深度：

> 我自以為世界上只有我一個人醒著
> 其實，醒著的還有酒
> 不管夜有多深
> 它總圓睜著它的眼睛

> 我自以為世界上只有酒醒著
> 其實，醒著的還有我
> 請不要說我的淚已乾
> 杯沿上依然掛著一滴露珠，苦的

　　在這部詩集裡所創造的酒神狄奧尼索斯〈註 1〉形象的
明確度上，似乎已將酒神的想像、聯想等透過形象思維規律
的延伸，透徹出詩人孤獨的本質的描繪。可見，形象思維確
是陳義海詩歌創作的生命；而浪漫觀念在其心底孕育，終結
成粒粒真珠。在這裡，詩人抒發了一種五味雜陳的複雜感情，
並表達了一種想要新生的欲望。如同法國著名詩人古爾蒙，
R.de 的代表作《西茉納》般，這首〈十四行的春天〉裡，作
者也延續了古爾蒙鮮明塑造出翹首企盼的情人形象來。此詩
裡的西茉納，很可能也是陳義海所愛好的名字；以見譬喻之
精巧，予人溫婉輕靈之感：

understands the world in images, and at the same time explains the depth of the world to people with the help of images:

I thought I was the only one awake in the world
In fact, there is still wine awake
No matter how deep the night is
It keeps its eyes wide open

I thought there was only alcohol in the world sober
In fact, I am the one who is awake
Please don't say my tears are dry
There is still a drop of dew hanging on the rim of the cup, bitter

In terms of the clarity of the image of Dionysus <Note 1> created in this collection of poems, it seems that the imagination and association of Dionysus have been extended through the law of image thinking to thoroughly describe the essence of the poet's loneliness. It can be seen that thinking in images is indeed the life of Chen Yihai's poetry creation; while romantic concepts are bred in his heart and eventually become pearls. Here, the poet expresses a mixed feeling and expresses a desire for a new life. Like the famous French poet Gourmont R. de's representative work *Simona*, in this song *Sonnet Spring*, the author also continued Gurmont's vivid and long-awaited lover image. Simona in this poem is probably also Chen Yihai's favorite name; seeing the ingenuity of the metaphor, it gives people a sense of gentleness and lightness:

生命之偶然如同一朵紅玫瑰
死亡之必然如同一朵紅紅的玫瑰
西茉納，請你從草葉上輕輕滴下
像絕望一樣完美，像完美一樣絕望
只有梨樹，站在絕望的那一頭
一邊盛開一邊朗誦下一段：

死亡之必然如同一朵紅玫瑰
生命之偶然如同一朵紅紅的玫瑰
西茉納，太陽在緩緩升起
露珠在溫柔地死去
只有最後的桃花
在水邊一邊凋零一邊朗誦上一段

西茉納，春天如一只頹廢的小羊
在我的憂鬱上快活地蹦著，唱著

　　此詩所用的藝術手法自然是擬人，其中，「愛情」自也
是「憂鬱的」；在舊有的意象中又派生出新的意象，加上又
有美麗繽紛的色彩反覆地點綴其間，令思念之情若現若隱，
更增添了美感力。詩行至最後一段，在一種迷離幽隱的意緒
中，忽然連結成不息的愛的節奏，反而帶來赫然有力的情感。
陳義海在這本集子共收錄詩歌 120 首，其中，有 20 首是出自
二十多歲時的詩作。雖自認是生澀，難免有「為賦新詞強說

The chance of life is like a red rose
Death is inevitable like a red rose
Simona, please let me drip from the blades of grass
perfect as hopeless, hopeless as perfect
Only the pear tree stands at the end of despair
Recite the next paragraph while blooming:

Death is inevitable as a red rose
The chance of life is like a red rose
Simona, the sun is slowly rising
Dewdrops are dying tenderly
Only the last peach blossom
Withering by the water's edge, reciting a passage

Simona, spring is like a decadent lamb
Jumping merrily on my melancholy, singing

The artistic technique used in this poem is of course anthropomorphic. Among them, "love" is also "melancholy"; new images are derived from the old images, and beautiful and colorful colors are repeatedly adorned in it, making people miss The feeling is looming, which adds to the beauty. In the last paragraph of the poem, in a blurred mood, it suddenly connects to the rhythm of endless love, which instead brings impressive and powerful emotions. Chen Yihai collected a total of 120 poems in this collection, among which 20 poems were written when he was in his twenties. Although he considers himself jerky, it is unavoidable to be suspected

愁」之嫌；但卻不失為清俊逸麗，又浪漫、奔放，洋溢著想
像的筆調。當詩人中年後，詩性更具有時間上的伸展性，又
具有空間上的廣闊性 如這首〈夜晚應該有一個自己的名字〉，
當詩人以濃重的色彩描繪了夜，交織著人們的希望，憂傷和
想像之後，又發出了深沉的嘆息：

　　　千萬年來，夜晚沒有一個自己的名字
　　　夜晚應該有一個屬於自己的名字
　　　而不是借用我的筆名

　　　夜晚應該有自己的國籍
　　　夜晚應該有自己的故鄉
　　　夜晚應該有自己的母親

　　　夜晚應該有自己的語法
　　　夜晚應該有自己的衣服
　　　夜晚應該有自己的情人

　　　夜晚應該有自己的詩歌
　　　夜晚應該有自己的酒杯
　　　而不是固執地附著在我的杯子上

　　夜，這戴著神秘面紗的姑娘，在作者筆下形成了紛呈凝
煉的「意象群」，以凸出「孤獨」之意。此詩比之於陳義海
過去的作品，思想更為深邃，精神境界更為宏闊。作者自己
強調，生命短暫，詩歌永恆。寫詩應該通過自己的心寫，陳

of "emphasizing sorrow for writing new words"; but it is still elegant, romantic, unrestrained, and full of imaginative writing style. When the poet is middle-aged, the poetic nature is more stretched in time and broad in space. For example, in the song *The Night Should Have Its Own Name*, when the poet described the night with strong colors, interweaving people's hopes, sorrows and imaginations, he sighed deeply:

For thousands of years, the night has not had a name of
　　its own
The night should have a name of its own
Instead of borrowing my pseudonym

The night should have its own nationality
The night should have its own hometown
The night should have its own mother

Night should have its own grammar
Night should have its own clothes
The night should have its own lover

Night should have its own poetry
Night should have its own wine glass
Instead of clinging stubbornly to my cup

　　The night, the girl wearing a mysterious veil, forms a diverse and condensed "image group" in the author's pen to highlight the meaning of "loneliness". Compared with Chen Yihai's past works, this poem has deeper thoughts and a more magnificent spiritual realm. The author himself emphasized that life is short, but poetry is eternal. Poems should be written with one's own heart. Chen Yihai's

義海的詩歌常與花草的舞動情狀或動物、四季的表情等，自
然地連結在一起，想像與取譬俱美。如這首〈寂寞的城〉，
就是作者誠摯情懷的抒發：

　　　　我總是在夜深人靜的時候上路
　　　　只有在夜深人靜的時候
　　　　耳朵才開始傾聽，只有
　　　　在夜深人靜的時候
　　　　沿街的房子才開始長出大大小小的耳朵

　　　　美麗的鮮花因為有了欣賞才格外嫵媚
　　　　清脆的馬蹄聲因為有了傾聽才格外美麗
　　　　夜色中的背影因為有了注視才格外孤寂
　　　　是啊，因為有了風
　　　　我的斗篷更像一面絕望的旗

　　　　夜深了，馬蹄聲激勵著我的孤寂
　　　　如果我的心是一座寂寞的城
　　　　我希望有你來居住
　　　　如果你的城是一顆寂寞的心
　　　　我希望你的心中有一座寂寞的城

　　抒真情，乃是詩生命。在中國北宋畫家郭熙的《林泉高
致‧畫意》書中，曾提出著名的「詩是無形畫，畫是有形詩」
〈註1〉的論斷。其論點，就是從藝術的目的——美上來要求。

poems are often naturally connected with the dancing scenes of flowers and plants, animals, and the expressions of the four seasons. Both imagination and analogy are beautiful. For example, this song *Lonely City* is the expression of the author's sincere feelings:

I always hit the road in the dead of night
Only in the dead of night
The ear begins to listen, only
In the dead of night
The houses along the street are only beginning to grow big and small ears

Beautiful flowers are extraordinarily charming because of appreciation
The crisp sound of horseshoes is extraordinarily beautiful because of listening
The back figure in the night is extra lonely because of the gaze
Yes, because of the wind
My cloak is more like a flag of despair

Deep in the night, the sound of hooves inspires my solitude
If my heart is a lonely city
I wish to have you to live in
If your city is a lonely heart
I hope there is a lonely city in your heart

Expressing true feelings is the life of poetry. In the book *Linquan Gaozhi · Painting Ideas* by Guo Xi, a Chinese painter in the Northern Song Dynasty, he once put forward the famous conclusion that "poetry is invisible painting, and painting is tangible poetry" (Note 1). The argument is to demand from the purpose of art —

陳義海也指出，正是狄奧尼索斯讓他找到了這本詩集的靈魂；換言之，他的這部詩集洋溢著他對酒神崇高美的想像與愛。他以一個中國詩人試圖突破時空的界限，循著藝術之神的光輝去描繪出心中每一感動之美。如這首〈孤獨有一張美麗的面孔〉，雖呈現出偏於調和性的陰柔風格，但情味綿渺，有著「孤獨」本然面貌的懷想：

　　孤獨有一張美麗的面孔
　　倒映在水中
　　像一朵水仙花
　　呢喃著水中的天空

　　天空流經之處
　　皆有河岸鉗制
　　致使天空不能自由散漫

　　孤獨有條不紊地流淌著

　　她的臉上刻著蒼老的年輕
　　她的皺紋青翠欲滴
　　她流淌在陽光下面

　　橋樑交流著此岸和彼岸的絕望
　　一葉輕舟
　　像個失敗的勸說者

beauty. Chen Yihai also pointed out that it was Dionysus who made him find the soul of this collection of poems; in other words, his collection of poems is full of his imagination and love for the sublime beauty of Dionysus. As a Chinese poet, he tries to break through the boundaries of time and space, following the brilliance of the god of art to describe the beauty of every emotion in his heart. For example, this song *Lonely Has a Beautiful Face*, although it presents a harmonious and feminine style, but the sentiment is weak, and it has the nostalgia for the original appearance of "loneliness":

Loneliness has a beautiful face
Reflected in the water
Like a daffodil
Whispering the sky in the water

Where the sky flows
Riverbank clamping
Causing the sky not to be free

Flowing orderly in solitude

Her face is engraved with old youth
Her wrinkles are verdant
She flows under the sun

The bridge communicates the despair of this shore and the
    other shore
A light boat
Like a failed persuader

航行在美麗的面孔上

也只有痛苦的美才能蠶食遠方

作者在追隨狄奧尼索斯的遨遊想像的宇宙之際，不免也會想像到自己孤獨的愁味。他認為，酒神精神在生活中，也是一種短暫的超脫，在文學中，卻能把情感、美感、性情的「狂喜」〈Ectasy〉，更符合生命本體地表現出來。幾乎和狄奧尼索斯一樣，作為雕塑的酒神狄奧尼索斯的表情是平和的，但有著時間藝術所獨有的美感力；陳義海的詩歌也同樣有同繪畫相通的那種繪畫美。然而，這種以感情注入物象的繪畫美，不僅體現在對多種畫面的描繪上，而且也從人物肖像的描繪上表現出來。如這首〈一個把憂傷描繪得無限美麗的人〉，或許是勾勒了詩人自己的外部形象：

一個把憂傷描繪得無限美麗的人
上帝一定會寬恕他

每當我走過考文垂郊外的紀念公園
我的腳步總會被那無名的小花喚住
是的，電台裡說，已經是春天了
他們告訴我說，我的憂傷青翠欲滴漫山遍野
一直伸展到艾汶河的那一邊
終於被沃里克城堡擋住去路

Sailing on a beautiful face

Only the beauty of pain can erode the distance

When the author follows Dionysus's journey into the imaginary universe, he can't help imagining his own loneliness and melancholy. He believes that the Dionysian spirit is also a kind of temporary detachment in life, but in literature, it can express the "ecstasy" of emotion, beauty, and temperament more in line with the ontology of life. Almost the same as Dionysus, Dionysus, the god of wine as a sculpture, has a peaceful expression, but has the unique aesthetic power of time art; Chen Yihai's poems also have the same kind of painting beauty as painting. However, this kind of painting beauty that injects emotion into objects is not only reflected in the depiction of various pictures, but also in the depiction of portraits. For example, this poem *A Person Who Describes Sadness Infinitely Beautifully* may outline the poet's own external image:

A man who paints sadness infinitely beautifully
God will forgive him

Whenever I walk through Memorial Park outside Coventry
My steps will always be called by that nameless little flower
Yes, the radio says, it's spring already
They tell me my sorrows are verdant
Stretches to the other side of the River Avon
Finally blocked by Warwick Castle

> 一個把憂傷描繪得無限美麗的人
> 可以飛行在天使的行列中
> 當我墜落
> 軌跡潔白如憂傷
> 憂傷如梨花在東方的一聲嘆息

　　沃里克城堡是一座位於英國中世紀風格的古堡，而艾汶河 AVON，是取自名詩人莎士比亞故鄉的河，兩岸綠柳成行，景致典雅。據作者自序，當「悲」和「憂傷」被藝術地表達時，其實，那也應該是一種符合酒神精神的「狂喜」。其實，詩人對他的內心是非常理解的，那孤獨絕塵的身影、不求名利的心情，以及對昔日自然美景的緬懷，透過詩人的懷想，形象鮮明的表現在文字裡；這使得整首詩中所欲塑造的詩人本然面貌，有更晰的展現。

　　總的說，陳義海詩歌的思想藝術，曾有多種評論，但最確切的恐怕是「深邃、絕塵」四字。儘管他在近些年來寫了不少翻譯詩歌，這恐怕更得力於他對外國詩歌的研究和借鏡。深邃和深沉是兩個不同的概念。深沉的詩，一般也較為含蓄；但含蓄的詩，有的可能是深沉的，有的也可能不是深沉的。陳義海詩歌的可貴之處，恰恰是把「深邃」和「絕塵」兩者結合起來了。他在藝術手法的運用及語言的音韻上，都有自己的特點，這就構成其藝術風格不可少的因素；而詩人總是自覺不自覺地把自己的孤獨情緒及想像糅入詩作中。

A man who paints sadness infinitely beautifully
May fly in the ranks of angels
When I fall
The trajectory is as white as sadness
Sad like a pear blossom sighing in the east

Warwick Castle is a medieval-style castle in England, and the Avon River is a river taken from the hometown of the famous poet Shakespeare, with green willows lining the banks and elegant scenery. According to the author's preface, when "sorrow" and "sorrow" are artistically expressed, in fact, it should also be a kind of "ecstasy" in line with the Dionysian spirit. In fact, the poet understands his heart very well. The lonely figure, the mood of not seeking fame and fortune, and the nostalgia for the natural beauty of the past are vividly expressed in the text through the poet's nostalgia. The original appearance of the poet to be portrayed in the poem is more clearly displayed.

Generally speaking, there have been many comments on the ideological art of Chen Yihai's poems, but the most accurate one is probably the four words "deep and dusty". Although he has written a lot of translated poetry in recent years, I am afraid that this is more due to his research and reference to foreign poetry. Deep and deep are two different concepts. Deep poems are generally more subtle; but some implicit poems may be deep, and some may not be deep. The value of Chen Yihai's poems is precisely the combination of "profound" and "juechen". He has his own characteristics in the use of artistic techniques and the phonology of language, which constitute an indispensable factor in his artistic style; and the poet always consciously or unconsciously incorporates his own loneliness and imagination into his poems.

註 1．書名的狄奧尼索斯(Dionysus)是古希臘的藝術之
　　神，也是葡萄酒與狂歡之神。據傳說，他是宙斯(Zeus)
　　和西姆萊公主(Semele)所生的兒子。在希臘國家博物
　　館的古幣館中陳列著一枚鑄有狄奧尼索斯頭像的
　　古希臘錢幣，他面帶希臘眾神所共有的平靜表情，
　　頭髮是用葡萄蔓結成髮髻，並有葡萄葉裝飾著他的
　　前額，猶如頭戴王冠，這是酒神狄奧尼索斯的象徵。
註 2．沈子丞，《歷代論畫名著匯編》，第 72 頁，文
　　物出版社。

—2013.5.17 作

—內蒙古《集寧師範學院學報》，2014 年第 3 期，第
　　36 卷，總第 126 期，頁 7-10。

Note 1 • Dionysus in the title of the book is the god of art in ancient Greece, as well as the god of wine and carnival. According to legend, he was the son of Zeus and princess Semele. An ancient Greek coin with the head of Dionysus is displayed in the ancient coin hall of the National Museum of Greece. Leaves adorn his forehead like a crown, a symbol of Dionysus, the god of wine.

Note 2 • Shen Zicheng, *Compilation of Famous Works on Painting in the Past Dynasties*, p. 72, Cultural Relics Publishing House.

7. 清靜淡泊的詩音——秦立彥詩歌的另類讀法

摘要：秦立彥在詩歌創作中，以虛靜的觀照和宏偉深邃的目光對新詩採取一種藝術視角來省思塵世浮生；既繼承了新詩通感的美學本質，又具有深刻的思想性，成為中國北方詩歌中一道引人注目的亮麗風景。

關鍵詞：秦立彥　新詩　美學　通感

一、其人其詩

　　一本出自谷羽編選的《當代女詩人詩讀本》，讓我有幸閱讀了秦立彥（1973-）的心靈詩影。她來自黑龍江省巴彥縣，美國聖地牙哥加州大學文學博士，現任北京大學文學院副教授。對閱讀其詩而言，品評其詩的情感同品評其詩的意象同樣重要，雖然其中寄托了不少詩人的孤寂與回憶，但寫得很輕靈，也有生活氣息。她在詩歌創作中，融入東方虛靜美學，讓心回歸單純與寧靜。她用宏偉深邃的目光對新詩採取一種藝術視角來省思塵世浮生，既繼承了新詩通感藝術的表現傳

7. Quiet and Indifferent Poetry — An Alternative Reading of Qin Liyan's Poems

Abstract: In her poetic creation, Qin Liyan adopts an artistic perspective on new poetry with a calm objective attitude to reflect on the worldly life; it not only inherits the aesthetic essence of the new poetry, but also possesses a profound ideological nature, and has created an eye-catching poetry scenery in northern China.

Key words: Qin Liyan, new poetry, aesthetics, synaesthesia

1. Her People and His Poems

Contemporary Female Poet Poetry Reader edited by Gu Yu gave me the honor to read Qin Liyan's (1973-) spiritual poetry. She is from Bayan County, Heilongjiang Province. She received a PhD in Literature from the University of California, San Diego, and is currently an associate professor at the School of Liberal Arts, Peking University. For reading her poems, appraising her emotions is as important as appraising the imagery in her poems. Although many of the poet's loneliness and memories are placed in them, the writing is light and full of life. In her poetry creation, she incorporates the oriental emptiness and tranquility aesthetics, allowing her heart to return to simplicity and tranquility. She adopts an artistic perspective on the new poetry to reflect on the worldly life with a grand and profound vision. She not only inherits the expressive tradition of the synaesthesia art of the new poetry,

統，又具有深刻的思想性，成為中國北方詩歌中一道引人注目的亮麗風景。

二、詩作賞讀

秦立彥的詩不僅有簡潔靈巧的特點，又學習了法國詩人波德萊爾（1821-1867）和美國愛倫・坡（1809-1849）等的一些象徵的手法。她往往用有質感的形象和暗示之筆來朦朧地揭示其弦外之音。如這首小詩〈寂寞〉：

寂寞如一條蛇，
昂著它美麗的頭，
閃著它灼灼的斑紋，
又纏上身來。

呂進曾說：「抒情詩的內容是像風飄過琴弦一樣，震動詩人心靈的瞬間體驗，」（注 1）這段話也恰恰說明了，僅管是小詩，但只要稱之為好詩，就能讓讀者同想像的聯繫更豐富。細緻探究此詩，從表面看來，似乎是詩人詠嘆生命的謳歌，但它又昇華了現實，讓思念之苦的意象疊加；而「閃」就是「自覺地審視體驗」透射出哲思之光，讓全詩從撲朔迷離的愁緒中，從而獲得了某種新生的力量。

隨著詩人生活閱歷的豐富和喜歡親近大自然的體驗，詩人不僅突破了個人自由的心理空間，也把每一首詩當作是自己心靈的活的雕塑。當秦立彥寫下〈鳥巢〉一詩，就已體現

but also has a profound ideological quality, and hasbecome a striking and beautiful landscape in northern China's poetry.

2. Appreciation and Reading of Poems

Qin Liyan's poems not only have the characteristics of brevity and dexterity, but also learned some symbolic techniques from French poet Baudelaire (1821-1867) and American Edgar Allan Poe (1809-1849). She often uses textured images and suggestive pens to vaguely reveal its overtones. Like this little poem *Lonely*:

> *Lonely as a snake,*
> *With its beautiful head held high,*
> *Glittering its blazing streaks,*
> *Wrapped up again.*

Lü Jin once said: "The content of a lyric poem is a momentary experience that shakes the poet's soul like the wind blowing over the strings." It can make the reader's connection with the imagination richer. Careful exploration of this poem, on the surface, seems to be the poet's eulogy of life, but it sublimates the reality and superimposes the image of the pain of longing; and "Shan" is "consciously examining experience" to transmit the light of philosophical thinking, so that the whole poem gained some new power from the confusing melancholy.

With the rich life experience of the poet and the experience of being close to nature, the poet not only breaks through the psychological space of personal freedom, but also regards each poem as a living sculpture

了她在美國學成歸國後，開始投入教學的良苦用心；詩裡含
有無限深意，在她眼中的北國，都染上了迷人的鄉土色彩，
而這也是她負笈遠方最思念的景物，哪怕是一棵棵雪中之樹
或充滿新生的小鳥，都讓詩人的眼睛漾出迷濛，而結尾一節
引發出詩人的翹首期盼，更耐人尋味：

> 冬天的樹高舉著一個個鳥巢，
> 彷彿獻給天空的禮物。
> 太陽的眼睛看到了每一個巢中，
> 而春天的葉子即將降臨，
> 千萬枚葉子將把那些鳥巢遮住。

　　另一首〈懷古〉中，詩人設想自己與古代詩人時空對飲，
讓想像力像生出了翅膀的馬，任意馳騁：

> 在唐人懷古的地方，
> 我懷念著唐人，
> 他們當時似乎並沒有想到，
> 唐朝之後還會有宋元明清。

> 在赤壁的江邊，
> 依然聳峙著亂石，
> 第一杯酒獻給三國的英雄，
> 第二杯酒獻給蘇軾。

of his own soul. When Qin Liyan wrote the poem *Bird's Nest*, it already reflected her hard work in teaching after returning to China after studying in the United States; the poem contains infinite deep meaning, and in her eyes, the Northland is dyed with charming countryside color, and this is what she misses the most when studying in a distant place. Even trees in the snow or birds full of newborns make the poet's eyes blurred, and the ending stanza arouses the poet's eager anticipation. Intriguing:

> *The winter trees hold high the bird's nests,*
> *Like a gift to the sky.*
> *The eyes of the sun saw in every nest,*
> *And the spring leaves are coming,*
> *Thousands of leaves will cover those nests.*

In another poem *Nostalgia*, the poet imagines himself drinking with ancient poets in time and space, letting his imagination gallop freely like a horse with wings:

> *In the place where Tang people nostalgia,*
> *I miss Tang Ren,*
> *They didn't seem to think at the time,*
> *After the Tang Dynasty, there will be Song Yuan Ming Qing.*

> *By the riverside of Chibi,*
> *Still towering rocks,*
> *The first glass of wine is dedicated to the heroes of the*
>   *Three Kingdoms,*
> *The second glass of wine is dedicated to Su Shi.*

懷古的人終於也成了古人，
一代代積累起來的是懷古的詩。

　　的確，此詩一開頭就讓我想起，創造出一種古今交融的
手法和歷史人物的穿插，雖然描繪了詩空截然不同的兩幅畫
面，但語加蘊藉，詩裡也寓含她對中國傑出的文學家及英雄
的悼念，這誠然也是一首對民族命運的關注，更是詩人奏響
的一曲愛國之音，內涵也很深邃。最後的這首〈春夜〉，描
繪出中國大陸北方春節年夜時 迎來爆竹一聲除舊歲的期盼，
以及由點燃到爆炸於夜空的炫目場景：

　　春夜的黑暗也是稀薄的，
　　一樹樹的花，
　　燒著紅的火把，黃的火把，
　　把周圍照徹。

　　整個世界都睡了，
　　只有花睜著灼灼的眼睛，
　　因為珍惜每一寸光陰，
　　因為經過了一年的等待，
　　才迎來這樣的良辰。

　　此詩給人們帶來了生活意趣和快樂，也反映出詩人深深
掛念的，其實是祖國同胞的文化和那片廣大土地上默默耕耘
的勞動者。詩人的感情真摯而自然，同樣在迎春的空曠的境

People who nostalgia finally become ancient people,
What have been accumulated from generation to
generation are nostalgic poems.

Indeed, the beginning of this poem reminded me of creating a blend of ancient and modern techniques and interspersed with historical figures. Although two completely different pictures of the poem and space are depicted, the language is more subtle, and the poem also contains her outstanding views on China. It is indeed a song of concern for the destiny of the nation, and it is also a patriotic voice played by a poet, with profound connotations. The last song *Spring Night* depicts the expectation of ushering in the sound of firecrackers to clear away the old year during the Spring Festival in northern China, and the dazzling scene from igniting to exploding in the night sky:

The darkness of the spring night is also thin,
A tree of flowers,
Burning red torches, yellow torches,
Light up the surroundings.

The whole world is asleep,
Only flowers open their burning eyes,
Because cherish every inch of time,
Because after a year of waiting,
Just ushered in such a good day.

This poem brings interest and joy to people's life, and also reflects that what the poet misses deeply is actually the culture of the compatriots in the motherland and the silent laborers on that vast land. The poet's feelings are sincere and natural, also in the empty state of Yingchun, although

界中，雖然她的詩少有那種大氣凜然、慷慨悲壯的抒情，但在其精緻的詩句背後，卻藏有清靜淡泊的詩音，自有其獨立存在的價值。

三、結　語

綜上所述，我認為秦立彥的詩歌風格形成的主客觀原因，歸根於她求學過程的刻苦經歷及自幼喜好文學、博聞強識，可說是形成她的藝術風格的基礎。但更重要的還是由於她受到歐美比較文學的薰陶，深耕有成，且懂得用她的全生命去歌唱，無論是回憶或者希望，痛苦或歡笑，都可以看出她的真情所在。她經常用另類眼光看世界，且詩歌裡永遠愛戀著她的故土的一草一木……倘佯在理性的思辯與文學的浪漫情懷中，讓心靈與自然相通。僅從這一點看，也顯示出她的思想純淨，彷若因詩而獲得了靈魂的新生。

注 1：本文譯作出自谷羽編選的《當代女詩人詩讀本》，漢俄對照中國詩歌系列，天津大學出版社，2020 年 2 月第 1 版，頁 214-220。

注 2：呂進著，《呂進詩學雋語》，曾心、鍾小族主編，秀威，臺北，2012 年 11 月一版，頁 215。

—臺灣《秋水》詩刊，第 190 期，2022.01，頁 69-71。

her poems seldom have the kind of majestic, generous and tragic lyricism, but behind her delicate lines, there is a quiet and indifferent poetic sound, with its own its independent existence.

3. Conclusion

To sum up, I think that the subjective and objective reasons for the formation of Qin Liyan's poetic style are rooted in her hard experience in studying, her love of literature since she was a child, and her knowledge and knowledge, which can be said to be the basis of her artistic style. But more importantly, it is because she was influenced by European and American comparative literature, she has been deeply cultivated, and she knows how to sing with her whole life. Whether it is memory or hope, pain or laughter, you can see her true feelings. She often looks at the world with different eyes, and in her poems, she always loves every plant and tree in her homeland... Wandering in rational speculation and romantic feelings of literature, let the soul communicate with nature. From this point alone, it also shows that her thoughts are pure, as if her soul has been reborn because of poetry.

Note ： This article is translated from *Contemporary Female Poet Poetry Reader* edited by Gu Yu, Chinese-Russian Contrasting Chinese Poetry Series, Tianjin University Press, 1st edition, February 2020, pp. 214-220.

Note 1. Lü Jin, *Lü Jin's Poetics*, edited by Zeng Xin and Zhong Xiaozu, Xiuwei, Taipei, November 1, 2012, p. 215.

8. 簡潔自然的藝術風韻——
讀余光中的鄉土詩

　　余光中〈1928-〉詩歌的偉大之處不只在於他的博學大家，專心致志地創新精神，得到許多敏感而認真的評論家一致的讚揚，而是在於他大部份作品中存有一種熱情、蘊含著浪漫主義衝動，且能從其寬宏本性中的一些心理波動顯現出來。說得更廣泛一點，其詩歌的藝術特點，是由表現的自由、注重聲律和語法完整性的密切關係構成的；它們優雅的冷色不時被清逸的筆觸變得富有生氣，而反映出詩人的心理世界、孤單的情思和以虛清堅定的心力獨往遠遊於遼闊天地之外。

　　在陳芳明選編的《余光中六十年詩選》中，將其詩創作分為臺北、香港及高雄時期，並撰寫了前言，筆法靈動而嚴密，讀來興味盎然。誠然，對余光中進行專門研究者不乏其人，但陳芳明的評述也多有創獲。細讀其間，尤以詩人的山水詩閑遠淡雅、觀察入微、意境新穎，由音節求神氣，由字句求音節的特殊手法 鮮明地體現了余光中的鄉土詩學思想。如 1972 年在墾丁寫下的〈車過枋寮〉，能切實掌握並提煉了他崇高美的觀念，在構思上做到簡潔巧妙，很受感動：

8. Concise and Natural Artistic Charm — Reading the Local Poems of Yu Guangzhong

The greatness of Yu Guangzhong's (1928-) poetry lies not only in his erudite masters and his dedicated and innovative spirit, which have been unanimously praised by many sensitive and serious critics, but in most of his works. Romantic impulsiveness can show some psychological fluctuations in its generous nature. To put it more broadly, the artistic characteristics of his poems are formed by the close relationship between freedom of expression, attention to rhythm and grammatical integrity; their elegant and cold colors are sometimes animated by clear brushstrokes, reflecting the poet's psychological world, lonely feelings and wandering far outside the vast world with a clear and firm heart.

In *Selected Poems of Yu Guangzhong in the Sixty Years* which was selected and edited by Chen Fangming, he divides his poetry creation into Taipei, Hong Kong and Kaohsiung periods, and a foreword was written. It is true that there are many people who have conducted special research on Yu Guangzhong, but Chen Fangming's comments are also very fruitful. In the process of careful reading, the poet's landscape poems are quiet and elegant, meticulously observed, and novel in artistic conception. The special technique of seeking spirit from syllables and syllables from words clearly embodies Yu Guangzhong's rural poetics. For example, *The Car Passing Fangliao*, written in Kenting in 1972, can truly grasp and refine his concept of sublime beauty, and the conception is concise and ingenious, which is very moving:

雨落在屏東的甘蔗田裏
甜甜的甘蔗甜甜的雨
肥肥的甘蔗肥肥的田
雨落在屏東肥肥的田裏
從此地到山麓
一大幅平原舉起
多少甘蔗，多少甘美的希冀
長途車駛過青青的草原
檢閱牧神青青的儀隊
想牧神，多毛又多鬚
在哪一株甘蔗下午睡

雨落在屏東的西瓜田裡
甜甜的西瓜甜甜的雨
肥肥的西瓜肥肥的田
雨落在屏東肥肥的田裏
從此地到海岸
一大張河牀孵出
多少西瓜，多少圓渾的希望
長途車駛過纍纍的河牀
檢閱牧神纍纍的寶庫
想牧神，多血又多子
究竟坐在哪一隻瓜上

Rain falls on sugarcane fields in Pingtung
Sweet sugar cane sweet rain
Fat sugar cane fat field
The rain falls on the fat fields in Pingtung
From here to the foothills
A large plain raised
How much sugar cane, how much sweet hope
The long-distance car drives through the green grassland
Inspecting the Faun Qingqing's guard of honor
Think of a shepherd, hairy and bearded
Which sugar cane to take a nap in the afternoon

Rain falls on watermelon fields in Pingtung
Sweet watermelon sweet rain
Fat watermelon fat field
The rain falls on the fat fields in Pingtung
From here to coast
A large river bed hatched
How many watermelons, how many round hopes
The long-distance car drives through the tired river bed
Examine the treasure trove of the Faun
Think of Mu Shen, bloody and son
Which melon are you sitting on?

> 雨落在屏東的香蕉田裏
> 甜甜的香蕉甜甜的雨
> 肥肥的香蕉肥肥的田
> 雨落在屏東肥肥的田裏
> 雨是一首濘濘的牧歌
> 路是一把瘦瘦的牧笛
> 吹十里五里的阡阡陌陌
> 雨落在屏東的香蕉田裏
> 胖胖的香蕉肥肥的雨
> 長途車駛不出牧神的轄區
> 路是一把長長的牧笛
> 正說屏東是最甜的縣
> 屏東是方糖砌成的城
> 忽然一個右轉，最鹹最鹹
> 劈面撲過來
> 那海

　　畫面是鹹鹹的海風剛剛吹拂而過的風光，描繪了大自然的莊嚴和奔放，藉以達到潔淨純樸的氛圍；詩人構思時情感的變化孕育在物象的變化之中。明顯地，詩人一絲不苟地詮釋大自然，他發現沿途原野直至望海的無限美麗之外，還使他有機會體悟到貧苦勞動農民和大地滋養的回饋；他心中對社會的悲憫增強了，這也是詩人內心情感的一種幅射。另一首是在 1988 年寫下的〈雨，落在高雄的港上〉，它表達了詩人與他居住的土地之間深刻的一致，他和心中那完美的世界

Rain falls on banana fields in Pingtung
Sweet banana sweet rain
Fat banana fat field
The rain falls on the fat fields in Pingtung
Rain is a wet idyll
The road is a skinny reed pipe
Blowing the rice paddies for ten miles and five miles
Rain falls on banana fields in Pingtung
Fat banana fat rain
Long-distance vehicles cannot drive out of Mushen's jurisdiction
The road is a long reed flute
It is said that Pingtung is the sweetest county
Pingtung is a city made of sugar cubes
Suddenly a right turn, the saltiest and the saltiest
Face to face
The sea

The picture is the scenery just blown by the salty sea breeze, which depicts the majesty and unrestrained nature, so as to achieve a clean and simple atmosphere; the emotional changes of the poet when conceiving is made in the changes of objects. Obviously, the poet interprets nature meticulously. He found that in addition to the infinite beauty of the wilderness along the way to the sea, he also had the opportunity to realize the rewards of poor labor farmers and the nourishment of the earth; A radiance of inner emotion. The other is *Rain, Falling on the Port of Kaohsiung* written in 1988, which expresses the profound unity between the poet and the land he lives in, and his

的交往是那麼愉悅、神聖；他和港都的夜雨以及寧靜的山海
是那麼協調：

> 雨落在高雄的港上
> 溼了滿港的燈光
> 有的浮金，有的流銀
> 有的空對著水鏡
> 牽著恍惚的倒影
> 雨落在高雄的港上
> 早就該來的冷雨
> 帶來了一點點秋意
> 帶來安慰的催眠曲
> 把幾乎中暑的高雄
> 輕輕地拍打
> 慢慢地搖撼
> 哄入了清涼的夢鄉
> 睡吧，所有的波浪
> 睡吧，所有的提防
> 睡吧，所有的貨櫃船
> 睡吧，所有的起重機
> 所有的錨鍊和桅杆
> 睡吧，所有的街巷
> 睡吧，壽山和柴山
> 睡吧，旗津和小港
> 睡吧，疲勞的世界

communication with the perfect world in his heart is so pleasant and sacred. He is so in harmony with the night rain in Hong Kong and the tranquil mountains and seas:

Rain falls on Kaohsiung's harbor
Wet the lights of Hong Kong
Some floating gold, some flowing silver
Some are empty facing the water mirror
Holding the trance reflection
Rain falls on Kaohsiung's harbor
Long overdue cold rain
Brings a little bit of autumn
Soothing lullaby
Kaohsiung who was almost sunstroke
Pat lightly
Shake slowly
Coaxed into a cool dreamland
Sleep, all waves
Sleep, all beware
Sleep, all container ships
Sleep, all cranes
All anchor chains and masts
Sleep, all the streets
Go to sleep, Shoushan and Chaishan
Sleep, Cijin and Xiaogang
Sleep, tired world

只剩下半港的燈光
有的，密擁著近岸
有的，疎點著遠船
有的流銀，有的浮金
都靜靜地映在水面
一池燦爛的睡蓮
深夜開在我牀邊

在港都雨夜的旋律中，余光中以自然寫實的筆觸烘托出
詩中的景物與空間，並將個人的孤獨與自然的溝通無間。在
遠景中變化多端的雨影，有的落在海邊多石的峭崖、船港或
清冷的街巷、山間，有的落在相思的心頭或夢鄉‧‧‧充分
表示了余光中鄉土詩的高度抒情風格和巨大的感染力；也使
詩變得更加真實，更具現代意義。最後這首在 2007 年寫下的
〈台東〉，是難得之作，在讀者心目中引起諸多聯想：

城比台北是矮一點
天比台北卻高得多

燈比台北是淡一點
星比台北卻亮得多

街比台北是短一點
風比台北卻長的多

飛機過境是少一點
老鷹盤空卻多得多

Only half of the lights left
Yes, close to the shore
Yes, light the distant ship
Some flow silver, some float gold
Silently reflected in the water
A pool of brilliant water lilies
By my bed late at night

In the melody of the rainy night in Hong Kong, Yu Guangzhong uses natural and realistic brushstrokes to highlight the scenery and space in the poem, and communicates personal loneliness with nature. In the distant view, the changing rain shadows, some fall on the rocky cliffs by the sea, the ship port or the cold streets and alleys, and the mountains, and some fall on the lovesick heart or dreamland. It fully expresses the highly lyrical style and great appeal of Yu Guangzhong's local poems; it also makes the poems more real and more modern. The last song *Taitung*, written in 2007, is a rare work, which arouses many associations in the minds of readers:

The city is a little shorter than Taipei
The sky is much higher than Taipei

The lights are a bit dimmer than in Taipei
The stars are much brighter than Taipei

The street is a bit shorter than Taipei
The wind is much longer than Taipei

The port is smaller than the west coast
The sea is much bigger than the west coast

　　人比西岸是稀一點
　　山比西岸卻密得多

　　港比西岸是小一點
　　海比西岸卻大得多

　　報紙送到是晚一點
　　太陽起來卻早得多

　　無論地球怎麼轉
　　台東永遠在前面

　　詩中畫面充滿明亮、靜止感，背景從城市生活的嘈雜到
潔淨、悠閒、鎮定的對真實社會的寫照的轉折；這種暫時的
寧靜 除了暗喻詩人藉由旅遊能卸除生活中的沉重壓力之外，
對詩人來說，純真的風光景色與人情味是極其寶貴的。他除
了試圖反映社會的不均之外，還要尋求環境保育的真實。這
是余光中要傳給後代、要讓他們思考並理解的寓意。晚年的
詩翁在鄉情及友情的照射下，仍繼續為追求的藝術實踐及現
代詩歌的發展，注入更多的活力，並專研於臺灣文學史而放
出新的異彩。

　　　　—2011.12.29 作
　　　　—臺灣《海星》詩刊，2012 年 9 月，第 5 期秋季號，
　　　　　頁 16-19。

People are a little rarer than the West Bank
The mountains are much denser than the west bank

The port is smaller than the west coast
The sea is much bigger than the west coast

The newspaper was delivered a little later
The sun rises much earlier

No matter how the earth turns
Taito is always ahead

The picture in the poem is full of bright and static feeling, and the background changes from the noisy city life to the clean, leisurely and calm portrayal of the real society; this kind of temporary tranquility is not only a metaphor that the poet can relieve the heavy pressure in life through travel. In addition, for poets, pure scenery and human touch are extremely precious. In addition to trying to reflect social inequality, he also seeks the truth of environmental conservation. This is the meaning that Yu Guangzhong wants to pass on to future generations and let them think and understand. In his later years, under the influence of nostalgia and friendship, the poet continued to inject more vitality into the pursuit of artistic practice and the development of modern poetry, and radiated new splendor by specializing in the history of Taiwanese literature.

9. 最輕盈的飛翔——淺釋
鍾鼎文的詩

摘要：鍾鼎文對詩歌最獨特的貢獻在對雕字琢句的審美。他的潛伏著的文思，苞放著意蘊與奇妙的詩才；而形象的聯想、藝術形式的生動，也往往使讀者沉入美感的藝術世界。

關鍵詞：鍾鼎文；詩美；意象主義；藝術次序；審美思維

臺灣著名詩人鍾鼎文〈1914—2012 年〉，安徽省舒城縣人。父親是律師，母親持家務；1933 年，父母在老家遭土匪殺害，其時正留學日本京都帝國大學攻讀哲學，驚聞噩耗，至為悲慟。回國後任教于國民黨南京中央軍校，繼任上海復旦大學教授，並主編《天下日報》。抗戰後任《廣西日報》總編等職。1949 年抵達臺灣，曾任《自立晚報》總主筆，創刊「新詩週刊」，開啟臺灣的新詩運動，《聯合報》主筆長達 35 年。

1954 年與覃子豪、余光中、夏菁、鄧禹平等人共創「藍星詩社」，主編《藍星季刊》等。他發起組建「世界詩人大會」，並任「世界藝術文化學苑」主席。詩作曾在英、美、菲、德、

9. The Lightest Flying — An Analysis of Zhong Dingwen's Poems

Abstract: Zhong Dingwen's most unique contribution to poetry lies in the aesthetics of carved characters and sentences. His latent literary thoughts are full of connotations and wonderful poetic talents; while the association of images and the vividness of art forms often make readers sink into the artistic world of aesthetic feeling.

Key words: Zhong Dingwen; aesthetics in poetry; imagism; artistic order; aesthetic thinking

Zhong Dingwen, a famous Taiwanese poet (1914-2012), was born in Shucheng County, Anhui Province. His father was a lawyer and his mother took care of housework. In 1933, his parents were murdered by bandits in their hometown. At that time, he was studying philosophy at Kyoto Imperial University in Japan. After returning to China, he taught at the Nanjing Central Military Academy of the Kuomintang, succeeded as a professor at Fudan University in Shanghai, and edited *World Daily*. After the Anti-Japanese War, he served as the editor-in-chief of *Guangxi Daily*. Arrived in Taiwan in 1949, served as chief editor of *Zi Li Evening News*, founded *New Poetry Weekly*, started new poetry movement in Taiwan, and served as chief editor of *United Daily News* for 35 years.

In 1954, together with Qin Zihao, Yu Guangzhong, Xia Jing and Deng Yuping, he founded the "Blue Star Poetry Club" and edited "Blue Star Quarterly". He initiated the establishment of the "World Poets Conference" and served

詩論《現代詩往何處去》等專書。曾獲殊榮無數及榮譽博士學位、中國名譽桂冠詩人獎,其傳記刊于英、美的世界名人錄。

　　鍾鼎文是被廣大的讀者選為當代詩界泰斗的詩人,他超逸溫雅,聖潔高遠;迄今依舊保存著他特有的風采。事實上,他已經用他獨特的意象主義〈註 1〉寫作證明了這一點;但他最獨特的貢獻還在他的對雕字琢句的審美。他的潛伏著的文思,苞放著意蘊與奇妙的詩才;而形象的聯想、藝術形式的生動,也往往使讀者沉入美感的藝術世界。因此,我們要理解鍾鼎文的詩的奧秘,既要把握社會歷史的視角,也必須重視時代的自然審美情懷。在這樣的背景下,研究鍾鼎文的詩論的價值凸顯。

詩的深層結構的發現

　　鍾鼎文的詩,以清心優雅的姿態尋找飽滿的精神內在,以灑脫的心態發現生活的實感經驗,進而激勵出現代詩的生命新美學。我認為,可以從心理學和社會學兩種不同的思考模式來解釋鍾鼎文的詩美論點。

as the chairman of the "World Academy of Arts and Culture". His poems have won many awards in Britain, the United States, the Philippines, Germany, Pakistan and other countries, and he is the most important promoter of the Taiwan poetry movement. He is the author of collections of poems such as *Bridge, Walker, Mountain and River Poems, White Flower Bouquet, Rainy Season*, etc., and special books on poetry *Where is Modern Poetry Going?* He has won numerous honors and honorary doctorates, China's Honorary Poet Laureate Award, and his biography has been published in the *Who's Who* in the World in Britain and the United States.

Zhong Dingwen is selected by the majority of readers as a leading poet in the contemporary poetry world. He is elegant, gentle, holy and lofty; he still retains his unique style so far. In fact, he has proved this point with his unique imagism <Note 1> writing; but his most unique contribution lies in his aesthetics of carved words and sentences. His latent literary thoughts are full of connotations and wonderful poetic talents; while the association of images and the vividness of artistic forms often make readers sink into the artistic world of aesthetic feeling. Therefore, in order to understand the mystery of Zhong Dingwen's poems, we must not only grasp the social and historical perspective, but also pay attention to the natural aesthetic feelings of the times. In this context, the value of studying Zhong Dingwen's poetic theory is highlighted.

The Discovery of the Deep Structure of Poetry

Zhong Dingwen's poems search for a full spiritual inner world with a pure and elegant attitude, and discover the real experience of life with a free and easy attitude, which in turn inspires the new aesthetics of life in modern poetry. In my opinion, Zhong Dingwen's poetic beauty argument can be explained from two different thinking modes of psychology and sociology.

　　從心理學的視角分析,以這首〈風雨黃山行〉為例,詩人並不描述黃山的奇松、雲海、怪石或溫泉的現象及其客觀法則,而是透過詩人的潛在次序,霎時間直聯及自己內心隱秘的經驗及情感等轉化為可見的、有深層意蘊的意象。在自我觀照與詩人心靈的交融中,凝成高潔的思維,以建構一種對自然的看法或圖像,去接近並引導出詩的藝術次序,而創作出佳篇來:

迎面的山風、颯颯,

> 迎面的山雨、濛濛,
> 迎面的山色,摻著曙色,
> 如夢的幽昧,蒼翠而朦朧;
> 三十六峰,還在睡眠中。
>
> 冒著迎面的山雨,
> 頂著迎面的山風,
> 我在風雨的山岰間獨步,
> 忽覺得這盤曲的山路,
> 通向米芾〈註2〉的畫圖中⋯⋯

　　這首詩閃現著感性與詩意的光輝,不難看出,含有這樣的旨趣:霎時的詩人在山岰間獨步沉思,細雨輕柔,卻遮掩不了翠峰老林的寂寞。此時,詩人在靜睡的樹下,欣喜而靈動,會悟了不曾神會過的生命意趣;也許是勾廓加皴的松樹姿態,也許是沉著臨風的怪石,也許是不自覺地走入水墨點

　　Analyzing from a psychological perspective, taking this poem *A Journey to Huangshan Through Wind and Rain* as an example, the poet does not describe the phenomenon of strange pines, sea of clouds, strange rocks or hot springs in Huangshan and their objective laws, but directly connects them in an instant through the poet's potential sequence. And the secret experience and emotion in one's own heart are transformed into visible images with deep meaning. In the blending of self-reflection and the poet's soul, the noble thinking is condensed to construct a view or image of nature, to approach and guide the artistic order of poetry, and create a good poem:

> *The oncoming mountain wind, rustling,*
>
> *Oncoming mountain rain, misty,*
>
> *The face of the mountains, mixed with dawn,*
>
> *The twilight of a dream, green and hazy;*
>
> *Thirty-six peaks are still sleeping.*
>
> *Braving the oncoming mountain rain,*
>
> *Against the oncoming mountain wind,*
>
> *I walk alone among the stormy capes,*
>
> *Suddenly feel that this winding mountain road,*
>
> *In the drawing leading to Mi Fu's* <Note 2>...

　　This poem is full of sensual and poetic brilliance, and it is not difficult to see that it contains such a purpose: the poet in a moment is meditating alone among the hills, and the drizzle is gentle, but it cannot hide the loneliness of Cuifeng and old forest. At this time, the poet, under the sleeping tree, is joyful and agile, and will realize the meaning of life that he has never understood before; maybe it is the outline of the wrinkled pine tree, maybe it

每走一小段就想把光陰擲染中的微笑。在這樣的氛圍，總誘得詩人禁不住停下腳步，回歷史。而生命的自然威力，彷佛直入空靈之境；在淨化的靈魂中，深藏著一顆虔誠的慧心，也引起了許多有趣的記憶。人間的紛紜煩憂，早已隨風自然流轉，在詩人面前掠過，只剩下書畫家米芾筆勢豪邁的想像，置身其間的詩魂綿邈低回，與詩人留戀往返的蹤跡了。

從社會學的視角分析，鍾鼎文喜歡旅遊，與大自然作近距離接觸；他向來反對為寫詩而寫詩，為藝術而藝術。這就是說，詩人應胸次高遠，要有社會責任感，有堅韌的意志和豐富的情感；而悲天憫人的襟懷則是詩人不趨炎附勢的昇華。因此，作者寄予詩人無限想像和期翼的、高於現實世界的理想境地，其所形成對自然景物的特殊情感反應，始終是作者心理反映的主題。〈橋〉就是一首以審美視野面對上海的蘇州河，直抒胸臆的心理描寫，可再度展示了作者才情橫溢，不易體察的愛國澄懷：

> 在寬闊的灰白色的天后宮橋下，
> 疲倦了的蘇州河在流著……
> 在我們寂寞的生命下
> 疲倦了的時間在流著……

but stop, and every time he walks for a short distance, he wants to throw time back to history. And the natural power of life seems to go straight into the ethereal realm; in the purified soul, there is a pious heart hidden deep, which also arouses many interesting memories. The various worries in the world have already flowed naturally with the wind and passed in front of the poet, leaving only the imaginative and bold strokes of the calligrapher and painter Mi Fu.

From a sociological perspective, Zhong Dingwen likes to travel and have close contact with nature; he has always opposed writing poetry for poetry's sake and art for art's sake. That is to say, a poet should have a lofty mind, a sense of social responsibility, a tenacious will and rich emotions; and a compassionate heart is the sublimation of a poet who does not follow others. Therefore, the author entrusts the poet with infinite imagination and expectations, which is higher than the real world, and the special emotional response to the natural scenery formed by it is always the subject of the author's psychological reflection. *Bridge* is a poem that faces the Suzhou Creek in Shanghai with an aesthetic perspective, and expresses the psychological description directly from the heart. It can once again show the author's patriotic and sincere feelings that are full of talent and hard to understand:

Under the wide gray and white Thean Hou Palace bridge,

The tired Suzhou River is flowing...

under our lonely lives

Tired time is passing...

　　　　日子是水一般地流去、流去，
　　　　問不了哪些是歡樂，哪些是苦惱：
　　　　剩下的，是這堅固的生命
　　　　立在時間的上面，如像是橋。

　　　　如像橋，在水面上映著陰影，
　　　　我們的生命，也有著黯淡的魂靈；
　　　　這生命底影啊，浮在時間的河流上，
　　　　隨著河流的動盪而不住地變形。

　　　　讓時間帶去我們的往日底戀吧，
　　　　讓時間帶去我們的歡樂與苦惱吧……
　　　　在時間的上面，是這悠久的生命
　　　　立著，憑空地立著；如像是橋。

　　蘇州河是黃浦江最大的支流，源於江蘇太湖，向東經江蘇省後經上海市，在外白渡橋處匯入黃浦江。在上海市政府大力整治下，已發展為觀光河。沿途遊船路線，主打「文化記憶之河」的歷史文化底蘊。讓沉醉的詩人尋出往日底戀的悲感，此外，在沉思中，重複將時間的河流動盪，築成一座靜默的長橋，不知是喜是憂。

　　但詩人在想什麼呢？雖然在綿延無盡的人生道上，惟有堅實的橋，才能得以暢行無阻；才能跨越時空，緬懷前人點滴奮鬥累積而成的歷史軌跡，使後人對於生命的起伏不定，能夠少走一些紊雜茫昧的岐路。

The days flow like water, flowing, flowing,
Can't ask which is joy and which is distress:
The rest is this solid life
Standing on top of time is like a bridge.

Like a bridge casting shadows on the water,
Our lives also have dim souls;
This shadow of life, floating on the river of time,
Constantly deformed with the turbulence of the river.

Let time take away our past love,
Let time take away our joys and sorrows...
Above time, is this long life
Standing, standing out of thin air; like a bridge.

Suzhou Creek is the largest tributary of the Huangpu River. It originates from Taihu Lake in Jiangsu Province, flows east through Jiangsu Province, passes through Shanghai City, and flows into the Huangpu River at the Waibaidu Bridge. Under the vigorous rectification of the Shanghai Municipal Government, it has developed into a sightseeing river. The cruise along the route focuses on the historical and cultural heritage of the "River of Cultural Memory". Let the intoxicated poet find out the sadness of the love in the past. In addition, in meditation, he repeatedly flows the river of time to build a long silent bridge, and he does not know whether it is joy or sorrow.

But what is the poet thinking? Although on the endless road of life, only a solid bridge can travel unimpeded; it can cross time and space, remember the historical track accumulated by previous generations, and make future generations less confused about the ups and downs of life.

　　詩人的人生已度過了多少的曲折？經歷了多少的轉變？都在時空想像的反復之中，正從一點一滴的回憶流露出來，使所有的憶往看來新穎，更有一種無可言喻的詩意。瞧，那謝晉元抗日，奉命率部死守上海四行昌倉庫的英跡，莫不令人敬佩，廣為傳頌。看看天后宮橋下那蘇州河的故事，是不是充滿了古典的情致？能在生活之中創造不同的感受，以思考構築學習的高塔，對於思緒的開展來說，也能收到嶄新的生活美學的效果；甚或是詩人最重要的是，它陪伴著詩人渡過許多歷史記憶。這靜定的永恆，存于瞬息萬變的現實人生；而詩人卻兀自站在自己的崗位上，屹立不搖，做著自己該做的事情。如一位經歷過風風雨雨，仍隨時負笈於道上的行者。

詩是剎那間的美的感動

　　詩的極致是把握情景交融的同時又領悟到它深層的意蘊；景到情到，自然氣韻悠然。寫詩超過８０年的鍾鼎文是個早慧的詩人，也是愛國詩人。抗日戰爭時，他投筆從戎，歷任第５戰區少將參議等職。曾被人密告，為擔心殃及上級長官，不惜翻山越嶺，花了一個月時間，面見前蔣中正總統說明原委，其誠感動于蔣委員長，後應召任職中央黨部文書處長；由此可見，詩人在真理面前，勇者無懼的精神。

How many twists and turns has the poet's life gone through? How many transformations have you experienced? It is all in the repetition of time and space imagination, and it is flowing out of memories bit by bit, making all memories look new and more poetic than words. Look, Xie Jinyuan's heroic deeds of resisting Japan and being ordered to lead his troops to guard the Shanghai Sixingchang warehouse are all admirable and widely praised. Look at the story of the Suzhou Creek under the Tianhou Palace Bridge, is it full of classical sentiments? It can create different feelings in life, build a tower of learning with thinking, and can also receive a brand-new effect of life aesthetics for the development of thoughts; even the most important thing for a poet is that it accompanies the poet through the many historical memories. This static eternity exists in the ever-changing real life; but the poet stands on his own post, standing firm, doing what he should do. Like a traveler who has experienced the ups and downs and is still on the road at any time.

Poetry is the touch of beauty in an instant

The acme of poetry is to grasp the blending of scenes and at the same time comprehend its deep implication; Zhong Dingwen, who has been writing poetry for more than 80 years, is a precocious poet and a patriotic poet. During the War of Resistance Against Japan, he joined the army and served successively as a major general counselor in the 5th theater. He was once informed by others. In order to worry about harming his superiors, he did not hesitate to cross mountains and ridges. He spent a month in front of former President Chiang Kai-shek to explain the whole story. He was sincerely moved by Chairman Jiang and was called to serve as the Secretary of the Party Committee of the Central Committee. It can be seen from this that the poet has a fearless spirit in front of the truth.

與夫人向荃是青梅竹馬，鶼鰈情深，故事更是充滿傳奇，譽為美談。然而，3 年前，其摯愛的夫人病逝，詩人悲傷地寫下〈送亡妻骨灰回故鄉入土〉一詩；字字真情盡現；其中，

> 君若天上有靈　請與我舊盟重溫
> 君若地下有知　應知我守誓不逾

讓天地為之動容，草木皆悲。這首〈留言〉寫盡作者豐富的情感世界，纖毫畢現地引領著讀者進入其精神視野，有著撼動人心的絕美力量：

> 讓我將我不朽的愛，留給世界。
> 將我難忘的恨，帶進墳塋。
> 一片浮雲飄過大海，是我的生命，
> 一片微風吹過花叢，是我的感情。
> 我祈禱的手將變作樹，伸向穹蒼，
> 我含淚的眼將變作星，俯瞰大地。
> 親愛的母親、親愛的故鄉，我太困倦了，
> 讓我回到你們的懷抱裏久久地安息吧。

走過近百年的歲月，作者情感的基礎架構，在當代詩歌中，具有鋒芒的審美思維，也顯現出其超凡脫俗的襟懷。詩人在回首中，不期然地想起了以前，自我意識的光亮中，時而彌望、

He and his wife Xiang Quan are childhood sweethearts, and they have a deep love for each other. The story is full of legends and is known as a good story. However, three years ago, his beloved wife died of illness, and the poet sadly wrote the poem *Sending the Ashes of His Dead Wife Back to His Hometown*; every word expresses his true feelings.

> *If you have a spirit in the sky, please revisit the old alliance with me*
> *If you know the world, you should know that I will keep my oath*

Let the world be moved, and the grass and trees are sad. This song *Message* has written the author's rich emotional world, leading readers into his spiritual vision in every detail, and has a beautiful power that shakes people's hearts:

> *Let me leave my immortal love to the world.*
>
> *Take my unforgettable hate into the grave.*
>
> *A cloud drifts across the sea, is my life,*
>
> *A breeze blowing through the flowers is my emotion.*
>
> *My praying hands will become trees and reach out to the sky,*
>
> *My tearful eyes will become stars, overlooking the earth.*
>
> *Dear mother, dear hometown, I am too sleepy,*
>
> *Let me return to your arms and rest in peace for a long time.*

After nearly a hundred years, the author's emotional infrastructure, in contemporary poetry, has a sharp aesthetic thinking, and also shows his extraordinary mind. When looking back, the poet unexpectedly thought of the past. In the light of self-consciousness, sometimes he was lost in hope and silence, and sometimes he called silently and had

凝寂，時而默喚、含淚。縱然敲過雲窗多遍，有否把一切的歸鄉情夢都斟滿，直到靜謐如井。然而，踏月的馬啼，如飄過一朵朵悠閒而去的晚雲，只剩微風輕輕地吹⋯⋯ 詩人總會在那脫盡塵埃的夜晚，輕輕地記起祖國家鄉的名字。

讀完此詩，我底眼睛竟瞬間漾成水雲。彷彿中，一生以愛來涵融生命中的悲歡離合的詩人，又攀上黃山山巔，一如真正的行者，在黎明前，依然把腰杆挺直，灑脫自在，時間卻停在雞鳴的晨光。在我心中，鍾鼎文老師的詩，有一種把天地萬物納入胸懷的大氣魄，把情感與理性在想像空間裏全方位展現，有生活美學的禪味，終將歷久彌新。他像只極輕盈的、優美的丹頂鶴，正盤旋飛舞在偌大的宇宙中⋯⋯

附註：1.意象主義〈 Imagism 〉提倡詩歌應著重清晰精確的語言，由意象產生情感，表達一瞬間的直覺和思維，而不是過多的涉及情感與表現。

附註：2.米芾為北宋著名書畫家和文物鑒賞家，與蘇軾、黃庭堅、蔡襄並稱宋代四家，他擅長楷、行、草、篆、隸等多種字體，尤以行草最為著名。

—安徽省《安徽師範大學學報》人文社會科學版，第 38 卷第 2 期，總第 169 期，2010 年 3 月，頁 168-170。

（照片：林明理／鍾鼎文）

tears in his eyes. Even though I have knocked on the cloud window many times, have I filled all the dreams of returning home until it is as quiet as a well. However, the crowing of the horse on the moon, like the evening clouds drifting away leisurely, only the breeze blows gently. The poet will always gently remember the name of his motherland and hometown on that night when the dust is completely removed.

After reading this poem, my eyes suddenly turned into water clouds. It seems that the poet who used love to cover the joys and sorrows of life in his life climbed to the top of Huangshan Mountain, just like a real traveler, before dawn, he still straightened his waist, free and easy, but time stopped at the time of cock crowing. morning light. In my heart, Mr. Zhong Dingwen's poems have a kind of grandeur that takes everything in the world into his heart, fully displays emotion and rationality in the imaginary space, and has the Zen flavor of life aesthetics, which will last forever. He is like an extremely light and graceful red-crowned crane, circling and flying in the vast universe....

> Note:1. Imagism <Imagism> advocates that poetry should focus on clear and precise language, generate emotion from imagery, and express a momentary intuition and thinking, rather than involving too much emotion and expression.
> Note 2. Mi Fu is a famous calligrapher, painter and connoisseur of cultural relics in the Northern Song Dynasty. Together with Su Shi, Huang Tingjian and Cai Xiang, he is known as the four masters of the Song Dynasty.

10. 鄭愁予——站在中西藝術匯合處的詩人

一、追求詩美與藝術的歌者

　　自幼在中國隨世襲的軍職父親征戰南北，受著喜愛中國古詩詞的日籍母親的教育和美國文藝的薰陶又轉返定居於古寧頭海邊追緬先祖的鄭愁予，血液裡早就奔湧著中西文藝的水流。在當代詩壇上，詩人的作品不論早期或現在，始終具有一種強烈的浪漫色彩，並將感情和思想濃縮於新奇的意象中，且取得卓越的成就。這位籍貫河北省寧河人的大詩人，生於山東濟南，抗戰時期隨父遷徙來台，成長於新竹。中興大學法商學院畢業後，在基隆港務局任職；卻於 37 歲選擇遠赴美國愛荷華大學進修，獲藝術碩士學位，並長期任教於耶魯大學。迄今著有詩集十餘本，其中，《鄭愁予詩集》被台北《聯合報》選出 50 年代的 30 部經典中，名列前茅。曾獲青年文藝獎（1966）、中山文藝獎（1967）、中國時報「新詩推薦獎」（1968）及「國家文藝獎」（1995）、第 19 屆金曲獎傳統暨藝術音樂類「最佳作詞人獎」。

10. Zheng Chouyu — A Poet Standing at the Confluence of Chinese and Western Art

1. Singers Who Pursue Poetic Beauty and Art

Since he was a child, he fought north and south with his hereditary military father in China. He was educated by his Japanese mother who loved ancient Chinese poetry and influenced by American literature and art. Zheng Chouyu, who returned to live on the coast of Guningtou to pursue his Burmese ancestors, has long been in his blood. There are surging currents of Chinese and Western literature and art. In the contemporary poetry world, no matter in the early stage or now, the poet's works always have a strong romantic color, and they condense their feelings and thoughts into novel images, and have achieved remarkable achievements. The great poet, who was originally from Ninghe, Hebei Province, was born in Jinan, Shandong. During the Anti-Japanese War, he migrated to Taiwan with his father and grew up in Hsinchu. After graduating from the School of Law and Business of Chung Hsing University, he worked in the Keelung Port Authority; but at 37, he chose to go to the University of Iowa in the United States for further study, obtained a master's degree in fine arts, and taught at Yale University for a long time. So far, he has authored more than ten anthologies of poetry, among which *Cheng Chou Yu's Anthology of Poems* was selected by Taipei's *United Daily News* among the 30 classics in the 1950s, ranking among the best. Won the Youth obtained a master's degree in fine arts, and taught at Yale University for a long time. So far, he has authored more than ten anthologies of poetry, among which *Cheng Chou Yu's Anthology of Poems* was selected by Taipei's *United Daily News* among the 30 classics in the 1950s, ranking among the best. Won the Youth Literature and Art Award (1966), the Zhongshan Literature and Art Award (1967), the China Times *New Poetry Recommendation Award* (1968) and the *National Literature and Art Award* (1995), the 19th Golden Melody Awards Traditional and Art Music "Best Lyricist" people award.

　　鄭愁予詩歌優雅，音律柔婉，能賦予愛情堅貞的意象，並捕捉到東方美學的內在蘊藉之氣。就他本人的美學思想，歸根究底是崇高人格的產物，又或許母親的影子也影響了早期詩作的形象性。他個性豪爽明快，有冒險家的堅持、也有仗義而行的遊俠傾向及飄泊宇宙的人生觀。這一切應與他身上流著延平郡王鄭成功第 14 代後裔子孫的血相關，也是詩風崇尚自由不羈的藝術風格、眉宇英氣又無限超越世俗的根本原因。在詩人特兀的靈魂裡所追求生命的韻味，也常能激起無數讀者探究詩人的熱情。

　　依我的揣測，鄭愁予的美學思維受其母親影響頗深，它扎根於中國古典詩詞的深厚土壤中，又移居美國 37 年，廣泛地攝取西方文藝的精華而攀上詩藝界的高峰。然而，為了尋根的夢想，他義無反顧地打包回國並遷移入金門縣金城鎮。但詩人並不滿足於「抒情詩大家」形象的塑造，而是期望解脫先祖曾是海盜名銜的鎖鏈，讓祖先的靈魂獲得了自由。他為此理想而四處奔波、執著地投入精神、無怨無悔。如果說，今年已 77 歲的詩人的晚年是他為實現尋根的理想而必須去經歷的一段人生過程；那麼，加諸在他身上的壓力則是他多年來背負先祖的歷史十字架。鄭愁予從 15 歲起寫詩，就是現代新詩的倡導者和實踐者。他的自由詩形式不受局限，但十分講究內在的節奏和音韻，讀來琅琅上口；有一種清新、淡雅之氣。從以下介紹的詩中，可以看出詩人美學觀與中西文化交匯的熔鑄冶煉之功。

Zheng Chouyu's poems are elegant and melodious, which can give the image of love and perseverance, and capture the inner spirit of oriental aesthetics. As far as his own aesthetic thought is concerned, in the final analysis it is the product of a noble personality, or maybe the shadow of his mother also affected the imagery of his early poems. He has a bold and bright personality, with the persistence of an adventurer, the tendency of a knight-errant who acts out of righteousness, and his outlook on life wandering in the universe. All of this should be related to the blood of the 14th generation descendants of Zheng Chenggong, the king of Yanping County. It is also the fundamental reason why the poetic style advocates free and unruly artistic style, heroic eyebrows, and infinitely transcends the world. The charm of life pursued in the soul of the poet Tewu also often arouses the enthusiasm of countless readers to explore the poet.

To my guess, Zheng Chouyu's aesthetic thinking was deeply influenced by his mother. It was rooted in the deep soil of Chinese classical poetry, and he immigrated to the United States for 37 years. However, in pursuit of his dream of finding his roots, he packed his bags back home without hesitation and moved to Jincheng Town, Kinmen County. But the poet is not satisfied with shaping the image of the "lyric poet", but hopes to break free from the chains of the ancestors who were pirates, so that the souls of the ancestors can be free. He ran around for this ideal, devoted himself to it persistently, and had no complaints or regrets. If the 77-year-old poet's old age is a life process that he must go through in order to realize the ideal of seeking his roots; then, the pressure on him is the historical cross he has carried his ancestors for many years. Zheng Chouyu has been writing poetry since he was 15 years old, and he is an advocate and practitioner of modern poetry. The form of his free verse is not limited, but he pays great attention to the internal rhythm and rhyme, and it is catchy to read; it has a fresh and elegant atmosphere. From the poems introduced below, we can see the fusion of the poet's aesthetics and Chinese and Western cultures.

二、詩意唯美 超塵絕俗轉

　　鄭愁予是個早慧的詩人。他寫詩題材大多是旅遊、抒情、懷鄉、景物等寫意方面。詩人的第一本詩集《夢土上》，其中〈殘堡〉是18歲時所寫，詩中把殘堡和戰爭年代聯繫起來，語言質樸平白，卻能以自己的反思觀照上一個時代的反思：

　　　　戍守的人已歸了，留下
　　　　邊地的殘堡
　　　　看得出，十九世紀的草原啊
　　　　如今，是沙丘一片……

　　　　怔忡而空曠的箭眼
　　　　掛過號角的鐵釘
　　　　被黃昏和望歸的靴子磨平的
　　　　戍樓的石垛啊
　　　　一切都老了
　　　　一切都抹上風沙的鏽

　　　　百年前英雄繫馬的地方
　　　　百年前壯士磨劍的地方
　　　　這兒我黯然地卸了鞍
　　　　歷史的鎖啊沒有鑰匙
　　　　我的行囊也沒有劍

2. Poetic and Aesthetically Pleasing

Zheng Chouyu is a precocious poet. The themes of his poems are mostly freehand, such as travel, lyricism, nostalgia, and scenery. The poet's first collection of poems *Dream Land*, in which *Remnant Castle* was written when he was 18 years old. The poem connects the remnant castle with the war years. The language is simple and plain, but he can use his own reflection to observe the past era reflection:

> *The guards have returned, stay*
> *Remnants of the Borderlands*
> *It can be seen that the grassland in the 19th century*
> *Now, it's a sand dune....*

> *Drowsy and empty arrow eyes*
> *Nails Hanging the Horn*
> *Worn by the boots of dusk and hope*
> *The stone stacks of Xulou*
> *Everything is old*
> *Everything is rusted by wind and sand*

> *The place where the hero was a horse a hundred years ago*
> *The place where the strong men sharpened their swords a*
> *　　hundred years ago*
> *Here I saddle sadly*
> *The lock of history has no key*
> *I don't have a sword in my bag*

要一個鏗鏘的夢吧
趁月色，我傳下悲戚的「將軍令」
自琴弦……

詩人以巨大的悲痛寫出望故鄉渺邈之情，富真切情感。可以說，年少時期的鄭愁予，即已體悟了先祖們四處飄泊、經歷了兵荒馬亂、坎坷的歲月。但詩人對故土及先人的愛始終不減，這也給了他無窮的動力，促使他去克服未來人生旅途上的層層難關；他常仰望自己於天涯，而去尋找心靈上的「淨土」。此詩感情的表達使用白描手法，有的是詩人深深的憂患和凝重的思索，在他早期之作少見的沉鬱之風；藉以描摩出百年前戰爭苦難的深淵中昇華出的藝術形象，引領我們體認詩人那種無言的吶喊和熱烈的抒情。

再如這首〈採貝〉是 26 歲詩人天才的靈感創作，有一種興發感動的質素，是創作中最有光彩的詩作之一：

每晨，你採貝於，沙灘潮落
我便跟着，採你巧小的足跡
每夕，你歸來，歸自沙灘汐止
濛濛霧中，乃見你渺渺回眸
那時，我們將相遇
相遇，如兩朵雲無聲的撞擊
欣然而冷漠……

Want a sonorous dream
Taking advantage of the moonlight, I passed on the sad
"General Order"
From the strings....

The poet wrote about the feeling of looking forward to his hometown with great grief, which is full of real emotions. It can be said that Zheng Chouyu, in his youth, had realized that his ancestors wandered around and experienced the rough and tumultuous years. But the poet's love for his homeland and ancestors has never diminished, which also gave him infinite motivation, urging him to overcome the difficulties in his future life journey. The expression of emotion in this poem uses the method of line drawing, some of which are the poet's deep sorrow and solemn thinking, and a melancholy style rarely seen in his early works; it is used to describe the artistic image sublimated from the abyss of war and suffering a hundred years ago, leading us Recognize the poet's wordless cry and passionate lyricism.

Another example is this poem *Caibei* which was inspired by a 26-year-old poet genius. It has a moving quality and is one of the most glorious poems in creation:

Every morning, you gather shellfish, the beach tide ebbs
I'll follow, following your tiny footprints
Every night, you come back, from the sand stall Xizhi
In the mist, I see you dimly looking back
Then we will meet
Meeting is like two clouds colliding silently
Glad yet indifferent....

這採貝是借助於大自然中的客體物象作為自己心靈感受的對應物，不但拓展了詩作的思想內涵，而且使之更富有詩意和質感。詩人明面寫採貝，實際寫愛人離開後相思的情懷；詩人畢竟是生於大陸並伴隨著戰爭的苦難和新生而成長起來的詩人，靈魂深處對生命的感觸與律動，都不曾減弱。儘管愛情已遠，但是卻因思念加以濃縮和約制，融進多彩的意象中，從而使此詩優美獨特的意象時時疊現，其思力沉摯之處，令讀者產生強烈的感情共鳴。

鄭愁予是在 2005 年歸籍金門縣金城鎮的。其實早在此之前，他已 5 度造訪金門，並寫下了五首詩；〈金門集〉、〈飲酒金門行〉、〈煙火是戰火的女兒〉、〈八二三響禮炮〉、〈大膽島童謠〉。其中，〈煙火是戰火的女兒〉是 2003 年中秋節前夕，鄭愁予應邀參金門和廈門共度中秋活動後，有感而作：

煙火是戰火的女兒，嚴父的火灼痛，女兒的火開花；花開在天空疑是星星也在撒嬌，彩光映在海上莫非波濤跟著巧笑……

> 哎，讓女兒自由地長大罷！讓她撒嬌，讓她巧笑，讓她
> 推開廣廈之門正是金色之門
> 洛陽兒女對門居呀！中秋月圓是歷史的舞臺，讓飲者演出那月老的浪漫，乾守望之杯！乾相助之杯！乾杯呀……

This collection uses objects in nature as the counterparts of one's own spiritual feelings, which not only expands the ideological connotation of the poem, but also makes it more poetic and textured. The poet writes Caibei openly, but actually writes about the lovesickness after his lover leaves; after all, the poet was born in the mainland and grew up with the suffering and rebirth of the war, and the feeling and rhythm of life in the depths of his soul have never weakened. Although love is far away, it is condensed and restrained by thoughts, and blended into colorful images, so that the beautiful and unique images of this poem appear from time to time.

Zheng Chouyu returned to Jincheng Town, Kinmen County in 2005. In fact, he had visited Kinmen five times before that and wrote five poems; Island Nursery Rhymes, among which *Firework is the Daughter of War* was written on the eve of the Mid-Autumn Festival in 2003. Zheng Chouyu was invited to participate in the Mid-Autumn Festival activities in Kinmen and Xiamen, and wrote:

Fireworks are the daughters of the flames of war, the flames of a strict father are burning, and the flames of a daughter are blooming; the flowers bloom in the sky, it seems that the stars are also acting like a baby, and the colorful light is reflected on the sea. Could it

Hey, let your daughter grow up freely! Let her be coquettish, let her smile cleverly, let her Pushing open the gate of Guangsha is the golden gate. The sons and daughters of Luoyang live opposite each other! The full moon in the Mid-Autumn Festival is the stage of history, let the drinkers perform the romance of the old moon, and drink the cup of watching! Do a cup of help! Cheers....

　　哎，兒女的自由長大不就是門當戶對了嗎？

　　此詩節奏感強，具有慷慨激昂的氣象，也是詩人在喚起兩岸人民和平共處的自覺；他跳脫了多數軍中詩人的悲壯抒懷，改把自己赤裸的靈魂捧給讀者。當兩岸中秋同步綻放煙火於夜空，對孤懸於海峽兩岸的「前線戰地」的金門人而言，心中自是五味雜陳的；於是，詩人內在心性的引發，用赤子之心看待兩岸關係，給人一種真誠、親切之感。

　　縱觀歷史，鄭成功是抗清名將，明朝時期被封為延平郡王。籍貫福建泉州，父親是海盜出身的南明將領鄭芝龍，母親為日本人；他在父親投降清朝而被俘虜後，領軍和清朝對抗 15 年，是主要的抗清勢力，曾一度以大軍包圍金陵，但功敗垂成。事後，他率軍渡過台灣海峽，擊敗荷蘭東印度公司的軍隊並接收其領地，建立台灣第一個漢人政權。當年，鄭愁予的先祖鄭成功就是以金門為起兵反清復明的基地，但因鄭氏家族曾降清，集體遷移大陸，後被迫分派各地軍職；可惜的是，當地金門人似乎對延平郡王祠不太熱衷。鄭愁予晚年則積極於追溯鄭氏家族的歷史，希望能找回鄭成功應有的歷史定位及尊崇。在這種心情交織下，遂而寫下〈飲酒金門行〉：

Hey, isn't it right for children to grow up freely?

This poem has a strong sense of rhythm and an impassioned atmosphere. It is also the poet's arousal of the awareness of peaceful coexistence between the people on both sides of the strait. When the Mid-Autumn Festival on both sides of the strait simultaneously blooms fireworks in the night sky, for the Kinmen people who are lonely on both sides of the strait in the "front-line battlefield", there are mixed feelings in their hearts; therefore, the poet's inner heart is triggered, and he looks at the relationship between the two sides of the strait with a pure heart, giving a sense of sincerity and intimacy.

Throughout history, Zheng Chenggong was a famous general who fought against the Qing Dynasty. During the Ming Dynasty, he was named the king of Yanping County. Born in Quanzhou, Fujian, his father was Zheng Zhilong, a Nanming general who was a pirate, and his mother was Japanese. After his father surrendered to the Qing Dynasty and was captured, he led the army against the Qing Dynasty for 15 years. He was the main anti-Qing force. He once surrounded Jinling with a large army, but false success. Afterwards, he led his army across the Taiwan Strait, defeated the army of the Dutch East India Company and took over its territory, establishing Taiwan's first Han regime. At that time, Zheng Chenggong, the ancestor of Zheng Chouyu, used Kinmen as the base to fight against the Qing Dynasty and restore the Ming Dynasty. However, because the Zheng family had surrendered to the Qing Dynasty and moved to the mainland collectively, they were forced to assign military positions to various places. The shrine is not too keen. Zheng Chouyu was active in tracing the history of the Zheng family in his later years, hoping to regain Zheng Chenggong's due historical positioning and respect. With this kind of mood intertwined, I wrote *Drinking Jinmen Tour*:

　　飲者乃有俠者之姿，豪興起時，大口吞浪如鯨之
嘯海
　　當懷思遠人，就閉目坐定，
　　輕啜芳洌猶吻之沾唇……

　　此詩剛猛有力，頗具鋒芒。隨潮汐遠去，詩人在追緬的
聯想中自己與鄭成功及先祖的某種微妙關係，則在看似品酒
的豪爽激昂中，其核心蘊藏著對未來的憧憬之情，並把一種
內在的使命感揭示出來了。

三、鄭愁予詩歌卓然有成

　　在描繪大自然壯麗山河或家鄉的詩作中，鄭愁予的詩常
以小見大的藝術概括力展現出更寬闊的自然境界，並寄以深
厚的情思。誠然，當我們欣賞一首好詩，是必須運用自己的
感官，透過感知與想像、理解與情感等心理機制；加以結合
自己的生活經驗，經過思維反復提煉，從而形成的一種審美
愉悅。這也是一個從藝術直覺到心靈頓悟的深化過程。其中，
尤為重要的是，鑒賞的同時也接受了詩人的藝術修養。意大
利美學大師克羅齊〈1866-1952〉也提及：「一切藝術品只有
對懂得他們的人，才顯得重要」《美學原理》〉。而歌德也
曾說：「藝術的真正生命正在於對個別特殊事物的掌握和描
述」。依我的看法，鄭愁予與生俱來即有一種本質上的審美

The drinker has the appearance of a chivalrous man. When
he is proud, he swallows the waves like a whale's
tsunami sea.
When thinking about people far away, just close your eyes
and sit still,
Gently sipping the fragrance is like a kiss on the lips....

This poem is fierce and powerful, quite sharp. As the tide goes away, the subtle relationship between the poet himself and Zheng Chenggong and his ancestors in the association of chasing Myanmar, in the boldness and passion that seems to be wine tasting, its core contains the longing for the future, and puts an inner A sense of purpose is revealed.

3. Zheng Chouyu's Poems Are Outstanding

In the poems depicting the magnificent mountains and rivers of nature or his hometown, Zheng Chouyu's poems often show a broader natural realm with his deep emotional thoughts through the artistic generalization of the small to see the big. It is true that when we appreciate a good poem, we must use our senses, through psychological mechanisms such as perception and imagination, understanding and emotion; combined with our own life experience, through repeated thinking, to form a kind of aesthetic pleasure. This is also a deepening process from artistic intuition to spiritual epiphany. Among them, the most important thing is that while appreciating, he also accepted the poet's artistic accomplishment. Italian aesthetic master Croce (1866-1952) also mentioned: "All works of art are only important to those who understand them." "Principles of Aesthetics". And Goethe once said: "The true life of art lies in the grasp and description of individual and special things." In my opinion, Zheng Chouyu is born with an

觀，他喜歡旅遊，與大自然作近距離的接觸，並習慣於從自己的經驗中感悟。他把體現的匠心融於詩中，是文人的理想自我的精神寫照；他的詩品和人品都為當今文藝界、或是整個華文詩歌都做出了卓越的楷模。

　　反觀台灣，自 1992 年 11 月 7 日解嚴後，時至今日，金門已轉而為兩岸觀光旅遊的新熱點。就在鄭愁予歸籍金門人滿三年，由金格唱片為詩人出版的《旅夢─碟兒詩話》：

> 風起六朝　沙揚大唐
> 宋秩一卷雲和月　明清兩京清明雨
> 風起六朝　沙揚大唐
> 風實是風騷惟在那園林　啊
> 沙卻是沙場　臥有醉漢
> 雲它遮了月　啊　喪廬失墓悲歌
> 清明雨霆　天下盡是斷腸人
> 這一碟詩話　由書生主烹　這五色作料
> 千古的氣候如火候
> 煮了一碟相思豆
> 煮了相思的詩話　一碟浪漫的紅豆

　　這首詩讓鄭愁予勇奪了最佳作詞人獎座。詩人直接從歷史的興衰中擷取意象，把自己渴望先人指點迷津、擺脫跋涉之苦的對白描繪得很逼真。到這裡，詩人對先祖的追悼及歷史的悲歌的無奈，其激情的噴湧似乎已找到了第一道出口了。

essential aesthetic sense. He likes to travel, to have close contact with nature, and is used to comprehend from his own experience. He integrates the ingenuity embodied in his poems, which is the spiritual portrayal of the ideal self of the literati; his poetry and character have set an excellent model for today's literary and art circles, or the entire Chinese poetry.

In contrast to Taiwan, since the lifting of martial law on November 7, 1992, Kinmen has turned into a new hotspot for cross-strait tourism. Just three years after Zheng Chouyu returned to Kinmen, Jinge Records published *Traveling Dreams-Die Er Shihua* for the poet:

The wind rises from the Six Dynasties Shayang Datang
A Roll of Clouds and Moon in Song Zhi, Qingming Rain in Ming and Qing Dynasties
The wind rises from the Six Dynasties Shayang Datang
The wind is really coquettish but only in the garden
The sand is a sand field, there are drunks lying down
The cloud covers the moon, ah, the sad song of losing the hut and the tomb
Qingming rains, the world is full of heartbroken people
This dish of poems is composed of five colors of ingredients by scholars.
The climate of the ages is like a fire
Cooked a plate of acacia beans
Cooked poems about lovesickness, a plate of romantic red beans

This poem made Zheng Chouyu win the best lyricist award. The poet directly extracts images from the ups and downs of history, and vividly portrays his dialogue that he longs for his ancestors to guide him and get rid of the pain of trekking. At this point, the poet's mourning for the ancestors

他的另一首成名詩〈偈〉：

不再流浪了
我不願做空間的歌者
寧願是時間的石人
然而，我又是宇宙的遊子

地球你不需留我
這土地我一方來
將八方離去

正是詩人人格的自我象徵。彷彿中，晚年的大詩人早已跳脫了世俗的塵事，過去，有多少舊夢已成雲煙，他汲汲營營追求的是宇宙那看不見的經卷。如今，年過 76 歲的詩人，仍風塵僕僕奔波於金門與美國、台灣三地；當他眺望在古寧頭海邊，想必又激起了許多馳騁想像。那清澈的碧海、晨光如月光、百姓的真樸豪爽，想必詩人晚年的心情是恬靜的，也是歡樂的。此刻，詩人追求的應是與大自然的融合，這才是心靈的經。他的生命便與空間時間一致而取得永恆的寧靜了。

—2010.5.21 作

—臺灣的「國圖」刊物，《全國新書資訊月刊》，2011年 3 月，第 147 期，頁 45-48。

His other famous poem "Gather":

No longer wandering
I don't want to be a singer of space
I would rather be a stone man of time
However, I am a wanderer in the universe

Earth, you don't need to keep me
I come to this land
Leave Bafang

It is the self-symbol of the poet's personality. It seems that the great poet in his later years has already escaped from the mundane affairs. In the past, how many old dreams have become clouds and smoke, and what he is eagerly pursuing is the invisible scriptures of the universe. Today, the 76-year-old poet still travels back and forth between Kinmen, the United States, and Taiwan; when he looks at the seaside in Guningtou, it must have aroused many imaginations. The clear blue sea, the morning light like moonlight, and the simplicity and boldness of the people, presumably the poet's mood in his later years was tranquil and joyful. At this moment, what the poet pursues should be the integration with nature, which is the sutra of the soul. His life will be consistent with space and time and obtain eternal tranquility.

11. 論周夢蝶詩中的道家美學──以〈逍遙遊〉〈六月〉二詩為例

摘要：周夢蝶是當代重要的詩人，他的詩用語豐富而多義，善以莊子思想撥見對其哲學與美學形成的敏感，在孤獨中鋪陳出不凡的思維與想像。以周夢蝶的《逍遙遊》、《六月》二詩為例,分析詩中所展露的道家美學的生命演出,進而建構出臺灣現代詩史上的新創價值。

關鍵字：莊子；美學；周夢蝶；道家；詩

　　周夢蝶〈1921.12.29-〉，本名周起述，河南淅川縣人；童年失怙，個性沉靜且獨善其身。自幼熟讀古典詩文，曾就讀開封師範、宛西鄉村師範學校；因戰亂，中途輟學。隨軍來臺時，家鄉遺有髮妻和二子一女。1952 年開始在報上發表詩集，十五歲時，偷偷替自己取筆名為『夢蝶』，其實是源自莊周夢蝴蝶，表示崇尚自由的無限嚮往。自軍中退伍，加

11. On the Taoist Aesthetics in Zhou Mengdie's Poems:
Taking *A Happy Excursion* and *June* as Examples

Abstract: Zhou Mengdie, an important contemporary poet, whose words in poems are rich and meaningful, is inspired by Zhuangzi to get insight into philosophy and aesthetics, and creates extraordinary thought and imagination in solitude. This paper analyzes Zhou Mengdie's *A Happy Excursion* and *June* as examples, as well as the Taoist aesthetic life in the two poems, to construct the creative value of modern Taiwan poetry history.

Key words:Zhuangzi; aesthetics; poet; Taoist; Zhou Mengdie

Zhou Mengdie (1921.12.29-), whose real name is Zhou Qishu, was born in Xichuan County, Henan Province. He lost his father in childhood, and has a quiet and independent personality. He has been familiar with classical poetry and prose since he was a child, and studied in Kaifeng Normal School and Wanxi Rural Normal School; he dropped out of school due to the war. When he came to Taiwan with the army, his wife, two sons and a daughter were left behind in his hometown. In 1952, he began to publish a collection of poems in newspapers. At the age of fifteen, he secretly took the pen name "Dream Butterfly" for himself. In fact, it originated from Zhuang Zhou's dream of a butterfly, expressing his infinite yearning for freedom. After retiring from the

入「藍星詩社」；後又於 1959 年起在臺北市著名的明星咖啡廳門前擺書攤渡日，長達 21 年。出版的第一本詩集《孤獨國》，被選為「台灣文學經典」。1962 年開始有佛禪、與莊子共融的明顯傾向，常默坐書攤前，成為「市景」一隅，晚年似「苦行僧」般，過著幾近孤隱的生活。

1980 年美國 Orientations 雜誌記者專訪於他，並以古希臘時期代神發佈神諭的 Oracle 為喻，撰文稱許他為「廈門街上的先知」（Oracle on Amoy Street）。同年因胃潰瘍開刀，以致歇業。曾獲臺灣「中國文藝協會」新詩特別獎、笠詩社「詩創作」獎、中央日報文學成就獎、第一屆「國家文化藝術基金會」文藝獎、「中國詩歌藝術學會」藝術貢獻獎等。著有《孤獨國》、《還魂草》、《周夢蝶世紀詩選》、《約會》、《十三朵白菊花》、《周夢蝶詩文集》等。他對作品的要求相當高，常透過「虛實相生」等方法使讀者的視覺與感知達到平衡，畫面空靈純淨；並以自我靈魂為起點，引禪意入詩，這是對莊子道家美學思想的藝術實踐。

army, he joined the "Blue Star Poetry Society". Later, he set up a book stall in front of the famous Star Cafe in Taipei City in 1959 for 21 years. His first collection of poems, "Lonely Country", was selected as "Taiwan Literature Classics". Beginning in 1962, he began to have a clear inclination towards Buddhist meditation and communion with Zhuangzi. He often sat silently in front of the book stand and became a corner of the "cityscape". In his later years, he was like an "ascetic monk", living an almost solitary life.

In 1980, a reporter from the American Orientations magazine interviewed him exclusively, and used the Oracle, which issued oracles on behalf of the gods in ancient Greece, as a metaphor, and wrote an article calling him the "Oracle on Amoy Street". In the same year, he was operated on due to a gastric ulcer, so he went out of business. He has won the Special Award for New Poetry from the "Chinese Literary and Art Association" in Taiwan, the "Poetry Creation" Award from the Li Poetry Association, the Literary Achievement Award from Central Daily News, the 1st "National Culture and Art Foundation" Literary Award, and the "Chinese Poetry Art Society" Art Contribution Award, etc. He is the author of *Lonely Country, Resurrection Grass, Zhou Mengdie's Century Poems, Dating, Thirteen White Chrysanthemums, Zhou Mengdie's Poems and Essays*, etc. He has very high requirements for his works, and he often uses methods such as "coexistence of virtual and real" to balance the reader's vision and perception, and the pictures are ethereal and pure; starting from his own soul, he introduces Zen into poetry, which is a reflection of Zhuangzi's Taoist aesthetics and artistic practice.

一、〈消遙遊〉與忘我美學

　　《莊子》書中不乏「超以象外」與具備詩意想像的畫面。其中，強調的包括「虛」與「實」需時時體現的，在概念上雖是相對立；但在創作中，周夢蝶對天地自然的感受和表達，則選擇語言超越了拘泥於物象的階段，而直入司空圖在《詩品》中提出了「超以象外，得其寰中，離形得似」的境界。

　　正是這種「超以象外」的創作方法，才能「得其寰中」，從而達到莊子美學中永恆追求的至極表現。如今，周夢蝶的詩是華人文學寶庫中的奇葩，單從畫面形式的表層意義上看，他常體現出自我美學素養來啓迪觀眾的思維，藉以享受審美愉悅。

　　正如莊子生於戰亂之世，認為「道」的性質即自然，它是虛無和永恆的、是一種心靈與精神的境界，也是萬物與生命之美產生和存在的本原。在〈至樂〉中，曾說：「人之生也，與憂俱生」，這就是莊子出於苦難而能超越苦難的生活美學。周夢蝶也在思考具體的物象與抽象之中，力求「美」與「真」的和諧統一，他接受《莊子》，也冀望借助《莊子·刻意》之說：「淡然無極，而眾美從之，此天地之道，聖人之德也。」他常透過對自然的細膩觀察，去瞭解美、尋找美、體悟美，從而使自己能夠減少痛苦，忘懷得失。也就是

1. *A Happy Excursion* and the Aesthetics of Selflessness

There are many pictures in Zhuangzi that are "beyond imagination" and poetic imagination. Among them, the emphasis is on the fact that "virtual" and "real" need to be manifested over time, although they are conceptually opposed; but in the creation, Zhou Mengdie's feelings and expressions of the nature of heaven and earth, choose language to go beyond the stage of sticking to objects, and Zhijin Sikongtu put forward the realm of "beyond the image, get the world, and get the likeness without the shape" in "Shipin". It is this creative method of "beyond imagery" that can "get the world", thus achieving the ultimate expression of the eternal pursuit of Zhuangzi's aesthetics. Today, Zhou Mengdie's poems are rare works in the treasure house of Chinese literature. From the superficial sense of the picture form, he often reflects his own aesthetic literacy to enlighten the audience's thinking and enjoy aesthetic pleasure.

Just as Zhuangzi was born in a war-torn world, he believes that the nature of "Tao" is nature, it is nothingness and eternal, it is a state of mind and spirit, and it is also the origin of the beauty of all things and life. In *Supreme Happiness*, it was said: "The life of a man is born with sorrow." This is Zhuangzi's life aesthetics that can transcend suffering out of suffering. Zhou Mengdie is also thinking about concrete images and abstractions, and strives for the harmony and unity of "beauty" and "truth". This is the way of heaven and earth, and the virtue of a sage. He often understands beauty, seeks beauty, and realizes beauty through careful observation of nature, so that he can reduce pain and forget gains and losses. That is

說，周夢蝶將體道為一種自我修養，其強烈的生命精神與澹泊的詩性、特有的直覺性，使他能處於清靜無為的境界中得以體驗天籟、地籟、人籟等萬殊聲音。其目的是為追求一種宇宙精神，追求物我相融的心態；又或許，也只有在自然的靜默中才是他對神聖感覺的最好回應。

然而，道家「物我俱忘」的思想也影響周夢蝶甚廣。在創作理念上，他看到了《莊子》的深刻本質，對現象世界的超越，亦必然是其推動藝術發展的根本動力。按莊子所言，道不僅存在於客觀世界中，更存在於得道者的心中。於是，周夢蝶也以詩尋求心靈的解脫為對策，在虛靜、孤寂而自由的生活中，終結出千古永垂的佳作〈消遙遊〉。他將「道」賦予了強烈的審美特徵，首先，題下先引《莊子・消遙遊》：「北溟有魚，其名為鯤。鯤之大，不知其幾千里也。化而爲鳥，其名爲鵬，鵬之背，不知其幾千里也，怒而飛……」其全詩如下：

> 絕塵而逸。回眸處
> 亂雲翻白，波濤千起；
> 無邊與蒼茫與空曠
> 展笑著如回響
> 遺落於我蹤影底有無中。

to say, Zhou Mengdie regards Taoism as a kind of self-cultivation. His strong life spirit, indifferent poetic quality, and unique intuition enable him to experience the sounds of nature, earth, and people in a state of tranquility and inaction. sound. Its purpose is to pursue a kind of cosmic spirit and a state of mind that blends things and me; perhaps, only in the silence of nature is his best response to the divine feeling.

However, the Taoist thought of "I forget everything" has also greatly influenced Zhou Mengdie. In terms of creative ideas, he saw the profound nature of Zhuangzi, and the transcendence of the phenomenal world must be the fundamental driving force for its artistic development. According to Zhuangzi, Tao not only exists in the objective world, but also exists in the hearts of those who have attained it. Therefore, Zhou Mengdie also used poetry to seek spiritual liberation as a countermeasure, and in the quiet, lonely and free life, he finally produced the eternal masterpiece *A Happy Excursion*. He endowed "Tao" with a strong aesthetic feature. First of all, he quoted *Zhuangzi • A Happy Excursion* under the title: "There is a fish in the north ocean, and its name is the great orc. The size of the orc is so big that I don't know how many thousands of miles it is. It is a bird, its name is the fabulous bird, and the back of the fabulous bird does not know how many thousands of miles away it is, so it flies away in anger..." The full poem is as follows:

> *Dust and escape. Looking back at*
> *The chaotic clouds turn white, and the waves rise a*
> *thousand;*
> *Boundless and boundless and empty*
> *Smile like an echo*
> *Lost in the bottom of my trace.*
> *Lost in the bottom of my trace.*

從冷冷的北溟來
我底長背與長爪
猶滯留着昨夜底濡濡；
夢終有醒時——
陰霾撥開，是百尺雷嘯。

昨日已沉陷了，
甚至鮫人底雪淚也滴乾了；
飛躍啊，我心在高寒
高寒是大化底眼神
我是那眼神沒遮攔的一瞬。

不是追尋，必須追尋
不是超越，必須超越——
雲倦了，有風扶著
風倦了，有海托著
海倦了呢？堤倦了呢？

以飛為歸止的
仍須歸止於飛。
世界在我翅上
一如歷歷星河之在我膽邊
浩浩天籟之出我脅下……〈註 1〉

　　從題下引言開篇寫景，細味卻不止是簡單寫景，同時還速寫出詩人的主觀感受原是渴求消遙；即著重視覺意象，藉

Come from the cold North Sea
My long back and long claws
Still lingering to see how wet last night was;
When the dream finally wakes up —
The haze was cleared away, and there was a thunderous
*　　roar from a hundred feet.*

Yesterday has sunk,
Even the snowy tears of the merman dripped dry;
Leap, my heart is in the alpine
Alpine coldness is Dahua's eyes
I am the moment when the eyes are not covered.

Not after, must be after
It's not beyond, it must be surpassed——
Tired of clouds, supported by the wind
The wind is tired, supported by the sea
Are you tired? Are you tired?

To fly
Still have to come down to flying.
The world is on my wings
Just like the history of the galaxy is by my side
The mighty sound of nature comes out of my side... 〈Note 1〉

Starting from the introduction under the title, the scenery is described in detail, but it is not only a simple description of the scenery, but also a sketch of the poet's

由自喻為鯤鵬的飄逸身影而給人於空靜中傳出動蕩的波濤、平淡中透出幽深而自在的印象。在詩人回眸處，看似寫眼前蒼茫與空曠之景，其實是把他的孤獨寫盡了；如同那鵬鳥高飛遠去，直至無影無蹤。而那展笑著如回響，造成懸疑落合的效果，正是情思所在。詩人開始回想起自己從彼岸跨海而來，以「我底長背與長爪」純然是鯤鵬的神奇英姿，以及「陰霾撥開，是百尺雷嘯」的遄飛氣勢，用誇張比喻，逸想自己生命中曾經有過濡濕的淚光、在飽經喪亂之後隨之而來的淒清與無可奈何的遣悶，使詩人陷入一個不可預知的陰霾……直到夢醒時，那羈旅他鄉、欲歸未得的愁思方得以獲得了片刻寧靜。

　　第三段，詩人繼以擬人手法，描摹「鮫人底雪淚」已滴乾的「善等待」與「我是那眼神沒遮攔的一瞬」的「愛凝望」，鮮明塑造出翹首盼望故鄉與愛人的癡情。詩行至第四段，已去掉了「沉鬱頓挫」的尾巴，透過移覺把視覺印象轉換為聽覺，呈現一種迷離憂傷的意緒。然而，「不是超越，必須超越──」，這遠近交錯的情感，能精妙傳神地烘托出一線「蕭散自然」的生機，而讓詩的傳意活動無礙自發的顯現。其深

subjective feeling, which is longing to be away; that is, it focuses on visual images, and the elegant figure of roc-bird, who describes itself as roc-bird, gives people a sense of tranquility. There are turbulent waves, and a deep and comfortable impression is revealed in the plain. When the poet looks back, he seems to write about the vast and empty scene in front of him, but actually writes about his loneliness; just like the bird flying away until it disappears without a trace. And the effect of smiling like an echo, causing suspense and Ochiai, is exactly where the emotion lies. The poet began to recall that he came across the sea from the other side, using "my long back and long claws" as the purely magical heroic posture of Roc-bird, and the flying aura of "thunder is a hundred feet away from the haze", using exaggerated metaphors. Yi thinks that there have been wet tears in his life, the desolation and helpless depression that followed after suffering from grief and chaos, which made the poet fall into an unpredictable haze... until he woke up, the wandering and lustful. The melancholy thoughts that have not been returned have been able to obtain a moment of peace.

In the third paragraph, the poet continued to use anthropomorphic techniques to describe the "waiting kindly" that has dried up in the "merman's snow tears" and the "gazing love" of "I am the moment when the eyes are not covered", clearly shaping the longing for the hometown and the lover's infatuation. In the fourth paragraph of the poem, the tail of "depressed and frustrated" has been removed, and the visual impression is converted into auditory sense through telepathy, presenting a blurred and sad mood. However, "it is not transcendence, it must be transcendence —", this intertwined emotion of far and near can subtly and vividly

含之意則暗示大化之中，已無過往的責難與懺悔，轉而渴望追求完全擺脫塵世之累的寧靜心境；在頻頻提問中，怎不動人心眼而啟遙念之思。詩至此，連結成不息的音韻與節奏，把「不是追尋，必須追尋」的愛整個流洩出來，反而有一種「渾然無雕飾」的清新之美。到了最後一段，「以飛為歸止的／仍須歸止於飛。」為全詩鋪墊了詩人藝術自覺追求的目標——超以象外，甚而想達到「世界在我翅上」的那種無限壯闊的天境。於是，詩人從有言、具象可感知的藝術空間，慢慢昇華到「一如歷歷星河之在我膽邊／浩浩天籟之出我脅下……」形象以外的「忘我」境界，思念至此已是徹底的形象化了。

二、〈六月〉的詩境與「道美」

要閱讀周夢蝶詩的唯美、意蘊，就得借重莊子美學的智識，記得《莊子·天道》曾說：「夫虛靜恬淡寂寞無為者，萬物之本也。」這也應驗了周夢蝶的詩風表現在文學創作上就是抒情樸真。其實樸就是淡雅，淡就是樸，就是自然；也正因為「心繫鄉土」的深厚情結，致使詩

express a line of vitality of "scattered nature", so that the conveying activities of the poem will not hinder the spontaneous presentation. Its deep meaning implies that in Dahua, there is no past blame and repentance, and instead longing to pursue a peaceful state of mind that is completely free from the burdens of the world; in frequent questions, how can one not move people's eyes and open up thoughts from afar. So far, the poem has been connected into an endless rhyme and rhythm, and the love that "is not to be pursued, but must be pursued" is fully released, but there is a fresh beauty of "no ornamentation". In the last paragraph, "What ends with flying / must still end with flying." This paves the way for the whole poem to achieve the goal of the poet's artistic self-conscious pursuit — beyond the imagination, and even wants to achieve "the world is on my wings". An infinitely vast sky. As a result, the poet gradually sublimated from the artistic space of words, representations and perceptions to the realm of "selflessness" beyond the image of "just like the stars and rivers of the past are by my side / the sound of the vast sky comes out of my side...". It is completely visualized.

2. The Poetic Scene and "Beauty of Taoism" in *June*

To read the beauty and connotation of Zhou Mengdie's poems, you have to borrow the knowledge of Zhuangzi's aesthetics. I remember that "Zhuangzi·Tiandao" once said: "A husband who is quiet, quiet, lonely and inactive is the foundation of all things." This also fulfills Zhou Mengdie's poetic style. In literary creation, it is lyrical and simple. In fact, simplicity means elegance and nature; it is precisely because of the deep complex of "heart for the countryside" that many of the

人的不少作品充滿了思辨的色彩。有時雖因形象發展常見以末段接回首段的「迴旋書寫」手法，似有趨於悲傷之勢，但通常到最後總能剎見曙光、體現出詩人對美好事物的嚮往。

由道出發的莊子美學自然也是「無言」的美學——「天地有大美而不言」（《莊子·知北游》）。然而，這種最高境界的美，如同《莊子·外物》所言：「言者所以在意，得意而忘言」，意旨詩歌之美，不僅在有盡之言，尤在「無聲勝有聲」或「無窮之意」的層面。這些道家的美學思想，也同樣深深影響著周夢蝶的思維方式及對生命哲學的把握。其中，莊子審美自由論集中體現在「神遊」的理論上，主要宗旨是，要實現對客觀世界的超越，「心遊」才是最重要的。它需要想像，讓精神在超越時空的宇宙中無拘無束的「逍遙」。這與前詩欣賞中的「消遙遊」對感覺的覺醒有其關聯性。莊子在《逍遙遊》中，構想了無功、無名、無我的神人、聖人、至人，又使他們成為他人生審美的對象——人融合於自然。也就是這個深刻思考，再度讓周夢蝶注入了全部思想、情緒、語言的花朵，而成為一個淵深的哲人。再就他的另一首早年之作〈六月〉，我們可以清楚地看到詩人欲解脫這形體束縛的莊蝶意象。一首詩的形神、平奇、隱

poet's works are full of speculative color. Sometimes due to the development of the image, the "convolutional writing" technique of connecting the last paragraph to the first paragraph seems to tend to be sad, but usually at the end, the dawn can always be seen, reflecting the poet's yearning for beautiful things.

Zhuangzi's aesthetics starting from the Tao is naturally also the aesthetics of "no words" — "there is great beauty in the world without words" (Zhuangzi ·Journey to the North). However, the beauty of this highest state is just like "Zhuangzi • Waiwu" said: "The reason why the speaker cares about it is that he forgets his words when he is proud." The level of "infinity", these Taoist aesthetic thoughts have also deeply influenced Zhou Mengdie's way of thinking and his grasp of life philosophy. Among them, Zhuangzi's theory of aesthetic freedom is concentrated in the theory of "mind wandering". The main purpose is that "mind wandering" is the most important thing to realize the transcendence of the objective world. It requires imagination, allowing the spirit to "relax" unrestrainedly in the universe beyond time and space. This is related to the awakening of feeling in *A Happy Excursion* in the appreciation of the previous poems. In *A Happy Excursion*, Zhuangzi conceived gods, sages, and perfect people who have no merit, no name, and no self, and made them the objects of his life's aesthetics — the fusion of man and nature. It was this deep thinking that once again injected Zhou Mengdie with all the flowers of thought, emotion, and language, and became a profound philosopher. As for another of his early works *June*, we can clearly see the poet's image of Zhuang Die trying to get rid of the bondage of the body. Whether a poem's form, spirit,

顯……等，是否能構成統一和諧的藝術整體，關係著詩
之所以優劣的主因；而從這兒也得到了最佳證明：

> 蘧然醒來
> 繽紛的花雨打得我底影子好濕！是夢？是真？
> 面對珊瑚礁下覆舟的今夕。

> 一粒舍利等於多少堅忍？世尊
> 你底心很亮，而六月底心很暖──
> 我有幾個六月？
> 我將如何安放我底固執？
> 在你與六月之間。

> 據說蛇底血脈是沒有年齡的！
> 縱使你鑄永夜爲秋，永夜爲冬
> 縱使黑暗挖去自己底眼睛……
> 蛇知道：它仍能自水裡喊出火底消息。

> 死亡在我掌上旋舞
> 一個蹉跌，她流星般落下
> 我欲翻身拾起再拚圓
> 虹斷霞飛，她已紛紛化爲蝴蝶。

> 　　【附注】釋迦既卒，焚其身，得骨子
> 　　　　累萬，光瑩如五色珠，搗之不碎。
> 　　　　名曰舍利子。〈註2〉

flatness, invisibility, etc., can form a unified and harmonious artistic whole is related to the main reason why the poem is good or bad; and here is the best proof:

Wake up suddenly
The rain of colorful flowers made my shadow so wet!
Is it a dream? is true?
Facing Jinxi, the shipwreck under the coral reef.

How much perseverance is one grain of relic equal to?
  World Honored One
Your heart is very bright, but at the end of June, your
  heart is very warm —
How many Junes do I have?
How shall I place my stubbornness?
Between you and June.

It is said that the blood of snakes has no age!
Even if you cast eternal night as autumn and eternal
night as winter
Even if the darkness gouges out my own eyes ....
The snake knows: it can still shout the message of fire
  from the water.

Death dances in my palm
One stumble, she falls like a meteor
I want to turn over, pick it up and put it together again
Hongduan Xiafei, she has turned into butterflies one after
  another.

【Additional Note】Since Sakyamuni died, burn his body and get his bones. There are tens of thousands of seeds, shining like five-color beads, which cannot be broken when smashed. Name Said the relic. <Note 2>

　　縱觀此詩氣韻生動，深遠難盡。一開始，詩人給我們描繪的就是他在創作時所進入的「物我相融」、「物我統一」的境界；其思想核心則是講求現實世界的「空」與超現實世界的「真如」。若就詩的結構而言，首先從聽覺起筆，花雨成全詩的底色，凸出詩人孤獨的身影、珊瑚礁、舟子這些圖景；也體現了「蘧然醒來」與夢境意象的空靈與超脫塵俗之美。這與道家美學首先表現在道的朦朧美和不可捉摸的神秘極為相似，但這種神秘却給人想像的聲響、一種美的享受；又似是人生幻化的莊周之蝶，是夢亦真中自我的物化，足見詩人意象經營之用心。

　　在《莊子‧齊物論》篇末「莊周夢蝶」：「夢飲酒者，旦而哭泣；夢哭泣者，旦而田獵。方其夢也，不知其夢也。夢之中又占其夢焉，覺而後知其夢也。且有大覺而後知此其大夢也，而愚者自以為覺，竊竊然知之。君乎，牧乎，固哉！丘也與女，皆夢也；予謂女夢，亦夢也。是其言也，其名為弔詭。萬世之後而一遇大聖，知其解者，是旦暮遇之也。」在這裡，或許周夢蝶將莊子具有濃重「超越」、「形上」、「虛靜無為」等意味和特點，從他心理的感受，蘊育出〈六月〉這首詩的背景。而這首詩亦有莊子美學思想「覺夢如一」

Throughout this poem, the charm is vivid, far-reaching and inexhaustible. At the very beginning, what the poet described to us was the realm of "integration of things and me" and "unity of things and me" that he entered in his creation; the core of his thought is to emphasize the "emptiness" of the real world and the "truth of the surreal world". As far as the structure of the poem is concerned, it starts with the sense of hearing, and the rain of flowers completes the background color of the poem, highlighting the lonely figure of the poet, coral reefs, and boats. Earthly beauty, this is very similar to the hazy beauty and intangible mystery that Taoist aesthetics first manifested in Tao, but this mystery gives people the sound of imagination and a kind of beauty enjoyment. Materialization, which shows the poet's intentions in image management.

In Zhuangzi's *Zhuang Zhou's Dream of Butterflies* at the end of "Qi Wu Lun": "Dreams of drinking, suddenly cry; dream of weeping, suddenly hunt in the field. Fang Qi dream, don't know the dream. The dream also occupies the dream, wakes up and then knows it's a dream. It's also a big dream after you have a great awakening, but a fool thinks he's aware of it, and he knows it secretly. You are a king, you are a herdsman, sure! Qiu Ye and women are both dreams. I call it a woman's dream. It is also a dream. It is its words, and its name is paradox. After ten thousand generations, you will meet the great sage once and know the solution, and you will meet him at night." Here, Zhou Mengdie may have Zhuangzi's strong "transcendence" and "formality". "Empty and inaction" and other meanings and characteristics, from his psychological feelings, cultivated the background of the poem *June*. And

的觀念呈現。如此說來，「莊周夢蝶」的審美化是無庸置疑的，周夢蝶亦是藉由夢覺狀態的不分來象徵認識主體與客體即「我」與物界限消融。亦即，以揚棄主體對於形軀、生死、人我之執著，進而覺知自由、超越的生命真境。

　　緊接著，自然又是一種道家之思了。「一粒舍利等於多少堅忍？」詩人默問著，也描寫出詩人在現實矛盾衝擊中造成的內心痛苦與失落。但這只是一種相對的圓〈你底心很亮〉與相對的寂〈我有幾個六月〉，正蘊含著詩人渴望明日的再生。詩人將「安放我底固執」，如同生命體的太陽，其沉落亦如佛僧之圓寂。由於此詩並沒有出現理語，又頗能彰顯現代詩這一體裁特有的音韻。但在第三段，則寄託主旨於言外，其力勢變化轉為由痛苦而沉靜、和緩，有著對生命獲得了悟的辨思。這裡，其深層次的含義，卻是以靜定之心，欲解脫情愛與死永恆搏鬥的主題，抵達無欲無求幸福的彼岸，恰如舟航。到了末段，「死亡在我掌上旋舞」及前兩句呈現的是偏於調和性陰柔風格。後兩句，則表現出詩人已把自我修持的疑惑與對罪惡、誘惑與慾望的恐懼，透過夢中幻化的頓悟

this poem also presents the concept of Zhuangzi's aesthetic thought of "feeling dreams as one". In this way, the aestheticization of "Zhuang Zhou's Dream Butterfly" is unquestionable. Zhou Mengdie also uses the indistinction of the dream state to symbolize the dissolution of the boundary between the subject and the object, that is, the "I" and the object. That is to say, to sublate the subject's attachment to the body, life and death, and self, and then perceive the free and transcendent real life.

Immediately afterwards, it was naturally a kind of Taoist thinking. "How much perseverance is equal to a relic?" the poet asked silently, and also described the inner pain and loss caused by the poet's conflicts in reality. But this is just a kind of relative circle (Your heart is very bright) and relative silence (How many Junes do I have), which contains the poet's longing for tomorrow's rebirth. The poet will "place my stubbornness" like the sun of the living body, and its sinking is like the death of a Buddhist monk. Since this poem does not appear rational language, it can quite show the unique rhyme of the genre of modern poetry. But in the third paragraph, the gist is placed outside the words, and its power changes from pain to calmness and gentleness, and it has a speculative thinking about the realization of life. Here, its deep meaning is to get rid of the theme of eternal struggle between love and death with a calm heart, and reach the other side of happiness without desire and pursuit, just like sailing. At the end, "Death is dancing in my palm" and the first two sentences present a harmonious and feminine style. The last two sentences show that the poet has transformed the doubts of self-cultivation and the fear of sin, temptation and desire. After the sudden enlightenment in the dream, the body has religiousized the love of the world, and it

之後，形體已把世俗之愛宗教化，亦含有人生必須經過痛苦的修行及磨難與血火冶煉，方能趨於永恆不滅的禪意。至此，詩人的心靈便得以自在遨遊。之後，詩人的作品，也常以莊子為宗師，著力描寫出一種「天人合一」中的東方哲人的智慧。

三、周夢蝶：以生命為詩的歌者

周夢蝶的一生，在藝術上，充滿了傳奇式的浪漫主義色彩。記得德國存在主義哲學家海德格（Heidegger, 1889-1976）曾說：「心境愈是自由，愈能得到美的享受。」個人以為，凡是優美的詩歌都是時代的鏡子和回聲，只有形象，才能給藝術以血液和呼吸。在過去的評論界，多認為周夢蝶是講究詩的形象化和多種修辭手段的運用，因而使人感到空靈逸秀，富有質感。他很少在詩中講些大道理，而總是通過形象化的描寫和語言的複雜變化來抒情。其詩的可貴之處，恰恰在於：他既能以澎湃的詩情為命運所帶來的痛苦與愛憐和追求光明的即將到來而高歌，又具有一種抑揚頓挫的節奏感以及以感情注入物象的繪畫美。而莊子美學不但體現了詩人所要表達的深層思想，又造成了一個完整的藝術世界。他總是運用自己豐富的想像力，使無形的變為有形，無聲的變為有聲，無色的使人可見，甚至把沒有生命的變為有生命。當然，從詩

also contains that life must go through painful practice and tribulation and smelting by blood and fire can lead to the eternal Zen. At this point, the poet's mind can travel freely. Afterwards, the poet's works also often use Zhuangzi as the master, focusing on describing the wisdom of an oriental philosopher in the "unity of man and nature".

3. Zhou Mengdie: A Singer Who Takes Life as a Poem

Zhou Mengdie's life is full of legendary romanticism in art. I remember the German existentialist philosopher Heidegger (1889-1976) once said: "The freer the mind, the more you can enjoy the beauty." Personally, I think that all beautiful poems are the mirror and echo of the times. Give art its blood and breath. In the past critics, it was mostly believed that Zhou Mengdie paid attention to the visualization of poems and the use of various rhetorical means, so that people feel ethereal, elegant and full of texture. He seldom talks about big truths in his poems, but always expresses emotions through visual descriptions and complex changes in language. The value of his poems lies precisely in that he can not only sing about the pain, love and pity brought by fate and the pursuit of light with surging poetic emotion, but also has a sense of cadence and rhythm and the beauty of painting that injects emotion into objects. Zhuangzi's aesthetics not only embodies the deep thoughts that the poet wants to express, but also creates a complete art world. He always uses his rich imagination to make invisible things visible, silent things into sound, colorless things visible, and even lifeless things into life. Of course, in terms of the content of the poem, its tone is deeply affectionate, gentle and

的內容上來講，其基調的深情低吟、溫婉淒美，也擅以矛盾
語法或用「蝴蝶」、「雪」、「火」來暗示禪機。似乎自苦
的詩心遠離了塵世，而生活又很早就鍛煉了他堅強的意志和
樸實；但是，從探求詩美來講，不能不使人讚嘆詩人的藝術
匠心。

　　事實上，周夢蝶的詩早期受莊子影響較深，對生死的感
悟，亦莊亦禪，是那樣深邃又空濛，使人讀後有一種惘然若
失之感，這正是詩的魅力所在。不過他對佛學、甚至回教可
蘭經中的哲學都用心研究過；而從小所受的古典文化的影響
也是潛移默化、形成一種新古典的語言風貌，進入到他靈魂
深處的。如〈消遙遊〉詩裡的前幾句，有宋詞的頓挫語音節。
所以，莊子美學是哲學，也是周夢蝶所尋求的精神家園；他
用自己的藝術實踐使得詩體獲得了新的生命。這點，與道家
美學本質上的要求是可以相匯通的。

　　正如德國哲學家康德(Immanuel Kant, 1724—1804)所說，
凡最高的美都使人惆悵，忽忽若有所失，如羈旅之思念家鄉。
也正是這種思鄉愁思反映在周夢蝶詩中便是追尋精神的超越
與失落情緒的並存，常直接藉由夢中或物我冥合所產生的經
驗，論證生命的片刻愉悅或自由精神之可得。這無異於符合

poignant, and it is also good at using contradictory grammar or using "butterfly", "snow", and "fire" to imply Zen. It seems that his self-sufficient poetic heart is far away from the world, and life has tempered his strong will and simplicity early on. However, from the perspective of seeking poetic beauty, one cannot but admire the poet's artistic ingenuity.

In fact, Zhou Mengdie's poems were deeply influenced by Zhuangzi in the early days. His perception of life and death, both Zhuangzi and Zen, is so profound and empty, which makes people feel lost after reading it. This is the charm of poetry. However, he has carefully studied Buddhism and even the philosophy in the Koran; and the influence of the classical culture he received since he was a child has subtly influenced him, forming a neo-classical language style, which has penetrated into the depths of his soul. For example, the first few sentences in the poem *A Happy Excursion* have the frustrating syllables of Song Ci. Therefore, Zhuangzi's aesthetics is philosophy, and it is also the spiritual home that Zhou Mengdie seeks; he uses his own artistic practice to give poetry a new life. This point is compatible with the essential requirements of Taoist aesthetics.

As the German philosopher Immanuel Kant (1724-1804) said, all the highest beauty makes people melancholy, and it seems to be lost all of a sudden, like a wandering man missing his hometown. It is this kind of nostalgia that is reflected in Zhou Mengdie's poems, which is the coexistence of the pursuit of spiritual transcendence and loss of emotion, and often directly demonstrates the momentary joy of life or the availability of free spirit through the experience generated in dreams

莊子美學的遊世情懷，也是詩人在詩美探索上企以達到「物化」即主客體相互泯合的境界或藝術追求。從總體看，詩人晚期之作更趨於寧靜、恬淡、感情轉向對人生哲理的開掘；在詩的形式上，韻律感增強。本文試圖運用莊子美學內涵作為現代詩〈消遙遊〉及〈六月〉的閱讀策略，並嘗試對文本中所透顯的詩性特質和生命情調作一詮釋。總之，無論是以此來探析長於形象描繪，或可加深瞭解字句多有來歷復有禪思的周夢蝶的詩歌。

　　　　　註 1.周夢蝶，《還魂草》，臺北，領導出版社，
　　　　　　　1978 年，頁 66-67。
　　　　　註 2.周夢蝶，《還魂草》，臺北，領導出版社，
　　　　　　　1978 年，頁 48-19。
　　　　　－2012.5.7 作
　　　　　－河南省《商丘師範學院學報》，2013 年第 1 期，
　　　　　　　頁 24-

or the fusion of things and me. This is tantamount to the wandering feelings in line with Zhuangzi's aesthetics, and it is also the poet's pursuit of "materialization" in the exploration of poetic beauty, that is, the state or artistic pursuit of the mutual obliteration of subject and object. On the whole, the late works of the poet tend to be more peaceful, tranquil, and emotionally turned to the exploration of the philosophy of life; in the form of poetry, the sense of rhythm is enhanced. This article attempts to use Zhuangzi's aesthetic connotation as a reading strategy for the modern poems *A Happy Excursion* and *June*, and tries to interpret the poetic characteristics and life sentiments revealed in the texts. In short, whether it is used to explore and analyze Zhou Mengdie's poems, which are good at image description, or to deepen the understanding of Zhou Mengdie's poems, which have many origins and meditation.

Note 1. Zhou Mengdie, *Resurrection Grass*, Taipei, Leader Publishing House, 1978, pp. 66-67.

Note 2. Zhou Mengdie, *Resurrection Grass*, Taipei, Leader Publishing House, 1978, pp. 48-19.

12. 追尋深化藝術的儒者——
楊牧詩歌的風格特質

博達深沉的精神內涵

　　楊牧〈1940-〉本名王靖獻，是臺灣著名的現代詩人、散文家。生於花蓮，獲美國柏克萊大學比較文學博士，曾任華盛頓大學教授，羈美多年，現任教於東華大學等校，2000年曾獲國家文藝獎。作者擅用滄桑的筆調探觸現實與理想的關照，以深化自己藝術生命為基點，自詩裡散發令人揮之不去的心底烙印。他的作品風神獨具，著重在精神意境的感悟，一方面源自中國古典文學的賦予，另一方面則是西方文化之生命義理；經過心靈形式的統合整理，將情感轉化為抽象的質素結構中，不僅給予具傳奇性的詩想空間，也同時飽蘊愛情的夢幻聯想與孤獨感。

　　楊牧的詩歌，給我的感覺是，優柔善感的線性之下，夾著悵惋凝重的沉澱色彩；能敏銳的捕捉生活經驗與想像溶入

12. Pursuing Confucianists Who Deepened Art

—the Style and Characteristics of Yang Mu's Poetry

Broad and Deep Spiritual Connotation

Yang Mu (1940-), whose real name is Wang Jingxian, is a famous modern poet and essayist in Taiwan. Born in Hualien, he received a Ph.D. in comparative literature from the University of Berkeley in the United States. He was a professor at the University of Washington for many years. He is currently teaching at Donghua University and other universities. The author is good at using vicissitudes of writing to explore the care of reality and ideals, and based on deepening his own artistic life, he exudes a lingering imprint in his heart from his poems. His works are unique in style and focus on the perception of spiritual artistic conception. On the one hand, they are endowed by classical Chinese literature, and on the other hand, they are the meaning of life in Western culture; through the integration and arrangement of spiritual forms, emotions are transformed into abstract quality structures. In it, it not only gives space for legendary poetic imagination, but also full of dreamy associations and loneliness of love.

Yang Mu's poems give me the feeling that under the soft and sensitive lines, there are sad and solemn precipitation colors; they can keenly capture life precipitation

創作，從而建構出以詩去解讀生命的現象、或記述與時間歷
史的抗衡，去呈現自己在外在環境所禁錮下的各種情境的心
理張力。其實，他的許多作品都深刻地去提揭詩藝創作的企
圖：營造一個靜默、超塵、極度精誠和完美的真境。看得出，
在凝望著時間和生命交互作用的記憶中，他在努力地以自身
生命的焠煉，表現出對追求超自我的崇高性。或者說，楊牧
的詩來自心靈國度之美，無論是自然的或是抽象的，他都坦
率地給讀者提供了一個「富有空間的穿透性」的想像空間。

以自然為師

　　楊牧 32 歲以前的筆名爲葉珊，之後，改名爲楊牧。在他
身上，有著許多浪漫主義的人格基因與兼含人文關懷的理想
主義。自 1972 年後改用楊牧作為新筆名後，其作品風格越來
越富於理性和關注社會寫實的論述。他的胸懷由孤獨沉鬱轉
而向批判社會、追求真理敞開。楊牧曾說：「變不是一件容易
的事，然而不變即是死亡，變是一種痛苦的經驗，但痛苦也
是生命的真實。」他開始直面人生，將現實性的理想渴求當是
一種高精神，對生命本真的抒寫裡，質樸而靈敏，意象語言
幽微而堅毅，更將他轉化為崇高人格的象徵符號。楊牧晚年，
回歸花蓮鄉土，在這裏，山海充沛的詩意，引領著他在藝術

colors; they can keenly capture life experience and imagination and integrate them into creation, thus constructing the phenomenon of interpreting life through poetry, or describe the confrontation with time and history, to present the psychological tension of various situations under the confinement of the external environment. In fact, many of his works profoundly reveal the intention of poetic creation: to create a quiet, supernatural, extremely sincere and perfect real environment. It can be seen that in the memory of staring at the interaction of time and life, he is trying hard to show the nobility of pursuing the superego with the refinement of his own life. In other words, Yang Mu's poems come from the beauty of the spiritual realm, whether they are natural or abstract, he frankly provides readers with an imaginary space "full of spatial penetration".

Learn from Nature

Before the age of 32, Yang Mu's pen name was Ye Shan, and later he changed his name to Yang Mu. In him, there are many romantic personality genes and idealism with humanistic care. After using Yang Mu as his new pen name in 1972, his work style has become more and more rational and concerned with social realism. His mind turned from being lonely and depressed to criticizing society and pursuing truth. Yang Mu once said: "Change is not an easy thing, but the same is death, and change is a painful experience, but pain is also the reality of life." He began to face life directly, and regarded the ideal of reality as a high spirit. In the true description of life, it is simple and sensitive, and the image language is subtle and firm, which turns him into a symbol of noble personality. In his later years, Yang Mu returned to the hometown of Hualien. Here, the abundant poetry of mountains and seas

追求的道路上，傾向探尋自然之序，再次獲得更單純、更撼人心魄的精神力度。我們不妨先摘引一首楊牧早期的詩〈雪止〉看看：

> 我不能不向前走
> 因為我聽見一聲嘆息
> 像臘梅的香氣暗暗傳來
> 我聽見翻書的聲音...
> 你的夢讓我來解析
> 我自異鄉回來，為你印證
> 晨昏氣溫的差距，若是
> 你還覺得冷，你不如把我
> 放進壁爐裡，為今夜
> 重新生起一堆火

此詩顯示出雪止與新火兩個意象的結合，構成一種沉靜幽深的白色與熾熱的爐火及光燄對比作為抽象背景，以襯托楊牧側身回首戀情的形象。當思念如潮，詩人的困境便在矛盾的兩難之中了。一時覺詩人發出的種種感情信息，就在遙遠的夢土傳來臘梅的暗香下，觸及得更深些。

楊牧在《楊牧詩集》「自序」中說：「此書包括 1986 年至 2006 年間的作品。物換星移，荏苒數十寒暑，偶爾有些陌生的警覺，但也不乏因為體會到其中一些雖不能盡知，卻多少也諳識有餘的奧秘，關於時間和空間，心靈的假象和神

led him on the road of artistic pursuit, tending to explore the order of nature, and once again obtain a more pure and soul-stirring spiritual strength. Let us first quote an early poem *Xue Zhi* by Yang Mu:

> *I can't move forward*
> *Because I heard a sigh*
> *Like the fragrance of wintersweet came secretly*
> *I heard the sound of flipping the book...*
> *let me analyze your dream*
> *I came back from a foreign land to testify for you*
> *The temperature difference between morning and evening, if*
> *You still feel cold, why don't you take me*
> *Put in the fireplace for tonight*
> *Rekindle a fire*

This poem shows the combination of the two images of Xuezhi and Xinhuo, forming a quiet and deep white contrast with the hot fire and flames as an abstract background, to set off the image of Yang Mu looking back at his love affair sideways. When longing is like a tide, the plight of the poet is in the dilemma of contradiction. For a moment, I felt that the various emotional messages sent by the poet touched deeper under the fragrance of wintersweet from the distant dream land.

Yang Mu said in the preface of *The Collected Poems of Yang Mu*: "This book includes works from 1986 to 2006. Things change and the stars move, and dozens of cold and summer, and occasionally there are strange vigilances, but there is no lack of awareness because some of them are not enough. The mysteries of time and space, the illusion of the mind and the truth of the mind, etc., which are well

志的真諦之類，一些屬於嚴謹縝密的詩的奧秘，所以招致的感慨，何曾忘懷。」我想，他所強調的是，像一切純情的藝術家，詩是楊牧抗拒現實的工具；在詩中他的生命之流得到了更多地自由釋放，是心靈的反努，它介乎孤獨與沉默意志的微妙頃間……，亦是美學範疇最純粹極致的實現。

比如我喜歡的<雷池>，楊牧以清新淡雅的筆風，將「時間—影像」凝止凍結在回憶的某個瞬間，正因為靜止，所以才能直接逼顯出愛情在時間的幻化中，只有詩的見證使不可見的時間成為可見。此詩畫面單純而意蘊雋永，有戀人間的真性羞澀的意趣：

> 我們像
> 擱淺的小舟被吹在一起
> 羞澀地招呼著卻不敢相識
> 怕——怕潮來時又把我們
> 送回那失去方向的大河
> 思念於憂傷怕不如淡忘於
> 孤獨的航行，於風波的隱喻
> 於一生的期待，一點驚喜
> 於一次不可能重逢的遭遇

當然這些浪漫主義的情詩，從《水之湄》到《花季》到《燈船》，在楊牧藝術生涯初期就已認定。在《有人》的後記，楊牧做了這樣的告白：「我對於詩的抒情功能，即使書

known, but more or less well understood, are mysteries that belong to rigorous and meticulous poetry, so the emotions they arouse have never been forgotten." I think, what he emphasized, like all pure artists, poetry is Yang Mu's tool to resist reality. In poetry, his life stream is released more freely, it is the rumination of the soul, it is between loneliness and the subtle moment of silent will... is also the purest and ultimate realization of aesthetics.

For example, in my favorite *Thunder Pool*, Yang Mu freezes "time-image" in a certain moment of memory with a fresh and elegant style of writing. It is precisely because of the stillness that he can directly show love in the illusion of time. Only the poetic witness makes visible the invisible time. The picture of this poem is simple but meaningful, and has the true shyness of lovers:

> *We are like*
> *Stranded boats blown together*
> *Greeting shyly but not daring to know each other*
> *Afraid — afraid that when the tide comes again we will be*
> *Send back the great river that has lost its direction*
> *Thinking about sadness is worse than forgetting*
> *A lonely voyage, a metaphor for storms*
> *In the expectation of a lifetime, a little surprise*
> *In an impossible encounter*

Of course, these romantic love poems, from *The Lake of Water* to *Flower Season* to *Light Boat*, have been recognized in the early stage of Yang Mu's artistic career. In the postscript, Yang Mu made this confession: "for me,

的是小我之情，因其心思極小而映現宇宙之大何嘗不可於精
微中把握理解，對於這些，我絕不懷疑。」然而，楊牧成熟
後的詩風，主要體現在他對家國情感的心緒至現實社會的黑
暗有更直接的悲愴之痛，從對家鄉的想望到書寫生命圓融、
族人簡樸、閑適的意趣，正是他晚年心境趨於平靜淡泊的一
種反映。

楊牧：詩人經典中的圖像

　　楊牧詩歌的特質是以「抒情沈靜」的基調來昭示藝術在
韶光流逝中的片刻，它寫盡俗世間最沒有矯飾的「詩生態」，
晚期作品更顯得面貌多樣，倒也頗吻合時代節奏性，而構成
一種清冷純淨的氣質，更積極於詩歌藝術之「純粹性」的探
求。楊牧曾說，花蓮是「我的秘密武器」，他對生長土地的情
感與關懷，是楊牧在一步一履痕的耕耘歷程中，既不刻意於
是鄉土的歌頌，也不以表現於詩論之成就為滿足；而是以更
沉潛的色彩、溫情而平和的生命內涵，表現出一個為詩歌開
拓藝術者的文人風範，也表現於他的逸筆下。比如這首<花
蓮>，就是品嚐楊牧詩歌以往未曾有過的美感：

　　你必須
　　和我一樣廣闊，體會更深；
　　戰爭未曾改變我們，所以
　　任何挫折都不許改變你

the lyrical function of poetry, even if the book is about personal feelings, because of its tiny mind, it reflects the vastness of the universe. Why can't I grasp and understand it in a subtle way? I have no doubts about these." However, Yang Mu's mature poetic style is mainly reflected in his more direct sorrowful pain from the emotions of his family and country to the darkness of the real society, from his longing for his hometown to writing about the harmony of life. The simple and leisurely taste of the family members is just a reflection of his calm and indifferent state of mind in his later years.

Yang Mu: Images in the Poet's Classics

The characteristic of Yang Mu's poetry is to use the keynote of "lyrical tranquility" to show the moment of art in the passage of time. It expresses the most unpretentious "poetic ecology" in the world, and form a cool and pure temperament, and more actively explore the "purity" of poetry art. Yang Mu once said that Hualien is "my secret weapon". His emotion and care for the growing land are the result of Yang Mu's cultivation process step by step. For satisfaction; but with more submerged colors, warm and peaceful life connotation, showing the style of a literati who pioneered art for poetry, and it is also expressed in his easy pen. For example, this song *Hualien* is to taste the beauty that Yang Mu's poems have never had before:

> *You must*
> *As broad as I am, deeper in experience;*
> *War never changed us, so*
> *No setbacks are allowed to change you*

　　這首詩在畫面中更趨自如，或許楊牧在緬舊的感懷之中，讓我們重溫到浪遊異國的漂泊心事與對花蓮部落的悲憫的那種情思蘊藉。詩人已將生命的精美片斷，以詩歌作為最終的心靈歸宿與完成；而我從中也感受到閱讀其詩歌的喜悅與豐足。

　　　　　　　　　　－2010.12.21 作

　　　　　　　－臺灣臺北「國圖」刊物，《全國新書資訊月刊》，
　　　　　　　　　2012 年 4 月，第 160 期，頁 27-30。

This poem is more comfortable in the picture. Perhaps Yang Mu, in his nostalgia for the past, allows us to relive the wandering thoughts of wandering in foreign countries and the kind of emotional connotation of compassion for the Hualien tribe. The poet has used poetry as the ultimate spiritual destination and completion of the exquisite fragments of life; and I also feel the joy and abundance of reading his poems.

13. 洛夫詩中的禪道精神

摘要：洛夫詩作的整個思維中有個基本元素：禪道精神。這個元素經不斷演繹而匯出其美學思想，還有待於深入進行研究和深化。

關鍵字：詩人；詩歌；莊子；美學；禪道

一、洛夫：現代詩的一代宗匠

洛夫（1928 年—2018 年），本名莫運端，湖南衡陽人，淡江大學英語系畢業，曾任教于東吳大學、北京師範大學、中國華僑大學。出版詩集、散文、評論、譯著等多種，獲臺灣"文藝獎"等殊榮，有"詩魔"之稱。洛夫詩作的整個思維中有個基本元素：禪道精神。這個元素經不斷演繹而匯出其美學思想，還有待於深入研究和深化。

在當代詩壇，洛夫是現代詩的一代宗匠。他先是向西方現代主義的注目，借鑒了與東方詩學極不同的藝術手法；中年以後，開始思考回歸傳統的問題，轉而對老、莊、禪道精神的吸收與超現實技巧的追求。尤以莊子思想影響最深，這

13. The Zen Spirit in Luo Fu's Poems

Summary: There is a fundamental element in Luo Fu's entire thought: the spirits of Zen and Taoism. After continuous transformation, this element has led to his aesthetics of poetry, and it needs to be studied further.

Key words: poet, poetry, Chuang Chou, aesthetics, Zen and Taoism

1. Luo Fu: A Master of Modern Poetry

Luo Fu (1928-2018), whose real name was Mo Yunduan, was born in Hengyang, Hunan. He graduated from the English Department of Tamkang University and taught at Soochow University, Beijing Normal University, and Huaqiao University. He has published a variety of poetry collections, essays, reviews, translations, etc., and has won Taiwan's "Literary Award" and other honors, known as the "Poetry Demon". There is a basic element in the whole thinking of Luo Fu's poems: the spirit of Zen. This element has been continuously deduced to bring out its aesthetic thought, which needs to be further studied and deepened.

In the contemporary poetry world, Luo Fu is a master of modern poetry. He first paid attention to Western modernism and borrowed artistic techniques that are very different from Eastern poetics; after middle age, he began to think about the problem of returning to tradition, and turned to the absorption of the spirit of Laozi, Zhuangzi,

便出現了具有中西文化合璧色彩的詩作。禪宗思想是講求現實世界的"空"與超現實世界的"真如",也就是外在世界的可感與永恆。而洛夫也常以直覺經驗和藝術感覺激發創作靈感,欲臻於和大自然融合匯通的空靈境界。所不同的是,詩人不同于古代的王維、孟浩然等詩人和山水自然擁抱時的純淨和禪悟時的心向專一,而是企圖訴諸具有穿透性的語言,去體現超越時空的生命自由、似也在追求一種禪意。因而,其詩歌具有如下的內涵:

(一)瞭解人與自然的親和關係,而不以對立的態度去超克它。《莊子》第一篇《消遙遊》中有"天之蒼蒼,其正色邪?其遠而無所至極邪?"說明了莊子的心胸是極為自然開闊、精神豁達。洛夫擅於由大自然的默察中而伸張無言之美,精神面貌,這與莊子是一致的。(二)瞭解時間接連的無限流動性與死生無常的變化性。莊子在《秋水》篇上雲:"夫物量無窮,時無止,分無常,終始無故。……故得而不喜,失而不憂,知分之無常也……"洛夫也瞭解無限時空中的死生得失之事,因而能培養出一種開朗曠達的心懷,用以開展高度的

and Zen and the pursuit of surreal techniques. In particular, Zhuangzi's thoughts have the deepest influence, and thus there are poems with the combination of Chinese and Western cultures. Zen thought emphasizes the "emptiness" of the real world and the "truth" of the surreal world, that is, the sensibility and eternity of the external world. And Luo Fu often inspires creation with intuitive experience and artistic sense, trying to reach the ethereal realm of integration with nature. The difference is that the poets are different from the ancient Wang Wei, Meng Haoran and other poets who embraced the nature of mountains and rivers when they embraced the purity and single-mindedness when they enlightened to Zen, but tried to resort to penetrating language to embody the freedom of life. It seems that he is also pursuing a kind of Zen. Therefore, his poems have the following connotations:

(1) Understand the affinity between man and nature, and not overcome it with an opposing attitude. In the first chapter of *Free Wandering* of *Zhuangzi*: "the sky is blue, but its righteousness is evil? It is far away and nothing is extremely evil?" It shows that Zhuangzi's mind is extremely natural and open-minded, and his spirit is open-minded. Luo Fu is good at exaggerating the silent beauty and spiritual outlook from the silent observation of nature, which is consistent with Zhuangzi. (2) Understand the infinite fluidity of continuous time and the variability of life and death. Zhuangzi said in *Autumn Waters*: "The quantity of things is infinite, the time is endless, the division is impermanent, and the beginning and the beginning are without reason...." So you don't like it when you get it, and you don't worry about it. The gains and losses of life and death in time and space can cultivate a kind of open-minded mind, which can be used to develop

人生境界。這點與莊子也有相通之處。本文想探討的,正是
洛夫詩的內在力度及其價值的表現所在。

二、詩作賞析

　　洛夫詩歌名震華語詩壇之因,是它吸取了中國道家美學
和禪宗文化的藝術精神,又把西方超現實主義詩歌取為己用
而掀起臺灣詩壇一種新的詩歌潮流。此外,他還追求詩的空
靈美。他講虛、講玄,但絕非故弄玄虛,而是透過自己的心
靈體味去揭示大自然的奧秘和延伸臺灣詩學的生長領域。比
如選自《洛夫詩鈔》(洛夫經典詩作手鈔本)的《春醒》:

　　　枯葉
　　　帶著蟲子
　　　飛

　　　歲月
　　　不驚

　　　蛺蝶
　　　從穢土中悠悠醒來

　　　一窩蛇
　　　剛換了新衣
　　　體香
　　　有桃花的味道

a high level of life. This point is also similar to Zhuangzi. What this article wants to explore is precisely the expression of the inner strength and value of Luo Fu's poems.

2. Poetry Appreciation

The reason why Luo Fu's poetry is famous in the circle of Chinese poetry is that it absorbed the artistic spirit of Chinese Taoist aesthetics and Zen culture, and took Western surrealist poetry for its own use, which set off a new poetry trend in Taiwan poetry circle. In addition, he also pursues the ethereal beauty of poetry. He talks about fiction and mysticism, but he is definitely not trying to be mystical. Instead, he reveals the mysteries of nature and expands the growth field of Taiwanese poetics through his own spiritual experience. For example, *Spring Awakening* from *Luofu's Poetry Notes*:

Dead leaves
With bugs
Fly

Years
Not surprised

Nymph
Waking up from the filth

Nest of snakes
Just got new clothes
Body scent
It smells like peach blossom

　　淡淡幾筆，就展現了春天到來的盎然生機，初期詩歌還比較淡遠，清悠；但也表現了洛夫詩想裡有一種素樸、醇厚的泥土氣息和情感的純真。

　　中年以後，洛夫執著地追求精神價值，菲薄物質享受；詩作有的選取古代的歷史人物直接吟詠，有的借古代的某些典故引發詩情。如原載 1956 年《創世紀》詩雜誌的早期之作《煙囪》，詩人則道出一種淡淡的情愁與人生滄桑的神秘感：

　　　蠹立於漠漠的斜陽裡，
　　　風撩起黑髮，而瘦長的投影靜止，
　　　那城牆下便有點寂寞，有點愴涼。
　　　我是一隻想飛的煙囪。

　　　俯首望著那條長長的護城河，
　　　河水盈盈，流不盡千古的胭脂殘粉，
　　　誰使我禁錮，使我溯不到夢的源頭？
　　　宮宇傾圮，那騎樓上敲鐘的老人依舊，
　　　鐘聲清越依舊。

A few strokes show the vitality of the coming of spring, and the early poems are relatively distant and clear; but it also shows that there is a simple, mellow earthy flavor and emotional innocence in Luo Fu's poetry.

After middle age, Luo Fu persistently pursued spiritual value and neglected material enjoyment; some of his poems chose ancient historical figures to sing directly, and some used some ancient allusions to arouse poetic sentiment. For example, the early work *The Chimney* originally published in the *Genesis* poetry magazine in 1956, the poet expresses a faint sense of melancholy and the mystery of the vicissitudes of life:

> *Standing in the deserted setting sun,*
> *The wind lifts the black hair, and the slender projection*
> * stands still,*
> *It was a little lonely and a little sad under the city wall.*
> *I am a chimney that wants to fly.*

> *Looking down at the long moat,*
> *The river is full of rouge residues that can't flow through*
> * the ages,*
> *Who imprisoned me and made me unable to trace the*
> * source of my dreams?*
> *The palace collapsed, but the old man ringing the bell on*
> * the arcade remained the same,*
> *The bell still rings clearer.*

我想遠遊，哦，那長長的河，那青青的山，

如能化為一隻凌雲的野鶴，

甚至一位微塵，一片輕煙……

而今，我只是一片瘦長的投影，

——讓人寂寞

　　在詩人筆下，「煙囪」其實是一個忍受了孤獨又想掙脫孤
獨的生命體，他把感情隱進具體意象中，給讀者留下更多的
思索空間。

　　再如這首 1983 年的《枯魚之肆》，「枯魚之肆」的解釋原
指無法挽救的境地。詩題源自中國古代戰國時代《莊子》外
物篇的片斷：“周曰：‘諾。我且南游吳越之王，激西江之水
而迎子，可乎？’鮒魚曰：‘吾失我常與，我無所處。吾得鬥
升之水然活耳，君乃言此，曾不如早索我於枯魚之肆！’”這
典故的背景是說，莊子家貧，所以去向監河侯借糧。監河侯
說：“好。等我收到地租，就借給你三百金，可以嗎？”莊子
見監河侯不願馬上借糧，有點生氣，臉色難看地說：“我昨天
來這兒的時候，聽到路上有個聲音在叫我。我回頭一看，只
見車輪碾過的車轍中，有一條鮒魚。我問：“鮒魚啊，你在這

I want to travel far, oh, that long river, that green mountain,
If I can turn into a wild crane that hovers over the clouds,
Even a speck of dust, a puff of smoke...
Now, I'm just a slender projection,
— It makes people lonely.

In the poet's writing, the "chimney" is actually a living being who has endured loneliness and wants to get rid of it. He hides his emotions in specific images, leaving more room for readers to think.

Another example is this 1983 song *The Place of the Dead Fish*. The interpretation of *The Place of the Dry Fish* originally refers to an irreparable situation. The title of the poem comes from a fragment of Zhuangzi in the Warring States Period in ancient China: "Zhou said: 'No. I will travel south to the king of Wu and Yue, and the water of the Xijiang River will meet my son. Is it possible?' Fish said: 'I If I lose my constant companion, I have nowhere to go. I have won the water of fighting and rising, but if you say this, it would be better to ask me to live in the dry fish!'" The background of this allusion is that Zhuangzi's family is poor, so go to Jianhehou to borrow food. The Marquis of Jianhe said, "Okay. When I receive the land rent, I can lend you three hundred gold, okay?" Seeing that Marquis Jianhe didn't want to borrow the grain immediately, Zhuangzi got a little angry, and said with an ugly face, "I came here yesterday. When I was walking, I heard a voice calling me on the road. I looked back and saw a squid in the rut where the wheels had run over. I asked, "Squid, what are you doing here?" The fish said, "I came from the East China Sea, and I'm stuck here." "Do you have a bucket or a liter of water to

兒幹什麼呢？"鮒魚說："我是從東海來的，被困在這兒了。您有一鬥或者一升水救活我嗎？"我說："好。我這就去遊說吳越之王 ，請他開鑿運河，把長江的水引過來救你，可以嗎？"鮒魚生氣地說："現在我都被困在這兒了，只需要一鬥或者一升的水就能活命。如果像你這麼說，不如早點到賣幹魚的店裡去找我好了！"洛夫則藉此詩題來反思人的處境：

　　每天路過
　　便想到口渴
　　想到鞭痕似的涸轍
　　以及魚目中好大的
　　一片空白

　　毋需掩鼻而過
　　或作不屑於問聞之態
　　斤斤計較的無非是去鰓去鱗
　　至於那些腐臭的鯉魚
　　何嘗不是一一躍龍門而來
　　只是他們的下游
　　止於砧板

　　洛夫說他每天路過賣魚幹的小店，「便想到口渴」，實際已道出他聯想到鮒魚在車轍中只要借鬥升之水即可活命，而如果去遊說吳越之王，開鑿運河，把長江的水引過來，鮒魚

save me?" I said: "Okay. I'm going to lobby the king of
Wuyue and ask him to dig a canal and draw the water from
the Yangtze River to save you, is that okay? The fish said
angrily, "Now I'm trapped here, and I only need a bucket
or a liter of water to survive." If it's like you say, why
don't you go to the shop selling dried fish and find me
sooner! Luo Fu uses this poem title to reflect on the
human situation:

Passing by every day
Think of thirst
Think of a dry rut like a welt
And the big fish eyes
Blank

No need to hide your nose
Or disdain to ask questions
The only thing that cares about is to remove the gills and scales
As for those rancid carp
Why didn't they jump over the dragon gate one by one
Just their downstream
Stop at the cutting board

Luo Fu said that when he passed by a small shop
selling dried fish every day, "I thought of being thirsty."
In fact, he has already said that he thinks that a carp can
survive in a rut by borrowing a bucket of water, and if you
go to lobby the king of Wuyue. The canals were dug to

早已渴死了。這個道理很簡單。但在我們的日常生活中,言過其實、形式主義豈不是比比皆是。洛夫將枯魚與砧板聯繫起來,感慨古今,表達了對現實中的魚肉鄉民與強權競爭下的處境與惋惜,頗具古典神韻。

洛夫崇尚簡約,從不對客觀事物做具體細緻的描摹。比如我所喜歡的這首小詩《窗下》,體現出一種內在的力度和浪漫情懷:

> 當暮色裝飾著雨後的窗子
> 我便從這裡探測遠山的深度
>
> 在窗玻璃上呵一口氣
> 再用手指畫一條長長的小路
> 以及小路盡頭的
> 一個背影
>
> 有人從雨中而去

詩中的童真和思情,是那些物欲味濃的詩無法比擬的。再如這首《河畔墓園——為亡母上墳小記》,就把我們帶入了一個悽楚的世界:

> 膝蓋有些些
> 不像痛的

bring the water from the Yangtze River, and the carp had already died of thirst. The reason is very simple. But in our daily life, exaggeration and formalism abound. Luo Fu connects the dead fish with the chopping board, feeling the past and the present, and expresses the plight and regret of the fish and meat villagers in reality under the competition of power, which is quite classical.

Luo Fu advocates simplicity and never makes specific and detailed descriptions of objective things. For example, my favorite little poem *Under the Window* embodies a kind of inner strength and romantic feelings:

When twilight adorns the windows after the rain
From here I probe the depths of the distant mountains

Breath on the window pane
Then draw a long path with your finger
And at the end of the path
A back view

Someone walks out of the rain

The childlike innocence and sentimentality in the poems are incomparable to those poems with a strong material desire. Another example is this song *The Cemetery by the River-A Little Note on Visiting the Grave for the Dead Mother*, which brings us into a sad world:

Some knees
Not painful

痛

在黃土上跪下時

我試著伸腕

握你薊草般的手

剛下過一場小雨

我為你

運來一整條河的水

流自

我積雪初融的眼睛

我跪著。偷覷

一株狗尾草繞過墳地

跑了一大圈

又回到我擱置額頭的土

我一把連根拔起

鬚鬚上還留有

你微溫的鼻息

　　詩裡那種對母親的追憶所付出的力量和達到的精神昇華，仍令人感傷。事實上，洛夫一生均未與愛情詩絕緣，如這首經典之作《因為風的緣故》，即寫出了青年時代約會時苦苦的等待：

昨日我沿著河岸

漫步到

Pain
When kneeling on the loess
I try to stretch my wrist
Hold your thistle hand
It just rained a little
I for you
Bring a whole river of water
Flow from
My snow-covered eyes

I kneel. sneak a peek
A foxtail skirts the cemetery
Ran a big circle
Back to the soil where I put my forehead
I uprooted
Still left on the mustache
Your warm breath

The strength and spiritual sublimation achieved by the memory of the mother in the poem are still sentimental. In fact, Luo Fu has never been insulated from love poems in his life, such as this classic *Because of the Wind*, which expresses the bitter waiting when dating in youth:

Yesterday I walked along the river bank
Stroll to

蘆葦彎腰喝水的地方
順便請煙囪
在天空為我寫一封長長的信
潦是潦草了些
而我的心意
則明亮亦如你窗前的燭光
稍有曖昧之處
勢所難免
因為風的緣故

此信你能否看懂並不重要
重要的是
你務必在雛菊尚未全部凋謝之前
趕快發怒，或者發笑
趕快從箱子裡找出我那件薄衫子
趕快對鏡梳你那又黑又柔的嫵媚
然後以整生的愛
點燃一盞燈
我是火
隨時可能會熄滅
因為風的緣故

　　這些感性的抒情詩句，不僅充分展現了洛夫內心世界對
愛情的忠貞不渝，而且也把故事情節一步一步向前推進，在
抒情與敘事的結合上達到了融合為一的境地。

Where the reeds stoop to drink
Chimney please
Write me a long letter in the sky
Scribbled
And my heart
It's as bright as the candlelight at your window
Slightly ambiguous
Inevitable
Because of the wind

It doesn't matter whether you understand this letter or not
Important is
You must be before all the daisies wither
Get angry or laugh
Quickly find my thin shirt from the box
Hurry up and comb your black and soft charm in the mirror
Then with a whole life of love
Light a lamp
I am fire
May go out at any time
Because of the wind

These emotional lyric lines not only fully demonstrate Luo Fu's inner world's unswerving loyalty to love, but also advance the storyline step by step, achieving a fusion of lyricism and narrative.

接著，這首《布袋蓮的下午》，是以幽默的口吻、機智的暗喻，探索人生的哲理：

> 下午。池水中
> 擁擠著一叢叢懷孕的布袋蓮
> 這個夏天很寂寞
> 要生，就生一池青蛙吧
>
> 唉，問題是
> 我們只是虛胖

由於詩人閱歷增多，思考也多了。這裡，像是在啟示他人，有時也要時時審視自己，可貴的是其中的自省與自律意識。在時下，是多麼需要的一種精神啊。最後推介這首《眾荷喧嘩》，禪境的體悟與荷相遇的機緣，令人莞爾：

> 眾荷喧嘩
> 而你是挨我最近
> 最靜，最最溫婉的一朵
> 要看，就看荷去吧
> 我就喜歡看你撐著一把碧油傘
> 從水中升起
>
> 我向池心

Then, this song *Afternoon of Budailian* explores the philosophy of life in a humorous tone and witty metaphors:

Afternoon, pool water
Crowded clumps of pregnant bagliapes
This summer is lonely
If you want to give birth, give birth to a pond of frogs

Alas, the problem is
We're just puffy

As the poet has more experience, he thinks more. Here, it seems to be inspiring others, and sometimes you have to examine yourself from time to time. What is valuable is the awareness of self-examination and self-discipline. Nowadays, what a spirit is needed. Finally, I would like to recommend this song *The Loudness of Many Lotuses*. The realization of the Zen realm and the chance of encountering lotuses make people smile:

All the noise
And you are the closest to me
The quietest, most gentle flower
If you want to see, let's see He
I just like to see you holding a green umbrella

Rising from the water I Xiang Chi Xin

輕輕扔過去一拉石子
你的臉
便譁然紅了起來
驚起的
一隻水鳥
如火焰般掠過對岸的柳枝
再靠近一些
只要再靠我近一點
便可聽到
水珠在你掌心滴溜溜地轉

你是喧嘩的荷池中
一朵最最安靜的
夕陽
蟬鳴依舊
依舊如你獨立眾荷中時的寂寂

我走了，走了一半又停住
等你
等你輕聲喚我

　　洛夫對詩神的摯愛隨著年齡而與日俱增，詩人不僅把山
河、大地、輕風、各種植物等自然景物用擬人化的手法把它
們寫活，或前景後情，或前情後景，或情景齊到，使人變得
與大自然更融合無間了。

Lightly throw a stone
Your face
Turned red
Startled
A water bird
Willow branches across the bank like flames
Come closer
Just come closer
Can be heard
Drops of water are rolling in your palm

You are in the noisy lotus pond
One of the quietest
Sunset
Cicadas are still singing
Still as silent as when you were alone among the lotus

I'm gone, I'm halfway there and I stop
Wait for you
Wait for you to call me softly

Luo Fu's love for the god of poetry grows with age. The poet not only anthropomorphizes natural scenery such as mountains and rivers, the earth, breeze, and various plants, or anthropomorphizes them, or foreground and background, or foreground and background, or the scene is here, making people more integrated with nature.

三、洛夫詩中的禪道精神

洛夫一生也有不少詩作是書寫對臺灣土地上生活的所見所思的，對臺灣思念之情仍是他身上的一根臍帶。如《蟋蟀之歌》、《美濃鄉村偶見》、《八斗子物語》、《平溪八行》、《行過墾丁草原》等。移民後的洛夫，仍經常往返於中國大陸以及中國香港和臺灣。這勇敢的種子，正是他永遠開出藝術探索之花的成因。在《莊子》中"生物進化"思想，雖然有些看似荒誕內容，如蝴蝶化鳥，馬生人之類。然而從生物進化論主要原理來看，有的可以從《莊子》書中找到原型思想。如生命起源于水中，由低級水草逐漸發展為植物、蟲、魚、獸、人，揭示生物演進的序列；同時也指出生物進化隨著生存環境變遷而變化等。凡此，說明了直到今天，莊子思想尚有它合理內涵與生命力。而洛夫詩歌中，也從"人"的自然原體性出發，他也跟莊子一樣，反對過分的享受與縱欲，也反對現代詩歌過度的思慮與謀劃。而且愈到晚年，越見其禪詩的光芒。如《夜宿寒山寺》、《背向大海》、《石濤寫意》等，這種禪道精神與現代詩的結合又非單純地復古或癡迷於某宗教，而是為禪道精神與現代主義的結合找到了一片綠茵。

3. The Zen Spirit in Luo Fu's Poems

Throughout his life, Luo Fu also wrote many poems about what he saw and thought about life on the land of Taiwan, and his nostalgia for Taiwan is still an umbilical cord in him. Such as *The Song of Crickets, Occasionally Seeing Meinong Village, The Story of Badouzi, Eight Lines of Pingxi, Walking Through the Kenting Grassland*, and so on. After immigrating, Luo Fu still often travels to and from mainland China, Hong Kong and Taiwan. This brave seed is the reason why he will always bloom the flower of artistic exploration. In *Zhuangzi*, the idea of "biological evolution" has some seemingly absurd content, such as butterfly turning into bird, horse giving birth to man and so on. However, from the perspective of the main principles of the theory of biological evolution, some of the original ideas can be found in the book *Zhuangzi*. For example, life originated in water, and gradually developed from low-level aquatic plants to plants, insects, fish, animals, and humans, revealing the sequence of biological evolution; at the same time, it also pointed out that biological evolution changes with the change of living environment. All this shows that until today, Zhuangzi's thought still has its reasonable connotation and vitality. In Luo Fu's poems, he also starts from the original nature of "human beings". Like Zhuangzi, he opposes excessive enjoyment and indulgence, and also opposes excessive thinking and planning in modern poetry. And as he got older, the more he saw the brilliance of his Zen poems. Such as *Night in Hanshan Temple, Back to the Sea, Shitao Freehand*, etc., this combination of Zen spirit and modern poetry is not simply retro or obsessed with a certain religion, but a combination of Zen spirit and modern poetry. The combination of doctrines found a piece of greenery.

　　綜上所述，洛夫詩歌之超越性美學的思想進路，在此撮其精義，概述其要：其一、洛夫詩歌中把禪宗的物化美學及無我之境等關係所含藏的核心思想與超越時空意象之美學轉化所代表的美學蘊含，闡述得更為明確、更完備；其二、洛夫順此理路，堅持走向與自然合一之路。其詩作常將莊子思想融入現代語境與當下生活之中，讓古典老、莊文本煥發新的現代意蘊，因此，研究莊子思想與其詩歌的關聯性，是有其必要性的。我認為，真正的詩人必須排除紛繁的矛盾與是非，以求得心靈解脫的途徑；而詩美的真義也必含時間、空間與心理的距離三方面的要素，且三者間有著不可分離的關係。研究洛夫詩歌價值觀念的取向不隨著不同時空的變遷而改變之因，是有其可取之處。當然，洛夫自我價值最後落腳點在於「真樸」。「真樸」是其主體意識自我覺醒，主體價值的自我裁定；而這種聯繫確定人與自然的承襲性，是洛夫從禪道精神中悟得自身價值的重要啟示。這或許就是其詩歌常受到東、西文學家的青睞，具有永恆不息的活力的原因吧。

　　　注・參見陳鼓應著，老莊新論，香港，中華書局，1993年2月重印，頁 253-255．

　　　—河南省《商丘師範學院學報》，2016 年第 2 期，第32 卷，總第 254 期，頁 9-11。

To sum up, here is a summary of Luo Fu's ideological approach to the aesthetics of transcendence in his poetry: first, the core of the relationship between Zen's materialized aesthetics and the state of no-self in Luo Fu's poems The aesthetic connotation represented by the aesthetic transformation of thoughts and images beyond time and space is expounded more clearly and more completely; secondly, Luo Fu follows this rationale and insists on the road of unity with nature. His poems often integrate Zhuangzi's thoughts into the modern context and current life, making the classical and Zhuangzi texts glow with new modern meanings. Therefore, it is necessary to study the relationship between Zhuangzi's thoughts and his poems. In my opinion, a real poet must get rid of the complicated contradictions and right and wrong in order to seek the way of spiritual liberation; and the true meaning of poetic beauty must also include three elements of time, space and psychological distance, and there is an inseparable relationship between the three. It is worthwhile to study the reason why the value orientation of Luo Fu's poetry does not change with the changes of different time and space. Of course, the final foothold of Luo Fu's self-worth lies in "authenticity". "Simplicity" is the self-awakening of the subject's consciousness and the self-judgment of the subject's value; and this connection confirms the inheritance of man and nature, which is an important revelation for Luo Fu to realize his own value from the spirit of Zen. This may be the reason why his poems are often favored by Eastern and Western writers and have eternal vitality.

Note: See Chen Guying, Lao Zhuang Xinlun, Hong Kong, Zhonghua Book Company, reprinted in February 1993, pp. 253-255.

14.席慕蓉的詩歌藝術

摘要：席慕蓉是近代中國詩史上影響深遠的女作家，其詩歌倍受讀者的青睞之因，在於其作品所抒發的細膩感人的真實情懷和對愛情的浮想聯翩，包羅萬有；在西方美學與浪漫思想的熔鑄下，透露出一種自然、清奇的氣逸。這裡，不想對她的思想傾向做進一步分析，僅想著重從其詩歌藝術本身，探索其對詩美的精湛創造和對新詩發展的貢獻。

關鍵字：席慕蓉，詩歌，藝術，浪漫思想

一、傳　略

　　席慕蓉（1943－），蒙古貴族出身，生於重慶，就讀於臺灣師範大學藝術系、比利時布魯塞爾皇家藝術學院畢業，曾任教東海大學於美術系。著有詩集、散文集、美術論著等多種。她是近代中國詩史上影響深遠的女作家，其詩歌倍受讀者的青睞之因在於作品所抒發的細膩感人的真實情懷和對愛情的浮想聯翩，包羅萬有；在西方美學與浪漫思想的熔鑄下，透露出一種自然、清奇的氣逸。這裡，不想對她的思想傾向做進一步分析，僅想著重從其詩歌藝術本身，探索其對詩美的精湛創造和對新詩發展的貢獻。

14. The Art of Xi Murong's Poetry

Abstract: Xi Mu-Rong is one of the women writers who has made a great impact on modern Chinese poetry. The true feeling and yarning for love expressed in her works are the main reason for gaining the admiration from her readers. Under the influences of Western aesthetics and romanticism, her poems reveal the tinges of natural freshness. This article concentrates on exploring the contribution of her creative poetry towards the development of modern Chinese poetry.

Key words: Xi Murong, poetry, art, romanticism

1. Biography

Xi Murong (1943-), born in Mongolian aristocracy, was born in Chongqing. She studied in the Art Department of Taiwan Normal University and graduated from the Royal Academy of Arts in Brussels, Belgium. She once taught at the Department of Fine Arts at Tunghai University. He has written a collection of poems, essays, art treatises, etc. She is a female writer with far-reaching influence in the history of modern Chinese poetry. The reason why her poems are favored by readers lies in the delicate and touching real feelings and imagination of love expressed in her works, which are all-encompassing. It reveals a natural and strange air. Here, I don't want to further analyze her thought tendency, but only want to focus on her poetic art itself, exploring her exquisite creation of poetic beauty and her contribution to the development of new poetry.

　　席慕蓉對於詩藝，著重於風格境界的研究；在特徵上更多體現在浪漫主義精神同詩歌絕致的融合。所謂風格是作為詩美的內在層面，也就是晚唐詩人、詩論家司空圖所謂的「味」。這是寄於語言、形象之外的，以詩人的情意為中心所創造出耐人尋味的藝術境界。司空圖曾說：「文之難，而詩之難尤難。」，這句涵義是說，沒有詩味的作品，就像無煙雲映襯的禿山，既單調又無生氣。因此，沒有真實的思想感情，藝術上也是蒼白無力的。

　　而席慕容在詩藝上的貢獻，對民初以來迄今的現代詩來說，應該是與名家鄭愁予、余光中並輩的佼佼者。多年來，她的詩歌仍受到廣大讀者的喜愛之因，首要一點，正是她在詩作中有了獨特的思想感情、有「情真、味長、氣勝」的藝術感染力、抒情的音韻效果以及充沛的激情等因素，容易激起人們感情的共鳴。她也是個美術論者、詩畫家。早期的詩歌裡有它獨自知道的別一個世界的憂傷與快樂；猶如一隻癡鳥，一邊唱著星月的光輝與小小的希望，一邊把自己柔軟的心窩緊抵著花叢上的枯刺，非到心血把雪地染紅她不住口。她曾自白：「寫詩，為的是紀念一段遠去的歲月，紀念那個只曾在我心中存在過的小小世界。」她的詩如空中之音，其妙處

For poetic art, Xi Murong focuses on the study of the realm of style; in terms of characteristics, it is more reflected in the perfect fusion of romantic spirit and poetry. The so-called style is the inner layer of poetic beauty, which is what Sikong Tu, a poet and poetic theorist in the late Tang Dynasty called "taste". This is an intriguing artistic realm created with the poet's affection as the center, which is beyond the language and image. Sikong Tu once said: "writing is difficult, but poetry is especially difficult." This sentence means that a work without poetry is like a bald mountain with no smoke and clouds, which is monotonous and lifeless. Therefore, without real thoughts and feelings, art is also pale and powerless.

Xi Murong's contribution to poetic art should be regarded as an outstanding figure in the same generation as Zheng Chouyu and Yu Guangzhong in terms of modern poetry since the early Republic of China. Over the years, the reason why her poems are still loved by readers is, first of all, that she has unique thoughts and feelings, artistic appeal of "truth, flavor, and vigor" in her poems and lyrical rhyme. Factors such as effects and abundant passion are likely to arouse people's emotional resonance. She is also an art theorist, poet and painter. In the early poems, there are the sorrows and joys of another world that it knows alone; like an idiot bird, while singing the brilliance of the stars and the moon and the little hope, while pressing its soft heart against the withered thorns on the flowers. She couldn't stop talking until she had painstakingly dyed the snow red. She once confessed: "Writing poems is to commemorate a long-gone time, to commemorate the small world that only existed in my heart." Her poems are like voices in the sky, and their subtleties are thorough an

透徹玲瓏；情意宛轉，帶有空明超脫之境。亦可宏偉奇崛，意趣高遠；尤擅說情。作品中浸潤西方美學，兼具東方禪家色彩，常透出一種人生無常的「幽情單緒」。所以，她詩裡的痛苦與歡樂是渾成一片的。

二、浪漫主義精神同詩歌絕致的融合

且看詩人的這首《我》，寫得情味超逸，不著跡象：

我喜歡出發　喜歡離開
喜歡一生中都能有新的夢想
千山萬水　隨意行去
不管星辰指引的是什麼方向

我喜歡停留　喜歡長久
喜歡在園裡種下千棵果樹
靜待冬雷夏雨　春華秋實
喜歡生命裡只有單純的盼望
只有一種安定和緩慢的成長

我喜歡歲月漂洗過後的顏色
喜歡那沒有唱出來的歌

我喜歡在夜裡寫一首長詩
然後再來在這清涼的早上

exquisite, with a state of emptiness and detachment. It can also be grand and strange, with high interest; especially good at intercourse. The works are infiltrated with Western aesthetics, and also have the color of Eastern Zen, often revealing a kind of "single emotion" that is impermanent in life. Therefore, the pain and joy in her poems are integrated.

2. The Perfect Fusion of Romantic Spirit and Poetry

Let's look at the poet's "I", which is written with a sense of elegance and no signs:

I like to go, I like to leave
I like to have new dreams in my life
Thousands of mountains and rivers, walk at will
No matter what direction the stars point

I like to stay for a long time
Like to plant a thousand fruit trees in the garden
Waiting for winter thunder and summer rain, spring
　　flowers and autumn fruits
I like that there is only pure hope in life
There is only one kind of stability and slow growth

I like the color after years of rinsing
Like the unsung song

I like to write a long poem at night
Then come again on this cool morning

　　逐行逐段地檢視
　　慢慢刪去
　　每一個與你有著關聯的字

　　當詩人文思勃發，把大千世界納入自己的藝術思維活動之中時；我們還是會驚歎於詩人的睿智以及她對生活觀察的細膩深刻。通過這首詩可以發現，她生存正處於漂泊的時期；但詩人的愛情價值觀是對一種美好理想的更廣闊的追求。那愛情的微妙與幻變無疑是詩人在東西方的美學碰撞中所開拓出的一個純美、幽深、寧靜的藝術世界。

　　她是一位無與倫比的浪漫詩人。寫詩，也是跟自己進行心靈的對話。比如《為什麼》一首，結尾處帶有較濃重的悲傷色彩：

　　我可以鎖住我的心　為什麼
　　卻鎖不住愛和憂傷
　　　在長長的一生裡　為什麼
　　歡樂總是乍現就凋落
　　走得最急的都是最美的時光

　　此詩既有真情，又有形象。雖不同於某些浪漫主義詩人赤裸裸的吶喊和直抒胸臆，但我們不能把它看作一首單純的愛情詩；因為，詩中已表現出席慕容為追求自由戀愛的勇氣的形象。從主體上講，她的詩也採用了局部的象徵來表達自

View line by line
Slowly delete
Every word associated with you

When the poet's literary thinking flourishes and he incorporates the vast world into his artistic thinking activities, we will still marvel at the poet's wisdom and her delicate and profound observation of life. Through this poem, it can be found that she is living in a wandering period; but the poet's love value is a broader pursuit of a beautiful ideal. The subtlety and illusion of love is undoubtedly a pure, deep and tranquil art world developed by the poet in the collision of Eastern and Western aesthetics.

She is an incomparable romantic poet. Writing poetry is also a spiritual dialogue with oneself. For example, *Why* has a strong sad color at the end:

I can lock my heart why
But can't lock love and sorrow
In a long life why
Joy always fades away
The most urgent time is the most beautiful time

This poem has both true feelings and images. Although it is different from some romantic poets' naked cry and direct expression, we can't regard it as a pure love poem; because the poem has already shown the image of Murong's courage to pursue free love. From the subject point of view, her poems also use partial symbols to express her own

　　己的思想感情，藉以獲得虛擬的一種精神上的昇華。如
這首〈致流浪者〉：

　　　　總有一天　你會在燈下
　　　　翻閱我的心　而窗外
　　　　夜已很深　很靜
　　　　好像是　一切都已過去了
　　　　年少時光的熙熙攘攘
　　　　塵埃與流浪　山風與海濤
　　　　都已止息　年也終於老去
　　　　窗外　夜霧漫漫
　　　　所有的悲歡都已如彩蝶般
　　　　飛散　歲月不再復返
　　　　無論我曾經怎樣固執地
　　　　等待過你　也只能
　　　　給你留下一本
　　　　薄薄的　薄薄的　詩集

　　　席慕容對世界各地豐美茂盛的大自然、山風與海濤以及
夜霧漫漫等視覺上的饗宴均留下深刻印象。然而最吸引她注
意力而反映在詩作上的，並非各種美麗景物等疊現情調的表
達，反而是詩歌藝術中抽象的朦朧情愫與時空感悟中的關係。
此詩當然有些絕望之感，但也表明了愛情的到來是要付出寂
寞的代價的。

thoughts and feelings, so as to obtain a virtual spiritual sublimation. Like this song *To the Vagabond*:

One day you will be under the lamp
Look through my heart and outside the window
The night is very deep and very quiet
It seems like everything is over
The hustle and bustle of youth
Dust and wandering, mountain wind and sea waves
It's all over, the years are finally getting old
Outside the window, the night is foggy
All the joys and sorrows are like butterflies
Flying away, the years will never come back
No matter how stubborn I was
I have waited for you, I can only
Leave one for you
A thin collection of poems

Xi Murong was deeply impressed by the visual feasts such as the rich and lush nature, mountain winds and sea waves, and long night fog all over the world. However, what attracts her most attention and is reflected in her poems is not the expression of overlapping emotions such as various beautiful scenery, but the relationship between the abstract and hazy emotions in the art of poetry and the perception of time and space. Of course, this poem has a sense of despair, but it also shows that the arrival of love comes at the price of loneliness.

　　再如〈七里香〉，也採用了含蓄的象徵手法：

　　溪水急著要流向海洋
　　浪潮却渴望重回土地

　　在綠樹白花的籬前
　　曾那樣輕易地揮手道別

　　而滄桑了二十年後
　　我們的魂魄却夜夜歸來
　　微風拂過時
　　便化作滿園的鬱香

　　內裡有無限悵然的弦外之音，結尾處，戀人的魂魄化作
滿園的鬱香，是一種浪漫主義的美麗的想像，也是一種動人
的象徵手法。接著，這首〈初相遇〉，描寫為愛情的誕生而忍
受著等待的煎熬與狂喜。這也是完成於她自己年輕時生命的
使命的時機：

　　美麗的夢和美麗的詩一樣
　　都是可遇而不可求的
　　常常在最沒能料到的時刻裏出現

　　我喜歡那樣的夢
　　在夢裏　一切都可以重新開始

Another example is *Fragrance of Seven Miles*, which also uses implicit symbolism:

The brook is rushing to the sea
The tide is eager to return to the land

In front of the hedge of green trees and white flowers
Waved goodbye so easily

And after twenty years of vicissitudes
Our souls come back every night
When the breeze blows
It turns into a garden full of tulips

There are infinite melancholy overtones in it, and at the end, the lover's soul turns into a garden full of tulips, which is a romantic and beautiful imagination and a moving symbolism. Then, this song *First Encounter* describes the suffering and ecstasy of waiting for the birth of love. It was also a time to fulfill a mission in her own young life:

Beautiful dreams are like beautiful poems
It's all possible
Often at the least expected moment

I like that dream
In the dream everything can start again

　一切都可以慢慢解釋
　心裏甚至還能感覺到所有被浪費的時光
　竟然都能重回時的狂喜和感激

　胸懷中滿溢著幸福
　只因爲你就在我眼前
　對我微笑　一如當年
　我真喜歡那樣的夢

　明明知道你已爲我跋涉千里
　却又覺得芳草鮮美　落英繽紛
　好像你我才初相遇

　　此詩中落英繽紛，象徵詩人年復一年等待的心緒；而後來感覺好像回到初相遇，又象徵詩人開始甦醒的愛情又變得鮮明的靈魂。〈悲歌〉中也描繪詩人在悲傷的愛情中仍懷著一種茫然的愁緒：

　今生將不再見你
　只爲　再見的
　已不是你

　心中的你已永不再現
　再現的　只是些滄桑的
　日月和流年

Everything can be explained slowly
I can even feel all the wasted time in my heart
To be able to return to the ecstasy and gratitude

Heart full of happiness
Just because you are right in front of my eyes
Smile at me like back then
I really like that dream

Knowing that you have traveled thousands of miles for me
But I feel that the fragrant grass is delicious and the
　　falling flowers are colorful
It's like you and I just met

The falling petals in this poem symbolize the poet's waiting mood year after year; and later it feels like returning to the first encounter, which also symbolizes the poet's awakening love and becoming a vivid soul. *Elegy* also depicts the poet still harboring a kind of dazed melancholy in his sad love:

I will never see you again in this life
Just for goodbye
Not you

The you in my heart will never reappear
The reappearance is just some vicissitudes
Sun, moon and year

　　此時，詩人無不在追求理想，追求愛情，也追求藝術上的創新。但愛情的折磨，使她感到迷惘與苦悶。又如，她的另一首成名詩《無怨的青春》，這也許是詩人一段感情的回憶；更擴大之，也可以理解為愛情道路上徬徨後的心跡：

　　　　在年青的時候
　　　　如果你愛上了一個人
　　　　請你一定要溫柔地對待她
　　　　不管你們相愛的時間有多長或多短

　　　　若你們能始終溫柔地相待　那麼
　　　　所有的時刻都將是一種無暇的美麗
　　　　若不得不分離
　　　　也要好好地說一聲再見
　　　　也要在心裏存著感謝
　　　　感謝她給了你一份記憶

　　　　長大了之後　你才會知道
　　　　在驀然回首的一剎那
　　　　沒有怨恨的青春　才會了無遺憾
　　　　如山崗上那靜靜的晚月

　　其實，席慕容詩的音樂美方面是下了功夫的。詩，對她而言，與音樂與美術都是同等同性質的；它都是詩人自身性靈裡的特殊表現。比如這首《樹的畫像》，其錯落有致的節奏，如詩人於風中吹奏的短笛：

At this time, poets are all pursuing ideals, love, and artistic innovation. But the torment of love made her feel confused and depressed. Another example is her other famous poem *Youth Without Complaints*, which may be the poet's memory of a relationship; more broadly, it can also be understood as the heart after wandering on the road of love:

At a young age
If you love someone
Please be gentle with her
No matter how long or how short you've been in love

If you can always be gentle with each other then
All moments will be a flawless beauty
If you have to separate
Say goodbye too
Also keep gratitude in my heart
Thank her for giving you a memory

You'll know when you grow up
In the moment when I suddenly look back
Youth without resentment will have no regrets
Like the quiet late moon on the hills

In fact, Xi Murong's poems have put a lot of effort into the musical beauty. Poetry, for her, is of the same nature as music and art; it is a special expression of the poet's own soul. For example, this song *Portrait of a Tree*, its patchwork rhythm is like the piccolo played by the poet in the wind:

　　當迎風的笑靨已不再芬芳
　　溫柔的話語都已沉寂
　　當星星的瞳子漸冷漸暗
　　而千山萬徑都絕滅蹤跡

　　我只是一棵孤獨的樹
　　在抗拒著秋的來臨

　　在這裡，詩人似乎已能因此開通思想，參悟到愛情其中的道理。而〈非別離〉詩中：

　　不再相見
　　並不一定等於分離
　　不再通音訊
　　並不一定等於忘記

　　只為　你的悲哀已揉進我的
　　如月色揉進山中　而每逢
　　夜涼如水　就會觸我舊日疼痛

　　詩人已能想到自己的苦難別人也曾熬受過，那言語的風兒一吹動，悲哀的夜色就憔悴。再如人們熟知的〈錯誤〉，婉轉而輕柔，一如她的詩的基調，更具有一種雅致的悲傷味道：

　　假如愛情可以解釋
　　誓言可以修改

When the windward smile is no longer fragrant
Gentle words are silent
When the pupils of the stars are getting colder and darker
And thousands of mountains and trails are extinct

I'm just a lonely tree
Resisting the coming of autumn

Here, the poet seems to have been able to open his mind and understand the truth of love. And in the poem *Not Parting*:

No longer meet
Does not necessarily mean separation
No more audio
Does not necessarily mean forgetting

Just because your sorrow has rubbed into mine
Rubbing into the mountains like moonlight, every time
The night is as cold as water, it will touch my old pain

The poet can already think of his own suffering and others have suffered it. As soon as the wind of words blows, the sad night is haggard. Another example is the well-known *Error*, which is tactful and gentle, just like the tone of her poems, and has an elegant and sad flavor:

If love can explain
Oath can be amended

假如　你我的相遇
可以重新安排

那麼
生活就會比較容易
假如　有一天
我終於能將你忘記

然而　這不是
隨便傳說的故事
也不是明天才要
上演的戲劇
我無法找出原稿
然後將你
將你一筆抹去

　　總之，她對詩歌音韻美的追求與對真愛追求的執著，是
應該肯定的。

三、席慕容：詩的繪畫師

　　席慕容在詩藝上的感人之處，還在於常以唯美的畫面創
造出動人的意境，並講究詩行的排列美。她是詩美的高級繪
畫師和建築師。如這首〈畫展〉，字句跳躍輕巧，造成一種獨
特的美感力：

If you and I meet
Can be rescheduled

So
Life will be easier
If one day
I can finally forget you

However this is not
Random legend story
Not tomorrow
Staged drama
I can't find the original
Then you
Erase you

In short, her pursuit of the beauty of poetry and the pursuit of true love should be affirmed.

3. Xi Murong: Painter of Poetry

What makes Xi Murong's poetry moving is that he often uses beautiful pictures to create a moving artistic conception, and pays attention to the beauty of the arrangement of lines of poetry. She is Shimei's senior painter and architect. For example, in this song *Painting Exhibition*, the words and sentences jump lightly, creating a unique beauty:

> 我知道
> 凡是美麗的
> 總不肯　也
> 不會
> 為誰停留
>
> 所以　我把
> 我的愛情和憂傷
> 掛在牆上
> 展覽　並且
> 出售

　　可見，她也是為排得長短錯落有致而經常苦吟的。接著，這首膾炙人口的〈鄉愁〉，詩情與意境的表達形式渾然一體，是那樣自然貼切：

> 故鄉的歌是一支清遠的笛
> 總在有月亮的晚上響起
>
> 故鄉的面貌卻是一種模糊的悵惘
> 彷彿霧裏的揮手別離
> 離別後
> 鄉愁是一棵沒有年輪的樹
> 永不老去

I know
Anything beautiful
Never
Won't
For whom to stay

So I put
My love and sorrow
Hanging on the wall
Exhibition and
Sell

It can be seen that she often groaned hard to make the rows arranged in a well-proportioned way. Then, in the well-known *Nostalgia*, the expression of poetic sentiment and artistic conception is integrated, which is so natural and appropriate:

The song of my hometown is a melodious flute
It always rings on a moonlit night

The appearance of my hometown is a kind of vague melancholy
Like waving goodbye in the fog
After parting
Nostalgia is a tree without annual rings
Never growing old

　　席慕容詩歌的另一特色，是它的形象化和多種修辭手段的運用，因而使人感到多彩多姿，富有質感。此詩感情是真摯而深沉的，最後一句，更渲染了鄉愁中憂傷靜謐的氣氛，給人們的官能上造成一種縈迴的旋律感。

　　過去的詩評家，大多針對席慕容反映生活和抒情狀物的特點、多種藝術手法的運用、清新婉約的藝術風格等方面做一分析。然而，席慕容的詩歌，在情景交融的描繪方面，也並非一種格式。像這首被唱紅海內外的《出塞曲》，是從情到景，又從景到情：

　　　　請為我唱一首出塞曲
　　　　用那遺忘了的古老言語
　　　　請用美麗的顫音輕輕呼喚
　　　　我心中的大好河山

　　　　那只有長城外才有的清香
　　　　誰說出塞歌的調子都太悲涼
　　　　如果你不愛聽
　　　　那是因為歌中沒有你的渴望

　　　　而我們總是要一唱再唱
　　　　想著草原千里閃著金光
　　　　想著風沙呼嘯過大漠
　　　　想著黃河岸啊　　陰山旁
　　　　英雄騎馬啊　　騎馬歸故鄉

　　Another feature of Xi Murong's poetry is its visualization and the use of various rhetorical devices, which make people feel colorful and full of texture. The emotion of this poem is sincere and deep, and the last sentence exaggerates the sad and quiet atmosphere of nostalgia, creating a lingering sense of melody on people's senses.

　　Most of the past poetry critics made an analysis of Xi Murong's characteristics of reflecting life and lyricism, the use of various artistic techniques, and his fresh and graceful artistic style. However, Xi Murong's poems are not a format in the description of the blending of scenes. Like this song *Out of the Fortress*, which has been sung popular both at home and abroad, it goes from emotion to scene, and from scene to emotion:

Please sing me a song
In the forgotten ancient language
Please call out with a beautiful vibrato
The great rivers and mountains in my heart

The fragrance that can only be found outside the Great Wall
Whoever says the tune of Sege is too sad
If you don't like to hear
That's because there is no desire for you in the song

And we always have to sing and sing
Thinking of the golden light shining thousands of miles
　　away in the grassland
Thinking of the wind and sand roaring across the desert
Thinking of the banks of the Yellow River, beside the Yin
　　Mountain
The hero rides a horse, rides back to his hometown

　　這首可以說是蘊聚著濃郁感情的長幅畫卷，詩中，展示了一幅廣闊的畫面;而詩人確如一個握著多色畫筆的畫家，把懷念中國大好河山、懷念故鄉的草原牛羊和各種英雄人物的動作神態都展現出來了。

　　身為一個詩畫家的席慕容，想像，恐怕是她最寶貴的財富了。在意象的選擇和運用方面，西方的意象派詩多是一組組獨立的意象，並不刻意追求藝術境界的完整;而席慕容則是想要融合中國古典美學所說的那種「意境的深邃完整」的藝術境界吧。比如這首《藝術家》，詩人用一組色調憂鬱的印象來表現自己的苦痛的情景，這些意象的創造和組接都是很有韻味的:

　　　你已用淚洗淨我的筆
　　　好讓我在今夜畫出滿池的煙雨

　　　而在心中那個芬芳的角落
　　　你為我雕出一朵永不凋謝的荷

　　　浮生若夢
　　　我愛
　　　何者是實　何者是空
　　　何去何從

　　同樣用的是意象的組合和剪接的經典之作，還有這首在1980年十月間寫下的〈一棵開花的樹〉:

This poem can be said to be a long picture scroll full of strong emotions. In the poem, it shows a broad picture; and the poet is indeed like a painter holding a multi-color brush, painting the grassland cattle and sheep that miss China's great rivers and mountains and hometown. And the actions and demeanor of various heroes are shown.

As a poet and painter, Xi Murong's imagination is probably her most precious wealth. In terms of the selection and application of images, Western imagist poems are mostly groups of independent images, and do not deliberately pursue the integrity of the artistic realm; while Xi Murong wants to integrate the "artistic conception" according to classical Chinese aesthetics. Deep and complete artistic realm. For example, in the song *The Artist*, the poet uses a set of melancholy impressions to express his painful scenes. The creation and combination of these images are very charming:

You have washed my pen with tears
So that I can draw a pond full of smoke and rain tonight

And in that fragrant corner of my heart
You carve for me a lotus that never fades

Floating like a dream
I love
What is real and what is empty
Where to go

Also using the classic composition and editing of imagery, there is also this song *A Flowering Tree* written in October 1980:

　　如何讓你遇見我
　　在我最美麗的時刻　為這
　　我已在佛前　求了五百年
　　求他讓我們結一段塵緣

　　佛於是把我化作一棵樹
　　長在你必經的路旁
　　陽光下慎重地開滿了花
　　朵朵都是我前世的盼望

　　當你走近　請你細聽
　　那顫抖的葉是我等待的熱情
　　而當你終於無視地走過
　　在你身後落了一地的
　　朋友啊　那不是花瓣
　　是我凋零的心

　　表面看來，似是詩人對美好愛情的追求，然而卻不是如
實地描寫，而是一種象徵和暗示，表達了一種對愛情追求那
可遇而不可得的惆悵情懷。意境是一種情景交融的藝術境地，
尤著重於客體物。比如這首〈異域〉，道盡了席慕容在比利時
留學歲月的孤寂情懷：

　　於是　夜來了
　　敲打著我十一月的窗

How to make you meet me
In my most beautiful moment for this
I have prayed for five hundred years before the Buddha
Beg him to let us form a relationship

Buddha then turned me into a tree
Grow by the road you must pass
Flowers are carefully blooming in the sun
Blossoms are my longing from the previous life

When you approach, please listen carefully
That trembling leaf is my passion of waiting
And when you finally walk by ignoring
Landed behind you
Friends, those are not petals
Is my withered heart

On the surface, it seems to be the poet's pursuit of beautiful love, but it is not a true description, but a symbol and hint, expressing a kind of melancholy feeling about the pursuit of love that can be met but not obtained. Artistic conception is an artistic state where scenes blend together, especially focusing on objects. For example, this song *Exotic Land* expresses Xi Murong's lonely feelings when he was studying abroad in Belgium:

So night came
Knocking on my November window

從南國的馨香中醒來
從回家的夢裡醒來
布魯塞爾的燈火輝煌
我孤獨地投身在人群中
人群投我以孤獨
細雨霏霏　不是我的淚
窗外蕭蕭落木

這其中情象流動的跳躍性，如細細揣摩，就可以使人去更多地咀嚼回味。在古今優秀的詩篇中，不變的是，感情總是和鮮明生動的具體藝術形象結合著。我認為，在席慕容的詩作中，溫婉真摯的感情，總是和清麗多彩的生活畫面、具體可感的藝術形象融為一體，形成她別具一家的風格。無疑，以其多彩的筆觸已為我們打開了一個繽紛的詩藝世界。探究其詩，對文壇的繁榮應會有促進作用的。

－2013.5.20
－內蒙古《集寧師範學院學報》，2015 年第 3 期，第
　37 卷，總第 130 期，頁 27-30。

Waking up from the fragrance of the Southland
Waking up from the dream of coming home
Bright lights in Brussels
I am alone in the crowd
The crowd voted me lonely
The drizzle is not my tears
Rustling trees outside the window

The jumping nature of the flow of emotion and imagery, if carefully pondered, can make people chew more aftertaste. In the excellent poems of ancient and modern times, what remains unchanged is that emotion is always combined with vivid and concrete artistic images. In my opinion, in Xi Murong's poems, the gentle and sincere feelings are always integrated with the beautiful and colorful life pictures and concrete and sensible artistic images, forming her unique style. Undoubtedly, with its colorful brushstrokes, it has opened up a colorful world of poetry and art for us. Exploring her poems should promote the prosperity of the literary world.

15. 夜讀鍾玲詩集《霧在登山》

　　鍾玲〈1945-〉是跨越臺、美、港三地的著名學者，更是擅長小說、散文的作家，也是在文學之路上跋涉的詩人。在她第二本《霧在登山》的詩集裡，人們從中可以不斷地揣摩其內心深層情感的秘密；也可以看到她對九位古典美人的造像與返思，其中的後記與箋注，是極有見地的。此外，還有為她敬愛的人及緬懷遊地景物等創作。豐富的內容和優美的詩的形式的結合，讓我看到的是一個孤獨的愛情守望者，在細雪的窗前感受著寂寞，在與心徘徊之後是渴盼恆定的力量和內心如秋葉般詩意的柔情。或許只有她自己才能深悟到行走中的痛苦，才能聽得見摯愛的人毫不留情地踏向死亡的足音。走進她一生感情的城池的疼痛，也促使她活得更加豐實且更有意義。現就我感受最深的幾首詩作略談體會。

　　首先是寫詩應有自己的深刻體驗，應全心地投入詩的構思和感受創作的過程。在她1999年十月寫下貼近現實，關注民生的〈安魂曲—致九二一地震的死難者〉，她感慨萬端，因

15. Night Reading of Zhong Ling's Poetry Collection

The Fog Is Climbing the Mountain

Zhong Ling (1945-) is a famous scholar across Taiwan, the United States, and Hong Kong. She is also a writer who is good at novels and prose, and she is also a poet who has been trekking on the road of literature. In her second collection of poems *Fog in Mountain Climbing*, people can constantly figure out the secrets of her deepest emotions; they can also see her portraits and reveries of nine classical beauties, and the postscript and notes are very special and insightful. In addition, there are creations for her loved ones and memory of the places she visited. The combination of rich content and beautiful poetic form, let me see a lonely watcher of love, feeling lonely in front of the snowy window, after wandering with the heart, longing for constant power and inner poetry like the tenderness of autumn leaves. Perhaps only she herself can deeply understand the pain of walking, and can hear the footsteps of the one she loves relentlessly stepping towards death. The pain of walking into the city of her life's emotions also prompted her to live a more fulfilling and meaningful life. Now I will briefly talk about some of the poems that I feel the most about.

First of all, writing poetry should have one's own profound experience, and one should devote oneself wholeheartedly to the conception of poetry and the process of feeling creation. In October 1999, she wrote *Requiem for the Victims of the September 21 Earthquake*, livelihood. She was so moved that she wrote a poem. What

而賦詩一首。其所表現的是她詩歌創作中的新的高度，是其
崇高人格和堅強生命力的放射。此詩曾由名作曲家黃友棣與
賴德和分別譜成曲：

　　　世界末日的震動晃醒你
　　　意識方脫離夢境
　　　磚塊石塊已經壓上身
　　　打破你的頭、折斷你的腿
　　　壓碎你的肋骨你的心
　　　飛來的黑色死亡
　　　像巨大的隕石壓下
　　　願親人長流的淚水
　　　洗淨你滿身的傷口
　　　願兩千萬人的心酸心痛
　　　沖淡你孤獨承受的驚恐

　　　如果這個島的罪孽深重
　　　重如堆在你身上如山的石塊
　　　你替我們大家承受天譴

　　　你累世的路
　　　今生最崎嶇
　　　可以起程了，不要驚怕
　　　前面是明亮的坦途

it shows is a new height in her poetry creation, and it is the radiation of her noble personality and strong vitality. This poem was once composed by famous composers Huang Youdi and Lai Dehe respectively:

Doomsday shocks that wake you up
Consciousness out of dream
Bricks and stones are already on the upper body
Break your head, break your legs
Crush your ribs your heart
Flying black death
Weighed down like a huge meteorite
May loved ones shed tears
Wash your wounds
May the hearts of 20 million people be heartbroken
To dilute the horror you bear alone

If the island is full of sin
As heavy as a mountain of stones piled upon you
You bear the wrath for all of us

Your way
The roughest life
It's time to go, don't be afraid
Bright road ahead

　　這可說是一首表達對社會悲憫的詩，而死難者意象象徵著人生的生存的本質，蘊涵著玄思和感慨。來自成長於臺灣的鍾玲的那份真摯與同情，卻不時流露出同胞間一種高貴的情操——彼此關懷，令人仰視。且讓死難者生命與死亡在同一墓中歇息，靈魂得以平靜，這正是鍾玲詩意之所在。

　　詩人自是多情客，高雄家鄉草木、異域風情等皆成為她詩歌中的華彩樂章，表達出她的感事傷懷。鍾玲認為，人是覺醒－成長－成熟，然後得到智慧。人的身體卅歲就開始衰退，但內心可不斷年輕和成長。它的啟示性是顯而易見的。雖然世人常道，鍾玲是個女強人。其實，她是個摯愛文學、做事極認真又感情執著的人。她自小希望能表現具有偉大抱負、廣闊視野；表現不倦地寫作精神、嚮往追求愛與美的崇高。而這種感情和風格，是體現出詩人一生的美學追求。如2001年秋，鍾玲寫下的〈你駐足的草地〉一詩，是為前夫名導演胡金銓上墳後而作：

　　　　來到這片你駐足的草地，
　　　　坐下遙望煙籠的洛杉磯，
　　　　你近到可以觸及我的手指，
　　　　卻遠隔一千個明暗的日子。

This can be said to be a poem expressing sympathy for the society, and the image of the dead symbolizes the essence of life, and contains deep thinking and emotion. The sincerity and sympathy from Zhong Ling, who grew up in Taiwan, reveals a kind of noble sentiment among compatriots from time to time — caring for each other, which makes people look up to. And let the life and death of the victims rest in the same tomb, so that the soul can be at peace, which is where Zhong Ling's poetry lies.

The poet is a passionate lover, and the vegetation and exotic customs of Kaohsiung's hometown have become the cadenzas in her poems, expressing her sentimental sadness. Zhong Ling believes that people awaken-grow-mature, and then gain wisdom. A person's body begins to decline at the age of thirty, but the heart can continue to be young and grow. Its revelation is obvious. Although people often say that Zhong Ling is a strong woman. In fact, she is a person who loves literature, works very seriously and is emotionally persistent. Since she was a child, she hoped to express her great ambitions and broad vision; to express her tireless writing spirit, and her pursuit of love and beauty. And this kind of emotion and style reflects the poet's lifelong aesthetic pursuit. For example, in the autumn of 2001, Zhong Ling wrote the poem *The Grassland You Stopped*, which was written for the grave of her ex-husband director Hu Jinquan:

Come to this meadow where you stand,
Sitting down and looking at Los Angeles in the smoke cage,
You're close enough to touch my fingers,
But a thousand days of light and darkness are far away.

想到你飄盪而鮮明的一生，
由北方的古都到南方的海域，
你的映像照亮五湖四海，
最後落腳煙籠的洛杉磯，
暮色四合中追逐一個夢想，
一個夢，刻畫異鄉人的飄盪。

一股力量催我來這片草地——
那十年同行、十年的糾結，
來整理兩人之間千絲萬縷：
什麼是以為付出其實收受，
什麼是以為脫離其實滲透。

來到你最後駐足的地方——
一片片碑石平鑲草地上
像千萬片巨廈的玻璃窗，
躺著望去一片也看不見，
一個名字一個日期也看不見，
你真的已經融入風景，
正像你鏡頭下的畫面。

穿越朝鮮看外景那年
你教我用眼睛框架山水；
二十年來你的色彩和構圖、

Thinking of your wandering and vivid life,

From the ancient capital in the north to the sea in the south,

Thy image illuminates the world,

Finally settled down in Los Angeles,

Chasing a dream in the twilight,

A dream depicts the wandering of foreigners.

A force urges me to this meadow —

Those ten years of colleagues, ten years of entanglement,

To sort out the inextricable clues between the two:

What is thinking that giving is actually receiving,

What is thought to be detached is actually infiltrated.

To the place where you last stood —

A piece of stele flat inlaid on the grass

Like the glass windows of thousands of huge buildings,

Lying down and looking, I can't see a piece of it,

Neither a name nor a date can be seen,

You really have melted into the landscape,

Just like the picture under your lens.

The Year I Traveled Through North Korea to Watch Locations

You taught me to frame landscapes with my eyes;

Twenty years of your color and composition,

你的叮嚀、滲透我的生命。
這一刻、在這寧靜的下午，
我依然用你的品味四顧。

我來到這片幽綠的草地
探訪到寧靜自得的你，
那不寧靜的出了遠門。

　　詩人目光東流，靜靜地坐在空寂之外；想像自己遇到了
前夫並與之交談。她看著記憶，與時間並肩行走……。詩中
有幽綠的草地、由北方的古都到南方的海域、巨廈的玻璃窗、
穿越朝鮮，意象的轉換幅度大，時空跳躍強，傳達出一種哀
思和憂鬱。越是在現實的世界裡，越是感到個人的無助與徬
徨，精神的困境因此而生。此刻，詩人的影子是靜的，只沉
浸在回憶與現實、自然與時空相交融的境界裡，其身姿也是
孤獨的。在靜穆的沉思中，她的心靈展開翅膀輕柔地在幽遠
的時空裡翱翔。而最後一段有兩層意義：一方面，象徵著死
亡，再者也有靈魂洗淨之意。這兩個意義是一體兩面。詩人
把幽綠的草地在時間上拉長，使節奏慢下來，類似電影中的
高速攝影所製造出來的慢鏡頭。這時詩人的心裡已被寧靜的
陽光曬暖，於是，她發現了自己未來該走的路。當年情感失
意時，鍾玲也曾在學佛、探求智慧的過程中了悟到，那深藏

Your exhortation penetrates into my life.
At this moment, in this quiet afternoon,
I still look around with your taste.

I came to this green meadow
To visit you who are peaceful and contented,
The restless one went far away.

The poet looks eastward and sits quietly in the emptiness; imagining that he has met and talked with his ex-husband. She looks at memory, walks side by side with time.... In the poem, there are green grasslands, the sea from the ancient capital in the north to the sea in the south, the glass windows of giant buildings, and crossing North Korea. The more you are in the real world, the more helpless and hesitant you feel, and the spiritual dilemma arises from this. At this moment, the shadow of the poet is still, only immersed in the realm where memory and reality, nature and time and space blend together, and his posture is also lonely. In quiet contemplation, her heart spreads its wings and soars softly in the remote time and space. And the last paragraph has two meanings: on the one hand, it symbolizes death, and on the other hand, it also has the meaning of soul cleansing. These two meanings are one and the same. The poet elongates the green grass in time to slow down the rhythm, similar to the slow motion produced by high-speed photography in movies. At this time, the poet's heart has been warmed by the quiet sunshine, so she found the way she should go in the future. When she was emotionally frustrated, Zhong Ling also realized in the process of learning Buddhism and seeking wisdom that the rhythm hidden deep in her

於內心的律動與在夜空中的憧憬，原本都是未完成的生命形
式。於今，她以往對心靈的信任，現已轉為佛教精義的信心。
此詩雖讓人看到「美麗得使人痛苦」的瞬間，但也有著禪家
智慧的妙語。她想像中的前夫已然獲得了寧靜，回到豐足永
恆的世界了。

　　中年以後的鍾玲，是個人教學與創作的強力放射時期。
她在2004年七月寫下的〈陌地生故居〉一詩的背景，據其自
述是在1967-1972年間於陌生地〈Madison〉就讀威士康辛大
學研究所，在那裡，她經歷過苦讀與情感的風暴。三十多年
後，詩人再度回到陌生地故居，有感而作：

　　　細雨怎會那麼黏人？
　　　不像記憶中爽身。
　　　我不得不踏著雨向南
　　　回到小紅樓前面。
　　　三十年前就是座老木屋
　　　如今竟一點也不肯傾斜，
　　　依舊棗紅同樣的棗紅。
　　　細雨靜靜裹住各式折騰：
　　　第一次心悸，第一次心許
　　　第一次折磨自己的淚水，
　　　接下去是半甲子重複
　　　心悸心許和淚水。
　　　紅樓是一種循環的起點。

heart and the longing in the night sky were originally unfinished forms of life. Today, her previous trust in the soul has now turned into the confidence in the essence of Buddhism. Although this poem allows people to see the moment of "beautiful so painful", it also contains witty words of Zen wisdom. Her imaginary ex-husband had found peace, returned to a world of abundance and eternity.

After Zhong Ling's middle age, it is a period of strong radiation for personal teaching and creation. The background of the poem *The Former Residence of Mo Di Sheng* written by her in July 2004, according to her self-report, was studying at the University of Wisconsin Graduate School in a strange place Madison from 1967 to 1972. There, she experienced hard study and emotional storm. Thirty years later, the poet once again returned to his former residence in a strange place, and wrote with emotion:

> *How can drizzle be so sticky?*
> *Not as refreshing as I remember.*
> *I have to walk south in the rain*
> *Go back to the front of the small red building.*
> *Thirty years ago it was an old wooden house*
> *Now I don't want to tilt at all,*
> *Still the same date red.*
> *The drizzle quietly covers all kinds of tossing:*
> *First heart palpitations, first heart palpitations*
> *The tears that tormented myself for the first time,*
> *Next is Banjiazi Repeat*
> *Heart palpitations and tears.*
> *The red building is the starting point of a kind of circulation.*

我看見一個女孩爬出前窗，
後門正激烈地搖晃，
她逃離的是生命的強烈。
有一天當我不再逃離，
我將打開門穿入小樓
走進茫茫的細雪。

　　這裡，暗示著詩人在喧嘩與回憶中的內心苦悶與孤獨。
鍾玲自美國威斯康辛大學取得比較文學博士學位後，1972 年
起曾在紐約、臺灣、香港等名校任教。此詩含蓋在她讀書時
的青春勃動期，充滿著對人生、愛情的美好嚮往，也有著青
年人的憂鬱和悲傷。她把自己最天真純摯的哀愁與熱情全注
入到喜愛的詩中，她的愛又是真誠的，深沈而傷感的。誠然，
詩歌理應借景抒情，托物言志。鍾玲也用歌聲親吻著陌地生
故居，她對昔時的生活與往事，縱是痛苦與歡樂參和著，又
是那樣懷念；所以說，沒有愛就沒有真正的詩人。

　　在這瞬息萬變的世上，鍾玲認為，她是靠自己堅強的個
性，想做的事就一定能做到，亦肯定世間存有真實的愛情。
如詩人在 2008 年六月寫下的這首〈太陽的面貌〉，讓讀者了
解，影響詩人一生的情感世界就存在於兩個重要的人之間：

I saw a girl climb out the front window,
The back door is shaking violently,
What she escaped was the intensity of life.
One day when I don't run away anymore,
I will open the door and enter the small building
Into the vast snow.

Here, it implies the poet's inner depression and loneliness in the noise and memories. After Zhong Ling obtained a Ph. D. in Comparative Literature from the University of Wisconsin in the United States, she has taught in prestigious universities in New York, Taiwan, and Hong Kong since 1972. This poem covers the vigorous period of youth when she was studying, full of beautiful yearning for life and love, as well as the melancholy and sadness of young people. She poured her most innocent sorrow and enthusiasm into her favorite poems, and her love is sincere, deep and sad. It is true that poetry should use scenery to express emotions and express aspirations through things. Zhong Ling also sang and embraced Modisheng's former residence. She missed the life and past events of the past, even though she was involved in pain and joy, and she missed it so much; therefore, there is no real poet without love.

In this ever-changing world, Zhong Ling believes that she can do what she wants to do with her strong personality, and she also affirms that there is true love in the world. For example, the poem *The Face of the Sun* written by the poet in June 2008 allows readers to understand that the emotional world that affects the poet's life exists between two important people:

我的世界有兩種太陽
有一個人雖然在遠方
卻恆久給我力量
溫暖我，用他對世界灑下的光熱

穩定我，像不動的太陽

有一個人
他的心總是在遊走
卻循著一定的軌跡
試探我，以變幻不定的光芒
扶持我，像風推動飄帆

這個宇宙有無數太陽
隱藏在心的深處
我們看不見的地方

　　鍾玲把感受和思考意象化，是此詩的核心；同時，亦將世俗和精神的愛混合起來，以證實自己對愛的哲學見解。當然，說它內裡寓含著對一位傑出的胡導演的悼念，是不可否認的。而與余光中師生間的知遇之情，是那樣真切感人，也是真實生活的寫照 從而將具體的形象與幻想化的精神融合，創造出富有張力的意象。鍾玲自己一再強調，她原來就想好好當一個作家。她的思想敏銳而寬廣，很顯然地，此詩的藝術情境也是展示得成功的。

　　　　─2013.2.23 作
　　　　─臺灣《海星》詩刊，第 12 期，2014.06 夏季號，頁
　　　　　15-頁 19。

There are two suns in my world
Although there is a person far away
Give me strength forever
Warm me, with the light and heat he sprinkled on the world

Steady me like the unmoving sun

There is a person
His heart is always wandering
Follow a certain track
Test me with changing lights
Hold me up like the wind pushes the sail

There are countless suns in this universe
Hidden deep in my heart
Where we can't see

Zhong Ling's imagery of feeling and thinking is the core of this poem; at the same time, she also mixes worldly and spiritual love to prove her philosophical views on love. Of course, it is undeniable that it contains a tribute to an outstanding director Hu. The acquaintance with Yu Guangzhong's teachers and students is so real and touching, and it is also a portrayal of real life, so that the specific image and the fantasy spirit are integrated to create an image full of tension. Zhong Ling herself has repeatedly emphasized that she originally wanted to be a writer. Her thoughts are sharp and broad, and obviously, the artistic situation of this poem is also successfully displayed.

16. 一棵不凋的樹──試析穆旦的詩三首

摘要：穆旦一生在教學與翻譯研究上成就斐然，但在逝世以前，很長的一段時間裡，也曾面對辛酸的命運與憂患艱難之苦。對一個自幼即滿懷愛國情操的穆旦而言，他以詩言志，凝聚文筆之力，滋養文學沃土之情，恰似一棵不凋的樹，為了守護尊嚴而獨立生存在陡峭的山頂；如今那棵樹已然蒼綠成蔭，而其血液裡流淌的詩句，也逐漸受到學界一致的肯定與尊崇。

關鍵詞：穆旦　詩歌　翻譯家

一、其人其詩

穆旦（1918-1977），原名查良錚，著名的詩歌翻譯家，曾任南開大學副教授，出版詩集有《探險隊》、《旗》、《穆旦詩選》，翻譯普希金抒情詩五百首及詩體小說《葉甫蓋尼‧奧涅金》、拜倫的長詩《唐璜》等多種。閱讀穆旦詩歌，能夠明顯感受到詩人一生耗竭心力，熬到最後一刻，仍孜孜不倦對

16. An Unfading Tree: Analysis of Three Poems by Mu Dan

Abstract: Mu Dan made great achievements in teaching and translation research throughout his life. But for a long time before his death, he also faced bitter fate and hardships. Full of patriotic sentiments ever since his childhood, Mu Dan used poetry and aspirations to nourish the soil of literature. Like an unfading tree, standing independently atop a steep mountain in order to protect dignity; now that tree is green and shady, and the poems flowing in its blood have gradually been affirmed and respected by academic circles.

Key words: Mu Dan, poetry, translator

1. His People and His Poems

Mu Dan (1918-1977), also known as Zha Liangzheng, a famous poetry translator, once served as an associate professor at Nankai University, published poetry collections including *Expedition*, *Flag*, *Selected Poems of Mu Dan*, and translated 500 lyric poems by Pushkin and the poetic novel *Eugene Onegin*, Byron's long poem *Don Juan* and so on. Reading Mu Dan's poems, one can clearly feel that the poet has exhausted all his life, until the last

於詩歌的翻譯與創作有一種獻身崇高的追求。在塵世漂泊裡，他一直與詩歌同行，與憂愁相遇；雖然有過金光燦爛或被頌揚誇耀的片段，但終其一生，他的詩歌的象徵意義是有價值的，這與其自幼年以來的滿腔愛國熱忱，應未曾改變。他就像一隻勇敢的飛鷹，展翼在烏雲的巨浪，但他只帶著堅強的心靈走向遠方……而遠方永不漆暗，渴望光明與寧靜的心也永不消失。

穆旦在赴美留學歸回祖國，任南開大學外文系副教授期間，除了專於教學與翻譯的創作實踐和詩歌研究，他以無比勇毅的擔當，把他的詩魂根植於人民的心目中；而普希金（A. C. Пушкин，1799—1837）賦予俄羅斯文學特有的貢獻與詩裡最純真的感情都構成了穆旦的書籍以及晚年大規模的詩歌創作的基礎。雖然文革開始，他在四十歲左右，曾被指為歷史反革命，全家被迫到農場接受勞動改造；而穆旦惘然告別了教書崗位，告別知心的親友與他嚮往呼吸真正自由的天空，轉調到圖書館和洗澡堂工作，先後十多年，受到批判與勞改。但穆旦仍抓住每一個永恆的瞬間，日夜以最積極的態度勤於翻譯工作，以供學子及學者研究；五十九歲那年，他因心臟病突發去世，兩年後，雖然得以平反，但為時已晚。

moment, he still has a dedicated and noble pursuit of poetry translation and creation. In the wanderings of the world, he has been walking with poetry and meeting with sorrow; although there have been golden or glorified fragments, but throughout his life, the symbolic meaning of his poetry is valuable, which is different since his childhood. Full of patriotic enthusiasm, it should not have changed. He is like a brave eagle, spreading his wings in the dark clouds and huge waves, but he only goes to the distance with a strong heart... and the distance is never dark, and the heart longing for light and tranquility will never disappear.

When Mu Dan went to study in the United States and returned to his motherland, when he was an associate professor in the Department of Foreign Languages and Literatures of Nankai University, in addition to his creative practices such as teaching and translating and poetry research, he took on the responsibility with incomparable courage and rooted his poetic spirit in the hearts of the people; Pushkin (А. С. Пушкин, 1799-1837) endowed Russian literature with unique contributions and the most pure emotions in poetry, which formed the basis of Mu Dan's books and large-scale poetry creation in his later years. Although the Cultural Revolution began, when he was about forty years old, he was accused of being a historical counter-revolutionary, and his family was forced to undergo labor reform on the farm; while Mu Dan left his teaching position in a daze, bid farewell to his close relatives and friends, and his longing for the sky of real freedom. Working in libraries and bathhouses for more than ten years, and was criticized and reformed through labor. But Mu Dan still seized every eternal moment, and worked diligently on the translation work day and night with the most positive attitude for the study of students and scholars. At fifty-nine, he died of a heart attack. Two years later, although he was rehabilitated, it was too late.

　　對一個自幼即滿懷愛國情操的穆旦而言，他以詩言志，凝聚文筆之力，滋養文學沃土之情，恰似一棵不凋的樹，為了守護尊嚴而獨立生存在陡峭的山頂；如今那棵樹已然蒼綠成蔭，而其血液裡流淌的詩句，也逐漸受到學界一致的肯定與尊崇。

二、詩作賞讀

一本出自谷羽編選的《當代詩讀本（一）》，讓我有幸閱讀了穆旦的心靈詩影。就在詩人垂暮之年，除了更進一步研究翻譯詩文以外，猶完整地保有一顆飽經憂患卻毫無枯竭於詩歌創作的心。在他死前的一年期間，曾大量創作他最後的詩歌作品，最後因病溘然長逝，迨兩年後，始得以平反。後來在詩人所愛的南開大學文學院校園的「穆旦花園」內，校方為他立了一座雕像，花園圍牆上鑄有「詩魂」兩個大字。他在中國詩歌翻譯史上的豐碑，鼓舞著許多後人，也讓我深信，「苦難」成就更多的愛，「苦難」也使他學會包容與寬恕。在「穆旦花園」的周邊，恍惚中，我看到了樹木和花朵都具有茁壯的生長跡象，我的目光停駐在雕像的穆旦臉龐，那是我認得的天使，他並不孤單，因為他遵循上帝旨意，將他的愛及留下的詩篇繼續傳播在轉動的地球上。

　　他在 1976 年 3 月寫下的《智慧之歌》（注 1），詩裡盡是他的回憶，每一字詞，都將他的一生追逐於所有的夢想與悲歡，或在黑暗裡看見自己眼眸的光芒，寫得十分真摯、坦誠，而回憶也是一種希望：

For Mu Dan, who has been full of patriotism since he was a child, he expresses his ambition with poetry, gathers the power of writing, and nourishes the fertile soil of literature, just like a tree that does not wither, living independently on the top of a steep mountain in order to protect his dignity. Now that tree is green and full of shade, and the verses flowing in its blood have gradually been unanimously affirmed and respected by the academic circle.

2. Appreciation and Reading of Poems

Contemporary Poetry Reader (1), edited by Gu Yu, gave me the honor to read Mu Dan's spiritual poetry. In the poet's twilight years, in addition to further research on the translation of poetry, he still has a heart full of worries but never exhausted in poetry creation. During the year before his death, he wrote a large number of his last poems, and finally died of illness, only to be rehabilitated two years later. In the following years, in the Mudan Garden on the campus of the College of Liberal Arts of Nankai University, which the poet loved, a statue was erected in his honor, and the two characters "Poetry Soul" were cast on the garden wall. His monumental achievements in the history of Chinese poetry translation have inspired many future generations, and convinced me that "suffering" has made more love, and "suffering" has also taught him to learn tolerance and forgiveness. Around the Mudan Garden, in a trance, I saw the signs of vigorous growth of trees and flowers. My eyes stopped on the face of the statue of Mu Dan. It was the angel I knew. He was not alone, because he is following God's will, continuing to spread his love and the psalms left behind on the rotating earth.

He wrote *Song of Wisdom* (Note 1) in March 1976. The poem is full of his memories, and every word is chasing all his dreams and sorrows and joys all his life, or in the dark seeing the light in my eyes. I wrote very sincerely and honestly, and memories are also a kind of hope:

我已走到了幻想底盡頭，
這是一片落葉飄零的樹林，
每一片葉子標記著一種歡喜，
現在都枯黃地堆積在內心。

有一種歡喜是青春的愛情，
那時遙遠天邊的燦爛的流星，
有的不知去向，永遠消逝了，
有的落在腳前，冰冷而僵硬。

另一種歡喜是喧騰的友誼，
茂盛的花不知道還有秋季，
社會的格局代替了血的沸騰，
生活的冷風把熱情鑄為實際。

另一種歡喜是迷人的理想，
他使我在荊棘之途走得夠遠，
為理想而痛苦並不可怕，
可怕的是看它終於成笑談。

只有痛苦還在，它是日常生活
每天在懲罰自己過去的傲慢，
那絢爛的天空都受到譴責，
還有什麼彩色留在這片荒原？

I have come to the end of my fantasy,
This is a forest with fallen leaves,
Each leaf marks a joy,
Now it's all piled up in my heart.

There is a joy that is youthful love,
At that time the brilliant shooting star in the distant sky,
Some disappeared, disappeared forever,
Some fell to their feet, cold and stiff.

Another joy is tumultuous friendship,
The lush flowers do not know that there is still autumn,
The pattern of society has replaced the boiling of blood,
The cold wind of life casts enthusiasm into reality.

Another joy is the charming ideal,
He has carried me far enough in the thorny way,
It is not terrible to suffer for ideals,
It is scary to watch it finally become a joke.

Only the pain is there, it's everyday life
Punishing myself every day for my past arrogance,
That splendid sky is condemned,
What color is left in this wasteland?

> 但唯有一棵智慧之樹不凋，
> 我知道它以我的苦汁為營養，
> 它的碧綠是對我無情的嘲弄，
> 我咒詛它每一片葉的滋長。

　　眾所周知，穆旦晚年飽受病痛之苦，但他仍打起精神譜寫出具有審美表現力的詩句。這首詩的魅力在於韻律，文字往往是具象的，更具濃重的感情色彩。這正好說明，詩人的胸襟是開闊而善良的，且對美好的時代來臨，存有精神的嚮往與希望。可見，他的精神世界不但和高尚堅毅的品格相連，也和對祖國的希望及嚮往純文學的創作緊緊聯繫在一起；而詩裡的疊字也強化了詩歌本身所要凸顯的「歡喜」的純然的感受，它的反復出現使此詩體現了對稱交錯的音韻，有如正在沉思的抒情旋律，莊嚴而美麗，直搗人心。

　　另一首在 1976 年 4 月寫下的《聽說我老了》，同樣巧妙地從生活中抒發真情和從美好的想像中醒來，但有別於許多強調寓意的象徵詩人，穆旦傾向擁有其獨特的形式，充滿其深邃的思想，也有甜蜜的夢幻色彩：

> 我穿著一件破衣衫出門，
> 這麼醜，我看著都覺得好笑，
> 因為我原有許多好的衣衫
> 都已讓它在歲月裡爛掉。

But only one tree of wisdom never withers,
I know it feeds on my bitter juice,
Its green is a merciless mockery of me,
I curse the growth of every leaf of it.

As we all know, Mu Dan suffered from illness in his later years, but he still cheered up to compose verses with aesthetic expression. The charm of this poem lies in the rhythm, and the words are often figurative and more emotional. This just shows that the poet's mind is open and kind, and he has spiritual yearning and hope for the coming of a beautiful era. It can be seen that his spiritual world is not only connected with his noble and resolute character, but also closely connected with his hope for the motherland and his longing for the creation of pure literature. Pure feeling, its repeated appearance makes this poem reflect the symmetrical and interlaced rhyme, just like the lyrical melody in meditation, solemn and beautiful, directly touching people's hearts.

Another song, *I Heard I'm Old*, written in April 1976, also subtly expresses the true feelings from life and wakes up from the beautiful imagination, but unlike many symbolic poets who emphasize meaning, Mu Dan tends to adopt a unique form, full of profound thoughts, but also sweet and dreamy:

I went out in a rag,
It's so ugly, I find it funny when I look at it,
Because I have many good clothes
Has let it rot over the years.

人們對我說：你老了，你老了，
但誰也沒有看見赤裸的我，
只有在我深心的曠野中
才高唱出真正的自我之歌。

它唱著：「時間愚弄不了我，
我沒有賣給青春，也不賣給老年，
我只不過隨時序換一換裝，
參加這場化裝舞會的表演。

「但我常常和大雁在碧空翱翔，
或者和蛟龍在海裡翻騰，
凝神的山巒也時常邀請我
到它那遼闊的靜穆裡做夢。」

　　早知穆旦是詩人、翻譯家，也知道他的詩歌必將一切交付想像靈感和其接觸的事物有所聯結，但我很難想像，一個詩人如何在艱難的環境下，仍固有榮譽，默默地為中國翻譯史獻出其力，猶冀望日子翻新，更熱忱於詩歌的愛。此詩也有許多意象，各有其不同的意涵，都代表著他尚未向別人敘說的故事，也顯見他孤單的步伐，依舊在許多關切的親友的血液中漫步。而往日，穆旦的譯作是許多學子的引導，今日，他的詩歌已逐漸在中國學界蔚成一股研究的風氣。詩裡，沒有直接表露其內心的世界，也沒有諷刺或哀怨的筆調，有的是表達從痛苦中淬鍊的新精神，對後學詩人也有重要的啟發性。

People say to me: you're old, you're old,
But no one saw me naked,
Only in the wilderness of my heart
To sing the true song of self.

It sings: "Time can't fool me,
I did not sell youth nor old age,
I just change clothes every now and then.
Take part in the performance of this masquerade ball.

"But I often fly with wild geese in the blue sky,
Or toss in the sea with the dragon,
The mountain of concentration also invites me from
*   time to time*
To dream in its vast stillness."

　　I knew that Mu Dan was a poet and a translator, and I knew that his poems must give imagination to everything and connect with the things touching him, but it is hard for me to imagine how a poet can still have his own honor in a difficult environment. I have devoted myself to the history of Chinese translation, and I still hope that the days will be refurbished, and I will be more enthusiastic about the love of poetry. There are also many images in this poem, each with its own different connotations, all of which represent the stories he has yet to tell others. It also shows that his lonely steps are still walking in the blood of many relevant relatives and friends. In the past, Mu Dan's translations were the guidance of many students, but today, his poems have gradually become a trend of research in Chinese academic circles. In the poems, there is no direct expression of his inner world, nor is there any tone of irony or sorrow, but some express the new spirit quenched from pain, which is also an important inspiration for later poets.

　　中國現代詩歌的發展告訴我們，真正堅持寫詩的詩人無論處在哪一個時代的洪流裡，從孤獨的行吟，直到對理想的追求，從青春年少到白髮蒼老，他們都能用赤子之心看待世界，對世間的紛紜與幻變，都能以心靈的愛之歌溫暖世界最深處的傷痛缺口。但當我看到穆旦在 1976 年 10 月寫下的這首《停電之後》，我便立即明瞭，它既是詩人自己在病痛中用淚水澆灌詩的萌芽，也是他唱起命運之歌、心卻全部為光明所照耀的真實寫照：

> 太陽最好，但是它下沉了，
> 擰開電燈，工程照常進行。
> 我們還以為從此驅走夜，
> 暗暗感謝我們的文明。
> 可是突然，黑暗擊敗一切，
> 美好的世界從此消失無蹤。
> 但我點起小小的蠟燭，
> 把我的室內又照得通明：
> 繼續工作也毫不氣餒，
> 只是對太陽加倍地憧憬。
>
> 次日睜開眼，白日更輝煌，
> 小小的蠟台還擺在桌上。
> 我細看它，不但耗盡了油，
> 而且殘留的淚掛在兩旁：
> 這時我才想起，原來一夜間，

The development of modern Chinese poetry tells us that poets who really insist on writing poems, no matter what era they are in, from chanting alone to the pursuit of ideals, from youth to gray-haired old age, they can use their innocence. Looking at the world with the heart, facing the diversity and changes in the world, all can warm the deepest pain in the world with the song of love in the heart. But when I read the song *After the Blackout* written by Mu Dan in October 1976, I immediately understood that it was not only the bud of the poet who watered the poem with tears in his illness, but also the song of his destiny when he sang the song of fate, but his heart was still. A true portrayal of everything illuminated by the light:

> *The sun is best, but it sinks,*
> *Unscrew the light, and the project continues as usual.*
> *We thought we drove away the night,*
> *Secretly thank our civilization.*
> *But suddenly, darkness overwhelms all,*
> *The wonderful world has since disappeared without*
>   *a trace.*
> *But I light a little candle,*
> *Light up my chambers again:*
> *Keep working without getting discouraged,*
> *Just looking forward to the sun doubly.*
>
> *Open your eyes the next day, the day is brighter,*
> *The small candle holder was still on the table.*
> *I looked at it, not only ran out of oil,*
> *And the remaining tears hang on both sides:*
> *Only then did I remember that one night,*

有許多陣風都要它抵擋。
於是我感激地把它拿開，
默念這可敬的小小墳場。

走過十多年的艱辛歲月，再回首，那是歷史無法抹滅的傷痛，但在穆旦的心靈卻乾淨得發亮，猶如不掉淚的蠟燭，不斷地嘗試燃燒自己，照亮別人，直至蠟炬成灰淚始乾。穆旦的艱忍與良善的溫柔，讓此詩除了張揚了詩歌的藝術的生命，更得以超越時空的界限，成了永恆不朽之作。

三、結　語

當穆旦的詩歌向我緩緩走來，讓我看到，讓我仰慕打從開始尊敬於心的詩人。從他的創作方法上看，由於他翻譯了許多普希金俄文與拜倫的英語詩歌，譯文的技巧也促使其詩從浪漫主義走向象徵主義的轉化，且具節奏悠揚，韻律優美的特質。在其晚年大量湧現許多真實地抒發詩人的感情的作品中，詩人的現實環境畫面雖然是桎梏的，但詩人的心靈卻是自由的。他的詩歌也敘述了夢中獲得了美好的世界的遐思，折射出文革年代帶給知識分子的憂患感與堅強的意志。但這些不足以道出他的詩歌最感人之處，是他用他的快樂或痛苦，回憶或希望去歌唱的心靈，是崇高而樸素的。我有幸在其詩歌中看到了一個詩人不斷努力以赴的堅毅氣息以及他用眼淚和歡笑合成的生命中去創造出更廣闊的藝術氛圍的詩句；然而這也是他奔湧在他血液裡的詩句，並且是有啟發意義的。

記得穆旦在死前的寫下一首《冥想》的詩裡說：

There are many gusts to resist.
So I gratefully took it away,
Meditate on this venerable little cemetery.

After more than ten years of hard times, looking back, it was a pain that history cannot erase, but Mu Dan's heart is clean and shining, like a candle that does not shed tears, constantly trying to burn himself and illuminate others, until the wax torch turns into ashes and tears dry. Mu Dan's forbearance and kind gentleness make this poem not only publicize the artistic life of poetry, but also transcend the boundaries of time and space, and become an eternal and immortal work.

3. Conclusion

When Mu Dan's poems came to me slowly, let me see, let me admire the poet whom I have respected from the very beginning. From the point of view of his creative method, since he translated many of Pushkin's Russian and Byron's English poems, the translation skills also facilitated the transformation of his poems from romanticism to symbolism, with melodious rhythm and beautiful rhythm. In his later years, a large number of works that truly express the poet's feelings emerged. Although the poet's real environment pictures are shackled, the poet's heart is free. His poems also narrate the dream of obtaining a beautiful world in his dreams, reflecting the sense of anxiety and strong will brought to intellectuals during the Cultural Revolution. But these are not enough to say that the most touching part of his poems is that the soul he sings with his joy or pain, memory or hope is noble and simple. I was fortunate enough to see in his poems a poet's perseverance in his constant efforts and the verses in which he created a broader artistic atmosphere in his life synthesized with tears and laughter. However, these are also the verses in his blood and it's instructive.

I remember that Mu Dan said in his poem *Meditation* before his death:

> 而如今突然面對墳墓，
> 我冷眼向過去稍稍四顧，
> 只見它曲折灌溉的悲喜，
> 都消失在一片亙古的荒漠。
> 這才知道我全部的努力不過完成了普通生活。

　　每一讀來，真讓人眼中隱隱有淚光閃動。他堅毅的骨子裡，其實仍充滿對大時代光明的渴望和為詩歌而努力以赴的精神。隨著中國經濟文化的崛起與飛速發展，我更有理由相信，穆旦不是時代的悲劇人物，人們看到的是畫面上處於艱忍環境下，為培育知識精英而堅守崗位的一個被下放的學者，但他在別人難以洞悉的心靈世界裡，其實是個像天使般純淨的氣質的詩人。德國詩人里爾克（Rainer Maria Rilke，1875-1926）曾寫下這樣豪邁而感性的句子：「只因我經歷過強大，／故我頌揚柔弱。」（注 2）我由衷地認為，那些加諸在穆旦身上無以名狀的痛苦，反而成就了他抵達繆斯的殿宇的真正力量，願以一詩《冥想》（Meditation）（注 3）向我尊敬的他，致上最深的、最後為了表達對詩人穆旦的敬意：

> 直到你能步入繆斯的殿堂
> 我才相信
> 你已生氣勃勃
> 歌詠著神妙的詩句
> 才能預感
> 你如大熊星清晰浮現

And now suddenly facing the grave,
I glanced coldly at the past for a while,
I saw the joys and sorrows watered by its twists
andturns,
All disappeared in an ancient desert.
Only then did I know that all my efforts were nothing
but the completion of ordinary life.

Every time I read it, I really have tears in my eyes. In his resolute bones, in fact, he is still full of longing for the bright era and the spirit of working hard for poetry. With the rise and rapid development of China's economy and culture, I have more reason to believe that Mu Dan is not a tragic figure of the times. What people see is a devolved person who sticks to his post in order to cultivate intellectual elites in a harsh environment. He is a scholar, but he is actually a poet with an angelic pure temperament in the spiritual world that is difficult for others to understand. German poet Rainer Maria Rilke (1875-1926) once wrote such a heroic and emotional sentence: "Only because I have experienced strength, / Therefore I praise weakness." (Note 2) I sincerely believe that those who impose the indescribable pain in Mu Dan's body, on the contrary, achieved his true power to reach the palace of the Muses. I would like to express my deepest and final thanks to him whom I respect with a poem *Meditation* (Note 3) In order to express respect to Mu Dan as a poet:

Till you can step into the halls of the muse
I just believe
You are alive
Singing wonderful verses
Ability to foresee
You are clearly emerging like a big bear star

躺在海面細品島嶼四季的流轉
驅走我心中的激蕩

而你行了一個奇蹟——
恰似一棵不凋的樹
當我走近　想畫你微笑的
姿態，自信，謙虛，還有
堅定的眼神。
在我眼睛深處，你的微笑如歌
不可思議卻令人開懷

注 1：　本文譯作出自谷羽編選的《當代詩讀本
　　　　（一）》，漢俄對照中國詩歌系列，天津
　　　　大學出版社，2020 年 2 月，第 1 版，頁
　　　　36-40。
注 2：　里爾克著，唐際明譯，《慢讀里爾克》，
　　　　臺北，商周出版，2015 年 9 月初版，頁
　　　　155。

—2022.08.29 完稿

—刊台灣（秋水詩刊），第 198 期，2024.01，頁
60-64。

Lying on the sea and savoring the four seasons of the island
Drive away the turmoil in my heart

And you performed a miracle —
Like a tree that never withers
When I get close, I want to draw you smiling
Posture, confidence, humility, and
Firm eyes.
In the depths of my eyes, your smile is like a song
Incredible but delightful

Note 1. This article is translated from *Contemporary Poetry Reader (1)* edited by Gu Yu, Chinese-Russian Chinese Poetry Series, Tianjin University Press, February 2020, 1st edition, pages 36-40.

Note 2. Written by Rilke, translated by Tang Jiming, *Slow Reading of Rilke*, Taipei, Shang Zhou Publishing, 1st edition in September 2015, p. 155.

林 明 理 專 書
Dr.Lin Mingli'smonograph

©作者：林明理 博士 Dr. Lin Mingli（1961-）專書封面

Author: Dr. Lin Mingli (1961-) Book cover

＊林明理專書 暨義大利出版的合著

Dr. Lin Mingli's monograph cum （Chinese-English Poetry Co-author published in Italy）

1.《秋收的黃昏》The evening of autumn。高雄市：春暉出版社，2008。 ISBN 986695045-X

2.《夜櫻-林明理詩畫集》Cherry Blossoms at Night。高雄市：春暉出版社，2009。 ISBN86695068-9

3.《新詩的意象與內涵-當代詩家作品賞析》The Imagery and Connetation of New Poetry-A
Collection of Critical Poetry Analysis。臺北市：文津出版社，2010。 ISBN 978-957-688-913-0 〔820〕

4.《藝術與自然的融合-當代詩文評論集》The Fusion Of Art and Nature。臺北市：文史哲出版社，2011。
ISBN 978-957-549-966-2

5.《山楂樹》HAWTHORN Poems by Lin Mingli（林明理詩集）。臺北市：文史哲出版社，2011。ISBN 978-957-549-975-4

6.《回憶的沙漏》Sandglass Of Memory（中英對照譯詩集）英譯：吳鈞。臺北市：秀威出版社，2012。ISBN 978-986-221-900-3

7.《湧動著一泓清泉—現代詩文評論》A GUSHING SPRING-A COLLECTION OF COMMENTS ON MODERN LITERARY WORKS。臺北市：文史哲出版社，2012。

ISBN 978-986-314-024-5

8.《清雨塘》Clear Rain Pond（中英對照譯詩集）英譯：吳鈞。臺北市：文史哲出版社，2012。 ISBN 978-986-314-076-4

9.《用詩藝開拓美－林明理讀詩》DEVELOPING BEAUTY THOUGH THE ART OF POETRY － Lin Mingli On Poetry。臺北市：秀威出版社，2013。 ISBN 978-986-326-059-2

10.《海頌－林明理詩文集》Hymn To the Ocean（poems and Essays）。臺北市：文史哲出版社，2013。
ISBN 978-986-314-119-8

11.《林明理報刊評論 1990-2000》Published Commentaries1990-2000。臺北市：文史哲出版社，2013。 ISBN 978-986-314-155-6

12.《行走中的歌者－林明理談詩》The Walking singer-Ming-Li Lin On Poetry。臺北市：文史哲出版社，2013。
ISBN 978-986-314-156-3

13.《山居歲月》Days in the Mountains（中英對照譯詩集）英譯：吳鈞。臺北市：文史哲出版社，2015。ISBN978-986-314-252-2

14.《夏之吟》Summer Songs（中英法譯詩集）。英譯：馬為義（筆名：非馬）（Dr. William Marr）。法譯：阿薩納斯 · 薩拉西（Athanase Vantchev de Thracy）。法國巴黎：索倫紮拉文化學院（The Cultural Institute of Solenzara），2015。
ISBN 978-2-37356-020-6

15.《默喚》Silent Call(中英法譯詩集)。英譯：諾頓 · 霍奇斯(Norton Hodges）。法譯：阿薩納斯 · 薩拉西（Athanase Vantchev de Thracy)。法國巴黎：索倫紮拉文化學院(The Cultural Institute of Solenzara），2016。 ISBN 978-2-37356-022-0

16.《林明理散文集》Lin Ming Li´s Collected essays。臺北市：文

史哲出版社，2016。　ISBN 978-986-314-291-1

17.《名家現代詩賞析》Appreciation of the work of Famous Modern Poets。臺北市：文史哲出版社，2016。　ISBN 978-986-314-302-4

18.《我的歌　MY SONG》，法譯：Athanase Vantchev de Thracy 中法譯詩集。臺北市：文史哲出版社，2017。
ISBN 978-986-314-359-8

19.《諦聽　Listen》，中英對照詩集，英譯：馬為義（筆名：非馬）（Dr. William Marr），臺北市：文史哲出版社，2018。
ISBN 978-986-314-401-4

20.《現代詩賞析》，Appreciation of the work of Modern Poets，臺北市：文史哲出版社，2018。　ISBN 978-986-314-412-0

21.《原野之聲》Voice of the Wilderness，英譯：馬為義（筆名：非馬）（Dr. William Marr），臺北市：文史哲出版社，2019。
ISBN 978-986-314-453-3

22.《思念在彼方　散文暨新詩》，Longing over the other side（prose and poetry〉，臺北市：文史哲出版社，2020。
ISBN 978-986-314-505-9

23.《甜蜜的記憶（散文暨新詩）》，Sweet memories（prose and poetry），臺北市：文史哲出版社，2021。
ISBN 978-986-314-555-4

24.《詩河（詩評、散文暨新詩）》，The Poetic River（Poetry review 、Prose and poetry），臺北市：文史哲出版社，2022。
ISBN 978-986-314-603-2

25.《Kurt F · Svatek Lin Mingli Giovanni Campisi 庫爾特·F·斯瓦泰克，林明理，喬凡尼·坎皮西詩選》（中英對照），《Carmina Selecta"（"Selected Poems"）by Kurt F. Svatek, Lin Mingli, Giovanni Campisi》，義大利：Edizioni Universum〈埃迪采恩

尼大學〉，宇宙出版社，2023.01。TEL. +0039 331 8444673

26.《紀念達夫尼斯和克洛伊 In memory of Daphnis and Chloe》（中英對照）詩選，作者：Renza Agnelli，Sara Ciampi，Lin Mingli 林明理，義大利：Edizioni Universum〈埃迪采恩尼大學〉，宇宙出版社，書封面，林明理畫作（聖母大殿），2023.02。TEL. +0039 331 8444673

27.《詩林明理古今抒情詩 160 首》《Parallel Reading of 160 Classical and New Chinese LyricalPoems》（漢英對照 Chinese-English），英譯：張智中，臺北市：文史哲出版社，2023.04。ISBN978-986-314-637-7

28.《愛的讚歌》《hymn of love》（詩評、散文 暨 新詩）（Poetry review 、Prose and poetry），臺北市：文史哲出版社，2023.05。ISBN 978-986-314-638-4

29.《埃內斯托‧卡漢，薩拉‧錢皮，林明理 和平詩選》（義英對照）（Italian-English），《Carmina Selecta" ("Selected Poems") by Ernesto Kahan, Sara Ciampi , Lin Mingli Peace-Pace》，義大利：Edizioni Universum〈埃迪采恩尼大學〉，宇宙出版社，2023.11。 ISBN 978-889-980-379-7

30.《祈禱與工作》，中英義詩集，"ORA ET LABORA" Trilogia di Autori Trilingue: Italiano, Cinese, Inglese 作者的三語三部曲： 義大利語、中文、英語 Trilingual Trilogy of Authors: Italian, Chinese, English，作者：奧內拉‧卡布奇尼 Ornella Cappuccini，非馬 William Marr，林明理 Lin Mingli，義大利，宇宙出版社，2024.06。

31.《名家抒情詩評賞》（漢英對照）《Appraisal of Lyric Poems by Famous Artists》，張智中教授英譯，臺北市：文史哲出版社，2024.06。出書中 ISBN978-986-314

譯者簡介

非馬(本名馬為義Marr)，詩人暨科學家。詩人兼藝術家，出版有23本中英文詩集，3本散文集及多本翻譯。他的詩被譯入上百種選集及合輯，中國、美國及德國等地的高中與大學裡皆選入他的詩。曾任美國伊利諾州詩人協會會長，在芝加哥及中國策劃過數次畫展及聯合展。

Dr. William Marr, a Chinese-American poet and artist, has published a total of 23 books of poetry. 3 books of poetry and several books of translations. His poetry has been translated into more than ten languages and included in over one hundred anthologies. Some of his poems are used in high school and college textbooks in Taiwan, China, England, and Germany. A former president of the Illinois State Poetry Society, he is a scientist by profession and has held several solo and group art exhibitions in the Chicago area and China

◎封面繪畫：林明理

本書詩集著者2017年初發海內外的詩畫作品百首，至裡內容由美國詩人非馬(馬為義譯Dr William Marr)擔心翻譯而成。還包括本詩翻英文學作國師友及其寫中教授，以名可醫師詩人及1985本獲諾貝爾和平獎的prof. Ernesto Kahan、法國詩人Athanase Vantchev de Thracy、義大利詩人Giovanni Campisi 的翻譯。

內容包括對鄉土的懷念、對老人的讚頌、地球與生態變遷的感慨、旅遊觀賞及感恩動物的謳歌、對戰爭與和平的反思等。可謂是愛意真切的世界，為詩愛好者最真摯的抒情寫照，供愛心的讀者。

This poetry collection includes 100 poems & paintings by the author, which were published domestically and overseas in 2017. Most of the pieces were translated into English by Dr. William Marr, a famous American poet; other translators include Dr. Zhang Zhizhong, professor from the Foreign Languages College of Tianjin Normal University, professor Ernesto Kahan, an Israeli physician-poet and winner of Nobel Prize in Peace 1985, Athanase Vantchev de Thracy, a French poet, and Giovanni Campisi, an Italian poet.

The themes of the poetry collection range from nostalgia, praise of celebrities, sighs over global and ecological changes, tourism landscape and protection of animals, as well as the reflection of war and peace, etc., which reveal the author's most sincere lyrical portrayal in the poetic world. This is an excellent reader for lovers of English poetry.

ISBN 978-986-314-401-4

諦　聽 中英對照詩集
Listen
Poetry Collection (Chinese & English)
林明理著　非馬(馬為義)譯
Author: Dr. Lin Mingli　Translator: Dr. William Marr

文史哲英譯叢刊
文史哲出版社印行
The Liberal Arts Press

Lin Ming-Li, short CV

Dr. Lin Ming-Li was born in 1961 in Yunlin, Taiwan. She holds a Master's Degree in Law and lectured at Pingtung Normal College. A poetry critic, she is currently serving as a director of the Chinese Literature and Art Association, the Chinese New Poetry Society, and Beijing's International Association of Chinese Poetry. On the 4th of May, 2013, she rose on the Creative Poetry Prize as the 54th Chinese Literature and Arts Awards. On the 21st of October 2013, she received a Doctor of Literature degree from America's World Culture and Art Institute. On the 9th of September 2012, the World Satellite IV Station in Taiwan broadcast her interviews, "Lin Ming-Li: The Heart that Pursues a Dream with Poetry and Painting". On the 22nd of August, 2016, FTV (FORMOSA TELEVISION) educated two poems by her, namely, "Songs of the Forest of Mt. Ali" (2016.12.24 premiere) and "Ode to the Orchid Island" (2016.11.19 premiere). "Love of the Bethlehem Stars" (2017.07.15 premiere).

林明理　1961年生，臺灣雲林縣人，法學碩士，曾兼任屏東師範學院講師、曾任職省政府編纂、中國文藝協會理事、中國新詩學會理事，現任北京《國際漢語詩刊》編委，2013.5.4獲「第54屆中國文藝獎章文學類詩歌創作獎」。2013.9.9人間衛視【知道】節目專訪【畫中有詩－林明理】。2012.10.21獲美國世界文化藝術學院頒發榮譽文學博士。其作品在山水及詩學詩畫集三本。2016年三立電視台FTV【福爾摩沙電視台】播出其【阿里山之歌】於2016.12.24首播及【蘭嶼頌】於2016.11.19首播。【伯利恆之星】於2017.07.15首播。...

現代詩賞析
Appreciation of the work of Modern Poets
林明理 著　author：Dr.Lin Ming-Li

現代文學研究叢刊
文史哲出版社印行

原野之聲
Voice of the Wilderness
Poetry Collection (Chinese & English)
林明理著　非馬(馬為義)譯
Author: Dr. Lin Ming-Li　Translator: Dr. William Marr

文史哲英譯叢刊
The Liberal Arts Press

思念在彼方 (散文及新詩)
Longing over the other side (Prose and poetry)
林明理 著　Author: Dr. Lin Mingli

文學叢刊
文史哲出版社印行

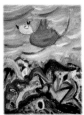

甜蜜的記憶 (散文及新詩)
Sweet memories (Prose and poetry)
林明理 著　Author: Dr. Lin Mingli

文學叢刊
文史哲出版社印行

詩　河 (散文及新詩)
The Poetic River
(詩評・散文暨新詩) (Poetry review・Prose and poetry)
林明理 著　Author: Dr. Lin Ming-Li

文學叢刊
文史哲出版社印行

Kurt F. Svatek
庫爾特・F・斯瓦德克
Lin Mingli
林明理
Giovanni Campisi
喬凡尼・坎皮西

CARMINA SELECTA
詩選

Edizioni Universum